What Art Is

What Art Is

The Esthetic Theory of
Ayn Rand

Louis Torres & Michelle Marder Kamhi

Open Court
Chicago and La Salle, Illinois

To order books from Open Court, call toll-free 1-800-815-2280.

For more information about *What Art Is*, see
<www.aristos.org/editors/booksumm.htm>.

Open Court Publishing Company is a division of Carus Publishing Company.

Designed by Iris Bell. The text face is Times, issued in digital form by Adobe Systems. The headings are in Optima, a font designed by Hermann Zapf in 1958 for the Stempel Foundry and also issued in digital form by Adobe Systems.

Library of Congress Cataloging-in-Publication Data

Torres, Louis, 1938-
    What art is : the esthetic theory of Ayn Rand / Louis Torres and Michelle Marder Kamhi.
        p.   cm.
    Includes bibliographical references and index.
    ISBN 0-8126-9372-8 (alk. paper) — ISBN 0-8126-9373-6 (pbk. : alk.)
    1. Rand, Ayn—Aesthetics. 2. Art and literature—United States—History—20th century. 3. Aesthetics, American. 4. Art in literature.   I. Kamhi, Michelle Marder.   II. Title.

PS3535.A547 Z9 2000
813'.52—dc21

                                                            00-037363

For Mom
whose indomitable spirit has been
a constant source of inspiration

Brief Contents

Part I   Ayn Rand's Philosophy of Art

Part II   Extension and Application of Rand's Theory

Detailed Contents

Part II Extension and Application of Rand's Theory

Preface

When we began a modest series of articles on Ayn Rand's philosophy of art for the readers of *Aristos* a decade ago, we little imagined that it would develop into a book of this length and scope. Still less did we expect, when we contracted with our publisher in December 1995 to deliver a manuscript for a book based on that series within a year, that the one year would stretch into more than five, or that the total number of words would be more than double our original estimate. Even so, we have omitted many points we had wanted to deal with, and have dealt with others in less detail than we would have liked. What we offer here is a beginning—to be supplemented and expanded by ourselves and others in the future.

As generalists covering many disciplines, in the sciences as well as in the arts, we have had to acquaint ourselves with a wide-ranging literature and we fully expect to have made some mistakes of fact or interpretation. We trust that specialists will be quick to point these out, and we look forward to refining our thesis in the light of such corrections. Yet we are also confident that any refinements that are needed will not alter the basic truth of the theory we present, in its key principles if not in all its details.

To sustain a long project of this kind has required intense personal motivation. On an almost daily basis, our sense of purpose has been renewed by fresh evidence of the insanity of the contemporary artworld—its degradation of the nature of art in both theory and practice. And we have been moved by a sense of profound injustice at the critical and public elevation of meaningless work to the status of art, while genuine artists (good friends among them) move on to other careers, or toil away unknown, their work unrecognized except by a few private collectors.

No amount of personal commitment could have enabled us to complete this study, however, without the support of the countless individuals who, over the past decade, have lent their time, ideas, and energy. To begin, we owe thanks to Tibor Machan, for his early encouragement to expand our *Aristos* series into a book, and for his recommendation of Mary Sirridge and Randall Dipert (who has become our friend) as philosophers in the academy who might offer comments and suggestions. Our thanks to them, in turn, and to Norris Clarke, Stephen Cox, Douglas Den Uyl, Murray Franck, John Hospers, and the late Ronald Merrill, and, for their comments on the series. We are also grateful to Victor Niederhoffer for his generous support of a colloquium to critique that first tentative effort of ours, and to Jurgis Brakas, Murray Franck, John Gillis, Randall Dipert, Peter Saint-André, and George Walsh, for their thought-provoking participation in the colloquium; and to Randy Dipert for later giving us the delightful opportunity to discuss Rand's work with his esthetics class at the U.S. Military Academy, and for his continued interest and support.

Additional thanks, for assistance with research and background materials, to Erin Dunkerly, Susan Kleinman, Art Smith, Katharina Strobel, Chris Tame, Anthony Teets, Wilfried van Damme, and especially to George Kline for his generous provision of information relevant to a possible link between Rand and the work of Hippolyte Taine.

For reading and commenting upon parts of the manuscript, we are grateful to Iris Bell, Christine Bluestein, Nathaniel Branden, Philippe Chamy, Frank Cooper, Randy Dipert, David Kelley, Kenneth Livingston, Diana McDonell, Douglas Rasmussen, and Barry Vacker.

Iraida Botshteyn, Sandra Giasulla, Max Kamhi, Olivia Czink Kamhi, Isobel Kleinman, and Hila Ratzabi helped with hours of word-processing. And Paul Kelley was a stalwart assistant during the harried final stages of readying copy for the typesetter. Without his help we could never have met our deadline. All their efforts are greatly appreciated.

Two academic readers—Stephen Cox and Chris Matthew Sciabarra—have offered steady support, as well as reading and offering suggestions on virtually the entire manuscript. We especially benefited from Steve's incisive, often questioning, remarks, which prodded us to think more deeply on the points he challenged. And Chris's encyclopedic knowledge of Rand's life and work has been an invaluable resource, not to mention the countless philosophic discussions we have had with him or his frequent exhortations to us not to weaken in our enterprise. Our third principal reader, Don Hauptman, helped us to clarify our language and thought in innumerable instances. The comments of all three readers leavened our task with humor, always much appreciated. Like most writers, however, we have not always heeded our readers' advice, and so must take full responsibility for any errors in fact or substance or lapses in style.

To Don and Chris, above all, we owe unbounded gratitude for support in countless ways. More constant and generous friends one could not find.

To our editor, David Ramsay Steele, our warmest thanks for his candor, patience, good counsel, and just plain hard work in shepherding this project through its long, and sometimes painful, gestation and birth.

Thanks are also owed to Barbara Branden, for use of the Ayn Rand photo on the cover, and for her encouragement. Special appreciation is due to our friend Iris Bell, for her patience and sense of style in designing a handsome book and cover.

To the loyal subscribers of *Aristos*, who have suffered long periods of suspended publication, our thanks for their unflagging interest in our work over the years; and our deep gratitude to those who have generously supported the Aristos Foundation, keeping our "gutsy" little journal afloat, and helping to cover the costs of writing this book.

Our lives and work have been enriched by the friendship of sculpture scholar Beatrice Proske, whose Yankee wit and wisdom continue to inspire us in this her hundred-and-first year.

In addition, Jacques Barzun's generous words of encouragement and advice over the past decade have spurred us on, as has his exemplary model of scholarship informed by deep humanity and solid sense. The influence of his ideas is apparent throughout this book.

Collaboration, especially of the spousal variety, is often fraught with difficulty. At many moments we were reminded of the actress Lynn Fontanne's rejoinder, when an interviewer, referring to her lifelong collaboration with her husband and fellow actor, Alfred Lunt, asked if she had ever contemplated divorce. "Homicide, frequently. Divorce, never," was her swift reply. Two friends, in particular—Edna and Larry Gabler—saved us from pursuing either of these dire alternatives. Their friendship and confidence in us, individually and jointly—not to mention the good times we have shared—have meant more than they can imagine.

Finally, our gratitude to the many family members and friends who have patiently borne our frequent ill humor and benign neglect. A saddening aspect of having taken so long to complete this work is that two people who were very dear to us will not see it—Dick Disbrow, whose friendship, homespun wisdom, and staunch support we sorely miss, and Jack Avruch, to whom the terms stepfather or father-in-law scarcely do justice. Happily, "Mom" (Ida Marder Avruch) is still with us, and to her we dedicate this book, with love.

Louis Torres
Michelle Marder Kamhi

My father, Allah, was the first person I knew who lived in the world of ideas, though I was scarcely appreciative of this as a child. And my mother, "Mimi," though untutored herself, always encouraged my intellectual pursuits to the end of her life. My gratitude also to my sister and brother, Maggie and Ed, for their constant love and support. Two teachers, in particular, inspired me to pursue the humanities: my high school English teacher, Beatrice van Campen, for whom I wrote my first serious paper, on the work of John Steinbeck; and the philosopher Houston Peterson at Rutgers University, who taught me to think philosophically, as well as to savor the pleasures of reading great fiction aloud.

L.T.

To my long-deceased father, Maurice "Macy" Marder, as well as to my mother, I owe everlasting gratitude for educational opportunities they never had themselves. And deep thanks to the teachers who believed in me and encouraged me to believe in my own abilities, in particular: Leroy Haley, an English teacher at Hunter College High School who taught me that being contrarian requires accepting the consequences; John A. Kouwenhoven, who never tolerated facile answers; and Howard McP. Davis, whose introduction to the humanistic values of the art of the Italian Renaissance was a transforming experience. Finally, to Max and Olivia, thank you for love and support in what often seemed to all of us an interminable undertaking.

M.M.K.

Introduction

Early in the twentieth century, for the first time in history, works purporting to be art were created that were not, in fact, art at all—bearing little or no resemblance to the painting, sculpture, literature, music, or dance that had come before. Whereas art had always integrated and made sense of human experience, this new work was invariably fragmented, disorienting, and unintelligible, often intentionally so. In many respects, it was more akin to madness, or to fraud, than to art.[1]

Such work did not lack its critics.[2] In a remarkably short time, however, new forms such as abstract painting and sculpture, and "experimental" work in the other arts, gained virtually complete acceptance among members of the arts establishment. By the end of the century, most critics and scholars had come to regard the legitimacy of every conceivable new form of art as beyond question, while "traditional" contemporary work was relegated to nearly total neglect[3]—a trend that has continued unabated into the new millennium.

As increasingly bizarre alleged art forms have proliferated at a dizzying rate, so has a body of impenetrable critical and scholarly literature professing to explain and justify them. Nonetheless, a substantial segment of the public, even among those repeatedly exposed to this work and to the arguments on its behalf, have failed to embrace it. While some merely express confusion and frustration, others are skeptical that there is anything in it to be understood or appreciated, and still others reject it outright, considering it beyond the pale of art. In the controversy that has ensued between experts and the public on this issue, we maintain that the ordinary person's view, based as it is largely on common sense, is the correct one. A principal goal of this book is to provide that common-sense view with the theoretical justification it warrants.

Traditional Meanings of the Term "Art"

To understand the source of the present chaos in the artworld,[4] it is helpful to know something of the history of both the concept and the term *art*. First, it is important to recognize that a term, or word, is not the same thing as a concept.[5] Like most terms, "art" has, over time, come to refer to a number of different, though related, concepts—which dictionary entries indicate as separately numbered definitions. Normally, the context in which the term appears makes clear which of its possible concepts is intended.

In its original and broadest sense, the term *art* (derived from the Latin *ars, artis*) dates back to antiquity. Synonymous with the Greek term *technê*, it refers to the concept of "skill," "discipline," or "technique." In that sense, it has long been applied to a wide range of human activities and products, from the "art of warfare" and the "art of medicine" to the "mechanical arts" and the "liberal arts." In all cases, it connotes an ability acquired by careful study and applied to a particular undertaking. This idea of "skill" is fundamental to the concept of *art* and is implicit in all the legitimate uses of the term.

The narrower use of the term *art* with which we are concerned is of much more recent origin, dating only from the late nineteenth century, when it began to be applied to the so-called *fine arts*, either collectively or individually. The term "fine arts," too, is of relatively recent date, having been coined only in the mid-eighteenth century, in reference to painting, sculpture, literature, music, dance, and drama.[6] When the ordinary person uses the term *art* without a qualifier, this is usually the sense that is intended. Moroever, it is this concept which the "avant-garde"[7] attempts to appropriate, for the benefits it bestows, while simultaneously undermining it.

Like all concepts, this concept of *art* did not arise in a vacuum. It was not a mental construct divorced from real experience, but developed out of a long tradition of observing similarities between the existing art forms, as well as differences between them and other human products and activities. Contrary to the frequent claim that such a generic concept of art originated only in the West in the eighteenth century, it has had a long genesis, dating back to the ancient Greek concept of the "mimetic (or imitative) arts." It is clearly implicit in the numerous comparisons between poetry and painting, song and dance, painting and sculpture, that have occurred in the writing of poets and philosophers since antiquity. The work of Aristotle, for example, is replete with comparisons of this kind. Nor are such observations limited to the West. They are also common in the thought of other cultures, just as the major art forms themselves are universal.

The primary significance of any concept is its "ostensive" meaning—that is, the particular things it refers to. Since the eighteenth-century, however, Western theories about the nature of art have tended to obscure this principle. In attempting to identify the essential qualities distinctive to art, theorists lost sight of the original referents of the term, and of their complex totality, and focused instead on certain attributes abstracted from the whole, such as "beauty" or "expression." In so doing, they ignored the attribute of *mimesis*, whose relationship to art they did not fully appreciate, though it was fundamental to the original concept.[8] This led, in turn, to their expanding the concept to include referents it had not originally subsumed—first and foremost, architecture, as we argue in Chapter 10. Though the conceptual breakdown began innocently enough as a direct consequence of mistaken theories, it is now exploited by an artworld seeking to further a variety of extra-artistic ends, from spurious political agendas to a desire for prestige and financial gain, however unearned.

What the Ordinary Person Thinks

Despite continual efforts on the part of alleged experts to "educate" the public on the merits of avant-garde, or "nontraditional," work, the majority of ordinary people remain unpersuaded. From time to time, this mostly silent majority makes its voice heard in letters to the editors of major newspapers and magazines. As one letter-writer protests: "A fundamental problem with 'art' in the late twentieth century [is that] we have, too permissively, accepted everyone's self-declaration of career as 'artist' at face value."[9] Another observes: "To refer to the childish banalities of Andy Warhol as 'art' illustrates conclusively how far the level of true art in the twentieth century has fallen."[10] In the words of yet another: "New music ([with] its total aural alienation of audiences, young and old). . . . has failed the listener. It is therefore ridiculous . . . to suggest that pre-concert lectures and plenty of program notes are going to correct that failure. (If a composer has to explain his work in print, he has already failed as a composer)."[11] Commenting on one of the Whitney Museum of American Art's controversial biennial exhibitions, a disgruntled art lover writes: "This vulgar collection of junk is an insult to museumgoers. Bundles of newspapers lying on the floor in three places with labels nearby finally kindled my irritation to the point that I demanded my admission money back. . . . This exhibition had nothing to do with art."[12]

Regarding postmodernist work, another observer notes that, while it "may at times be difficult to judge the fine borderline where art ceases to be what it claims to be and instead becomes but a commodity of the marketplace . . . the displacement of all artistic sensibility by rhetoric might be considered one reliable guideline."[13]

The *Truisms* of "conceptual artist" Jenny Holzer—which consist of banal inscriptions such as "Raise Boys and Girls the Same," "What Urge Will Save Us Now That Sex Won't," and "Boredom Makes You Do Crazy Things"[14]— provoke the following judgment: "Her name is Jenny Hoaxer, not Holzer. Give her credit: she even took in the Guggenheim [Museum]. Inscribing [her words] on marble benches does not elevate them above contradictory, ungrammatical, . . . gibberish. At best, . . . Holzer is a frustrated preacher. This is art?"[15]

Finally, a reader of *Investment Vision* comments ironically: "It was stated [in a previous issue] that Brice Marden's 'Untitled' sold for a record $1.1 million. My issue was defective: it showed a rectangle of two shades of mud divided by a straight line."[16]

The Cartoonists

A clear reflection of the public's attitude is the frequent derision of both modernist and postmodernist work in cartoons and comic strips in the popular press. "If you have to ask what it means," says a bearded painter angrily to a meek-looking couple standing before the inscrutable abstraction on his canvas, "you can't afford it."[17] Another painter confides to a female companion viewing his abstract work in progress: "It has no meaning yet. The critics will take care of that."[18] In another cartoon, a prosperous-looking couple visiting a museum are standing before a huge canvas covered with spidery lines and chaotic blotches; while the wife earnestly seeks enlightenment in the catalogue, the husband barks: "I know what he's trying to say—he's trying to say that he can't paint worth a damn!"[19] In yet another, a frumpy pair of museum-goers confront a vast black circle on a white canvas. While the wife stares at the painting, the husband, seeking enlightenment from the wall label, announces: "It's called, 'Humongous Dot.'"[20] Still another cartoon depicts two men with briefcases gazing at a large, abstract, riveted-metal sculpture in an outdoor plaza; a live bird is perched atop the piece. One of the men says to the other: "I had hoped we could get rid of that eyesore, but now I notice it's home to a spotted owl."[21]

While abstract painting and sculpture are the most frequent butt of ridicule, postmodernist work also comes under fire. A cartoon in the *Chronicle of Higher Education* depicts a defendant and his lawyer before a judge, with the caption: "My client stole what he thought was merely an old automobile tire, and used it as such, unaware that it was—as the museum now claims— a major work of art!"[22]

The literary avant-garde, too, is a target. In a trenchant cartoon that appeared in *Punch* several decades ago, a rapt theater audience watches two cleaning women scrubbing the stage, one of whom pauses to inquire of the other: "Shouldn't we tell them the play's been over for an hour and a half?"[23]

Comic strips can of course go beyond the simple situations and one-line humor of cartoons. Bill Watterson, creator of the widely syndicated "Calvin and Hobbes," regularly seized the opportunity to satirize and deflate the art-world's pretensions. In one episode, six-year-old Calvin explains his new abstract snow sculpture to his imaginary tiger-friend Hobbes: "This piece is about the inadequacy of traditional imagery and symbols to convey meaning in today's world. By abandoning representationalism, I'm free to express myself with pure form. Specific interpretation gives way to a more visceral response."[24]

The Journalists

Prominent journalists also frequently call the artworld to task for its indiscriminate promotion of every form of would-be art. In a *Wall Street Journal* op-ed commentary on the National Endowment for the Arts, for instance, Irving Kristol, co-editor of the journal *Public Interest*, sharply censures the "'arts community,' consisting of artists themselves but also and especially . . . [of] critics, art professors, art dealers [and] museum directors" for its embrace of every novelty, however outrageous, and for its "contempt for 'art' in any traditional sense of the term." Kristol also criticizes the media, for reverentially deferring to "anything declared to be 'art'" by such experts.[25]

Columnist George Will similarly laments, in *Newsweek*, that "nowadays almost anything may, without serious challenge, be said to be a work of art." He further observes: "Today the question 'Is it art' is considered an impertinence and even a precursor of 'censorship,' understood as a refusal to subsidize. Today art is whatever the 'arts community' says it is, and membership in that community involves no exacting entrance requirements."[26]

In an article entitled "Remember the Fine Arts?" nationally syndicated columnist William Rusher observes that many twentieth-century artists have aimed "to shock viewers with a brand-new vision of 'reality'—or even to abandon the depiction of reality altogether, in favor of pure abstraction. The result has been to leave a great many well-meaning people unable to relate to most twentieth-century art. I include myself in that unhappy number. I have always enjoyed the great dynastic arts of China . . . and . . . the great Dutch and Italian masters. But most 'modern' (or postmodern) art simply doesn't speak to me."[27]

So, too, economist and syndicated columnist Thomas Sowell writes: "For centuries art, music and literature have been treasured for the grace, beauty or exaltation they have brought into people's lives. But add the word 'modern'. . . and these things are far more likely to produce puzzlement, boredom or disgust."[28]

R. Emmett Tyrrell, Jr., editor of *The American Spectator*, refers to photographers Andres Serrano and the late Robert Mapplethorpe as "artistic blanks" whose fame is due to "political clout masterfully applied." In Tyrrell's unequivocal judgment: "Mere naughtiness in our age sells, but it is not art."[29]

In his column in *U. S. News and World Report*, senior editor John Leo exposes the fraudulence of "victim art"—the sort of politically motivated, artistically empty work that depends on eliciting pity for the alleged oppression or the illness of the "artist." In his view: "We have reached the point where almost any victim complaint is passed off as art." Among other examples, he cites "a large puddle of plastic vomit" by a feminist "outraged about female eating disorders in an oppressive patriarchal culture," exhibited at a Whitney Museum Biennial.[30]

Pulitzer prize-winning columnist and humorist Dave Barry begins one of his syndicated pieces by observing: "Like many members of the uncultured, Cheez-It-consuming public, I am not good at grasping modern art. I'm the type of person who will stand in front of a certified masterpiece that looks . . . like a big black square, and quietly think: 'Maybe the actual painting is on the other side'. . . . I especially have a problem with modernistic sculptures, the kind where you . . . cannot be sure whether you're looking at a work of art or a crashed alien spacecraft."[31]

Finally, *Boston Globe* columnist Jeff Jacoby repeatedly excoriates the National Endowment for the Arts (NEA) for subsidizing offensive and spurious contemporary work. Observing that the endowment's "partisans . . . maintain that art is supposed to 'challenge our most sacred values,' that the artist's role is to 'shatter preconceptions' and 'provoke society,'" he argues that such definitions "reduce the idea of art to little more than self-indulgent rudeness. It is a sign of how badly the currency of contemporary culture has been debased that so many artists and arts bureaucrats insist that debauchery and degeneracy are compatible with art—insist, even, that they *are* art."[32] On another occasion, he notes that "NEA handouts have encouraged scabrous pseudo-artists to keep churning out 'art' that the public doesn't like and would never willingly support."[33]

Prime-Time Television

Even more remarkable than such opinions rendered in the print media is the position taken by Morley Safer on the CBS network newsmagazine *60 Minutes*. In September 1993, Safer reported a segment entitled "Yes . . . But Is It Art?"—in which he exposed the fraudulence and pretension of much of the work promoted by today's artworld.[34] Covering a sale at the prestigious auction house of Sotheby's, a sardonic Safer commented on items ranging from Cy Twombly's *Untitled*, "a canvas of scrawls done with the wrong end of a paint brush" (which sold for $2,145,000),[35] to a work by Jeff Koons consisting of three real basketballs in a real fish tank, which sold for $150,000—"giving [as Safer quipped] new meaning to 'slam dunk'." Koons explained, in part: "This is an ultimate state of being. . . . I was giving a definition of life and death. This is the eternal. That is what life is like also, after-death."

After deriding Koons's "artspeak," Safer observed that such work "would be worthless junk without the hype of the dealers and, even more important, the approval of the critics," whose impenetrable discourse "might as well be in Sanskrit." As could be expected, Safer brought down the wrath of the art establishment; and a heated debate followed in the media during the succeeding weeks.[36]

Early in 1994, a brilliantly satirical episode of the popular CBS sit-com *Murphy Brown* aired which was clearly inspired by the *60 Minutes* segment and its aftermath.[37] In one scene, the show's eponymous TV anchorwoman faces off against "art" experts on a public television talk show (a scene modeled on Safer's appearance on the *Charlie Rose* show), and heaps scorn on a work aptly entitled *Commode-ity*, which is simply a toilet affixed to a wall. (*Commode-ity* is no more bizarre, of course, than the real-life commodities of Robert Gober, whose "artworks" consisting of plumbing fixtures had been featured on the *60 Minutes* segment—recalling the urinal that the notorious early modernist Marcel Duchamp had presented in 1917 as a "readymade" artwork he entitled *Fountain*.[38])In another scene, Murphy demonstrated the absurdity of abstract expressionist art, by successfully passing off as the mature work of an unknown artist a painting by her eighteen-month-old son— a scene that might well have been inspired by an event that occurred in Manchester, England, and was widely reported on in the British and American press.[39]

The Ubiquitous Question: "But Is It Art?"

The pervasiveness of public skepticism regarding what passes for "contemporary art" is further suggested by the frequency with which the question "But is it art?" (or variants thereof) crops up in headlines or in book or lecture titles—pertaining to virtually anything, from "conceptual art" to pottery, tattoos, and furniture.[40] That the *60 Minutes* segment cited above was entitled "Yes . . . But Is It Art?" is not surprising, therefore—though it is somewhat atypical, since Safer's answer was clearly in the negative. More often, the crucial question is merely posed rhetorically, as if anticipating a skeptical response to the "difficult" or bizarre work under discussion. Thus the book *But Is It Art? The Spirit of Art as Activism* extols work that "refram[es traditional] notions of the meaning of art itself" and "agitates for progressive social change."[41]

Headline variations on the theme "But is it art?" have even appeared in the business section of the *New York Times*—as in "If It's Commercial, Is It Really Art?" The writer concludes that what is most interesting about the graphic design field is "the ways in which it confounds conventional notions of what art is."[42]

Predictably, the phenomenon of "furniture art" inspires frequent headline equivocation. Examples include "Art or Furniture? A Little of Both" and "If a Chair Is a Work of Art, Can You Still Sit on It?" An article reporting on an exhibition of furniture by an "influential and irreverent" Italian architect is captioned "Sottsass' Oversize Collection: Is It Furniture or Art?" According to the reporter (not an art critic), the pieces in question "are sure to add life to [the] debate over whether furniture can be art." Yet there is little debate in the article itself, and the reporter concludes that "the prices put them in the class of artworks rather than furniture."[43]

Pottery, tattoos, and furniture as art? How about *stuff*? As in "Just Stuff. Just Art?"—about a museum exhibition of the ordinary furnishings and everyday clutter on loan from an anonymous New Yorker's apartment: items ranging from his refrigerator and kitchen utensils to his sneakers, washed but "grungy" T-shirts and underpants, and a spray bottle of tile cleanser.[44] Or, how about *dead meat*? As in "Is It Art, or Just Dead Meat?"—a color-illustrated feature article about Damien Hirst, the prize-winning "conceptual artist" whose installations of animals preserved in formaldehyde were included in the recent *Sensation* exhibition, which created a public furor at the Brooklyn Museum of Art in New York City.

A refreshing exception to the foregoing headlines appeared in the London *Times* a few years ago: the caption "*Art—Or Just a Hollow Sham?*" The more pointed question "Has the Tate [Gallery] pulled off a gigantic hoax on the public?" appears above the headline. The article reports on a "conceptual" art work entitled *Mneme*, occupying three rooms, the first of which contains a display case "filled with condensation." In the second room, a visitor walks through suspended sailcloth, then takes an elevator to a seventy-foot-long gallery, empty except for a hand-turned record player, through which a human voice emits phonetic sounds, accompanied by the howling and whistling of wind. The meaning of it all? According to the Tate, the work creates "an experience of relationships which are sought rather than grasped."[45]

The Experts Speak

The artworld's obfuscation of the nature of art is especially apparent in the purportedly expert views of art historians and critics.

The Art Historians

Recognizing the gulf separating the public and the artworld on the issue of what art is, authors of major art historical surveys and popular art books in recent decades have often begun their exposition rather self-consciously with the question, What is art? or variations thereon. H. W. Janson, for example, introduced his *History of Art* (long regarded as the standard survey of the subject) by envisioning the ordinary man asking "Why is this supposed to be art?" He then lamented the "fateful" belief among the uninitiated that "there are, *or ought to be*, exact rules by which we can tell art from what is not art."[46] The Introduction for the book's third through fifth editions (1986–1995), revised by his son, Anthony Janson, begins by directly asking "What is art?" and then continues: "Few questions provoke such heated debate, yet provide so few satisfactory answers."[47]

The noted Renaissance scholar Frederick Hartt, too, began his survey, *Art: A History of Painting, Sculpture, Architecture* (now in its fourth edition), by asking "What is art?" Much of the answer offered in his Introduction, entitled "The Nature of Art," attempted to justify modernist art—in particular, abstract painting and sculpture. Hartt's first edition, for example, included this somewhat patronizing advice:

> I clearly remember periods in my youth when works of . . . contemporary art seemed remote, strange, and even repulsive. It is easy for me to put myself in the place of today's student, who may at first experience many of the same reactions. Even after many years of looking at contemporary art, I found it difficult to accept immediately the work of [the abstract expressionist] Jackson Pollock. . . . . *The only cure for hostile reactions is constant exposure, study, and analysis.*[48]

For Hartt, as for other art historians (and the entire art establishment), the term *contemporary art* is equated, misleadingly, with nontraditional work—that is, with avant-gardism.[49] Thus he claimed that people make art today because, in large part, they enjoy "the triumph of translating their sensory impressions of the visible world into a *personal language* of lines, surfaces, forms, and colors"[50]—a statement clearly alluding to the inscrutable character of abstract painting and sculpture. So, too, he virtually ignored the requirement of objective content and meaning with respect to contemporary work, although he referred to "the forces in [the] human environment" that *earlier* artists reflected in their work.

In a similar vein, the eminent art historian Ernst Gombrich begins his survey *The Story of Art* (now in its sixteenth edition) with the rather dubious assertion: "There is really no such thing as Art. There are only artists." He goes on to reassure the reader that there is "no harm" in calling something art, "as long as we keep in mind that such a word may mean very different things in different times and places."[51]

Finally, in a book itself entitled *What Is Art?* (not a history of art, strictly speaking, but rather a book on art appreciation) John Canaday—an art historian who taught at various universities and also served as art critic for the *New York Times* for nearly two decades—states at the outset: "The only way to begin this book is to make clear that we are not going to arrive at any single answer to the question, What is art?" Consistent with that view, Canaday concludes the book by observing: "The only answer to the question, What is art? is that art, *whatever its definition*, is an inexhaustible enrichment of life."[52] Not surprisingly, all these writers treat avant-garde work as an essential part of the art historical continuum, while they give short shrift to so-called traditional figurative painters and sculptors of the late-nineteenth and twentieth centuries.[53] Moreover, none of them offers what the question What is art? implicitly requires, and what the reader might naturally expect: *an objective definition.*

As unsatisfactory as these standard art histories are with respect to the twentieth century, they do at least offer a reasonable survey of earlier art, presenting key monuments of Western painting and sculpture, and often interpreting the works in relation to the salient values of their respective cultures.[54] Yet even the transmission of this artistic legacy is now being compromised. Revisionist art historians who dominate the profession are completely "rethinking" the standard survey of Western art, introducing "experimental alternatives" which focus on political issues of "gender, race, and sexual preference" and are corrupted by the linguistic distortions of decontructionism.[55] In "reconsidering" the canon of works covered in both textbooks and course curricula, these academics are questioning not only "the traditional hierarchy of the arts" but also, more astonishingly, "the distinction between art and ordinary 'imagery.'"

By eliminating the "elitist esthetic sensibilities" reflected in the standard surveys by Janson, Gombrich, and Hartt, the new textbooks presumably will be more appropriate to "a postmodern world characterized by aesthetic relativism and cultural pluralism."[56] One such text, Marilyn Stokstad's *Art History*, purports to be "inclusive and comprehensive . . . [and] determinedly even-handed": "Arts previously ignored or given minor accreditation—

pottery, weaving and textiles, jewelry, enamelwork, armour and other metal-work—are detailed alongside the traditional arts of painting, sculpture, and architecture."[57]

What other assumptions underlie the "advanced practices of art history" today? As one writer indicates, the belief that some works are "more deserving and rewarding of attention" than others is suspect; the notion of a "common culture" is a "chimera"; and chronology is "a kind of machinery that can be likened to, or [is an] actual expression . . . of, the quest for (male) sexual release." Masterpieces—the "*so-called* key monuments of art history"—are deemed worthy of study only for what they reveal about "art history's unacknowledged agendas and investments." A prime concern of art history should instead be with "the interpretation of culture in contemporary politics."[58]

Nothing the revisionists have yet conceived is more startling, or more patently absurd, however, than the recommendation that art historians should now concern themselves directly with "*images that are not art*"; that they should "question" (i.e., challenge or disregard) "the distinction between art and ordinary imagery"—the very distinction that lies, logically, at the base of their discipline. Yet such a recommendation is developed at excruciating length in the December 1995 issue of *Art Bulletin*. The author, James Elkins, argues that "the interests of art history" should be expanded to include "images principally intended . . . to convey information," from graphs, maps, and official documents, to astrological charts, technical and engineering drawings, and "scientific images of all sorts, . . . in other words, the sum total of visual images that are not obviously either artworks or religious artifacts." In Elkins's view, all these non-art images "are fully expressive, and capable of *as great and nuanced a range of meaning as any work of fine art.*" In conclusion, he advises his fellow art historians against "preserving the differences between the histories of art, science, and mathematics," and advocates, instead, "writing the history of *images* rather than of art."[59]

The Critics

Rare is the critic today who dares to suggest that a given work does not qualify as art.[60] What is the fundamental assumption shared by the majority of critics today? To discover this, one need only turn to the arts pages of the *New York Times*. Roberta Smith, for example, has candidly declared that she cut her "art-critical eye-teeth" on the dictum "If an artist says it's art, it's art."[61] So, too, Jack Anderson subscribes to the admittedly "extreme" view that "dances are dances and ballets are ballets simply because people who call themselves choreographers say they are."[62] Another writer, Rita Reif, cites art historian Robert Rosenblum, a leading twentieth-century specialist, as an authority for the opinion that (as she puts it) "if an artist makes it, it's art, regardless of the artist's intentions."[63] In the view of Grace Glueck, something is a work of art if it is "intended as art, presented as such, and . . . judged to be art by those qualified in such matters."[64]

In other words, *anything* can be art—if a reputed artist (or other expert) *says* it is.

Need for a Valid Theory and Definition of Art

As Jacques Barzun suggested two decades ago, the "incessant verbalizing" about art, far from clarifying the present confusion, has only beclouded it further, because art is now "an institution without a theory. No coherent thought exists as to its aim or *raison d'être*."[65] Moreover, the lack of a consistent, objective view of what art is, and of what purpose it serves, has compromised the authority of would-be custodians of art, from art critics and historians to curators and museum directors—not to mention their counterparts in music, literature, and the performing arts.

By the middle of the twentieth century, when modernist trends were well established in all the arts, a pervasive lack of critical standards was already evident. It prompted the philosopher Eliseo Vivas to charge that "contemporary American criticism suffers from a serious defect: it ignores, sometimes truculently, the need for a systematic philosophy of art." What the enterprise of criticism requires from philosophy, Vivas stressed, is a clear idea of such underlying issues as "the nature of art, its relation to other modes of activity, . . . and its function." His essay was aptly entitled "The Objective Basis of Criticism."[66]

What Vivas complained of nearly half a century ago, holds even more true today, as we have seen. Because contemporary critics and scholars lack a proper theoretical foundation, they compromise the validity of their judgments as to artistic merit, and render their opinions arbitrary and subjective. Since they cannot discriminate between "art" and "non-art," they cannot be relied upon to discriminate properly between "good" art and "bad." If a critical judgment is based on a mistaken notion of the nature of art, as distinct from that of other human endeavors, it necessarily forfeits its claim to respect or consideration.

Those who deplore the present trends in the arts may nonetheless doubt that a *theoretical* understanding of art is called for—much less a formal definition. Even a discriminating critic such as John Simon (who reviews theater for *New York* magazine and film for *National Review*), for example, has expressed a fundamental suspicion of "theory." "I don't believe in theory in any field in the arts," he has unequivocally stated. "If there were one, it would be there only to be cast aside." When Simon explained his approach to critical writing to an interviewer, however, a number of operative esthetic principles did emerge—among them, the following: (1) "all art must address itself to central human concerns"; (2) art should "alert, sensitize, awaken" us to something we were not aware of before; and (3) "artistic representation doesn't ignore reality [but rather] uses it as a starting point; literal reality should be included [in art] but should also be transcended."[67] No critic can function without such guiding premises, implicit or explicit. And a theory is simply a coherent, integrated set of premises. The question is not whether a critic bases his judgments on premises of some kind but whether those premises are valid and coherent.

The Default of Philosophy

As Vivas emphasized, the task of clarifying *what art is* properly falls neither to artists nor even to critics or art historians, but to *philosophers*. The roots of the twentieth-century chaos and disintegration in the arts lie in philosophic assumptions. Although the critics' statements we have cited regarding the identity of art may seem patently illogical from a common-sense viewpoint, they are directly traceable to comparable notions in the philosophic literature.

In a study of recent attempts to define art, Stephen Davies argues, for example, that Marcel Duchamp's "readymade" *Fountain* should be regarded as a work of art "even if he did not make the urinal he appropriated in creating that work." Why? Because

> art historians and critics talk about the piece; it is constantly pictured and referred to in books on the history of modern art and in courses on recent art history. Moreover, artists have been influenced by Duchamp's readymades and frequently allude to them, not only in their manifestos but also in their own artworks. In brief, *Fountain* and its kin are treated as artworks (indeed, as important artworks). . . . It is implausible to think that . . . [one] could seriously deny [their] impact . . . on the theory, history, and practice of art.[68]

This statement, of course, sounds remarkably like critic Grace Glueck's contention, cited above, that something is a work of art if it is "intended as art, presented as such, and . . . judged to be art by those qualified in such matters."

Such views appear to represent the dominant tendency within the profession—as indicated in a 1993 position paper presented to the American Council of Learned Societies by a representative of the American Society for

Aesthetics. According to that statement, two "seemingly intractable" central issues pose a threat to the very "utility, status, and integrity" of esthetics as a philosophic discipline. First, the central question of esthetics—What is art?—is regarded as "increasingly frustrating as the energies of artists and would-be artists are directed in increasingly *unconventional* ways" (emphasis ours). Second, an equally "intractable" question is "whether any satisfactory account of art must be generalizable across all [art forms], or whether the discussion of art may or must always be art-specific."[69] In other words, can one speak about "art" at all, or only about the individual art forms? What, if anything, do the various art forms have in common? Or is it futile and inappropriate to use *art* as a generic term? In short, having failed to define art objectively, even in terms of its proper referents, philosophers of art now find themselves doubting the very validity of the concept.

Ayn Rand's Theory of Art

In marked contrast to the prevailing relativism and subjectivism of twentieth-century art theory and criticism, the philosopher-novelist Ayn Rand (1905–1982), best known as the author of *The Fountainhead* and *Atlas Shrugged*, proposed a uniquely objective esthetic theory—one that provides compelling answers to the reputedly intractable questions cited above. Between 1965 and 1971, she published a series of brief essays setting forth the basic principles of her philosophy of art, defining the essential nature and function of art in relation to the conceptual nature of the human mind.

In one important respect, Rand's concept of *what* art is—in the sense of *which entities the concept properly comprises*—is a traditional one, largely consistent with ideas of the "fine arts" that have had wide currency since the eighteenth century. For her, much as for Tolstoy and for the nineteenth-century philosophers in general (and for most ordinary people today), "art" means primarily painting, sculpture, music, and literature (fiction, poetry, and drama).[70] For her, too, art is essentially mimetic, albeit in a highly selective and often stylized manner.

Although Rand offers a strong justification for what are often termed "traditional values" (as opposed to modernism and postmodernism) in the arts, her defense of the traditional art forms, unlike that generally offered by cultural conservatives,[71] does not rest on the mere authority of the past. Indeed, she properly regarded such a defense as anathema in a free society.[72] Nor does she ever characterize the principal art forms as "traditional." Instead, she seeks to understand the identity of art in relation to man's nature as a thinking and valuing being. She explains *why* the major art forms came into being and why they have persisted in virtually every human culture—why they are the only forms consonant with essential features of human nature, both physical and psychological.

Rand not only sheds light on why the various art forms exist, she makes clear what it is that they have in common, and she offers an objective generic definition of art. Moreover, she offers a psychologically astute account of *how* works of art function, both for their creators and for others. She makes clear that the "traditional" art forms are not arbitrary conventions (as modernists and postmodernists have often argued), but are a natural development, rooted in the requirements of human psychology and physiology.

While Rand retains the traditional classification of art—as well as the idea that the arts are essentially mimetic in nature—she rejects the traditional view that the primary purpose of art is to afford pleasure and convey value through the creation of *beauty*, which she does not regard as a defining attribute. In her view, the primary purpose of art is much broader: it is the meaningful objectification of whatever is metaphysically important to man. For Rand, every art work—whether of painting, sculpture, literature, music, or dance— is a "selective re-creation of reality" that serves to objectify, in an integrated form, significant aspects of its creator's basic "sense of life."

Further, Rand holds that the distinctive character of each of the major branches of art derives from—is determined by—a specific mode of human perception and cognition. As a consequence, she argues that, technological innovations notwithstanding, no truly new categories of art are possible, only recombinations and variants of the primary forms which have existed since prehistory.[73]

According to Rand, art serves a vital psychological need that is at once cognitive and emotional. Only through art, in her view, can man summon his values into full conscious focus, with the clarity and emotional immediacy of direct perception. For Rand, then, art is a unique means of integrating the physical and psychological aspects of human existence. Thus she not only identifies what art *is*, in terms of essential characteristics, she also provides an enriched appreciation of the importance of art in human life. Moreover, in so doing, she makes clear why much of what the artworld has promoted as the art of the past hundred years is, by objective standards, a perversion of the very concept.

Rand's esthetic theory forms an integral part of her total philosophic system, which she termed *Objectivism*—a neo-Aristotelian philosophy of individualism based on reason and an objective view of reality.[74] As an integrative thinker, she considered all aspects of human existence to be interrelated; and her thought encompassed all the major branches of philosophy: "*metaphysics*— the study of existence as such or, in Aristotle's words, of 'being qua being'"; "*epistemology*, the theory of knowledge, which studies man's means of cognition"; "*ethics*, or morality, [which] defines a code of values to guide man's choices and actions"; "*politics*, which defines the principles of a proper social system"; and "*esthetics*, the study of art."[75]

Thus, the term *esthetics*, as Rand uses it, is synonymous with "the philosophy of art"; it does not mean "the study of beauty and related concepts," the much broader sense in which it has been generally understood. Her usage is not without precedent, however. The nineteenth-century German philosopher G. W. F. Hegel, for example, emphatically argued that the term be used to mean "the philosophy of (fine) art."[76] As we shall see, Rand's theory of art shares other important points of correspondence with earlier thinkers—most notably, Aristotle—although she integrates such views into an original totality, informed by a more accurate understanding of human cognition and emotion.

Owing to the integrated nature of Rand's philosophic system, her esthetic theory cannot be isolated from her answers to more fundamental philosophic questions: What is reality? What is knowledge? How does man acquire knowledge of reality? What is the relationship between consciousness and reality? mind and body? reason and emotion? How are concepts formed, and what is the role of definitions in human knowledge? What is the nature of "spiritual values," and why does man need them? As we shall note, every significant aspect of Rand's esthetic theory—from her definition of art to her analysis of art's essential function—is tied to her position on these fundamental questions.[77]

The Status of Rand Studies

As a thinker, Rand has attained a remarkably polarized status in contemporary culture. On one hand, her novels and collections of nonfiction essays have for decades attracted a large popular readership worldwide. In addition, her ideas have generated a multifaceted philosophic movement, which has had a discernible influence on political and economic thought in American culture at large. She is widely credited with substantially contributing to the revival of classical liberal thought in the past two decades, for example—a revival that has gained broad visibility and influence through such organizations as the Reason Foundation and the Cato Institute.[78]

On the other hand, Rand is still regarded with a mixture of suspicion and contempt by many intellectuals, including most academics. In truth, such negative feelings were, in large measure, mutual during her lifetime, for she began her career as a popular author and, like Tolstoy and other well-known Russian writers, she deliberately pursued her literary and philosophic goals from the position of an academic outsider.[79]

Herself born in Russia, in the first decade of the twentieth century, Rand spent her early youth in relative comfort and security, as the precocious eldest daughter of a bourgeois Jewish family. She then experienced the tumultuous years of the Bolshevik revolution, developing a deep revulsion for every form of collectivism, whether religious or secular—a conviction which subsequently alienated her from intellectuals on both the right and the left. Having resolved at an early age to become a writer, she attended the State Institute of Cinema Arts for two years after graduating from the University of Leningrad, where she had completed a three-year course combining historical and philosophical studies. In 1926, she emigrated to the United States, working in Hollywood—first as an extra, then as a writer of scenarios and screenplays—while she honed her command of English and her skills as a novelist.

Rand articulated her philosophy gradually, as she enhanced the scope and complexity of her fiction—from the anti-collectivist themes of her semi-autobiograpical first novel, *We the Living* (1936), and her dystopian short novel *Anthem* (1938), to what she characterized as her "projection of the ideal man" in *The Fountainhead* (1943) and *Atlas Shrugged* (1957). To fully concretize that ideal, and the conditions that would enable such a human being to flourish, Rand eventually outlined a complete philosophic system, which she first presented in a fictional context—as the sixty-page-long speech delivered toward the end of *Atlas Shrugged* by the novel's hero, John Galt. This passage subsequently formed the core of her first volume of strictly philosophic writings, *For the New Intellectual: The Philosophy of Ayn Rand* (1961), which also included a long introductory essay by her on the history of philosophy, and other philosophic excerpts from her fiction.

By the late 1950s, Rand was the center of a coterie of mostly youthful admirers who had been attracted to her ideas through her novels. With her approval, one of these disciples, Nathaniel Branden, with Barbara Branden (then his wife), formed an institute in his name to sponsor lectures and publications on Rand's philosophy. In 1962, *The Objectivist Newsletter*, edited by Rand and Nathaniel Branden, was founded, succeeded in 1965 by a small magazine, *The Objectivist*. Rand wrote the vast majority of her philosophic essays for these publications, aimed at an audience already familiar with and sympathetic to her ideas. When she subsequently reprinted the most important of the essays, in the several volumes of her collected nonfiction (including *The Romantic Manifesto*—her essays on art and literature), she did not revise them in any way for a wider audience. They are often polemical in tone, and give short shrift to the ideas of other thinkers, as we note in subsequent chapters.

Although Rand accepted invitations as a guest speaker on numerous college campuses in the 1960s (usually under student rather than faculty auspices), her status as an outsider never altered, for she was relentlessly and severely critical of the leftist tendencies of mainstream academic and intellectual thought. Both the polemical style of her presentation and the radical content of her philosophy set her apart. And, as we note in an article on the critical neglect of her esthetic theory,[80] political bias often distorted assessments of her work. Nevertheless, some aspects of Rand's philosophy were debated in scholarly journals even during her lifetime, and her ideas have begun to be dealt with in the academy. In part, this is due to the maturation of a new generation of scholars who have pursued advanced academic degrees, supplementing their university coursework with nonacademic study of Objectivism.[81] A number of them have entered the teaching ranks. Since Rand's death in 1982, her ideas have also begun to be included (if not always accurately interpreted) in widely used introductory philosophy textbooks and anthologies on ethics and politics.[82]

In the past five years, Rand studies have accelerated, owing largely to the work of Chris Matthew Sciabarra, a visiting scholar in the department of politics at New York University.[83] A major turning point was the publication, in 1995, of his *Ayn Rand: The Russian Radical* by Penn State Press. The first scholarly analysis of Rand's work, it illuminates the historical and intellectual context of her youth during Russia's Silver Age. Sciabarra persuasively argues that Rand adopted from the European philosophic tradition an integrative, dialectical approach, which she applied to the forging of a radically new individualist, libertarian philosophy. In 1999, Sciabarra co-edited, with Mimi Reisel Gladstein (Associate Dean of Liberal Arts at the University of Texas, El Paso), *Feminist Interpretations of Ayn Rand*, in Penn State Press's "Re-Reading the Canon" series, which places Rand in the company of major philosophers from Plato to Nietzsche. Sciabarra is also a founding editor of the new *Journal of Ayn Rand Studies*, the first peer-reviewed, interdisciplinary periodical devoted to Rand's life and work. In addition, *The Fountainhead: An American Novel*, by philosopher Douglas J. Den Uyl—the first scholarly book on Rand's fiction—is a recent title in the "Twayne's Masterwork Studies" series. Entries on Rand have also been appearing in major reference works, such as the *Routledge Encyclopedia of Philosophy*. Finally, feature articles on the recent spate of Rand scholarship have been published in *Lingua Franca* and the *Chronicle of Higher Education*, two highly respected periodicals aimed at the scholarly community.[84]

Before our own monograph on the subject was published, however (see below), Rand's philosophy of art had received scarcely any serious attention—in marked contrast to the substantial consideration given to other aspects of her work. The neglect of her esthetics, even by those interested in the larger body of her thought, is all the more remarkable and lamentable in that she was a novelist. Art, in the form of fiction was the medium in which she first chose to present her philosophic ideas.

Ironically, the cause of this neglect lay in no small measure with Rand herself, for she tended to subordinate her theory of art to her literary theory, and to her personal literary esthetic.[85] Moreover, to the extent that Objectivist scholars have been interested in the arts at all, they have tended to focus on literature, as she did, since it is conceptual and verbal in nature and therefore closer to philosophy than are the visual arts, music, or dance. Finally, the value of Rand's theoretical analysis is often obscured by idiosyncratic pronouncements on individual artists, works, or styles.

Overview of the Present Study

This book grew out of a monograph we published serially in 1991 and 1992 in *Aristos*, the arts journal we co-edit. As in that preliminary study, our aim here is to identify and evaluate the basic principles of Rand's theory of art—as distinct from her literary theory and her personal esthetic preferences. Focusing on her four key essays on esthetics (the first four chapters of *The Romantic Manifesto*), we supplement them with material from other sources.[86] We also seek to assess her ideas by comparison with those of other thinkers, past and present. While we have geared our presentation to the intelligent general reader, we have aimed to offer substance enough for specialists as well.

In our analysis of Rand's theory, we have avoided the critical extremes that have too often marred assessments of her work—from the claim that she was an infallible thinker who owed little to the ideas of others to the view that she was merely a pop novelist and ideologue whose thought merits no serious consideraton. We argue instead that, shortcomings in detail notwithstanding, her esthetic theory is, in its fundamental principles, coherent, substantial, and *valid*, constituting a major contribution to the literature on the philosophy of art. For this reason, the title of our book is a deliberate inversion of the question in Tolstoy's famous study *What Is Art?*—published a century ago.

In Part I we offer a critical examination of Rand's esthetic theory, beginning with a close analysis (in Chapters 1–4) of her four key essays on the subject, the main ideas of which have been subject to distortion or misunderstanding even by Objectivists well versed in her philosophy. In Chapter 5, we consider Rand's analysis of music, offering a reconciliation of its apparent contradictions. We devote Chapter 6 to an in-depth assessment of Rand's definition of art, contrasting it with contemporary philososophic approaches to the issue. Finally, since Rand's theory of art is based on a view of man's nature as a being of conceptual consciousness, and should be consonant with knowledge gained from the human sciences, in Chapter 7 we present data and theoretical insights from such disciplines as anthropology, cognitive science, and clinical psychology, which tend to corroborate her basic assumptions and conclusions.

In Part II, we expand upon important issues that Rand touched on only briefly, if at all. These include a consideration of the nature of photography, architecture, and the decorative arts, as well as an application of her ideas to an analysis of major trends in modernist and postmodernist work, beginning with abstract art. While the analysis we offer in these chapters is largely our own, it proceeds from, and is consistent with, the basic principles of Rand's esthetic theory. Finally, in Chapter 16, we examine the implications of her theory for issues of broad public concern, from corporate and government support of the arts to art law and arts education.

Part I

Ayn Rand's Philosophy of Art

1

"The Psycho-Epistemology of Art"

"While physics has reached the level where men are able to study subatomic particles and interplanetary space, a phenomenon such as art has remained a dark mystery, with little or nothing known about its nature, its function in human life or the cause of its tremendous psychological power." Yet art is of "passionately intense importance and profoundly *personal* concern to most men" and it has existed since the dawn of mankind, prior even to written language.[1] So Rand observes at the outset of "The Psycho-Epistemology of Art,"[2] the first and most fundamental of her four essays on esthetics.

The title of the essay is itself significant: Rand's use of the term "psycho-epistemology" (rather than simply "psychology") indicates the emphasis she places on the cognitive role of art. *Psycho-epistemology*, she explains, pertains to the interaction between conscious and subconscious mental processes in human cognition. (18) And it is in relation to the dynamic interaction between these complementary levels of mental activity—an interaction she regarded as crucial in human consciousness—that she analyzes the nature and purpose of art.

The Purpose of Art

Contrary to the view that art serves a mainly social function, Rand argues that the primary function of art pertains to a need of the *individual*. "Art belongs to a non-socializable aspect of reality, which is universal (i.e., applicable to all men) but non-collective: [that is, it pertains] to the nature of human consciousness." (16) She continues:

> One of the distinguishing characteristics of a work of art (including literature) is that it serves no practical, material end, but is an end in itself; it serves no practical purpose other than contemplation—and the pleasure of that contemplation is so intense, so deeply personal that [one] experiences it as a self-sufficient, self-justifying primary. [16]

Two aspects of this passage require elaboration. First, Rand offers no clue as to the particular kinds of works she has in mind when she speaks of *art*— apart from revealing, parenthetically, her special concern with literature. Nor does she state elsewhere in the essay what forms of art she is considering. She seems to assume that the reader will know what kinds of work she has in mind. Only in her later essay "Art and Cognition" does she make clear that by "art," she means the forms traditionally regarded as the *fine arts* (though she does not use that term).[3]

The second point of potential confusion arises from Rand's statement that art is "an end in itself,"[4] serving "no practical purpose other than contemplation." At first glance, her proposition might be mistaken for a conventional "art for art's sake" view, such as that articulated by the influential critic Clive Bell, an early champion of modernist painting. The confusion can be quickly dispelled, however. Unlike Bell, Rand does not detach art's meaning and purpose from life itself. Quite the contrary. Whereas Bell held that a work of art possesses "an intense and peculiar significance of its own . . . *unrelated to the significance of life*,"[5] Rand emphasizes that art is profoundly related to human life. In her view, "art *does* have a purpose and *does* serve a human need; only it is not a material need, but a need of man's consciousness." For her, art is "an end in itself" only in the sense that its primary purpose is not "practical" (or material), but *spiritual*.[6] A work of art is not comparable to a tool such as a hammer or to an article of clothing such as a raincoat—each of which is designed to perform a practical, *physical* function. Art is not "utilitarian" in this sense. But it does have an important *psychological* function.[7]

The fundamental purpose of art, according to Rand, pertains to the conceptual, integrative nature of the human mind—to the fact that "man acquires knowledge and guides his actions, not by means of single, isolated percepts, but by means of *abstractions*."[8] (17) Her theory of art is therefore integrally related to her theory of knowledge. Just as language serves to convert conceptual abstractions into the "equivalent of concretes" and thereby condenses a vast sum of knowledge, so art, too, satisfies the cognitive need for condensation and "unit-economy"[9]—in a crucially important sphere: the realm of human values and value-judgments. (18)

Metaphysical Value-Judgments

According to Rand, the most important value-judgments each individual forms are *metaphysical* in nature.[10] They are conclusions about the fundamental nature of reality from a specifically human perspective—that is, about oneself, the world, and one's fellow human beings. Because they pertain to the basic aspects of reality that have the greatest impact on human existence, such judgments are crucial to the phenomenon of art. In Rand's view, these "metaphysical value-judgments" implicitly answer certain fundamental questions that are profoundly relevant to human life. For example: "Is the universe intelligible to man, or unintelligible and unknowable? Can man find happiness on earth, or is he doomed to frustration and despair? Does [he] have the power . . . to choose his goals and to achieve them . . . or is he the helpless plaything of forces beyond his control? Is man, by nature, to be valued as good, or to be despised as evil?"[11] The answers to such questions are *metaphysical value-judgments.*[12] (19)

Metaphysical abstractions involve "such a vast sum of knowledge and such a long chain of concepts that no man could hold it all in the focus of his immediate conscious awareness," Rand continues. Yet each human being requires the "comprehensive view of existence" such abstractions provide, whether they are held consciously or subconsciously, explicitly or implicitly.[13] Without such a view, he cannot "integrate his values, . . . choose his goals, . . . [or] maintain the unity and coherence of his life." Here Rand identifies what she considers to be the distinctive function of art: it is the means by which man can summon into "full, conscious focus" his fundamental view of reality. (19)

Although the concept of metaphysical value-judgments is central to Rand's analysis and definition of art, she offers no further explanation or clarification of the concept in "The Psycho-Epistemology of Art." As a result, the reader is apt to be somewhat baffled. While one can easily grasp the idea of metaphysical value-judgments as personally relevant conclusions about the fundamental aspects of reality, it is difficult to understand how the specific questions Rand poses would pertain to any art form but literature—unless the given work had a literary or narrative base (biblical, historical, mythological, or fictional) known to the viewer or listener. A full grasp of David's famous painting of the *Death of Socrates*, for example, requires a knowledge of the historical event: without it, one can only sense that some event of great moment is occurring, one cannot guess what values are at stake in the action depicted.[14]

Nor do ethics and moral values appear to be essential to any other art forms. Indeed, this is the first of many instances in which Rand's focus shifts from art in general to the art forms that most interested her: that is, to fiction and drama.

The concept of metaphysical value-judgments, and its relevance to all the arts, becomes clearer in Rand's subsequent essays, however, in which she articulates her concept of *sense of life*, the psychological form in which such judgments are integrated and retained. For now, suffice it to say that, in the broadest terms, metaphysical value-judgments constitute what psychologist Edith Packer has termed "core evaluations"[15] about oneself and about one's relationship to reality and to other human beings.

Rand's Definition of Art

Having introduced her concept of metaphysical value-judgments, Rand defines art as follows:

> *Art is a selective re-creation of reality according to an artist's metaphysical value-judgments.*[16] [19]

Like her analysis of metaphysical value-judgments themselves, Rand's initial explanation of what she means by "a selective re-creation of reality" is stated in the broadest terms:

> [A]rt isolates and integrates those aspects of reality which represent [the artist's] fundamental view of himself and of existence. Out of the countless number of concretes—of single, disorganized and (seemingly) contradictory attributes, actions and entities [in reality]—an artist isolates the things which he regards as metaphysically essential [i.e., fundamental] and integrates them into a single new concrete that represents an embodied abstraction.[17] [19–20]

Through this process of selective re-creation, the work comes to reflect the artist's "fundamental view" of life, for it embodies or objectifies those aspects of reality that are of greatest personal importance to him. (19–20) When concretized in a work of art, the complex metaphysical abstractions implicit in the artist's view of life can be grasped with unequaled immediacy and emotional intensity.

To illustrate this principle, Rand contrasts two hypothetical sculptures representing man: "one as a Greek god, the other as a deformed medieval monstrosity. Both are projections of the artist's view of man's nature; both are concretized representations of the philosophy of their respective cultures."[18] This elemental contrast between the art of ancient Greece and that of the Middle Ages is one to which Rand will return in a later essay. While the starkness of her comparison does not do justice to the complexity of either culture, it does make her point clear. Each figure reflects the *dominant* metaphysical outlook of the culture in which it was created.[19] For Rand, in sum: "Art is a concretization of metaphysics." (20)

While distinctive and thought-provoking, Rand's definition of art in terms of "metaphysical value-judgments"—or, for that matter, as "a selective re-creation of reality"—is by no means self-evident. As the keystone of her theory of art, it warrants a detailed explication and critique. Since her intended meaning will become clearer in the light of her full analysis of the nature of art, we will reconsider her definition in Chapter 6, after we have presented her theory in its entirety.

The Cognitive Function of Art

Rand's view of the function of art is closely linked to her realist epistemology, her view that all human knowledge is based ultimately on sensory-perceptual experience.[20] She analyzes the nature of art in relation to cognition as follows:

Art brings man's concepts to the perceptual level of his consciousness and allows him to grasp them directly, as if they were percepts.[21]

Rand emphatically concludes: "*This* is the psycho-epistemological function of art and the reason of its importance in man's life (and the crux of the Objectivist esthetics)."[22] (20)

As Rand has indicated, however, it is not with just *any* concepts that art is primarily concerned but, rather, with the basic value-judgments about reality that most profoundly bear upon the individual's life. Only when concretized in a work of art do these important abstractions "acquire the full, persuasive, irresistible power of reality." (23) Like language, then, art serves the basic cognitive need to condense and integrate knowledge and experience into graspable concretes. "Just as language converts abstractions into the psycho-epistemological equivalent of concretes, into a manageable number of specific units—so art converts man's metaphysical abstractions into the equivalent of concretes, into specific entities open to man's direct perception."[23] (20) The old adage that "art is a universal language" is, in this sense, "literally true," Rand observes.[24] (20)

The Creative Process

If art is "a selective re-creation of reality," as Rand maintains, what is the precise nature of the creative, or "re-creative," process in her view? As she explains in another context: "By 're-creation,' I don't mean *copying*, but neither do I mean *creation*, in a mystical sense. I do not mean going contrary to reality. . . . I mean creating *that which could be real*, . . . *that which is consistent with reality*."[25] Her conception of re-creation therefore differs significantly from Plato's notion that what the artist does is equivalent to merely holding "a mirror up to nature."[26] Though Rand does not refer to Aristotle in her analysis of the phenomenon of the "selective re-creation of reality," her conception of this process is comparable to Aristotle's understanding of artistic *mimesis* ("imitation"). Whereas Plato had used the term "imitative arts" in a disparaging sense, suggesting a slavish copying of nature (a pejorative connotation that persists in modern English usage), Aristotle broadened and deepened the meaning. For him, as for Rand, artistic "imitation" involved not a literal transcription of reality but rather a process of selecting and transforming aspects of human experience and awareness so that the "likeness" produced conveys through its particular appearance a more general (universal) significance. Rand's term "selective re-creation" suggests more clearly than "imitation," however, the complexity of the process involved, illuminating its purposeful nature.

Literary characterization affords "the best illustration of the psycho-epistemological process" in the creation of art, Rand suggests, since fiction and drama most fully capture the complexity of human character. (20) As a simple instance of the creative process involved in concretizing a particular type of human being, she cites Sinclair Lewis's creation of the eponymous protagonist of his novel *Babbitt*. According to Rand's analysis, Lewis would have selected—from among innumerable traits he identified and evaluated in innumerable men "of a certain type"—those traits he considered most representative, and would have then integrated them into the fictional character of Babbitt. The result so effectively concretizes the idea of a small-town businessman unable to break out of the mold of provincial conformity that, as she points out, the name "Babbitt" has entered the language as a generic term to denote such a person.[27] (21) Rand's analysis of the creative process Lewis probably followed is an intuitive one, informed by her own experience as a novelist.[28] The process she describes in relation to literary characterization applies, in principle, to the kinds of steps every artist goes through, whether he is fully aware of them or not, in the "selective re-creation of reality." The painter or sculptor, too, selects from nature those aspects best suited to his creative purpose.

Art, Religion, and Philosophy

In Rand's view, art, religion, and philosophy are closely related phenomena, in that each serves to provide man with "a comprehensive view of existence." Noting that, historically, art was at first "an adjunct (and, often, a monopoly) of religion"—which was, in her view, "the primitive form of philosophy"—Rand further observes that the art of primitive cultures was "a concretization of their religion's metaphysical and ethical abstractions."[29] (20)

Whether the abstractions objectified by an art work derive ultimately from religious doctrine or belief or from secular philosophic thought, the essential function of art remains the same, in Rand's view. Neither philosophy nor religion could ever fully replace or dispense with art. Owing to the distinctive nature of their cognitive and emotional processes, human beings will always need art to experience their values and their view of life in objectified form.[30] By the same token, art is not "a substitute for philosophical thought."[31] (22) According to Rand, art depends ultimately on *ideas* and *values*, which are the product of human cognition and evaluation. Even religious abstractions "are the product of man's mind, not of supernatural revelation."[32] Whether an art work concretizes beliefs or values widely held in a given culture, or the revolutionary ideas and values of an individual artist, it is a characteristically *human* product of *human* cognition. While Rand thus rejects the idea of divine inspiration, she nonetheless regards art as profoundly spiritual in its nature and function.

Rand's view of the relationship between art, religion, and philosophy inevitably invites contrast with the thought of Hegel, who has exerted an incalculable influence on art historical theory and criticism.[33] Like Hegel, Rand emphasizes that art, religion, and philosophy are significant products of *mind*, or *intellect*, and serve to convey the highest *spiritual* values. But the resemblance between their views on this triad ends there. Rand's understanding of "mind" and "spirit" could not be more different from Hegel's. For Hegel, "Mind" or "Spirit,"[34] is a *metaphysical absolute*, a higher level of reality which has its own existence and gradually becomes manifest in the human realm through art, religion, and philosophy. Whereas Hegel regards these phenomena as hierarchically related stages of spiritual self-consciousness, Rand completely rejects his metaphysics of spirit. For her, the mind or spirit is to be understood, as the human faculty of awareness and understanding.[35] She views art as uniquely answering a particular cognitive and emotional need of human nature as such, whereas Hegel postulates an historical progression in which human self-awareness will eventually achieve spiritual perfection through philosophy—the highest manifestation of "absolute Mind." According to Hegel, art will then cease to be a "supreme need of the [human] spirit."[36] Contrary to that view, Rand holds that the need for art will remain a constant in human life: "so long as men exist, the need of art will exist, since that need is rooted . . . in the nature of man's consciousness."[37]

Art and Ethics

Rand argues that the need for concretization through art is especially urgent in the realm of ethics. No theoretical treatise—no "list of virtues," however lengthy and detailed, she emphasizes—could adequately convey the concept of an ideal man, for the human mind cannot deal with such a vast number of abstractions. No one could "retranslate all the abstractions into the perceptual concretes for which they stand—i.e., connect them to reality—and hold [them] all in the focus of [his] conscious awareness." Moreover, any such purely theoretical treatise would be "sterile [and] uninspiring," for its ethical principles would remain mere disembodied abstractions, unfathomable and unattainable.[38] (21) That explains why each religion has its own mythology— "a dramatized concretization of its moral code embodied in the figures of men who are its ultimate product."[39] (21) According to Rand: "*Art is the indispensable medium for the communication of a moral ideal.*" (21) Without art, she argues, "ethics remains in the position of theoretical engineering: *art is the model-builder.*" (22, emphasis ours) The work of art serves as a model by embodying the relevant moral principles in clearly perceptible form.[40] Rand employs the same metaphor in an earlier essay, "The Goal of My Writing" (1963), in which she writes: "*Art is the technology of the soul.*[41] . . . Ethics is the applied science that defines a code of values to guide man's choices and actions—the choices and actions which determine the course of his life; ethics is the engineering that provides the principles and blueprints. Art creates the final product. *It builds the model.*" (169, emphasis ours)

Although Rand uses the generic term *art* in these passages, it is important to recognize that her remarks on the ethical "model-building" aspect of art works in fact apply primarily, if not exclusively, to the art of *literature*— in particular, to fiction and drama. Commenting on Rand's proposition that art "builds the model," Peikoff correctly argues that not all art performs this function, since "literature . . . alone is able to depict the richness of man in action across time, making choices, pursuing goals, facing obstacles, exhibiting not merely an isolated virtue, but a whole code of them. . . . *The modelbuilding aspect, therefore, . . . is not a universal attribute of art*; and even where it is present, it is not a primary."[42]

Apparently aware, with good reason, that some readers may incorrectly infer from her discussion that the primary focus of "art" (more precisely, literature) is ethical, Rand quickly adds that "moral values are inextricably involved in art, . . . only as a consequence, *not* as a causal determinant: the primary focus of art is metaphysical, not ethical." Art is "the concretization of a moral ideal," she argues, "not a textbook on how to become one." In her view: "The basic purpose of art is *not* to teach, but to *show*—to hold up to man a concretized image of his nature and his place in the universe." And again: "*Art is not the means to any didactic end.* This is the difference between a work of art and a morality play or a propaganda poster."[43] (22) Once more, while Rand's emphasis on the primarily metaphysical (as contrasted with ethical) content of art is appropriate, her view of art as the "concretization of a moral ideal" applies only to some literature and to art works in other media which rely on a literary or narrative base.

Romanticism and Naturalism

To elucidate her view that "the place of ethics in any given work of art" depends on the metaphysical view of the artist, Rand briefly introduces two concepts—Romanticism and Naturalism. These concepts figure prominently in her personal esthetic of literature but are misleading in the context of her theory of art, and have led to much confusion in the meager Objectivist literature on her esthetics. (23) Her analysis of these concepts—both in "The Psycho-Epistemology of Art" and in an essay she wrote four years later, "What Is Romanticism?" (as well as in several other essays reprinted in *The Romantic Manifesto*)—is almost exclusively in terms of fiction and drama, and she fails to indicate how her analysis would apply to other art forms.

Rand argues as follows: If an artist believes that man possesses volition, his work will be value-oriented; this is the essence of *Romanticism*. If, on the other hand, an artist is a determinist, holding that human life is controlled by external forces, his work will have an "anti-value" focus; Rand identifies this approach with *Naturalism*. Romantic art, according to Rand, projects "the values man *is to seek*" and presents "the concretized vision of the life he *is to achieve*."[44] (23, emphasis ours) In contrast, Naturalistic art "assert[s] that man's efforts are futile" and presents "the concretized vision of defeat and despair as his ultimate fate."[45]

Rand's initial focus on the concept of value-orientation as a defining characteristic of Romanticism is particularly confusing in the context of her theory of art. As she argues elsewhere, *all* art (not just Romantic art), necessarily involves values: "It is inconceivable to have an art divorced from values. . . . Values cannot be separated from any human activity. . . . It is impossible . . . to write a book [for example] without some kind of selectivity. . . . Every time a man has to exercise a choice, he is directed by some kind of values, conscious or not."[46]

Delving further into the question in the essay entitled "What Is Romanticism?," Rand offers the following definition: *"Romanticism is a category of art based on the recognition of the principle that man possesses the faculty of volition."* (99, emphasis ours) Although she employs the generic term "art" in this definition, her subsequent argument explicitly refers only to "the field of literature." (99ff.) Moreover, the attributes she regards as *defining* Romanticism are again specific to fiction and drama and cannot be validly generalized to other art forms. It is clear that by the phrase "recognition of the principle that man possesses the faculty of volition," Rand does not mean simply that the artist exercises volition during the creative process. As we have just noted, *all* art-making, in her view, entails volition. What she means instead is that the principle of volition is objectified in the art work itself. As Rand herself argued in another context, the only way the principle of volition can be fully and clearly objectified is through the presentation of characters engaged in the choice and pursuit of values over time; that is, through their purposeful, on-going actions to gain or to keep their values in the face of obstacles or conflicts, whether internal or external.[47] The only art forms in which that principle can be concretized are narrative and dramatic literature—as Peikoff's previously quoted remarks on the "model-building aspect" of art confirm.[48]

Notwithstanding her numerous references to Romantic "art," Rand offers few clues as to what she considers to be the defining attributes of Romanticism in the visual arts or music.[49] Those she does offer bear no relation to her own definition of Romantic art in terms of the "principle of volition." In her early essay "The Goal of My Writing," for example, she cites a scene from *The Fountainhead* in which the architect-protagonist Howard Roark explains to the sculptor Steven Mallory that he wants Mallory to create a sculpture for the Stoddard Temple because his figures "have a magnificent respect for the human being" and represent "the heroic in man." Rand explains that, in this passage, she "was consciously and deliberately stating the essential goal of [her] own work" as a "Romantic Realist." (168) But surely one could attribute "respect for the human being" and a sense of "the heroic in man" to any number of works predating the nineteenth century—for example, various classical Greek sculptures, Renaissance works such as Michelangelo's *David*, or numerous figures by Bernini and other Baroque sculptors, to cite but a few. These works could not properly be termed "Romantic," however, since Romanticism was an historical phenomenon, a product of a unique set of forces in the Western world of the nineteenth century, as Rand herself emphasizes.[50]

Rand's only other reference to Romanticism in the visual arts occurs in the context of her criticism of the "virulently intense antagonism of today's esthetic spokesmen to any manifestation of the Romantic premise in art." (102) She argues not only that they resent plot structure in literature for its "implicit premise of volition (and, therefore, of moral values)" but also that

> [t]he same reaction, for the same subconscious reason, is evoked by such elements as heroes or happy endings or the triumph of virtue, or, in the visual arts, beauty. Physical beauty is not a moral or volitional issue—but the *choice* to paint a beautiful human being rather than an ugly one, implies the existence of volition: of choice, standards, values.[51] [102, emphasis in original]

Rand's attribution of "the *choice* to paint a beautiful human being rather than an ugly one" to "the Romantic premise [of volition] in art" is mistaken on several counts, however. Most obvious is that artists long before the Romantic era chose to paint beautiful subjects. More troubling, however, is Rand's apparent implication that the choice to paint a physically *ugly* human being necessarily indicates an *absence* of volition or values. She fails to consider how the individual artist's context and hierarchy of values might affect the significance of his depiction of beauty or ugliness in a given painting. Consider, for example, the insightful portraits Velazquez (1599–1660) painted of the dwarfs of the Spanish court. Although he realistically depicted their physical deformity, that aspect is transcended by the depths of character he captured in each subject—qualities ranging from the serene confidence of his *Don Diego de Acedo* to the fierce pride of his *Don Sebastian de Morra*. Here, as elsewhere, meaning in art resides not merely in the ostensible subject portrayed but, more crucially, in *how* it is portrayed—a principle Rand herself recognizes in other contexts (see Chapter 3).

"Efficacy of Consciousness"

In the concluding paragraphs of "The Psycho-Epistemology of Art," Rand returns to a key question she raised early in the essay: Why is art of such "profoundly *personal* significance" for man? Surprisingly, she introduces an entirely new point here—one of dubious validity, in our view. "[A]ccording to whether an art work supports or negates [an individual's] fundamental view of reality," she asserts, "*art confirms or denies the efficacy of a man's consciousness.*" (24, emphasis ours) Since she offers no elucidation, one can only speculate as to her intended meaning. In her later essay "Art and Sense of Life," Rand repeats this proposition. Since it can be most profitably examined in that context, we defer our discussion of this point to Chapter 3. For now, let us simply repeat Rand's previous claim that art is important because it gives one the power to grasp fundamental ideas about life directly "as if they were percepts." As she unequivocally stated in a proposition we quoted earlier: *"This* is the psycho-epistemological function of art and the reason of its importance in man's life (and the crux of the Objectivist esthetics)."

2

"Philosophy and Sense of Life"

Although Rand did not originate the term *sense of life*, she appears to have been the first writer to analyze the concept in depth and to give it a precise definition:

> A sense of life is a pre-conceptual equivalent of metaphysics, an emotional, subconsciously integrated appraisal of man and of existence.[1] [25]

While Rand's initial analysis of the nature of art in "The Psycho-Epistemology of Art" conspicuously omitted any discussion of the crucial role of the emotions in art, in her concluding paragraphs she introduced the subject, with respect to *sense of life*—the psychological phenomenon which she regards as the integrating factor in both the creation of and the response to art. (24) In "Philosophy and Sense of Life," she analyzes this central concept from a broad philosophic perspective before proceeding to explain its relation to art.

Developing her idea that art is a "concretization of metaphysics" (that is, an embodiment of the artist's fundamental view of reality as it pertains to man), Rand explains that few individuals have an *explicit* metaphysics—a carefully thought-out, systematically integrated view of reality—much less a complete philosophy. Nevertheless,

> Long before he is old enough to grasp such a concept as metaphysics, man . . . acquires a certain *implicit* view of life. Every choice and value-judgment [he makes] implies some estimate of himself and of the world around him—

most particularly of his capacity to deal with the world. He may draw conscious conclusions, which may be true or false; or he may remain mentally passive and merely react to events (i.e., merely feel). Whatever the case may be, his subconscious mechanism sums up his psychological activities, integrating his conclusions, reactions or evasions into an emotional sum that establishes a habitual pattern and becomes his automatic response to the world around him. What began as a series of single, discrete conclusions (or evasions) . . . becomes a generalized feeling about existence, an implicit *metaphysics* with the compelling motivational power of a constant basic emotion—an emotion which is part of all his other emotions and underlies all his experiences. *This* is [his] sense of life. [25–26]

Nathaniel Branden further characterizes *sense of life* as the emotional form in which a person experiences his deepest view of existence and of his own relationship to existence. It is, in effect, the emotional corollary of a metaphysics—of a *personal* metaphysics—reflecting the subconsciously held sum of his broadest and deepest implicit conclusions about the world, about life, and about himself.[2]

The concept of sense of life articulated by Rand and Branden can be compared to what the Spanish philosopher José Ortega y Gasset terms a "metaphysical sentiment," which he characterizes as the "essential, ultimate and basic impression which we have of the universe." For Ortega, this sentiment "acts as a foundation and support for our other activities, whatever they may be. No one lives without it, although its degree of clarity varies from person to person. It encompasses our primary, decisive attitude toward all of reality, the pleasure which the world and life hold for us. Our other feelings, thoughts, and desires are activated by this primary attitude and are sustained and colored by it."[3] As will become clear, however, the genesis Rand postulates for an individual's sense of life differs fundamentally from the origin of "metaphysical sentiment" according to Ortega. He regards metaphysical sentiment as a wholly innate tendency—as the product of what he terms one's "primogenital clay."[4] In contrast, Rand holds that sense of life is the cumulative product of the individual's experiences, and of his characteristic way of responding to them.[5] As Branden explains, in the course of his development from childhood, a human being encounters certain fundamental facts of reality—facts about the nature of existence and the nature of human life—to which he can respond with varying degrees of appropriateness. The cumulative sum of these responses constitutes a person's distinctive sense of life."[6]

Like Rand, Branden regards the individual's customary methods of thinking as an important component of his sense of life. A variety of attitudes are involved in the formation of this complex totality. For example, one may develop a policy of independent thought and action, or one may passively follow the judgments and convictions of others. One may develop the capacity to defer gratification for the sake of long-term goals, or one may demand the immediate fulfillment of one's desires. One may regard suffering as an aberration or as the very essence of existence. Finally, one may regard irrationality as a departure from human nature or as characteristic of one's fellow men. These are but a few of the possible basic attitudes encompassed by a person's sense of life. Moreover, as Branden emphasizes, they may be present in varying proportions and degrees in the psyche of a given individual.[7]

Edith Packer, a psychologist closely associated with Objectivism, coined the apt term "core evaluations" to refer to the "basic conclusions, [the] bottom-line evaluations" that are held subconsciously in the form of an individual's sense of life. These evaluations are the subconscious equivalents of metaphysical value-judgments pertaining to three fundamental areas of life: oneself, other people, and the broader world.[8] Because core evaluations are held subconsciously, they function as if they were "self-evidently true."[9] They therefore affect one's fundamental emotional tenor. In Packer's view, they also "influence every aspect of our method of thinking, the way we integrate reality in the present, and, ultimately, the way we behave."[10]

Rand's concept of sense of life has a cultural as well as an individual dimension. As she argues in a later essay, "A culture, like an individual, has a sense of life or, rather, the equivalent of a sense of life—an emotional atmosphere created by its dominant philosophy, by its view of man and of existence. This emotional atmosphere represents a culture's dominant values and serves as the leitmotif of a given age, setting its trends and its style."[11] Nathaniel Branden further argues that many of an individual's most important cultural beliefs and assumptions are acquired from the social environment at this implicit, inarticulate level of awareness. Such ideas "can be harder to call into question," Branden emphasizes,

> precisely because they are absorbed by a process that largely bypasses the conscious mind. Everyone possesses what might be called a "cultural unconscious"—a set of implicit beliefs about nature, reality, human beings, man-woman relationships, good and evil—that reflect the knowledge, understanding, and values of a historical time and place. I do not mean that there are no differences among people within a given culture in their beliefs at this level. Nor do I mean that no one holds any of these beliefs consciously or that no one challenges any of them. I mean only that at least some of these beliefs tend to reside in every psyche in a given society, and without ever being the subject of explicit awareness.[12]

Branden clearly reflects Rand's view that individuals tend to absorb the dominant ideas and attitudes of their cultural environment, and that such ideas may contribute to their sense of life, often in an unarticulated form.[13] Yet Rand also held that (as Branden suggests) the individual need not be a passive recipient of the *Zeitgeist*. In this and other important respects, her view of history and human progress bears a striking similarity to that of the nineteenth-century French historian and critic of literature, Hippolyte Taine— who argued that culture was the product of the cumulative labors and achievements of exceptional individuals, transcending their immediate cultural context.[14]

Emotional Abstraction

According to Rand, one's sense of life is formed by a process of "emotional generalization." Unlike other types of generalization or abstraction, "it consists of classifying things *according to the emotions they [e]voke*"[15] (27)—i.e., of tying together, by association or connotation, all those things which have the power to make an individual experience the same (or a similar) emotion."[16]

To illustrate this process, Rand offers two contrasting sets of experiences and phenomena:

> [For a child]: a new neighborhood, a discovery, adventure, struggle, triumph— or: the folks next door, a memorized recitation, a family picnic, a known routine, comfort.
>
> On a more adult level: a heroic man, the skyline of New York, a sunlit landscape, pure colors, ecstatic music—or: a humble man, an old village, a foggy landscape, muddy colors, folk music. [27]

Rand maintains that the emotions evoked by such things depend ultimately on the individual's estimate of himself. In her view, an individual possessing self-esteem will necessarily feel "admiration, exaltation, a sense of challenge" in response to the first set of examples in each case, and "disgust or boredom," to the second; whereas an individual *lacking* self-esteem will respond with "fear, guilt, resentment" to the first set, and will feel relieved, reassured, and safe in response to the second. (27)

No doubt, the emotions Rand here associates with the possession of self-esteem correspond to the sorts of feelings she herself would have experienced in such circumstances, while the contrasting feelings (for the individual lacking self-esteem) appear to be deduced by her as the antithesis of her own responses. But she is mistaken to generalize her personal responses into a universal phenomenon. In so doing, she violates a principle she herself rightly held to be paramount: *the importance of context in all human cognition and valuation.*[17] As she properly stresses, every value implies a valuer, whose specific context influences the values that evoke his emotional responses. By assigning a specific value-meaning to the experiences she enumerates in her illustration of emotional generalization, and by suggesting that such a value-meaning would apply to every individual, dependent only on his level of self-esteem, without regard to countless other aspects of his personal context or of the specific circumstances, Rand falls into the fallacy of "context-dropping" she adamantly opposed.[18] Her proposition is belied not only by the basic tenets of Objectivism but by common sense: one can easily imagine circumstances in which, for example, a child of high self-esteem might find a new neighborhood boring, the "folks next door" interesting, reciting poetry from memory pleasurable, and an agreeable household routine satisfying— just as there are circumstances in which an adult of high self-esteem might enjoy a "foggy landscape," or in which a person of low self-esteem might take pleasure in "pure colors." It is important to identify and reject Rand's context-dropping here, because the same fallacy frequently mars her value-judgments on specific works and styles of art.[19] In sum, the process of emotional generalization involved in the formation of one's sense of life—which in turn affects one's emotional responses to art—is far more complex and individualized than Rand's simplistic illustration suggests.

That her specific illustrations are inappropriate, however, does not invalidate Rand's argument that the emotional abstractions which form an individual's sense of life are rooted in his "view of *himself* and of *his own* existence." (28) The criteria for forming one's emotional abstractions about life can be expressed in the statements "That which is important to *me*" and "The kind of universe which is right for *me*, in which *I* would feel at home." (28) The key concept here—*important*—is not necessarily synonymous with "good"; it is used instead in the essentially *metaphysical* sense of "entitle[d] to attention or consideration." Which aspects of reality are most entitled to attention or consideration, according to Rand? Those that have the greatest implications for one's life—in particular, those pertaining to man's nature, since they serve as a bridge between reality (the realm of metaphysics) and a code of values (the realm of ethics). Rand regards as paramount the answers to questions about free will and the human capacity for valid knowledge and efficacious action. As in her previous essay, she states that the answers to such questions constitute "metaphysical value-judgments," since they "form the base of [one's] ethics."[20] "It is only those values which he regards . . . as 'important,' those which represent his implicit view of reality, that remain in a man's subconscious and form his sense of life," Rand argues. "The integrated sum of a man's basic values is his sense of life."[21] (28-29)

Philosophy and Sense of Life

Rand maintains that, beginning in early childhood, each individual forms his sense of life automatically, without conscious effort, and that his "early value-integrations . . . remain in a fluid, plastic, easily amendable state." (29) By adolescence, however, cognitive capacity is sufficiently developed for the individual to begin to form a fully explicit philosophy, a clearly articulated system of principles by which to live. Ideally, the transition to an explicit philosophy occurs as the growing child consciously validates and corrects what he previously only *sensed* about the nature of existence and his relationship to it. Yet Rand is quick to point out that *an articulated philosophy does not take the place of one's sense of life.* Rather, the two co-exist, one's sense of life continuing to serve the crucial function of automatically integrating one's values on an emotional level. In Rand's view, however, the individual's explicitly formulated philosophy gradually comes to determine the *criteria* for his emotional responses. Instead of continuing to rely on a metaphysical outlook which is merely implicit in his value-judgments, he now bases conscious value-judgments on an explicitly articulated philosophic viewpoint. "The mind leads, the emotions follow." (30) In other words, he becomes aware of the connection between his fundamental metaphysical premises and the value-judgments underlying his emotions.

Although Rand argues that an individual's sense of life, once formed, is not immutable,[22] she stresses that it "always retains a profoundly personal quality; it reflects a man's deepest values. . . . It is involved in everything about that person, in his every thought, emotion, action . . . in his every choice and value . . . in his manner of moving, talking, smiling, in the total of his personality." (31) An individual's sense of life, then, is experienced by him (and by others) as integral to his very identity. As such, it appears to be an "irreducible primary." Yet one's sense of life, as Rand emphasizes, is a "very complex sum"; it can be felt automatically, effortlessly, but it can be identified and understood only through analysis, identification, and conceptual verification. (32) In these psychologically astute observations on the complex nature of an individual's sense of life, Rand seems to be focusing, appropriately, on the unarticulated, emotional quality of the phenomenon—a quality that tends to remain constant throughout one's lifetime—however much one may alter one's consciously chosen values.

Sense of Life and Character

Rand maintains that one's sense of life—i.e., one's implicit metaphysics— "sets the nature" (i.e., determines) not only one's emotional responses but also "the essence of [one's] character."[23] (25) Though she does not define what she means by "character," she appears to adhere to standard usage, stressing moral qualities. Indeed, that is the sense specified by Leonard Peikoff:

> "Character" means a man's nature or identity insofar as this is shaped by the moral values he accepts and automatizes. By "moral values," I mean values which are volitionally chosen, and which are fundamental, i.e., [which] shape the whole course of a man's action, not merely a specialized, delimited area of his life. . . . So a man's character is, in effect, his moral essence—his self-made identity as expressed in the principles he lives by.[24]

In connecting sense of life to character, Rand echoes a prior claim in "The Psycho-Epistemology of Art"—that one's answers to certain metaphysical questions *determine* the nature of one's ethical or moral values (19)—a proposition she did not elaborate or substantiate. Once again, she neglects to offer any substantiation for the automatic cause-and-effect relationship she posits between one's view of reality (albeit implicit) and one's moral values. Yet she will frequently allude to such a relationship in her analysis of art.

Contrary to Rand's claim, a simple and direct causal connection between sense of life and moral values seems neither self-evident nor probable. While she correctly argues that moral values can be derived, through reason, from an understanding of reality (most particularly, of human nature), she herself emphasizes that few individuals consistently carry out such a process.

> For most men, the transition [to a rational philosophy] is a tortured and not fully successful process, leading to a fundamental inner conflict—a clash between a man's conscious convictions and his repressed, unidentified (or only partially identified) sense of life. Very often, the transition is incomplete, as in the case of a man whose convictions are not part of a fully integrated philosophy, but are merely a collection of random, disconnected, often contradictory ideas, and therefore, are unconvincing to his own mind against the power of his subconscious metaphysics. In some cases, a man's sense of life is better (closer to the truth) than the kind of ideas he accepts. In other cases, his sense of life is much worse than the ideas he professes to accept but is unable fully to practice. [30]

For most individuals, then, the choice of moral values is likely to be a less predictable process than Rand suggests. In reality, it is a process influenced not only by one's implicit or explicit metaphysical assumptions but by a host of psychological and cultural factors as well, many of them below the level of immediate conscious awareness.[25] Contrary to Rand, we suggest that, because sense of life is a subconsciously integrated emotional phenomenon, the underlying premises of which tend to remain unarticulated, it has less influence on one's conscious choice of moral values (and therefore on one's character) than do such factors as cultural norms and practices, which are inculcated at an early age, often without a full understanding of their underlying premises. Nonetheless, sense of life does appear to have a profound influence on *personality*, as that concept is generally understood.[26]

Sense of Life in Love and Art

Two crucial aspects of human experience, Rand notes, are the "special province and expression" of one's sense of life. They are *romantic love* and *art*, both of which involve the fullest integration of intellect and emotion, of values and feelings. Stressing that romantic love is "a response to values," Rand maintains: "It is with a person's sense of life that one falls in love—with that essential sum, that fundamental stand or way of facing existence, which is the essence of a personality." (32)

Rand continues: "One falls in love with the embodiment of the values that formed a person's character, which are reflected in his widest goals or smallest gestures, which create the style of his soul." Here, again, we think her emphasis on moral implications and character is misleading. The notion that a person's "smallest gestures" reflect any aspect of his character seems especially dubious. Such nonverbal forms of expression seem, rather, to be a manifestation of *personality*. And aspects of personality (as distinct from character) form an important component of romantic love.[27] In attempting to understand emotional responses solely in terms of their underlying philosophic and moral premises, Rand grossly oversimplifies the psychological complexity of the human individual, as Nathaniel Branden argues in his essay "The Benefits and Hazards of the Philosophy of Ayn Rand."[28] In his view: "Our souls are more than our philosophies—and certainly more than our conscious philosophies."[29] (62)

Rand concludes "Philosophy and Sense of Life" with the following provocative conjecture (echoing her observation in "The Psycho-Epistemology of Art"): "Of all human products, art is, perhaps, the most *personally* important to man and the least understood." (33) In her subsequent essay, "Art and Sense of Life," she will analyze the role of sense of life in the creation of, and the response to, art. Just as her consideration of romantic love mistakenly focuses on moral values, however, so, too, she will argue in her subsequent essay that one's choices in art bear moral implications. That error notwithstanding, her analysis offers many valuable insights into the nature of art.

3

"Art and Sense of Life"

To dramatize the role that sense of life plays in the emotional response to art, Rand begins her essay "Art and Sense of Life" with a hypothetical contrast, which she frames in characteristically overstated yet instructive terms: If one were to see, in reality, a beautiful and elegantly attired woman with a cold sore on her lip, one would disregard the blemish, attaching no importance to it; but a painting depicting such a woman would prompt feelings of revulsion and outrage. Such a painting "would be a corrupt, obscenely vicious attack on man, on beauty, on all values—and one would experience a feeling of intense disgust and indignation at the artist." That emotional response would be "instantaneous, much faster than the viewer's mind could identify all the reasons involved." (34)

The "psychological mechanism which produces that response" is the individual's *sense of life*. The same mechanism is involved in the creation of art, for it is the *artist*'s sense of life that "controls and integrates his work, directing the innumerable choices he has to make, from the choice of subject to the subtlest details of style."[1] (34–35) In Rand's view:

> The emotion involved in art is not an emotion in the ordinary meaning of the term. It is experienced more as a "sense" or a "feel," but it has two characteristics pertaining to emotions: it is automatically immediate and it has an intense, profoundly personal (yet undefined) value-meaning to the individual experiencing it. The value involved is life, and the words naming the emotion are: "*This* is [or is not] what life means to *me*."[2] [35]

The implicit meaning of any work of art, therefore, is *"This* is life as *I* [the artist] see it"; and the meaning of one's response to a work is *"This* is (or is *not)* life as I see it." (35) What an art work "expresses," according to Rand, is not an emotion *per se*, but rather a concretized view of life, which has emotional significance for the artist, and has the power to elicit an emotional response in others.

Emotion and "Expression" in Art

Rand's view of the role of emotion in artistic creation and response is distinctive, and can best be appreciated in contrast with various forms of "expression theory"—the widely held view that art directly "expresses" emotional or feeling states.[3] An early exponent of this viewpoint was Tolstoy. In his frequently cited book *What Is Art?* he defines art as "a human activity, consisting in this, that one man consciously, by means of certain external signs, hands on to others feelings he has lived through, and that other people are infected by these feelings, and also experience them."[4] According to Tolstoy, the purpose of art is the direct communication by the artist to his fellow men of his personal feelings and emotions. Moreover, a necessary condition for art, in Tolstoy's view, is that even a simple, uneducated person could experience the feelings conveyed. Indeed, Tolstoy goes so far as to maintain that any work which fails to transmit the artist's feelings to the common man does not qualify as art.[5]

A far more influential version of the "expression theory" was first proposed by the Italian philosopher Benedetto Croce in the first quarter of the twentieth century and subsequently elaborated by the British philosopher R. G. Collingwood.[6] While Tolstoy sought to discredit the nascent modernist tendency to indulge in self-expression at the expense of intelligibility, Collingwood offered a purported justification of that tendency, arguing that the purpose of art is not the "arousal," or evocation, of emotions in others, but rather the artist's clarification of his own emotional "perturbation or excitement" for himself.[7] According to this theory, artistic "expression" is essentially a process of self-exploration. It need not even be externalized in a form perceptible or accessible to others.[8] Although Croce, Collingwood, and their critics alike devote considerable attention to explicating and critiquing the notion of "expression," they (unlike Rand) do not analyze the nature or source of *feelings* or *emotions*—the purported focus of artistic expression.

In contrast, Susanne Langer, presenting yet another view of the "expressive" nature of art, does explain what she means by the crucial term *feeling*. In *Problems of Art*, she states: "A work of art is an expressive form created for our perception through sense or imagination, and what it expresses is human feeling . . . , meaning *everything that can be felt*, from physical sensation, pain and comfort, excitement and repose, to the most complex emotions, intellectual tensions, or the steady feeling-tones of a conscious human life."[9] For Langer, much as for Tolstoy, then, what the work of art "expresses" is not merely emotions but, rather, the whole range of human feeling, including all forms of sensory experience. In her view, art conveys "the *subjective aspect* of experience, the direct feeling of it," which constitutes "what we call the 'inward life' of human beings."[10] Unlike both Tolstoy and Collingwood, however, Langer argues that what an artist expresses need not be feelings he has himself experienced, but rather "what he *knows* about human feeling." (26, emphasis ours) In her view, a work of art "objectifies the subjective realm" of human experience; it "expresses a conception of life, emotion, inward reality. But it is neither a confessional nor a frozen tantrum; it is a developed metaphor, a non-discursive symbol that articulates what is verbally ineffable—the logic of consciousness itself." (26) Langer further argues, in contrast with Tolstoy, that the feelings objectified in a work of art are intended "for our contemplation"—"for our understanding," rather than for the purpose of evoking the same feelings in us. (25)

Rand's view of art is closer to Langer's than to other variants of "expression theory." Yet it differs in fundamental respects. Rand eschews the idea that all the arts are primarily a vehicle for the "expression" or objectification of feelings or emotions as such.[11] Instead, she emphasizes the implicit reference to external reality that evokes the emotions in art.[12] Consistent with her view of emotion as an implicit estimate of things and events in reality, she regards the emotions involved in the experience of art as a response to the nature of the physical reality objectified in works of visual art and literature, or suggested by emotionally charged melodic movement (see Chapter 5). Moreover, she understands that the emotional response to a given work depends not only on objective features of the work itself but also on the personal context and values of the individual respondent.

"Communication" in Art

In sharp contrast with Tolstoy, and with many contemporary critics of modernism, Rand argues that the artist's primary purpose is not "communication"[13]—as that word is properly understood[14]—but, rather, *objectification*. That is, the artist's implicit focus during the creative process is "to bring his view of man and of existence into reality," for *himself*.[15] Yet Rand adds this crucial qualification: "but to be brought into reality, it has to be translated into objective (therefore, communicable) terms." (35) Thus, the apparent "communication" effected by an art work is only *indirect* on the part of the artist—a by-product, as it were, of his successful objectification. If he is in touch with reality, his work will have meaning for other human beings —since, as members of the same species, they share the same basic faculties of sense perception and cognition, the same basic needs and emotions, and so on.

Rand's distinction between artistic creation and "communication" is crucial, as she indicated in a 1946 journal entry: "[T]he idea of writing a philosophical non-fiction book bored me; in such a book, the purpose would actually be to teach others, to present my ideas to *them*. In a book of fiction the purpose is to create, for myself, the kind of world I want and to live in it while I am creating it; then, as a secondary consequence, to let others enjoy this world . . . and to the extent that, they can."[16] As Rand suggests, communication and artistic creation employ fundamentally different kinds of focus. Yet, to say that the artist creates *for himself* does not mean that he does not care whether others appreciate his completed work. It simply means that such a concern does not govern the act of creation.[17] While Rand deals only fleetingly with this principle in her essays on art, it is the theme of her short story "The Simplest Thing in the World" (the only work of fiction she included in *The Romantic Manifesto*)—about a talented but impoverished writer who attempts to write something "commercial" but cannot because it belies his sense of life.[18]

Although Rand's view of the artist's focus differs substantially from Tolstoy's idea of "communication," both writers regard *intelligibility* as essential to art. In emphasizing the importance of this attribute, Rand, too, was reacting against the inscrutability of modernist art—which, by her time, had exceeded anything Tolstoy could have imagined. But Rand clearly recognizes that there is an *indirect* "process of communication" between the artist and the "viewer or reader,"[19] which she analyzes in cognitive terms as follows:

> . . . [T]he artist starts with a broad abstraction [concept] which he has to concretize, to bring into reality by means of the appropriate particulars; the viewer [or reader] perceives the particulars, integrates them and grasps the abstraction from which they came, thus completing the circle. . . . The creative process resembles a process of deduction; the viewing process resembles a process of induction.[20] [35]

In order to objectify his values, the artist must translate them into concretes, into forms appropriate to the nature of reality as perceived by the human mind.[21] When concretized, these values are made accessible to the responder. Thus, Rand's analysis of the indirect process of communication involved in art reinforces the fundamental connection between her theory of art and her theory of knowledge. Human cognition, she emphasizes, requires "dancing back and forth" between the abstract and the concrete.[22] One must always ground one's abstractions in real concretes, and one must always try to understand the abstract principles or concepts implicit in all concretes. As Rand suggests, art may be the pre-eminent activity in which that process is carried out with regard to the most important abstractions of human life.

The Significance of Artistic Selectivity

According to Rand, the artist does not merely simulate reality: "he *stylizes* it."[23] (36) That is, he "condense[s it] to essential characteristics." By "essential," here as elsewhere, Rand means *fundamental*. The artist

> selects those aspects of existence which he regards as metaphysically significant—and by isolating and stressing them, by omitting the insignificant and accidental, he presents *his* view of existence. . . . His selection constitutes his evaluation: everything included in a work of art—from theme to subject to brushstroke or adjective—acquires metaphysical [i.e., fundamental] significance by the mere fact of being included, of being *important* enough to include. [36]

Whereas cognitive abstractions pertain to what is "epistemologically essential to distinguish one class of existents from all others," and normative abstractions pertain to "what is *good*," esthetic abstractions, in Rand's view, pertain to "what is *important*."[24] (36)

Further, in defining art as a mode of "*re*-creation" of reality, Rand indicates that the artist does not create his work *ex nihilo* but, rather, bases it on objective, perceptible reality. Her views on this crucial point contrast sharply with those of modernist theorists, who regard the artist as free of all such "constraints."[25] As she states in another context:

> The power to rearrange the combinations of natural elements is the only creative power man possesses. It is an enormous and glorious power—and it is the only meaning of the concept "creative." "Creation" does not (and metaphysically cannot) mean the power to bring something into existence out of nothing. "Creation" means the power to bring into existence an arrangement (or combination or integration) of natural elements that had not existed before. (This is true of any human product, scientific or esthetic: man's imagination is nothing more than the ability to rearrange the things he has observed in reality.)[26]

In stating that the artist "presents *his* view of existence" in his work, Rand appears to mean that the artist's *comprehensive* view of existence is implicit in—and, as she subsequently suggests, inferrable from—his work, regardless of the medium or the scale. As she elsewhere indicates, however, the capacity of an art work to project such a view varies greatly in degree, according to the nature and scope of the medium and the particular genre.[27] Individual works of painting and sculpture, for instance, confined as they are to representing only the visual and tactile aspects of experience at a single moment, are inevitably limited in scope, compared with, say, a novel. They can at best only suggest complex issues such as human motivation and morality. In any case we would argue that no work of art, however comprehensive, presents the artist's "view of existence." Rather, each work embodies his view of an *aspect*, or *aspects*, of existence. In sum, while we agree with Rand's proposition that the artist's sense of life governs his selectivity, inferences cannot be reliably drawn from his work, concerning so complex a psychological totality.[28]

In emphasizing the significance of selectivity, Rand illuminates a principle that has been recognized since antiquity. Aristotle, for example, praised Homer for omitting episodes incidental to the main narrative of his epics, "[f]or a thing whose presence or absence makes no visible [perceptible] difference is not an organic part of the whole."[29] Early in the twentieth century, the painter-critic Kenyon Cox wrote of the "selective imitation" involved in the art of painting.[30] Similarly, Langer observed that a work of art, though an "imitation" of natural forms, "is never a *copy* in the ordinary sense. . . . It records what [the artist] finds significant."[31] Statements of this principle can easily be multiplied.

More than most theorists, Rand is concerned with identifying and articulating the basic philosophic premises that inform artistic choices. To illustrate the role of implicit premises in the creation of art, she returns to the contrast between ancient Greek and medieval sculpture which she touched upon in the simplest of terms in "The Psycho-Epistemology of Art." She argues that an artist who, like the sculptors of ancient Greece, chooses to depict man as "a god-like figure,"

> is aware . . . that men may be crippled or diseased or helpless; but he regards these conditions as accidental, as irrelevant to the essential nature of man—and he presents a figure embodying strength, beauty, intelligence, self-confidence, as man's proper, natural state. [37]

Similarly, an artist who, like many of the sculptors of the Middle Ages, depicts man as. . . . "a deformed monstrosity," is aware that there are men who are healthy, happy or confident; but he regards *these* conditions as accidental or illusory, as irrelevant to man's essential nature—and he presents a tortured figure embodying pain, ugliness, terror, as man's proper, natural state. [37]

Crudely drawn though her art-historical analogies may be, the images Rand thereby conjures up vividly illustrate a dominant aspect of both the art and the metaphysical outlook of each culture. Yet, as we indicated in Chapter 1, the reader should not make the mistake of regarding such statements as adequately representing the complexity of either Greek or medieval culture.[32]

Rand now returns to the question of *why* the painting of a beautiful woman with a cold sore would evoke a more intense response than would such a woman in reality. That minor affliction, she argues, engaging once again in exaggeration, "acquires a monstrous metaphysical significance by virtue of being included in a painting. It declares that a woman's beauty and her efforts to achieve glamor (the beautiful evening gown) are a futile illusion undercut by a seed of corruption which can mar and destroy them at any moment— that this is reality's mockery of man—that all of man's values and efforts are impotent against the power, not even of some great cataclysm, but of a miserable little physical infection." (37) Rand's rhetoric aside, the principle of her argument is no doubt valid: particular details do assume greater significance in a work of art than they would possess in reality, because the viewer is at least subliminally aware that their presence is *intentional*, and that the artist must therefore have considered them important. But in her specific application of this principle, linking beauty and glamor to "all of man's values and efforts," she surely overstates the case.

In response to those who might defend such a painting as being "true to life," Rand counters that, unlike a news report, "art is not concerned with actual occurrences or events as such, but with their metaphysical significance to man." (37) This important distinction—between "journalistic information" and fiction—is one that she repeatedly draws upon. While the reporter can exercise selectivity in his "manner" of presentation and in determining which *details* of an event are most relevant, he is expected to do so as objectively and accurately as possible, without altering or inventing them. But the "range of selectivity" for the fiction-writer includes altering "the events themselves." He need not, indeed should not, merely stick to the facts. He must not only re-create the events appropriate to his story, he must know what "he wants to say by means of that story." Though he may not be fully conscious of his reasons for a particular choice in the heat of creation, he should, Rand insists, be able to identify them on reflection.[33]

The Response to Art

In Rand's view, the distinction between art and strictly factual types of representation has important implications for the responder.[34] While a news article is a "concrete from which one may or may not draw an abstraction . . . relevant to one's own life," a work of fiction is an "abstraction that [implicitly] claims universality, i.e., application to every human life."[35] (37–38) This implicit premise accounts for an apparent paradox: one may remain indifferent to the article, despite its reality, Rand argues, whereas "one feels an intensely personal emotion," whether positive or negative, in response to a work of fiction—and, as she implies, to other forms of art. "The emotion may be positive, when one finds the abstraction applicable to oneself—or resentfully negative, when one finds it inapplicable and inimical." (38) Oddly, Rand fails to note that responses to art actually range, in fact, from complete indifference to varying degrees of positive or negative response, and even to ambivalence. Her polarized alternatives and her reference to the applicability to a reader of the abstraction in a work of fiction suggest that here, once more, she is focusing on the moral values conveyed by literature.

The value a person seeks from a work of art, Rand stresses, is neither information nor moral direction ("though these may be involved as secondary consequences"), but rather

> the fulfillment of a more profound need: a confirmation of his view of existence—a confirmation, *not in the sense of resolving cognitive doubts,* but in the sense of permitting him to contemplate his abstractions outside his own mind, in the form of existential concretes. [38, emphasis ours]

This proposition—that art enables man to experience his most important abstractions, his conception of reality and his fundamental values, in concrete, perceptual form—is central to Rand's theory.

Rand does not argue that in order for the work to qualify as art its "view of existence" must conform to a particular value system. She recognizes that art can encompass the broad spectrum of human perspectives, and that each work has the potential to find its audience, according to the values it projects. But she does consider certain kinds of art to be objectively superior, as she now makes clear. To begin, she argues that art plays an especially important role in the life of a "rational" individual, whose long-term goals are difficult to achieve and require persistent effort over a lifetime ("the higher the values, the harder the struggle"). For such an individual, art that projects his values can give him the instantaneous "sense of living in a universe where [they] have been successfully achieved." (38) What purpose does art serve for an "irrational" person? For such an individual, "the concretized projection of his malevolent sense of life serves, not as fuel and inspiration to move forward, but as permission to stand still: it declares that values are unattainable, that the struggle is futile." Moreover, "his kind of art gives him a moment's illusion that *he* is right—that evil is metaphysically potent." Rand concludes: "Art is man's metaphysical mirror; . . . what an irrational man seeks to see is a justification—even if only a justification of his depravity, as a last convulsion of his betrayed self-esteem." (39)

The principle to be abstracted from Rand's argument is that *each person seeks to find his own view of life concretized in art.* But her overstatement and her moralistic tone are unfortunate, as is her tendency to oversimplification. First, she seems to imply that irrationality—which she elsewhere characterizes as "the act of unfocusing [one's] mind, . . . the [deliberate] refusal to see, . . . to know"—necessarily implies a "malevolent sense of life."[36] As we argued earlier, however, one cannot posit a cause-and-effect relationship between an individual's sense of life and his morality.[37] Most disturbing is Rand's attempt to link one's personal response to a particular kind of art not only with "irrationality"[38] but with moral "depravity" and a belief in the power of "evil." Even Peikoff, while generally uncritical of Rand's views, has emphatically rejected the notion that one's sense of life entails specific moral implications, or that valid moral judgments can be drawn from an individual's sense-of-life responses to, or preferences in, art. As he has unequivocally stated, one "can respond to tragedy without having a tragic sense of life," one "can have a tragic sense of life without being in any way immoral, corrupt, or evil," and one "can have a tragic sense of life and still be one hundred percent honest, rational, and moral."[39]

Rand's dubious moralizing aside, she offers valuable insights into the nature of the response to art. She regards the individual viewer, reader, or listener as actively engaged in the process—epistemologically, in grasping the meaning of the work, and emotionally, in reacting to it on the basis of his personal values. Further, she avoids the common pitfall of confusing the concept of *art* with that of "good art."[40] As we shall see more clearly in Chapter 4, her criteria for denying the status of art to certain works are based on her view of the nature of reality and human cognition, not on a particular code of values, whether esthetic or moral.

Subject and Meaning in Art

According to Rand, the meaning conveyed by a work of art is projected through "two distinct, but interrelated" aspects: the subject ("*what* an artist chooses to present") and the style ("*how* he presents it"). Her brief analysis of these

key concepts in "Art and Sense of Life" is frustratingly incomplete and problematical, however. Even when supplemented with material from other sources,
the account that emerges is confusing and inconsistent. Rand glosses over
fundamental distinctions, and the examples she offers do not always support
her sweepingly categorical assertions. Nonetheless, as is so often the case,
her ideas warrant consideration.

On the fundamental issue of meaning in art, Rand, much like Aristotle
(*Poetics*, ch. 2), clearly holds that all art pertains, implicitly or explicitly, to
human concerns. As she explains, art is the objectification of values, and the
"most important values [are] those affecting [oneself] and, therefore, other
human beings."[41]

With regard to the way in which an art work conveys meaning, Rand holds
that the "subject" is the principal consideration. In her view, the subject indicates "what aspects of human existence the artist regards as important—
as worthy of being re-created and contemplated." The nature of the subject "expresses a view of man's existence" and, in so doing, "reveals" the
artist's metaphysical outlook.[42] She also maintains that the artist's "selectivity in regard to subject" is "the primary, the essential, the cardinal aspect
of art."

> In literature, this means: *the story*—which means: the plot and the charac-
> ters—which means: the kind of men and events that a writer chooses to
> portray.
>   The subject is not the only attribute of art, but it is the fundamental one,
> it *is the end to which all the others are the means.*[43]

Contrary to "most esthetic theories," in which "the end—the subject—is omitted from consideration, and only the means are regarded as esthetically relevant," Rand insists on the primacy of the subject.[44]

While Rand is justified in rejecting the excessive emphasis on style in
much modern criticism, her reaction leads her to the opposite pole of a false
dichotomy. Thus her emphasis on the subject matter of art prompts her to
deprecate Vermeer's choice of everyday domestic subjects, for example, which
suggest to her "the bleak metaphysics of Naturalism." (41) Here "subject"
for her apparently means those aspects of external reality which constituted
the artist's starting point, as it were; that is, what he chose to "selectively re-
create" in his work. In this instance, she seems to regard such *external* subject matter as the "end" to which all the other attributes of the work, including
its style, are the "means."

At other times, however, Rand more appropriately argues that the ultimate "end" of an art work is the meaning embodied by the finished work in

its entirety, as a result of the artist's particular concretization and stylization of the subject. For example, in "Art and Sense of Life," she states that "it is the subject (qualified by the theme) that projects an art work's view of man's place in the universe"; she further notes, without elaboration, that the *theme* (the work's abstract meaning) is the "link uniting . . . subject and style." (40) In "Basic Principles of Literature," moreover, she emphasizes that a novel is an *integrated whole*, whose effect (and meaning) depends on the "indivisible sum" of its attributes, which are not discrete parts but are only conceptualized separately for analysis. (80) In that essay, she also stresses that the *theme* serves as the "integrator" of a novel by "defin[ing] its purpose," "set[ting] the writer's standard of selection," and directing the writer's "innumerable choices." (81) Although she is referring primarily to fiction and, secondarily, to drama, her remarks also apply, in broad principle, to the visual arts (though not to music, a fact she fails to mention[45]). As she observes in "Art and Cognition," all the elements of painting—not only subject, but theme, composition, and style as well—"are involved in projecting an artist's view of existence." (49) In all these instances, then, she appears to properly differentiate between the nominal "subject" and the *ultimate content, or meaning, of the work as a whole*—and it is the latter that she regards as corresponding to "the artist's view of existence."

Rand's occasional confusion of external *subject matter* (the existential phenomena a work nominally "refers to" or "is about") with the ultimate *content* of a work of art, at times leads her to grossly misconstrue individual works, especially in the visual arts—as in the case of Vermeer. While she admires his "brilliant clarity of style," she derisively characterizes his subject matter as "the folks next door . . . to kitchens"—mistakenly implying that his subjects are essentially banal. Only one of his paintings, *Maidservant Pouring Milk*, even suggests the vicinity of a kitchen. Most of his work, in fact, depicts figures engaged in thoughtful or creative pursuits: reading or writing letters, music-making, and painting, for example. Several works are pure portrait studies, with no genre subject at all. Finally, two paintings—*The Astronomer* and *The Geographer*—celebrate the decidedly non-domestic realms of science and exploration.[46] More important, Rand fails to grasp the full significance of Vermeer's treatment of even the most mundane of his subjects. Through his masterly technique and extraordinary sensitivity, he transcends the seeming triviality of simple acts such as the reading of a letter or the pouring of milk, and thereby suggests, among other things, the depth and worth of the individual human soul.

Rand's error regarding subject matter is a common one,[47] and does not diminish the value of her insistence on the centrality of *meaning* in art. Another philosopher, Louis Arnaud Reid, offers a subtler analysis of subject matter, which can serve to supplement hers on this important issue.[48] Like Rand, he holds that meaning in art is of fundamental importance, but he offers a clearer account of where that meaning resides. To begin, he points out that the terms "subject" or "subject matter" properly apply only to the visual and literary arts, not to music, since they imply that "what is 'represented'" can be conceptualized and verbalized apart from the representation itself.[49] With respect to the representational arts (literary as well as visual), Reid differentiates between "primary," "secondary," and "tertiary" subject matter.[50] In his view, existential events or phenomena experienced by or known to ("cognized by") an artist constitute his *"primary* subject-matter"—for example, a landscape in nature as observed by a painter. (230–31) The *"secondary* subject-matter" is the landscape as the artist begins to transform it (to "selectively re-create it," Rand would say). (233) Finally, the *"tertiary* subject-matter," according to Reid, is the subject "as it finally appears when the whole embodiment is complete." Simply stated, the tertiary subject matter is the *content* of the work—that is, "the subject-matter imaginatively experienced ['re-created'] in the work of art."[51] (234–37)

Reid's analysis helps to illuminate Rand's judgments regarding the "subject" of particular artworks. In focusing, in effect, on the "primary" subject, she often misses the ultimate content (Reid's "tertiary" subject matter). Thus a work that she regards as trivial or bleak because of its primary subject, may, in its ultimate meaning, be far from that.

Style

On the topic of *style*, Rand remarked that she did not "know of anyone who ever said anything sensible" about it. Candidly admitting that she was "not a very wide reader" in esthetics, she declared that what she would say about it was solely the result of her own thinking.[52] Though her analysis has important points in common with the ideas of other theorists, she makes her own distinctive contribution to the subject, but only as pertaining to the field of literature. Rand observes in "Art and Sense of Life" that style is "the most complex element[53] of art, the most revealing and, often, the most baffling psychologically." (41) Unlike plot, characterization, and theme, it is the one attribute of literature that "cannot be synopsized."[54] She holds that an artist's style—his "particular, distinctive or characteristic mode of execution"—is the "product of his own psycho-epistemology"; that is, of his habitual ways of thinking and feeling. (40) She is by no means alone in holding such a view. Numerous literary critics and art historians have attempted to analyze stylistic features in terms of an artist's attitudes and habits of mind[55]—although they of course do not use Rand's term "psycho-epistemology."

Rand differs from other theorists primarily in attempting to uncover and articulate the fundamental epistemological and metaphysical assumptions underlying works of art.[56] But the manner in which she pursues this goal is questionable. It is one thing to recognize that the style of a work is the product of an artist's way of thinking, and quite another to attempt to *infer* his psycho-epistemology from his work.[57] Yet Rand insists that the style of an art work "reveals" the artist's psycho-epistemology, just as the subject "reveals" his metaphysics. (40) Accordingly, she does not hesitate to base broad judgments on minimal evidence, with the result that her analyses sometimes depreciate the meaning and artistic value of particular works, and deprive the unwary reader who uncritically accepts her dicta of the pleasure he might reasonably derive from the works in question.

As our critique of Rand's analysis of subject matter has indicated, her dichotomy between subject and style—as the "what" and the "how," the "metaphysics" and the "psycho-epistemology," of an art work—is itself a misleading oversimplification. Style inevitably affects the content, or the "what," of a work.[58] Similarly, aspects of the subject matter often figure in an artist's style, as she herself at times acknowledges. In "Basic Principles of Literature," for example, she argues that literary style involves not only *choice of words* ("particular words and sentence structures") but also *choice of content* ("those aspects of . . . description, narrative or dialogue" that a writer "chooses to communicate"). (94) Even the choice of different words to convey an idea tends to alter meaning, since no two words carry precisely the same connotation (which is crucial to both style and ultimate meaning), although their denotation may be roughly synonymous.[59]

In analyzing fictional treatments of similar subject matter, in order to highlight their stylistic differences, Rand attempts to draw out the psycho-epistemological implications of those differences.[60] To cite one example, which she includes in "Basic Principles of Literature," she quotes brief narrative descriptions of New York City from Mickey Spillane's *One Lonely Night* and Thomas Wolfe's *The Web and the Rock*, arguing that they are virtually polar opposites in their approach. Spillane creates "a mood of desolate loneliness" by describing carefully selected perceptual *concretes*: the "misty . . . foglike" rain, the "cold gray" atmosphere, the "pale ovals of white that were faces locked behind the steamed-up windows of the cars that hissed by," and a "few sleepy, yellow lights off in the distance."[61] (95–96) Wolfe, on the other hand, offers no concrete details, visual or otherwise, to characterize New York. He "asserts that the city is 'beautiful,' but does not tell us *what* makes it beautiful," Rand observes. "Such words as 'beautiful,' 'astounding,' 'incomparable,' [and] 'lovely' are estimates; in the absence of any indication of what aroused these estimates, they are arbitrary assertions and meaningless generalities." Whereas Spillane's style in the sample passage is "reality-oriented and addressed to an objective psycho-epistemology," the excerpt from Wolfe is "emotion-oriented and addressed to a subjectiv[ist][62] psycho-epistemology: he expects the reader to accept emotions divorced from facts, and to accept them second-hand." (96) In Rand's view, the Wolfe passage is badly written, because it does not conform to the way the human mind best functions. Instead of concretizing abstractions by means of carefully selected particulars, Wolfe presents "floating abstractions" and emotional responses disconnected from the objective reality that give rise to them. He therefore requires the reader to intuit the appropriate concretes from the connotations of his vocabulary. While all good writing depends to a considerable extent on careful attention to the connotations of words, to their implicit as well as their explicit meanings, Rand argues, Wolfe virtually ignores denotation in favor of connotation.[63]

Rand's unforgiving judgment of Wolfe's style is troubling on several counts, its critical interest notwithstanding. First, the excerpted passages are taken out of context. By her own admission, moreover, she had "not read much of [Wolfe], in fact very little."[64] Most disturbing is her unfortunate subtext, of a kind that infects many of her judgments about particular works and styles of art: an implicit *moral* condemnation, not only of the artist in question but of anyone who might respond positively to work in such a style.[65]

In Rand's view, an individual "whose normal mental state" is one of "full focus, will create and respond to a style of "radiant clarity and ruthless precision—a style that projects sharp outlines, cleanliness, purpose, an intransigent commitment to full awareness and clean-cut identity."[66] In contrast, an individual who

> is moved by the fog of his feelings and spends most of his time out of focus will create and respond to a style of blurred, 'mysterious' murk, where outlines dissolve and entities flow into one another, where words connote anything and denote nothing, where colors float without objects, and objects float without weight—a level of awareness appropriate to a universe where A can be any non-A one chooses, where nothing can be known with certainty and nothing much is demanded of one's consciousness. [40–41]

Given the primacy of rationality in Rand's ethics, it is clear that moral condemnation and contempt lurk between the lines of such a passage. Indeed, its judgmental implications become explicit in the concluding paragraph of "Art and Sense of Life": "When one learns to translate the meaning of an art work into objective terms," declares Rand, "one discovers that nothing is as potent as art in exposing the essence of a man's character. An artist reveals his naked soul in his work—and so, gentle reader, do you when you respond to it."[67] (44)

Style and "Efficacy of Consciousness"

According to Rand, an artist's style is not only the "product of his own psycho-epistemology" but also "by implication, a projection of his view of man's consciousness, of its efficacy or impotence, of its proper method and level of functioning." (40) She offers no evidence in support of this sweeping assertion.[68] In concluding her discussion of style, however, she elaborates on a proposition she introduced toward the end of "The Psycho-Epistemology of Art": she declares that style is of "profoundly *personal*" importance because it is "an expression of that level of mental functioning on which the artist feels most at home. . . . To the artist, it is an expression, to the reader or viewer a confirmation, of his own consciousness—which means: of his efficacy—which means: of his self-esteem (or pseudo-self-esteem)." (42) As we argued in Chapter 1, such a proposition seems to be fundamentally at odds with Rand's emphatic declaration that what a person seeks from a work of art is "a confirmation of his view of existence . . . *not in the sense of resolving cognitive doubts, but in the sense of permitting him to contemplate his abstractions outside his own mind, in the form of existential concretes.*" (38, emphasis ours) Rand's contention that "art confirms or denies the efficacy of a man's consciousness, according to whether an art work supports or negates his own fundamental view of reality" (24) can only mean that if an art work supports (corresponds to) an individual's sense of life, it confirms (validates) the efficacy of his consciousness. If an artwork negates (contradicts) one's fundamental view of reality, it denies (invalidates) the efficacy of his consciousness.[69] Our own experience suggests that such claims are simply not true. For example, we loathe the grotesquely tortured view of life projected by the work of the British painter Francis Bacon,[70] but his paintings do not prompt us to doubt our own mental efficacy. Instead, we infer a profound psychological disturbance on his part.

Esthetic Judgment

Rand insists that, although one's "sense of life" forms the basis for one's deepest responses to art, it is not an appropriate criterion for judging art. A work of art cannot be properly evaluated as "good" or "bad" on the basis of a sense-of-life response. She thus draws a crucial distinction between *esthetic response* (though she does not use that term) and what she terms *esthetic judgment.*[71] The former is a spontaneous, emotional reaction to the work as a whole. The latter is a function of intellectual appraisal; it is a dispassionate evaluation of the success with which the artist projects his intended theme. Whether one shares or does not share an artist's fundamental view of life, Rand explains, "is irrelevant to an *esthetic* appraisal of his work *qua* art."

> One does not have to agree with an artist (nor even to enjoy him) in order to evaluate his work. In essence, an objective evaluation requires that one identify the artist's theme, the abstract meaning of his work (exclusively by identifying the evidence contained in the work and allowing no other, outside considerations), then evaluate the means by which he conveys it—i.e., taking *his* theme as criterion, [one must] evaluate the purely esthetic elements of the work, the technical mastery (or lack of it) with which he projects (or fails to project) *his* view of life.[72] [42]

Note that, in Rand's view, the theme is to be discovered "in the work" itself, not through any biographical evidence, commentary, or other "outside considerations." Since every work of art is an *objectification* of *fundamental* values, its meaning should be discernible to individuals other than its maker—at least to those who share the same culture. (As to the specific "esthetic principles . . . which must guide an objective evaluation," Rand explicitly places them "outside the scope of this discussion," for she is mainly concerned with the issue of the nature and function of art.)

In Rand's view one may well say: "This is a great work of art, but I don't like it," or "I love it, even though it isn't a great work of art"—recognizing that the concept of "greatness" refers to objective qualities, apart from one's personal response. To illustrate the deeply personal nature of a response to art based on a sense-of-life affinity, Rand confides that she loves the work of Victor Hugo, for example, for the grandeur of his sense of life, although she disagrees with virtually all of his explicit philosophy. Yet one can enjoy art in other than sense-of-life terms, she explains. She likes the work of Dostoevsky "for his superb mastery of plot structure and for his merciless dissection of the psychology of evil." Yet his sense of life, "almost diametrically opposed" to her own, gives her "the feeling of entering a chamber of horrors"—albeit "with a powerful guide." Through these and other frankly personal observations, Rand vividly evokes the psychological complexity of the response to art, without attempting to generalize her own responses into absolutes.

Rand's brief remarks on "esthetic judgment" in "Art and Sense of Life" do not exhaust her views on the issue of evaluating art, however. As her analysis of the subject matter of art suggests, her ultimate criteria pertain not merely to how well the artist realizes his theme (whatever it may be) but also to the depth, universality, and moral compass of that theme.[73] Consistent with that view is her evaluation of the "top rank" of Romantic novelists and dramatists—writers such as Hugo, Dostoevsky, and Schiller. In addition to their "purely literary genius," she lauds them as "unmatched in the brilliant ingenuity of their plot structures." Most important, they are "concerned with man's soul (i.e., his consciousness)." (107)

> They are *moralists* in the most profound sense of the word; their concern is not merely with values, but specifically with *moral* values and with the power of moral values in shaping character. . . . The events of their plots are shaped, determined and motivated by the characters' values (or treason to values), by their struggle in pursuit of spiritual goals and by profound value-conflicts. Their themes are fundamental, universal, timeless issues of man's existence— and they are the only consistent creators of the rarest attribute of literature: the perfect integration of theme and plot, which they achieve with superlative virtuosity.[74]

Once again, Rand's position is comparable to that of Louis Arnaud Reid, who held that the greatest art deals with values that are "profound and lofty and broad and far-reaching in the complexity of their implications"—"the greater the values, and the more of great values we have, provided they are united into one coherent meaning, the greater is the work."[75] For Rand, too, the content or meaning of art is primary, and no work can be judged great that is neither profound nor complex in its meaning.

4

"Art and Cognition"

Rand begins her fourth and final essay on esthetics, "Art and Cognition,"[1] by asking this fundamental question:

> What kind of objects may be properly classified as works of art? What are the valid forms of art—and why these? [45]

No issue of esthetics is more basic, of course—or has been more beclouded in the twentieth century. In her three preceding essays, Rand did not deal with this question directly, though she clearly implied that by art she meant the major categories traditionally designated as the *fine arts*, a term she did not use.[2] In "Art and Cognition," she at last offers a justification for this system of classification.

Before analyzing the principal branches of art, Rand restates the core of her esthetic theory:

> Art is a selective re-creation of reality according to an artist's metaphysical value-judgments. Man's profound need of art lies in the fact that his cognitive faculty is conceptual, i.e., that he acquires [and retains] knowledge by means of abstractions, and needs the power to bring his widest metaphysical abstractions into his immediate perceptual awareness. Art fulfills this need: by means of a selective re-creation, it concretizes man's fundamental view of himself and of existence.[3] [45]

Rand then differentiates the major branches of art according to "the specific . . . media they employ"[4] and their relationship to man's cognitive faculty. *Literature* re-creates reality through language and "deals with the field of concepts"; *painting* employs color on a flat surface and "deals with the field of sight"; *sculpture* employs solid materials, in three-dimensional form, and deals with "the combined fields of sight and touch"; and *music*, which employs "sounds produced by the *periodic* vibrations of a sonorous body," deals with the field of hearing—it does not re-create visual or tactile reality but rather "evokes man's sense-of-life emotions." As for *architecture*, Rand notes that it "is in a class by itself, because it combines art with a utilitarian purpose and does not re-create reality, but creates a structure for man's habitation or use, expressing man's values." Although that proposition clearly suggests that architecture does *not* qualify as art, according to her own definition, Rand then states: "Architecture, *qua* art, is close to sculpture: its field is three-dimensional, i.e., [that of] sight and touch, but transposed to a grand spatial scale." (46) Despite the puzzling contradictions implicit in these remarks, she says nothing further about the nature of architecture in "Art and Cognition"—apart from a passing reference in her discussion of sculpture,[5] and this cryptic allusion to her novel *The Fountainhead*: "I shall not include architecture in this discussion—I assume the reader knows which book I will refer him to." (50) Her fictional treatment of architecture in *The Fountainhead* cannot take the place of a formal philosophic consideration of the subject, however. In Chapter 10, we consider architecture in relation to Rand's esthetic theory, and conclude that, in spite of her contradictory statements in "Art and Cognition," architecture is not *art*, by her own definition of the concept.

Elaborating on the relationship between art and man's cognitive faculty, Rand briefly summarizes her view that human cognition begins with the ability to perceive *things* (i.e., *entities*) directly, through the faculties of *touch* and *sight*.[6] Whereas the other senses (hearing, taste, and smell) give only partial information, pertaining to the *effects* or *attributes* of entities, sight and touch provide direct awareness of the entities themselves.[7] Since "It is by perceiving entities that man perceives the universe," Rand insists, he can *"concretize his view of existence [only] by means of concepts (language) or by means of his entity-perceiving senses (sight and touch)."*[8] (46) Yet music, Rand observes, "does not deal with entities" in this sense: it does not concretize *things*. (46) Unlike the representational arts (painting, sculpture, and literature), music does not re-create tangible, visible aspects of reality. How, then, does it qualify as art? Rand maintains (mistakenly, in our view) that "its psycho-epistemological function is different from that of the other arts."

Rand's insistence that art must concretize a view of reality by means of either concepts or visible and tactile entities, and her claim that the psycho-epistemological function of music differs from that of the other arts, might lead one to conclude that her concept of art does not, in fact, include music (since music "does not deal with entities"). The difficulty stems from her overly narrow definition of *concretization* in this context. In implying that concretization requires entities, she ignores the important distinction she draws, in her *Introduction to Objectivist Epistemology,* between "concretes" and the much narrower concept "entities." In that context, she states: "The first concepts man forms are concepts of entities—since entities are the only primary existents," attributes, motions, and relationships are all dependent on entities. (15) Equating "existents" with "concretes," Rand explains that they subsume not only *entities* but also attributes, actions, and relationships— "everything that exists on which you can focus, anything which you can [mentally] isolate." (241) Thus, existents include *events* as well as what contemporary philosophers call "states of affairs," or situations. Since music does deal with concretes, although not with entities, its psycho-epistemological function is not essentially different from that of the other arts, and it is properly subsumed by Rand's definition of art—as she herself indicates in her fuller discussion of the nature of music (to which she devotes by far the greatest space in "Art and Cognition," allocating four times as many pages to it as she does to any of the other arts). Given the length and complexity of that discussion, we consider it separately, in Chapter 5.

In "Art and Cognition," Rand analyzes (albeit briefly) the nature of each of the major art forms, beginning with a comparison of literature and the visual arts. Although literature "re-creates reality by means of words, i.e., concepts," while the visual arts "produce concrete, perceptually available" objects, she emphasizes, the various forms of these arts are all fundamentally *conceptual* in nature. "All are products of and addressed to the conceptual level of man's consciousness, and they differ only in their means." These art forms ultimately serve the same function, that of *cognitive integration*: each of them "integrates man's forms of cognition [i.e., perception and conception], unifies his consciousness and clarifies his grasp of reality." (47)

Literature

Rand's analysis of literature in "Art and Cognition" is brief and highly abstract. She observes that the conceptual nature of the literary art forms is most easily grasped, because in re-creating reality literature employs conceptual material directly, through the medium of language. Yet literature, like the visual arts, must appeal to the sensory-perceptual level of awareness as well. To be effective, it must employ language to convey not merely broad abstractions but vivid, *concrete* images of characters, situations, events, and places—by describing their "specific sights, sounds, and textures." This is what Rand means when she states that literature "starts with concepts [in the form of words] but integrates them [in]to percepts." (47)

This brief account can be supplemented with material from Rand's essay "Basic Principles of Literature" (1968)—in which she analyzes the fundamental attributes of the major literary forms, with the exception of poetry[9]— and from her *Lectures on Fiction-Writing* (1958).[10] Although her discussion focuses exclusively on her primary interest, the novel, Rand emphasizes that her analysis applies "with appropriate qualifications" to all forms of fiction, including "novels, plays, scenarios, librettos, [and] short stories"—in other words, to those forms of literature which involve plotted action.[11] (80–81) Stephen Cox observes that Rand's literary theory is a "unique combination" of Aristotelian and Romantic principles: like Aristotle, she regards literature as a product of rational human selection and design; at the same time, she renews the Romantic emphasis on the role of the individual artist as the integrating force in the creative process.[12]

Rand's debt to Aristotle is evident in the following remarks, with which she chose (however regrettably, as we shall see) to preface her analysis of the nature of literature:

> The most important principle of the esthetics of literature was formulated by Aristotle, who said that fiction is of greater philosophical importance than history, because "history represents things as they are, while fiction represents them as they might be and ought to be."

This purported citation of Aristotle has long served as an esthetic rallying cry among Objectivists, frequently repeated by Rand and others as a justification for morally idealized fiction.[13] Unfortunately, she misquotes Aristotle and misrepresents his intent.[14] In Chapter 9 of the *Poetics*, he states:

> The distinction between historian and poet . . . consists really in this, that the one describes the thing that has been, and the other a kind of thing that might be. Hence poetry[15] is something more philosophic and of graver import than history, since its statements are of the nature rather of universals, whereas those of history are singulars [i.e., particulars]. By a universal statement I mean one as to what such or such a kind of man will probably or necessarily say or do.[16]

Neither in this passage nor anywhere else does Aristotle state or imply that all poetry (or even all worthwhile poetry) presents life as it *ought to be*. Indeed, in Chapter 25 of the *Poetics*, he makes clear his view that poetry which presents life as it "ought to be" is but one of three possible types.[17] By suggesting that Aristotle was advocating idealization in literature, Rand is arguing for the sort of fiction she wrote and most valued; she is not stating a proposition true of all fiction. Nor is her stress in the opening paragraph of "Basic Principles of Literature," on things "as they ought to be," reflected in the body of the essay. Instead, she presents a largely straightforward account of the four "essential attributes" of fiction—*style, theme, plot*, and *characterization*—without regard to idealized content. (80–81) Since we have already noted her ideas regarding the role of *style* (see Chapter 3), we will limit ourselves to summarizing her analysis of the other three attributes. On the whole, her account is not original, although she does offer some distinctive observations on plot and characterization, which sharpen and deepen the conventional view.

As Rand notes, the *theme* of a novel (as of any work of art) is its "abstract meaning." It need not be philosophic in nature. In her view, a novel may present a "narrower generalization," such as the "portrayal of a certain society in a certain era." But if a novel has "no discernible theme," it is a failure, because its events "add up to nothing": it lacks *integration*—an essential attribute of all art.[18] (81) An original aspect of Rand's analysis of literature is her concept of "plot-theme":

> The link between the theme and the events of a novel is an element which I call the *plot-theme*. . . . [It] is the central conflict or "situation" of a story— a conflict in terms of action, corresponding to the theme and complex enough to create a purposeful progression of events.
>
> The *theme* of a novel is the core of its abstract meaning—the *plot-theme* is the core of its events.
>
> For example, the theme of . . . *Les Misérables* is: "The injustice of society toward its lower classes." The plot-theme is: "The life-long flight of an ex-convict from the pursuit of a ruthless representative of the law.". . .
>
> The integration of an important theme with a complex plot structure is the most difficult achievement possible to a writer, and the rarest. Its great masters are Victor Hugo and Dostoevsky. . . . [T]he events of their novels proceed from, express, illustrate and dramatize their themes. [85–86]

Since a novel is a "re-creation of reality" pertaining to human existence, Rand argues, its meaning must be concretized in terms of human *actions*, the "ultimate form of expression" of all man's "thoughts, knowledge, ideas, [and] values." These actions are presented in the form of a *plot*. Like Aristotle, who held that the plot is "the first principle and, as it were, the soul of a tragedy,"[19] Rand regards plot as the "crucial attribute of a novel." She defines it as "a purposeful progression of logically connected events leading to the resolution of a climax."[20] (81–82) As she explains:

In real life, only a process of final causation[21]—i.e., the process of choosing a goal, then taking the steps to achieve it—can give logical continuity, coherence and meaning to a man's actions. . . .

Contrary to the prevalent literary doctrines of today, it is *realism* that demands a plot structure in a novel. All human actions are goal-directed, consciously or subconsciously; purposelessness is contrary to man's nature: it is a state of neurosis. . . . [I]f one is to present man *as he is*—as he is metaphysically, by his nature, in reality—one has to present him in goal-directed action. [82–83, emphasis in original]

Since goals are not achieved automatically, goal-directed action must be dramatized through *conflict*—either the "inner conflict" of a character or the "conflict of goals and values between two or more characters." The clash or struggle arising from such conflict should never be a "purely physical one," however. Physical action should always be rooted in "psychological conflict or intellectual value-meaning." In Rand's view, "ideas or psychological states divorced from action" and "physical action divorced from ideas and values" are the two sides of the "mind-body dichotomy that plagues literature." (86–87)

Although Rand (like Aristotle) emphasizes the importance of plot, she also recognizes that plot must "proceed from and be consistent with the nature of [the story's] characters." *Characterization* is, in her formulation, "the portrayal of those essential traits which form the unique, distinctive personality of an individual human being," with the emphasis on "essential."[22] Given the complexity of human beings, the writer must be extremely selective in choosing the essentials, and "then proceed to create an individual figure, endowing it with all the appropriate details down to the telling small touches needed to give it full reality. That figure has to be an abstraction, yet look like a concrete; it has to have the universality of an abstraction and, simultaneously, the unrepeatable uniqueness of a *person*."[23]

Characterization is achieved primarily through *action* and *dialogue*; in other words, in externalized form. Descriptions of a character's appearance and manner, and passages dealing with his thoughts and feelings, are "merely auxiliary means," of far less value than showing "what he does and what he says."[24] (87) Most important, an author must never resort to simple assertions about the nature of his characters, without supporting his assertions through significant actions. "[O]ne action is worth a thousand adjectives." Further, Rand emphasizes that a crucial aspect of creating believable and intelligible characters is to reveal their *motivation*—the "basic premises and values that form [their] character and move [them] to action." By the end of any novel, in Rand's view, "the reader must know *why* the characters did the things they did."[25] Whereas the criminal in a simple detective story may be motivated by nothing more than simple greed, a profound novel such as Dostoevksy's *Crime and Punishment* "reveals the soul of a criminal all the way down to his philosophical premises." In the portrayal of motivation, moreover, *consistency* is essential. A character may hold inconsistent premises and be "torn by inner conflicts," but the author must be fully aware and in control of such contradictions, integrating them into the overall characterization. (88)

Finally, all the major elements of a novel (as of any work of art) must be fully integrated. "[A] good novel is an indivisible sum." Its theme can be conveyed only through the plot, and the events of the plot depend on the nature of the characters who enact them; their characterization is, in turn, achieved only through the plot, which itself depends on the theme. It does not matter which of these elements a writer begins with in the creative process, "provided he knows that all three attributes have to unite into so well integrated a sum that no starting point can be discerned."[26] (93–94)

Painting and Sculpture

In contrast to literature, the visual arts convey abstract (conceptual) meaning through directly perceptible physical entities; thus, both painting and sculpture "start with percepts and integrate them [in]to concepts." (47) In other words, the painter or sculptor creates visually and/or tactilely perceptible forms to convey, or concretize, an abstract meaning. Rand's emphasis on the ultimately conceptual, integrative nature of painting and sculpture is fundamental. She explains:

> The visual arts do not deal with the sensory field of awareness as such, but with *the sensory field as perceived by a conceptual consciousness.* The sensory-perceptual awareness of an adult does not consist of mere sense data . . . , but of automatized integrations that combine sense data with a vast context of conceptual knowledge.[27] [47, emphasis in original]

Rand here implies that so-called abstract art is not art at all, since it reduces the visual field to "mere sense data," in effect, by eliminating the representation of objects or entities.[28] Rand's stress on the fundamentally "conceptual" nature of art should not be viewed as legitimizing the postmodernist phenomenon of "conceptual art," however, which we discuss in Chapter 14.

Through the selectivity of the creative process, the visual artist forms an image that reveals his conceptual focus. In everyday experience, individuals attend to and remember different aspects of the innumerable entities in their range of perception. And what they remember is not necessarily what is metaphysically most important. In place of their "countless random impressions," the artist provides a *"visual abstraction"*—an integrated sum of the aspects or details he has identified as significant.[29] (48) The apples in a still-life painting, for example, may seem, at normal viewing distance, to possess a "heightened reality"—although the illusory nature of that appearance may become evident on close examination. The artist has isolated "the essential, distinguishing characteristics of apples" and integrated them "into a single visual unit." He has performed the process of concept-formation in purely visual terms.[30] (47–48) The painter concretizes the *idea* of an apple (that is, of apples in general)

> by means of visual essentials, which most men have not focused on or identified, but [which they] recognize at once. What they feel, in effect, is: "Yes, that's how an apple looks to me!" In fact, no apple ever looked that way to them—only to the selectively focused eye of an artist. But, psychoepistemologically, their sense of heightened reality is not an illusion: it comes from the greater clarity which the artist has given to their mental image. The painting has integrated the sum of their countless random impressions, and thus has brought order to the visual field of their experience.

As Rand adds, the same process of visual abstraction is at work whether the subject is a simple still life or a complex composition involving the human figure. (Though she is here focusing exclusively on the purely *cognitive* aspect of art, the affective, or emotional, aspect, which she analyzed in "Art and Sense of Life" is also relevant, of course.)

"The closer an artist comes to a conceptual method of functioning visually," Rand concludes, "the greater his work." As an example, she cites Vermeer, arguing that he "raised perception to the conceptual level"—in contrast with the Impressionists, who "attempted to disintegrate perception into sense data." (48–49) On Rand's analysis of Vermeer's work, we have already commented in Chapter 3. We should now note an apparent inconsistency in her views. The seeming disintegration of form for which she criticizes Impressionist paintings occurs mainly at close range—much as in her hypothetical example of the painting of the apple discussed above—and it is often resolved, to a large degree, when the images are viewed at the appropriate distance. If Impressionists seemed to "disintegrate perception into sense data," it was not with the intent of dissolving form, as Rand charged, but rather of seeing forms through the atmospheric effects of light, as one normally experiences them.[31]

Rand devotes less than a page to the subject of sculpture, and her brief analysis is marred by a number of misstatements and erroneous implications. Referring to sculpture as a "more limited" art form than painting, she asserts that it is "restricted by the necessity to present a three-dimensional shape as man does *not* perceive it: without color." (49, emphasis in original) Her negative emphasis is both surprising and misleading. Whereas one might expect her to analyze sculpture in terms of its distinguishing attributes—that is, its tactile and spatial qualities—she focuses instead on a nonessential element, color. Further, she mistakenly implies that color is never used to enhance the naturalism, or verisimilitude, of sculpture. Contrary to common belief, even the ancient Greeks often painted their figures or otherwise sought coloristic effects, as in the practice of using inlaid work in bronze sculptures to simulate the natural appearance of the eye.[32] The prevalence of monochromatic sculpture is, in fact, a relatively recent phenomenon, the exception rather than the rule in the history of art.

In any case, the issue of color is beside the point. The primary focus of sculpture is, as Rand herself previously stated, three-dimensional form. From the standpoint of epistemology, moreover, one could certainly argue that the form of a thing is more significant than its color.[33] Rand's apparent implication that the sculptural medium is not merely different from but also inferior to painting, because it is deficient in color, is therefore inappropriate.[34] She might as well have argued that painting is "more limited" than sculpture because it re-creates reality in only two dimensions. Oddly, however, she fails to observe that sculpture is "more limited" than painting with respect to scope. Painting can concretize more complex situations and relationships, by representing figures in more fully delineated contexts than are possible in sculpture. Yet a work of sculpture can seem more *real*, precisely because it is three-dimensional and inhabits the same space as the viewer, whereas the space re-created in a painting is entirely illusory. The important principle, in our view, is to understand how each art form's distinctive means of re-creating reality determines which aspects of reality can be most effectively re-created within that form.[35]

Rand further errs when she declares that sculpture "expresses an artist's view of existence through his treatment of the human figure . . . . [O]nly the figure of man can project a metaphysical meaning."[36] (49–50) While it is true that the human figure projects greater metaphysical complexity than the figure of an animal, Rand's categorical proposition belies the expressive power of much animal sculpture. Consider, for example, the magnificent horses' heads flanking the sculptural group of the Parthenon's east pediment, or the pair of lions that dignify the entrance to the New York Public Library.

Finally, although Rand praises the subtlety with which skin texture is rendered in Michelangelo's *Pietá*, for example, she subsequently implies that no sculpture of worth has been created since antiquity. While declaring that a "Renaissance is always possible" in the future, she ignores that Italian

Renaissance sculptors themselves often rivaled, even surpassed, the ancient Greeks both in technical virtuosity and in the power and beauty of their work, or that anything of value was created in succeeding centuries, including our own. Most regrettably, she completely overlooks the many fine works that American sculptors have created—such as Augustus Saint-Gaudens's Sherman Monument in New York City; Daniel Chester French's *Mourning Victory* for the Melvin Memorial in Concord, Mass. (a marble copy of which is in the Metropolitan Museum of Art, New York), or his seated *Lincoln* for the Lincoln Memorial, Washington, D.C.; Anna Hyatt [Huntington]'s *Joan of Arc* and other works; or Harriet Whitney Frishmuth's *The Vine* (Metropolitan Museum of Art), a female nude that compares favorably with any sculpture from classical antiquity.[37]

The Performing Arts

Rand briefly considers the *performing arts*: that is, "acting, playing a musical instrument, singing, [and] dancing." According to Rand, the performing arts do not in themselves "re-create reality"; rather, they each "implement the re-creation made by one of the primary arts."[38] As she puts it, the performing arts "translate a primary work of art into existential *action*, into a concrete event open to direct awareness."[39] (64–65) The performing arts, as well as the large-scale collaborative art forms such as opera or film, are all based on the primary arts of music or literature, or both—which provide the content, the metaphysical meaning, that is essential for art. Without a solid musical or literary foundation, she insists, "a performance may be entertaining, . . . as [in] vaudeville or the circus, but it has nothing to do with art."[40] (70) The quality of performance and production—as in drama or opera, for example—can enhance, clarify, and illuminate the meaning of the primary work, but it cannot supply meaning or value when the literary text or musical score is deficient. (66) Rand maintains that, while the performing arts are "an extension of and dependent on" the primary arts, they are in no way "secondary in esthetic value or importance;" that is, performers are not to be considered "mere 'interpreters.'" The performing artist contributes his own "creative element." As she further explains:

> The basic principles which apply to all the other arts, apply to the performing artist as well, particularly stylization, i.e., selectivity: the choice and emphasis of essentials, the structuring of the progressive steps of a performance which lead to an ultimately meaningful sum. The performing artist's own metaphysical value-judgments are called upon to create and apply the

kind of technique his performance requires. For instance, an actor's view of human grandeur or baseness or courage or timidity will determine how he projects these qualities on the stage. A work intended to be performed leaves a wide latitude of creative choice to the artist who will perform it.[41] [65]

As she clearly implies, the performer's interpretation must be consistent with the intent of the primary artist. "He becomes a partner, almost a co-creator—if and when he is guided by the principle that he is the means to the end set by the work." When the performance is "perfectly integrated in meaning, style, and intention" with the primary work, it yields a complete concretization of the values projected by that work, creating an event of compelling psychological immediacy.[42] (64–65) When, on the other hand, the performance departs from the meaning, style, or intention of the primary work, "it gives the audience an experience of psycho-epistemological disintegration."

Dance

In her consideration of the performing arts, Rand devotes particular attention to dance. Notwithstanding certain reservations we note below, she offers important insights into the fundamental nature of dance as an art form. Most significant, in our view, is her insistence that dance is "the silent partner of music." (66) As she emphatically declares: "Music is an independent, primary art; the dance is not. . . . [The art of] dance is entirely dependent on music. . . . Music sets the terms."[43] (69) Whereas music "presents a stylized version of man's consciousness in action,"[44] Rand argues, dance "presents a stylized version of man's body in action." (66) By "stylized," she reminds the reader, she means "condensed to essential characteristics." (67) More specifically, dance "presents an abstraction of man's emotions in the context [through the medium] of his physical movements."[45] (67) Its proper goal is not the mere projection of "single, momentary emotions, *not* a pantomime version of joy or sorrow or fear, . . . but a more profound issue: . . . the use of man's body to express his sense of life."[46] (67) Rand's further explanation identifies the natural mimetic foundation of meaning in dance:

Every strong emotion has a kinesthetic element, experienced as an impulse to leap or cringe or stamp one's foot. . . . Just as a man's sense of life is part of all his emotions, so it is part of all his movements and determines his manner of using his body: his posture, his gestures, his way of walking, etc. We can observe a different sense of life in a man who characteristically stands straight, walks fast, gestures decisively—and in a man who characteristically slumps, shuffles heavily, gestures limply. This particular element—the overall manner of moving—constitutes the material, the special province of the dance. The dance stylizes it into a *system of motion* expressing a metaphysical view of man. [67]

For Rand, such a stylized *"system of motion"* is "the essential element of the precondition of the dance as an art." (Though she does not here mention *rhythm*—which is generally considered essential to dance[47]—it is implied, since it is a fundamental attribute of music, on which she insists dance depends.)

Although we agree with the basic thrust of Rand's argument—that dance is fundamentally dependent on music; that dance movement is meaningfully stylized; and that its stylization, like that of the other arts, is reflective of a sense of life—all these factors are more complex, subtle, and variable than Rand suggests. First, she places too much emphasis on the significance of the *"system of motion"* per se, implying that a given system can express only one sense of life or metaphysical view of man. We would argue that many such views are possible within each school or style of dance. Ballet, for instance, can reflect sensibilities as disparate as the ethereal spirituality of Fokine's *Les Sylphides* (1909) and the passionate impetuosity of Kenneth MacMillan's *Romeo and Juliet* (1965).[48]

Further, the dependence of dance on music allows for more creativity on the part of the choreographer than Rand envisions. Regarding the creative process in dance, she mistakenly compares the work of a choreographer to that of a stage director. Although she concedes that the choreographer's creative role is "more demanding," she argues that, just as the director "translates a primary work, a play, into physical action," the choreographer "translate[s] a primary work, a composition of sounds, into another medium," that of movement. (70) According to Rand, "the task of the dance is to follow [the music], as closely, obediently and expressively as possible." (69) Contrary to her view, however, choreographers do far more than translate music into movement or follow it obediently. The inspiration they draw from music is often realized in unpredictable ways that, while true to the spirit of the music, could never be characterized as mere *translation*. As a composer who collaborated with Martha Graham observed, her work "stems from the music but then goes off into areas that are hers alone. The work becomes a real duet."[49] Choreography "at its best," another composer notes, can add "an extra dimension that the music itself cannot have."[50] Nonetheless, it is significant that even Graham—who often commissioned new music for a dance she was conceiving (as in the case of *Appalachian Spring*)—choreographed the movements based on the music.[51] As further evidence of the correctness of Rand's insistence that dance is dependent on music, Copland's score for *Appalachian Spring* has a life of its own in the concert hall, but no one would think of performing Graham's choreography without the music.

Rand errs, however, in claiming that "music is the primary work [dancers] perform—with the help of . . . the choreographer." (70) More accurately, dancers perform the steps and movements devised by the choreographer. Furthermore, the dancer often contributes to the creative process by inspiring new ideas through the uniqueness of his own personality and musical sensibility, or by offering specific suggestions. Yet, as we shall argue in Chapter 12, "dance" movement in silence, while perhaps not quite "meaningless gymnastics" (as Rand put it), certainly does not constitute the *art* of dance, which requires the emotional underpinning of music to be fully expressive.

As is often the case with Rand, her observations regarding specific genres of dance are less valuable than her identification of basic theoretical principles. For example, she claims, in typically sweeping fashion, that "[m]ost dance performances" do not "qualify as art," because they are not sufficiently stylized. (67) Citing no examples, she asserts that such performances are not consistent systems of movement, but rather "conglomerations of elements from different systems and of random contortions, arbitrarily thrown together, signifying nothing." She is especially critical of what she refers to as "random movements" such as "skipping, jumping or rolling," which she contends are "no more artistic" than "children romping in a meadow." (67) Though, again, Rand offers no examples, her remarks appear to allude to modern dance.[52] Indeed, in a subsequent passage, she explicitly condemns "so-called modern dance," perfunctorily dismissing it as "neither modern nor dance" (70), without further explanation. In rejecting all of modern dance, however, she misses much that is of value. She also ignores that some modern choreographers—most notably, Graham (whom she could have had ample opportunity to observe, as her contemporary)—created new systems of movement of great expressive power.

In contrast with her distaste for modern dance, Rand appears to have admired ballet. Yet her comments on it mingle valid observation with error. She correctly notes that, by creating the illusion of weightlessness, ballet projects ethereal, spiritual qualities. But she mistakenly insists that ballet cannot also project strong passions, negative emotions, or sexuality. (68) Contrary to her claim, strong passions and negative emotions figure importantly in such nineteenth-century classics as *Giselle* and *Swan Lake*,[53] as well as in major ballets created in the twentieth century. A notable example is the aforementioned *Romeo and Juliet*, which centers on the passionate character of Juliet—whom the choreographer regarded as a strong-minded girl defying the conventions of her society.[54] Moreover, even plotless ballets can be powerfully expressive of sexuality.[55]

To illustrate her concept of dance as a *stylized system of motion*, Rand contrasts ballet with Hindu dance forms. Here, again, her remarks are not entirely reliable. For example, she maintains that ballet, unlike Hindu dance, "does not distort man's body" (68)—a claim that ignores the unnatural technique of *turn-out*, for example, which is fundamental to ballet. Moreover, while she accurately characterizes the dominant movement style of Indian dance as one of "flexibility, undulation, writhing," her interpretation of its meaning is inferred from her vantage point as a Westerner ignorant of the associations such movements have in the context of Indian culture.[56]

Rand offers a more appreciative analysis of the dance form that was her personal favorite—tap dancing. Emphasizing that it is "completely synchronized with" and "responsive . . . to the music,"[57] she captures the spirit of the form when she observes: "It conveys a sense of purpose, discipline, [and] clarity . . . combined with an unlimited freedom of movement and an inexhaustible inventiveness that dares the sudden, the unexpected, yet never loses the central integrating line: the music's rhythm."[58] (69) As Rand argues, however, the emotional range of tap dancing tends to be limited. While her claim that "it cannot express tragedy or pain or fear or guilt" may be too categorical; it is true that what it best expresses is "gaiety," the "joy of living."[59] (69) This limited emotional range no doubt explains why—contrary to her claim that it "possesses the key elements on which a full, distinctive system [of movement] could be built" (68)—it has never developed into a major dance form and has always remained in the realm of entertainment rather than art.

The Role of the Director

Rand's all too brief remarks on the art of directing are also of value. Neither a "primary" nor a "performing" artist in the usual sense of those terms, the director is the "crucially important . . . esthetic *integrator*," who (much like a musical conductor) unites primary and performing arts. His task is to coordinate the cast, the scenic designer, the cameramen (in the case of film), and other collaborators in the "translation of the primary work [the play] into physical action as a meaningful, stylized, integrated whole," consistent with its original intent. (71) Directorial skill requires not only an understanding of all the production components involved but also a high degree of "abstract thought" and "creative imagination." Most important, the director must avoid "the twin pitfalls of abdication and usurpation." (71) His goal is to impose an integrated vision on the whole; but that vision must always be consistent with, and in service to, the playwright's (or screenwriter's) fundamental intent. (On the primary role of the screenwriter, see our discussion in Chapter 13.) The director must not indulge in "a hodgepodge of clashing intentions," nor should he engage in "senseless tricks unrelated to or obliterating the play."[60]

As an example of great direction, Rand cites the work of Fritz Lang, whose early silent feature films (notably *Siegfried*) she particularly admired—for their style, not their content or meaning. In Rand's view, Lang was unique in the extent to which he comprehended that *"visual* art" is intrinsic to the art of film and involves more than "the mere selection of sets and camera angles."[61] As the term "motion pictures" suggests, cinematic art depends, in part, on "stylized visual composition in motion." With respect to Lang's *Siegfried*, she remarks:

> It has been said that if one [were to] . . . cut out a film frame at random, it would be as perfect in composition as a great painting. Every action, gesture, and movement . . . is calculated to achieve that effect. Every inch of the film is *stylized,* i.e., condensed to those stark, bare essentials which convey the nature and spirit of the story, of its events, of its locale. [72]

Rand further notes that Lang was said to have hung a sign in his office stating: *"Nothing in this film is accidental"* (emphasis ours). The same principle, she stresses, underlies *all* great art. Indeed, one could say that this is a cardinal principle of her theory of art: the creation of art necessarily involves purposeful selectivity by the artist in every stage and aspect of the creative process. As we shall argue in Part II, that principle has profound implications for much of the alleged art of the twentieth century.

The Art of Film

Rand's views on the nature of film are of particular interest and value. Contrary to the widespread view that the director is the primary artist, she insists:

> In motion pictures or television, literature is *the* ruler and term-setter. . . . Screen and television plays are subcategories of the drama, and in the dramatic arts *"the play is the thing."* The play is that which makes it art; the play provides the end, to which all the rest is the means.[62] (71)

Rand was enthusiastic about the artistic possibilities of film and television. From her youth in Russia on, she was not only personally enamored of film but also recognized its potential as an art form. And at the time of her death, she was working on the script for a television miniseries of *Atlas Shrugged*. Having worked as a screenwriter, however, Rand knew first-hand the pitfalls of the medium, and the difficulty of actualizing the potential of a form that requires the "synchronization of so many esthetic elements and so many different talents." She saw no impediment to artistry in the fact that work in a mass medium such as film or television must appeal to a broad audience to be commercially viable. For her, the problem lay, rather, in the "philosophical-cultural disintegration" of our time. To be "art," a film must present an integrated view of man. Rand not only insisted that such a presentation depends, first and foremost, on a literary base, the screenplay;[63] she also argued that it can be fully realized only when the "many different talents" involved are "united, not necessarily by their formal philosophical convictions, but by their fundamental view of man, i.e., their sense of life." (72–73) In Chapter 13, we will amplify Rand's implication that the screenwriter, not the director, is the primary creative artist in film—just as the playwright, not the director, is in drama.

The Arts and Cognition

Returning to the question she raised at the outset of her essay, *What are the valid forms of art—and why these?* Rand answers:

> The proper forms of art present a selective re-creation of reality in terms needed by man's *cognitive faculty,* which includes his entity-perceiving senses[;] and [they] thus assist [in] the integration of the various elements of a *conceptual* consciousness. [73]

Each of the major art forms, in its own particular way, *"bring[s] man's concepts to the perceptual level of his consciousness and allow[s] him to grasp them directly, as if they were percepts."* The literary forms do so through the verbal concretization of concepts; the visual arts through the senses of sight and touch, or the visual evocation of touch; music through hearing. The performing arts "are a means of further concretization," through the "medium" (as Rand termed it) both visual and auditory, of a performer's body and voice— or, as we noted above, of a performer playing a musical instrument. Rand argues, unequivocally, that

> all the arts were born in prehistoric times, and . . . man can never develop a *new* form of art. The forms of art do not depend on the *content* of man's consciousness, but on its *nature*—not on the extent of man's knowledge, but on the means by which he acquires it. [73]

This proposition, too, has profound implications for the assessment of the twentieth century's countless "new art forms."

Since Rand previously characterized film as a potentially "great art," is she now contradicting herself by arguing that all the art forms came into being in prehistory? Not at all. In her view, the "unlimited growth" that occurs in the arts as a result of science and technology can generate only new *variants* or *subcategories* of the primary arts, which are determined by the nature of man's cognitive and perceptual faculties. As we have noted, she regards film as a *subcategory* of drama (which is, in turn, a subcategory of literature). Such a subcategory, or variant, requires "new methods, new techniques, but *not* a change of basic principles." (73) "[D]ifferent techniques are required to write for the stage or screen or television; but all these media . . . are subject to the same basic principles."

Although Rand regards motion pictures as an art form (albeit one that is rarely fully realized), she insists that photography itself is not art—since it is not a selective re-creation of reality. In contrast, motion pictures, while employing a photographic medium, *are* art, because the *story* (the screenplay) "provides [the] abstract meaning which the film concretizes." (74) Given the prominence of both photography and film in contemporary culture, much more needs to be said about their distinctive attributes and the question of their status as art. For our further comments, see Chapters 9 and 13.

Finally, Rand's analysis of art and cognition includes a few brief comments on the nature of the decorative arts. Since this, too, is a subject of growing confusion in the contemporary artworld, we defer our discussion (and extension) of Rand's position to Chapter 11.

"Modern Art"

In the final pages of "Art and Cognition," Rand delivers a brief but scathing polemic on the role philosophy has played with respect to "modern art."[64] (76–79) She begins with this analogy, characteristically harsh in its imagery: "If a gang of men—no matter what its slogans, motives or goals—were roaming the streets and gouging out people's eyes, people would rebel and would find the words of a righteous protest. But when such a gang is roaming the culture, bent on annihilating men's minds, people remain silent." (76) Immoderate though Rand's rhetoric may be, her basic argument is sound. In her view, "the essence of art is integration, a kind of super-integration in the sense that art deals with man's widest abstractions, his metaphysics," and thus extends the range of his consciousness. In contrast, the "keynote and goal of modern art," she argues, is nothing less than "the disintegration of man's conceptual faculty."[65] (76) "To reduce man's consciousness to the level of sensations,[66] with no capacity to integrate them, is the intention[67] behind the reducing of . . . painting to smears, of sculpture to slabs, of music to noise."(76–77) While Rand cites no specific works, we will offer examples to confirm her argument in Part II.

Rand excoriates modern philosophy, with its "war against reason," as the "sponsor and spawner" of the "gang" of modernists who have ravaged the culture. In her view, the philosophers who destroyed logic by abolishing definitions, eliminated "the first line of defense against the chaos of mental disintegration." Because "works of art—like everything else in the universe—are entities of a specific nature," she argues, "the concept requires a definition by their essential characteristics, which distinguish them from all other existing entities." (78) Alluding to the implicit premise underlying modernist art, she emphatically states: "'Something made by an artist' is *not* a definition of art." Absurd though this hypothetical example may seem in its obvious circularity, it accurately reflects the way in which contemporary thinkers have defaulted on the issue of defining art—from philosopher George Dickie's "institutional theory" to art historian E. H. Gombrich's claim: "There is really no such thing as Art. There are only artists."[68]

Rand concludes "Art and Cognition" with the following exhortation:

> There is no place for the unknowable, the unintelligible, the undefinable, the non-objective in any human product. This side of an insane asylum, the actions of a human being are motivated by a conscious purpose; when they are not, they are of no interest to anyone outside a psychotherapist's office. And when the practitioners of modern art declare that they don't know what they are doing or what makes them do it, we should take their word for it and give them no further consideration. [79]

Lest the reader conclude that Rand is indulging in empty rhetoric regarding "the practitioners of modern art," it is worth citing two of its most celebrated figures, John Cage and Samuel Beckett—both of whom we discuss in Part II. Cage once declared: "Modern art has no need of technique. We are in the glory of not knowing what we're doing."[69] On another occasion, he announced: "I have nothing to say and I am saying it."[70] In a similarly nihilist vein, Beckett once alluded to himself as possessing "nothing to express, nothing with which to express, nothing from which to express, no power to express, [and] no desire to express."[71]

Contrary to Rand's admonition, however, artworld figures such as Cage and Beckett have received generous "consideration" in contemporary culture. Rather than being dismissed outright, they have been championed by critics, scholars, and cultural institutions.[72] If most people "remain silent," unable to articulate their incredulity or outrage at such folly, Rand laments, it is because "the words they need can be supplied only by philosophy," and modern philosophy has failed them.

5

Music and Cognition

The unique qualities of music—its abstract character and profound emotional power—present a challenge to any theory of art, especially to one based, as Rand's is, on the idea that art re-creates reality. As we indicated in Chapter 4, her analysis of music is often problematical, even appearing at times to be inconsistent with her theory of art. Yet, as we also suggested, the apparent discrepancies are due to errors in her analysis of music, rather than to flaws in her esthetic theory. In fact, music does correspond in essential respects to Rand's broad conception of art. Our purpose in this chapter, therefore, is to summarize and critique her analysis and to clarify how music is (like the other arts) a "selective re-creation of reality."

Music and Emotion

At the outset of her analysis, Rand emphasizes the emotional content of music. She begins by proposing that music is experienced "as if it reversed man's normal psycho-epistemological process"—"*as if it had the power to reach man's emotions directly.*" (50, emphasis ours) While the sequence of mental processes in experiencing both literature and the visual arts is "from the perception of the object,[1] to the conceptual grasp of its meaning, to an appraisal in terms of one's basic values, to a consequent emotion," she argues that the process in listening to music is essentially reversed. Though we begin with perception, we then "experience" an immediate "emotion," prior to any conceptual abstraction or evaluation.[2] (50) Rand emphasizes that the steps involved in this emotional response are completely automatized, requiring no conscious analysis or evaluation. One is not aware of them as separate, distinguishable phases; instead, they "are experienced as a single, instantaneous reaction, faster than one can identify its components." (50–51)

On the crucial issue of *how* music conveys its emotional content, Rand is equivocal. At first, she maintains that music "induces an emotional state" in the listener (51)—a proposition that implies (perhaps unwittingly) an *arousal* theory of musical expression. According to such a theory, the music automatically awakens emotions in the listener that correspond directly to the emotional tenor of the given work. In a subsequent passage, however, Rand states that, in the act of musical perception, "one grasps the suggestion of a certain emotional state" (53)—a proposition that clearly implies a *cognitive* theory of musical expression. In the cognitive view, the listener "recognizes" (at least subconsciously) the expressive properties of the music, much as one might recognize the emotional implications of a person's countenance, posture, or quality of movement. (The "recognition" need not be articulated or verbalized; it may be merely intuited, or "sensed," on a nonverbal level.)[3] And each listener's emotional response to what he hears in the music then varies, dependent on his own personal context.[4] Although Rand's initial account emphasizes the "fundamental difference between music and the other arts" (50), premised on an arousal theory, that "difference" subsequently collapses, when she interprets the emotional power of music according to a cognitive theory.[5] Moreover, the reader's confusion is increased by the fact that, in both accounts, Rand alternately uses arousal terms and cognitive terms.[6]

Notwithstanding such ambiguities, Rand appropriately emphasizes that music differs from the other arts with respect to the aspects of existence it can re-create, or concretize. She explains:

> Music cannot tell a story,[7] . . . it cannot convey a specific existential phenomenon, such as a peaceful countryside or a stormy sea. . . . Even concepts which, intellectually, belong to a complex level of abstraction, such as "peace," "revolution," "religion," are too specific, too *concrete* to be expressed in music. All that music can do with such themes is convey the emotions of serenity, or defiance, or exaltation. Liszt's "St. Francis de Paul Walking on the Waters" was inspired by a specific legend, but what it conveys is a passionately dedicated struggle and triumph—by whom and in the name of what, is for each individual listener to supply.[8] [52]

Although Rand continues to employ terms rather loosely here,[9] the gist of her argument is clear. The emotions or states of mind suggested by a musical composition are far less specific than those depicted in a work of literature or visual art, since music cannot indicate the existential contexts that evoke particular emotions or mental states.

What music conveys, many writers have suggested, are certain attributes of emotional states, rather than specific emotions themselves. That is, through particular qualities of tone, tempo, rhythm, and timbre, music "imitates" or "re-creates" the vocal and behavioral expressions associated with emotional states and with emotionally charged movement. As the philosopher Peter Kivy has observed, music is expressive "in virtue of its resemblance to expressive human utterance and behavior."[10] Through such qualities, and through the intricacies and interplay of melodic lines, as well as through structural elements such as recapitulation, music can also suggest or metaphorically "re-create" other aspects of experience, such as struggle or return. In Susanne Langer's view:

> The tonal structures we call "music" bear a close logical similarity to the forms of human feeling—forms of growth and of attenuation . . . conflict and resolution, speed, arrest, terrific excitement, calm . . . —not joy and sorrow perhaps, but the poignancy of either and both—the greatness and brevity and eternal passing of everything vitally felt. Such is the pattern, or logical form, of sentience; and the pattern of music is that same form worked out in pure, measured sound and silence. *Music is the tonal analogue of emotive life.*[11]

What music presents, then, are certain *auditory concretes*—particular combinations of sounds—that have emotive and existential significance. That is why music, in Rand's analysis, possesses an *objective*, albeit generalized, core of meaning. Even individuals "who hold widely divergent views of life," she maintains, will usually agree on "whether a given piece of music is gay or sad or violent or solemn."[12] (52)

Music and Sense of Life

Although Rand at first states that music directly "induces" emotions in the listener, she subsequently offers an interpretation that is more consistent with her theory of art.

> Music communicates emotions,[13] which one grasps, but does not actually feel; what one feels [i.e., "grasps"] is a suggestion, a kind of distant, dissociated, depersonalized emotion—*until and unless it unites with one's own sense of life.*[14] [52, emphasis ours]

Rand adds that, since the emotional content of the music is neither "communicated conceptually" (that is, verbally) nor "evoked existentially" (that is, visually), the listener "feel[s] it in some peculiar, subterranean way." (52) Thus "grasping" the emotional content does not entail making an explicit verbal or conceptual identification. Yet Rand clearly implies that a form of *perceptual* cognition is involved.[15] Moreover, her concept of sense of life helps to explain why listeners differ in their emotional response to the perceived content of a piece of music (though she unwittingly confuses the issue by continuing to employ both arousal and cognitive terms). While music "conveys the same categories of emotions to listeners who hold widely divergent views of life," she argues, and those listeners therefore "experience the same emotions in response to the same music,"[16] they differ radically in "how they *appraise* this experience—i.e., how they feel about these feelings." (52)

> Psycho-epistemologically, the pattern of the response to music seems to be as follows: one perceives the music, *one grasps the suggestion of a certain emotional state* and, with one's sense of life serving as the criterion, one appraises this state as enjoyable or painful, desirable or undesirable, significant or negligible, according to whether it corresponds to or contradicts one's fundamental feeling about life.[17] [53, emphasis ours]

According to this view, then, one's response to a work of music—like the emotional response to the other arts—is based on an implicit (subconscious) appraisal, and varies accordingly. If the emotive content of the music is consonant with the listener's sense of life, the response will be a positive one. Conversely, if the emotive content of the music is "irrelevant" to the listener's sense of life, or contradicts it to some degree, the work will engender, in Rand's view, such responses as "boredom" or "resentment." Thus listeners may report sharply contrasting reactions to the same piece—for example: "'I felt exalted because this music is so light-heartedly happy,'" versus "'I felt irritated because this music is so light-heartedly happy and, therefore, superficial.'" (53)

Since Rand holds that all emotions are dependent on values, one may well wonder on what basis the emotional states initially "grasped" in music can be appraised, in the absence of a particular existential context or any conceptual content in a work of music. Her explanation is that, when "music induces an emotional state without external object, [the listener's] subconscious suggests an internal one."[18] (51) On a subconscious level, music evokes, as it were, a random, fragmented sequence of images, scenes, events, or experiences, which seems "to flow haphazardly, without direction, in brief, random snatches, merging, changing and vanishing, like the progression of a

dream. But, in fact, this flow is selective and consistent: the emotional meaning of the subconscious material corresponds to the emotions projected by
the music."[19] (51) That subconscious process (which can be confirmed by
introspection) is analogous to saying: "I would feel this way if . . . ," with
each listener completing the sentence according to his own response to the
musical passage. It is, in effect, a spontaneous, largely subliminal process of
deeply personal free association triggered by the work, if one "suspend[s]
one's conscious thoughts and surrender[s] to the guidance of one's emotions."[20] (51) Implicit in the formation of these imaginary associations, Rand
emphasizes, is a process of *emotional abstraction*, comparable to the process
by which one's sense of life is formed. Consistent with her theory of art, Rand
concludes that it is "in terms of his fundamental emotions—i.e., the emotions
produced by his [subconsciously held sense of life]—that man responds to
music." (52)

Rand's Mistaken Hypothesis

Yet the issue is both more complex and "more specifically *musical*" than simply preferring happy music or sad music, Rand argues. What matters, in her
view, is "not merely *what* particular emotion a given composition conveys,
but *how* it conveys it." (53) Such a proposition is not peculiar to music, however; it applies to all the arts. As we argued in Chapter 3, the manner or style
of presentation substantially contributes to the significance of any work of
art. Nonetheless, Rand proposes (mistakenly, we think) that, while music is
like the other arts in affording "a concretization of [one's] sense of life," it
differs in that "the abstraction being concretized is *primarily epistemological*, rather than metaphysical." (59, emphasis ours) Thus she insists that an
individual's response to a given piece of music depends mainly upon whether
the work "*confirms, or contradicts, his mind's way of working.*"[21] This dubious proposition echoes her claim, in "The Psycho-Epistemology of Art" and
"Art and Sense of Life," that a work of art "confirms or denies the efficacy
of a man's consciousness." (24, 42) As we indicated in our discussion of those
essays, we emphatically reject such a proposition.

Rand begins her tentative hypothesis regarding the nature of man's response
to music, "from the standpoint of psycho-epistemology," by observing: "If
man experiences an emotion without existential object, its only other possible object is *the state or actions of his own consciousness.*" (57, emphasis
ours) The reader may feel confused here, since this proposition, which Rand
states as if it were entirely new, partly echoes a proposition she stated only a
few pages earlier—i.e., that, "when music induces an emotional state with-

out external object, [the listener's] subconscious suggests an internal one," and that he subconsciously "appraises" the imagined "object[s]" according to his sense of life. (51) Yet she now argues that the meaning of a work of music does not lie primarily in the sort of subconscious associations it evokes but, rather, in "the kind of work it demands of a listener's ear and brain" in the process of "hearing and integrating a succession of musical tones." (58) In so arguing, Rand seems to have been influenced, directly or indirectly, by the formalist emphasis of the nineteenth-century music theorist Eduard Hanslick and, more explicitly, by a similar emphasis in the work of his contemporary the eminent physiologist Hermann Helmholtz.

Based partly on Helmholtz's demonstration—in his pioneering work *On the Sensations of Tone*—that (as she puts it) "the essence of musical perception is mathematical," Rand hypothesizes that music alone "permits an adult to experience the process of dealing with pure sense data,"[22] because "single musical tones are not percepts, but pure sensations." (57–59) According to Rand, music (in contrast with the other art forms) involves a process of integration at the sensory level, and musical tones "become percepts only when integrated [into a melody]." (58–59) This erroneous view appears to derive, at least in part, from an insufficiently critical reading of Helmholtz,[23] who similarly argued that music "stands in a much closer connection with pure sensation than any of the other arts." According to Helmholtz, "the sensations of tone exist for themselves alone, and produce their effects independently of anything [i.e., any external reference or meaning] behind them,"[24] whereas the literary and visual arts aim "to excite in us the image of an external object of determinate form and colour." (2–3) However, while Helmholtz characterized the auditory experience of tones as a "sensation," rather than as a "perception," his analysis of their auditory features clearly indicates that tones are, in fact, heard as integrated units of discriminated awareness— thereby implying that they should be regarded as *percepts.*[25]

As Kelley argues in *The Evidence of the Senses* (160), *all* sounds (including musical tones) should be regarded as percepts, because we hear them "as particulars, discriminated from the background of other sounds. . . . The[ir] qualitative features . . . —pitch, loudness, duration, pattern—are experienced as attributes of particular items in the auditory context. And we experience modulations of sound as changes in a single item discriminated over time." Since we perceive sounds (even though they are not solid objects) as having attributes and undergoing change, Kelley persuasively argues that the concept of *entity* should be understood as including such auditory phenomena, in addition to solid physical objects, which are the "paradigmatic" entities.[26]

The Importance of Melody

While Rand is mistaken in her view of musical tones as "pure sensations," she is correct in emphasizing the importance of integrating single tones into the higher-level entity of a *melody*, for melody is, as she elsewhere observes, the "fundamental aspect" of music.[27] Since music is a temporal art made up of discrete tones, a composition requires melodic structure in order to be perceived as a unity. In her discussion, however, Rand offers neither an analysis of the basic characteristics of melody nor a definition of the concept. *Melody* is the "rhythmically organized and meaningful succession of single musical notes or tones [pitched sounds] having a definite relationship one with the other and forming an esthetic whole."[28] The essential attribute of melody is the illusion of movement created by the rhythmic succession of related tones. For this illusion to occur, the relationships between successive tones must fall within a range discernible to the human ear and mind. For example, successive tones must vary sufficiently in pitch for a change to be audible, and the time lapse between them must be small enough for them to be perceived as part of a continuum, rather than as isolated, unrelated entities. As Helmholtz observed (252), melody "has to express a motion, in such a manner that the hearer may easily, clearly, and certainly appreciate the character of that motion by *immediate perception*." Since melodic motion is "change of pitch in time," the alterations in both time and pitch must "proceed by regular and determinate degrees" in order to be discernible. As Helmholtz emphasizes, moreover, rhythm, "as the measure of time, belongs to the inmost nature of [musical] expression."[29]

Although rhythm is as essential to musical structure and effect as tonal relationships are, Rand does not consider it in her hypothetical speculations regarding melodic integration.[30] Nor does she consider the *expressive* characteristics of melody. She focuses, instead, solely on the mathematical aspect of tonal relationships, taking her cue from Helmholtz's analysis of the mathematical ratios of tones—that is, of their frequency of vibration—which determine dissonance and consonance in harmonics (tones sounded simultaneously). Moreover, she considers only one characteristic of this aspect: its relative simplicity or complexity. She says nothing about the particular quality of movement conveyed by a melody or the role of rhythm in the overall effect.

To illustrate her view of the integrative process involved in listening to music, Rand calls to mind a range of compositions varying in melodic complexity, from those that require the "active alertness needed to resolve complex mathematical relationships" to those that "deaden the brain by means of monotonous simplicity" or that "obliterate the process [of integration]" by presenting "a jumble of sounds" that cannot be mathematically or physiologically integrated and are thus perceived as "noise," not music. (58) According to Rand, the listener's response will be determined mainly "by the level of cognitive functioning on which he feels at home." A person with an "active mind," in her view, will enjoy music that is complex but intelligible, will be bored by monotonous, repetitive compositions, and will be angered and repelled by jumbled, unintelligible sequences of sound, which he experiences "as an attempt to destroy the integrating capacity of his mind." Other reactions will vary according to the character of the music and the diverse cognitive habits of individual listeners. (58–59)

While mathematical relationships are indisputably involved in both the rhythmic and the tonal aspects of music, and contribute to the intelligibility of musical compositions, we regard as entirely mistaken Rand's claim that those relationships are the primary focus in the experience of music. Mathematical relationships pertain to the structure of music, and therefore belong to the technical means of musical expression, but Rand seems to elevate them to the ultimate end, or purpose, of music. Nor do we agree with her claim that a listener with an "active mind" will necessarily enjoy music whose melodic line "requires a process of complex calculations and successful resolution," or that he will be "bored by too easy a process of integration, like an expert in higher mathematics who is put to the task of solving problems in kindergarten arithmetic." (58) Many more factors are involved than Rand's analysis suggests.

Contrary to Rand's emphasis on mathematical relationships, all that is essential for a meaningful experience of music is that the listener be sensitive to its *expressive* character.[31] And this capacity appears to be independent of mathematical ability, even among professional musicians. As the cognitive psychologist Howard Gardner suggests in his study of the diverse modes of human intelligence:

> [T]he task in which musicians are engaged differs fundamentally from that which preoccupies the pure mathematician. The mathematician is interested in forms for their own sake, in their own implications, apart from any realization in a particular medium or from any particular communicative purpose. He may choose to analyze music . . . ; but from the mathematical point of view, music is just another pattern. For the musician, however, the patterned elements must appear in sounds; and they are . . . put together in certain ways not by virtue of formal consideration, but because they have expressive power and effects.[32]

Rand claims as "evidence . . . on the psycho-existential level" for her hypothesis regarding the primarily epistemological significance of music that

certain musical traditions—in particular, "primitive music and most Oriental music"—have a "paralyzing, narcotic effect" on the mind, resulting in
"the dissolution of self and of consciousness." In contrast, she argues, the tradition of diatonic music that developed in the West[33] affords the listener "an
intensely personal experience[34] and a confirmation of his cognitive power."
Each type of music, in her view, evokes the kind of psycho-epistemological
state regarded as "proper and desirable for man," according to the culture's
dominant philosophy.[35] (62–63)

Although Rand began her discussion of music by emphasizing the emotional aspect of musical experience, she ends by completely subordinating
it, insisting that "the epistemological aspect . . . is *the fundamental*, [though]
not the exclusive, *factor*, in determining one's musical preferences." (61,
emphasis ours) True, the expressive nature of music still constitutes, for her,
"the concretized abstraction of existence—i.e., a world in which one feels
joyous or sad or triumphant or resigned, etc."—to which one responds,
according to one's sense of life: "'Yes, *this* is *my* world and *this* is how I
should feel!' or: 'No, this is not the world as I see it.'" (61) Yet Rand deems
this aspect less important than the *process* of integration itself—that is, "the
concretized abstraction of one's consciousness." In our view, such an emphasis is as mistaken as if she were to argue that one's enjoyment of a novel
depends more on an abstract appreciation of its intricacies of plot than on
the particular nature of the characters and value-conflicts involved in the
plot. Ironically, it is as if Rand, while unequivocal in her criticism of formalism in the other arts, had gone over to the formalist camp with respect
to music.

The Composer's Viewpoint

As the reader may have inferred by now, Rand's analysis of music, even
more than that of the other arts, is almost exclusively from the vantage point
of the responder. She says little of the composer or of the creative process
involved in musical composition, though her theory of art implies that the
composer works in a manner essentially comparable to that of other creative
artists. Like the painter or the poet, he, too, re-creates aspects of reality that
reflect his deepest feelings about life; only the means are different: his medium
is that of sound. Aaron Copland similarly observes that the composer creates "patterns of sound that represent the central core of [his] being,"[36]
embodying the "fullest and deepest expression of himself . . . and of his
experience."[37] So, too, the critic Harold Schonberg observes, in his *Lives of
the Great Composers*:

[A] man's music is a function of himself, and is a reflection of his mind and his reaction to the world in which he lives. Just as we see the world through the eyes and mind of a Rembrandt . . . when we look at [his] paintings, so we experience the world through the ears and mind of a . . . [composer] . . . when we hear [his] music. We are in contact with a mind. [9]

Indeed, of all the arts, music could be said to provide the most direct concretization of a *"sense* of life," in that it comes closest to re-creating the personally *felt* experience of life. As Deryck Cooke suggests in *The Language of Music*—and as Rand's concept of sense of life itself indicates—what the composer "expresses" in music are "his deep, permanent, significant emotions, not the superficial fleeting ones called forth by trivial pleasures and disappointments."[38] (16) Similarly, J. W. N. Sullivan, in his classic study *Beethoven: His Spiritual Development*, argues that the composer's music expresses "his personal vision of life," a vision that is "the product of his character and his experience." (vii) In Sullivan's view, "Beethoven does not communicate his perceptions or experiences" but, rather, "the attitude based on them." (17) Finally, the British psychologist Anthony Storr observes:

[W]hen a composer . . . succeed[s] in penetrating the hidden regions of the psyche, he not only encounters his deepest emotions but also ways of bringing those emotions into consciousness by converting them into those ordered structures of sound which we call music. . . . Although music is not a belief system, . . . its importance and its appeal also depend upon its being a way of ordering human experience.[39]

All these observations, then, and others like them in the musical literature, testify that the composer, no less than other artists, guided by his fundamental life values. Moreover, as Storr's comment suggests, the composer can be thought of as bringing certain concepts (specifically, emotional and emotive concepts) "to the perceptual level of . . . consciousness," allowing the listener "to grasp them directly as if they were percepts," much as Rand argues the other arts do.[40]

Music as a "Re-Creation of Reality"

On the crucial question of how music can be said to "re-create reality"— which, according to her definition, all the arts do—Rand is conspicuously silent in "Art and Cognition." At the outset of the essay, in fact, after she has indicated how each of the other arts re-creates reality, she states only that music "evokes man's sense-of-life emotions." And, as we have noted, she never explains how those emotions are evoked, apart from vague references to their being "induced," "expressed," or "conveyed." (46, 52) On the question of how music "communicates emotions," how it conveys its emotional meaning, she states only that "there are no criteria for identifying the *content*, i.e., the emotional meaning of a given piece of music." (55)

Yet the validity of Rand's concept of art, including her definition, seems to depend on these very issues. While it is relatively easy to understand how literature and the visual arts "re-create reality," the mimetic basis of music is far less evident. Indeed, music has often been cited as cause for rejecting the once-prevalent theory of art as "imitation."[41] A common mistake in seeking to understand music as a mimetic art is to view it in literary or visual terms— to regard it as "telling a story" or as "painting a picture."[42] Both approaches are inappropriate, since the medium of music is neither verbal-conceptual nor visual; it is aural—more specifically, it is composed of tonally and rhythmically organized sounds. Since music consists of *sounds*, the only aspects of reality it can sensuously "re-create" are *auditory* in nature—although the meaning of music is far deeper and wider than that of mere "sounds."

What, then, are the aspects of reality music "selectively re-creates"?[43] And how does it accomplish this? Entire books have been devoted to such questions, and we will attempt only to highlight some basic principles.[44] First, we should note that many modern observers, from Hanslick on, have argued that the meaning and value of music bear little or no relation to "reality," residing instead in an abstract intricacy and beauty of design—to be enjoyed in much the same way one enjoys the shifting colored patterns of a kaleidoscope, as Hanslick famously but mistakenly suggested.[45]

In considering such "formalist" views, however, it is important to recognize that they pertain mainly to the instrumental secular music that has developed in the West since the eighteenth century.[46] Only with this relatively recent historical development has the issue of music's connection to existential reality been called into question. As long as music remained tied to the voice in song and to bodily movement in ritual or ceremonial dance— as it did for most of human culture—its expressive meaning was apparent. That an objective relationship existed between music and life was not doubted. As Storr has noted: "One consequence of the separation of music from words is to render the meaning of music equivocal. . . . When music accompanies words, or is closely associated with public events such as triumphs or funerals, questions of its meaning hardly arise."[47] Music's "meaning," or reference to reality, in such cases is self-evident, embedded in the implicit knowledge of every culture. The qualities that render a piece of music appropriate or inappropriate to a particular poetic sentiment or dance movement (or, by the same token, to a specific dramatic situation) are imbued with implicit meanings, based on their resemblance to and association with emotionally charged aspects of vital experience—to "felt life," borrowing Henry James's phrase.[48]

The question then remains, Does the purely instrumental ("absolute") Western music of recent centuries retain the same sorts of meanings? In our view, it does. Indeed, as many theorists have argued, and as music's close kinship with song and dance suggests, the two main aspects of experience from which music derives its vital meaning—and which it "selectively re-creates"—are *vocal expression and the sonic effects of emotionally charged movement*. Even Hanslick, the most influential exponent of the formalist view, recognized that music can "represent" the "dynamic properties" of feeling—"the motion accompanying psychical action, according to its momentum: speed, slowness, strength, weakness, increasing and decreasing intensity."[49]

We can "hear" these qualities in musical sound, because we naturally perceive pitched sounds in terms of vocal expression, and we are innately attuned to its varieties of meaning in our human context. Moreover, we expect that music, as a product of human creation, will make sense in *human* terms. Helmholtz observed that the power of music to convey emotional meaning derives, in large part, from "*the instinctive modulations of the voice that correspond to various conditions of the feelings.*" (370, emphasis ours) As he further remarked, and as the etymological kinship of the two terms indicates, *emotion* and *motion* are closely allied. Further, the quality of physical movement under the influence of a given emotion has its counterpart in the "rhythm and accentuation" of vocal utterance. To cite an obvious example, mournful speech, like mournful movement, lacks vital energy—it is low in register and intensity (since greater effort is required to elevate either tone or volume), and slow in pace—whereas joy energizes the mind and body, producing rapid, higher-pitched speech, just as it lends a bounce to the step. Both the motor and the vocal aspects of emotional expression, then, have their roots in human physiology[50]—which helps to explain why overt as well as subtle *physical* responses to music so often constitute an integral part of both the listening and the performing experience.[51]

In considering the relationship between music and speech, it is important to remember that speech has two components: one, verbal and explicit; the other, nonverbal and implicit. In every culture, the *tone* of the spoken word powerfully affects the implicit meaning of what is said. While variations of tone become most pronounced under the influence of strong emotion, even everyday speech has its "musical" aspect (more marked in some languages than others)—a fact delightfully played upon in the scene from *My Fair Lady*, for example, in which Higgins demonstrates on the xylophone the properly genteel and ingratiating inflection with which Eliza should intone "How *kind* of you to let me come." In the course of civilization, the verbal component of speech, with its superior capacity to convey factual information and propositional thought, has become dominant, being developed to a high degree of complexity and subtlety.[52] Yet the nonverbal, or *prosodic*, aspects of vocal expression retain their pre-eminence in the communication of emotion, and are maximally exploited in the realm of music.[53]

Music is often said to be the most "abstract" of the arts. Under the influence of modernist thought on the visual arts in the twentieth century, that term has unfortunately come to mean "non-objective," reinforcing the false notion that music bears no essential relation to extra-musical reality. Music *is* abstract, but in the true sense of the word, which implies an objective basis in reality: *it selects and stylizes meaningful aspects of our aural experience— isolating (abstracting) them for our clearer perception, and emphasizing those qualities having the greatest expressive effect.*

In discussions of the "abstractness" of music, formalists frequently claim that the splendid contrapuntal compositions of Bach are prime examples of music devoid of vital meaning—magnificent tonal constructions having no significance beyond the awesome beauty of their design.[54] Bach himself emphasized the emotional import of music, however. "If we know one thing about Bach," Schonberg tells us, "it is that he was a passionate man and a passionate performer," who insisted that one must not merely play the notes of a composition, but must express its emotional significance as well.[55] Commentaries by the renowned harpsichordist Wanda Landowska on the forty-eight preludes and fugues of Bach's *Well-Tempered Clavier* underscore the emotional range and depth of his purportedly abstract compositions. Her lifelong study of Bach's keyboard oeuvre led Landowska to conclude that, in his hands, "erudite fugues [became] poems. . . . What has destroyed the human relation between us and the fugue is having valued only the skill with which it is constructed and having denied it all capacity for emotion and expression."[56]

In sum, Western instrumental music of the past three hundred years (excluding the twentieth century's "avant-garde" experiments) has not fundamentally altered the nature of music, notwithstanding the greatly altered contexts in which it is performed and heard. Its great achievement has consisted, instead, in the unprecedented realization of the expressive potential inherent in the medium—a development which has gone hand in hand with the invention of diverse forms and instruments.[57]

The Symphony Orchestra

Even the modern symphony orchestra can be understood as a logical extension of human expressive capacities. It has been suggested, for example, that the entire range of musical instruments have their precursors in the natural ways in which human beings produce sound: string instruments correspond to voice production by the vocal chords; wind instruments, to vocalization and whistling; and percussion, to clapping and foot stamping and tapping. If this supposition is valid, then the vast number of instruments that have been devised in various cultures since prehistory have merely been means of imitating and extending the musical qualities of the innate modes of human expression.[58] While the development of the modern orchestra has greatly diversified the sound palette (the variety of tone "colors," or *timbres*) available to the composer, the overall range of tonal frequency has remained essentially within that of the human voice, although the full human auditory range is much broader. Moreover, the string instruments, which are most closely analogous to the voice, form the core of the orchestra.[59]

Thus the meaning of instrumental sound remains substantially rooted in vocal expression. With its diversity of instruments of varying timbres, and its well-developed percussion and brass sections, however, the orchestra permits almost infinitely subtle variations in tonal color and texture, as well as complex and well-defined rhythmic patterns. Strong rhythmic effects require sharply accented sounds, with a clear beginning and end, which cannot be produced by the vocal cords (or by bowed strings). The enhanced rhythmic capacity of a full orchestra allows for a richer evocation of movement, since rhythm constitutes, as we have suggested, the motor of music.[60]

The remarkable development of the symphony orchestra which occurred from the seventeenth through the nineteenth century in the West may therefore be viewed as objectively based in reality; though artificial, it springs from human nature (as Rand insisted all art does), and is not an arbitrary invention.[61] However stylized instrumental music composed in this tradition may have become, ordinary listeners continue to understand it, implicitly, in human terms. They "know" what it means, even if they are unable to say *how* they know it.[62] Skeptics might argue, of course, that the characteristics we have outlined are merely holdovers from the long period of predominantly vocal music, and that nonvocal music need not remain bound by such restrictions. Our reply would be to cite the example of avant-garde composers, who have attempted to "liberate" music from these "stale conventions," only to find that their efforts repeatedly fall upon deaf ears.

We have thus far commented almost exclusively on the broad dimensions of musical perception and experience. We have not dealt with the more difficult, technical issue of precisely why or how certain combinations of tones create emotional effects. Rand herself regarded this as music's "great, unanswered question."[63] (54–55) Though she was keenly aware of the need to define these "axioms of musical perception," she was unable to do so. Happily, research in the past two decades has shed much light on the matter, and we shall explore this important question further in Chapter 7.

Avant-Garde "Music"

Rand concludes her analysis of music with "a brief word about so-called modern music." As is so often the case, she cites no specific examples—alluding only to work that incorporates "noise," i.e., unpitched sounds such as those "of street traffic or of machine gears or of coughs and sneezes." The "introduction of [such] nonperiodic vibrations" into a would-be work of music, she insists, "eliminates it automatically from the realm of art." (64) Although Rand's meaning is not entirely clear in the absence of examples, we take her to be referring to so-called *musique concrète* or "noise music", which is made up entirely of unpitched environmental sounds.

Rand's answer to those who advocate "conditioning" the ear to appreciate such compositions has implications for all the arts. Regarding the "perpetrators" of this kind of work, Rand observes:

> Their notion of conditioning is unlimited by reality and by the law of identity; man, in their view, is infinitely conditionable. But, in fact, you can condition a human ear [only] to different types of music (it is not the ear, but the *mind* that you have to condition in such cases); you cannot condition it to hear noise as if it were music; it is not personal training or social conventions that make it impossible, but the physiological nature, the *identity,* of the human ear and brain. [64]

The point Rand is making here—that the meaningful range of creativity in the realm of music (as in all the arts) is delimited by human physiology, by the requirements of the faculty of hearing—recalls her general philosophic emphasis on the fundamental distinction between "the metaphysical and the man-made." Human physiology belongs to the realm of nature, that is, to the *metaphysically* given; music, while belonging to the realm of the *man-made*, must conform to the laws of nature.[64] The issue of musical perception is but one of numerous instances in which this essential distinction between the metaphysical and the man-made is relevant to would-be innovations in the arts. In the realm of music, Rand's argument applies not only to "noise music" but also, if less obviously so, to avant-garde work such as serial music which employs musical tones yet creates an effect utterly alien to most listeners.

The overwhelmingly negative public response to such work can be understood in terms consistent with Rand's esthetic theory—in particular, with the
principle that music, like the other arts, is an expression of the composer's
sense of life (which in the case of avant-garde work is often antithetical to
that of the listener), and with her insistence that music, like all art, must be
intelligible; that it must conform to the laws of human cognition. We shall
explore these ideas further in Chapters 7 and 12.

6

The Definition of Art

In the preceding chapters, we have examined Ayn Rand's esthetic theory in detail, explicating her analysis of the nature of art in relation to human cognition and emotion. The linchpin of Rand's theory, undoubtedly, is her definition of art, which now merits closer consideration. A full appreciation of that definition, however, requires some awareness of the philosophic climate in the second half of the twentieth century, as well as a consideration of why definitions are essential to meaningful human discourse, and what rules govern their formulation.

Anti-Essentialism in Contemporary Philosophy

As we noted in Chapter 4, Rand concluded her final essay on the philosophy of art, "Art and Cognition" (1971), with a scathing indictment of contemporary philosophers for having abandoned the attempt to formulate an objective definition of art—that is, a definition in terms of *essential*, or fundamental, characteristics.[1] Her indictment was entirely justified. By the 1950s, many philosophers had been led to "despair of the possibility of defining 'art,'" as the esthetician George Dickie has noted.[2] In an influential article published in the *Journal of Aesthetics and Art Criticism* in 1956, Morris Weitz declared, for example, that "the very expansive, adventurous character of art, its ever-present changes and novel creations, makes it logically impossible to ensure any set of defining properties."[3] Two years later, W. E. Kennick further argued that "traditional aesthetics" rests on a mistake—the mistake of trying to define art. Since art has no definite function, he claimed, it cannot possibly be defined. In his view, "the search for essences in aesthetics"—that is, for "characteristics common to all works of art"—is a "fool's errand."[4] By 1975, the Polish scholar Wladyslaw Tatarkiewicz observed: "Our century has come to the conclusion that a comprehensive definition of 'art' is not only very difficult but impossible to achieve."[5]

The anti-essentialist bias in contemporary esthetics[6] is traceable to several factors. First, all prior attempts at an essentialist, or "analytical,"[7] definition of art had failed, for they had focused on criteria that were neither common to all art works nor unique to art—criteria such as beauty, "esthetic quality," and expression.[8] Further, most philosophers after mid-century were influenced by the anti-essentialism of Ludwig Wittgenstein, who held that the referents of many familiar concepts do not actually share any common or universal feature but are united only by a series of "family resemblances" observable among them, and that they therefore cannot be defined in terms of an essential common denominator.[9] Although Wittgenstein did not apply this argument to the concept of *art* (the specific example he used was *game*[10]), philosophers influenced by him—most notably, Weitz—did so.[11] Moreover, as the century wore on, increasingly diverse objects and events had been put forward, and accepted, as art—no doubt, in part, because no valid definition had been formulated. The ever-greater diversity of purported art works, to which Weitz unwittingly alluded, posed an insurmountable barrier to a meaningful definition, since the supposed referents shared no commensurable characteristics. Finally, the school of thought known as "linguistic analysis" had became the dominant approach in Anglo-American philosophy, with the result that most philosophers merely examined the way words are *used*, rather than attempting to formulate objectively valid definitions of important concepts. Indeed, they even denied that a definition can be either true or false.[12]

The "Institutional" Definition of Art

Having despaired of identifying any essential attributes by which art might be defined, most contemporary estheticians have embraced open-ended theories regarding its nature. Such theories have in turn generated a profusion of spurious definitions in terms of non-essentials. The most influential of these, the *"institutional" definition*, was first proposed by George Dickie in 1969,[13] and again, in somewhat revised form, in his 1974 book *Art and the Aesthetic*:

A work of art in the classificatory sense is (1) an artifact (2) a set of the aspects of which has had conferred upon it the status of candidate for appreciation by some person or persons acting on behalf of a certain social institution (the artworld).[14] [34]

Although Dickie regarded this as a formal definition, refuting Weitz's claim that art cannot be defined, it violates virtually every principle governing the construction of a rigorous definition (see "The Rules of Definition" later in this chapter). Beginning with the not very informative stipulation that a work of art is an "artifact"—a very broad concept that is further broadened by his promiscuous definition of it[15]—Dickie's formulation is essentially circular and therefore vacuous, in spite of subsequent attempts on his part to invest it with meaning.[16] Logically, the concept *artworld*—an idea he borrowed from Arthur Danto, who had introduced it in 1964[17]—must depend on the concept *art*, the term being defined. Thus Dickie's attempt to define *art* in terms of the *artworld* is profoundly mistaken.

In response to criticisms of his original version, Dickie published in 1984 a substantially revised, "improved" version of the institutional theory, with the following definition:

A work of art is an artifact of a kind created to be presented to an artworld public.[18]

Though it has the virtue of brevity, and abandons the absurd idea that something becomes art by having that status "conferred" upon it, this later incarnation of the institutional definition of art is as fundamentally circular as the previous version. Dickie himself seemed to sense something more was needed to buttress it, for he appended four additional definitions—two, of terms that appear in the main definition; the other two, of concepts that are implicit in it:

An *artist* is a person who participates with understanding in the making of a work of art. A *public* is a set of persons the members of which are prepared in some degree to understand an object which is presented to them. The *artworld* is the totality of all artworld systems. An *artworld system* is a framework for the presentation of a work of art by an artist to an artworld public. [92]

In his most recent book, Dickie maintains that the five definitions taken together "provide the leanest possible description of the institution of art and thus the leanest possible account of the institutional theory of art."[19] To us, they provide the leanest possible evidence of the utter emptiness of his theory, owing to its blatant circularity. They fail to tell us anything about the actual nature of art works or how they differ from other human artifacts.

Dickie acknowledges that his definitions of art are circular, but claims that they are not "viciously" (or fundamentally) so, for they constitute, in his view, "a logically circular set of terms" which are *inflected,* "bend[ing] in on, pre-suppos[ing], and support[ing] one another," thus reflecting the "inflected nature of art." (92) "What the definitions reveal," Dickie explains, "is that art-making involves an intricate, co-relative structure that cannot be described in the straightforward, linear way envisaged by the ideal of noncircular definition." Furthermore, "the inflected nature of art is reflected in the way that we learn about art." Thus the poor reader who is lost in the opacity of all this prose can be taught "how to be a member of an artworld public"—"how to look at pictures that are presented as the intentional products of artists." (93)

In the nearly three decades since Dickie first promulgated the institutional theory, it has been repeatedly discussed and revised by other philosophers. Yet the resulting "definitions" of art have retained the same fundamentally circular thrust: all of them imply, in effect, that virtually *anything* is art if a reputed artist or other purported expert *says* it is. Moreover, the basic assumptions of the institutional theory have persisted, even in the thought of philosophers who claim to reject it in whole or in part. In *Art and Nonart* (1983), for example, Marcia Eaton pointed to "serious weaknesses" in Dickie's definition (though she nonetheless considered it "the most careful and clearest working out of such a definition"). (82) She subsequently offered her own version of what art is:

> [Something] is a work of art if and only if . . . [it] is an artifact and . . . [it] is discussed in such a way that information concerning the history of [its] production . . . directs the viewer's attention to properties which are worth attending to.[20] [99]

Note that Eaton's implied discussants, who direct our attention to properties of artifacts they deem "worth attending to," bear an uncanny resemblance to the "person or persons acting on behalf of . . . the artworld"—who anoint certain artifacts as "candidate[s] for appreciation"—in Dickie's original definition. Moreover, the determinative role of the "artworld" becomes even more obvious in the revised definition proposed by Eaton in *Aesthetics and the Good Life* (1989).[21] Eaton strives to retain what she refers to as the "aesthetic value" of art. But her definition of this concept[22] sheds no light on the distinctive value of *art,* as compared with other "aesthetic" objects. In any case, Eaton accepts the institutional theory's basic premises. As Ralph Smith has observed, the *discussion* emphasized by Eaton enables "a thing that otherwise would not be regarded as art [to be inducted] into the world of art": thus such things as "[b]oulders, pieces of driftwod, or ditches" that "get talked about in relevant terms . . . in effect become works of art" according to Eaton's theory.[23]

Another prominent philosopher, Richard Wollheim, promisingly begins a sometimes insightful critique of the institutional theory, in his book *Painting as an Art,* by noting the theory's "fundamental implausibility," and by further suggesting that revision does not reduce any of "the very serious difficulties that attach to it." That the theory is popular in some circles, he astutely remarks, derives from the enhanced power and enlarged self-esteem it imparts to those "tempted to think of themselves as representatives of the art-world." In their view, Wollheim observes, "[p]ainters make paintings, but it takes a representative of the art-world to make a work of art." (13–14) Nonetheless, like Eaton, he ultimately embraces the basic assumptions of the institutional theory.

Though Wollheim does not offer a definition of art (notwithstanding his concern with painting "as an *art*"), one need only read between the lines of his work to see that his concept is little removed in essence from those of Dickie and Eaton. "The experience of art," Wollheim explains, rather opaquely, "takes the form. . . of coming to see the work that causes the experience as in turn the effect of an intentional activity on the part of the artist." Further, the artist's intention involves, in part, his belief that

> when a particular intention is fulfilled in his work, then an *adequately sensitive, adequately informed,* spectator will tend to have experiences in front of the painting that will disclose this intention. [8, emphasis ours]

What is one to make of Wollheim's reference to "an adequately sensitive, adequately informed, spectator"? Imagine a poor, befuddled "spectator" standing before an abstract painting in a museum and confiding to Wollheim that he discerns only geometric forms, color, and texture which *represent* nothing. He therefore questions whether the work is, in fact, art. Wollheim would no doubt inform him that the work is actually "at once representational and abstract" (as he argues later in his book), and that it is indeed a work of art. When the hapless spectator, now "adequately informed," nonetheless fails to discern the alleged artist's "intention," and continues to doubt that the work is art, he would then be judged "inadequately sensitive"—according to Wollheim's version of the "experience of art." In effect, Wollheim is a representative of the artworld he purports to disparage.

In *Definitions of Art* (1991), Stephen Davies remarks that Dickie's original proposition "struck some people as preposterous" (78)—owing, no doubt, to its obvious circularity. Yet all the succeeding approaches which Davies examines can be seen, when stripped of the obfuscating jargon in which they are often cast, to be nothing more than variations on the institutional theory. Indeed, after describing and commenting in detail on the definition of art "as it has been discussed in Anglo-American philosophy over the past thirty years,"[24] Davies himself offers "not a new theory but rather a new perspective," culminating in the following conclusion:

> Something's being a work of art is a matter of its having a particular status. This status is conferred by a member of the Artworld, usually an artist, who has the authority to confer the status in question by virtue of occupying a role within the Artworld to which that authority attaches.[25] [218, emphasis ours]

How does Davies define the crucial concept "Artworld"? It is, he explains somewhat murkily, an "informal institution" arising from "(noninstitutional) social practices related to the function of art and . . . continu[ing] to develop through time," which is "structured in terms of its various roles—artist, impressario, public, performer, curator, critic, and so on—and the relationships among them." Of these many roles,[26] Davies defines only the first:

> An artist is someone who has acquired (in some appropriate but informal fashion) the authority to confer art status. By "authority" I do not mean "a right to others' obedience"; I mean an "entitlement successfully to employ the conventions by which art status is conferred on objects/events." This authority is acquired through the artist's participation in the activities of the Artworld.[27] [87]

Thus Davies's "new perspective" merely combines and reshuffles the elements of the two versions of Dickie's definition for a result that, in our view, is equally nonsensical.

Regarding the *purpose* of art, and the question of why art plays "so significant a role in the lives of so many people" (50), Davies notes only that its "primary function . . . is to provide enjoyment."[28] Unlike Rand, he offers no suggestion of what might be the *source* of the pleasure derived from art. He notes only that the "wider social functions" art serves—"providing employment, securing the value of [financial] investments, and so on"—tend to influence the Artworld "to operate in a way that often is at odds with the function of art." With no further comment on his part, however, the reader is left to guess at his precise meaning. (220)

Just how entrenched anti-essentialism and the assumptions of the institutional theory have become in scholarly and critical circles is evident from an article in the *New York Times*,[29] in which nearly a score of prominent "art-world participants" answer the fundamental question of esthetics, "What is art?"—as well as the frequently appended question "Who decides?" A typical response is that of Thomas McEvilley, professor of art history at Rice University and a contributing editor of *Artforum*. McEvilley prefaces his answer by recalling a visit to the Houston "Media Center," where an assortment of laundry hanging from clotheslines attached to posts, "as in a back yard," was immediately recognizable by him as a work of art "because of where it was." He concludes:

> It is art if it is called art, written about in an art magazine, exhibited in a museum or bought by a private collector.
>
> It seems pretty clear by now that more or less anything can be designated as art. The question is, Has it been called art by the so-called "art system"? In our century, that's all that makes it art. [30]

In so stating, McEvilley echoes the critical dictum of Roberta Smith, quoted in our Introduction. Similarly, *Time* magazine's art critic Robert Hughes (known also through his televised surveys of art history and related books) avers: "As far as I am concerned, something is a work of art if it is made with the declared intention to be a work of art and placed in a context where it is seen as a work of art." William Rubin, director emeritus of painting and sculpture at the Museum of Modern Art in New York City, sounds an equally familiar refrain when he claims that "no single definition of art [is] universally tenable." And Arthur Danto, Johnsonian Professor of Philosophy emeritus at Columbia University and art critic for *The Nation*, even more bluntly declares: "You can't say something's art or not art anymore. That's all finished."

Most disturbing is the opinion of Robert Rosenblum—professor of art history at New York University's Institute of Fine Arts, and a curator at the Guggenheim Museum in New York City—who disdainfully presumes: "By now the idea of defining art is so remote I don't think anyone would dare do it."[31] Since Rosenblum surely knows of on-going attempts at an institutional "definition" by his peers in the artworld, he must mean that no one would dare to propose an *essentialist* definition, framed according to the rules of logic. As this book testifies, however, he is much mistaken. In any case, the pedagogical implications of Rosenblum's remark are disconcerting, for it is all too easy to imagine the intimidating influence his attitude might have on students inclined to even raise the question of an objective definition of art in the classes he teaches.

The "Appeal to Authority"

The institutional theory, in all its manifestations, resorts to the logical fallacy known as the "appeal to authority."[32] But the rules of logical argument demand that adequate evidence be given in support of a claim or theory. As Kelley points out in *The Art of Reasoning*, it is entirely appropriate to rely on expert testimony, provided that "the conditions of credibility are satisfied": (1) the alleged authority must, in fact, be an expert in the field under discussion; and (2) he must be objective. Moreover:

> The use of authorities . . . is appropriate only when the issue in question requires specialized knowledge or skill that the ordinary person does not possess. If the issue is *not* a technical one—if it is a matter of common sense, . . . then the ordinary person is capable of understanding the evidence for it, and . . . should simply be given the evidence, not asked to rely on someone else's judgment. Why should [one] settle for secondhand knowledge, when [one] could have firsthand knowledge? [119–120]

Contrary to the artworld's authoritarian "experts" cited above, we would insist that the general nature of art is decidedly *not* a technical issue requiring specialized knowledge beyond the grasp of the ordinary person.[33] As Jacques Barzun has admonished: "Talk and thought about art must conform to the canons of common sense, because art offers itself to the senses and the mind not as an idea or an abstraction, but as a piece of concrete experience. Nor does common sense here mean conventional opinion but thought free of jargon."[34]

Since the institutional theory in all its forms depends on the appeal to authority, we refer to it as the "authoritarian theory of art," a term that more accurately indicates its true nature, and to the various definitions subsumed under it, as "authoritarian definitions" of art.

The Rules of Definition

Given the overwhelming trend away from essentialist, or analytical, definitions in contemporary philosophy, Rand deserves credit, at the outset, for insisting on the need for such a definition with respect to art. In so doing, she continued an established practice of inestimable value. The virtues of precise definition, and the rules governing its construction, had been a commonplace of intellectual discourse in the first half of the twentieth century.

As late as 1948, for example, the *Encyclopaedia Britannica* carried a succinct entry on "definition," written from an essentialist perspective.

Refering to *definition* as "a logical term used popularly for the process of explaining, or giving the meaning of, a word," the entry went on to cite a set of rules "generally given as governing accurate definition."[35] In his classic introductory text *Logic* (first published in 1950), Lionel Ruby observes that "when we speak of 'definition,' we usually refer to this type of definition" (99). He further notes that such a definition is valuable because it tells us that "something belongs to a general class of things and that it is distinguished from other members of its class by certain characteristics." (100–101) Ruby aptly begins his discussion with a trenchant bit of dialogue from *Lady Windermere's Fan*, by Oscar Wilde, in which the Duchess implores: "Do, as a concession to my poor wits, Lord Darlington, just explain to me what you really mean," and Darlington candidly replies: "I think I had better not, Duchess. Nowadays to be intelligible is to be found out." As Ruby explains: "When we define our terms we explain 'what we really mean,' with all the risks attendant thereto. But if we desire to avoid obfuscation and discussions which move at cross-purposes, we must give definite and precise meanings to our terms." (88)

Regarding the process of constructing a proper definition, Ruby acknowledges that it can be very difficult, "particularly when there is controversy over the 'proper' meaning of a word." (119) As it happens, one of the controversial concepts with which he chooses to illustrate the process is *art*, for it is precisely such "vague or ambiguous terms" that most require an analytical definition, which helps to clarify the objective nature of the concept's referents. (100) According to Ruby:

> We should first stipulate that the word ['art'] will denote certain referents: . . . [i.e.,] productions in the fields of painting, sculpture, architecture,[36] literature, and music. . . . Our next task is to analyze the nature of the referents . . . [and to] seek for the characteristics which are common and peculiar to paintings, poems, etc., so that our definition will have the virtue of equivalence. [119–120]

Kelley, too, discusses the definition of the concept *art*, emphasizing that "the more abstract a concept is, and the longer the chain of other concepts that link it to its referents, the more important a definition is."[37] (35)

In her *Introduction to Objectivist Epistemology*, Rand argues that, though a definition is often said to state the meaning of a word or term, it really identifies "the nature of the [referents] subsumed under a concept." She explains: "A word is merely a visual-auditory symbol used to represent a concept; a word has no meaning other than that of the concept it symbolizes, and the meaning of a concept consists of its [referents]. It is not words, but concepts

that man defines—by specifying [the fundamental attributes of] their referents." The purpose of a definition, she emphasizes, is "to distinguish a concept from all other concepts and thus to keep its [referents] differentiated
from all other existents."[38] (40) A useful definition can therefore be based
only on a rational system of classification,[39] and one cannot merely "stipu-
late" (as Ruby might seem to suggest) the referents being defined. "When in
doubt about the meaning or the definition of a concept," Rand counsels, one
should seek the referents that "gave rise to the concept."[40] (51) In the case of
art, this means pre-modernist works of painting, sculpture, literature, music,
and dance. Since the process of concept-formation itself depends on a recognition of fundamental similarities and differences,[41] a re-examination of these
original referents would yield more reliable information than a consideration
of avant-garde work. Thus the approach taken by contemporary theorists,
who focus on such phenomena as "dadaism, pop art, found art, and happenings,"[42] is completely mistaken.

As outlined by both Ruby and Kelley, as well as by the brief *Encyclopaedia
Britannica* article cited above, a proper definition is constructed according
to a prescribed set of principles, or rules, the most important of which are the
following: (1) it includes a *genus* (the general class of things to which the
referents of the concept being defined belong) and a *differentia* (the principal characteristic[s] distinguishing the concept's referents from other things
in that class); (2) it is neither too broad nor too narrow; (3) it identifies the
essential attributes or characteristics of the concept's referents; (4) it avoids
circularity (it must not employ a synonym or cognate of the concept being
defined) and (5) it is clear—avoiding, in Kelley's words, "vague, obscure, or
metaphorical language."[43]

Rand's Definition of Art

How well does Rand's definition of art as *"a selective re-creation of reality
according to an artist's metaphysical value-judgments"* satisfy the criteria
enumerated above? Let us examine each point, in turn:

(1) Rand's definition does include a *genus* ("a selective re-creation of reality") and a *differentia* ("according to an artist's metaphysical value-judgments"). Further, the genus conveys, as it should, important information about
the larger class of things to which art works belong.[44] As we suggested in
Chapter 1, Rand's genus broadly corresponds to the concept of *mimesis* [45]
(imitation) in ancient Greek thought. In our present-day context, Rand's concept of "selective re-creation" subsumes a wide variety of man-made objects
and activities, many of which are not works of art. Among the non-art examples are dolls, toy cars, model ships, billboard advertisements, magazine

illustrations, children's play-acting,[46] and celebrity impersonations. In each instance of mimesis, the principal criterion for the selective re-creation of reality is suitability for the intended purpose, or function, of the object or activity. The designer of toy cars or dolls, for example, seeks to delight and instruct children. The billboard designer aims to catch the eye of people traveling at some speed on a highway and motivate them to purchase commercial goods or services, for example, or to support some cause. The celebrity impersonator's goal is to entertain an audience by mimicing the vocal and physical mannerisms of well-known personalities, often by exaggerating them as in a caricature.

The criterion of selectivity on the part of the artist is also dependent upon the ultimate function of the work—which is to objectify fundamental values and a view of life. In contrast with the individuals cited above, however, the artist need not be aware of that ultimate function at all, and surely not to the degree explicated by Rand.[47] Though it governs his choices, it does not necessarily form part of his conscious intention. Nor does the artist focus, during the creative process, on the work's relation to other people. His intentional focus is on the work itself, on its intrinsic importance for him, as we emphasized in our discussion of "communication" and art in Chapter 3. He is guided primarily by the standard of what he holds—on the deepest, emotionally integrated, subconscious level—to be *important* in life.[48] This is what Rand's *differentia* of "metaphysical value-judgments" is meant to convey, but the full meaning of that term and its relationship to art are far from transparent. On that issue, see (5) below.

(2) To test whether Rand's definition is too broad or too narrow, one must seek possible counterexamples: would it include some things that are clearly *not* art? might it exclude anything that one would reasonably classify as art? To our knowledge, her definition subsumes all, and only, those works that commonly fall under the traditional category of ("fine") art—with the exception of architecture, the exclusion of which is justified, as we argue in Chapter 10. We can think of nothing whose status as art is undisputed that would be excluded by it.[49] The only works excluded are precisely those that have been regarded as "controversial" or "avant-garde" in the twentieth century—that is, those which have been arbitrarily granted art status by the "artworld." In our view, their exclusion is a major virtue of Rand's definition.

(3) Does the definition identify the *essential* attribute(s) or characteristic(s) of all works in the major art forms? As we have indicated in (1) and (2), we think that Rand's concept of a "selective re-creation of reality" does indeed identify a fundamental attribute of all authentic instances of art. Moreover, her criterion of selection "according to an artist's metaphysical value-judgments" (at least as it is elaborated by her in terms of her concept of sense

of life) is valid, in our view, although we have reservations about the term as such—on which, again, see (5) below. Taken as a whole, Rand's definition accounts for the salient features of the rich diversity of art works in various cultures from prehistory onward, while also allowing ample possibility for future creativity—even as technology advances—within the limits set by the requirements of human nature.[50] It not only points to the distinctive attributes of art works but also suggests why art can be of profound personal significance for both creator and responder, as well as being culturally significant. In sum, it answers three of the principal objections commonly raised against an essentialist definition: first, that such a definition would foreclose creativity; second, that works of art share no perceptible common features; and third, that such a definition could not be a guide to distinguishing art from non-art.[51]

Nonetheless, the objection has been raised that Rand's definition is inadequate, because it fails to specify the function of art.[52] On the face of it, this may seem to be a legitimate objection, since human artifacts are usually defined in terms of their function, which determines their characteristics.[53] Rand herself emphasizes that a distinctive characteristic of art is that it serves a unique psychological function—that of concretizing or objectifying what one deems to be important in life. A persistent problem in attempting to define art in terms of its purpose, however, is that an art work often serves multiple purposes. While the cognitive function identified by Rand constitutes the ultimate purpose for which art exists, secondary functions may readily coexist with it. And, as we have stressed, the cognitive function of art does not ordinarily form part of an artist's conscious intention.[54]

According to Rand's definition, it matters little whether the conscious purpose or intention of a Renaissance painter depicting a Madonna and Child, for instance, was to pay homage to the Virgin, while satisfying his patron's wish to do the same—perhaps hoping thereby to insure intercession with God. As evidenced by the widely varying treatments of such religious subjects, a different artistic temperament shaped each one, and each work projects a distinctive sense of life. Nor do we need to know whether Dante's motivation for writing *The Divine Comedy*, for example, was to save the souls of his fellow Christians. What counts is that, in every case, the individual sensibility of the artist is embodied in the work itself. Because Rand's definition identifies the essence of art works as such, without stipulating their function, it need not exclude those works intended or employed for ritual or religious purposes.[55] Regardless of the purposes for which such works may have been intended or enjoyed, they presented a selective re-creation of reality which held deep personal significance for the artist and for countless others as well, down to the present day.[56]

In any case, it is important to remember that a definition need not specify *all* the important characteristics of the concept's referents, but should focus instead on those that have the greatest explanatory power. In our view, Rand's definition of art does this, notwithstanding any reservations we express below about the key term of the differentia.

(4) At first glance, the objection could be raised, that Rand's differentia violates the rule of non-circularity, since it employs the term "artist," a cognate of the term or concept being defined. On closer examination, however, this objection evaporates. Rand's definition is not fundamentally circular, since one might easily substitute the term "maker" or creator" without altering the essential meaning of the statement (though we much prefer the term "artist").[57] In other words, one does not need know to what an "artist" is in order to understand what "art" is, according to Rand's definition. Authoritarian definitions of art, by contrast, are fundamentally circular. Their meaning ultimately depends on one's knowledge of what an "artist" or the "artworld" is, which in turn requires that one know what "art" is.

(5) Finally, we must consider whether Rand's definition is sufficiently clear, whether it avoids vagueness and obscurity. The key term of her differentia, "metaphysical value-judgments," might well be obscure to persons not steeped in philosophy.[58] As we noted in Chapter 1, her own discussion of the concept is cursory, and the examples she cites seem to have little relevance to art forms other than literature. Her fullest explication of *metaphysical value-judgments* as it pertains to the arts is in terms of *sense of life*, as we indicated in Chapters 2 and 3. Why, then, did she not use that concept in her definition?

The likely answer is that, while less obscure, the term "sense of life" would be far more vague, in the absence of Rand's explication and analysis. Though the phrase is often used in everyday discourse, no one unfamiliar with Rand's thought could be expected to be aware of the complex layers of meaning she ascribes to it, as "a pre-conceptual equivalent of metaphysics"—"an emotional, subconsciously integrated appraisal of man and of existence." In the light of her analysis of sense of life and its role in art, however, it is clear that the term "metaphysical value-judgments," without further modification, may be somewhat misleading as the criterion of artistic selectivity, since it can be taken as referring to conscious value-judgments, whereas "sense of life" refers to the subsconsciously held value-judgments that are crucial to emotional response.

In our previously published introduction to Rand's philosophy of art, we proposed the following reformulation of her definition: *Art is a selective re-creation of reality according to an artist's fundamental values.* Such a formulation gains some support from Rand's own comments in "Philosophy and Sense of Life." For example, she observes that "it is only those values which he regards or grows to regard as 'important,' those which represent his implicit view of reality, that remain in a man's subconscious and form his sense of life." (28) And: "The integrated sum of a man's *basic values* is his sense of life." (29, emphasis ours) Further, she maintains that an individual's sense of life reflects his "deepest values." (31)

When we proposed our revision of Rand's definition, we were unaware that she had originally employed the term "values" though in her definition and had then replaced it with "metaphysical value-judgments."[59] In reconsidering this point, one of us (M.M.K.) has had a change of mind; the other (L.T.) has not. we offer both our views below for our reader's consideration.

[*M.M.K.*] Certainly, the concepts of "values" and "metaphysical value-judgments," while related, are by no means equivalent for Rand. She defines a *value* as "that which one acts to gain and/or to keep," not "fundamental" or "basic" values—and implicit in that definition is the standard sense of that which one esteems as a good. In contrast, a *metaphysical value-judgment* might be defined (based on her analysis) as "an assessment of a fundamental aspect of reality in relation to its import for one's life." Whereas *values* pertain to everything that a man regards as a good (and therefore seeks to gain and to keep),[60] *metaphysical value-judgments* comprise both negative and positive assessments, since they pertain to fundamental aspects of existence—that which is deemed *important*, for better or for worse.

With respect to art, in particular, the concept of metaphysical value-judgments has broader relevance than that of values alone. An artist who chooses to depict human suffering and misery, for example, cannot reasonably be supposed to be guided in the creative process by his fundamental *values*, if by "values" one means "that which he deems as a good." Rather, he is guided by what he considers to be metaphysically *important*. Because he regards suffering as a salient and inescapable aspect of human existence, he makes it the subject of his art. The medieval painters who depicted the horrors of the plague in fourteenth-century Italy (or the patrons who commissioned such scenes), for instance, did not "value" the Black Death, but they deemed it to be an event of shattering importance, of which one must remain mindful, and therefore sought to give it concrete expression. Indeed, Rand herself stresses, *which includes his deepest values*. in her analysis of the role of sense of life in art, as we have previously noted. In replacing "values" with "metaphysical value-judgments" in her definition of art, Rand may have recognized that the former term would include such works. To translate her definition into simpler language that accurately reflects her concept of sense of life. I therefore now propose: *Art is a selective re-creation of reality according to an artist's fundamental view of life, which includes his deepest values.*

[*L.T.*] In substituting "metaphysical value-judgments" for "values" in her definition of art, Rand may have realized that the term is, by her own account, far too inclusive, since it encompasses literally *anything* one acquires (or seeks to acquire), or store or preserves in some manner—from seashells and ice cream to picture postcards and freedom. But the term *value* occurs repeatedly in Rand's thought on art, most often preceded by such qualifiers as "metaphysical," "deepest," "basic" or "fundamental," so it is worth examining further, especially in relation to the above-mentioned notion of its "being esteemed as a good."

As defined by Peter A. Angeles (*Dictionary of Philosophy*), "value" is, indeed, "that which is . . . regarded highly, or a good"—but, as he adds: "the opposite of a positive value is . . . 'negative value.'" More germane, in *The Philosophic Thought of Ayn Rand* (64), Douglas Den Uyl and Douglas Rasmussen note that, for Rand, "*Value* is a morally neutral term." Finally, as Nathaniel Branden has observered: "If a man regards a thing (a person, an object, an event, a mental state, etc.) as good for him, as beneficial in some way, he values it—and, when possible and appropriate, seeks to acquire, retain and use or enjoy it . . . As a being of volitional consciousness, [however, man] is not biologically 'programmed' to make the right value-choices automatically. He may select values that lead him to suffering and destruction. But whether his values are life-serving or life-negating, it is a man's values that direct his actions" ("Emotions and Values," *The Objectivist*, May 1966.)

Most importantly, in the first of her *Fiction-Writing* lectures, Rand elaborated on her concept of art. "The mere fact of what you select to present and how you present it, will express your fundamental values," she remarked, adding: "When I say 'fundamental,' I mean 'metaphysical.' I mean your view of the nature of reality, or man's relation to it."

In light of the above, I offer again the revised definition we proposed in 1991 (since the alternative suggested above strikes me as insufficiently clear and overly broad): "*Art is a selective re-creation of reality according to an artist's fundamental values.*"

[*M.M.K.* and *L.T.*] We hasten to stress that, our differences on this point notwithstanding, we consider Rand's original definition of art) and either of our reformulations of it) preferable to any other definition we know of in the critical literature.

7

Scientific Support for Rand's Theory

Ayn Rand's theory of art is rooted in her view of human nature—its perceptual faculties, its cognitive needs and capacities, and its often baffling emotional complexity. Her analysis of art as a function of man's nature, physical as well as psychological, thus constitutes an essentially *biocentric* theory—though she never refers to it as such.[1] As we have suggested, the basic principles of her theory are not only internally coherent but objectively valid as well. If so, one should be able to substantiate both its fundamental premises and its main conclusions by direct appeal to the relevant scientific disciplines.[2] In our view, support for Rand's main ideas can indeed be found in fields ranging from archeology and anthropology to cognitive science and psychology. Moreover, to a remarkable degree, she anticipated ideas that are now gaining scientific acceptance. While a comprehensive examination of such material is beyond our scope, we shall touch upon some key points which tend to corroborate her theory.

Human Evolution and Prehistoric Art

Rand's view that art is both a product and a need of human consciousness rests in part on her twofold premise that "art has existed in every known civilization [and culture], accompanying man's steps from . . . his prehistorical dawn," and that the basic forms of art "were born in prehistoric times."[3] As we noted earlier, the arts she has in mind are those she analyzes in "Art and

Cognition"—painting, sculpture, music, dance, and literature.[4] In stating that "art" existed in prehistory, as we also noted, Rand does not mean that early man had formed such a *concept*[5]—merely that he engaged in these activities, and that they served the same primary psychological function as they have ever since: that of integrating and objectifying experience in an emotionally meaningful way. How justified, one may ask, are such assumptions?

The most compelling evidence is found in painting and sculpture.[6] This is not surprising, since artifacts of this kind are durable, in contrast with music, oral literature, and dance—temporal forms, which, in the absence of notational systems, are ephemeral in nature. Yet even those arts have left some trace. The existence of some type of musical activity, for example, has been reasonably inferred from the remains of primitive flutes, dated to at least 30,000 years ago, concurrent with the earliest visual representations.[7] Remarkably, the holes in at least one of these early flutes are spaced so as to produce regularly stepped tones comparable to the pentatonic scale—which is still used in some types of Hindu and Japanese music, as well as in Anglo-Saxon folk melodies.[8] (That some flute fragments have been found on the floor of caves containing art has led to the speculation that, as Robert Payne puts it in his splendid survey of art, "the Paleolithic artists, like Leonardo da Vinci, enjoyed painting to music."[9]) Substantial evidence also remains for the existence of dance. Dancers are clearly depicted in cave paintings of Africa and southern Europe that are some 20,000 years old. And patterns of footprints found at more than one prehistoric site further indicate that dance played a significant part in the life of early man.[10]

Finally, even the likelihood of story-telling can be inferred with some confidence from many of the images left by Paleolithic man, as the archeologist Alexander Marshack persuasively argues in *The Roots of Civilization,* his provocative inquiry into the cognitive capacities of prehistoric man. One of the earliest-known sculptured figures, for example, is an ivory carving of a lion-headed human, found at Hohlenstein in Germany and dated to 30,000–33,000 years ago. Whether this figure, or others like it, represents a shaman engaged in a ritual or an animal spirit of some sort, it strongly implies an underlying explanative narrative, or story, actual or imagined.[11] Other prehistoric paintings and engravings also imply such narratives. The simplest of them apparently constitute seasonal scenes—ancient precursors, as it were, of the calendar pages traditionally included in a medieval Book of Hours.[12] According to Marshack, such scenes suggest a "story" in the most fundamental sense, for they embody a meaning that is both "time-factored and relational"—indicating a sequence of causally related events occurring over time.[13]

The question remains, of course, whether these prehistoric images served what Rand identifies as the purpose of art. The earliest theory regarding their original intention was that proposed by the abbé Henri Breuil, who maintained that the purpose of the cave paintings was mainly to endow the hunters with magic powers over their prey—a thesis that could be viewed as arguing against their status as art. While Breuil's interpretation still persists in discussions of Paleolithic culture, it has in recent years been challenged, for a number of reasons. First, as Marshack and others have emphasized, the inaccessible locations chosen for much of the work in question is inconsistent with such a purpose.[14] Perhaps more significant, had the sole or main purpose of the images been simple magic, early man would probably not have devoted so much care to their creation. The crudest representations would have sufficed.

Although Paleolithic paintings and engravings vary widely in quality, the best of them exhibit an exquisite delicacy of touch and a profoundly sensitive perception of nature, as well as a relatively high level of technical mastery.[15] Not only are the creatures rendered in such accurate detail that particular species or seasonal anatomical features can often be clearly discerned[16] but, more important for our purposes, they possess an extraordinary emotive power. As the British archeologist Steven Mithen has implied, they employ line and color to convey "not just a record of what is seen but [the artist's] feelings for it."[17] If they served, in part, an "information-storing" function (as Mithen and others have speculated[18]), the information so stored was emotionally charged and esthetically treated. The very quality of the prehistoric images, then, suggests that they were an embodiment of important values, rather than mere instruments of magic. As one observer has remarked: "The way [the] animals are drawn . . . is evidence of something sacred."[19]

Consider, for example, the remarkable image from the Font-de-Gaume cave in southern France, in which a male reindeer seems to watch over a recumbent pregnant female either wounded or about to give birth.[20] The importance this scene must have held for the artist is implicit in the finesse with which the deer are drawn—the sweeping curve of the antlers, the undulating outlines of the creatures' bodies, the fragility of their spindly legs. The full focus of the image, moreover, is on the tender solicitude of the male for the female in her vulnerable state. In answer to the question posed by art historian Ernst Gombrich—will we ever be able to tell what the purposes of such images were?[21]—we would argue that they served the same *ultimate* purpose that art still serves, though it is not one that the earliest artists are likely to have been aware of. To judge from the poignant Font-de-Gaume image, and from others of equivalent artistry, prehistoric man in some manner identified with the creatures who shared his world and, as Rand's theory suggests, he needed to objectify such sentiments by fixing them in visible form. Thus it is likely that, as Robert Payne speculated, prehistoric artists painted the animals "out of reverence and fellowship, with a deep compassion for them, knowing themselves to be sharers of the same kingdom," and that "they filled the [cave] walls with them *because their minds were filled with them.*"[22]

The Fundamentality of Mimesis

Although archeologists and cognitive scientists have proposed a variety of theories regarding the meaning and purpose of prehistoric art, all agree that the arts are among the evolutionary developments that "embody the very essence of what it means to be fully human."[23] Moreover, most theorists distinguish between Paleolithic "art" and the abstract symbols and notations which emerged around the same time in the prehistoric record.[24] The fundamentally *mimetic* character of art[25]—in contrast with the abstract nature of symbolic and notational systems—has been highlighted by the Canadian neuropsychologist Merlin Donald, who offers a profoundly illuminating theory regarding its significance. In his *Origins of the Modern Mind*, Donald persuasively argues that mimesis played a crucial role in human cognitive evolution, serving as the primary means of representing reality among the immediate ancestors of *Homo sapiens*, just prior to the emergence of language and symbolic thought. For Donald, the term "mimesis" refers to *intentional means of representing reality that utilize vocal tone, facial expression, bodily movement, manual gestures, and other nonlinguistic means.*[26] In his view, it is "fundamentally different" from both *mimicry* and *imitation.* Whereas mimicry attempts to render an exact duplicate of an event or phenomenon, and imitation also seeks to copy an original (albeit less literally so than mimicry), mimesis adds a new dimension: it "re-enact[s] and re-present[s] an event or relationship" in a nonliteral yet clearly intelligible way.[27] Donald's concept of *mimesis* is therefore closely comparable to Rand's concept of "selective re-creation of reality."

Donald emphasizes that mimetic representation, though a vestige of an earlier cognitive stage, remains "a central factor in human society" and is "at the very center of the arts." (169) While it is logically prior to language, it shares certain essential characteristics with language, in his view, and its emergence in prehistory would have paved the way for the subsequent evolution of speech.[28] (171) Yet mimetic behavior, he insists, can be clearly separated from the symbolic and semiotic devices of modern culture. Not only does it function in different contexts, it is still "far more efficient than language in diffusing certain kinds of knowledge . . . [and in] communicating emotions."[29] (198–99) Moreover, he argues that

mimetic representation remains [fundamental] . . . in the operation of the
human brain. . . . When [it] is destroyed [through disease or injury], the [indi-
vidual] is classified as demented, out of touch with reality. . . . But when language alone is lost, even completely lost, there is often considerable residual
representational capacity.[30] [199]

Repeatedly stressing the importance of mimetic representation in the arts,
Donald notes that even literature, which employs the symbolic medium
of language, is "ultimately mimetic" (170)—since (as Rand emphasized) it
recreates concrete characters, events, and situations. He suggests, further, that
story-telling and the construction of myths, which arose out of a need to
describe and explain events and objects, were themselves the "basic driving
force" behind the acquisition of language by early man. (257) Noting that
narrative thought (as contrasted with abstract-theoretic thought, which evolved
later) continues to be the dominant mode in primitive societies, he emphasizes that its "supreme product" in such societies is the myth, which plays
an essential role in the formation of a sense of tribal, as well as personal,
identity.

The myth is the authoritative version, the debated, disputed, filtered product
of generations of narrative interchange about reality. In conquering a rival
society, the first act of the conquerors is to impose their myth on the conquered. And the strongest instinct of the conquered is to resist this pressure;
the loss of one's myth involves a profoundly disorienting loss of identity. The
myth stands at the top of the cognitive pyramid in such a society; it not only
regulates behavior and enshrines knowledge, but it also constrains the perception of reality and channels the thought skills of its adherents.[31] [258,
emphasis ours]

Donald's emphasis on the importance of myths in primitive culture accords
with Rand's view that mythology in such cultures and art in civilized societies serve essentially the same function, that of concretizing and objectifying core values, whether societal or personal. Of even more fundamental
significance, with respect to Rand's theory of art, is Donald's insistence on
the "ultimately mimetic" basis of all the arts, and his view that its roots lie
in a deeply embedded, prelinguistic mode of human thought. Such a view
goes a long way toward justifying Rand's conviction that all art "selectively
re-creates reality" in a way that is immediately intelligible, "present[ing]
man's concepts as if they were percepts." It also lends theoretical support
for the principle (articulated by many writers in addition to Rand, of course)
that literature must "show," not merely "tell." If, as Donald argues, mimetic
thought is indeed a powerful cognitive mode distinct from analytic-symbolic-

theoretic thought processes, then art can be viewed (consistent with Rand's theory) as a means of integrating knowledge and experience from these disparate modes into a seamless, emotionally meaningful whole. Such a perspective renders all the more compelling her proposition that the various arts serve the same psycho-epistemological function, that of "integrat[ing] man's forms of cognition, unif[ying] his consciousness and clarif[ying] his grasp of reality."[32]

Anthropological Perspectives

As we have indicated above, speculations about the meaning and purpose of prehistoric art rely heavily on analogies drawn with modern-day hunter-gatherer societies. Such primitive[33] societies, as Steven Mithen emphasizes in *The Prehistory of the Modern Mind*, tend to view man and beast, animal and plant, organic and inorganic realms, as participants in an integrated, animated totality. (164–66) The dual manifestations of this tendency are *anthropomorphism* (the practice of regarding animals as humans) and *totemism* (the practice of regarding humans as animals), both of which pervade the visual art and the mythology of primitive cultures. Thus the natural world is conceptualized in terms of human social relations.[34] When considered in this light, the visual preoccupation of early humans with the nonhuman creatures inhabiting their world becomes profoundly meaningful. Among hunter-gatherers, animals are not only good to eat, they are also *good to think about*, as anthropologist Claude Lévi-Strauss has observed. In the practice of totemism, he has suggested, an unlettered humanity "brood[s] upon itself and its place in nature."[35] Through their observation of other species, primitive peoples find ways of conceptualizing human relationships.

The role of art in primitive societies has been explored in depth by the anthropologist Ellen Dissanayake in two highly illuminating books, *What Is Art For?* and *Homo Aestheticus*. In fundamental respects, Dissanayake implicitly corroborates Rand's view of the purpose of art, though that fact is at times obscured by her failure to recognize two important distinctions: first, between the major and the minor (i.e., "decorative") arts; and second, between "traditional" Western and "avant-garde" art. If one reads between the lines, however, one finds that both distinctions (which are explicit in Rand) are implied by Dissanayake, however unwittingly.

Dissanayake, like Rand, begins by emphasizing that art is a universal human phenomenon. In her Introduction to *What Is Art For?* Dissanayake observes:

> Although no one art is found in every society, or to the same degree in every society, there is found universally in every human group that exists today, or

that is known to have existed, the tendency to display and respond to one or usually more of what are called the arts: dancing, singing, carving, dramatizing, decorating, poeticizing speech, image making.[36] [6]

As her inclusion of "decorating" in this passage indicates, Dissanayake defines *art* much more broadly than Rand, characterizing it, in behavioral terms, as the tendency to estheticize (she terms it "making special") important aspects of individual and social life.[37] Stressing that art in primitive societies is always integral to the activities of life, she (much like Rand) is properly critical of Western formalist notions of "art for art's sake," which claim that the significance of art is detached from life, belonging instead to a realm of pure esthetic contemplation.[38] Because such notions originated with the concept of *fine art* in eighteenth-century theories of esthetics,[39] Dissanayake seems to assume that the category of "fine art" must itself be invalid, since the notion of esthetic detachment (or "disinterestedness") associated with it is mistaken. Thus she tends to view purely decorative practices—such as body ornamentation and the ritual display of food—in much the same light as the full-fledged art forms.[40] Nevertheless, she notes that "[w]hat we are accustomed . . . to call [fine] art (painting, carving, dancing, singing, and the like—or pictures, sculptures, songs, and dances) is certainly widespread in primitive societies," and she recognizes that the ubiquitous "arts" also include "dramatizing" and "poeticizing speech" and story-telling. (44, 6, and 115) Although she never characterizes the primitive manifestations of these forms as "*fine* arts"—a concept she associates exclusively with civilized cultures—nor otherwise explicitly distinguishes them, she does at times imply that they constitute a special category. Moreover, she observes that civilized peoples presumably need "*these aesthetic manifestations of their worldview, not simply the worldview itself*," though she seems not to recognize that such a "psychological need" is, in fact, universal. (34, emphasis ours)

Dissanayake proposes a "biobehavioral," or biocentric, view of art that has many points in common with the view implicit in Rand's esthetics. As indicated by the title of her second book, *Homo Aestheticus*, she regards the making and experiencing of art as an evolved human behavior no less fundamental to the species than language or tool making.[41] Since the experience of art is universally pleasurable, she argues that it must have been biologically advantageous. If it did not provide some adaptive benefit to the human species, she maintains, it would not have evolved as a deeply satisfying human experience, since the pleasure-pain mechanism (a flexible alternative to the instinctive patterns of specific behaviors in lower animals) operates to ensure actions conducive to survival and reproduction. Regarding the pleasure-pain principle in the life of civilized societies, however, Dissanayake cautions against assuming that every activity that is now pleasurable is necessarily advantageous. Whereas behavioral mechanisms evolved over a relatively long timespan, she argues, human culture has radically altered the environment in so brief a period that once-adaptive behavioral tendencies may now mislead us.[42] Dissanayake therefore distinguishes between the "ultimate" reasons (which are biologically based, and unconscious) for engaging in a behavior and the "proximate" reasons (which are conscious and voluntary). (31–31) According to such a distinction, emotional enjoyment is only the *proximate* reason for creating and experiencing art, not the *ultimate* reason for its existence as a fundamental part of human life. Rand implies a similar distinction when she analyzes and defines art in relation primarily to its cognitive function, rather than to its pleasurable effects. Her focus should serve as a reminder that, while the emotional experience of art is *felt* to be psychologically primary, it is not *metaphysically* primary, since it is dependent on the underlying cognitive function for its very existence.

While Dissanayake does not explicitly distinguish between the major art forms and the decorative arts, she does so implicitly, when she argues that art in preliterate societies serves to embody and integrate, in emotionally compelling ways, the essential knowledge and principal values of the group. Significantly, the specific arts she mentions in this context are poetry, music, dance, and painting—rather than such practices as body decoration, basket weaving, or ritual displays of food. (152–55) Thus she appears to imply that the major art forms constitute a distinctive category. Dissanayake even acknowledges as "legitimate" the question, "What differentiates the 'fine arts' from the other objects that are decorated, or have rhythmic form, or give sensuous pleasure?"[43] (39) (Regrettably, she does not attempt to answer it, however, because she regards it as the province of "philosophers of art, not biologists"— insufficient reason, in our view, since the focus of her work is on the nature of art.) Further, Dissanayake argues that the "behavior of art" evolved with the capacity for conceptual thought and the growing awareness of self, which are related, in turn, to both the capacity and the need for voluntary action and long-range planning—a view entirely consistent with Rand's. (118) Moreover, Dissanayake argues that the emotional *response* to art was as crucial in the evolution of this behavior as the *creation* of art works themselves. In fact, she regards the affective experience of art as "indispensable," both in the life of the individual and in human evolution. "It is from our emotions that we recognize our values: what moves [us] is what [we] seek as good or avoid as bad," she emphasizes (131–32)—an emphasis consistent with Rand's view of the emotions.

Dissanayake concludes that "what the arts [are] for" is the "embodiment and reinforcement of socially shared significances." (200) Owing in part to her admitted bias in favor of "traditional rather than modern peoples and ways of life" (44), however, she cannot reconcile such a primarily "social" purpose of art with what she regards as the excessive individualism of Western art. Because she fails to distinguish between genuine art in the West and the spurious art of the "avant-garde,"[44] she does not seem to recognize that Western art, while highly individualistic, nonetheless presents important "significances," which are often "socially shared." In contrast, Rand (who properly relegates the twentieth-century avant-garde to the realm of non-art) grasps the psychological importance of art for the *individual*, yet also makes clear in what respects art relates to a shared social and cultural context as well.

The Cognitive Psychology of Music

Just as anthropology has documented the forms of art common to all cultures, so studies by ethnomusicologists have provided evidence that the music of diverse cultures, distinctive and disparate as it may seem,[45] nonetheless exhibits certain universal characteristics. Having reviewed the ethnomusicological literature in depth, John Sloboda, a pre-eminent researcher in the cognitive psychology of music, suggests in his book *The Musical Mind* that the common features discernible in the various musical traditions of the world derive from "some universal cognitive basis for music which transcend[s] individual cultures." (253)

Lending credence to Rand's conviction that the essential attributes of music conform to the requirements of human perception and cognition, Sloboda argues that many of the principal features often identified with Western music are, in fact, common to all cultures to a considerable degree, and probably have a basis in biologically defined aspects of musical perception. These features therefore relate to the overriding principle of *intelligibility* emphasized by Rand, and to her insistence that one "cannot condition [the ear] to hear noise as if it were music."[46] According to Sloboda, for example, both the theory and the practice of music in various cultures tend toward tonality. Although tonality as it exists in the West "is by no means universal," he observes, analogous features exist "in most cultures."[47]

Another researcher, Roger Shepard, whose work is prominently cited by Sloboda, reports that, "[f]ar from being a recent Western invention, the diatonic [seven-note] scale has in fact been traced back to the most ancient tuning systems so far deciphered from archaeological records."[48] Moreover, even in cultures where the musical scale is divided into a large number of tones, a subset of only five or seven tones (comparable to the Western pentatonic and diatonic scales) forms the basis for the central musical structure, while the additional tones are used merely for melodic ornamentation. Finally, as

Sloboda points out, many pentatonic scales are based on a subset of the full diatonic scale, and can easily be converted by the addition of two notes. All these observations, "support the centrality of the diatonic scale." (257)

In addition, Sloboda identifies certain shared principles of temporal, or rhythmic, organization. "Just as reference pitches [or tonal centers] seem universally important," he observes, "so do reference *times*, important moments in relation to which other sounds are organized," and which are marked by the sounding out of a regular pulse or meter, with intermittently accented beats that provide a sense of location within the on-going pulse.[49] (257–58) In Sloboda's view, "scale and rhythm perform the same essential function, that of dividing up the pitch and time continua into discrete and re-identifiable locations." They thus provide a backdrop against which all the basic musical effects (such as tension and resolution, motion and rest) on which musical meaning depends can be created. (259)

Sloboda's identification of such "musical universals" provides evidence that Western music (excluding the avant-garde) does not differ fundamentally, in kind, from other musical traditions. As we argued in Chapter 5, its difference lies mainly in the degree to which composers, instrument makers, and performers have exploited universal principles of musical intelligibility to create works of unprecedented depth, variety, and expressive range. Chief among these principles are the tonal and rhythmic features that contribute to melodic coherence. In the light of the evidence marshaled by Sloboda, tonality and melody are more than "time-honored traditions"[50]: they are the linchpins of musical intelligibility, and are therefore essential to the nature of music as such—as Rand suggested.

The Integrative Nature of Perception

Fundamental to Rand's esthetic theory is her proposition that art brings man's "concepts to the perceptual level of his consciousness and allows him to grasp them directly, as if they were percepts." The validity of such a proposition of course depends, in large part, on the validity of its underlying epistemological premises. Most relevant here is Rand's view that perception constitutes the all-important foundation of human cognition, on which conceptual understanding is based, and to which it must constantly be referred. According to that view, as stated by Robert Efron—a neurophysiologist closely associated with her in the late 1960s, when she was writing her essays on esthetics—perception is man's "primary form of cognitive contact with the world around him," and "all conceptual knowledge is based upon or derived from this primary form of awareness."[51]

The view of perception advocated by Rand and Efron was in the distinct minority at that time. Since then, neurological research has greatly expanded the scientific understanding of perceptual processes, and has tended to confirm their broad view[52]—that perception is the first step in the process of cognitive integration which human beings, by nature, continually engage in; and that it is a spontaneous process, requiring no conscious effort. Because the process occurs automatically and nonvolitionally, we are generally unaware of it. Only when normal perception is impaired, can we begin to grasp the extraordinary complexity of integration achieved at the perceptual level.

The primary perceptual faculty in human beings, as in all primates, is *vision.* Much of the improved understanding of perceptual processes has therefore derived from the neurobiology of visual perception. As Semir Zeki, a principal researcher in the field, has observed, the study of vision is a "profoundly philosophical enterprise," for it constitutes an inquiry into "how the brain acquires knowledge of the external world, which is no simple matter."[53] Until the 1970s, Zeki points out, neurological models of perception were heavily influenced by the mistaken philosophic view, probably traceable to Kant, that "sensing" reality and "understanding" (grasping) it are fundamentally disparate phenomena.[54] Now, however, through sophisticated techniques for studying both normal subjects and patients who have suffered various impairments of brain function, we know that normal perception entails simultaneous "seeing" and "understanding." Specialized areas of the brain not only detect visible attributes such as color, form, and motion but also "identify" and integrate them into a unified, coherent "picture." The integration of visual information that results constitutes both sensory perception and recognition of the visual world.[55]

The realization that normal vision entails simultaneous *seeing* and *understanding* has profound implications for the arts of painting and sculpture, as Rand recognized when she insisted, in "Art and Cognition," that a work of visual art "*has to be representational;* its freedom of stylization is limited by the requirement of intelligibility; if it does not present an intelligible [i.e., recognizable] subject, it ceases to be art." (75, emphasis ours) The requirements of pictorial intelligibility have been illuminated by the work of James J. Gibson, a psychologist who proposed, in the 1960s and 1970s, a revolutionary theory of visual perception.[56] Rejecting the old theory that vision involves sheaves of light reflected in a straight line from points on the surface of objects in the environment to corresponding points on the retinal image of the eye, Gibson argued that the light reflected by objects in the environment is a complex and highly structured "array" which surrounds the perceiver. According to Gibson, the structure of this ambient array of light is determined by the attributes of objects in the environment. These attributes affect not only wavelength and intensity—perceived, as has long been known, in terms of color and brightness—but other characteristics as well. As Kelley explains, in *The Evidence of the Senses*: "The array of light striking the retina . . . is reflected from objects with different shapes, slants, sizes, colors, and textures. As a result, it is structured into visual solid angles with . . . relational properties . . . specific to the attributes of the objects reflecting the light." The "information" that is contained in the structure of the light itself thus enables us to perceive external objects directly and noninferentially. (66–67)

Gibson's theory of perception prompted him to reject earlier views of the nature of pictorial representation. Prior *mimetic theories* had assumed that the objects represented in a picture are recognizable because the light "come[s] from the picture to the spectator's Eye in the very same manner as it would do from the Objects themselves [in reality]," as one eighteenth-century theorist wrote.[57] According to such theories, no special knowledge is required for the recognition of images of ordinary objects; all that is required is normal perceptual capacities. In contrast, *symbolic* (or *semiotic*) *theories* of representation, such as that developed by the philosopher Nelson Goodman in his *Languages of Art*, hold that pictures are composed of symbolic forms, determined by cultural convention, and that one must learn to "read" them much as one learns to read a written text. The implications of such assumptions for twentieth-century painting and criticism were clear to Gibson:

> [I]f painting is a language, then just as a new language can be invented (. . . like Esperanto, for instance) and can be learned by mastering its vocabulary and grammar, so a new mode of visual perception can be learned by all of us if we succeed in mastering its elements. This revolutionary belief is, indeed, what motivates a good many modern painters [and critics]. They intend not merely to educate our visual perception of the world but to give us a radically different kind of perception and make us discard the old kind. [Rudolf] Arnheim, for example, in *Art and Visual Perception* asserts boldly that only a kind of "shift of level" is needed "to make the Picassos, the Braques, or the Klees look exactly like the things they represent." These paintings do not now represent things for us, he seems to admit, but they will come to do so.[58]

According to Gibson, the symbolic theory of pictorial representation is profoundly mistaken. But he does not accept earlier mimetic theories either. What he proposes instead is a more subtle account of mimesis. A two-dimensional image can never precisely replicate the optical stimulus of an equivalent scene in reality, he argues, but it can provide some of the same *essential informa-*

tion about the objects represented.[59] Thus one's *perception* can be fundamentally similar in both cases although the underlying *physical stimuli* are not the same.[60] Because a picture conveys "the distinctive features of things," an intelligible depiction—even one as sketchy as a caricature—is not "a *reduction* of the information in a natural [optic] array but an *enhancement* of it,"[61] since the artist selects and emphasizes the characteristic aspects by which we recognize things. Pictorial mimesis, according to Gibson's analysis, therefore involves a process of "visual abstraction" very much analogous to that postulated by Rand in "Art and Cognition."[62]

The Psychology and Physiology of Emotion

The view that emotion involves a process of subconscious cognitive evaluation or appraisal—an idea central to Ayn Rand's esthetic theory—is now generally accepted among psychologists, and the neural mechanisms involved are beginning to be identified.[63] In the years when Rand was consolidating and articulating her philosophy, however, behaviorist views still dominated psychological theory in academic circles, predicating that all human emotion results from an automatic response to a given stimulus, with no intervening evaluative component.[64]

The growing understanding of the interrelationship between emotion, cognition, and reason offers considerable support for Rand's concept of *sense of life* as a "pre-conceptual equivalent of metaphysics" and an "emotional, subconsciously integrated appraisal of man and of existence," as well as for her view of the role of the individual's sense of life in both the creation of and the response to art. Although current theories differ in detail, virtually all psychologists and neuroscientists now agree that emotions arise from some kind of subsconscious appraisal or evaluation of a perceived or imagined "stimulus" in relation to stored information about similar stimuli or events the individual has experienced in the past.[65] An important component of this stored information is its emotional significance, its personal meaning or relevance, for the individual.[66]

Moreover, because such information derives mainly from the individual's personal experience, it retains an idiosyncratic character that profoundly affects the emotional coloration of the individual's behavior and responses. As the neurophysiologist Antonio Damasio explains in his illuminating book *Descartes' Error*, these acquired mental "representations" about the world "embody knowledge pertaining to how certain types of situations usually have been paired with certain emotional responses." They therefore embody your unique experience of such relations in your life. Your experience may be at subtle or at major variance with that of others; it is yours alone. Although the relations between type of situation and emotion are, to a great extent, similar among individuals, unique, personal experience customizes the process for every individual. [136–37]

Current scientific thought regarding brain function and mental processes also supports Rand's view of the early formation and relative constancy of an individual's sense of life. Learning and memory are now widely thought to involve the strengthening of synaptic connections between neurons, and much evidence suggests that early childhood is a crucial period for structuring these neural pathways, which are incompletely set at birth. As one neuroscientist has explained: "Associations early in life help choose which synapses live or die." Thus the individual's most important emotional brain circuits may be largely defined in the first two years of life.[67] Additional evidence that emotional memories, once formed, are "relatively permanent," is offered by Joseph LeDoux, a leading neurobiologist. According to extensive studies related to the fear/defense response, emotional memory persists—even when reverse conditioning seems to extinguish the original response—and can reappear spontaneously or in the presence of an unrelated stressful experience. As this phenomenon indicates, the memory is never fully erased but is only overridden by other mental processes.[68]

Also relevant to Rand's distinctive analysis of the emotional significance of art are studies illuminating the powerful role of emotion in human choice and action. As documented by Damasio, individuals with severed or impaired connections between the "rational" and "emotional" areas of the brain suffer from chronic indecision as well as from a lack of vital affect. Unable to appraise alternatives in emotional terms, they cannot make rational choices, even though their capacity for abstract reasoning is apparently intact and unimpaired. The emotions may thus be seen as an essential biological mechanism for keeping the motor of life functioning[69]—calling to mind Rand's emphasis on the emotional "fuel" provided by the experience of art. In this light, the emotional response to art may be regarded as an intensely personal, physically felt reminder of one's values and one's fundamental view of life.

Research on another basic aspect of the biology of emotion has shed light on the expressive means used by artists in the process of concretizing and objectifying their own emotionally charged view of life—a process that is central to Rand's esthetic theory. The neurophysiology of the emotional system in human beings (and in other mammals) is such that both the physical expression of the basic emotions and their recognition are biologically determined.[70] In fact, the same areas of the brain that control the production of emotion and its various modes of expression also govern its recognition. When a given emotion is triggered, one's normal spontaneous response follows a complex genetically programmed pattern of muscular, hormonal, and cardiovascular changes. Unless the individual deliberately attempts to suppress or dissimulate the emotion, it is outwardly expressed in specific characteristics of posture, facial expression, and movement that are immediately recognizable by other human beings, regardless of race or culture.[71] This instinctive reciprocal system is of obvious benefit to social animals such as humans, since it contributes to the accurate communication of emotional states. These universal patterns of emotional behavior are exploited by artists as prime components of the objective content of art. As the painter and teacher Gary Faigin emphasizes, in the Introduction to his *Artist's Complete Guide to Facial Expression* (8–11), the face is "the center of our entire emotional life" and is, therefore, of crucial importance in art. In this connection, he quotes Leon Battista Alberti's handbook for artists, written at the height of the Florentine Renaissance. A painting, wrote Alberti, "will move the soul of the beholder when each man painted there clearly shows the movements of his own soul." Faigin adds: "The power of the face will always inspire artists to explore its expressive possibilities, and pictures that capture emotions in a striking way will always be notable. Moments of strong emotion are rare, in the humdrum of daily life, and we're instinctively drawn to the image of the face when the 'movements of the soul' are clear."

Through facial expression, then, as well as through bodily attitude in figurative painting and sculpture, and through the emotionally charged kinetic movement of dance and drama, and the expressive dynamics of music, much of the meaning in art is conveyed. All of these features belong to the deeply innate mimetic mode of representation emphasized by Merlin Donald as the foundation of art. Unlike the recondite content ascribed to abstract art, for example, they require no expert interpretation. Under normal conditions, they belong to the instinctual repertoire of every human being.[72] Thus such features greatly contribute to the universality of works of art, enabling them to transcend the particular culture in which they were created.[73]

Neurological Case Studies

A further point emphasized by Rand, in her fiction as well as in her essays on esthetics, is the psychologically integrative power of art, and its dependence on personally relevant meaning.[74] No scientist offers more compelling testimony to these principles than the clinical neurologist Oliver Sacks, who has articulated, with extraordinary sensitivity, the central importance of art in the lives of diverse patients. In numerous case studies, he has emphasized the practical and theoretical importance of art in the integration and normalization of neurological function.

The case of Rebecca, a severely retarded nineteen-year-old woman whose case history is told in *The Man Who Mistook His Wife for a Hat*, offers a particularly poignant illustration. Sacks recounts that, while Rebecca's retardation in the abstract cognitive sphere was painfully apparent in remedial classes and workshops focusing on this capacity, it was wholly eclipsed in experiences with music, poetry, and drama, to which she was extraordinarily responsive. Nature, too, gave her great pleasure, he relates, but it was not sufficient—it was too "mute." As he explains:

> She needed the world re-presented to her in verbal images, in language, and seemed to have little difficulty following the metaphors and symbols of even quite deep poems, in striking contrast to her incapacity with simple propositions and instructions. The language of feeling, of the concrete, of image and symbol, formed a world she loved, and to a remarkable extent, could enter. Though conceptually (and "propositionally") inept, she was at home with poetic language, and was herself, in a stumbling, touching way, a sort of "primitive," natural poet. [179]

For Rebecca, as for other mentally defective patients, much as for children, Sacks emphasizes, stories can provide *"a sense of the world*—a concrete reality" in narrative form, when abstract thought is beyond comprehension.[75] (184)

Rebecca herself explained one day in a moment of profound self-revelation, after vowing she would attend "'no more classes, no more workshops'":

> "They do nothing for me. They do nothing to bring me together. I'm like a sort of living carpet: I need a pattern, a design, like you have on [the office] carpet. I come apart, I unravel, unless there's a design. . . . I must have meaning. . . . The classes, the odd jobs have no meaning. . . . What I really love . . . is the theatre." [185]

Rebecca's reference to "pattern" and "design" should of course be taken metaphorically. As her subsequent statements makes clear, what she desires is not an abstract visual pattern but, rather, purpose and direction—meaningful, as opposed to random, activity. Sacks reports that he heeded her plea for "no more classes" and she was enrolled, instead, in a special theater group, where she would become, in each part she played, "a complete person, poised, fluent, with style," so that when one saw her on stage, no hint of her retardation was evident. As Sacks further observes, with regard to the exceptionally talented young autistic artist Stephen Wiltshire, whom he writes about in *An Anthropologist on Mars*: "[T]here are forms of health, of mind, other than the conceptual, although neurologists and psychologists rarely give these their due. There is mimesis—itself a power of mind, a way of representing reality with one's body and senses, a uniquely human capacity no less important than symbol or language." (240) Not surprisingly, Sacks cites the work of Merlin Donald, whose speculations about the mimetic mode of cognition in primitive man constitute, in his view, "one of the most powerfully argued and imaginative reconstructions" of human mental evolution. Like Donald, Sacks emphasizes the fundamentality of mimesis to the arts—which reminds us once more of Rand's concept of art as a "re-creation of reality."

In all his work, Sacks attests to the particular power of music in integrating and normalizing neurological function.[76] He recounts in *Awakenings*, for example, that a patient with Parkinson's disease once confided to him that in music "the feeling of movement, of living movement, is communicated. . . . And not just movement, but existence itself." (282) Sacks has empirically corroborated subjective reports of this kind through electroencephalograms and videotapes which demonstrate, in his words, "the awakening and modulating powers of art." He emphasizes, however, that the effect of music or the other arts in such cases is dependent upon the particular receptivity of the patient—"no scale, no measure, no rule can work, unless it works, personally, livingly." (284) While the power of music to integrate the otherwise erratic movement of Parkinsonian patients is both fundamental and universal, he has observed, not every kind of music will work with every patient. In the case of Miss D., for example, Sacks reports that

> "[t]he only music which affected her in the right way was music she could *enjoy;* only music which moved her 'soul' had this power to move her body. *She was only moved by music which moved her.* The 'movement' was simultaneously emotional and motoric."[77] [60–62n45]

In relation to this principle, he subsequently quotes the novelist E. M. Forster: "'The Arts are not drugs. They are not guaranteed to act when taken. Something as mysterious and capricious as the creative impulse has to be released before they can act.'" (283) In Rand's view, of course, that "mysterious" something would stem from the individual responder's sense of life, just as the artist's creative impulse stems from his own sense of life. Indeed, Sacks himself may be adumbrating such a view, when he writes: "I think the integrative power of art—which I continually see, and continually write about—is not something superficial, but evokes (the neural bases of) 'self' in a fundamental way."[78]

Sacks also clearly suggests that art conveys *abstract meaning* in an emotionally compelling *concrete* form. In his view, the concrete "is readily imbued with feeling and meaning—more readily, perhaps, than any abstract conception. It readily moves into the aesthetic, the dramatic, the comic, the symbolic, the whole wide deep world of art and spirit." Moreover, it is the concrete that "makes reality 'real,' alive, personal and meaningful. All of this is lost if the concrete is lost."[79] He further emphasizes:

> I cannot think of anything intellectual that is not, in some way, also sensible—indeed the very word "sense" always has this double connotation. Sensible, and in some sense "personal" as well, for one cannot feel anything, find anything "sensible," unless it is, in some way, related or relatable to oneself.[80]

The dependence of both emotion and cognitive judgment on the concrete, the particular, is poignantly illustrated by Sacks in the case of "Dr P."—the subject of the title chapter of *The Man Who Mistook His Wife for a Hat*. Dr P. was a distinguished musician and teacher suffering from a rare form of visual agnosia, in which he could see but not recognize or identify the objects in his visual field. So it was that he would reach for his wife's head, mistaking it for his hat. Faces became "abstract puzzles" to him. Similarly, when handed a splendid red rose, he could react to it only as kind of morphological specimen: a "convoluted red form with a linear green attachment"—"[a]bout six inches in length." (13) As Sacks reports, Dr P.'s "absurd abstractness of attitude—absurd because unleavened with anything else" rendered him incapable not only of recognizing particular entities but of forming judgments as well. Sacks explains: "[O]ur mental processes, which constitute our being and life, are not just abstract and mechanical, but *personal*, as well—and, as such, involve not just classifying and categorising, but continual judging and feeling also. If this is missing, we become computer-like, as Dr P. was." (20, emphasis ours)

Another aspect of Dr P.'s case is particularly relevant to Rand's theory of art. Having been a gifted amateur painter, Dr P. continued to pursue this avocation while his neurologic condition deteriorated, and he thereby unwittingly produced a striking visual record of his growing disorder. Whereas all his earlier work had been vividly realistic, "finely detailed and concrete" with a strong sense of "mood and atmosphere"—Sacks observes—the later paintings were increasingly abstract, "even geometrical and cubist," until, finally, they became "nonsense, . . . mere chaotic lines and blotches of paint." (17) When Sacks remarked on this pictorial deterioration to Dr P.'s wife, however, she chided him for being a "Philistine," unable to see her husband's *artistic development*—how he [had] renounced the realism of his earlier years, and advanced into abstract, nonrepresentational art." Sacks comments ironically to the reader:

> [Dr P.] had indeed moved from realism to nonrepresentation to the abstract, yet this was not the artist, but the pathology, advancing . . . towards a profound visual agnosia, in which all powers of representation and imagery, all sense of the concrete, all sense of reality, were being destroyed. This wall of paintings was a tragic pathological exhibit, which belonged to neurology, not art.[81] [17]

Regrettably, Sacks does not pause to reflect on the cultural significance of the twentieth-century phenomenon of "abstract art"—though it seems to cry out for comment in the light of his remarks on Dr P. As we shall see below in our discussion of "Madness and Modernism," however, clinical psychologist Louis Sass has vividly illuminated this phenomenon (albeit obliquely), so that its unfortunate cultural implications become disturbingly clear.

The Modular Mind and the Diversity of the Arts

Still another remarkable aspect of Dr P.'s case is that, while his visual function steadily declined, his musical capacity remained entirely unimpaired. Not only did he successfully continue to teach music until his death, he was also able, through a constant stream of sung or hummed *melody*, to negotiate the simple daily tasks of dressing, eating, and bathing that were otherwise impossible for him. (16–17) Such striking disparities of mental function, frequently noted by Sacks and widely reported elsewhere in the neurological and psychological literature, consitute a major category of evidence for a "modular" view of both the brain and the mind.[82] According to such a view, now generally accepted, the brain is not a homogeneous organ, giving rise to a unitary "general intelligence," but is, rather, a modular system of distinctive, and largely independent, neural networks productive of particular capacities or faculties.

Numerous versions of the modular view have been propounded,[83] the most extensive and provocative of which is that proposed by the cognitive and developmental psychologist Howard Gardner, in his seminal work *Frames of Mind: The Theory of Multiple Intelligences* (1983) and subsequent studies. Drawing on evidence from the fields of developmental and experimental psychology, evolutionary biology, and psychometric testing, as well as from neurology, Gardner proposes that the modular structure of the brain gives rise to six major modes of mental function, which he terms "intelligences"—sets of skills and capacities for apprehending and coping with important features of the human environment. In his view, these capacities, while present to a degree in all members of the human species, vary from population to population and individual to individual both in the degree of their potential and in their actual development and expression. Moreover, even individuals whose neural systems are intact and free of pathology can exhibit extraordinary powers in one or more spheres, and quite unremarkable, sometimes deficient, capacities in others. Rare are the cases of exceptional talent in all spheres.

Of the six "intelligences" postulated by Gardner (linguistic, musical, logical-mathematical, spatial, bodily-kinesthetic, and personal), four are relevant to the principal forms or modes of art emphasized by Rand—the same arts conceptualized in antiquity as the "mimetic arts," and in the eighteenth century as the "fine arts." Gardner's "linguistic intelligence" pertains to literature; the "musical," to music of course; the "spatial," to the visual arts; and the "bodily-kinesthetic," to drama and, especially, to dance. Thus he seems to confirm Rand's view that the major art forms are profoundly dependent on the distinctive ways in which human beings make sense of and represent their experience of the world.

Certain inconsistencies and ambiguities are discernible in Gardner's specific comments on the various arts, however, and are equally informative. Having written widely on the psychology of art, he exhibits throughout his work a profound respect and admiration for individual creativity, which leads him to accept, uncritically, the twentieth-century trend toward arbitrary new forms of "creativity" in the arts. Thus he never doubts the legitimacy of modernist and postmodernist departures from the "traditional" art forms, and he is unquestioning in his acceptance of "avant-garde" work as art. Although he stresses, for example, that dance involves body movements that are both "purposeful" and "intentionally rhythmical" (222), and that music is "the most important partner in dance" (224), he implicitly approves the work of Merce Cunningham, despite the fact that Cunningham "has cut the knot between music and dance" in order to present "movement pure and simple." (225) Nor does Gardner question Cunningham's use of random methods, such as the rolling of dice, to determine the nature of the movements and their sequences— procedures that make a mockery of notions of purposefulness.[84]

Further, Gardner's remarks on "spatial intelligence" contain significant contradictions relevant to the nature of visual art. To begin, he emphasizes correctly that "the plastic arts begin with a painstaking observation of the every-day world," and he argues that "[i]n contradistinction to logical-mathematical knowledge, which [involves] increasing abstraction, spatial intelligence remains tied fundamentally to the *concrete world*, to the world of objects and their location in a world."[85] (204, emphasis ours) Nonetheless, he fully accepts the modernist tendency toward "increasing abstraction" in the visual arts. Thus he refers approvingly both to "abstract art" and to cubism, as if they were simply new forms of creative expression, entirely consistent with man's natural "spatial intelligence." As the case of Dr P. suggests, however, the tendency toward extreme "abstraction," or nonobjectivity, in the visual arts may be viewed as a symptom of profound pathology. While Dr P.'s pathology was completely involuntary, neurologically induced by a growing tumor or by some degenerative process, we would argue (as Rand herself suggested) that the *voluntary* creation of nonobjective works of visual "art" which are intended to be more than merely decorative, ultimately stems from different sorts of "pathology" or dysfunction—either in the would-be artist's personal psychology or resulting from the intellectual error involved in a kind of cultural pathology.

Clinical Psychology—Madness and Modernism

The pathological implications of "abstract art" and other twentieth-century avant-garde phenomena (implications to which we alluded in the opening paragraphs of this book) have been documented in exhaustive detail by the clinical psychologist Louis Sass, in a monumental work entitled *Madness and Modernism: Insanity in the Light of Modern Art, Literature, and Thought.*[86] Sass shares our view that postmodernism is, at root, an extension of modernism. Thus he uses the term *modernism* "in a fairly broad sense, one that includes what is called postmodernism as a somewhat-difficult-to-define subgenre." He explains:

> I view postmodernism, rather than as a deviation in some radically new direction, either as being an *exaggeration* of central modernist tendencies (of modernism's reflexivity and detachment), or as involving certain *dialectical reversals* occurring within a shared framework defined by these same tendencies. In either case, postmodernism looks less like an adversary than like an offspring—or, perhaps, a sibling—of the . . . high modernist period and sensibility.[87]

As Sass vividly illustrates, various tendencies of modernist and postmodernist "art" correspond to the characteristic manifestations of schizophrenia—the most severe form of mental illness, in which the patient becomes dissociated from objective reality and retreats into a solipsistic world of pure consciousness. According to Sass, the schizophrenic typically experiences a complete "loss of the concrete," and engages instead in increasingly abstract thought turned inward on the self. The faculty of consciousness (which evolved to enable the organism to survive in the world) becomes more and more reflexive in its focus, concerned not with the individual's interactions in the world but with his "inner reality." The requirements of reality—from the law of cause and effect to the rules and conventions of one's social milieu— are variously denied, flouted, or derided. Like the modernist or postmodernist artist, the schizophrenic defies authority and engages in the ironic destruction of social norms and values. Further, in schizophrenia as in both modernist and postmodernist art, a coherent sense of chronological and narrative sequence is replaced by a chaos of contingent associations.

Most remarkable—and most disturbing—about Sass's book, however, is the conclusion he draws from the "eerie likeness" between madness and modernism (i.e., *"all those trends in twentieth-century culture that have undermined traditional values,"* as one reviewer put it[88]). In Sass's view, this uncanny similarity suggests not that modernism is, at root, a pathological cultural phenomenon (as Rand argued) but, rather, that schizophrenia, which was formerly regarded as involving an extreme deficit of rationality, should now be understood as a disease of *hyperrationality.* The egregious fallacy of that view lies in accepting the mistaken Cartesian and Kantian equation of "rationality" with pure, abstract thought, divorced from sentient experience. (90–91) In contrast, Rand emphatically rejected that inadequate view—insisting instead that human reason must always remain rooted in perceptual reality, in the concrete evidence of the senses.[89] And, as we have indicated throughout this chapter, recent science has borne out the correctness of her view.

By implication, then, though certainly not intentionally or explicitly, Sass's work lends powerful support for one of Rand's most provocative conclusions—that radically modernist "art" is, in fact, *the antithesis of art,* for it subverts both the integrative function and the basis in objective reality that are essential to art.[90] As Sass compellingly demonstrates, the work of the so-called avant-garde, whether modernist or postmodernist, rejects reality— deliberately *dis*integrating and fragmenting perceptions of, and thought about, the world—to indulge in a detached mode of abstraction, cut off from existential experience. It is, in a very profound sense, *insane* (lit. "unsound"). In Part II, we will further explore the far-reaching implications of Sass's work

Part II

Extension and Application of Rand's Theory

8

The Myth of "Abstract Art"

The phenomenon of "abstract art"[1] was original to the twentieth century. Though nonrepresentational forms and designs had been employed since time immemorial to ornament or decorate items of practical use, never before had they been the focus of work whose sole purpose was to be contemplated. There is simply no historical precedent for the nonobjective painting and sculpture that began to be produced in Europe and the United States after 1910.[2]

In many respects, abstract art was the quintessential expression of twentieth-century modernism. Since visual perception is basic to human cognition, the abandonment of objective representation in the visual arts was perhaps the most profound of modernism's many departures from tradition.[3] Moreover, both through the example of their work and, perhaps more important, through the countless manifestoes, periodical articles, exhibitions, and other means they employed to explain and justify it, abstract painters and sculptors assumed a vanguard position in the modernist movement, exerting a powerful influence on work in other media, as well as on the public perception of modernism in general.[4]

From its inception, abstract art was theory-driven, dependent on an evergrowing body of philosophic and critical discourse for its very existence, not to mention its legitimization.[5] Occult beliefs about the nature of the universe and of man's place in it led the first abstract artists to their own radical break with reality. And, since that break defied all prior practice, the artists recognized that public acceptance of their work would depend in large measure upon the articulation of a convincing theory to support it. As a consequence, theory and practice are so intertwined in abstract art that one cannot adequately consider one without the other. The inseverable link between creating and writing about abstract painting, in particular—fittingly derided by Tom Wolfe in *The Painted Word*—is not limited to the latter half of the century, which he dealt with; it is endemic to the phenomenon of abstract art from the beginning.

The stylistic diversity of abstract art is bewildering, the more so since each new style or *ism*—from the Neo-Plasticism of Mondrian to the Abstract Expressionism and later Minimalism of the New York School—carries its own distinctive theoretical baggage, sometimes reversing the claims of previous practitioners. Yet, different as they are in detail, the various styles share certain fundamental characteristics and mistaken premises. Moreover, the seeds of later trends can be readily discovered in philosophic errors inherent in the phenomenon from its inception. As we shall see, however, while art historians and critics in recent years have begun to acknowledge the flawed theoretical assumptions underlying abstract painting and sculpture, they have failed to take the next logical step—that is, to question their legitimacy as art.

Like Rand, we insist upon taking that step, in order to restore the coherence and viability of the concept of art in contemporary culture. In this chapter, therefore, we apply the principles of Rand's philosophy—principles that are rooted in a scientifically sound view of human nature—to a critique of the major theoretical and critical claims for abstract art. Focusing on the work of prominent modernists, we analyze in far greater detail than Rand did in her brief comments on "modern art" in *The Romantic Manifesto* and elsewhere why the very concept of abstract art is invalid.

Pioneers: Kandinsky, Malevich, and Mondrian

To a large degree, the credit or discredit for the purported legitimization of abstract painting belongs to Vasily Kandinsky (1866–1944), Kazimir Malevich (1878–1935), and Piet Mondrian (1872–1944)—owing as much to their theoretical writings as to their paintings.[6] All three artists have been the subject of important exhibitions in American museums in recent years, and their influence is repeatedly cited. Vastly different though these men were in background and temperament, as well as in the style of their work and the details of their theories,[7] they were remarkably alike in their basic assumptions about the nature of reality, and in their aspirations for art and human society. Moreover, those assumptions and aspirations were shared by a broad segment of the early twentieth-century avant-garde.[8]

Given the eventual critical and scholarly acceptance of abstract art,[9] one might expect that its initial rationale would have been intellectually rigorous and compelling. When one analyzes the arguments put forward by these seminal figures, however, one can see that the whole abstract edifice rests on the flimsiest of intellectual foundations, weakly cemented by dubious premises incompatible with modern science. Those unsubstantiated claims, often originating in occultist beliefs, pertain not only to the ultimate nature of reality but also to the sources of human knowledge and emotion, as well as to the function of art. In the spirit of Rand's customary advice, therefore, let us "check the premises"[10] underlying the artistic innovation that many claim is one of the supreme achievements of twentieth-century culture.

Mind Divorced from Matter:
The "Primacy of Consciousness"

In an essay entitled "Whither the 'New' Art?" published in Russia in 1911, the year in which he produced his first completely abstract painting, Kandinsky declared: "Our epoch is a time of tragic collision between matter and spirit and of the downfall of the purely material worldview."[11] His declaration reveals the basic metaphysical fallacy of the early abstract movement—that spirit and matter, mind and body, are fundamentally opposed—and the related belief that a new era was dawning in which the superior spiritual realm would triumph over base material reality. Reacting against the one-sided materialism that had dominated European thought in the late nineteenth century, the early proponents of abstract art embraced the opposite pole of the mistaken mind-body dichotomy: the "primacy of consciousness" premise that Rand emphatically rejected.[12] For them, the material world of perceptible objects in three-dimensional space had no connection with the world of spirit, and must therefore be eliminated from an art seeking to convey the highest spiritual values. Before the "awakening soul" could complete its evolution, Kandinsky proclaimed, it must be liberated from the "nightmare of materialism" still holding it in thrall.[13]

For his part, Mondrian repeatedly insisted that the natural appearance of objects is deceptive, merely distracting us from the direct intuition of their "inward" spiritual essence. He maintained that all subject matter "*must be banished* from art," because "representation [of physical objects] . . . is fatal to pure art," which must henceforth embody only "pure relationships."[14] Only through the "annihilation" of objective reality, and of time and space, could art express the "new consciousness" toward which humanity was evolving.[15] And, as Carel Blotkamp has emphasized in his exhaustive monograph on Mondrian's life and work, the idea of spiritual evolution was closely bound up with that of destruction: the destruction of the old material forms was a condition for the creation of the higher spiritual forms.[16]

Such ideas owed much to German speculative philosophy and to Platonism, as well as to the occultist principles of Theosophy, a quasi-religious movement that attained wide popularity and influence in the final quarter of the nineteenth century and the beginning of the twentieth.[17] That these ideas had no empirical basis whatever is a point ignored not only by the pioneers of abstraction but by many of its later, purportedly soberer, advocates as well. Nor has anyone offered any justification for the naïve assumption that "soul" or "spirit" as such could be represented visually. Artists for centuries have known better—as did Socrates, who instructed that it is only indirectly, through the careful depiction of facial expression and bodily postures and gestures, that the "soul," which "has neither proportion nor color" and "is altogether unseen," can be represented in the visual arts.[18]

Collectivist Aspirations: The "Universal" vs. the "Individual"

It is one of the ironies of abstract art—which was eventually thought of as a bastion of individual freedom—that the originators of the "new art," who considered themselves harbingers of the "new consciousness," were profoundly collectivist in their outlook and explicitly aspired to the eventual submersion of the "individual" in the "universal," in art as in society and politics. Firmly believing that art "marches in the vanguard of psychic evolution," as Malevich declared, they insisted that man's inevitable progress toward the new state of consciousness would be manifested in abstract form in the arts.[19] For them, the "universal" was not merely an epistemological concept; it was endowed with metaphysical reality, comparable to that ascribed to Plato's ideal "Forms," which were thought to exist in a higher plane of being. Proponents of the "new art" deprecated the "individual" as the dominating force in the old world order, which mankind must move beyond. According to the 1918 manifesto of *De Stijl* (the influential modernist journal which Mondrian co-founded), "the struggle between individual and universal" had been evident in the First World War, and "contemporary artists throughout the world [had] united in a world war against the dominance of the individual . . . to create international unity in Life, Art, and Culture."[20]

In art, attainment of the universal meant escaping from the "circle of things," as Malevich put it."[21] In direct opposition to the essence of what art had always been, Mondrian advised that artists must avoid the danger of "express[ing] something 'particular,' therefore human."[22] Both the new art and the new life he envisaged would require "freeing ourselves from the personal, from the individual."[23] "[W]hat we understand by 'life,'" he maintained, "is not the subjective life of the individual but the manifest social life of at least a *group*." As for the personal "hand of the artist," formerly deemed "all-important," it was, for him, merely an aspect of the old art which "derives from an individualistic orientation . . . no longer important for the more universal conception of the future."[24] Kandinsky was similarly critical of those who value "the personality, individuality, and temperament of the artist."[25] In his view: "The more abstract is form, the more clear and direct [is] its appeal."[26]

Absolute Subjectivism

Although the pioneers of abstract art rejected all human subject matter, they nevertheless insisted that "emotion" or "feeling"—which they did not define—is conveyed by their work. Malevich was most explicit in predicating such a notion of contextless feeling. In his treatise *The Non-Objective World*, for example, he declared that "the visual phenomena of the objective world are, in themselves, meaningless; the significant thing is feeling,[27] as such, quite apart from the environment in which it is called forth." (67) His own "desperate attempt to free art from the ballast of objectivity" led him, he relates, to "[take] refuge in the square form," and he consequently exhibited "a picture which consisted of nothing more than a black square on a white field." (68) Dubbing his new approach "Suprematism," Malevich intended to create "an altogether new and direct form of representation of the world of feeling"—the first form in which "non-objective feeling" was expressed— through a limited "vocabulary" of starkly geometric, two-dimensional shapes; namely, rectangle, circle, triangle, and cross.[28] The black square in his first Suprematist painting, he cryptically declared, "= feeling," while the white field "= the void beyond this feeling." Not surprisingly, the public and critics alike saw in his work "the demise of art," and they lamented (as he recalls): "'Everything which we loved is lost. We are in a desert. . . . Before us is nothing but a black square on a white background.'" (76, 68) Malevich then adds: "But a blissful sense of liberating non-objectivity drew me forth into the 'desert,' where nothing is real except feeling . . . *and so feeling became the substance of my life*."[29] (68, emphasis ours) His declaration epitomizes the complete subjectivism of abstract art, its final and complete detachment from reality—a detachment symptomatic, once again, of what Rand rejected as the "primacy of consciousness."

Though Mondrian, too, intended to attain a transcendent realm of spiritual feeling through an art free of all existential associations, he differed from Malevich in his focus. Concerned not with "feeling, as such," but with the issue of "aesthetic emotion," he claimed that the "essence of art expresses or evokes our emotion of *beauty*."[30] Through his art of "pure relationships," he hoped to create a "moving expression of beauty." (303) "[T]hrough complete negation of the self," he wrote, "a work of art emerges that is a monument of Beauty: far above anything human; yet most human in its depth and universality!"[31] When we free ourselves from everything "personal" and "individual," we can then "create a direct expression of beauty—clear and as far as possible *'universal'* . . . expressed exclusively through lines, planes, or volumes and through color—a beauty without natural form and without representation . . . *purely abstract beauty.*"[32]

For his part, Kandinsky maintained that familiar emotions "such as fear, joy, grief, etc. . . . will no longer greatly attract the [new] artist," who will instead endeavor to awake subtler emotions, as yet unnamed." The work of such new artists will give *"to those observers capable of feeling them,"* he predicted, "lofty emotions beyond the reach of words."[33] Toward this end, he attempted to codify an entire "language of form and color" apart from any representational imagery.[34] (27–45) A marked disparity between his color interpretations and those offered by Malevich and Mondrian, however, demonstrated the impossibility of such a project.[35]

"Decoration" vs. Art

A persistent concern of the pioneers of abstract art, and of many of their successors, was that, in the absence of representational imagery, their work would seem to lack meaning and would therefore be only "decorative" in its effect.[36] Thus they fully accepted the principle that art, as opposed to "decoration," conveys metaphysical meaning—as Rand emphasized.[37] Kandinsky, Malevich, and Mondrian alike repeatedly asserted that their work was more than decoration, because it possessed spiritual meaning. While it did not represent visible, tangible reality, they insisted that it represented the invisible metaphysical reality underlying or transcending material existence.[38] (36–37) As early as 1911, Kandinsky warned that, if artists broke the ties binding them to natural appearances before they had sufficiently grasped the "inner harmony of true colour and form composition," they would "produce works which are mere decoration, . . . suited to neckties or carpets." Further, he emphasized that *"Beauty of Form and Colour is no sufficient aim by itself,* despite the assertions of pure aesthetes . . . , who are obsessed with the idea of 'beauty.'"[39] The "new art" must appeal "less to the eye and more to the soul."[40]

Blotkamp points out that for Mondrian, as for the other early abstract painters, "there was the constant danger of falling into the abyss of meaningless ornament." In Blotkamp's view, all of Mondrian's theorizing was dominated by his "need to prove to himself and to others that . . . his art was not just decoration."[41] Mondrian argued in his initial treatise "The New Plastic [i.e., Form] in Painting" (1917), for example, that the "growing profundity of the whole of modern life" can be purely reflected only in *"pictorial*, not *decorative* painting." By *pictorial* he did not mean "representational," as one might expect, but painting in which, as he claimed, "naturalistic expression . . . become[s] more inward, . . . essentialized into the abstract."[42] For Mondrian, this essentialization consisted of reducing the entire universe of meaning to his austere arrangements of horizontal and vertical black lines, interspersed with rectangles of the three primary colors. So severe was his view that the mere introduction of a diagonal or the use of a double instead of a single line became events of shattering importance for him.[43] That he failed to create a truly "pictorial," as opposed to "decorative," way of painting, however, can be gauged by the frequency with which his signature style has been successfully adapted for use in clothing and various product designs, as well as in interior decoration.[44]

Utopian Aspirations

At the heart of the early abstract movement was a profound and explicit yearning for release from, or resolution of, the struggles and discords of material existence. Such utopian aspirations recur as a leitmotif throughout the theoretical writings of the three pioneers we focus on. For example, Malevich characterized the "objectless world" he sought to reflect in his paintings as a timeless condition of absolute rest.[45] In his 1924 essay "Through My Experience as a Painter," he declared: "I want to traverse all nature, all existence, in complete peace and calm. I do not want enmity and oppression." That he was not referring simply to release from *political* oppression but, rather, conceived the idea in *metaphysical* terms is revealed by his succeeding sentence: "I want to squeeze my battle-flushed brain into nature and dissolve in it."[46]

Similarly, the ideas of equilibrium and the reconciliation of opposites that pervade Mondrian's theory of "Neo-Plasticism" are invested with metaphysical significance, evidencing his profound desire to transcend the alleged dualities of human existence by attaining a higher state of being.[47] "Art has always sought to establish universal equilibrium," he wrote—*"universal* equilibrium and not . . . individual equilibrium. . . . The search for particular equilibrium (personal interest) thrives on hate, produces death. . . . All the tendencies of the new art . . . have unconsciously led to . . . the exact realization of universal equilibrium."[48] Nor was Mondrian's quest for perfect equilibrium limited to the esthetic sphere. "In our disequilibrated society," he wrote in 1926, "everything drives us to search for that pure equilibrium which engenders the *joie de vivre*. To achieve this, the 'painting' of purely abstract art is not enough;

its expression must necessarily be *realized in our material environment*, and thus prepare the realization of pure equilibrium in society itself. Only then will 'art' become 'life.'"[49]

Such aspirations call to mind the influential thesis of the art historian Wilhelm Worringer regarding the psychological factors involved in the genesis of abstract art. In his seminal work, *Abstraction and Empathy* (1908), Worringer maintained that, historically, the tendency toward geometric abstraction in art stemmed from "immense spiritual dread" of the real world, from an "instinctive fear conditioned by [the] feeling of being lost in the universe." (15–16) By means of abstraction—"the life-denying inorganic"; that is, "crystalline" or geometric forms—artists sought "to wrest the object[s] of the external world out of [their] natural context, out of the unending flux of being," to render them absolute and immutable. (4, 16) According to Worringer:

> The less [man] has succeeded, by virtue of . . . cognition, in entering into a relation of friendly confidence with the appearance of the outer world, the more forceful is the dynamic that leads to the striving after this highest abstract beauty. . . . [I]t is because he stands so lost and spiritually helpless . . . , because he experiences only obscurity and caprice in the inter-connection and flux of the external world, that the urge is so strong in him to divest the things of the external world of their caprice and obscurity . . . and to impart to them a value of necessity and . . . regularity. [17–18]

As to the forms chosen toward that end, Worringer explained that the "simple line and its development in purely geometrical regularity" were the most appealing to men "disquieted" by existence. "For here the last trace of connection with, and dependence on, life has been effaced, here the highest absolute form, the purest abstraction has been achieved: here is law, here is necessity, while everywhere else the caprice of the organic prevails." (20)

A muted echo of Worringer's thesis is discernible in the comment by Hilton Kramer that the source of abstract art's "powerful appeal" lies precisely in its "profound distaste for the world it inhabits." For Kramer, such work

> shuts out the world, in all its imperfections and vulgarities and commonplace emotions, and offers us instead an aesthetic utopia in which nothing that is merely contingent need ever be considered in the human equation. . . . [A]ll quotidian realities are dissolved into the vapors of aesthetic sensation and all earthly pain triumphantly transmuted into the untroubled pleasures of the mind.[50]

Other viewers do not necessarily share such a grim sense of life, however, and may doubt the ultimate value of an endeavor that "shuts out the world" and dissolves all into "the vapors of aesthetic sensation."

A Flawed View of Human Perception and Cognition

Kramer's allusion to the pleasures of "aesthetic sensation" relates to yet another set of dubious assumptions underlying abstract art. In addition to their unsubstantiated claims regarding the essential nature of reality and the alleged dichotomy between matter and spirit, the pioneers of abstract art based their approach to painting on certain erroneous premises about human perception and conceptual knowledge. To begin, they shared the view, expressed by the Futurist sculptor and theorist Umberto Boccioni, that "the true reality is sensation."[51] This mistaken view—that sensation (rather than perception) is the basic mode of human sensory experience—pervaded both the scientific and the philosophic thought of the early twentieth century, and was readily taken up by artists eager to surrender themselves to feeling, emotion, and the involuntary promptings of their subconscious, and to avoid the necessity of dealing with the realities of existence.

The sensory experience of color was a particular focus of scientific research at the time, and was invested with great significance by the early abstract artists, owing in large part to their fundamental misunderstanding of its physical nature.[52] Not surprisingly, given their rejection of objective reality, they failed to recognize that color is *an attribute of material objects*—and that the experience of color is therefore dependent on the physical properties of those objects, as well as on the psychology of human sense perception.[53] Instead, they entertained vague notions of color as a kind of formless energy, somehow activated in the mind by the vital energy of the world. Such notions led Boccioni to speculate that, with the evolution of the new psyche envisaged by the early abstractionists, "[t]he human eye will see colours as feeling materialized. Colours . . . will not need forms to be understood, and pictorial works will become whirling musical compositions of enormous coloured gases. On a stage free of horizons, these works will excite and electrify the complex soul of a crowd we cannot yet conceive of."[54]

Thus etherealized, color took on a wholly spiritual aspect that was explicitly divorced, in theories of abstract art, from the material nature of forms and objects. Although Kandinsky recognized that color, unlike form, "cannot stand alone; it cannot dispense with boundaries of some kind," he nonetheless maintained that, in one sense, form "is nothing but the separating line between surfaces of colour."[55] Similarly, Malevich conceived of "dynamic color" as existing prior to form, and he attempted to show how movement and color could be conveyed without the representation of objects.[56] Mondrian, too, abstracted color from the objective contexts that contribute to its meaning and emotional impact. He explicitly advocated the elimination of "images and boundaries," because "[b]oundaries cloud what is true."[57]

In sum, far from understanding that (as Rand recognized) visual *perception* is the very foundation of human cognition, and that the essence of perception is *the discriminated awareness of entities* (that is, the differentiation of objects from their surroundings), the early modernists sought to escape from the reality of perceptual forms, either by dissolving the objects of real experience into a relatively amorphous sea or "symphony" of color (as in the case of Kandinsky's *Compositions*) or by reducing them to a limited repertoire of rigidly geometric forms (as in the case of Mondrian's Neo-Plasticism and Malevich's Suprematism).[58] Moreover, the importance they ascribed to color and form in ordinary perception, as well as in the experience of art, was the reverse of what it is in actuality.[59] With regard to human epistemology and cognition—and to the emotions dependent on cognition—the experience of color is far less fundamental than the perception of form. As Oliver Sacks has observed: "One could live very richly in a world without color"—but not in one without form. In comparison with the hapless "Dr. P" (the eponymous "man who mistook his wife for a hat" cited above in Chapter 7), whose life was tragically constrained by his inability to recognize objects in his visual field, the subjects of Sacks's book *The Island of the Colorblind* are able to lead quite normal lives. Even the colorblind painter whose case Sacks recounts in *An Anthropologist on Mars* managed, in time, to adjust to the traumatic onset, late in life, of complete achromatopsia, although the experience of color had been of the utmost importance to him—not only personally but professionally as well, since he had had a career as an abstract painter. As his case demonstrates, color incalculably enriches perceptual experience but is by no means essential to human cognition and well-being. Indeed, artists of the past were well aware that representational form is much more significant than color. Thus the great Venetian painter Titian, renowned as a colorist, is said to have observed that "[i]t is not bright colors but good drawing that makes figures beautiful."[60] Much the same idea underlies the famous dictum of Ingres: "Drawing is the probity of art."[61]

Misconceptions about the perception of color, and its relation to the emotions, are also involved in the analogies frequently drawn between abstract art and music. The special importance Kandinsky placed on color in his theory of painting was closely bound up with his profoundly mistaken conviction that the "best teacher" for all the arts, including painting, was music—"the art which has devoted itself not to the reproduction of natural phenomena, but rather to the expression of the artist's soul."[62] For Kandinsky, who appears to have been born with the rare perceptual anomaly known as *synesthesia*,[63] colors had precise sensory counterparts in musical tones and timbres, and vice versa. Thus his claim that colors produced a "correspondent spiritual vibration" may have been literally true for him, and would help to explain his emphasis on a complete analogy between visual and musical composition.[64] For the vast majority of individuals, however, correspondences between sound and color are far weaker (if they exist at all) than in Kandinsky's experience. Furthermore, the analogy between music and painting is marred by a more fundamental distinction. As E. H. Gombrich emphasized forty years ago, since painting "lacks the dimension of time . . . , its combinations of shapes and colors should not be compared to a symphony but to a chord."[65] Recall that the essence of music is (we argued in Chapter 5) not harmony but melodic movement—the succession of tones over time. While a painting taken in at a glance may weakly suggest "rhythms" through the repetition or variation of formal and linear elements, it cannot begin to equal music's capacity to concretize the varying qualities of on-going movement in all its subtlety and complexity.[66]

"Intuition" in Place of Reason and Objectivity

The abstract artists' abandonment of representational forms in favor of color, and their mistaken focus on sensation as the primary mode of awareness, were the epistemological consequence of their metaphysical rejection of the material world. So, too, they abandoned the rational thought processes by which cognition proceeds from information acquired in perceptual contact with reality. In place of reason, the exercise of which requires effort and is necessarily subject to human fallibility and error, they substituted a more direct and presumably certain avenue to spiritual truth: an infallible "intuitive" process, requiring no conscious thought or effort. Just as their utopian vision of a higher metaphysical reality promised a state of pure repose and harmony, free of all strife, toil, and discord, their conception of a "higher" form of human consciousness envisioned effortless insight—immune from error—into the fundamental truths of existence. This process was variously characterized. Mondrian referred to a "higher intuition" that would guide him in realizing the beauty and harmony of pure relationships in his painting.[67] "[This] pure intuition becomes conscious through long culture and creates pure abstract art, which arises neither from intellect nor from vague intuitive feeling."[68] It was, in Mondrian's view, a more evolved form of consciousness. Boccioni similarly alluded to "a psychic force that empowers the senses to perceive what has never been perceived before." "What needs to be painted," he insisted, "is not the visible, but what has hitherto been held to be invisible, that is, what the clairvoyant painter sees."[69] Malevich and other Russian "Cubo-Futurists" characterized this capacity of the evolved psyche as *zaum*, "beyond reason." The *zaum* state was believed to confer not only clairvoyance but also the ability to see through solid objects.[70]

Counterfeit Elitism and "The Emperor's New Clothes"

Not everyone was capable of achieving the *zaum* state, of course. As we have noted, the early abstract painters regarded themselves as a spiritual elite, endowed with psychic powers not yet attained by the majority of humanity. Like the great artists before them, Kandinsky claimed, these "solitary visionaries" stood at the apex of a spiritual triangle, and were doomed to be "abuse[d] as charlatan[s] and madm[e]n" until their fellow men, crowded into the broad lower segments of the triangle, had evolved sufficiently to ascend to their level.[71] "Creative workers are . . . always a step ahead of the general public— they show it the road of progress," declared Malevich—an innocuous claim until one realizes that it was made in the context of his treatise *The Non-Objective World* (34), which was profoundly alienated from reality. For his part, Mondrian emphasized that those who had broken sufficiently free of matter to be "receptive to abstract art"—particularly to his "New Plastic style" of painting—belonged to a very small "elite."[72] In contrast: "Ordinary vision is the vision of the individual who cannot rise above the individual. As long as materiality is seen individually, style cannot be perceived. Thus ordinary vision obstructs all art: it does not *want* style in art, it demands a detailed reproduction."[73] According to Mondrian, the more evolved "elite" will eventually "make its influence felt upon the [ordinary] masses, and in the end life itself will evolve as well. But this is [so slow as to be] almost indiscernible. So, to retain one's faith in human evolution, one must constantly look to that elite."[74]

Elitist premises are essential to the phenomenon of abstract art,[75] since it flouts the rules of normal perception. In the early days, the people who did not "get it" were characterized as spiritually less "evolved." Now they are disdained as "philistines"—the dread epithet in the argument-by-intimidation employed by modernist critics.[76] The alleged philistines—correctly perceiving that nothing is there, objectively speaking, to be "gotten"—have repeatedly responded by invoking Hans Christian Andersen's tale of "The Emperor's New Clothes." The height of human folly, Andersen's tale reminds us, is to deny the evidence of one's senses—to pretend to see what is invisible, and to deny seeing what one does, in fact, see.

Freedom, Spontaneity, and "Cognitive Slippage"

Another idea central to the theory and practice of abstract art from its inception is that of *freedom*.[77] As we suggested above, the term was used not merely in its essentially political sense but in a broader *metaphysical* sense. In seeking to liberate themselves from objective reality, to free their art from what they mistakenly regarded as the mere imitation of nature, the early abstract artists expected to attain complete spiritual freedom, which would be expressed in the uninhibited spontaneity of their work.[78] Throughout the twentieth century, these related concepts—*freedom* and *spontaneity*—recur with the frequency of a mantra in abstract art manifestoes and in the writing of sympathetic critics. What they reveal goes far deeper than a simple quest for personal autonomy on the part of the artists; they are symptomatic of a profound desire to escape the material conditions of existence, to evade the exigencies of mundane reality.[79]

Both in their overabstractness of thought and in their attempt to escape from life's objective constraints, the pioneers of abstract art exhibited a type of "cognitive slippage" that is characteristic of schizophrenia. As Louis Sass argues in *Madness and Modernism*, a common feature of schizophrenic thought is its "pathological freedom"—its "failure to adopt the practical perspective of everyday, commonsense reality, which normally attunes one to the . . . canonical properties of objects and situations."[80] (127) Schizophrenics are often preoccupied with issues of "cosmic or totalistic proportions—about the nature of existence in general or its fundamental relationship to the self." (190) In the depths of their illness, they are likely to seem "almost entirely detached from their literal circumstances, engaged almost exclusively with hypothetical actions in their delusional or quasi-delusional worlds." That tendency may lead them at times to engage in seemingly "woolly or empty philosophizing" (191)—a phrase that can be applied to much of the theoretical and critical writing on abstract art we quote throughout this chapter.

We are by no means suggesting that all abstract artists suffer from schizophrenia, or from other forms of mental illness—although evidence certainly exists that at least some of its more prominent practitioners did.[81] But we do mean to challenge the view of critics such as Kramer—who sees in the work of Mondrian, for example, "a dazzling demonstration of a first-class intelligence working out its special destiny" and evidence of "a powerful mind . . . expressing itself through the pictorial inventions of a powerful sensibility."[82] Contrary to such extravagant claims, we emphasize that this type of painting (and sculpture), long regarded by many scholars and critics as the most "advanced" or "progressive" art of this century,[83] does not resemble the products of a mind functioning at the peak of its powers, but rather (in Mondrian's case, and in that of others we cite here) the workings of a profoundly pathological state of consciousness—or at least of a consciousness selectively out of touch with reality for any number of psychological or philosophic reasons. That fact, in turn, raises disturbing questions of much broader import. What can be concluded about the health of a society in which such an inversion of values is institutionally encouraged and supported?[84] Can a phenomenon that is clearly pathological for the individual be regarded as beneficial for society and culture at large? What is the impact of insisting on the value of such work in arts education programs aimed at children in their formative years?

Theoretical Revisionism

We have focused on Kandinsky, Malevich, and Mondrian in order to document the fallacies inherent in the "fateful leap into abstraction" (to borrow Kramer's words about Kandinsky). Though scores of other artists, some quite well known, were involved in the movement to varying degrees from the early years on, these three may be taken as prototypical. Not only do their theoretical statements express many of the principal ideas shared by other early abstract artists, but their paintings are also broadly representative of the two poles of abstraction: on one hand, the freer, looser, "expressionistic" style, initially employed by Kandinsky; on the other, the more geometric, often "hard-edged" style, typical of Malevich, Mondrian, and Kandinsky's late phase. Abstract artists throughout the century have continued to work in these styles, with infinite variations on, and admixtures of, the two.[85]

Nevertheless, in the course of the century, substantial revisionism has occurred with respect to the theory and intent of abstract art. Whereas the pioneers aimed in both theory and practice to convey metaphysical values through their work (however mistaken they were in their basic assumptions and approach), many latter-day artists and critics instead emphasized either "personal expression" or "exploration" of the painterly medium. These two perspectives—as markedly different from each other as from the theoretical viewpoint of the first abstract artists—owe their currency in America largely to the work of two men: the art historian Meyer Schapiro (1904–1996) and the critic Clement Greenberg (1909–1994). Their thought on abstract art and their activism in promoting it have greatly influenced its theory and its practice and have also contributed to its institutional legitimization. Both Schapiro and Greenberg eschewed the occultist metaphysics that had inspired the early abstract artists. Yet their fundamental premises were equally flawed.

Meyer Schapiro

More than any other individual, Meyer Schapiro brought academic respectability to abstract art in America.[86] A brilliant, wide-ranging scholar, and an impassioned, charismatic lecturer, he served on the faculty of Columbia University for many decades, taught at New York University and the New School for Social Research, and contributed articles to influential left-wing publications as well as to important academic journals. Unlike many modernist critics of his day, Schapiro did not adopt a narrowly formalist approach to art, but a broader, more humanistic perspective. For him, a work of art—from any era—was a meaningful expression of the mind and personality of its maker, and also a reflection, filtered through the artist's imagination, of his cultural and social context. For example, he insisted that still life paintings, which were often interpreted in exclusively formalist terms, are an expression of the "values [and] outlook" of the artist, both in the choice of objects and in the style in which they are painted.[87] And he saw them as reflecting the fact that our direct perception of objects "is the model or ground of all knowledge." (19) Thus he appeared to recognize that this process is fundamental to human cognition and, therefore, crucial in art.

Nonetheless, Schapiro enthusiastically championed abstract art. Ignoring the epistemological requirements of visual perception and representation, and the extent to which these must determine the nature of painting, he focused on the purported social and political implications of abstract art. Indeed, his first major article on the subject, "The Nature of Abstract Art," was published in the premier issue of *The Marxist Quarterly*, a journal of which he was a founding editor.[88] As Rosenthal emphasizes (94), this article challenged the "strictly formalist, ahistorical view of abstraction" promoted by Alfred Barr (the Museum of Modern Art's influential founding director) and others. Here, Schapiro first indicated his view that abstract art continues the tradition of modernist painting since 1885—"as an assertion of personal freedom in the face of the increasing oppressiveness and depersonalization of individual life brought about by capitalist institutions" (to borrow art historian Linda Nochlin's characterization).[89] Painting after 1885 was, Schapiro maintained, "an ideal domain of freedom" in the "stultifying . . . advance of monopoly capitalism." (192) He did not consider the twentieth-century tendency toward "extreme subjectivism and abstraction" in the arts to be a product of philosophic trends—which he characterized as "the renewed ideological oppositions of mind and nature, individual and society." Instead, adhering to Marxist theory, he saw both tendencies as jointly "proceed[ing] from social and economic causes." (194-95) In abstract art, Schapiro maintained, "personality, feeling and formal sensibility are absolutized." Further, he argued that, in "seek[ing] freedom outside of nature and society and consciously negat[ing] the formal aspects of perception—[such as] the connectedness of shape and color or the discontinuity of object and surroundings," abstract painters gain "an active sovereignty over objects."[90] (198) If the resulting work resembles the products of children or madmen, he proposed, it is because the artist's goal of "imaginative freedom" shares a fundamental kinship with the "spontaneity and technical insouciance of the child, who creates for himself alone, without the pressure of adult responsibilty and practical adjustments.[91] And similarly, the resemblance to psychopathic art . . . rests on their common freedom of fantasy, uncontrolled by reference to an external physical and social world." (199–200) Here Schapiro echoes the two key values we noted above—*freedom* and *spontaneity*—the more extreme manifestations of which are linked by Sass with schizophrenic thought patterns.

These related concepts crop up frequently in Schapiro's other writing on abstract art and have since become clichés of modernist criticism and art history. They recur throughout Schapiro's 1957 essay "The Liberating Quality of Avant-Garde Art."[92] In that context, he also emphasizes the "more deeply personal, more intimate character" of abstract art (213)—a claim that fundamentally contradicts the express intent of Kandinsky, Malevich, and Mondrian to expunge everything "individual" and "human" from their paintings. Yet Schapiro himself implicitly acknowledges the essential antithesis between abstraction and human individuality when, toward the end of the essay, he asks: "[H]ow can a complete personality leave out of his life work so much of his interests and experience, his thoughts and feelings? Can these be adequately translated into the substance of paint and the modern forms with the qualities I have described?" (225) These questions—which, he notes, "arise repeatedly, [and] are latent within modern art itself"—he never adequately resolves. The ultimate justification he offers is thinly drawn from insubstantial analogies with architecture and music—analogies that ignore the more significant differences between these endeavors.[93] Alluding to photography, he also observes that representation is now accomplished "through other means than painting and with greater power than in the past," thereby implying that literal representation was the sole objective of traditional painting. That implication is not only mistaken but surprising, since Schapiro himself had previously insisted that representation in art is not "passive, [or] 'photographic'" but, rather, "proceeds from [the artist's] values," which "shape the image."[94] Here, again, Schapiro's view of abstract painting is inconsistent with his broader theory of art.

Finally, Schapiro contradictorily claims that abstract painters, having "freed themselves from the necessity of representation," opened up "new possibilities of imaginative representation."[95] We would argue, first, that it was not in their power to so "free themselves," since the dependence of human cognition on perception is biologically determined. The perceptual requirements of representation are therefore not amenable to alteration. Nor can abstract art be properly thought of as a type of "imaginative representation," since that term implies the very *images* that abstract artists have abandoned.[96] In the absence of such images, their work remains inscrutable, especially in the terms postulated by Schapiro. So he, too, must ultimately rely on a spurious elitist perspective with regard to the appreciation of abstract work—an elitism based not on the early abstractionists' concept of spiritual evolution but, rather, on the requirement of *esthetic sensitivity*. "Only a mind . . . sensitized by experience and responsive to new forms and ideas," he claims, "will be prepared for the enjoyment of this art."[97]

Clement Greenberg

The subjectivist elitism that constitutes a minor corollary of Schapiro's theory of modern art becomes the principal focus of Clement Greenberg's critical writing. In his early championing of abstract art, Greenberg was mainly concerned with differentiating between "high culture" and "kitsch"—as he characterized them in "Avant-Garde and Kitsch" (1939), the essay that launched his career as a critic but which he repudiated late in life.[98] He argued that modernist avant-garde work—"in particular, 'abstract' or 'non-objective' art"—constitutes "high art," because it aims at the esthetically "absolute," as if trying "to imitate God by creating something valid solely on its own terms." (8) Thus perpetuating the dogma of "art for art's sake" without offering any evidence that it is, in fact, a valid principle, Greenberg promulgated a purely formalist view of esthetic value, in which "subject matter or content becomes something to be avoided like a plague." In the process, he grossly misrepresented the intent of the originators of abstract art. He claimed, for instance, that Mondrian, Kandinsky, and other early modernists "derive[d] their chief inspiration from the medium they work[ed] in,"[99] and that their art is purely preoccupied with "the invention and arrangement of spaces, surfaces, shapes, colors, etc." (9) Thus he (like Barr) ignored the metaphysical significance that those artists insisted was essential if their work were not to be reduced to mere decoration. In a further historical distortion, in an essay written twenty years later, Greenberg claimed: "Abstract art is not a special kind of art; no hard-and-fast line separates it from representational art; it is only the latest phase in the development of Western art as a whole. . . . The old masters stand or fall, their pictures succeed or fail, on the same ultimate basis as do those of Mondrian or any other abstract artist."[100] For Greenberg, representation was simply one of the "*expendable* conventions" of painting.[101]

In essays such as "'American Type' Painting" (1955), "The Case for Abstract Art" (1959), and "Modernist Painting" (1960), Greenberg presented his theory of the "ineluctable flatness" of pictorial art, and its relation to abstract painting—the theory so mindlessly echoed by subsequent critics and art historians, and so effectively debunked by Tom Wolfe.[102] As he wrote in *The Painted Word*:

> When Greenberg spoke, it was as if not merely the future of Art were at stake but the very quality, the very *possibility,* of civilization in America. . . . He saw Modernism as heading toward a certain inevitable conclusion, through its own internal logic, just as Marxists saw Western society as heading irrevocably toward the dictatorship of the proletariat and an ensuing nirvana. . . . And just what was this destination? On this point Greenberg couldn't have been clearer: *Flatness.* . . .
>
> . . . The question of what an artist could or could not do without violating the principle of Flatness—"the integrity of the picture plane," as it became known—inspired such subtle distinctions, such exquisitely miniaturized hypotheses, such stereotactic microelectrode needle-implant hostilities, such brilliant if ever-decreasing tighter-turning spirals of logic . . . that it compares admirably with the most famous of all questions that remain from the debates of the Scholastics: "How many angels can dance on the head of a pin?" [48–50]

According to Greenberg, modernism in art conformed to a tendency of Western thought and culture that had originated with Kant—a tendency which he opaquely defined as "the use of characteristic methods of a discipline to criticize the discipline itself, not in order to subvert it but in order to entrench it more firmly in its area of competence."[103] Just as Kant had done this in philosophy, Greenberg insisted, modernist artists were pursuing the same approach in painting. What did this mean, in practice? Since "flatness alone was unique and exclusive to pictorial art," modernist painters would concern themselves with emphasizing the "integrity of the picture plane." (87) That many of the painters themselves adamantly rejected the reduction of their work to such trivial concerns, and instead averred its deep metaphysical significance, did not deter Greenberg in the least.[104]

According to Louis Sass, the very qualities that Greenberg most praised in "modern [i.e., abstract] painting" are analogous to the "disturbances of distance" that constitute a major form of the "cognitive slippage" symptomatic of schizophrenia. Whereas normal perception necessarily focuses on the familiar objects and events relevant to one's practical needs and activity, schizophrenics tend to lose this sense of perspective and focus. Either they draw "so close to the world of sensory or material particulars as to lose [themselves] in . . . infinite minutiae," or else they move, in their mental framework, "so far away from particular objects or sensations as to lose touch with their conventional meanings or practical significance." Such "disturbances of distance" are manifested, in part, in their perception of visual form. (149) In Sass's view, "visual art's intense reflection on itself in the twentieth century," including the "famous quality of flatness" which Greenberg posited as the ultimate goal of modern (i.e., avant-garde) painting, "has engendered forms analogous to the schizophrenic disturbances of distance."[105] (170)

On what basis should such paintings be judged, in Greenberg's view? Here his counterfeit brand of elitism was absolute. There were no rules or principles, only "intuitive judgments." "You don't start to analyse pictures and find meaning and so forth; it's just good, bad—all the rest is bullshit," he told an interviewer. Intellect, he insisted, had no place in the esthetic realm.[106] Ultimately, it boiled down to "people with good eyes and [people with] bad eyes and that's all" (27)—a phenomenon as mysterious and ineffable, we might add, as the "evolved consciousness" of the early abstract artists. Nor did Greenberg—who never doubted the reliability of his own eyes—attempt to distinguish (as Rand did) between esthetic *judgment* and esthetic *response*. For him, "evaluation coincide[d] with aesthetic experience," which was simply a spontaneous, intuitive response of "liking [or] not liking" the work. Yet Greenberg's criticism held sway in the artworld for a generation, and continues to influence critics even today.[107] In the forties and fifties, reputations rose or fell according to his oracular pronouncements. And the ascendancy of abstract expressionism was in no small measure due to his critical attention and support.[108]

Abstract Expressionism

Three decades ago, Hilton Kramer proclaimed that Abstract Expressionism—the modernist "school" of painting and sculpture that flourished in New York City in the late 1940s and 1950s—is among the outstanding achievements of American culture in this century, "by virtue of the worldwide critical esteem [its artists] have enjoyed and the crucial artistic influence they have wielded."[109] Although postmodernist scholars and critics have in recent years challenged such an exalted view, the work of leading Abstract Expressionists continues to occupy a pre-eminent status in twentieth-century culture, and still influences contemporary abstract painters. Their typically oversized canvases and "sculptures" are enshrined in major public and private collections, and command exorbitant prices on the world art market; their work regularly receives renewed attention in retrospective exhibitions; and a commemorative stamp was issued in their honor in 1999 by the U.S. Postal Service as part of its "Celebrate the Century" series. Yet their reputation, like that of the pioneers of abstract art, has rested on a remarkably insubstantial foundation, composed of invalid assumptions and vacuous claims, rarely questioned by the artworld until recently—though ordinary people have not been so easily gulled.

Also known as the "New York School," the Abstract Expressionists were actually too diverse a group to constitute a true school. Their work ranged in style from the impulsively "gestural" canvases of the so-called Action painters, such as Willem de Kooning, Franz Kline, and Jackson Pollock, to the more controlled, minimalist "field" compositions of Mark Rothko and Barnett Newman.[110] Yet they were united by a shared set of assumptions and aspirations. Reacting against the soulless formalism that had dominated American abstract art in the 1930s, they insisted on the profound importance of content and subject matter in their work. In so doing, they necessarily relied heavily on verbal statements and manifestos to convey their meaning and justify their acceptance—just as the first abstract artists had done, and for the same reason: in the absence of representation, no objective content or meaning was discernible. Remarkably ignorant of the lofty metaphysical meanings the pioneers of abstract art had claimed for their work, the Abstract Expressionists presented themselves as creating a completely new art. So Barnett Newman, one of their principal spokesmen for the "new American painting," as it was often called, asserted that, in contrast with "pure abstractionists" such as Mondrian—who had insisted, according to Newman, on a "purist world of forms and color"—the new art would be "abstract yet full of feeling, capable of expressing the most abstruse philosophical thought."[111] Unwittingly echoing Mondrian, he further declared:

> The new painter is . . . the true revolutionary, the real leader who is placing the artist's function on its rightful plane of the philosopher and the pure scientist who is exploring the world of ideas, not the world of the senses. Just as we get a vision of the cosmos through the symbols of a mathematical equation, just as we get a vision of truth in terms of abstract metaphysical concepts, so the artist is today giving us a vision of the world of truth in terms of visual symbols.[112]

The fallacy in Newman's argument, of course, is his failure to recognize that the "idea" conveyed by a mathematical equation depends on a system of symbols whose meanings are fixed by cultural convention and are, therefore, universally accessible. The abstract forms employed by Newman and his fellow-painters have no such meanings—as evidenced by the widely disparate interpretations they invariably engender.

The Abstract Expressionists differed from the pioneer abstract artists in several key respects. The most obvious difference is the colossal size of their canvases—intended to virtually immerse the viewer in the painting. More significant is the fact that, contrary to the pioneers, who had adamantly rejected any sense of individuality in their work, the New York School elevated solipsism to the level of a guiding principle. In contrast with Rand's view that every work of art declares, in effect, "This is life as I (the artist) see it," the Abstract Expressionists declared in their work: "'This is Me! Me! Me!'"— as David and Cecile Shapiro put it in the illuminating introduction to their anthology on Abstract Expressionism.[113] In Newman's words: "Instead of making [art] out of Christ, man or 'life,' we are making it out of ourselves, out of our own feelings."[114] In each case, the search for self-expression culminated in what critics generously term a "major breakthrough" to a signature style—such as Rothko's luminous color fields, Pollock's drips and spatters, and Newman's "zips," or stripes.[115]

One of the most bizarre aspects of Abstract Expressionism was that many of its artists adopted the dubious Surrealist practice of *automatism*, or "automatic writing,"[116] which they carried to an unprecedented extreme. The Surrealists had, at least, never wholly dispensed with the representation of objective forms. Seeking to tap their subconscious emotions directly, the Abstract Expressionists not only suspended conscious control and direction but eliminated all "intermediary narrative, forethought, known symbol, [and] formal design. . . . The artist became, in a sense, only the [passive] conduit, the [involuntary] brush by means of which . . . emotion [was transmitted] onto an external object, the painting surface."[117] That such an approach constituted the negation of art—which, at root, involves the intentional application of skill—fazed neither the artists nor the critics who championed them. Nor did the fact that many of the resultant products of their subconscious could scarcely be distinguished from paintings produced by chimpanzees (and, more recently, by elephants). Least of all did anyone question whether the theory of mind underlying the concept of automatism had any validity. In sum, as the Shapiros note, during the heyday of the New York School "reasoned arguments attacking its assumptions" were few and far between. John Canaday, then chief art critic of the *New York Times*, was almost alone among his colleagues in complaining that

anyone, literally, can paint in a kind of abstract expressionist idiom. Sweet innocence of technical fetters may even give the most unconsidered daub an individual character. Witness the highly personal work of Betsy the Ape. . . . Of course Betsy's work was not art, but it was certainly abstract and, in its own way, quite expressive of her own gay, outgoing self.[118]

... The question is why so many painters have adopted a form of art that should seem pointless except to the recondite, . . . and why are we taking them so seriously?

"[To] the most wonderful and terrible time of history," concluded Canaday, "the abstract expressionists have responded with the narrowest and most lopsided art on record. Never before have painters found so little in so much."[119] After searching for "something deeper than surface movement and color" in their work, Canaday came up empty-handed, concluding that universal "human values . . . are non-existent in the painting of the New York School"—even in "the best of it."[120]

What was it that encouraged so many other members of the cultural establishment to find so much in so little with respect to the Abstract Expressionists? The answer is indicated, in part, by an official statement prepared by three prominent American institutions concerned with contemporary art.[121] First, they regarded the new work as part of the tradition of "courageous exploration and creative achievement" begun by modernists at the turn of the century—a tradition whose validity they never doubted. (231) Second, they noted that most of the valued art of the past century and a half had been publicly misunderstood or neglected, and they wanted, at all costs, to avoid making the same mistake.[122] Finally, and above all, they regarded the very diversity of viewpoints and styles as symptomatic of the freedom of expression inherent in a democratic society." (230–31) The "advanced artist," they argued, must be honored as "true to his personal vision." (232)

Thus abstract art, which had originated in the explicitly collectivist rejection of all that was personal and individual, was transformed, in theory, into the last bastion of individual liberty. At the height of the Cold War, this was no small issue, and it was exploited for political purposes. Moreover, although contemporary abstract artists had abandoned the human figure as "the central element of art," their work was regarded as "humanistic" because, in exploring "newly discovered levels of consciousness, new concepts of science and new technological methods," it was "helping humanity to come to terms with the modern world, not by retreating from it but by facing and mastering it." It thereby contributed to "the dignity of man." (232) (Whether such fields of exploration are, in fact, within the range of visual art was not questioned. Nor was it explained how contemplating the drips and spatters of a Jackson Pollock, say, would enable one to "face and master the world.") Finally, it was argued that "the so-called 'unintelligibility' of some modern art" was merely "an inevitable result of its exploration of [these] new frontiers." "We do not believe," the museum administrators declared, "that many artists deliberately aim to be unintelligible, or have voluntarily withdrawn from the public." (231) Such an assertion (which implicitly acknowledged the inscrutability of abstract art) completely ignored the elitism endemic to abstract art from its origin, as well as the explicitly anti-social attitude of leading Abstract Expressionists. Rothko, for example, complained of the public's cruelty and vulgarity. Another prominent Abstract Expressionist, Adolph Gottlieb, characterized abstraction as being "at war with society" and as declaring to the public: "'You're stupid. We despise you. We don't *want* you to like us—or our art.'"[123]

Last but not least, there can be no doubt that the claims of critics such as Greenberg—and, later, Kramer—regarding the "difficulty" of high art and the superiority of those individuals capable of appreciating it were a powerful factor in effecting their rapid acceptance. Such claims served, as the Shapiros have suggested, to make the enjoyment of so-called difficult art a "cultural test," to be met by people with "upwardly mobile cultural aspirations."[124] Ironically, these critics, who played so important a role in creating the reputation of the Abstract Expressionists, regarded their work in purely formalist or essentially decorative terms, blatantly disregarding the artists' own intentions.

Mark Rothko

The Russian-born color-field painter Mark Rothko (1903–1970) is widely considered one of the most important Abstract Expressionists, and one of the most enigmatic.[125] Although he began by doing figurative work in a Surrealist vein, by the late 1940s he had reduced his paintings to a few broad, flat planes of color, which have prompted widely diverse interpretations. Rosenthal characterizes their form and content as follows:

> A typical Rothko composition . . . consists of two or three soft-edged [horizontal] rectangles of highly saturated color, stacked vertically, with the largest usually presented as the central focus and the other colors subtly balancing the dominant one, creating an atmosphere of weight and mystery. Rothko used a range of color, thinly painted and applied with great nuance, . . . giving his reductive compositions a vulnerable, even human, dimension, which is magnified by the blurred edges of his forms. The effect is theatrical, for Rothko was a master at creating a physical impact, and his evocation of infinity, or the sublime, is palpable.[126]

For Rosenthal, then, Rothko's work conveys, through color alone, a variety of profound metaphysical concepts. In a somewhat different vein, Anthony Janson finds in Rothko's paintings the "purest contemplative stillness" and the "mysterious power to move us"—a power which he claims arises from

the "delicate equilibrium, . . . strange interdependence, [and] subtle variations of hue" of the colored rectangles. For viewers who respond to such qualities, Janson suggests, "the experience is akin to trancelike rapture."[127] Other
writers conclude that, in the end, we do not really know what Rothko's work
is about. To Michael Kimmelman, for example, it "has always remained obsti-
nately vague."[128] And art historian Dore Ashton, who knew the artist for 18
years and wrote a book about him, notes that the meaning of his work eluded
even the "single-minded quest" of the scholar who compiled his catalogue
raisonné. Rothko, she emphasizes, "remains mysterious."[129]

Rothko himself professed exalted, if often contradictory, aims as a painter.
Harking back to the dubious theories of Kandinsky, he believed that color
could directly evoke feelings of spiritual transcendence. To an even greater
degree than the early abstract painters, he subordinated form to color. So, too,
his urge for spiritual transcendence, for submerging the self in a primal state
of union with the universe, was more extreme than the similar impulses of
the first abstract painters. This desire appears to have been related to the psychological difficulties that led to his eventual suicide, at the age of sixty-
seven—death representing "the ultimate loss of self," as one writer has noted.[130]
Yet the peaceful aura of "contemplative stillness" inferred from Rothko's
work by Janson, and by many other viewers, is far removed from the artist's
express intentions. "[T]o those who think of my pictures as serene," Rothko
countered, "I have imprisoned the most utter violence in every square inch
of their surface."[131]

Rothko once declared that his work demonstrated "'a clear preoccupation
with death.'"[132] The British painter Simon Morley correctly argues, however,
that Rothko was mistaken in asking something "visually minimal and reductive to carry the weight of deep and complex emotions and ideas." He rejects
James Breslin's claim, written "in the sort of inflated language that Rothko's
work seems to attract," that the paintings "grieve," "portend," and "exalt,"
and "transform hollowness and despair into transcendence and nurturing
beauty."[133] (18) As Morley notes, many have failed to make such associations
and have often considered Rothko's paintings "exquisite decorations."[134] (18)
Notwithstanding his lofty metaphysical claims, Rothko was painfully aware
that his signature paintings might be viewed as merely decorative. In 1957,
in fact, he began to darken his palette, apparently in a futile attempt to avoid
that fate.[135]

Even Breslin acknowledges that Rothko's paintings are "'virtually empty'"
and that he is "'the least autobiographical of painters'" (326)—facts that made
the writing of his life daunting. Yet this quality of emptiness, so central to
Rothko's work, must have attracted Breslin. "My idea of utopia," he confided

to an interviewer, "would be to own a Rothko and come down each morning and spend a half-hour drinking a cup of coffee in front of it."[136] More revealing, perhaps, of the biographer's complex emotional tie to his subject—and of the appeal Rothko's work may exercise for viewers receptive to it—is Breslin's response to the somber maroon and black murals in the Rothko chapel in Houston, which he characterizes as (in part) "amorphous fields of color, devoid of any reference to external, remembered reality." (475) Astonishingly, Breslin studied these vacant murals "for several hours a day . . . over a period of five days." (476) He relates:

> the dark rectangle in the rear-wall painting pulled me in, holding my attention for long stretches of time. . . . [T]he black attracts precisely because it can't be possessed, because it pulls toward something beyond personality, something that can't be owned. . . . When the black looks solid, it thwarts entry. When the black dematerializes, it draws the viewer into an amorphous, empty, anonymous, all-absorbing—in fact, annihilating—darkness.
> . . . [T]hese murals are spiritual only in the sense that they renounce the world—the world of material objects, of historical time and social pressures. Decorating a public, sacred space, they express a private and very human desire: a despairing wish to withdraw *from* the human. [482]

As we have argued, such concerns as *renouncing the world* can be represented in painting only through reference to the human form, and to other tangible percepts of reality. We can only speculate that Breslin was fantasizing when he conjured up the awesome powers he ascribes to "the dark rectangle" in the passage quoted above. Perhaps he stared at it too often, and for too long, during his stay at the Rothko Chapel, projecting his own psyche onto its emptiness—identifying, on some level, with the painter's deeply troubled personality. How else could he be so powerfully drawn to work he describes in such uncompromisingly bleak terms?

Kramer, too, is much drawn to Rothko's work, but for very different reasons. Focusing on the earlier paintings, which employ a brighter palette, he admires the fact that Rothko "gives to color and the scale necessary to sustain its power . . . an audacious priority over every other pictorial consideration."[137] Alluding to "visual magic," Kramer finds that in Rothko's paintings "the eye is more and more ravished by an experience unlike anything to be found in the work of other painters": his color is "seductive"—"soft, luminous, almost cloudlike," enchanting and captivating.[138] (148–49).

Kramer's discussion of color in Rothko's work expands into the realm of esthetic theory. Emphasizing that "Rothko himself was adamant in insisting that his art went 'beyond' color—that its fundamental purpose was religious and spiritual," and that "the subject [of painting] is 'crucial,'" he reflects that Rothko's work "raises in the most extreme form the whole question of exactly how a purely abstract art may be construed as having—or as expressing—a subject matter that somehow exists beyond the visual boundaries of the object itself." (149) How indeed. Dismissing as "nonsense" fanciful critical speculations as to the subject of Rothko's work, Kramer nevertheless acknowledges that "the question of 'meaning' in [his] art . . . cannot be avoided," since Rothko himself insisted on the importance of subject matter yet denied that the subject of his paintings is color—although it is the dominant element in them. Kramer observes: "He had carried painting to a point of extreme reduction, and had made something extraordinary out of what remained, and yet he still yearned for the world of meaning that painting had jettisoned on its way to colonizing its extreme position." (150) Given his sympathy for this "extreme position," however, Kramer fails to grasp that such a yearning on Rothko's part would have stemmed from a subconscious recognition that meaning is essential to art.[139]

Inspired by the 1998 Rothko retrospective at the Whitney Museum, other critics, too, have waxed hyperbolic over the painter's color. James Gardner recalls coming "face to face with one of those chromatic harmonies that almost overwhelm you with their sheer presence. They do not speak to you: you are overhearing them."[140] For Calvin Tomkins, Rothko's "euphorically beautiful" paintings convey "deep, oceanic pleasures" in which the "reverberating pulse of color makes your spine tingle . . . not colors harmonized, or orchestrated for a predetermined effect, but color itself, color liberated and breathing within the alternative world of the picture."[141] Warming to his subject, Tomkins urges the reader: "Stand close to the painting, as Rothko advised[142] . . . and you feel color as a physical sensation: close your eyes, open them, and register the slight vibrating movement of the blurred rectangles on the retina." (103) Kimmelman similarly rhapsodizes:

> [The paintings] are astonishingly, breathtakingly moving. The colors all seem to be ecstatic and springlike: chartreuse, pink, peach, orange, saffron, lavender and white, layered in veils with the quality of breath on a pane of glass.
> They radiate light. The images seem to project off the walls. You stand in front of them as if before the sun, basking. There is a sense of surrender by Rothko to some exquisite and mysterious new discovery—a feeling akin to new love.[143]

Despite all the talk about the primacy of color in Rothko's painting, of its almost mystical powers, what remains foremost in our minds is his own poignant insistence that his paintings were about so much more. "You might as well get one thing straight," he once declared, "I'm *not* an abstractionist. . . . I'm not interested in [mere] relationships of color or form. . . . I'm interested only in expressing basic human emotions."[144]

As Kramer reminds us, Rothko's denial that he was an abstractionist—in the face of incontrovertible evidence to the contrary—was not an isolated case:

> It has long been one of the curiosities of abstract art that so many of its practitioners have denied that they were in fact abstract artists. To have created works of art that were seen to be "merely" a mode of abstraction has been, for these artists, a considerable vexation, and some have gone to great lengths to—in their view—set the record straight on this question. But whether they actually succeeded in this project of denial or only added further impediments to our understanding of abstract art—including their own—remains a matter of debate.[145]

For our part, we do not find such a denial at all curious. Here, again, Kramer misses the point: in disavowing their art as "abstract," Rothko and others implicitly acknowledged (much as the pioneers of abstract painting had) that art must convey *meaning*, that painting must involve more than mere *color*, however "ravishing" and "seductive."

Jackson Pollock

World renowned for his signature "drip" paintings,[146] Jackson Pollock is the quintessential practitioner of the style of Abstract Expressionism dubbed "action painting" by the critic Harold Rosenberg. Beginning with a major article in *Life* magazine in 1949 documenting his unorthodox style of painting, and culminating with the issuing by the U.S. Postal Service in 1999 of a stamp celebrating his contribution to Abstract Expressionism, Pollock has been elevated to the status of a cultural icon,[147] thanks in part to effusive critics. Clement Greenberg, the first to champion his work, esteemed him the "greatest painter of [his] generation."[148] Subsequent critics have enlarged that assessment.[149] "There is a sense that no one, not even post-modernists who reject everything he stands for, knows how to cut him down to size. . . . [H]e remains the great presence in American art, and no one else is close."[150] "Pollock is our chief symbol of the culmination of abstract art—the bad-boy revolutionary who painted without a brush, like God."[151] "Pollock is the dark, liberating angel at the shoulder of postwar art: his drip paintings blew traditional notions of academic skill to smithereens."[152] "Pollock is one of the legends of modern art. . . . [He] remains the prototypical American modernist, the one who not only 'broke the ice' . . . but set a canon of intensity

for generations to come."[153] "During the five short years between 1947 and
1952, he created a body of work whose primal ferocity, spirituality and beauty
should assure him a place among the best of the twentieth-century American
painters."[154] Finally, according to Kirk Varnedoe, who organized (with Pepe
Karmel) a major Pollock retrospective at the Museum of Modern Art in
1998–99, he "profoundly altered or even obliterated the concept of painting
handed down within the Western tradition, reinvented it as a different kind
of activity and object, and established a new 'point of no return'" within modern art, ultimately giving "permissions" to a whole generation of postmodernist artists in various media.[155] Varnedoe's estimation is reflected in the
exhibition brochure, which characterizes Pollock as "the most celebrated,
and controversial, artist of the twentieth century"—an "embodiment of avant-
garde provocation," whose "'allover' abstractions . . . opened up freedoms
for artists of all kinds . . . not just in painting but throughout the new forms
of sculpture and performance art that arose after him."[156]

Though Pollock is indelibly identified with the "drip" technique, it did not
originate with him. Yet he carried it to an unprecedented extreme,[157] and its
mystique was enhanced both by his belligerent personality and by the numerous photographs and films by Hans Namuth and others documenting his working method—clutching paint can in one hand and brush or stick in the other,
rhythmically pouring, dripping, or spattering paint while doing what one writer
has characterized as his "strenuous grapevine dance step" around the canvas,
which was stretched out on the floor of his studio or outdoors.[158]

According to Rosenthal, Pollock's working method, which "courted chance
and spontaneous effects," was "akin to a masterful accident of the hand"—a
contradiction in terms if ever there was one. Rosenthal finds in the "densely
woven filamented lines and textures that overlap and interweave" in Pollock's
"mature" work such as *Number 1, 1950 (Lavender Mist)*, "an allover compositional format in which space, or the possibility of visual penetration,
appears to be invited and then denied"[159]—a fanciful statement that, in any
case, has nothing to do with Pollock's professed intentions of self-expression, on which we comment further below.

If Pollock's paint-spattered studio was "a raw environment where important ideas were born"[160]—as one writer suggested on a visit to the house (now
a National Historic Landmark) that Pollock shared with his beleaguered wife,
Lee Krasner—one may well wonder what those ideas were. Ascribing meaning to Pollock's canvases is a daunting task even for seasoned critics and art
historians, however. After conceding that "his cryptography begs to be decoded"
and that his work stands for "everything that the ordinary person can't understand in contemporary art," Kay Larson declares: "It's almost impossible to

reduce a Pollock picture to a verbal analogy—those who try usually resort to silly adjectives." Yet she then proceeds to compare his quality of line to "fireworks popping in a black sky far above your head."[161] Carter Ratcliff argues that Pollock's "paint-slinging" is remembered precisely because it "generated a power that overwhelms understanding."[162] Pollock's biographers Steven Naifeh and Gregory Smith characterize his abstractions as consisting of "unreadable skeins of paint . . . an 'alien code.'"[163] Michael Kimmelman suggests that Pollock "pursued something so wild, untested and mysterious that its full meaning was unclear even to him," and advises that "it's a fool's game to try to attribute specific meanings to [his painterly gestures]." He laments that "pure abstract painting, which [Pollock] brought to a peak, remains the most difficult art for many people to grasp because content is still commonly mistaken for subject matter, as if a picture with no recognizable images in it can't be about anything." Nonetheless, as if frustrated in his own search for meaning, Kimmelman asks "Yet what is a Pollock about?" and repeats: *"The question troubled even him."*[164]

In sharp contrast, Varnedoe contends that Pollock's work is not "especially 'difficult.'" For him, the "'drip' or 'poured' paintings seem to expose the way they were made, and in significant part to be *about* that process."[165] The only question is "whether the energies poured out of Pollock's head or his body." According to one of the pro-head theories, "the vectors of enamel are flung out in trancelike unawareness, and represent the lineaments of psychic knots, cathartically untangled and expelled in a healing ritual." Another proposes that Pollock's canvases reflect "the precarious balance of randomness and order that is the excitement and anxiety of modern urban life." (54) Alternative theories, focusing on "bodily functions," are even more absurd. Rosalind Krauss and Yve-Alain Bois, for example, link Pollock's "downward spillage of liquid paint [onto the horizontal canvas] to a radical tradition of formlessness in art associated, psychically, with bodily excretion."[166] Another bodily metaphor which critics have resorted to in attempting to explain Pollock's work—and which Pollock himself encouraged—is that of intercourse. According to Varnedoe, when Pollock was asked how he knew a painting was completed, he retorted, "'How do you know when you're through making love?'"—on which Varnedoe comments:

That equation of painting with love-making is hardly original, but it may have specific usefulness here, not just because of the horizontality and the impulsion of fluid, but for the physical and psychic opposites it embraces: the orchestrated and the intuitive; driving impulse and give-and-take responsiveness; urgent thrust and repetitive caress; aggressive personal catharsis and

hunger for communication outside the self. To the connotations of waste and
defilement it also adds implications of insemination that . . . may be appropriate—even where the spermatic look of the pouring . . . is not so evident.
[55]

Attempts to read meaning into Pollock's paintings do not rest there, however. In a more exalted vein, his work has been repeatedly, if groundlessly,
compared to the poetry of Walt Whitman. For Robert Hughes, Pollock's work
reflects "a deeply set strain in American culture, the vision of landscape as
transcendental"—in particular, "the Edenic expanse of its plains, apostro-
phized by Walt Whitman as 'that vast Something, stretching out on its own
unbounded scale, unconfined, which there is in these prairies, combining the
real and the ideal, and beautiful as dreams.'"[167] Ratcliff develops the analogy, claiming that

> Pollock's loops and swirls of color draw the imagination into a region of
> boundless space. Evoking a sense of limitless possibility, the best of his can-
> vases give us—for the first time—a pictorial equivalent of the American infi-
> nite that spreads through Walt Whitman's *Leaves of Grass*. Depicting neither
> landscape nor figure, Pollock pointed the way into a realm as vast as Whit-
> man's, and his gesture made him one with it.[168]

Contrary to Ratcliff, Pollock's randomly abstract canvases cannot be a "*pictorial* equivalent" for anything (much less for the vivid imagery and astonishing range of subject matter and theme in Whitman's poetry), since they
depict nothing—a point we have made regarding abstract art throughout this
chapter. Moreover, the unwitting irony of the Whitman-Pollock analogy is
evident in the Namuth film of Pollock painting out of doors, turning his back
on the Edenic expanse of eastern Long Island to immerse himself in the
painterly expression of his inner turmoil.[169] Critics who insist upon the Whitman analogy, moreover, completely ignore the pathetically narrow solipsism
of the painter's professed intentions. According to Pollock, he and other "modern artist[s]" were directly "expressing an inner world . . . the energy, the
motion, and other inner forces."[170] If his work reflects anything, therefore, it
is not the American landscape's "sense of infinite possibility" but, rather, the
severe limitations of his own confused mind. Yet Varnedoe lends further credence to the analogy, claiming that Pollock, like Whitman, stands apart from
other American artists "as someone powerfully understood, at home and
abroad and for better and worse in his grandeur and in his misery, to represent the core of what America is."[171] Even if one were to agree with Varnedoe's ambivalent view of America (which we do not), one must surely question

his assessment of Pollock. "Misery," indeed, but "grandeur"? The very suggestion that this pathologically abusive and self-destructive individual represents America's "grandeur," much less its "core," strikes us as verging on the obscene.[172]

Barnett Newman

The work of Barnett Newman, whose carefully controlled stripes and flat areas of color could not be more unlike Pollock's drips and spatters, offers particularly illuminating evidence of the gaping disparity between artworld claims and the common-sense responses of ordinary people toward abstract painting. Certainly, few works have provoked as much public furor as his *Voice of Fire*, which was purchased in 1989 by the National Gallery of Canada in Ottawa for 1.8 million Canadian dollars. A starkly minimalist, symmetrical composition of wall-sized proportions (18 feet high by 8 feet wide), it consists simply of a broad vertical stripe of deep cadmium red flanked by two vivid ultramarine blue stripes of identical width.[173] As reported in the *Wall Street Journal* by Sarah Jennings, a Canadian writer and broadcaster, the gallery's curators judged the painting "'a modern masterpiece, a mystical work for a secular age.'"[174] The general public did not view it that way, however. Outraged at the hefty price paid for Newman's work (in a time of fiscal crisis), most citizens were not reassured by what Jennings characterized as the "unintelligible art jargonese" the gallery offered in defense of it. "For ordinary Canadians looking at the three blank stripes of color," Jennings noted, "being told that 'the painting helps take us away from the devastating cares of everyday life' has not been enough."[175] And the draft version of a brochure the curators were preparing to explain to visitors what the Newman painting was about was "alarmingly bogged down in the language so favored by contemporary art experts"—"peppered with references to the picture as an 'objectification of thought' that 'floods our consciousness with a sublime sense of awe and tranquility.'" As Jennings facetiously concluded, "maybe those worrisome thoughts of everyday life are forgotten for a moment and one is suspended in time and space. Still, back on Earth, it's comforting to know . . . that the word 'top' is marked on the back of the picture so that anyone hanging it can be quite certain which end is up."

About six months after the initial furor had subsided, the National Gallery attempted to mollify the public by convening a symposium to which it was invited. Six years later, that event was extensively documented, along with media coverage of the original controversy, in a volume aptly titled *Voices of Fire: Art, Rage, Power, and the State*. As the editors of the volume—Bruce Barber, Serge Guilbaut, and John O'Brian—point out, political and economic factors had contributed to the unprecedented intensity of the controversy. Yet they also recognize that more was involved than public concern over fiscal irresponsibility in a gravely failing economy. At root lay "the peculiar and paradoxical character of abstract art in general and the problems it consistently poses for viewers." (viii) On this phenomenon, the volume offers potent, if sometimes unwitting, testimony. Not only do the editors thoroughly document the common-sense reaction of ordinary people; more tellingly, their analysis of that reaction reveals their own blindness to the primary issues involved—a condition often exacerbated by their condescending attitude toward the public.

In his Introduction, for example, O'Brian (a professor of art history at the University of British Columbia at Vancouver) acknowledges "the public's aversion to abstraction in general and [to] the paintings of Newman in particular," yet rather patronizingly claims that gallery visitors experienced *Voice of Fire* as "bewildering in its reductiveness." (19) What their comments reveal, in fact, is not bewilderment, but derision and contempt. Typical reactions were "It looks like the ribbon on a military medal," or "'A flag of a country somewhere'"; "Looks like something my son'll do in daycare"; "I wouldn't pay a dollar [for it]"; and "I would put it in the garbage."[176] The member of parliament who headed the House of Commons Standing Committee on Communications and Culture at the time of the controversy quipped: "'It looks like two cans of paint and two rollers and about ten minutes would do the trick.'"[177]

In an essay entitled "Who's Afraid of Barnett Newman?" O'Brian again suggests that "the animosity directed at [*Voice of Fire*] reflected a long-standing popular mistrust of abstract art, in particular its failure to give value for money in terms of skilled labor." (134) Critical of the National Gallery for not dealing effectively with "the difficulties that abstract art . . . habitually poses for viewers," he cites Brydon Smith's vacuous claim that the painting's "soaring height, strengthened by the deep cadmium-red centre between dark blue sides, is for many visitors an exhilarating affirmation of their being wholly in the world and in a special place where art and architecture complement each other." To this specimen of artspeak, O'Brian retorts: "Little wonder . . . the anti-abstraction brigade queried: exhilaration at being in *what* special place? a place where the wall is covered in stripes?" Yet he fails to pursue such an observation to its logical conclusion and suggests, instead, that "Smith might have been better advised to insist on Newman's craftsmanly skills as a painter." (134)

Where O'Brian saw "Newman's mastery over his medium" (133), however, the press saw only "'wallpaper'" and "a giant striped panel."[178] For most Canadians—who weren't "in the artistic know," quipped one writer in the

Kamloops Daily News—Voice of Fire would only conjure up thoughts of P. T. Barnum: "'There's a sucker born every minute and they saw us coming.'"[179] Nor were journalists taken in by the National Gallery's brochure purporting to explain the painting. For example, Stephen Godfrey, writing in the *Globe and Mail*, derided the gallery's claim that the painting's three stripes are, as he puts it, "a metaphor for oppression and national identity," as well as the artist's claim that they would give the viewer "'the feeling of his own totality, of his own separateness, of his own individuality, and at the same time of his connection to others who are also separate." As for the brochure's author, Brydon Smith (then the assistant director of collections and research at the gallery), who confided that it was difficult to put the painting's impact into words, Godfrey wrily comments that, "for some viewers, the text of [his] brochure may prove him right."[180]

Another *Globe and Mail* writer, Bronwyn Drainie, astutely identified the source of popular resentment toward Newman's work—and toward Abstract Expressionism in general:

> Why do we, as a society, hate this red-and-blue striped painting so much? To put it crudely, Canadians don't like *Voice of Fire* because it doesn't like them. In fact, it wants nothing to do with them. It is an imposing symbol of one of the haughtiest, most elite art movements in world history, the New York school of abstract expressionism, . . . [whose] baleful influence continues to this day. . . .
>
> The Abstract Expressionists—besides Newman the big names are Jackson Pollock, Willem de Kooning, Mark Rothko, Franz Kline—devised a definition of art that was completely self-referential. "All great art is about art," pronounced one of the revered theorists of the day, Leo Steinberg, and Barnett Newman himself described his canvases as "non-relational," filled with nothing but color and "drained of the impediments of memory, association, nostalgia, legend, myth, or what have you." In other words, drained of anything that might relate them to other human beings who had not taken an academic course in abstract expressionism.[181]

In conclusion, Drainie opines that *Voice of Fire* represents "a once powerful but dead-end artistic movement which is, one can only hope, gone forever."

Equally revealing were the numerous cartoons inspired by the controversy, and unanimously critical not only of the painting and of the gallery's purchase of it but also of abstract art in general. That Bruce Barber, one of the editors of *Voices of Fire*, utterly failed to grasp this last point is suggested, in particular, by his analysis of a cartoon depicting two men standing in front of *Voice of Fire*. One, wearing a beret, points at the painting and, turning to a scowling bare-headed man in a plaid sweater next to him, announces:

"I see it as an abstract expression of our country divided. The blue background symbolic of the potential harmony between English and French isolated by a blazing red-neck stripe . . . A contemporary mirror. What do you see?" To which the scowling man tersely replies: "$1.8 million down the toilet."[182] Contrary to Barber's obtuse gloss,[183] the figure in the beret is not so much a "cultured Québécois" as a quintessential member of the artworld public, pretentiously echoing the claims of the gallery's brochure about the painting. Nor is his dour-faced companion an "Anglo-Canadian philistine," but rather an ordinary citizen, properly outraged at the evident waste of taxpayers'—and *his*—money for an object of so little worth.

Barber similarly misses the point of another cartoon, depicting an artist intently painting a canvas of humongous polka dots, in a studio full of similar paintings, while his wife, seated with her back to him, reads a newspaper headline announcing the National Gallery's extravagant purchase price for a "striped painting" and exclaims: "For thirty years I said 'Why don't you try stripes . . . just once . . . for variety?' . . . but *noooo*. . . ."[184] According to Barber, this cartoon "brings together the purchase price of the painting with a potential domestic struggle over the value of creative work." The issue is not "the value of creative work," however—an especially ludicrous claim, in this case. Rather, it is the absurdity of the painter-husband's obsessive devotion to a single, and arbitrary, minimalist formula—an obsession comparable not only to Newman's preoccupation with stripes (he called them "zips")[185] but to numerous other real-life counterparts in the twentieth century, from Ad Reinhardt's fifteen-year fixation on all-black canvases to Robert Ryman's four decades of painting all-white canvases.[186]

Other cartoons depicted opportunists attempting to cash in on the success of the *Voice of Fire* formula. In one, an artist phones the National Gallery to offer a bargain: "Two red stripes on a blue background. Worth at least 3.6 million . . . I can let you have it for a mere 3 mill. . . ."[187] This cartoon, too, had its real-life counterparts. In one example, albeit more forthright in spirit, a woman saw *Voice of Fire* on television and exclaimed to her husband, John Czupryniak, a house painter: "'Hey, anybody could paint this, even a painter.'"[188] He then proceeded to create a facsimile of *Voice of Fire*. Using plywood instead of canvas, because he was unfamiliar with the technique of painting on such a surface, and choosing his colors on the basis of a newspaper illustration, since he had not seen the painting in person, Czupryniak is reported to have produced a fairly accurate reproduction. Completing it in about seven hours, he propped it up in front of his house, with a "For Sale" sign on which he had scrolled his telephone number. Regarding Czupryniak's choice of a title for his painting, art historian Thierry de Duve notes that he "hesitated for some time between *Voiceless, No Voice at All, Whose Voice, Voice of Anger,*

Voice of Stupidity, Voice of Amazement, Voice of Laughter, Voice of the Aghast, Voice of the Disillusioned, and *Voice of the Confused,* before opting finally for *Voice of the Taxpayer.*" (83) As for his price, Czupryniak declared: "'If you're with the government, . . . it's $1,800,000. If you are a private individual, you can have it for $400'"—a figure he forthrightly, if not very accurately, estimated on the basis of $190 spent on materials and seven hours' work at $45 per hour.[189] (91)

The intelligent response of ordinary people to Barnett Newman's work—a response documented in sweeping scope in the *Voice of Fire* controversy—was, on the whole, to call a *stripe* a "stripe."[190] Much the same response was documented on a more intimate scale in a remarkably revealing article published the following year in the "Metro" section of the *New York Times,* about the private musings of the guards at the city's Museum of Modern Art. Written by John Tierney, the article was entitled "Defender, Critic, Watcher: All in One at the Modern" (20 November 1991) and bore the apt subhead: "After Years of Walking Museum's Galleries, Guards Know Their Art and What They Like." As Tierney suggests, the guards were "singularly qualified" to judge modern art, since they scrutinized it all day long, spending "close to 2,000 hours a year in the galleries, . . . probably longer than any art historian—or any entire department of art history." Of particular interest was the reaction of Alec Sologob (then a fifteen-year veteran of the museum) to Newman's purported "masterpiece" pretentiously entitled *Vir Heroicus Sublimis* (Heroic Sublime Man)—a 17-foot-wide bright red canvas divided by five thin vertical stripes ranging in color from white to maroon and black. As reported by Tierney, Sologob "could not discern how the Newman work provided, in the words of the official museum guidebook, 'direct, intimate contact' with the viewer as well as an 'affirmation of Newman's somewhat mystical sense of the human condition with all its tragedy and dignity.'" In Sologob's words:

> I don't see it. . . . With Cézanne or Bonnard, there's intimate contact because you can feel yourself walking into the painting, into that wooded area with the men chopping firewood. With [Andrew] Wyeth you always find something new. In *Christina's World* you see the details in her hands, you find cracks in the wooden boards of the house, you get a marvelous sense that this really is her world. . . . But this Newman has never looked to me like anything. This is a blank wall with stripes, and I don't like the color red to begin with.[191]

According to Sologob, abstract art, in general, did not wear well with the museum's guards. "'You've seen one Pollock, you've seen them all,'" he remarked.[192] "'And Rothko. I remember the time one couple looked at *Red, Brown, and Black.* She was in a rapture, she was ecstatic, and he said, "Hey, it looks like our old TV set." I kind of sympathized with the man, because at the time I had an old TV set myself.'"

In marked contrast with Sologob's jaded response to abstract art was his love of Impressionist painting, that of Monet in particular. As Tierney touchingly relates, "he often arrived for work early, before the museum opened, and would spend the free time sitting in the second-floor gallery overlooking the museum's courtyard, in front of Monet's *Water Lilies.* "'It is so peaceful,'" Sologob explained. "'You know, during the day many people come here and stay for three or four hours with *Water Lilies.* They say it calms them down and it's cheaper than a psychiatrist. I can see what they mean. You come with your nerves raw, and then you just drift into the painting. It really soothes you.'"

Abstract Sculpture

Until now, we have confined our remarks about abstract art to painting, which is far more familiar to most people, and has generated a more extensive body of theoretical and critical literature. Abstract sculpture ultimately rests on the same basic fallacy as abstract painting: the supposition that meaning can be conveyed visually without the representation of objective reality. Owing to its three-dimensional character, however, it has prompted its own set of theoretical and critical claims.

Like abstract painting, abstract sculpture has varied greatly in style—ranging from the biomorphic forms of early modernists such as Henry Moore and Constantin Brancusi (for the most part employing traditional sculptural techniques and materials)[193] and the mechanical-looking contrivances of Constructivism[194] to the "pieces" of American minimalist sculptors of the 1960s and 1970s, such as Donald Judd and Carl Andre, typically utilizing prefabricated industrial materials.[195] Rather than attempt a survey, however, we focus on the critically acclaimed American sculptor David Smith (1906–1965)—whose most characteristic works are his *Zig* sculptures, composed of flat rectangles and circles of painted steel, and his *Cubi* series, constructions of asymmetrically stacked cubes and cylinders of burnished stainless steel.[196] Since Smith's work was largely inspired by the example of the European avant-garde and also paved the way for the more extreme reductivism of the Minimalists, it can serve to illustrate aspects of the whole range of abstract sculpture.

A contemporary of the Abstract Expressionist *painters* (with whom he is generally identified, owing to shared assumptions and goals regarding art as a means of direct self-"expression"), Smith has been characterized as the "most original and influential American sculptor of his generation" and "a towering modern master."[197] According to Hilton Kramer, he is "the greatest of all American artists," whose body of work is not only "among the truly greatest artistic productions of this century" but is also "the most eloquent and complex and deeply sustained any American artist has yet produced."[198] Yet Smith's career, much like that of the abstract painters discussed in this chapter, testifies to the gaping disparities between artistic intention, artworld interpretation, and objective reality. Like Jackson Pollock, he has become a mythic "larger-than-life American artist-hero," whose personality (as one admiring critic has acknowledged) looms far larger than his work.[199]

To begin, although Smith is regarded as a sculptor, his work—like that of many other abstract sculptors—is not, technically speaking, sculpture at all. Whereas "sculpture" (from the Latin *sculpere*, "to carve") properly refers to the carving or molding of human or animal forms out of a three-dimensional mass—either by cutting into a solid block of wood or stone or by shaping a mass of clay or other malleable material—Smith *constructed* his abstract pieces by welding together iron and steel elements of various shapes, often incorporating so-called found objects such as industrial parts and scrap metal.[200] This medium naturally attracted him because, as he said, "nothing technical was involved outside of [the] factory knowledge" he had acquired during a summer's employment in a Studebaker motor plant, and it therefore enabled him to become "a sculptor, with no formal training in the sculpture tradition."[201] Indeed, Smith's entire training in art, formal or otherwise, consisted of a few years' study in *painting* at the Art Students League in New York, where he was introduced—as Kramer approvingly relates—"to the art of the great European modernists."[202] That Smith never attained a mastery of the human figure, the primary subject of sculpture, is evident from his drawings: even the best of them are relatively crude, while the worst could be taken for a child's finger paintings.[203]

Regarding his artistic approach and intent, Smith himself declared: "The equipment I use, my supply of material, comes from factory study and duplicates as nearly as possible the production equipment used in making a locomotive. . . . My aim in material function is the same as in locomotive building: to arrive at a given functional form in the most efficient manner."[204] Just what that "functional form" is in each of his pieces, however, is anybody's guess. Smith's *Hudson River Landscape*, for example, said to be one of his "finest works," is scarcely recognizable as a work of sculpture, much less as a landscape.[205] It looks more like a free-form spatial doodle made of oversized wire coat hangers, with the addition of various indeterminate metal elements.[206] Since it neither conveys any of the particular spatial, atmospheric, or other qualities of the Hudson River landscape nor even faintly evokes the emotional impact they might have on a viewer, it renders vacuous Kramer's claim that "the pastoral beauty of the American landscape" was an element of Smith's inspiration. (50) If it was an inspiration, it had no perceptible embodiment in his work.

Equally vacuous is the frequent claim that Smith's constructions suggest "personages" and presumably reveal a major preoccupation with the human figure on his part. Michael Kimmelman, for example, reviewing a major outdoor exhibition of Smith's signature work at the Storm King Art Center in Mountainville, New York, writes: "Some of the sculptures . . . suggest . . . headstrong figures striding purposely [sic] across the lawn. . . . [U]pright, they gain a tension and an alertness and a physical presence that one associates with another person. When you stand next to them they seem to be standing next to you, too."[207] Similarly, Karen Wilkin views Smith's *Lectern Sentinel* (1961)—one of a series of works by him purportedly on the theme of the sentinel, or "watcher"—as conjuring up an "animate presence."[208] Without the title, however, who would reasonably perceive such a piece (a vertical stacking of steel plates, set at varying angles, topped with a horizontal bracketlike element, capped on one side by a hollow cylinder) as an "animate" object, much less as a human sentinel? More to the point, even if one were to take the leap of imagination required to view it as a sentinel, what sort of sentinel is it meant to be? The mere suggestion of an "animate presence" counts for nothing, absent the qualities of human character which can be conveyed solely through body posture and facial expression. Like any abstract work, Smith's "figure" is devoid of such qualities, as is obvious in comparison with any truly figurative work. Consider, for example, Daniel Chester French's *Minute Man*—aptly described by Wayne Craven as "poised, alert, and confident . . . handsome, rugged, and square-shouldered, with one hand on a plow and the other . . . holding his rifle . . . a man of homespun philosophy, common sense, and determination"—a monument to the "genius and resourcefulness" of the people of New England.[209]

Questions of meaning become especially arbitrary with respect to Smith's famous *Cubi* series. Among his "greatest masterpieces," according to Craven (628), these angular geometric constructions are composed of boxes and cylinders of welded steel in varying configurations. Inspired as he was by industrial technology, Smith claimed that the *Cubis* evoked "the great quiet of stopped machines." For H. W. Janson, however, they seem to represent a "triumph over gravity," while Craven views them as "twentieth-century votive images" that testify to "man's ability to find beauty . . . in the harmony of pure geometric forms." Finally, Kramer, who characteristically eschews any such suggestion of transcendent values, is transported simply by their "brilliantly polished surfaces [which] absorb the light with a stunning intensity, dissolving their bold geometric masses into a weightless and variable and purely optical poetry of the eye."[210]

Clearly, critics and scholars are unable to agree, even approximately, on the meaning of Smith's work, or on why one should value it. As Wilkin observed in her 1984 monograph: "Every year [his] reputation grows a little. Every new showing of his work makes him loom larger, yet he remains an elusive artist." (7) Even for those critics who most admire Smith's work, it continues to be "resistant to easy interpretation," to borrow Kramer's words (41), belying his subsequent claim that it is remarkably "eloquent" (49)—a term connoting forceful clarity and, therefore, *intelligibility*. As Wilkin uneasily acknowledged:

> If our ideas about Smith seem haunted by confusion, it is not always the fault of our perceptions. The work is astonishingly difficult. It is uningratiating and contradictory, resisting precise definitions. The best pieces are often at once radically abstract and uncannily anthropomorphic, aggressively robust and surprisingly sensitive. . . . Like their maker, they cannot easily be categorized. (8)

Here Wilkin resorts to a device frequently employed by nonplused critics in the face of avant-garde work: she characterizes it in terms of polar opposites. All bets are covered, and only the reader who pauses to think, mindful of Aristotle's law of noncontradiction and the promptings of common sense, is likely to question her.

But why should anyone hope to understand Smith's work when he himself could not? As he declared in a speech at Ohio University in 1959:

> I've made it because it comes closer to saying who I am than any other method I can use. This work is my identity. There were no words in my mind during its creation, and I'm certain words are not needed in its seeing; and why should you expect understanding when I do not? That is the marvel—to question but not to understand. Seeing is the true language of perception. Understanding is for words.[211]

In so arguing, of course, Smith ignored that the "true language of perception" depends precisely on the presence of perceptually recognizable objects, which he had eliminated from most of his pieces. For this reason, they are not just "difficult," they are incomprehensible. That is why any analyses of it, apart from those that are strictly formalist, are inevitably incoherent, since no one can coherently explicate something that is itself unintelligible.[212]

In the end, the only rational way to regard wholly abstract work, be it painting or sculpture, is in purely formal and sensory terms. This logical if unintended implication of Smith's work was soon made explicit by the Minimalists, who adopted his formal approach, while rejecting the sorts of metaphysical and expressive meanings he claimed for them. Smith's *Five Units Equal* (1956), for example, is clearly echoed in the work of Donald Judd, who is noted for his blandly repetitive arrangements of industrially fabricated slabs and cubes. Unlike Smith, however, Judd insisted that his constructions were devoid of any meaning beyond their sensory physical properties. As characterized by Craven, Judd's principle was that his works

> exist in and of themselves, without reference to anything else: they are exactly what they are, nothing more, nothing less, and they do not symbolize anything, stand for anything, represent anything in illusionistic fashion, or imply any social or cultural connections. . . . They are noniconic, nonsymbolic, nonanthropomorphic forms.[213]

To state this, however, is to argue, albeit unwittingly, that they are not art. Whereas Smith had at least *claimed* that his work served the kind of spiritual or psychological function properly associated with art works, the Minimalists implicitly rejected the very idea of art, for they deliberately aimed to create objects that would so blend with the surroundings as to be ignored. Carrying this goal to its extreme, Carl Andre created "floor pieces" that were intended to be walked upon. Such objects, we would argue, belong to the realm of *anti-art*,[214] since the whole point of a work of art is to focus attention on things that are deemed to be important in human life. In view of the intentional meaninglessness of Minimalist "art," we consider it profoundly ironic that Smith is credited, among other things, with having influenced Judd and others like him—as if their dehumanized work were a praiseworthy contribution to civilization.[215]

Polling the People

Evidence that ordinary people find abstract art fundamentally alien and inscrutable—utterly devoid of the various meanings ascribed to it by the artworld—is not limited to the sort of scattered anecdotal reports we cited in relation to Barnett Newman. More systematic evidence is forthcoming from a series of surveys conducted in the 1990s to assess public opinion and tastes regarding visual art, especially painting. In 1993, two Russian émigré "conceptual artists" named Vitaly Komar and Alexander Melamid commissioned a public-opinion research firm in Boston to conduct the first statistical survey ever undertaken of Americans' likes and dislikes in painting.[216] Partly financed by The Nation Institute (affiliated with *The Nation* magazine), the telephone poll was eventually replicated in other countries throughout the world, with remarkably similar results.[217]

As documented in the whimsically titled volume *Painting by Numbers: Komar and Melamid's Scientific Guide to Art*, edited by JoAnn Wypijewski (a senior editor at *The Nation*), 1,001 persons from diverse economic, educational, and social strata across the nation responded to a broad range of questions regarding their preferences in visual art. While one may quarrel with the wording of some of the questions,[218] the results are nevertheless illuminating—in particular, with respect not only to "abstract art" but to landscape painting as well. Though the term "abstract" was not used in any of the questions, it was clearly implicit in several of them. Regarding the selection of "pictures, photographs or other pieces of art" for their home, for example, respondents replied as to whether they tended to prefer "traditional" (64%) or "modern" (25%) styles; and "realistic-looking" (60%) or "different-looking" (30%) images. Another question alluded to the issue of intelligibility, asking respondents if they agree (77%) or disagree (22%) with the proposition "Art should be relaxing to look at, not all jumbled up and confusing."

The survey was actually just the first phase of a work of so-called conceptual art by Komar and Melamid entitled *The People's Choice*.[219] Based on the survey data, they created two composite paintings—*America's Most Wanted* and *America's Most Unwanted*—illustrating, in literal terms, the key preferences indicated by the poll.[220] Since the majority of respondents said they liked paintings of, among other things, outdoor scenes, landscapes with bodies of water, groups of fully clothed active people, a historical figure (preferably from the distant past), some animals, and the color blue, *America's Most Wanted* depicts an idyllic wilderness scene with an expansive cloud-tinged blue sky, blue-tinted hills, and a bluish lake mottled with white. A relaxed George Washington stands in the center foreground, while a family group in contemporary dress strolls toward the edge of the lake, seemingly oblivious to the presence of Washington; and a pair of deer standing in the shallow water seem ready to bolt off the lower right edge of the large canvas. More relevant to our concerns here, *America's Most Unwanted*, not surprisingly, is an abstract painting: a small, multicolored, mostly yellow and orange oil-and-acrylic composition of sharply angled geometric forms, whose surface is thickly textured in places. And, though stylistic details differed, the "most unwanted" painting in all the countries surveyed, with one exception, was abstract and angular.[221]

Komar and Melamid did not intend their composite images as art, much less as good art. They are well aware that, as Arthur Danto argues, "No one who wants a painting of wild animals *or* . . . a painting of George Washington wants a painting of George Washington *and* wild animals."[222] Still, their tongue-in-cheek concoctions drove their point home—a point that was inspired, in part, by their respect for ordinary people and by an impatience with the arbitrary elitism of the artworld, in which "there is no objective truth," as Melamid puts it in an interview with *The Nation*.[223] In focus groups and town meetings held before and after the poll, as he recounts, he was struck by the genuine need of those he spoke with "to talk about art . . . for hours and hours."[224] Noting that it was "hard to stop them," he adds: "Nobody ever asks them about art." The "blue landscape" turned out to be "more serious" than he and Komar had expected. "Almost everyone you talk to directly [has] this blue landscape in their head. It is there and it is not a joke." Perhaps the blue landscape is "genetically imprinted in us," he speculates. Further, he notes that the people he spoke to seemed to be "looking for words to express themselves . . . it was foreign territory. . . . [T]hey were very passionate. . . . But they don't have the words. . . . There needs to be written . . . a book."[225] Above all, Melamid rejects as "the wrong premise" the idea that people "need some special historical knowledge in order to appreciate art."

Predictably, the artworld derided the Komar and Melamid project. As noted by Wypijewski, for example: "The *Philadelphia Inquirer*'s art critic, Edward J. Sozanski, sniffed: '. . . [If] much contemporary art has little to say to ordinary people . . . [it's only] because Americans want to be soothed and reassured, not stimulated. They want decoration, not intellectual challenge. Sixty percent of the respondents agreed with this statement: *I only like to look at art that makes me happy.* There just isn't much of an audience for any kind of art . . . that traffics in ideas.'" (61) Wypijewski comments that sheer *pleasure* in art did not figure "in the cognoscenti's discussion of this project"; they tended to agree that "what people 'like' (always in quotation marks) is simplistic, illegitimate, even cynical as a line of inquiry." (75) In a panel discussion by artworld experts about the poll, at the School of Visual Arts in New York City in 1994, David Ross (then director of the Whitney Museum) observed that when you ask questions about preference, you are "'playing with people's predispositions and presumptions about what . . . art . . . is'"; but this has "'nothing'" at all to do with art, in his view.[226] Wypijewski, herself an "ordinary person" in relation to the artworld, is understandably troubled by the unrelenting condescension of such rhetoric:

Certainly, those New York panelists all made a lunge in the direction of something they called democracy and the responsibility of the artist to an audience. But I couldn't help hear the scold of Authority in the one's declaration of 'the idiocy of these blue landscapes,' [in the others'] analogy between the poll's questions and 'asking illiterate people to judge poetry.'

Illiterate people judged Shakespeare all the time in his day. They had little patience for *Troilus and Cressida* . . . just like so many critics . . . today. They loved *Lear*, which has lost none of its honor over the centuries. Why should painting be so different? Why the assumption that public taste must be base, possibly evil, perhaps even irrelevant? If "literate people" could love landscapes without fear of ridicule a hundred years ago, why should a preference for "outdoor scenes," for "realistic-looking" pictures, for representations of "lakes, rivers, oceans, and seas," now be, as one cybercritic put it, a sign of "how dismal this country's view of art is"? . . . . Why did so many readers of *The Nation* and visitors to the Dia Center's World Wide Website[227] on the art poll—in both cases disproportionately well-educated, liberal, and museum-loving—see in the poll results a "mandate for missionary work among the backward masses"? [76]

In contrast with such readers—who belong, in effect, to the "artworld public" we alluded to in Chapter 6—Wypijewski respects the taste of ordinary people like herself, viewing it as a sign of "landscape's special power to invite the viewer in—and perhaps [of] its special *pleasure* as well."

Art in the Home

By an odd coincidence, at about the same time that Komar and Melamid released the results of their "People's Choice" project, the sociologist David Halle published *Inside Culture*, an unprecedented study of ordinary people's taste in the visual arts, which largely corroborated the key findings of their poll.[228] Halle's method was simple and direct: with a research assistant, he visited people in their homes, walked through the rooms, noted the art displayed, and interviewed the owners regarding the meaning it held for them. He selected 160 homes in urban and suburban neighborhoods in and around New York City, ranging from Manhattan's affluent Upper East Side to working-class and immigrant sections of Brooklyn and Long Island. Halle's findings, as Wypijewski noted, "animate the ['People's Choice'] poll's plain numbers." What they show, in part, is that, as she put it, "across class and race and profession, people like landscapes best"—and abstract art least. (78)

The impetus for Halle's study—which was informed by a familiarity with art history and criticism (including the problematic definition of art)—was the knowledge that, for every period prior to the modern, art has been studied mainly in relation to the context in which it was originally displayed and viewed. Historically, in Western culture, the primary context for contemporary art has been, increasingly, the private home, yet there have been few studies of the visual arts in this context.[229] With respect to the twentieth century, Halle accurately observes, major developments in the history of taste have not been sufficiently explained. "We do not fully understand why abstract art took hold, why the painted portrait declined, . . . [or] why landscape depictions took a particular form." And we know very little about the "audience" for abstract painting and sculpture or "the actual meaning of abstract art to those who purchase and view it." (1–3) Twentieth-century art history has focused on the role of artists, and has tended to "deduce the meanings [art] must have" for ordinary people, while critics tend to "ratify" as "art" any works produced by "artists."[230] (5) In the process, no one has adequately accounted for phenomena such as the "apparent inaccessibility to an ordinary audience of much twentieth-century painting." (8)

Halle's findings regarding ordinary people's responses to "abstract art"[231] are, consistent with the argument we have developed in this chapter. First, an outright dislike of abstract art was widespread—prevalent in all but one of the neighborhoods studied, and even there it was shared by a sizable minority of the individuals interviewed. As illuminating as the statistical distribution of responses were the comments and reasons offered: respondents in all groups repeatedly expressed the view that abstract art is a fraud perpetrated by people who cannot really draw or paint. Such a view, often derided as unsophisticated by critics, was by no means limited to working-class individuals. An architect residing on the Upper East Side of Manhattan, for example, declared:

> Abstract art? It's a zero! It's something foisted on us by charlatans and sold by charlatans. . . . [Adolph] Gottlieb, [Robert] Motherwell, they're frauds. Jackson Pollock is the worst. Abstract art became a highly intellectual thing. But art has to have an immediate feeling. If I see a Rembrandt, it has an immediacy. You don't have to have someone writing a book about it. [127]

A woman residing in suburban Manhasset was equally irreverent: "I stand looking at two blobs, trying to find a meaning in it." The charge that abstract art is meaningless was, in fact, the objection most often raised by upper-class Manhattanites who disliked it. Other respondents complained that it is "cold," "harsh," and "unemotional."

Even more revealing than such negative judgments, however, were the specific comments of respondents who *like* abstract art. Not surprisingly, the only neighborhood in which a majority of individuals expressed such a liking and displayed abstract art in their homes, was both affluent and urban. Presumably, such individuals are among the "elite" whom theorists of abstract art often allude to (as we have noted above): that is, those rare individuals of superior intelligence, education, and taste who have the capacity to appreciate the purported depth and complexity of abstract painting and sculpture. The surprise is that, when asked *why* they like it, more than half of these individuals pointed not to any profound meaning but to decorative qualities—the dread specter that abstract artists have perennially inveighed against.[232] "[T]hey're colorful. They brighten up the wall." "I like the colors. . . . I think of how it will blend into the room." "To me it's . . . basically design." "I love Mondrian. . . . I see balance and color in the paintings." Finally, a respondent who happened to be a friend of the abstract painter Helen Frankenthaler's declared that he likes "[t]he colors, the total look" of her later paintings. "They don't mean anything to me," he added. "I don't know if they're meant to mean anything."[233]

Also striking was Halle's finding that "[d]epictions of the landscape[234] pervade the houses studied. Hills and mountains, meadows, oceans, rivers and bays, trees and bushes, skies that are clear—such scenes, in endless combinations, are the most popular [subject] of the pictures on the walls of all social classes." (59) Why are individuals drawn to such paintings? Overwhelmingly, respondents cited "the tranquility of the subject matter." They liked these pictures "because they are 'calm,' 'restful'; they offer 'solitude' and 'quiet'; they soothe."

The overwhelming preference for landscape paintings documented by Halle, as well as by the Komar and Melamid poll, seems to point to a basic human need—something more significant than the banal suggestion offered by Arthur Danto: that people are familiar with images of landscapes from their frequent use on calendars and that they simply prefer what is familiar to them.[235] In our view, the value of *solitude* (and related states of being), cited or implied by many respondents, suggests a powerful motivation for being drawn into a peaceful landscape setting. As it happens, two books on the subject published in recent years indirectly shed light on this issue. Though neither author mentions landscape painting as such, it is surely no accident that the cover of each book features a painted landscape. As the British psychiatrist Anthony Storr persuasively argues in *Solitude: A Return to the Self*, solitude must be cultivated "if the brain is to function at its best, and if the individual is to fulfill his highest potential. . . . Learning, thinking, and maintaining contact with one's own inner world are all facilitated by solitude." (28) The painting on the cover of Storr's book—*Max Schmitt in the Single Scull* (1871) by Thomas Eakins[236]—depicts a single figure in the foreground, drifting in a small racing boat on a river, who turns slightly to peer over his shoulder at the viewer. Though a few other figures in shells are visible in the distance, in addition to a bridge indicating the presence of civilization, the aura of tranquility is palpable, and one has the sense that Schmitt, though momentarily distracted, will soon be alone again with his thoughts.

Even more relevant to the Halle survey is the cover illustration for *Solitude: A Philosophical Encounter*, a richly reflective study by Philip Koch—who characterizes solitude as "the luminous silent space of freedom, of self and nature, of reflection and creative power . . . [where] we feel and see and contemplate with a freshness scarcely to be believed." Appropriately, a luminous landscape, *The Coast of Labrador* (1866), by the American painter William Bradford,[237] is featured on the cover of Koch's book. In the lower left foreground, a solitary fisherman sits in his rowboat in a calm, protected cove, sheltered by imposing bluffs beneath a great expanse of misty sky. Such depictions of solitude in natural settings suggest that landscapes (with or without people) appeal to viewers, in part, because one can project one's self into the scene and experience, vicariously, a psychological state that is profoundly necessary for the most private and deeply personal workings of the mind.

Killing the Messenger

For those who regard abstract art as a sacroscant feature of high modern culture, Halle is the bearer of systematically culled bad tidings. Thus it is little suprise that a review of his book by Roger Kimball,[228] a confirmed apologist for the genre, simple ignores his most salient findings—that the majority of ordinary people intensely dislike abstract painting, many even regarding it as fraudulent; and that those who do like it, collecting and displaying it in their homes, tend to regard it as decoration. Unable to rebut the evident implication of such data—that abstract painting may not be art—Kimball mainly resorts to *ad hominem* argument by innuendo.[229]

Kimball begins his piece with a gratuitous anecdote about "poor Jedediah Buxton," an obscure eighteenth-century *idiot savant* who was obsessed with the counting of things, such as the number of words spoken by an actor or the number of steps executed by dancers in a performance, and whose knowledge was otherwise "extremely limited." While reading Halle's book, Kimball was often reminded of that pathetic figure. Halle's "statistical approach to artistic phenonmena," he declares, is in some respects "reminiscent of Buxton's." In truth, Halle did much more than mindlessly tally what he saw and heard—but the poor reader dependent on Kimball's account would not know this.

"Halle thinks that up until now we have all misunderstood the social context of modern art," Kimball continues. "We have listened far too much to what artists and critics say about art and have not devoted enough attention to investigating what people—real people like you and me—look at in their homes." Never mind that Kimball is not the "real" person he pretends to be, but is among the very "critics" people have "listened far too much too." Indeed, his entire review offers singular evidence of the counterfeit elitism that has tainted critical thought about abstract art since its inception.

After depreciating Halle's motives and methodology, at length, Kimball focuses on some of his minor findings, devoting an entire paragraph to an analysis of an admittedly flawed interpretation of a decline in popularity of images of the Last Supper. He also dismisses what he characterizes as Halle's contention that "the rise of abstract art is associated with the 'decline' of elaborately decorated wallpaper"—falsely implying that Halle attributes the creation of abstract work to this trend, when, in fact, he clearly stipulates that he is referring only to its domestic purchase.

Finding Halle's book to be "very funny indeed," Kimball ends his piece with a distorted account of an incident Halle relates in his acknowledgements—concerning an unpleasant encounter with the prominent modernist architect I. M. Pei, whose name happened to have been included in the random sample of subjects for the study. Owing to an unfortunate set of circumstances, in which Halle was in no way at fault, he and his assistant were, as he relates, "summarily evicted and rebuked" by Pei for "trying this kind of research." Kimball's account of the incident conveniently ignores the latter phrase, as well as the chance events that had contributed to the misunderstanding. Having begun by impugning Halle's intellect, he concludes with this veiled slur on his integrity: "I've always admired Mr. Pei as an architect. I am pleased now to have a reason to admire his judgement of character as well."

Kimball's piece contrasts sharply with another review of Halle's book, by Maureen Corrigan. As she correctly observes, it challenges the "reductive ideas about art, taste and class" too long promulgated by the by the "snooty guardians of culture"—among whom Kimball must surely be included. Corrigan (who teaches literature at Georgetown University and reviews books for a variety of publications) concludes with a sympathetic nod to the majority of readers: "Halle has written a fascinating book that will open the eyes of anybody who's ever glibly said about art, 'I know what I like.' After reading *Inside Culture*, they'll also know a little bit more about why.[230]

9

Photography:
An Invented "Art"

Soon after the invention of photography in the first half of the nineteenth century, the question arose as to whether this new means of picture-making should be considered an art form. Despite numerous arguments pro and con, the matter has never been fully resolved—largely owing, no doubt, to the lack of a clear understanding of the concept of art itself. In recent decades, the view that photography *is* art has been rapidly gaining acceptance in the artworld.[1] Yet the nagging question persists, "Is photography art?" Many people still doubt that photography is an art form, though they may not be able to say exactly why. Rand's argument, in "Art and Cognition" and elsewhere, that photography is *not* art, is essentially correct, in our view, but it is only briefly stated and therefore apt to be dismissed. In this chapter we expand upon that argument in relation to her theory of art, and apply it to a critique of recent attempts to elevate photography to the status of art—in the light of historical considerations regarding its classification.

Rand's Argument

In distinguishing photography from the art of painting, Rand focuses on the process by which the photographic image is formed:

> [Photography] is a technical, not a creative, skill. Art requires a selective re-creation. A camera cannot perform the basic task of painting: a visual conceptualization, i.e., the creation of a concrete in terms of abstract[ed] essentials.

The [photographer's] selection of camera angles, lighting or lenses is merely a selection of the means to reproduce various aspects of the given, i.e., of an existing concrete.[2]

Several brief remarks on photography which Rand made in earlier contexts help to illuminate her argument here. In the first of her lectures on fiction-writing, for example, she pointedly contrasted photography and journalism with painting and fiction, arguing that, unlike painting,

> Photography is a mechanical means of reproducing whatever is put in front of the camera. When you speak of an "artistic" photograph, what you mean is that the photographer exercised [some] choice in his [selection and] arrangement of the material which his camera is to reproduce. . . . But the mere process of photographing, the mechanical part of it, is not art, because no choice is involved: the camera operates the same way regardless of the nature of the material.[3]

In contrast, painting is an art, Rand explains, "because everything about it is selective; not only the subject and the way in which it is going to be executed, but [also] the process of execution, is a process of constant choice." This is a crucial distinction, for what emerges from that process, as Rand emphasizes in "Art and Cogniton," is a *visual conceptualization*—a concrete image that stands for a broader idea pertaining to the artist's fundamental values or view of life.

In both "What Is Romanticism?" and "The Goal of My Writing," Rand again referred to photography, implying that—unlike fiction, which selectively re-creates reality according to the writer's values, through a process of imaginative integration—photography in effect *documents* reality through a "lens directed at the range of the immediate moment." (117) It reproduces, "indiscriminately and unselectively," an aspect of "given concretes" as they actually are.[4] Like the reporter or the historian, the photographer records, or captures, things as they exist in "real life." (164)

Rand's emphasis on the process of execution as the primary criterion for distinguishing between photography and painting is neither trivial nor arbitrary. Even theorists who claim that photography is art readily acknowledge that the mechanical means by which photographs are produced is absolutely essential to their nature. As we shall see, what one writer characterizes as the "mechanical and mindless"[5] nature of the photographic process not only determines the fundamental relationship between reality and the images formed but also profoundly influences the way in which photographs are interpreted and experienced. Rand herself did not pursue these important implications.

But other thinkers have done so in depth—among them, Susan Sontag and Roger Scruton. While providing a fuller and subtler analysis of the essential nature of photography than Rand did, each corroborates her view that it is not art—though neither unequivocally draws that conclusion, which would require a clearly defined concept of art.[6] In the discussion that follows, we shall refer frequently to their ideas.

What Photography Is

Nearly all writers who analyze the nature of photography concur with Rand in emphasizing the limitations of the photographer's role as compared to the painter's. Since photography is, as she stated, a "mechanical means of reproducing whatever is put in front of the camera," the photographer is constrained in both his choice of subject and his treatment of it. First, he can select his subject only from the actual objects and events accessible to him. Whereas a painter imaginatively "constructs" an image, Sontag observes, a photographer merely "discloses" something that exists. (92) In contrast with a work of art, which is created by its maker "on a 'blank slate' bit by bit over time,"[7] the photographic image is formed more or less instantaneously, by the action of light on a chemically sensitized surface. The photographer—unlike the composer, painter, sculptor, or poet—does not select and shape every minute detail of the work. Though he may choose, for instance, the angle or perspective from which he will photograph a given subject—a person, say—unlike a painter he cannot modify or rearrange various features, such as a strand of hair or the set of the mouth.[8] Once the photographer releases the shutter, the camera takes over, indiscriminately recording everything reflected in the light caught by the lens. So, too, the variables of the print process (type of light, exposure time, quality of paper, and so on) affect the final image in an indiscriminate manner. Finally, such choices—as well as the photographer's decisions regarding type of lens and film, lighting conditions, and exposure time—will uniformly affect the entire subject: he cannot selectively control their impact on each element of the image.

Moreover, since any visual field exceeds an individual's capacity to perceive it in full detail, the camera always captures more on film than the photographer can be aware of. But a painter is able to check back and forth between the subject and the evolving image on his canvas, and select or alter details at each stage. As noted by William Henry Fox Talbot (1800–1877), the British inventor of the first direct photographic process on paper, the camera lens "often discloses a multitude of minute details, which were previously unobserved and unsuspected" and "the operator himself discovers on examination, perhaps long afterwards, that he has depicted many things he had no notion of at the time."[9] As Talbot further observed, such details are often irrelevant. Consequently, the viewer cannot be certain which details of a given image were deliberately chosen by the photographer because he deemed them significant, and which were merely accidental and unintentional—a point also emphasized by Scruton.[10] While a painting, too, may take on a meaning that the artist was unaware of or did not intend, the viewer may at least assume that the work owes its ultimate physical appearance to the artist's intentional actions. Even elements dictated by tradition or by the wishes of a patron are mediated through the mind and hand of the painter. While many outstanding photographs are "lucky accidents," a compelling work of art is always the product of an artist's deliberate application of skill, talent and imagination.[11] For all these reasons, Scruton explains, a photographic image is properly regarded not as a representation or "an interpretation of reality" but rather as a "presentation of how something looked. In some sense looking at a photograph is a substitute for looking at the thing itself."[12] (588)

Unlike a photograph, Scruton emphasizes, a painting does not prompt us to assume that its subject actually existed or that, if it did exist, it is necessarily represented as it was in every detail. (578–79) Instead,

we are dealing with an object that is manifestly the expression of thought. . . . [T]o understand a painting involves understanding thoughts [which] are, in a sense, communicated by the painting. They underlie the painter's intention, and at the same time, they inform our way of seeing the canvas. [580–81]

When we look at an equestrian portrait, for example,

We see not only a man on a horse but a man of a certain character and bearing. And what we see is determined not by independent properties of the subject but by our understanding of the painting. It is the way the eyes are painted that gives that sense of authority, the particular lie of the arm that reveals the arrogant character. . . . The picture presents us not merely with the perception of a man but with a thought about him, a thought embodied in perceptual form. [581]

Scruton's "thought embodied in perceptual form" strikingly recalls Rand's idea of a *visual conceptualization,* as well as her dictum that "*Art brings man's concepts to the perceptual level of his consciousness and allows him to grasp them directly, as if they were percepts.*" (see above, Chapter 1). Since an artist's thoughts are conveyed not merely by the subject but by the way he renders it, the question of style is a major consideration in painting, while (as both Scruton and Sontag emphasize) it is of lesser significance in photography, in which the subject (what the image is *of*) is always of primary importance. That is why Sontag is correct to observe: "It makes senses that a painting is signed but a photograph is not (or it seems bad taste if it is). The very nature of photography implies an equivocal relation to the photographer as *auteur*." As she further notes: "Many of the published photographs by photography's greatest names seem like work that could have been done by another gifted professional of their period." (133–34) Such a statement could never be made about masterpieces of painting.

Because a painting (like any work of art) is the product of intentional selectivity in all its details, "the question, Why?"— as Scruton argues—"can be asked of every observable feature, even if it may sometimes prove impossible to answer." (593) No such search for meaning is justified with respect to a photograph, however, since there are few, if any, ways in which the photographer can reveal his intentions. Only the sort of selective representation and stylization of a subject that occurs in painting offers such clues to intended meaning. As the "expression of a process of thought," Scruton concludes, a painting

> can be understood in isolation from the special circumstances of its creation because each and every feature . . . can be both the upshot of an intentional act and at the same time the creation of an intentional object. The interest in the intentional object becomes an interest in the thought which it conveys. A painter can fill his canvas with meaning in just the way that a writer may fill his prose. That is what makes painting and literature into representational arts: . . . they . . . can be . . . understood in terms of a descriptive thought which they articulate. [597]

Historical Considerations

As Sontag emphasizes, photography began as a scientific invention, "a means of easing the burden of ever accumulating information and sense impressions." She notes that "the earliest photographers talked as if the camera were a copying machine; as if, while people operate cameras, it is the camera that sees." (87–88) In fact,

> The camera suggested itself to Fox Talbot as a new form of notation whose allure was precisely that it was impersonal—because it recorded a "natural" image; that is, an image which comes into being "by the agency of Light alone, without any aid whatever from the artist's pencil." [88]

Thus the photographer was thought of as, in Sontag's words, "an acute but non-interfering observer—a scribe, not a poet." (88) As another writer, Hans Koning, has put it, the invention of photography was inspired by the wish to get nature "to draw her own portrait with light as her pencil." Unlike Sontag, however, he argues that *"surely what isn't art at its conception cannot be made into art by the passing of years or even centuries."*[13] As we shall note in later chapters, the fallacy that an activity or product which was *not* an art form at its inception could "become," or be elevated to, the status of art at a later date pervades twentieth-century esthetic theory and criticism. In contrast, Rand was correct to argue that the primary art forms are determined by human nature, not by technological advances or authoritarian fiat.

Soon after its invention, as we have noted, the question of whether photography is an art (as well as the related question of the criteria by which its images should be judged) became an issue; and it has been debated ever since. As early as 1851, one photographer deemed himself an artist, exhibiting his work in the fine arts section of the Great Exhibition of Works of Industry of All Nations, held in England, while his soberer colleagues displayed theirs in the section devoted to "Philosophical Instruments and Objects Depending on their Use"—that is, in exhibits pertaining to such physical phenomena as optics and light.[14]

Both positions were reflected in an 1855 editorial in the journal of the Photographic Society of London. The writer argued that photography was a fine art insofar as the "true photographic artist" shared with the painter an appreciation of "the pictorial value of natural effects, and . . . of the beautiful and the sublime in nature"; but that, with respect to the printing of the images, which required only "skilful mechanical manipulation," it belonged with the manufacturing arts, sharing with them "the capability of indefinite multiplication and wide diffusion of their products."[15] Eventually, the idea emerged that photography should be classified as "an independent art" (that is, apart from both the mechanical and the fine arts)—a term that employed the word "art" in its broad sense of discipline or skill.[16]

In subsequent years, the debate over the status of photography shifted from a focus on the photographic process to an emphasis on the images produced and the qualities they shared with paintings. Toward the end of the nineteenth century in America, for example, a group of photographers eager to be recognized as artists deliberately emulated painterly effects by utilizing soft-focus techniques and manipulating the negatives and the print process. Borrowing esthetic ideas from the paintings of Whistler, Symbolist literature, French philosophy, and Japanese art, these "Pictorialists" produced romantically sensuous images, printed on textured paper. Then, as now, however, some critics objected that the sort of manipulation they employed violated the essence of the medium and undermined its unique value.

Ironically, one of the leading Pictorialists was Alfred Stieglitz,[17] who relentlessly campaigned to have their work recognized as art. Around 1910, he abandoned Pictorialism in favor of the "straight' (or "pure") photography for which he became famous—sharp-focused images which were not altered in any way.[18] Nonetheless, he claimed that these images, which looked more like photographic records of reality than painterly re-creations, were "art" as well—a claim that no doubt opened the door to the eventual consideration of photojournalism, fashion photography, and scientific photography, among other genres, as art, too.

In the course of the twentieth century, museums of art have elevated every variety of photographic image, however mundane, to the status of art. Although Stieglitz had to struggle for nearly a decade to persuade an American museum that photographs were worthy of exhibiting and collecting as art, after 1910 (when the Albright Knox Gallery in Buffalo was the first to capitulate to his claims) virtually every major American museum of art followed suit. The first photographic department in an American museum had actually been established in 1889, in the Brooklyn Museum; but its photographic collection was merely documentary and archival, for the museum was then devoted primarily to natural history and anthropology. Remarkably, much of even that collection is now regarded as art.[19]

Similarly, the Department of Photographs of New York's Metropolitan Museum of Art—which was established as an independent curatorial department in 1992—seems to include any type of photograph as art. Its collection of over 15,000 images ranges from straightforward photojournalism subjects, such as the 1937 explosion of the dirigible Hindenburg, to austere abstractions by modernist photographers. The Solomon R. Guggenheim Foundation has likewise embarked on a course of action to establish photography as a full-fledged art form. In 1992, it entered into a "permanent association" with the Robert Mapplethorpe Foundation—which had been formed by the controversial photographer in the year before his death, and which aims, in part, "to further the recognition of photography *as an art form as important as painting and sculpture*."[20] Finally, in perhaps the most blatant case of elevating photographs to the status of art, the Museum of Modern Art in New York (which is credited with being the first museum to systematically collect and exhibit photography in the same manner as painting) in 1997 exhibited a series of identification photographs that the Khmer Rouge had taken of their hapless torture victims.[21]

Contemporary Critical Views

As we have indicated, the artworld's virtually unanimous classification of photography as art[22] (like its legitimization of "abstract art") rests on the flimsiest of premises. Often the assumption of art status is merely asserted, with no argument whatever—yet another expression of what we term the authoritarian theory of art. Grace Glueck, for example, writing about Mapplethorpe's photographs, pronounces them art because they "are intended as art, presented as such, and are judged to be art by those qualified in such matters."[23] Hilton Kramer, too, considers them works of art, albeit reluctantly, explaining: "I know of no way to exclude them from the realm of art."[24] And some of the century's most acclaimed photographers—such as Dorothea Lange and Henri Cartier-Bresson—have been dubbed "artists" by the artworld despite their own vigorous denials.[25] As an amateur painter who well understands at first hand the essential difference between the two activities, Cartier-Bresson has been particularly outspoken in declaring that *no* photography is art. "There are no more craftsmen," he laments. "Now everybody's an 'artist.' What rubbish! Photography—it's an artisan's thing."[26]

Yet Lange and Cartier-Bresson are exceptions. Other photographers may sense what these two openly declare, though they proclaim the opposite. As Sontag observes:

> Like other steadily aggrandizing enterprises, photography has inspired its leading practitioners with a need to explain, again and again, what they are doing and why it is valuable. . . . Nothing is more acceptable today than the photographic recycling of reality, . . . as a branch of high art. Yet something about photography still keeps the first-rate professionals defensive and hortatory: virtually every important photographer right up to the present has written manifestoes and credos expounding photography's moral and aesthetic mission. [115]

The "something" that Sontag alludes to, of course, is the very nature of the photographer's craft, with all its limitations.

Despite concerted efforts by such photographers, as well as by critics, curators, and other members of the artworld, photography's alleged status as an art form "remains clouded over with residual doubts" among ordinary people, as Deborah Solomon acknowledges in an article entitled "But Is It Art?"— about Maria Morris Hambourg, the chief curator of photography at the Metropolitan Museum of Art.[27] Solomon tentatively attributes these doubts to the fact that photography is "a democratic medium," further noting: "Most people don't paint or draw, but most everyone owns a camera." We would add that most people also possess enough sense to know that something that virtually anyone can do without an ounce of talent or skill cannot be art. Astonishingly, Solomon's observation that "[a]mateurs have taken pictures that can hold their own beside the work of acknowledged masters" does not lead her to question their status as art. And she does not hesitate to accept as "'fine-art' photographs" the examples in an album entitled "Girls I Have Known," one of Hambourg's shrewd purchases for the Metropolitan. A collection of forty-eight photos taken by an amateur photographer of high-school girls he admired, the album is, according to Solomon, "a humble, unsung example of folk photography."[28] (64) As for Hambourg's rationale (she eschews theory—as she explains, she simply "'likes to look at pictures'"), the "Girls I Have Known" album attracted her because "'it really allows you to track the mind of a nut.'" Such inanity notwithstanding, Hambourg has been rumored as a potential successor to the director of the world-renowned museum.[29]

Postmodern Photography

Since the 1970s, a purportedly new movement in photography has developed, loosely subsumed under the catchall term "Postmodernist," though precedents for it can be found in earlier twentieth-century avant-garde experiments. According to Andy Grundberg and Kathleen Gauss, co-curators of *Photography and Art: Interactions since 1946*, however, what distinguishes the new movement is the photographers' use of the medium for the "expression of their personal visions" rather than for "objectively recording the world."[30] Absurdly attributing the documentary character of photography not to the fundamental nature of the medium as such but, rather, to a "modernist agenda" that chose to separate it from the art of painting, Grundberg and Gauss argue that "it no longer seems appropriate to distinguish them as two categories of expression, or to view photography as a medium unto itself," adding that such a distinction "may have been unnecessary in the first place." (15)

Yet, as Grundberg himself points out in his essay "Conceptual Art and the Photography of Ideas" in the exhibition catalog, the new "photographic art" merely employs photography as a means of recording or documenting a variety of allegedly artistic (more often "conceptual") concerns or activities. Examples range from Edward Ruscha's pseudo-documentary books of photographs, such as *Twenty-Six Gasoline Stations*, to Cindy Sherman's photographs of herself in various costumes and guises intended to make some kind of feminist statement. Since there is art neither in the photographic process, however, nor (as we shall argue in Chapter 14) in the "conceptual art" documented by the images, there is no justification for regarding such work as *art*.

10

Architecture: "Art" or "Design"?

Architecture is endowed with a special importance in Rand's fiction. As the profession of *The Fountainhead*'s hero, Howard Roark, it is a subject that she researched in some depth, even working in the office of a prominent New York architect for six months in the late 1930s.[1] In her preparatory notes for the novel, she wrote that architecture is "the most important of the arts."[2] Both implicitly and explicitly, *The Fountainhead* exalts the value of architecture, and represents Roark as a paragon of human creativity.[3] Rand's dedicatory note reads, in part: "to the great profession of architecture and its heroes who have given us some of the highest expressions of man's genius." In one scene of the novel, she compares architecture to music, characterizing the homes designed by Roark for his Monadnock Valley resort village, as "variations on a single theme, like a symphony played by an inexhaustible imagination," further suggesting that the buildings are "the promise of [certain] music . . . made real" and that "architecture [is] music in stone."[4]

Yet, in her essays on art, which were written nearly a quarter of a century after *The Fountainhead*, Rand says virtually nothing about either the theory or the practice of architecture. Her remarks are limited to a few cursory and problematic statements in "Art and Cognition," including this allusion to the novel: "I shall not include architecture in this discussion—I assume the reader knows which book I will refer him to." Contrary to her implication, however, a fictional treatment cannot take the place of a philosophic analysis. Moreover, what little she does say about the nature of architecture in "Art and Cognition" is obviously inconsistent with her theory of art. Since the resultant contradictions are not likely to have escaped her notice, it is reasonable to surmise that she simply avoided confronting them (contrary to her own strictures against evasion), for it would have required her to radically revise either her theory of art or her estimate of architecture, in which she had so largely invested in *The Fountainhead*. Anyone seeking to assess her theory of art, however, must examine her conflicting claims regarding architecture.

Rand's Theoretical Position

In her principal statement on architecture in "Art and Cognition," Rand clearly holds that it differs from the major arts in fundamental respects, and that it should therefore not be classified among them:

> Architecture is in a class by itself, because it combines art with a utilitarian purpose and does not re-create reality,[5] but creates a structure for man's habitation or use, expressing man's values. [46]

This proposition is flawed in several respects, however. First, Rand's claim that architecture is "in a class by itself" is meaningless in any but a loosely colloquial sense, meaning "unique," since the term "class" refers, by definition, to a set of entities sharing certain characteristics. In any case, the claim is invalid, for architecture *is* comparable (in kind though not in scale) to many other man-made entities that combine utility with esthetic and psychological appeal, as we shall argue below. Furthermore, given Rand's definition of art, the contradiction implicit in her proposition about architecture is evident—particularly so if the genus of her definition is substituted for the term "art." Her statement would then read, in part: *Architecture . . . combines a selective re-creation of reality with a utilitarian purpose and does not re-create reality.* Rand further confounds the issue when she observes that, in relation to the human cognitive faculties, "architecture, *qua art*, is close to sculpture" because "its field is three-dimensional, i.e., [that of] sight and touch, but [it is] transposed to a grand spatial scale." (46) Since architecture "does not re-create reality," however, it can be compared only to *abstract* sculpture, which Rand properly excludes from the realm of art. Still more confusing is the fact that she subsequently refers to architecture (along with painting and sculpture) as one of the "visual arts"—all of which, she argues, "start with percepts and integrate them [in]to concepts." (47) Not surprisingly, she offers no examples of what such percepts consist of in architecture, and no explanation as to how architecture would effect such an integration.

In addition, Rand had argued at the outset of "The Psycho-Epistemology of Art" that the primary purpose of art is not "material" (i.e., utilitarian), but *psychological*. "[O]ne of the distinguishing characteristics of a work of art . . . is that it serves no practical, material end, but is an end in itself; it serves no purpose other than contemplation." (16) Moreover, in "Art and Cognition" (74) she categorically maintains that "utilitarian objects cannot be classified as works of art."[6] Architecture cannot *combine* "art with a utilitarian purpose," therefore, since the two concepts are mutually exclusive, according to her own definition.[7] As Rand emphasizes in her *Introduction to Objectivist Epistemology*, "the requirements of cognition . . . forbid the arbitrary integration of concepts into a wider concept by means of obliterating their *essential* differences" (71). Thus, one must either substantially revise her definition of art or reject her characterization of architecture.[8]

Batteux's Classification

Rand's problematic claim that architecture belongs in "a class by itself, because it combines art with a utilitarian purpose" calls to mind the classification proposed by an eighteenth-century French theorist, abbé Charles Batteux, whose treatise *Les Beaux-Arts réduits à un même principe* (The fine arts reduced to a common principle) offered the first systematic account of the subject and played a seminal role in the genesis of the concept of art. Like many Enlightenment thinkers, Batteux attempted to identify the essential nature of the fine arts in relation to human skill of all kind—that is, to "the arts in general." Consequently, he (unlike Rand) began by defining "art" in this broad sense—as "a collection or compilation of rules for making well that which can be made [either] well or badly."[9] Such a definition fittingly recalls Aristotle's concept of *technê*, and thus serves as a reminder of the wider sense in which the term *art* was originally understood—a sense that we have argued remains implicit in the narrower meaning of the term at issue here.

Batteux divided "the arts in general" into three categories: the "mechanical arts," serving to fill man's physical needs; the "fine arts," serving only to give pleasure; and a *"third type"*—"which have as their object both usefulness and pleasure at once." Into this third category he placed *architecture* and *rhetoric*, observing that "need has brought them forth, and taste has perfected them: they are something in between the two other kinds [of art]: they partake of both pleasure and utility."[10] (82) Focusing on their relation to the fine arts, he wrote:

[T]hey owed their birth first to necessity; but, having known how to clothe themselves with pleasing ornament, they placed themselves alongside those

[arts] which we call "fine arts." It is thus that architecture, having transformed into pleasant and commodious dwellings the caves which necessity had hollowed out to serve as a shelter for man, merits among the arts [in the broad sense] a distinction which it had not previously had.[11] (103)

Whereas the fine arts—which, for Batteux, comprise "music, poetry,[12] painting, sculpture, and the art of movement, or the dance"—afford pleasure solely through the *imitation* of nature, architecture and rhetoric "employ" nature, "polishing" and "adorning" it for usefulness and pleasure. Though his phrase "employ[ing] nature" is not quite clear, his concept of "imitation" evidently corresponds to the traditional idea of *mimesis*, which is surely not an attribute of architecture in his view, just as Rand clearly states that architecture "does not re-create reality."

D'Alembert's Error

The confusion and equivocation evident in Rand's account of architecture are by no means unique to her. Such contradictions abound in the scholarly literature. In a recent introductory esthetics text, for example, the British philosopher Gordon Graham notes that the "undisputed usefulness of architecture" raises the question of "whether it is properly called an art [i.e., a fine art] at all"—yet he proceeds to analyze it "as an art."[13] Similarly, the *Oxford Dictionary of Art* (1997) uncritically observes that the term "fine arts," which refers to the "nonutilitarian arts," is commonly understood to include architecture "even though [it] is obviously a 'useful' art." The *Dictionary* then cites Batteux's tripartite classification—with architecture included among the arts that "combin[ed] beauty [*sic*] and utility."[14] Why had Batteux's straightforward and sensible classification been superseded by one so obviously illogical? According to the *Dictionary*'s cryptic and inadequate explanation: "Soon after, in Diderot's *Encyclopédie*, the philosopher D'Alembert (1717–83) listed the fine arts as painting, sculpture, architecture, poetry, and music. This list established itself."[15]

The crucial text cited here was the *Preliminary Discourse* (1751) which Jean Le Rond d'Alembert wrote for Denis Diderot's great *Encyclopedia*. D'Alembert's introductory essay set the tone for the entire encyclopedia project, eloquently conveying the spirit of the intellectual revolution underway; it also defined the categories of knowledge that would be covered in the work. His own interests and expertise lay mainly in scientific, mathematical, and practical pursuits, however, not in the fine arts.[16] While he no doubt relied on other authorities regarding these products of the "creative imagination," he ignored certain essential distinctions that earlier writers had drawn between architecture and the "imitative" or "fine" arts.

Contrary to all prior tradition (and to common sense as well), d'Alembert classified architecture as an *imitative* art.[17] Whereas fundamental similarities between the imitative (mimetic) arts of poetry, painting, sculpture, music, and dance had long been observed and analyzed by philosophers, poets, and visual artists, architecture had been traditionally omitted from this group.[18] Moreover, the necessarily flimsy justification d'Alembert offered for including it so attenuated the concept of imitation as to empty it of descriptive or explanatory value. Acknowledging that the imitation of nature in architecture is "less striking and more restricted than in Painting or Sculpture," since the latter "express all the parts of [Nature] . . . without restriction" (a proposition that considerably exaggerates the mimetic range of sculpture), d'Alembert held that architecture "is confined to imitating the *symmetrical arrangement* that Nature observes." (38, emphasis ours) Thus the mimetic quality that is directly and naturally expressive of vital meaning in all the arts is reduced, in his conception of architecture, to the abstract, impersonal property of symmetry.[19] Further, although earlier theorists had appropriately emphasized the *practical* function of architecture in contrast with the *nonutilitarian* nature of the imitative arts, d'Alembert entirely disregarded this fundamental distinction, focusing instead on the shared attribute of imaginative invention. (43, 51) As is often the case with later theorists who nominally include architecture among the fine arts, d'Alembert omitted it when he cited specific examples of art in a comparative context (as does Rand)—no doubt for the simple reason that it is fundamentally incommensurable with them, and therefore does not lend itself to comparative analysis.[20]

D'Alembert's *Preliminary Discourse* became the virtual manifesto of the French Enlightenment and, as such, had an incalculable influence on subsequent art theorists.[21] As Paul Oskar Kristeller observed, "the *Encyclopédie*, and especially its famous introduction, codified the system of the fine arts . . . and through its prestige and authority gave it the widest possible currency all over Europe."[22] Later theorists accepted d'Alembert's classification of architecture as one of the fine arts, while largely ignoring his claim that it is an imitative art—although that claim constituted one of the two criteria for his classification (the other being imaginative invention). Contrary to d'Alembert, they instead emphasized architecture's *abstract* nature, which they then inappropriately compared to the abstract character of music—and, in time, to abstract sculpture.[23]

By historical accident, then, rather than by superior argument, it was d'Alembert's classification, not Batteux's, which became the basis for the "traditional" concept of fine art. Despite d'Alembert's dubious rationale, the idea that architecture is a "fine art" gained wide currency owing simply to his intellectual prestige. Remarkably, the scholars who have most thoroughly traced the origins of the concept of *art* have often blurred the important distinctions between Batteux's common-sense classification and d'Alembert's muddled revision of it.[24] Failing to note the weakness of d'Alembert's argument, they have unquestionably accepted his inclusion of architecture among the fine arts.

The Nature of Architecture

Conceptual clarity is necessary in order to fully understand and appreciate both art and architecture, and to establish rational standards by which each sphere of undertaking may be judged. Anyone wishing to understand the nature of architecture and the fundamental ways in which it differs from art should consider the probing analysis offered by Roger Scruton in his book *The Aesthetics of Architecture*, to which we shall refer frequently in this chapter.[25] Scruton's analysis (which goes far deeper than our few brief references can suggest) tends strongly to corroborate our critique of Rand's statements on architecture, including our conclusion—based on her esthetic theory—that architecture is not art. Nonetheless, like virtually all other writers on the subject, Scruton tacitly accepts the classification of architecture among the fine arts, though he astutely identifies the many respects in which architecture differs from painting, sculpture, music, and literature. Rather than question that classification, he instead questions the validity of theories about art that apply to the major art forms but that, in effect, exclude architecture.[26]

From the outset Scruton acknowledges that architecture presents an "immediate problem" for any esthetic theory, since "through its impersonal and at the same time functional qualities [it] stands apart from the other arts, seeming to require quite peculiar attitudes, not only for its creation, but also for its enjoyment." (5) More specifically, he observes that

> representational arts, such as painting, drama, poetry and sculpture, give rise to an interest unlike the interest aroused by such abstract arts as music and architecture.[27] But . . . music has expressive, sensuous and dramatic powers in common with the representational arts. Only architecture seems to stand wholly apart from them, being distinguished from the other arts by certain features that cannot fail to determine our attitude towards it. [5]

Utilitarian Function

"First among [architecture's] distinguishing features," as Scruton emphasizes, "is utility or function," which accounts for its "strong asymmetry with other forms of art." (5) No one denies that this practical function is the primary factor in architecture—not even those who argue that architecture is art. With the rare exception of memorial structures, the primary impetus for the creation of architecture (in contrast with a work of art) is, invariably, a physical need:

> The utility of a building is not an accidental property; it defines the architect's endeavour. . . . The functional qualities of a building are of its essence, and qualify every task to which the architect addresses himself. . . . The value of a building simply cannot be understood independently of its utility. It is of course *possible* to take a merely 'sculptural' view of architecture; but that is to treat buildings as forms whose aesthetic nature is conjoined only accidentally to a certain function.[28] [6–7]

Whatever "expressive" purposes they may also serve, buildings are created, first and foremost, to provide a sheltered space and facilities for domestic activities, or for such pursuits as industry, business, recreation and religion. A building that does not suit its practical function is unsuccessful, even if it delights the eye or inspires the mind.[29] As one architectural historian has said: "[A]n architect may design an office building that looks beautiful. But if people cannot work comfortably and efficiently in it, the building fails architecturally."[30]

By the very nature of his work, then, the architect is far less autonomous than the composer, painter, poet, or sculptor. Typically, he builds for others, not for himself. The needs and preferences of the client must, in any case of conflict, take priority over his own desire to "express" his values. As Scruton emphasizes, the architect is "constrained at every point by influences which forbid him the luxury of a self-consciously 'artistic' aim." (17) He does not "create architecture in a vacuum"; he requires "real human beings to be sheltered," the "real contours" and "definite vistas" of a site to be reckoned with, and even a knowledge of allowable costs.[31]

Furthermore, successful architectural design is thoroughly integrated with, and largely dependent upon, its surroundings, as well as upon its intended function. It is, in a real sense, *site-specific*. Ideally, the design of a building takes account of salient environmental features, whether *natural*, as in a rural setting, or *man-made*, as on an urban site. An "art work remains intact, an entity complete in itself, an achieved, realized, immovable fact of reality"— as Rand observed in "The Goal of My Writing," (170). A work of architecture is *not* an entity complete in itself, however—contrary to her claim.[32] As Scruton argues, buildings (unlike works of art) cannot undergo a change of site "without absurd and disastrous consequences."[33] (10) In sum, to "talk of architecture as though it were a self-dependent art form" is entirely inappropriate, in his view. "Once again," he adds, "we seem to have discovered a factor which leads away from the manner in which we are commonly held to appreciate art." (12)

Scruton further stresses that works of architecture "are also affected to an incalculable extent by changes in their surroundings" (10), since much of the impact of a building depends on its site—which the architect exploits but does not create. As Frank Lloyd Wright noted, for instance, the site "determined the features and character" of the home he designed at Taliesin.[34] And the dramatic effect of his acclaimed *Fallingwater* owes at least as much to the spectacular natural setting as it does to his skill in harmonizing the forms and materials of the structure with the horizontal platforms of bedrock and the dramatic cascades of water. Indeed, the integration of buildings with nature was what Wright envisioned in his celebrated theory of "organic architecture."[35] In that integration, nature, not art, establishes the terms.

Finally, on any given project, the architect must devote much of his attention to a multitude of mundane practical considerations, from engineering problems to plumbing, heating, and ventilation—concerns that are not readily integrated or reconciled with the expression of the sort of spiritual values or emotional states with which the arts are exclusively concerned.[36] Moreover, owing in part to the variety of functions which most buildings, public or private, must serve, the major esthetic impact of a work of architecture is largely confined to the most prominent part of the building, such as the façade or the principal interior space. These parts are the most expressive of the building's character, while the subsidiary rooms and spaces are often blandly functional by comparison. In the case of Wright's Guggenheim Museum, for example, it is the soaring, light-filled, domed interior space with its upward-spiraling ramp that delights visitors—not the adjoining gallery spaces or the low-ceilinged corridors connecting them. With few exceptions (most notably, Gothic cathedrals), therefore, the building as a whole is rarely experienced as an integrated esthetic entity— in contrast with works of art.

Architecture and Values

Those who hold that architecture *is* art claim that esthetically designed buildings produce the same kind of pleasure as works of art do. For traditional theorists, who tend to identify art with the creation and perception of beauty, that pleasure can be found in the harmonious proportions and sensuous materials of architecture, with no need of representational or expressive meaning. From the perspective of Rand's esthetic theory, however, the primary pleasure derived from art does not depend on such abstract factors but on the concretization or expression of fundamental values. In what respect can this be true of architecture? Rand's brief statement in "Art and Cognition" characterizes architecture as "expressing man's values," but she does not explain what she means by "expressing" in this context, nor does she offer any examples of the values involved. Scruton holds that "it would be a gross distortion to assume that architecture is an 'expressive' medium in just the way that sculpture [is]"[37] (7)—a view in which we certainly concur.

What sort of values did Rand envision architecture as conveying? We can only surmise these from her fiction. Significantly, the terms in which she describes Roark's sketches, buildings, and architectural goals in *The Fountainhead* are rather abstract. The structures in his student sketches are "austere and simple" (19); and the house he designs for Austen Heller has "integrity," in that "the relation of masses were determined by the distribution of space within" and "the ornament was determined by the method of construction" (136). Similarly, Roark tells a real-estate magnate that a building should look as if it has a "purpose" (165–66); he explains to the directors of a bank that "an honest building" has to be "of one piece and one faith" (197); the Monadnock Valley homes are "variations on a single theme" (505); the Enright House sketch exhibits a "severe, mathematical order" in which each of the dwelling units is joined to the others "like a single crystal [held] to the side of a rock" (235). Finally, and perhaps most significantly, the Stoddard Temple, the most "spiritual" of Roark's buildings—it was to capture in stone "the heroic human spirit"—depends for its meaning on the figurative sculpture at its center.[38]

The mere suggestion of values is, in any case, insufficient reason to equate architecture with art, least of all from Rand's viewpoint. In other contexts she compellingly argued that all material production is an expression of spiritual values—in the sense that it depends upon the same virtues that art may embody, and externalizes them by translating them into something of practical worth to man. Indeed, *Atlas Shrugged* was an extended fictional celebration of such ideas. Yet even in that fictional context, in which Rand occasionally pushed the analogy between art and industry to invalid extremes,[39] she never concluded or suggested that industry is *art*. Since she was concerned in the novel with showing the connection between the practical, material realm and the "spiritual" realm of values, she paid little attention, in that context, to how material production *differs* from art. Nor did she deal with this question in *The Romantic Manifesto*—except by implication, through her emphasis on the mimetic and non-utilitarian character of art.

As Rand's fictional descriptions indicate, and as emphasized by Scruton, architecture—nonmimetic as it is—does not concretize values through the *representation* of reality, as do literature, painting, and sculpture. Nor does it convey values through the imitation of the expressive qualities of the human voice and movement, as do music and dance. Whereas the mimetic arts are organic and lifelike in quality, encompassing a broad spectrum of expressive possibilities, architectural forms are typically inorganic and abstract, and thus very limited in their repertoire of "expression."[40] Architecture does not "present itself self-consciously as art," Scruton observes, since it is "a natural extension of common [and practical] human activities." (17) He characterizes it as a "public art," one in which "expression cannot have the significance . . . it may have in the private arts of poetry, painting and music." (13) "The expressive features of architecture are not, and cannot be, of this private kind" (13–14), he rightly contends, noting that architectural expression "does not lie in the imaginative rendering of individual feeling." (195–96)

Architecture and Abstract Sculpture

A lamentable consequence of the claim that architecture is a fine art is the tendency to treat buildings primarily as abstract sculptural forms (into which metaphysical significance is often read), and, conversely, to regard abstract sculpture as architectural form. This tendency has vitiated the practice and criticism not only of architecture but of sculpture as well.[41] Scruton aptly cites the Spanish architect Antonio Gaudì, whose work "tries to represent itself as something other than architecture"—in the case of his Chapel of the Colonia Guëll, as "a form of tree-like growth rather than balanced engineering. . . . [T]he accidental has become the essential, and what purports to be architecture can no longer be understood as such, but only as a piece of elaborate expressionist sculpture seen from within." (8)

The art-historical literature is replete with such references. In *What Is Art?*, for example, John Canaday argues that the concept of "negative volumes," or "shaped space," applies equally to abstract sculpture and to architecture; and he characterizes architectural space as "the conscious . . . creation of the architect, which makes him a kind of abstract sculptor on the grand scale." (139–40) Mark Rosenthal, who cites several modern architects in *Abstraction in the Twentieth Century*, emphasizes the close kinship between architecture and abstract art.[42] A contributor to that volume notes that the "pure forms" of modern architecture are regarded as analogous to the "lack of observable referents" in abstract paintings and sculptures.[43] And H. W. Janson refers to the "space-articulating function that distinguishes [minimalist sculptures] from all previous sculpture and relates them to architecture."[44]

A prominent instance of contemporary architecture viewed sculpturally is Frank Gehry's postmodernist Guggenheim Museum in Bilbao, Spain. As described by Michael Kimmelman, for example: "The building seems a conglomeration of vast, diverse, occasionally disorienting spaces, punctuated by paintings and sculptures. It never altogether cedes the stage and sometimes hogs the spotlight. But then, as a work of *architectural sculpture*, it is more compelling than much of the art inside."[45] Another critic similarly describes the building as "resembling a huge sculpture from afar."[46] We would argue, however, that Gehry's building is neither sculpture (i.e., art) nor successful architecture, since his attempt to make a bold formal statement results in structural incoherence—as evidenced by the "disorienting spaces" cited by Kimmelman, and by the fact that the building subverts its primary function by detracting attention from the works exhibited.

Architecture as Design

Rand's characterization of architecture as one of the "visual arts" (along with painting and sculpture), while not valid in the sense she intended, calls to mind an earlier term—the sixteenth-century Italian concept of *Arti del disegno* ("arts of design"), which similarly referred to painting, sculpture, and architecture.[47] In this phrase, however, as in Batteux's usage, the term "art" referred not simply to the fine arts but to the broader category corresponding to the Greek concept of *technê*. As emphasized by Scruton, early Renaissance theorists such as the great Florentine architect Leon Battista Alberti regarded design as not merely a decorative addendum but as inseparable from the act of building as a whole. The task of architectural design, wrote Alberti, was "to appoint to the edifice and all its parts an appropriate place, exact proportion, suitable disposition and harmonious order, in such a way that the form of the building should be entirely implicit in the conception."[48] As Scruton explains, Alberti viewed the architect's work as a process through which such esthetic values permeated the whole enterprise. (25)

Sharing Alberti's view, Scruton characterizes architecture as a "special class of the activity of design,"[49] arguing that it "derives its nature not from some activity of representation or dramatic gesture, but from an everyday preoccupation with getting things right, a preoccupation that has little to do with . . . artistic intentions" of a personally expressive nature. (259) By "getting things right," Scruton means designing a building appropriate to its purpose and to its physical and cultural context, including a desired "style of life." Like other things which give us esthetic pleasure, Scruton emphasizes, architectural structures help to remind us of the kinds and quality of our human aims and pursuits. (16, 23, 35–36)

The concept of design is basic to discussions of architecture and of the graphic, industrial, and decorative arts, whose primary functions are utilitarian—but not to discourse on the fine arts. One customarily speaks of *designing* a book cover, an automobile, an evening gown, a lamp, or a build-ing, for example, but not a novel, a piano sonata, or a landscape painting. Thus, an architecture critic writes that the aim of most architectural compe-titions is not so much "to pick a design as to pick a designer."[50] The reviewer of a book on the work of Frank Lloyd Wright appropriately refers to him as a "skillful and sensitive designer."[51] And the noted urban scholar Witold Rybczynski draws a parallel between architecture and fashion design by point-ing out that "Like the couturier, the architect is involved in the complicated task of mating beauty with utility."[52] Yet Rybczynski, like Scruton and most other writers, does not draw the obvious conclusion that architecture should not be classified as art. Our own conclusion to this effect is based squarely on Rand's esthetic theory, her conflicted pronouncements on architecture notwithstanding.

11

Decorative Art and Craft

A decade ago the American Craft Museum in New York City held a symposium that exemplified the cultural trend we analyze in this chapter: the artworld's increasing tendency to deny the distinction between *art* and *decorative art* or *craft*.[1] Attended by nearly 300 art historians, museum directors, curators, dealers, critics, and craftsmen, the symposium aimed to clarify how museums "might better serve the growing crafts field, [by] bringing greater attention to its history, its esthetic issues, its living artists and, above all, its shifting relationship to the so-called fine arts"—art critic Roberta Smith reported in the *New York Times*.[2] The keynote of the event was sounded by George A. Kubler, Sterling professor emeritus at Yale University—an art historian whose 1962 book *The Shape of Time* began by proposing that "the idea of art can be expanded to embrace the whole range of man-made things."[3] In his address, Kubler offered an example of what such an open-ended concept might encompass. Comparing an antique wood chest made by an anonymous Mexican craftsman to an image of *St. Peter* by the seventeenth-century Spanish painter Jusepe de Ribera,[4] he equated "the 'strong Colonial surface' of the chest's solid wood planks and beautifully aged patina [with] the time-tested integrity of the saint," as Smith uncritically reported. Kubler's analogy—suggesting that the purely sensuous (and partly adventitious) properties of a piece of antique furniture are equivalent in significance to Ribera's representation of human character—typifies the distorted reasoning prevalent in today's artworld. Many arts professionals now view the traditional distinctions between fine art, craft, decorative art, and design as mere "visual prejudices" (as a curator of modern art approvingly observed at the craft symposium), while the arts themselves have become "more craftlike and the crafts more artlike."[5]

Rand's View

Unlike the contemporary critics and scholars we have just cited, Ayn Rand insisted on an essential distinction between *art* and the utilitarian objects that she termed "decorative arts," and that they refer to as "craft."[6] Though she commented only briefly on the decorative arts in "Art and Cognition," the relevant principles can be fleshed out from her larger theory of art and are applicable to craft and design as well. According to Rand's analysis, the utilitarian objects of decorative art differ fundamentally from works of art, not simply in having a primarily physical function, but also in their lower level of cognitive integration and in their distinctive relationship to the hierarchy of human values. In her view, the ornamentation of such objects "is a valuable task, [one] often performed by talented artists, but it is not an art in the esthetic-philosophical meaning of the term" because, in contrast with painting and sculpture, it is not essentially conceptual in its focus but is primarily sensory and perceptual.[7] For Rand, "an art in the esthetic-philosophical meaning of the term" re-creates reality in a manner that objectifies what the artist regards as important in life. Thus a work of visual art always implies a meaning broader than the particular image represented, whereas an object of decorative art need not have any significance beyond the object itself.[8] (75) Rand was not the first to suggest such a distinction, of course. Many writers have noted that meaningful content is essential to art.[9] Yet her analysis of the cognitive role of art in integrating and concretizing human experience lends heightened significance to the traditional distinction between "decorative" and "fine" art.

From the perspective of Rand's theory, it is a crucial consideration that the Mexican chest cited by Kubler, for example, was not intended to mean anything beyond itself: the goal of the craftsman who made it was simply to fashion a useful object that would also be pleasing to look at and to touch. The meanings Kubler ascribed to it are of his own invention, and could be ascribed to any piece of time-worn, well-crafted furniture. In contrast, Ribera's image of *St. Peter* is an intentional embodiment of human character— that of the saint who was the founder of the Catholic Church. In relation to a hierarchy of human values, therefore, the chest and the painting are widely disparate. While admirable as a practical and pleasing object of everyday use, the chest is scarcely commensurate with Ribera's concretization of moral piety.

According to Rand's view, the criterion of practical utility is crucial in determining the nature of an object. Most important, it determines the level of mental integration and focus involved—first, on the part of the craftsman or the artist during the creative process; and afterward, in the viewer's experience of the completed work. An implicit corollary of this principle is that the form and content of any representation (whether two- or three-dimensional) in a work of decorative art or craft is subordinated to the utilitarian features of the object. Often, as Rand noted, decorative images are highly stylized and abstracted—with a minimum of narrative, dramatic, or emotionally expressive content. But when representations are realistic or expressive, in a well-conceived object they are adapted to its shape and to the use for which it is intended.[10] Finally, while representational elements employed in a decorative or utilitarian context sometimes possess symbolic or allusive significance, such meanings tend to remain in the background of awareness. Consider, for example, the metal bosses in the shape of a lion's head that were often used for attaching rings or handles on luxurious articles of furniture—as compared with a sculptor's representation, such as the lions by Edward Clark Potter that benevolently guard the New York Public Library, which we cited in Chapter 4. Unlike the sculptures, the decorative lion's heads do not focus attention on the lion's significance as an embodiment of power and majesty.[11] If one is aware of such symbolic associations at all, they remain on the periphery of consciousness. As E. H. Gombrich emphasizes, one is always aware that a work of art "is meant to be focussed [upon] and contemplated. Painting [or sculpture], like speaking, implicitly demands attention." (116)

In sum, whereas decorative art is experienced primarily on the sensory-perceptual level, a painting or sculpture demands a conceptual level of mental focus and integration: one is aware not simply of a pleasing object or percept but of a representation integrating many aspects of reality and concretizing a broader meaning. Just as a painting *of* a Chinese vase would convey a significance beyond the vase itself, one's pleasure in the painting is of a different order, which derives, in part, from this wider significance. If one were to view a painting, however beautiful, merely as a visually pleasing "object," with no awareness of its meaning, one would not fully experience it as art. What matters is not merely the abstract "beauty" of the painted image but, more fundamentally, what it conveys of the artist's thought and feeling about the thing represented, his sense of its distinctiveness and its value and importance in life.[12] And, as Rand reminds the reader in "Art and Cognition," the "essence of art is integration, a kind of super-integration in the sense that art deals with man's widest abstractions, his metaphysics," and serves to expand the breadth and depth of his consciousness. (76)

Historical Influences

Several misconceptions have undermined the long-standing distinction between works of art and utilitarian objects of decorative art or craft.[13] Historically, the most important of these is the mistaken notion that the essential source of pleasure in visual art is *beauty*. According to this view, art presents "beauty for its own sake," while decorative art combines beauty with utility.[14] In time, the misplaced theoretical emphasis on beauty as an abstract concept, with no consideration of the particular contexts in which it appeared, led some critics to conclude that objects that were useful as well as beautiful should be valued more highly than fine art—which, they thought, had no purpose other than the projection of beauty. Such an argument was, for example, advanced by the influential English artist and poet William Morris (1834–1896).[15] Failing to recognize the unique cognitive and emotional function of painting and sculpture, Morris deprecated them as useless luxuries of the upper classes. In their place, he advocated cultivating the decorative arts and crafts—the "art of the people": "Have nothing in your house that you do not know to be useful and think to be beautiful," he advised. His egalitarian esthetic philosophy—valuing the simple, useful crafts "of the people" above art—was related to his deep commitment to political egalitarianism and socialism. As we shall see, a similar egalitarianism underlies many of today's attempts to elevate the crafts to the status of art.

Morris was a leading figure in the Arts and Crafts Movement, which emerged during the second half of the nineteenth century as a reaction against industrialization.[16] Through the establishment of small workshops, the revival of old techniques of handicraft, and a reverence for simple, pre-industrial household objects, this informal movement deliberately aimed to invert the traditional hierarchy of the arts, in which painting and sculpture had been regarded as superior to the "humble" crafts, such as wood-working and glass-making. Ignoring that the arts serve a profoundly important psychological human need, the Arts and Crafts Movement tended to dismiss them as symbolic of mere social and political elitism. In so doing, it set an influential, albeit misguided, precedent for many of today's advocates of crafts as art.

Although more elitist in spirit than the essentially populist Arts and Crafts Movement, the "Aestheticism" embraced by writers and critics such as Oscar Wilde and Walter Pater in the final decades of the nineteenth century also blurred the distinction between decorative and fine art—once again, through a mistaken emphasis on beauty as the primary attribute of art.[17] This tendency was perpetuated in the formalist esthetics of Clive Bell, for example, who indiscriminately applied his concept of "significant form" to a Persian bowl, a Chinese carpet, the architecture of the Hagia Sophia (the magnificent sixth-century Byzantine church in Istanbul), and the fresco masterpieces of Giotto or of Piero della Francesca.[18] In denying that content, or meaning, is essential to art, Bell's "aesthetic hypothesis" dealt a near-fatal blow to the valuable distinction between decorative and fine art. If all that was needed in art was "significant form," devoid of all representational or emotional content, then a porcelain vase might be just as admirable as Michelangelo's Sistine Chapel ceiling frescos. Finally, the eventual acceptance of "abstract art" offered additional justification for regarding the forms and designs of decorative and craft objects as art.

Another factor that has undermined the distinction between art and craft is a widespread misconception regarding the concept of creativity. From the eighteenth century on, theorists and critics placed increasing emphasis on creative invention, as contrasted with technical skill. Thus, art came to be associated with "creativity," while craft was identified with the old idea of skill in producing objects to fulfill a specific practical function. From the perspective of Rand's theory of art, this dichotomy was a false one, however, since the psychological function of art places its own limits on the creative freedom of the artist just as surely as the functional requirements of craft objects constrain the artisan's creativity. Western culture is now reaping the unfortunate consequences of this false dichotomy, as many craftsmen attempt to emulate the "creativity" they impute to the modern artist, while they completely disregard purposeful function. In an article on craft for the *Encyclopedia of Aesthetics*, Larry Shiner traces the recent history of this trend:

> The convergence of fine art and [so-called] studio craft began in the late 1950s when . . . a few craftspeople adopted the latest art-world styles to make nonfunctional objects in clay or fiber. Critics, galleries, and art museums responded enthusiastically and by the 1970s potters were being called "ceramic sculptors," weavers were renamed "fiber artists," and the new kind of craft was collectively designated "art in craft media" or "crafts-as-art." At the same time, feminists were attacking the exclusion of domestic crafts such as quilts and embroidery from fine art and soon quilts were promoted to art status and fiber artists began turning out "art quilts."

American Indian Artifacts

The growing tendency to regard craft objects as art not only influences the work of contemporary craftsmen; it also affects the way in which objects from the past are classified and interpreted. This tendency is particularly striking with regard to American Indian artifacts,[19] which in recent years have received increasing attention under the rubric of "multiculturalism." As indicated by a major exhibition of the "art" of the Plains Indians at the Minneapolis Institute of Arts in the early 1990s, such work comprises articles of practical function—from clothing, storage bags, and tepees to the paraphernalia of warfare and of ceremonial dance.[20] Among the artifacts in the Minneapolis exhibition were a crane-headed stick that served as an official insignia, a blackstone pipe bearing the carving of a bear, stone tools, a tobacco bag, a cradleboard and cover, and pipe bags. The representations of human beings, plants, and animals that appear on, or are part of, such objects, tend to be highly abstracted and stylized, often according to strict pictographic conventions, with little expressive content or variation. And much of the decoration is not representational at all, but purely geometric.[21]

In claiming the status of "art" for such objects, scholars and critics emphasize that, since many of the designs have symbolic or ritual significance, they should be regarded as evidence of the "intellectual and spiritual depth" of Native American cultures, as one writer put it.[22] Such arguments miss an essential difference, however, between the mimetically expressive character of *art*, on one hand, and the conventionalized modes of symbolic or pictographic representation that predominate in American Indian tribal artifacts, on the other.[23] (A similar distinction is applicable in Christian culture, for example, between a simple cross and a painting or sculpture of the Crucifixion: the former is merely a symbol, the latter is a work of art.) Nonetheless, Gaylord Torrence suggests in his book *The American Indian Parfleche*, for example, that the painted images on these objects—containers of folded or sewn rawhide, decorated with mostly abstract painted designs, and used to store and transport food and personal possessions—are "works of art" (27), some even "masterworks" (20); and he repeatedly refers to their makers as artists. Nonetheless, he observes that the painted images on these objects are "so conventionalized that they could be constructed without thought or intended meaning" (253). While they are "intended to represent tangible, objects, specific scenes or incidents, abstract concepts, or sacred associations," he further observes, some of the paintings are "indistinguishable from paintings intended as purely formal and decorative exercises without meaning." Yet, owing to such "symbolic content" (253) and to purported "associative meanings" (256), he considers the parfleches to be art. Not surprisingly, his book bears the subtitle *A Tradition of Abstract Painting*, clearly alluding to modern "abstract art."[24]

Quilts and Feminist Art History

Art historians in recent years have similarly attempted to elevate quilts to the status of art, arguing that they often held deep significance for their makers—

who were invariably women, with few other opportunities for "creative" artistic expression. Thus the authors of *The American Quilt: A History of Cloth and Comfort 1750–1950* claim that "women's primary reason for making quilts was to satisfy the need to make something beautiful. . . . Quilts were to their makers what canvas and oils were to the Impressionist painters."[25] Such a broad claim mistakenly equates making "something beautiful" with making art, and falsely implies that the Impressionists were concerned solely with beauty. True, quilts can be both beautiful and creative in their use of form and color.[26] As a review of *The American Quilt* by Patricia O'Conner (herself a quilter and textile collector) inadvertently reveals, however, the idea of "Art to Snuggle Under" (the title of her review) is absurd, especially in the light of the historical perspective O'Conner offers on the uses to which quilts were customarily put:

> There was a time when Americans came into the world swaddled in quilts and left it in the same way, wrapped in a favorite old quilt or "comfort" and laid into a rough board coffin, tucked in for all eternity. When Americans moved west, quilts went with them, padding the floors and insulating the sides of covered wagons, lining the walls of sod huts or log cabins. Quilts [also] went to war, and at least one—mailed home . . . to the grieving mother who made it—became the tattered and stained memorial to a soldier's final hours.[27]

While it is also true that quilts often "tell a story,"[28] that fact does not warrant designating them as an art form equivalent to painting. Their main physical properties are determined by their practical purpose; and the observer remains conscious of that purpose even when they are displayed on a wall. Moreover, quilts do not allow the subtlety or complexity of representation that is possible in painting. Like the parfleche designs, therefore, quilt patterns tend to be highly stylized and geometric, often following established conventions. Even those that employ individualized representations are typically schematic and simplified, owing to the limitations of the medium.

Nonetheless, feminist art historians insist that quilt-making merits equal consideration with "high art." In their view, the distinction between art and craft (or decorative art) has no objective justification, but merely reflects a male bias in art and art history.[29] In an influential article published in the *Feminist Art Journal* in 1973, Patricia Mainardi even claimed that quilts are "The Great American Art."[30] Her argument referred mainly to nonessential or even spurious attributes of art, however. "Women exhibited their quilts, and still do, at state and county fairs, churches and grange halls, much as our contemporary 'fine' art is exhibited." (331) "[T]he women who made quilts knew and valued what they were doing: frequently quilts were signed and dated by the maker." (332) "In designing their quilts, women not only made beautiful and functional objects, but expressed their own convictions on a wide variety of subjects in a [symbolic] language for the most part comprehensible only to other women." (338) Art, we would simply point out, is not primarily "symbolic," but *mimetically* expressive, and therefore comprehensible by men as well as women. Moreover, the contradictions in Mainardi's own concluding statement clearly reveal her confusion of categories: "[W]omen succeeded . . . in building a *design* tradition . . . which must today be acknowledged as The Great American Art." (345, emphasis ours) In elevating that design tradition to the status of *art*, feminist scholars not only trivialize the work of male painters and sculptors, they also diminish the achievement of women artists, by implying that a Mary Cassatt pastel of a mother and child, say, or Anna Hyatt Huntington's stalwart *Joan of Arc*, or Harriet Whitney Frishmuth's ecstatic figure of a maenad in *The Vine*, have no more to offer the viewer than a handsomely designed, well-crafted quilt.[31]

The Art and Artifacts of Africa

A landmark exhibition co-organized in 1995 by the Royal Academy of Arts in London and the Guggenheim Museum in New York offers further striking evidence of the conceptual confusion we have been analyzing. Entitled *Africa: The Art of a Continent*, it included objects ranging from obviously utilitarian artifacts, such as snuff containers and headrests, to powerfully realized works of figurative art, such as several magnificent portrait heads from the ancient Yoruba culture.[32] As the eminent scholar of African culture K. Anthony Appiah noted in the catalog's opening essay, all these objects were presented for "the particular form of respectful attention we accord to art," although many of them "had primary functions that were, by our standards, non-aesthetic, and would have been assessed, first and foremost, by their ability to achieve those functions."[33]

Owing in part to an intimate familiarity with African art and artifacts acquired during his childhood in what is now the republic of Ghana, Appiah is very nearly an ideal guide. His observations about the goldweights featured in the exhibition are particularly illuminating. Of these small brass objects cast in representational forms or geometric shapes, he writes: "The figurative goldweights are wonderfully expressive: they depict people and animals, plants and tools, weapons and domestic utensils, often in arrangements that will remind an Asante who looks at them of a familiar proverb." Yet, as he further points out,

quite often among these elegant objects, so obviously crafted with great skill and care, [there is] one that has a lump of unworked metal stuffed into a crevice, in a way that seems completely to destroy its aesthetic unity; or, sometimes, a well-made figure has a limb crudely hacked off. These amputations and excrescences are there because, after all, a weight is a weight:[34] and if it doesn't weigh the right amount, it can't serve its function. If a goldweight, however finely crafted, has the wrong mass, then something needs to be added (or chopped off) to bring it to its proper size. . . .

Goldweights . . . have many of the features that we expect of works of art. In Ashanti itself, they were appreciated for their appeal to the eye, or for the proverbial traditions they engaged. But in the end, as I say, they were weights: and their job was to tell you the value of the gold dust in the weighing pan. [46]

Although the best of the goldweights were "among the splendors of African creativity," and their "decorative elegance was something prized and aimed for," it was "an ornament, an embellishment, on an object that served a utilitarian function," Appiah rightly insists, and "in appreciating and collecting these weights *as* art we are doing something that their makers and the men and women who paid them did not do."[35] (46)

Nonetheless, Appiah uncritically accepts the fundamental rationale of the exhibition. "In presenting these objects as art objects," he writes, "the curators of the exhibition invited us to look at them in a certain way, to evaluate them in the manner we call 'aesthetic' . . . [that is,] to attend to them in the way we have learned to attend in art museums." He therefore concludes that "what's important isn't whether or not they are art or were art for their makers: what matters is that we are invited to treat them as art." (50) In one sense, Appiah is correct, of course: whether or not their makers *considered* these objects "art" (or had some comparable concept) is irrelevant. Whether or not they *are* art—that is, whether they share the fundamental attributes of what we term "art"—does matter, however. In claiming otherwise, Appiah embraces the authoritarian (institutional) theory of art, which we discussed in Chapter 6. To foster a genuine understanding and appreciation of African art and artifacts, he would do well to trust his own better judgment. He would then insist that objects such as goldweights and headrests, primarily intended for mundane practical functions (however pleasing to the eye and hand or suggestive of meaning beyond the task at hand), belong in a different category from the Yoruba heads we cited above—the overriding purpose of which appears to have been the embodiment of important spiritual values.[36]

Appiah concludes that "what made [the exhibition] wonderful was that the eye could linger with pleasure on the forms, the shapes, and the surfaces, the patination and the pigment, and engage each object with whatever [one] happened to know of its materials, its history, its origin." To do so, he claims, was to respond "naturally to these African artifacts *as* art." As he makes clear, however, to view so diverse a collection of objects "aesthetically" could only mean to view them in terms of their abstract formal properties. To view them in such terms, we would argue, is not to respond to them "*as* art" at all but, rather, as meaningless artifacts detached from their cultural context. Moreover, when Appiah attributes such a purely formalistic esthetic focus to the European Enlightenment, he presents only half of the picture, missing the distinction that many eighteenth-century thinkers drew between utilitarian objects and the nonutilitarian nature of art—though he uneasily alludes to the "important distinction between the fine and the decorative arts" since the nineteenth century, and to the idea of "fine art as 'art for art's sake.'"[37] That that last idea is flawed even in the context of Western culture he seems not to recognize. (48)

Appiah's remarks on the "Western" concept of art are symptomatic of a common fallacy of contemporary art theory: the claim that, since the concepts of decorative art and craft originated in European culture in relation to the concept of fine art, they are invalid for other cultures, which lack such concepts. (This claim would be rather like arguing that the concept of *gravity* did not apply to primitive man because, though he well knew that when he shook fruit from the trees it would fall to the ground, he had no *concept* comparable to "gravity.") Rather than understanding the decorative-fine art distinction in relation to a universal hierarchy of human physical and psychological needs, contemporary theorists often dismiss it as an attempt to establish the superiority of Western cultural achievements over the arts of non-Western, especially primitive, cultures. Motivated in part by an egalitarian impulse, such arguments have the ultimate effect not of elevating the artistic achievements of the neglected and the downtrodden but of reducing the value of all art to the lowest common denominator.

Though the distinction between fine and decorative art (or craft) has only become explicit in the West since the eighteenth century, it is implicit in other cultures, as we have noted in our discussion of Ellen Dissanayake's work in Chapter 7. African societies, for instance, accord the highest status to the art forms and works of art which most fully integrate and perceptibly embody the primary values of the society.[38] An implicit distinction between merely decorative imagery and representations that are invested with deep significance is evident in the West African culture of the Baule people, for example. Private devotional sculptures known as "spirit figures" (small wooden sculptures representing the "spirit" husband or wife believed to be left in the other world before birth) depict a Baule ideal of physical beauty and social perfection,[39] and are much more highly valued than the diverse utilitarian objects whose ornamental figures lack profound meaning or "content," serving only to afford esthetic pleasure and to bring prestige to their makers and their owners.[40] According to the principles of Rand's esthetic theory, we would argue that the spirit figures clearly qualify as works of *art*, although the language of the Baule lacks a comparable term.[41]

In contrast, the Western tendency to regard African masks as autonomous objects of "fine art," in isolation from their intended cultural context, is mistaken. Such masks are created as dramatic props, or dance regalia, meant to be seen as but one element of a complex esthetic experience incorporating music, poetry, and dance. Typically, they are not intended to be experienced apart from such a ceremonial or entertainment context, and should therefore not be regarded as works of art.[42]

Contemporary Crafts as "Art"

While conceptual confusion regarding artifacts from cultural traditons other than our own is to some degree understandable, because of differing contexts, the efforts of some contemporary American craftsmen (as well as of their dealers and collectors) to cloak their work in the mantle of art cannot be excused. Their motivation is clearly suggested by one curator's candid remark: "The nice thing about collecting crafts is that they're generally affordable when they're called crafts. . . . The minute you call it art, the price goes way beyond."[43] Driven by a desire for unearned prestige and financial gain, efforts to equate craft objects with art not only affect the way such objects are classified and appraised; they also spur the production of bizarre and useless articles that, by any objective standard, qualify as neither art nor craft.[44] Complicit in this process, of course, are gallery owners, such as one who claimed that his show of new "art furniture"—featuring chairs that are meant to be looked at rather than sat on—was "about chairs as they work themselves into the lexicon of contemporary art."[45]

Although the contemporary "studio" (or "art") craft movement ostensibly gains legitimacy from the nineteenth-century Arts and Crafts Movement (the flawed premises of which we noted above), many of its exponents are guided by aims diametrically opposed to those of the earlier group. What William Morris and his allies advocated in the crafts was the principle of honest functionality. In contrast, many of today's "studio craftspeople" aim for creativity and originality above all else, often completely disregarding function, and they eagerly misappropriate the term "art" for their often absurd products. Instead of furniture-making, glass-making, and weaving, they engage in "furniture art," "glass art," and "textile art."

One of the trailblazers in the studio furniture movement, for example, is the "furniture artist" Wendell Castle (b. 1932)—who is credited with having "given new meaning to being a craftsman in America" by "consistently [seeking] to tear down the barriers that divide the fine and the applied arts." He has been called "an American phenomenon," "one of the finest contemporary artists in America." [46] In 1989, Castle was the subject of a retrospective exhibition at the Detroit Institute of Arts (DIA), which several years earlier had commissioned a piece from him for its permanent collection. Entitled *Bench* (1987–88), it is a bizarre concoction of disparate forms, which quite defies description and is certainly not designed to welcome a sitter.[47] Castle's work is said to have gradually moved into the realm of fine art by becoming "sculpture," abandoning function entirely. If, as we argued in Chapter 8, however, abstract sculpture does not qualify as art, Castle's bastardized "furniture" surely does not. According to Davira S. Taragin, curator of twentieth-century decorative arts and design at the DIA, and co-curator of the retrospective, "Castle encouraged fellow craftspeople to move . . . to an emphasis on concept and meaning."[48] But just what the meaning of *Bench* might be is impossible to discern. Rather than attempt to interpret it, Taragin resorts to one of the meaningless clichés of today's criticism, asserting that Castle "does what all great artists do. He *challenges* us to see something we think we know in an entirely new light." (3A, emphasis ours)

Another highly influential figure in the studio craft movement is the "glass artist" Dale Chihuly (b. 1941), the subject of an hour-long PBS documentary in 1998, *Chihuly over Venice*. His oversized blown-glass installations, mostly in the shape of flowers, shells, and free-form baubles, are pure decoration at best and meretricious ornamentation at worst. Yet he has been celebrated as a "glass sculptor" and creative genius, and has been awarded a MacArthur Fellowship, as well as a string of honorary degrees. A 1997 monograph on his work features an 18,000-word encomium by the art historian and esthetician Donald Kuspit who argues: "It is the very ambiguity of Chihuly's objects that makes them art, even as it makes us uncertain as to whether they *are* art. . . . [T]hey put us in the position of being unable to decide whether they are craft or art, creating a Gordian knot of aesthetic consciousness."[49] In characteristically turgid postmodernist jargon, Kuspit continues:

> Glass in its molten state is feminine, yielding; in its hardened state it is masculine, phallic. But its feminine state is primary; its masculine state derivative. In working with glass, Chihuly is struggling with his female side, which remains evident in the fluid shapes his hard glass takes. . . . [H]is various glass spheres—"biomorphic bulbs of glass"—are emblematic of female containment, and as such unconsciously show a man's profound appreciation of the redemptive powers of woman.[50] [34]

In arguing for the distinction between *art* and decorative art or craft that Rand insisted upon, we do not mean to deprecate the value of well-conceived and carefully made objects. Such objects *are* important, for they help to create a sensually stimulating and emotionally gratifying human environment. As Ellen Dissanayake has persuasively argued, the universal human tendency to beautify or estheticize objects of everyday practical use, is in its way profoundly significant: it is the simplest and most direct means of enhancing the daily activities they relate to, and of thereby enriching the quality of life of those who use them.[51] For these reasons, the decorative arts are worthy of serious consideration in their own right.[52] In the "rush to graduate the crafts to the level of art," however—as a few brave souls suggested at the craft symposium we cited at the outset of this chapter—"the craftsman's responsibility to the tradition of designing beautiful everyday objects" has been abandoned.[53] Rand's esthetic theory provides a foundation for restoring that venerable tradition.

12

Avant-Garde Music
and Dance

Like painting and sculpture, the arts of music and dance have been radically debased by the avant-garde[1] during the past hundred years. In rejecting the purportedly arbitrary conventions of the past, in favor of entirely novel forms of creativity, "experimental" composers and choreographers have repudiated the essential characteristics of their art form. Just as abstract painters and sculptors have ignored or denied that the basis of visual art lay in the representation of perceptible objects, avant-garde composers have divorced their work from music's proper basis in human vocal expression and movement. Similarly, avant-garde choreographers have attempted to dissociate dance from its emotive basis in musical expression and in a culturally shared mimetic repertoire. Flouting the requirements of human perception and cognition[2] that Rand correctly emphasizes are central to art, these reputedly advanced artists have produced work that is inscrutable and alien to the vast majority of the public. Our aim in this chapter is to trace the main avant-garde currents in the fields of music and dance, and to explain why they are essentially invalid as forms of artistic expression.

Avant-Garde Trends in Music

Avant-gardism in the field of music has pursued two widely different approaches. The first of these retains musical tones but drastically alters the way in which they are organized in a composition. This tendency—which in our view encompasses not only atonality and serialism but minimalism as well—began in an effort to enlarge musical expression. But it evolved into an increasingly abstract, formulaic control of the compositional process, largely abandoning the organically expressive sense of melody that lies at the heart of musical meaning. The other avant-garde approach—which is termed "noise music"—minimizes or dispenses with the use of musical tones to embrace the realm of nonmusical sound.

Atonality

The more complex and difficult to analyze of the two broad avant-garde approaches is the one that appears to remain within the realm of music, since it retains pitched tones. This avant-garde tendency was first manifested in the phenomenon known by the rather confusing term *atonality*. "Atonal" composers did not abandon tones as such, however; what they abandoned was the use of scales possessing a clear "tonic" (or keynote). Such scales are crucial, since they anchor the music in a clearly perceptible reference point, to and from which melodic movement can be grasped. The father of the musical avant-garde was Arnold Schoenberg (1874–1951), who wrote his first wholly atonal composition in 1908. Ironically, he regarded himself as a traditionalist, convinced that he was simply pursuing the logical course of musical evolution implicit in the legacy of the great German composers. Indeed, atonality did appear to be anticipated by previous musical practice— in the increased use, for expressive effect, of "chromaticism."[3] Baroque and Romantic composers such as Bach and Chopin had employed chromaticism—but always within a tonal framework. They had thereby heightened expressive contrasts without destroying the overall intelligibility of their compositions. Schoenberg's descent into complete atonality—like that of Kandinsky, Malevich, and Mondrian into total visual abstraction—was inspired by a misguided desire to expand the expressive range of his art. Much like them, he aimed to convey what he termed "'a prophetic message revealing a higher form of life toward which mankind evolves.'" He was also convinced that his compositional techniques represented "'a more evolved type of thought.'"[4]

In contrast with abstract art, which abandons meaningful visual percepts, atonal music retains a significant connection to objective auditory reality. But the aural reality it projects is bizarre and disjointed, as exemplified by Schoenberg's seminal work *Pierrot lunaire* (1912)—a vocal and instrumental setting of twenty-one brief surrealist poems. In this composition, he fully realized what he viewed as "the emancipation of the dissonance."[5] The eerily swooping and sliding vocal line of the music vividly evokes the ghastly, corrupted world envisioned by the poet, for the dissonance of atonality is ideally suited to the expression of such morbid pessimism.[6] Schoenberg soon came to recognize, however, that extended atonal compositions would always be dependent on a vocal text for their coherence.

Serialism

In an attempt to bring a semblance of order to atonal instrumental music, Schoenberg devised his "serial" technique in the early 1920s. Each serial composition is based on an arbitrary basic set, or "series," of notes selected from the chromatic scale, such that no single note in the set is repeated. The series (also termed a "tone-row") then functions as a musical theme or motif which, after an initial statement, is manipulated by being played upside down, backwards, or backwards and upside down. Few people possess the ability to perceive such complexities, however. Ironically, Schoenberg himself said that the system should be of no concern to the listener, who must respond to the work *as music.*[7]

What, then, does one hear in such music? Typically, the melodic line, often set in exceptionally high or low registers, is disjointed, containing wide leaps and lacking recognizable themes. Since one interprets music in human terms, if such compositions are grasped at all by ordinary listeners, they tend to be perceived as "insane"[8]—for the simple reason that human speech normally remains within the middle registers and rarely undergoes such abrupt alterations in pitch. One cannot help thinking that only a madman would speak, or move, in the disjointed way such music sounds. It is disordered, chaotic, and (to most listeners) profoundly disturbing. Perhaps most important, it lacks coherent melodic themes—tonal and rhythmically memorable sequences that have a distinctive emotive character (beyond that of madness), and whose subsequent transformations can be grasped, suggesting a directed movement, an aural "journey" toward a final resolution or destination.

In spite of, or perhaps because of, its essentially alien qualities, serialism became *de rigueur* among "advanced" composers in the decades following World War II. Two prominent serialists, Pierre Boulez and Milton Babbitt, extended it to every element of musical composition—duration, dynamics, and timbre, as well as pitch. Scores became so complex in the intricacies of their structure that even musicians found them daunting and virtually unplayable, much as audiences found them unlistenable. The irony was that, as critic Harold Schonberg notes, "the more totally organized a piece became, the more chaotic it sounded to the lay listener."[9] Such compositions could be grasped only by trained musicians studying and expounding upon the written score—a phenomenon that gave rise to the term *Augenmusik* ("music for the eyes"), akin to the "painted word" in the world of visual art.

When serial works failed to attract an audience, the composers found refuge in the universities, from which they responded with predictable disdain to the public's rejection of them. Though Arnold Schoenberg had confidently predicted in 1910 that atonality would soon triumph, by 1947 he concluded (in delusions of grandeur much like those of the pioneers of abstract art) that the required "evolution" had not yet occurred. "[A] full understanding of my works cannot be expected before decades," he asserted. "The minds of the musicians, and of the audiences, have to mature ere they can comprehend my music." Nor did he for a moment doubt that the course on which he had set musical composition was inevitable. (602)

Later serialists were equally arrogant in their claims. In an article entitled "The Composer as Specialist" (which the editor of *High Fidelity Magazine* provocatively, if tendentiously, retitled "Who Cares If You Listen?"), Babbitt argued that the unpopularity of "'serious,' 'advanced,' contemporary music" was due only to the listener's insufficiently prepared "perceptual capacities." Why not recognize, he asked,

> that contemporary music has reached a stage long since attained by other forms of activity? The time has passed when the normally well-educated man without special preparation can understand the most advanced work in, for example, mathematics, philosophy, and physics. Advanced music, to the extent that it reflects the knowledge and originality of the informed composer, scarcely can be expected to appear more intelligible than these arts and sciences to the person whose musical education usually has been even less extensive than his background in other fields.[10]

Babbitt's conception of music as analogous to theoretical mathematics, philosophy, and physics is no doubt a reflection of his own background: he was trained and worked as a mathematician before turning full-time to music. This helps to explain why his complex serial work has held little appeal for most music lovers. Having turned musical composition into a quasi-mathematical procedure, he has lost touch with the emotive wellspring that is the primary source of its meaning.

As Harold Schonberg notes, the off-putting tendencies of serial music—total dissonance, rejection of melody and harmony, and an abstract remoteness from human expression—are shared by much non-serial music as well, most notably, by the prodigiously "difficult" work of Elliott Carter.[11] What critic Bernard Holland has observed about Carter's work might also apply to the response of many listeners to serial music. Holland has speculated: "I have often wondered why so much of Mr. Carter's music has disturbed my mind and frozen my heart." The customary explanation—"Telling people that they have not listened hard enough or summoned sufficient intelligence"—is not the answer, Holland insists. Observing that Carter's work tends to be "built from layers of opposing forces, each with its irreconcilable agenda, each moving according to its own clock and pace of life," he suggests that, while some listeners "revel in the conflict" and "find in it powerful metaphors for the complications of twentieth-century culture," others (like himself) are "repelled by this warring spirit," for they value order and "seek in music the solace of reconciliation." The latter group have accurately perceived the music, he concludes, but "simply do not like" what they hear.[12] Surely Rand's concept of "sense of life" is relevant here.

Minimalism

In the 1960s, one reaction against the unintelligible complexity of academic serialism took the form of a new approach to composition. Based on the systematic repetition of extremely simple, quasi-tonal motifs, this approach is aptly if unflatteringly termed *minimalism*. Its chief practitioners have been Steve Reich, Philip Glass, Terry Riley, and John Adams. Though their work "has proved too simple-minded to be of enduring interest," *Commentary* music critic Terry Teachout has argued, "its popularity nonetheless served to clear the way for the restoration of tonality as the lingua franca of Western classical music."[13] In truth, however, the practice of tonal composition had been kept alive during the preceding decades by numerous composers— from Rachmaninov and Prokofiev to Samuel Barber and Joaquín Rodrigo. These composers early recognized the poverty of atonality and serialism and had continued to write tonal music, at the cost of being labeled reactionaries. Moreover, contrary to the widely held view, minimalism is not resolutely tonal,[14] and is thus closer to serialism than its obvious simplicity might at first suggest.

In addition to its often ambiguous tonality, minimalism is comparable to serialism in another respect. It is dependent on formulaic compositional practices—on a systematic pattern of repetition that is rigid and arbitrary, in contrast with the vital nature of true artistic creativity. Basing their work on such schemes, minimalist composers often employ electronic devices to produce, by automatized means, the seemingly endless repetitions that characterize their work. At the same time, they share with the "noise-music" avant-garde a penchant for incorporating elements of recorded speech and various incidental sounds in their compositions, thereby blurring the distinction between music and nonmusic, or noise. Consider, for example, Steve Reich's *Different Trains* (1988). To produce this work, which alludes to the Holocaust, Reich first tape-recorded the wartime reminiscences of various individuals, including survivors. From these he isolated evocative phrases such as "from Chicago," "fastest train," "1941," and "Germany invaded Hungary," and developed bits of music based on their melodic shape. The spoken phrases were then electronically transferred into a newly invented "digital sampling keyboard," from which they were manipulated and synchronized with train whistles, sirens, and several overdubbed string quartets, a process which reduced the spoken word to virtual gibberish, as is often the case in minimalist works. The boringly repetitive "musical material" that resulted from all this technical sophistication resembles much other minimalist work in sounding like the sort of background music once used in films in shots of speeding trains—though in this piece it is at least thematically appropriate. *Different Trains* is also typically minimalist in the arbitrary abruptness of its beginning, its internal shifts, and its ending. Lacking integration and a sense of meaningful direction toward some climax or resolution, it suggests a piece of patterned fabric that is never shaped into a garment. Any emotional impact the piece might have would derive primarily from the piece's textual references to the Holocaust, rather than from any musical qualities in Reich's minimalist score.[15]

Similarly, Philip Glass's 1992 *The Voyage* (commissioned by the Metropolitan Opera for the unprecedented fee of $325,000) is, to quote *New York* critic Peter G. Davis, "a pageant of abstractions and moods rather than a plotted drama in which action is propelled by music." As Davis further observes, the composer's usual style—his "locomotive rhythms, wispy melodies, arpeggiated chords, [and] primitive syncopations"—produces a score of "stupefying banality" (a phrase apt for all minimalist work). Apart from Glass's incompetence in writing for the voice, Davis notes, the "opera's characters have virtually nothing of interest to sing [about]," and scarcely a word of the text is intelligible. On the whole, the singers seem "like additional bits of scenic decoration, inanimate objects to be manipulated by a pretentious, passionless, repellent piece of musical machinery."[16]

Minimalism is "pseudo-classical music" (in Schonberg's words) for a generation raised on rock-'n'-roll. It shares with rock music its predilection for mind-numbing loudness, its dependence on electronic instruments and synthesized sound, its simplistic approach to composition, and its penchant for repetitive patterns broken by abrupt shifts and endings, "as if a radio had been arbitrarily switched off."[17] As Teachout has observed, minimalism's hypnotic quality is "comfortably familiar to baby boomers raised on rock (especially those in the habit of using loud music as an accompaniment to the ingestion of mind-altering drugs)."[18] Indeed, as Terry Riley observed, the intent of early minimalist pieces was explicitly "'psychedelic,'" aimed at producing altered "'states of consciousness, out-of-the-body experiences, and so on.'"[19] This is no doubt the sort of music Rand had in mind when she wrote that "certain kinds of music have a paralyzing, narcotic effect on man's mind"—though she was mistaken in suggesting that all "[p]rimitive music and most Oriental music fall into this category."[20]

The mind-numbingly repetitive character of American minimalism is largely shared by the work of three contemporary European composers who have gained wide popularity—Henryk Górecki (b. 1933), Arvo Pärt (b. 1935), and John Tavener (b. 1944). Owing to their similar musical styles and shared commitment to religious orthodoxy, they have been dubbed the "holy minimalists." Their best-known work is Górecki's Third Symphony (1976) for soprano and orchestra. While decidedly tonal, and even sumptuous in its sound at times, it is, on the whole, a ponderous succession of chords that creates little sense of melodic movement or development. The sound appears to go nowhere, instead hovering ominously in space, prompting one critic to complain that "it is less a symphony than a miasma."[21] Devoid of melodic movement, this piece demonstrates that tonality and harmony alone cannot sustain genuinely musical interest.[22]

Melody, as we have argued, is the essential attribute of music. Tonality is important not in itself but as the basis for melodic (and, therefore, musical) intelligibilty. It is melody that conveys musical meaning—in part because, as Edward Rothstein has suggested, "it is associated with the listener's own private voice. The melody's turns and twists become expressions of mental and emotional life, a source of identification; its sojourn through a composition becomes the listener's adventure as well."[23] Although minimalist composers and critics often claim that minimalism recalls the tradition of medieval "plainsong" (of which Gregorian chant is the most familiar variety), nothing could be further from the truth.[24] For all its striking simplicity, plainsong does *not* lack melody. On the contrary, it is, to quote the eminent musicologist Percy Scholes, "pure melody."[25] In virtually abandoning melody, the minimalists, holy or otherwise, have in effect abandoned the art of music.

John Cage

Decades before the American minimalists employed tape-recorded speech and extramusical sounds in their work, attempts had been made to create works based wholly or partly on noise. Such "noise music" had been introduced by the Italian Futurists early in the century. But its most influential practitioner was John Cage (1912–1992)[26]—though, oddly, the term "noise music" is not often applied to his work. At the tamer end of the noise-music spectrum is Cage's most notorious, if somewhat atypical, piece—*4'33"* (1952)—a work inspired by the postmodernist "artist" Robert Rauschenberg's all-white canvases.[27] In it, the pianist simply lifts the lid on the piano keyboard and sits motionless for four minutes and thirty-three seconds—except for shutting and opening the lid at a point in the middle to signify a break between the first and second "movements"—while the audience listens to whatever ambient sounds happen to be audible. At the other extreme from *4'33"* Cage devised cacophonous multimedia pieces such as the perversely titled *HPSCHD* (1967–69), pronounced "harpsichord." Whereas *4'33"* defies the principle of selectivity in art (a principle Rand correctly emphasizes is essential to art) by briefly calling attention to random ambient sounds as if they constitute music, Cage's "harpsichord" piece makes a mockery of selectivity by presenting a plethora of simultaneous but unrelated sounds and images, over a period of four and a half hours. In performance, seven harpsichordists played computer-mixed music of Mozart, Beethoven, Chopin, Schoenberg, and Cage, while audio-tapes, slides, and film images were amplified or projected by means of fifty-two tape players, fifty-nine loudspeakers, sixty-four slide-projectors, and eight moving-picture projectors. As described by one reviewer, the result was "an atonal and structural chaos . . . continually in flux."[28] No human mind could process such a din, and the mind that went to such lengths to conceive and produce it, we would insist, cannot have been entirely sane.

Indeed, Cage's bizarre manifestations of iconoclasm were the expression of an eccentric personality that over time exhibited many of the schizophrenic or schizoid traits identified by psychologist Louis Sass in *Madness and Modernism*.[29] At the very least, Cage's unorthodox tendencies—which sympathetic critics have attributed to a boldly inventive imagination—appear in a very different light when viewed in the context of his personal history and Sass's account of the schizoid personality. Although he was precocious as a youth, and dabbled in a number of artistic fields—painting, dance, and architecture, as well as music—Cage appears to have had no marked talent or passion for any of them, including music. By his own admission, he "wasn't very gifted on the piano" and "had no feeling for harmony."[30] In 1937, he took a position as accompanist at the Cornish Dance School in Seattle, where he met the young dancer Merce Cunningham, who would become his lifelong collaborator and fellow iconoclast. At Cornish, Cage organized a percussion orchestra and began to compose works for it—thus obviating the need to deal with harmony. There, too, he "invented" the so-called *prepared piano*, by inserting assorted mundane objects (such as screws, bolts, rubber bands, bamboo slats, and hairpins) between the strings at various distances from the damper, thus converting the piano into the equivalent of a percussion orchestra for a single player—albeit one whose effects could not be anticipated by either the composer or the performer.[31] Moreover, since the prepared piano and many percussion instruments produce sounds of indeterminate or extremely complex pitch, Cage organized his compositions for them on the basis not of tonal (pitch) relationships but of rhythmic patterns.[32] He thereby eliminated a major constituent of melody.[33]

In the 1930s and early 1940s, Cage still aimed to compose pieces that would be musically expressive. To his dismay, however, he discovered that they elicited responses far removed from his intentions. Of his "Perilous Night," a composition in which he had attempted to convey a sense of "loneliness and terror," for example, one critic wrote that it sounded like "'a woodpecker in a belfry.'"[34] Emotionally shaken by this and other signs of his failure as a composer,[35] as well as by the breakup of his marriage and the devastating events of World War II, Cage sought solace in Eastern philosophy. Under the purported influence of Zen Buddhism, he proceeded to develop his *aleatory*, or chance, approach to composition, in which the elements and sequence of a piece are largely or wholly determined not by the composer's intentional choices, but by such practices as rolling dice and consulting the *I Ching*, an ancient Chinese book of divination.[36] "[M]y purpose is to remove purpose," he once declared. But the real motivation underlying his embrace of chance procedures is obvious: "If I have a particular purpose, and then a series of actions comes about, and all I get is an approximation of my purpose," he confided to an interviewer, "then nothing but a sort of compromise or disappointment can take place."[37] By minimizing or eliminating intentionality, Cage avoided both the risk of failure, with its potential for pain, and the moral burden of personal responsibility. He also avoided confronting the likelihood that he lacked the talent to be a composer and might be better suited to some other line of work. What some have praised as bold exploration on his part, then, seems little more than a pathetic attempt to guard against the consequences of failure and rejection.[38] As Nathaniel Branden has emphasized in an essay on alienation in the modern world, "*fear* of choices and decisions is a basic symptom of mental illness."[39]

One of Cage's rationalizations for his aleatory approach was his claim that "by eliminating purpose" in his pieces, "awareness increases."[40] Such a claim is absurd, since the random sort of awareness it presupposes (as in *4'33"*, for example) is antithetical to the very point of art, which is to focus attention on those aspects of existence deemed most important. For Cage, however, all sounds, of any quality and from any source, were equally "interesting in themselves," so much so that he even sought, through various means, to strip language of its meaning and reduce it to pure sound. He often declared that, as *4'33"* implied, "everything we do [and hear] is music."[41] Even "primitive" African tribesmen know better, however. Anthropologist Alan Merriam argues that the Bala people of West Africa, for example, implicitly confirm the principle that "if no distinction can be made between music on one hand and nonmusical sounds on the other, there can be no such thing as music."[42] Unlike Cage, they clearly understand that music is not the same as noise, that it is created only by humans, that it is a product of thought, and that it is never random but must always be purposefully organized. (272–74) As Sass suggests in *Madness and Modernism* (151), Cage's "glorifying of the unique and the random" constitutes a variety of mental aberration "very common" among schizophrenics. Exhibiting what Rand would have referred to as an extreme "concrete-boundedness,"[43] such patients, Sass further notes, exhibit an "abnormal interest" in the particular aspects of perceptual objects and "balk at defining things in terms that strike them as too general."

Another profoundly dysfunctional feature of Cage's work and thought involves his distrust of all emotion, not merely in the arts, but in life itself. "Emotions do not interest me," he told one interviewer. "Emotions have long been known to be dangerous. You must free yourself of your likes and dislikes."[44] On another occasion, he declared that "responding emotionally" is one of the things that concertgoers should most resist doing.[45] Here, again, Cage's attitude and theories bear a disturbing similarity to behavior exhibited by both schizoid and schizophrenic individuals. The former, Sass notes, characteristically seem "detached," displaying an extreme "'emotional flatness'"—as expressed in one schizoid person's statement: "'I have taught myself to dissociate from emotion.'"[46] According to another authority, such a "peculiar and fundamental want of any *strong feeling of the impressions of life*" may well be the most characteristic symptom of this form of mental illness.[47] (We are reminded here of the importance of emotion to psychological well-being, which we discussed in Chapter 7 in relation to Rand's theory of art.) At the same time, schizophrenics often exhibit a tendency toward inappropriate laughter, which is entirely joyless and is related to their "famous empty smile"[48]—aspects of behavior often displayed by Cage himself during videotaped conversations and interviews and in photographs, contributing to the disturbing impression that he was strangely out of touch with reality.[49]

Finally, there is Cage's often-cited claim that his compositional procedures were inspired by Zen Buddhism. To our knowledge, that claim has remarkably gone unchallenged, as if purporting to lend legitimacy to his and Cunningham's work.[50] In fact, it involves an egregious misrepresentation of the principles of Zen esthetics. Zen dicta regarding artistic creation are actually closer to Rand's theory of art than to Cage's absurdist, chaotic aims and arbitrary procedures—though Rand would have been surprised to learn it.[51] The most celebrated Zen-inspired tracts on esthetics, for example—treatises on Japan's traditional *no* theater by Zeami Motokiyo (1363–1443)—deal with such principles as discipline, intentionality, careful observation and stylized imitation of nature, intelligibility, integration, and the contextuality of meaning,[52] all principles which are ignored or rejected by Cage. In striking contrast with Cage, Zeami (who was a playwright, actor, and head of a theatrical troupe) insists upon meaningful integration of all the elements of performance. In the art of *no*—which combines drama, music, and dance—both movement and song (chant) are to be used "in the service of all that is suggested by the text." (27) For Zeami, then, "the play's the thing" around which all else revolves. Further, contrary to Cage's eschewal of both meaning and emotion, Zen artists focus on emotionally charged subjects and themes related to such elemental human concerns as love, death, beauty, and nobility. In sum, while Zen-inspired art strives for a total integration of purpose and the disciplined mastery of skills, in order to capture with the greatest clarity and economy of means the essence of the person or object represented, Cage's aleatory procedures produce only disintegrated complexity and an absence of intelligible content. "I try to make a music which I don't understand," he declared, "and which will be difficult for other people to understand, too."[53]

Ironically, although most of Cage's work was the antithesis of music, the *New Grove Dictionary of Music* credits him with "a greater impact on world music than any other American composer of the twentieth century" (and, despite the profoundly irrational character of Cage's thought, also identifies him as a "philosopher").[54] Cage's greatest influence was not on music, however. It was on the visual and performing arts, through his collaboration with Merce Cunningham and with such avant-garde visual "artists" as Rauschenberg.[55] In 1952, years before Cage's *HPSCHD*, the three had collaborated on a similarly chaotic piece assembled by Cage at Black Mountain College in Virginia. Though dubbed a "concerted action" (a term implying cooperative integration), the Cage event was, in fact, a cacophony of simultaneous yet disparate activities. Among other activities, Cage, on a stepladder, recited Zen-related and medieval texts.

> Then he performed a "composition with a radio." . . . Rauschenberg played old records on a hand-wound gramophone and David Tudor played a "prepared piano." . . . Cunningham and others danced through the aisles chased by an excited dog. Rauschenberg flashed "abstract" slides . . . and film clips projected onto the ceiling. . . . In a corner, the composer Jay Watt played exotic musical instruments and "whistles blew, babies screamed and coffee was served by four boys dressed in white."[56]

According to dance historian David Vaughan, this "untitled theater piece" was a "seminal work in the history of contemporary art."[57] Indeed it was. But what it gave rise to is scarcely worthy of celebration. The event served as a model for the bizarre "live art" and "happenings" that became the focus of the New York avant-garde in the late 1950s and 1960s, as well as for the sort of "dance" pieces Cage and Cunningham would subsequently produce together—work that would inspire a whole new generation of freakish "experiments" in the world of dance and so-called performance art. And Cage's antirational "esthetic" of chance has been appealing in recent years to an even younger generation of admirers.[58]

Avant-Garde Dance: Merce Cunningham

In the long partnership between Cage and Cunningham, which spanned more than four decades, Cage was clearly dominant. Cunningham not only embraced Cage's addled ideas about art and life, including his rejection of emotion and goal-directed intention; he also adopted Cage's chance procedures for his choreography. Moreover, in keeping with Cage's notion that artistic "collaborators" could develop their contributions to a piece independently and then simply appear together for the public performance, Cunningham insisted that music is not essential to dance, and accordingly set his choreography to silence—though he always employed some sort of sound, or "score," in performing the finished piece.[59]

Cage's eccentric influence on Cunningham is palpable. In *Variations V* (1965), for example, a profusion of moving and still images which had no relation to the choreography were projected onto the stage. What passed for sound accompaniment was generated by the dancers themselves—as their movements, read by electronic sensors placed at various points onstage, were translated into audible signals, in no discernible pattern or meaningful order.[60] *Winterbranch* (1964) employed a "sound score" and lighting scheme so punishing to the senses that they "drove audience members out of the theater."[61] Such works prompted dance critic Marcia Siegel to remark: "In his goodnatured way, Cunningham has always been in the forefront of the rape-the-audience crowd."[62] *Roaratorio: An Irish Circus on Finnegans Wake* (1983) presents Cunningham's choreography with a text adapted by Cage (the punning title is his as well) from James Joyce's most inscrutable work of fiction, as well as an unintelligible "score" consisting, in part, of a complex collage of sounds recorded in locales Joyce cites. Even *Summerspace* (1958)—a relatively early and far less aggressively iconoclastic work that became part of the New York City Ballet repertory in 1999—is dehumanized, abstract, and lacking in dramatic point or focus. This effect is not surprising, since Cunningham choreographed the piece by chance methods, independent of the score by Morton Feldman (which itself sounds like aimless musical doodling). Further, the costumes and decor, which Rauschenberg designed in an all-over pointillist pattern, served to camouflage the dancers, "as though they were [merely] elements of the decor" (as Cunningham put it), rather than setting off and enhancing their movement.[63] For one dance writer, this "lyric" piece evoked "winged insects in a summer landscape." But Cunningham claims it is simply "about space"—a characteristically abstract notion on his part, devoid of human significance or emotional nuance, and analogous to claims that abstract painting is "about" form or color.[64] He similarly characterizes *Winterbranch* as a dance "about falling."[65] "I am more interested in the *facts* of moving . . . than my feelings about them," he explains. "I am interested in experimenting with movements."[66] Echoing Cage's emotional detachment, he prefers random methods to decisions based on "likes and dislikes."[67] The basis for his dances is simply "the human body moving in time-space. . . . The ideas of the dance . . . are in the movement. It has no reference outside that. . . . This non-reference of the movement is extended into a relationship with music. It is essentially a non-relationship."[68]

In contrast with the "plotless" ballets of modern choreographers such as George Balanchine—which are often inaccurately termed "abstract"—Cunningham's use of human movement is wholly abstract—in the same sense that "abstract art" is in the use of form and color. As Clive Barnes has emphasized, Cunningham's approach depends on "having people behave in unlikely—therefore 'abstract'—fashion, with the fragmentation of movement and dance phrases in gobbets and clusters rather than lines . . . [and] on chance and happenstance. It all created a sense of the unreal and the, yes, abstract. Logic had . . . gone out the window and with it some sense of anthropomorphic dancing."[69] Cunningham's pieces thus lack not only the narrative plot that integrated the classic ballets of the nineteenth century; in contrast with Balanchine's work, they also lack the logical and emotional coherence of movement rooted in a musical score.[70] Their arbitrary clusters of movement are neither meaningful in themselves nor intelligible in relation to each other. "If we think we discern meaning in Mr. Cunningham's choreography," *New York Times* dance critic Anna Kisselgoff reminds us, "that is because we have attached [our own] interpretations to what we see."[71] Any such readings, as another writer aptly suggests, are "only the products of [a] pattern-seeking mind, eager for a structure [and significance] Mr. Cunningham and his colleagues never intended."[72] What is the point of his "dances of non-sequiturs"? asks Kisselgoff. "The point is no point"—other than that "through unorthodox ways of putting steps together," he "creates images and postures we have never seen before." Consequently, just as art critics write of "pure form" and "pure color" in abstract art, Kisselgoff views Cunningham's work in terms of "pure movement"[73]—thereby echoing his own claims.

Like Cage, Cunningham violates the essential principles not solely of dance but of the normal processes of human thought and action. In place of purposeful focus, meaningful selectivity, integration, and clarity, he cultivates lack of focus, the arbitrary and the random, disunity, and meaningless complexity. "One reason [my] dances are particularly difficult to see is that they are not constructed linearly," he claims. "One thing doesn't lead to another. As a student in dance composition, I was taught that you lead up to something, some climax. That didn't interest me very much. I rather liked the idea of things staying separate, something not leading up to something else."[74] According to Cunningham:

> In most conventional dances there is a central idea to which everything adheres. . . . What we have done in our work is to bring together three separate elements in time and space, the music, the dance and the decor, allowing each one to remain independent. The three arts don't come from a single idea which the dance demonstrates, the music supports and the decor illustrates, but rather they are three separate elements each central to itself. [137]

What Cunningham dismisses as merely "conventional" is, on the contrary, essential not only to dance but to viable human thought and action—as Rand repeatedly emphasized. Indeed, the insistence by both Cage and Cunningham on disparateness for its own sake—on assemblages of random, disconnected elements unrelated to any central idea or purpose—resembles yet another characteristic feature of schizophrenia Sass notes in *Madness and Modernism*. It is the

> loss of the normal hierarchical organization and goal-directedness of thought, . . . caused by an interruption or loosening of the normal threads of [conceptual] association. . . . [These] thought disorders . . . concern not so much the content of thought . . . as the patient's entire mode or style of thinking—including aspects of categorization, concept formation, and logical inference, as well as anomalies in the temporal or spatial ordering of experience. [121]

Sass's reference to "style of thinking" corresponds precisely to Rand's concept of *psycho-epistemology*, which is central to her theory of how art is created and experienced. His observations lend implicit support to her charge that "modern art" is symptomatic of profoundly dysfunctional cognitive processes. In the light of Sass's clinical observations, and the deliberate pointlessness of Cage's and Cunningham's work, Rand's remark at the conclusion of "Art and Cognition" bears repetition: "This side of an insane asylum, the actions of a human being are motivated by a conscious purpose; when they are not, they are of no interest to anyone outside a psychotherapist's office."

What is it that enthusiastic critics primarily respond to in Cunningham's inscrutable pieces?—the sight of technically accomplished dancers performing complex and difficult movements with masterly control. Cunningham's total commitment to technical perfection of movement constitutes his one important departure from Cage—who characteristically declared: "Modern art has no need of technique." A superlative dancer himself (he performed with Martha Graham for five years before striking out on his own), Cunningham developed a distinctive technique combining balletic movements with modern elements both derived from Graham and of his own invention.[75] Critics are seduced by the mere technical perfection of his dancers.[76] "Strip them of their technique," Arlene Croce has candidly declared, "and you have something which . . . comes close to saying, 'Art is bunk.'"[77] "One is entertained solely by the formal values of [their] dancing," she emphasizes. "[T]hose who get pleasure from the sheer physical act of dancing and from its cultivation by experts will find their pleasure taking an endless variety of forms, and, . . . they may even be moved to ecstasy."[78] (There is a particular irony in such an emphasis, however, when one considers that modern dance began as a rejection of the mere technical virtuosity of much classical ballet of the time.) Untroubled by the meaninglessness of Cunningham's virtuosity, the majority of critics acclaim him a "great artist" [80]—albeit one who, in the words of dance historian Walter Sorell, "has set the artistic clock ahead to an hour that some of us cannot yet read."[79] Croce goes so far as to argue that the virtue of Cunningham's choreography lies precisely in "its capacity to seem to be anything the viewer takes it for on any given night." Equally perversely, she insists (131) that Cunningham's work is "no more haphazard than the work of any other fine choreographer. Basically, [he] works from the materials he has—the capabilities of his dancers combined with formal or technical concerns that seem to him in need of development. The results of this labor may be illuminated or organized by chance discoveries, but what Merce Cunningham does is not determined by chance."

In the absence of a meaningful relationship to music, however, the formal values of Cunningham's work do not cohere into an objectively intelligible whole, expressive of something significant about human life. According to the principles of art identified by Rand, they constitute neither dance nor a new form of art. In their deliberate randomness and contingency, Cunningham's pieces are not simply failed art: they are the very antithesis of art— since the main point of art is to integrate human experience and focus attention on its significant aspects. There must be some point, some potential relevance for one's life—not in the sense of a didactic lesson but, as Rand emphasized, in the sense of "this is important." To quote Martha Graham (whose esthetic Cunningham rejected to his detriment): "No art ignores human values, for therein lie its roots." In art, moreover, such values must engage the emotions, as Graham further stressed: "[A]rt is not [merely] to be *understood*, . . . but is to be *experienced*. To experience means that our minds and emotions are involved. For primarily it is the nervous system [i.e. sensory perception] that is the instrument of experience. This is the reason music, with its sound and rhythm, is universally the great moving force of the world"[81]—and, therefore, of dance.

Dance: The "Silent Partner of Music"

As Rand stressed, dance is the "silent partner of music"; it is not "an independent, primary art."[82] And in the partnership between them, music "sets the terms." Cunningham and his followers aside, her view is widely shared in the dance world. As one composer noted: "Music and dance are allied arts. Dance may not be a lesser art, but it has no life of its own dissociated from music. It derives its stimulus from music." The task of the choreographer, therefore, is "to capture the emotional essence of the music."[83] So, too, George Balanchine advised that, because music is "the heart of a dance," a choreographer "ought to know this art professionally so that he or she can analyze the works and not only use the most obvious part—the melody—but all of its structural characteristics."[84] Dance is dependent on rhythmic organization, Balanchine emphasized, but the "choreographer can't invent rhythms, he only reflects them in movement. . . . [T]he organizing of rhythm on a grand scale . . . is a function of the musical mind."[85]

Dancers and choreographers alike acknowledge that music provides the *emotional* core of dance as well as its structure. Isadora Duncan, one of the pioneers of modern dance, improvised her performances in direct response to the emotional thrust of instrumental works by classical composers, and thereby established a complementary relationship between dance and music that has had an incalculable influence on ballet choreographers. The first plotless ballet—Michel Fokine's *Les Sylphides*, to music by Chopin—was inspired by her approach.[86] "Everything is born out of the music," the Italian ballerina Carla Fracci has declared. "I always try to imagine what the composer wanted to say with each piece, and then I breathe with the phrase."[87] The dancer-choreographer William Carter, exceptional for his equal mastery of classical ballet, modern dance, and Spanish dance, affirmed: "[F]or me, music is always the foundation."[88] Whenever possible, he would list the composer's name first on programs for works he choreographed. Finally, Moira Shearer (the Scottish ballerina who starred in the 1948 film *The Red Shoes*) rightly observed that ballets without music are "a contradiction of what dancing is about" and that it is surely music that "makes one want to dance."[89]

In an illuminating biography of the modern dancer-choreographer Mark Morris, Joan Acocella analyzes his profound musicality. "[T]he whole pattern of his mind—his intelligence, his emotions, his worldview—[is] woven on the web of music." His choreography "is not just accompanied by the music; it is a reading of the music . . . a physical act of musical understanding." (160–62) Morris tends to choose his music for its clarity, but an emotional connection for him is also essential. "'You can't just choose any old piece of music and lay choreography over it,'" he explains. "'The choice has to be motivated.'" (168) Morris loves Baroque music, in particular, for its expressiveness: "that emotional stuff that just hits you in the face. . . . The more you listen to it, the more secret and rich things you can find dramatically.'"[90] As Acocella recounts, Morris begins his creative process by "listening to the music very hard, analytically."

> [A]s he does so, an emotion is being born in his mind, an emotion that gradually eats the music, makes it his. That emotion, and not the music, is what he then mirrors in the dance. . . . [It] follows the lines of the music, but it is not a direct translation. . . . The choreography is a translation of the emotional idea or—because he is a choreographer and thinks in movement images—[of] the emotion/movement idea generated in his mind by the musical structure.[91]

Like Morris and Taylor, Jerome Robbins (1918–1998)—who choreographed in the classical ballet idiom, and was also noted for his work for the musical theater—repeatedly found rich inspiration in the complexities of baroque music, in his case that of J. S. Bach. Regarding Robbins's 1971 ballet setting of Bach's great keyboard work, the *Goldberg Variations*, Anna Kisselgoff observed: "At heart, it is [his] response to the music. Essentially, he hears music in unexpected ways, preferring the surprising dramatic image to a strict visual counterpart to the score's structure. . . . The choreography's relationship to the music is complex. . . . But Mr. Robbins's view of human relationships also comes to the fore."[92] In a rare interview with Deborah Jowitt a year before his death, Robbins explained his affinity for Bach's music: "'It's something you want to dance. . . . I find [its] richness very, very exciting, thrilling, and disturbing in a way. . . . He's taking strange journeys while searching out all the things he wants to find out.'"[93]

The ballets of Boris Eifman, a critically acclaimed contemporary Russian choreographer in the classical tradition, are also inspired by music. "Using the movements of the body, [I] try to express the protagonist's inner life, his emotions," Eifman stresses. I have always striven for . . . the physicalization of emotions of the soul." For him, as for Morris, that creative process begins with the music. "I am constantly in the world of music," he says. "Not only do I hear it, I also see it. It gives birth to my ideas."[94]

The contemporary dancer-choreographer Twyla Tharp offers candid further testimony of the centrality of music to dance. Of her early years as a member of the post-Cunningham avant-garde, she ironically recalls: "[W]e were not corrupt enough to perform [to] music. Some avant-garde taboos were . . . too powerful to break."[95] While she stops short of acknowledging that her youthful "explorations" of movement in the absence of music were something other than dance, it is clear that her mature work is musically inspired. Having abandoned any Cunningham-influenced notions that dance is merely about "dance" or "movement," her choreography now expresses more metaphysical concerns.[96] "I think of music as fuel, its spectrum of energy governed by tempi, volume, and heart," she wrote in 1992.[97] In *Grosse Sonate* (1999), set to Beethoven's "Hammerklavier" sonata, she accordingly took the lead from the music's drama—from its "assertive opening theme" (to quote dance critic Jack Anderson) to its "mighty concluding fugue." And just as the music, "though often stormy, ultimately conveys a sense of cosmic joy," the dancers, too, "seemed to attain a state of exaltation."[98]

Cunningham's Progeny

By seeming to legitimize the notion of dance as the mere "exploration of movement," independent of music, Merce Cunningham opened a Pandora's box that has yet to be closed. Consistent with the Cage-Cunningham dictum that "Everything is permitted," the avant-garde movement they influenced went even further than Cunningham in jettisoning the fundamental attributes of dance.[99] Self-styled choreographers even rejected the few characteristics that were, according to David Vaughan, Cunningham's work's remaining tenuous links to the realm of dance—"its technical finish, its theatricality, the fact that Cunningham himself remained firmly in control."[100]

Often referred to as *postmodern dance* (a term we shall say more about below), this movement gained momentum from a series of workshops in the early 1960s on the chance procedures of Cage and Cunningham.[101] Just as the audience for such work was drawn from people more interested in the visual arts than in dance, so too many of the students in the workshops were painters, rather than dancers or even musicians. Since what they were doing did not constitute dance, lack of training in dance or music scarcely mattered. Workshop participants soon began to stage public presentations of their often-improvised pieces at the Judson Memorial Church in New York's Greenwich Village, where the performing groups loosely allied themselves as the Judson Dance Theater.

Two of the principal Judson choreographers were Trisha Brown and Yvonne Rainer, both of whom had studied with Martha Graham as well as with Cunningham and the West-coast iconoclast Anna Halprin. Rainer, in particular, became notorious for her explicit rejection of every "traditional" aspect of dance represented by choreographers like Graham and even, albeit to a minimal degree, by Cunningham:

> NO to spectacle no to virtuosity no to transformations and magic and make-believe no to the glamour and transcendency of the star image no to the heroic no to the anti-heroic no to trash imagery no to involvement of performer or spectator no to style no to camp no to seduction of spectator by the wiles of the performer no to eccentricity no to moving or being moved.[102]

What did this leave? Not much. Typical early works by Rainer were *Parts of Some Sextets* (1965), which she called "a dance for 10 people and 12 mattresses"; and *Room Service* (1963), featuring two performers carrying a mattress up an aisle of the theater, out one exit, and then back in through another.[103] The movement in these pieces was deliberately banal, in no way stylized or intensified. Brown's similar "experiments in 'anti-gravity and ordinary movement in extraordinary circumstances'" included *Walking on the Wall* (1970)—in which the performers, hanging perpendicular to a wall by means of a harness, attempted to move as if they were in a normal upright position.[104]

Following Cunningham's example, the role of music was either trivialized or entirely eliminated. Rainer's "sound score" for her three-part solo *Three Seascapes* (1962), gave equal status to an excerpt of music by Rachmaninov, the sounds of a chair being dragged across a wood floor, and her own screams. The young Paul Taylor, who had danced with Cunningham's nascent company at Black Mountain College in 1953, staged a piece that was a counterpart, in "movement," to Cage's *4'33"* in the realm of "sound." In his ironically titled *Epic* (1957), Taylor simply walked onto the stage, stood still for approximately ten minutes while telephone time signals were played, and then walked off—a provocation that famously prompted Louis Horst to respond with a blank page where his review should have appeared in *Dance Observer*.[105]

Among the Judson Church performers was Meredith Monk, who began as a dancer-choreographer but has more recently been characterized as "a composer-choreographer-singer-dancer-filmmaker . . . and a vanguardist in all these roles."[106] Monk's vanguardism was evident in her first important solo, *Break* (1964), in which she wore a clear plastic raincoat over tights and a leotard, and moved about the stage to the sounds of an automobile. Possessing an unearthly vocal range, she soon began to add sung elements to multimedia theatrical pieces that often included film clips and *quasi* mime as well. Although she correctly claims that "'voice and body form parts of a single expressive instrument'"[107] (as our discussion of the interconnectedness of vocal and bodily expression in Chapters 5 and 7 suggests), both modes of expression are essentially incoherent in her work. Her movement consists "primarily of mime-style gesture disconnected from specific meaning" (to quote Tobi Tobias), while her "unearthly form of primal song [consists of] strings of repeated syllables that never form words, intoned in a voice that slides from the guttural to the angelically pure."[108]

Monk has the audacity to call what she does *opera*.[109] Critics should know better, however, as should opera directors. Yet Jack Anderson raises no objection to Monk's calling herself a composer—despite his finding her "music [to be] of a startling sort that requires singers to wail, cackle, chant, croon, hoot or moan." Nor does he question the judgment of the Houston Grand Opera management in commissioning and accepting a work from her—although he notes that the commissioned piece, *Atlas* (1991), is "an opera that surely only a choreographer could have conceived," since it has "almost no text whatsoever. Instead the cast sings wordless syllables, conveying the dramatic action through movements and tone of voice."[110] What Tobias has written about the current fad for "multimedia" presentations is surely applicable to Monk's work: "you wonder whether the artist isn't spreading himself thin over several genres because he's incapable of mastering a single one."[111] "Many postmodern-dance-makers use fragments of spoken text, either incorporating words as an element in the collage they're constructing or relying on speech to communicate ideas, emotions, even atmospheres they can't engender through dance alone."[112] (We have already noted much the same practice among minimalist "composers.") Whereas "traditional" collaborative art forms such as opera and ballet aim to integrate their components into an intelligible whole, today's avant-gardists, following the lead of Cunningham and Cage, offer mere simultaneity of various media. More often than not, each of the components is itself disordered or unintelligible; the inevitable effect is one of chaos and confusion.

Initially a fringe phenomenon ignored or rejected by critics, "experimental dance" and its cousins are now respectfully reviewed on a regular basis, and even influence the theoretical considerations of estheticians. Although classified as "postmodern dance," such performances are neither postmodern nor dance. They are not really *post*modern, since most of their departures from long-established forms and practices had been attempted either by Cunningham—whose own work was more closely linked to early avant-garde ballet than to "modern dance" (though critics often mistakenly associate with him with the latter)—or by early modern varieties of "performance art."[113]

In any case, whatever one terms it, the "post-Cunningham" avant-garde is worlds apart from the now classic tradition of modern dance exemplified by Martha Graham, José Limon, Pearl Lang, and Alvin Ailey. That tradition, as Tobias argues, honored "sound craft . . . coupled with humanistic concerns

and values"—whereas so-called postmodern dance rejects "clear logical structure" and (if it does not eliminate content entirely) "tends to 'dis' life, representing it as disjunctive and discordant, with personal relationships chronically
dysfunctional." Classic modern dance recognizes

> that life is not simple or easy, but its governing attitude is optimistic. *You can
> engage with trouble*, the classical modernists tell us, *and emerge triumphant,
> or, if you're defeated, at least go down with your flags flying. Mutual under-
> standing is possible. A community based on common ideals exists. Problems
> can be examined and resolved. Life at its darkest is still worth living.*[114]

Moreover, Tobias emphasizes:

> In works of this kind, you know just where you are; situations and feelings
> are painted boldly and clearly. There may be subtlety . . . but there's little
> ambiguity. Pain is pain; rage, grief, hope, and ecstasy are represented unequiv-
> ocally. *The world is knowable, and it makes sense, these dances tell us.*[115]

Most important, classic modern dance (in contrast with the post-Cunningham avant-garde) "bears some message about human character and human
relationships, reflecting and illuminating the viewer's personal experience."[116]
In sum, it deals in an intelligible and ultimately uplifting way with the sort
of humanly relevant metaphysical concerns that Rand emphasizes lie at the
core of art.

One variety of "postmodern dance"—so-called *dance theater*[117]—seems
fraught with "messages" about life, but they are mostly unintelligible. And
the work falls short of dance in other essential respects, as Tobias has tren-
chantly observed. Writing about one of its leading practitioners, the German
avant-gardist Pina Bausch, Tobias notes:

> [Her world] consists of semi-inscrutable, absurdist vignettes involving, in
> equal parts, physical messiness on a grand scale, cruelty (usually sexual, often
> misogynist), and intimations of doomsday. Clothing (vintage-style gowns,
> stiletto heels, underwear) and foodstuffs, along with spoken text and screams,
> play secondary but significant roles. . . . Bausch's natural modes are the nihilis-
> tic, the melodramatic, and the Dadaist.[118]

"But is it dancing?" Tobias asks, and opines: "Sometimes, the answer to
[that] query must be a firm no—when, say, rhythmic motion and a sense of
the body in space and time are not central to a work's concerns."[119] For this
reason, Bausch's "extravaganzas," like those of her Belgian counterpart Anne
Teresa De Keersmaeker, "certainly can't be termed dance; they're closer to

theater, [and] distantly related to that murkily defined genre performance art
. . . . They get previewed and reviewed by the dance press because the artists
creating the material got their start in the dance field and, I suspect, because
the theater critics refuse to be bothered with their stuff."[120]

If It Moves, It Must Be Dance

Many of the events now regularly reviewed by dance critics are more akin
to competitive or recreational sports or to the circus. But rare is the critic
either astute or intrepid enough to say so. Consider, for example, the critical
response to the group known as "Pilobolus," which was formed in 1971 by
four Dartmouth College students with minimal dance training. When they
premiered their act in New York that year, Anna Kisselgoff reviewed it in the
Times, dubbing it a "dance group" and describing what would become its singular style: the formation of "witty and theatrical shapes through various
linked groupings of their bodies." After praising the performers' "enthusi-
asm" and "amazing physical fearlessness," she tentatively ventured that there
"were times when it seemed they were in danger of confusing athletics [and
'fun'] with art." "Was this gymnastics disguised as dance?" she wondered.
"Perhaps. But it worked."[121] A responsible critic would have added "*as entertainment,*"[122] and would have refrained from referring to the four students as
a "dance group."

More than a quarter-century later, the "Pilobolus Dance Theatre"—as it
is billed in the *International Encyclopedia of Dance*—thrives.[123] And critics
have continued to hedge, ignoring that a large part of their job is to make
informed judgments. "Is it a parable, or simple play?" asks Jennifer Dunning
in a 1996 review of a new piece by the company. "With Pilobolus, one is
never quite sure." When the "understated message" that often seems to be
"lurking" beneath the surface of the group's antics never materializes, however, she willingly "settles for sheer playfulness"—just as "the cheering,
whistling audience clearly did."[124]

Less diverting than the Pilobolus brand of popular entertainment is Elizabeth Streb's aptly named "Ringside" company—which has won critical
acclaim for its "bone-wrenching gravity-defying movements."[125] Kisselgoff
regards Streb as "an experimental choreographer, exploring new movements."[126] Typically, these "explorations" involve employing formidable pieces
of equipment, such as a 19-foot-tall aluminum box that is rigged to serve as
"a portable launching pad," run by four one-ton chain motors.[127] According
to dance historian and critic Robert Johnson, the Ringside performers (he
calls them "dancers") attempt to "test the laws of physics" when they "hurl
themselves against walls, roll on the floor and dive from scaffolds." "'I'm

interested in human flight,'" he quotes Streb as saying. "'Everything I've done on some level has been an attempt to fly.'" Johnson proposes that Streb's intent is to "take dance formalism to a new level." But by "miking the surfaces against which her dancers collide, she [also] hopes to rouse the public to kinesthetic empathy." In Streb's words: "'I want them [the audience] to feel like they slammed into the wall, had bodies over their head, and screamed with us.'"[128] Streb is but one exemplar of what Kisselgoff calls "the suspended-in-air mania"[129] that has swept the dance world in recent years. While giving rise to such new categories as "aerial choreography" and "trapeze dances,"[130] this fad is not really new. Much of it is merely an extension of the sort of movement "experiments" attempted by post-Cunningham choreographers such as Trisha Brown in the 1970s—in some cases, with the addition of expressionist affectations. In fact, this type of performance derives from traditional circus acts, with movie-like stunt work thrown into the mix in Streb's case.

Yet another form of popular entertainment that contemporary critics treat as dance (or theater) is in fact merely a pretentious form of circus spectacle, despite the inflated claims of critics and of the performers themselves. According to John Rockwell (now editor of the New York Times "Arts & Leisure" section), the Paris-based Zingaro company, for example, is an "equestrian circus and theater troupe" that blends "conventional circus excitement (acrobats leaping on and off galloping horses, a clown) with moments—the best moments—that [are] indistinguishable from art."[131] Bartabas, the troupe's founder and "mastermind," insists that Zingaro is "'a little theater, a little music, a little dance and not at all circus'"[132]—a claim that Rockwell seems to confirm by adding: "and in fact Zingaro's shows are supported by the [French] Ministry of Culture's theater department, not its circus department." Though nominally a theater critic, the Times's Stephen Holden also reviews the circus as art, not only referring to the Zingaro performers as "artist athletes and theatrical conjurers" but, echoing Rockwell, further asserting that "at its best the company elevates circus into a high theatrical art."[133] To that fatuous claim, he adds this not-so-subtle observation: "and it is all done without words." Never mind that "high theatrical art" means theater, and that theater consists of plays, which are made of words, not equestrian circus acts.

Fortunately, however, not all critics are so easily gulled. On the subject of Zingaro, Vincent Canby, former chief theater critic at the Times, sounds the right sardonic note:

While in the pitch-dark tent, sitting on a backless wooden plank . . . , trying to breathe oxygen through incense as thick as cigar smoke at a stag party, I was under the impression that I was simply watching some rather impressive horsemanship. . . . Not till I got home and read the very extensive program notes did I realize that I hadn't been at the circus at all. I had been watching a man's "journey to his imagined origins—a journey to Rajasthan, the mythical home of all gypsies." Most members of the audience . . . were entranced. I felt bamboozled, though one lesson was learned: from now on, if I can smell a show before it begins, I'm leaving.[134]

Constrained Movement as Dance

In stark contrast to current attempts to elevate acrobatics and movement spectacle into the art of dance (or theater) are recent efforts to create "dances" in which the performer's body is severely constrained either by the "choreography" or by a physical handicap.[135] An example of the first type is a piece by Sally Hess that Tobias characterizes as "a vigorous, grotesque *dance for the face*, with the rest of the body, rooted center-stage, playing obbligato." In her brief review, Tobias claims that the piece is an "odd and oddly satisfying study [which] seems to depict one of those loud, vulgar people convinced of the righteousness of their opinions," and adds that "there's an Aunt Marilyn of this ilk in every family. Hess's achievement rests in making her poignant."[136] Such a fancifully detailed interpretation could never be supported by facial expressions alone, however.

That a critic of Tobias's acumen seems to legitimize the notion of a "dance for the face" is regrettable enough. Far more troubling is the proposition, by philosopher Francis Sparshott, that "There could be dances of eyes, or of fingers," and that a "finger-dance . . . might (however unlikely) be the harbinger of a dance practice in which only the fingers were dancing parts."[137] His argument that "a developed art of dance" need not be "a dance of the whole body" commits a fallacy common in the esthetic speculations of "analytic" philosophers. In this case, Sparshott deals with the concept of dance as if it were a floating abstraction, divorced from the referents that gave rise to it. But the concept of dance, as we have argued, is not a mere mental construct; it is based on actual instances of a natural mode of human expression—the salient characteristics or which are determined by fundamental aspects of man's nature—from his primary means of locomotion to his basic ways of expressing emotion and communicating ideas mimetically. Whatever one might do with one's fingers, eyes, or face, it could never be properly construed as *dance*.

Similar considerations apply to the recent phenomenon of "wheelchair dance." On a personal level and figuratively speaking, the claim that someone in a wheelchair "cannot walk, yet she can dance"[138] may have inspirational and even therapeutic value. But if it refers to the *art* of dance, it is a blatant contradiction. As Rand properly argued in "Art and Cognition," the whole point (*the metaphysical meaning*) of dance emerges from a stylization of the body's natural capacities. To choreograph a "dance" for someone who cannot walk is rather like composing a "song" for someone who cannot speak. The serious critical attention that has been paid to groups such as the CandoCo—described in *Dance Magazine* as "Britain's most successful group of abled and disabled dancers"[139]—has little to do with "what dance is really about" (to quote the article's author) and everything to do with misplaced egalitarianism and a refusal to deal realistically with the vast differences that inevitably exist in individual capacities, owing to inborn or circumstantial factors. Compassionate "awareness of people with special needs" and respect for their courage and perseverance[140] may take many legitimate and useful forms. Redefining the nature of *dance* is not one of them.

"Discussing the Undiscussable"

As Joan Acocella has observed, extra-artistic "political considerations" now make it "very hard" to offer dance-related criticism where politically charged issues—such as AIDS, racism, or physical disability—are involved.[141] That such considerations enter into heated debates about the nature of dance (and other art forms) was dramatically demonstrated by the controversy surrounding Arlene Croce's provocative essay "Discussing the Undiscussable" in the *New Yorker* a few years ago.[142] Croce's subject was the choreographer Bill T. Jones's *Still/Here*, a multimedia work that prominently featured videotaped excerpts from "Survival Workshops" Jones had held with individuals suffering from terminal illnesses.[143]

"I have not seen . . . *Still/Here*, and have no plans to review it," Croce announced. She regarded Jones's inclusion of the video material as beyond the pale of art: "People are asking whether Jones's type of theatre is not a new art form," she noted. "Dying an art form? . . . If I understand *Still/Here* correctly, . . . it is [rather] a kind of messianic traveling medicine show, designed to do some good for sufferers of fatal illnesses." As Croce explains, she had decided not to view the piece because, as a critic, she felt

excluded by reason of its express intentions, which are unintelligible as theatre. . . . [But] it is as theatre, dance theatre, that I would approach it. And my approach has been cut off. By working dying people into his act, Jones is putting himself beyond the reach of criticism. I think of him as literally undiscussable—the most extreme case among the distressingly many now representing themselves to the public not as artists but as victims and martyrs.

Croce continues:

> In theatre, one chooses what one will be. . . . [But] the sick people whom
> Jones has [videotaped]—have no choice other than to be sick. The fact that
> they aren't there in person does not mitigate the starkness of their condition.
> . . . They are the prime exhibits of a director/choreographer who has *crossed
> the line between theater and reality*—who thinks that victimhood in and of
> itself is sufficient to the creation of a [work of art].[144]

The key point of Croce's argument—that "in theatre, one chooses what
one will be"—implies an important principle (which Rand emphasized): that
art does not simply *present* reality but, rather, *selectively re-creates* it. It was
not Jones's subject matter per se to which Croce primarily objected; it was
the fact that the subject matter was not transformed into art. Most critics
and writers failed to grasp this distinction, however, focusing instead on
extra-esthetic issues.[145] That there is (as novelist Joyce Carol Oates argued
in the *New York Times*) "a long and honorable tradition of art that 'bears witness' to human suffering,"[146] is beside the point. For the problem with
Still/Here was precisely that it was not Jones's *art* that bore witness to suffering, but rather the patients themselves. Nor was Croce's stand based, as
Clive Barnes charged, on "blind prejudice."[147] What it involved, first and
foremost, was adherence to an objective critical principle regarding what art
is—and is not.

Ice Dancing

The aforementioned critical principle pertains to a question raised by the
growing popularity of ice dancing[148] in recent years. Is it primarily a form of
dance (and therefore art) or an essentially athletic activity (and therefore
mainly a competitive sport) or is it a form of entertainment? That ice dancing often displays an appealing grace, as well as an expressive response to
music, is undeniable. For some critics, these characteristics are sufficient to
deem it art. "By now," Kisselgoff disdainfully proclaimed in 1994, "the debate
over whether ice dancing is a sport or an art is just one big yawn." For her,
the question had long ago been decided by the "dazzling creativity" and "artistic expression, even in rules-burdened international competition," of skaters
like Torvill and Dean.[149] For many, however, the question is not so peremp-
torily decided. *Dance Magazine* contributing editor Susan Reiter observes,
for example, that though the routine of skaters who specialize in ice dancing
"has much in common with that of dancers," they "look anxiously up to a
scoreboard rather than bask in the applause" of an appreciative audience.

"Artists or athletes? Skaters who dance or dancers who skate?" asks Reiter. "The debate rages on in figure skating publications and leaves audiences confused and frustrated."[150] The answer seems clear. If the primary focus is winning a competition bound by arbitrary rules, the activity is more akin to sport than to art, despite the fact that it incorporates "artistic" elements. The absurdity that can result from confusing art with athletics is evident in a *New York Times* editorial proclaiming the "marriage of athletics and art" when top figure skaters (or "artist-athletes") compete. According to the *Times*: "Skating the role of Salome, minus the head of John the Baptist, [Michelle Kwan] seemed to float across the ice, her hands and arms carving the air in balletic movements. Almost effortlessly, she landed seven triple jumps, one more than [her rival], including a difficult triple toe jump she adventurously added at the end."[151] Was it any wonder that, with judges scrutinizing her every move, Kwan omitted carrying the Baptist's severed head, during all those triple jumps?

Some might argue that the efforts spearheaded in the 1970s by Olympic gold medalist John Curry took ice dancing out of the realm of competition and into that of a "theater art capable of complexity of thought and design and of generating and sustaining a body of lasting work, such as exists for drama and dance."[152] Here the answer depends on an understanding of the nature of dance as an art form. Ice dancing is not *dance* because the ability to glide and to "achieve lean, or edges"[153] that is essential to figure skating is not part of the natural repertoire of human locomotion. As one dance theorist has emphasized: "In dancing, stepping from one foot to the other is the foundation from which step patterns are built, while in ice skating the foundation lies with the gliding from one foot to the other."[154] The natural response to, or struggle against, gravity—which underlies all dance—is minimized in skating. Hence Clive Barnes's observation that the "lack of friction" in ice dancing makes it "both too easy and too monotonous."[155] Finally, not only does the gliding motion of ice dancing require the use of special equipment, boots equipped with blades, but the rigidity of the boot also places limits on the skater's flexibility and fluidity.[156]

Such considerations, however, do not deter the ardent proponents of ice dancing from proclaiming it an art form. In recent years, for example, a group called the Next Ice Age, founded by disciples of Curry, has performed at the American Dance Festival in Durham, North Carolina and at the Kennedy Center Opera House. For Charles and Stephanie Reinhart, the Kennedy Center's artistic advisors for dance, "it's another way of pushing the envelope for what modern dance has traditionally done, which is to break new ground," she declares. To that he adds: "I put this in the category of what Elizabeth Streb and Pilobolus have done; when people first see them they ask, 'Is that dance?'"[157]

13

The Literary Arts
and Film

Since Ayn Rand was a novelist, (as well as a screenwriter and playwright) before she turned to philosophic essays and cultural criticism, it is not surprising that the only avant-garde art forms she dealt with in any detail were literary. What is perhaps surprising, since she is often charged with lacking a sense of humor, is that her criticism often took the form of satire in her fiction.[1] In both *Atlas Shrugged* and *The Fountainhead*, she skewered the literary avant-garde and the critical establishment that supports it, in deftly drawn caricatures of art world figures and of their theories and practices: their rejection of objective standards, their unremittingly bleak sense of life, their perpetual undermining of human dignity and achievement, and their concomitant embrace of collectivism and statism.

The acknowledged "literary leader" of the fashionable social set Rand delineates in *Atlas Shrugged*, for example, is Balph Eubank, who declares that "Plot is a primitive vulgarity in literature" and whose novels (such as *The Heart Is a Milkman*) project his conviction that the essence of life is "defeat and suffering." (133–34) Another minor character is a novelist named Gilbert Keith-Worthing, whose fame derives from writing books that no one reads. At one point early in *Atlas Shrugged*, the heroine, Dagny Taggart, exhausted and discouraged, walks through the city streets, longing for some sign of hope, and sees in a store window a stack of new novels entitled *The Vulture Is Molting*. (64)

But it was in *The Fountainhead* that Rand had given fullest expression to her satire of the literati, developing a whole circle of minor characters around the novel's antagonist Ellsworth Toohey (the collectivist-minded architecture and culture critic for Gail Wynand's newspaper *The Banner*) and the avant-garde writer Lois Cook, whom Toohey champions as "the greatest literary genius since Goethe." (232) The character of Toohey is modeled, in part, on Lewis Mumford, while Gertrude Stein clearly provided the inspiration for Lois Cook. Cook's three published works, Toohey explains, are "not exactly novels" or "collections of stories either" but "just Lois Cook—a new form of literature entirely" (233), as exemplified by this passage from her *Clouds and Shrouds*, described as a record of her world travels: "'. . . toothbrush in the jaw toothbrush brush brush tooth jaw foam dome in the foam Roman dome come home home in the jaw Rome dome tooth toothbrush toothpick pickpocket socket rocket . . .'" (234)

Rand also lampoons the audience for such work—people who puff them-selves up by pretending to appreciate the essentially inscrutable, The social-climbing architect Peter Keating, for example, is certain that *Clouds and Shrouds* is "a profound spiritual experience," because he does not understand it. In his view

> "A thing is not high if one can reach it; it is not great if one can reason about it; it is not deep if one can see its bottom"—this had always been his credo, unstated and unquestioned. This spared him any attempt to reach, reason or see; and it cast a nice reflection of scorn on those who made the attempt. So he was able to enjoy the work of Lois Cook. He felt uplifted by the knowl-edge of his own capacity to respond to the abstract, the profound, the ideal. Toohey had said: "That's just it, sound as sound, the poetry of words as words, style as a revolt against style. But only the finest spirit can appreciate it, Peter." Keating thought he could talk of this book to his friends, and if they did not understand he would know that he was superior to them. He would not need to explain that superiority—that's just it, "superiority as superiority"—auto-matically denied to those who asked for explanations. He loved the book. [234]

It was for people like Keating that the work of the members of the Council of American Writers, organized by Toohey, was aimed. Headed by Cook, the group included "a woman who never used capitals in her books, and a man who never used commas; a youth who had written a thousand-page novel without the a letter o, and another who wrote poems that neither rhymed nor scanned; a man with a beard who was sophisticated and proved it by using every unprintable four-letter word in every ten pages of his manuscript; a woman who imitated Lois Cook, except that her style was less clear; when asked for explanations she stated that this was the way life sounded to her, when broken by the prism of her subconscious. (306)

Rand also depicts fashionable parties, at which sophisticates discuss the latest avant-garde dicta. Cook's view is that "words must be freed from the oppression of reason"; that "the stranglehold of reason upon words is like the exploitation of the masses by the capitalists"; and that words "must be permitted to negotiate with reason through collective bargaining." And the *Banner* drama critic, Jules Fougler, predicts that "in the world of the future the theater will not be necessary at all," since "the daily life of the common man is as much a work of art in itself as the best Shakespearean tragedy. . . . The critic will simply observe the life of the masses and evaluate its artistic points for the public." (588)

However exaggerated Rand's fictional satires may seem, they are no more absurd than the actualities that inspired them. In this chapter, we shall touch on three prominent exponents of the literary avant-garde, and will then turn to a brief examination of the art of film (which many regard as the quintessential contemporary art form), in the light of Rand's theory that it is, at root, a form of literature.

James Joyce

When critics are asked to rank twentieth-century fiction, James Joyce's *Ulysses* (1922) is invariably at the top of the list. And Joyce himself has been regarded as the greatest master of the English language since Shakespeare or Milton.[2] As characterized by one scholar, Joyce (1882–1941) was "one of the most radical innovators of twentieth-century writing, who dedicated himself to exuberant exploration of the total resources of language."[3] As Stuart Gilbert, one of his many explicators, observed, however, a "large number" of the people who have attempted to read *Ulysses* without the benefit of a critical guide have given it up, "as making too great demands on their attention, memory and endurance."[4] By contrast, Homer's *Odyssey*, which partly inspired Joyce's work, is "quite easy reading"—even in the original, to someone with a "smattering of Greek," according to Gilbert (vii). How is it that a work composed nearly three millennia ago, in a culture worlds apart from our own, is more accessible to modern readers than Joyce's acclaimed novel, which requires a commentary of some 400 pages to disclose its mysteries and unlock its pleasures? How can an acclaimed master of the English language have failed so miserably to communicate to his own age?

On the face of it, *Ulysses* is a simple tale. As summarized by Gilbert, the narrative spans just one "perfectly ordinary" day (16 June 1904, to be precise) in the life of Leopold Bloom, a Dublin salesman "undistinguished by any particular virtue or vice" (3, 19); Stephen Dedalus, who previously appeared as the largely autobiographical protagonist of Joyce's *Portrait of the Artist as a Young Man* (1916); and Molly Bloom, Leopold's adulterous wife. The episodic thread of the narrative, much of it in the stream-of-consciousness style, takes the characters through a series of incidents representative of Dublin life, ironically paralleling the principal episodes of the *Odyssey*. Joyce not only incorporates numerous allusions to the Greek epic, some of them arcane, but also draws liberally upon other aspects of his encyclopedic store of knowledge, including fluency in several languages (not least, Latin) and a prodigious familiarity with world literature. In addition to "echoes of writers of all races, of all times" throughout the work, one episode is a "chapter of parodies," and another satirizes the hair-splitting precision of medieval theologians. (76)

In the view of J. I. M. Stewart (the author of books on both Joyce and Shakespeare):

Although [*Ulysses*] can be represented as elaborately schemed and patterned at half a dozen levels, [it] is essentially an immense and exuberant exploration of the resources of language. Nothing in it need be taken very seriously except this. When it is boring—and it is often boring—it is because the artist in Joyce has succumbed to the philologist. When it is exhilarating . . . it is because the English language is being used with a vigorous creativeness unexampled since Shakespeare.[5]

Joyce himself is reported to have told a befuddled reader that the value of his book—which was understood by only "a few writers and teachers"—lay in its "new style."[6] Indeed, it is no exaggeration to say that Joyce's style, his "manipulation of language" (as critics often refer to it), became in effect the substance of his work, exploited for its own sake, rather than as a medium for communicating a view of the world or of human character and values. In *Ulysses,* to quote Gilbert again (76), *le style c'est le thème* (just as Rand charged in her criticism of esthetic theories that emphasize style over content, as we noted in Chapter 3).

That perverse attitude toward language found its ultimate expression in Joyce's sequel, *Finnegans Wake* (1939)—a book that "cannot in any common sense be read."[7] The entire work purports to present the subconscious mental processes of a single unexceptional character, yet attempts to touch upon the whole of human history, incorporating wide-ranging mythological, literary, scientific, and historic references, not to mention numerous Joycean neologisms, the comprehension of which requires familiarity with half a dozen languages. The contrived abstruseness of *Finnegans Wake* is evident from its first line (also repeated as its last): "riverrun, past Eve and Adam's, from swerve of shore to bend of bay, brings us by commodius vicus of recirculation back to Howth Castle and Environs." Or consider the following passage, which begins the chapter entitled "Here Comes Everybody," included in *The Portable James Joyce*:

Yet may we not see still the brontoichthyan form outlined aslumbered, even in our own nighttime by the sedge of the troutling stream that Bronto loved and Brunto has a lean on. *Hic cubat edilis. Apud libertinam parvulam.* Whatif she be in flags or flitters, reekierags or sundyechosies, with a mint of mines or beggar a pinnyweight. Arrah, sure, we all love little Anny Ruiny, or, we mean to say, lovelittle Anna Rayiny, when unda her brella, mid piddle med puddle, she ninnynannygoes nancing by. Yoh! Brontolone slaaps, yoh snoores. Upon Benn Heather, in Seeple Isout too. [711]

No wonder that *Finnegans Wake* has been characterized as "admired more often than read, when read rarely read through to the end, when read through to the end not often fully, or even partially understood."[8] The "literary experiments" embodied in *Finnegans Wake* had engaged Joyce's exclusive and unremitting labor for seventeen years of his life. In it, Daniel Boorstin suggests in *The Creators*, he reached (we would say, passed) "the outer limits of intelligibility." (700) *Ulysses* was "simple clarity" compared to *Finnegans Wake*, in which "the admiring reader of Joyce meets his match, and is reluctantly driven to a heavy reliance on interpreters. Even the puzzled serious student comes to feel that he is trying to understand the ground plan of an elaborate filigreed castle in a treatise by its architect written in an only partly intelligible code." (710–11) Asks Boorstin: "Why has so eloquent and [once] lucid a writer as Joyce spent his energies teasing us with a book of colossal proportions, of 628 dense often-unparagraphed pages, with its puzzling plenitude of invented words, multiple puns, and onomatopoetic inventions? Is it inconceivable that this master of the comic may have launched the biggest literary hoax of history?"

Boorstin is not the only writer to propose that Joyce's late style may have been intended to deceive the public. In marked contrast with *Ulysses* and *Finnegans Wake*, the novelist's early work had been conventionally and lucidly written, but had repeatedly provoked would-be censors, owing to its unorthodox content.[9] "Inhibited from writing naturally of natural instincts," suggested Harry Levin, "Joyce ended by inventing an artificial language of innuendo and mockery."[10] Stewart similarly argued that, with *Finnegans Wake*, "the writer who had found himself continually harassed by censorship throughout his literary career, made it the supreme task of his life to evolve as elaborately 'censored' a work as was ever achieved by man." (648) H. L. Mencken suspected that Joyce had "concocted [*Ulysses*] as a vengeful hoax"—not to evade censors but to attract serious critical attention.[11]

Nonetheless, interpreters have for decades pored over the enigmas of *Finnegans Wake*, generating a plethora of critical studies. According to Levin, they had, by 1947, "already arrived at rough agreement as to its methods and premises, its characters and situations"— testifying, in his view, to Joyce's "artistic sincerity and intellectual rigor" (a claim that seems to contradict Levin's prior speculation regarding the author's "innuendo and mockery"). In any case, the style of the work is so impenetrable that, as even Levin concedes, "it cannot yet be considered readable in the sense of an ordinary novel." (709)

Whatever Joyce's motivation, the result was "fiction" from which human action—the most significant element of any story, as Rand emphasized), had been completely eliminated. The tendency was already evident in *Ulysses*, in which, for all its length and complexity, the main characters *do* very little. In most of the novel's incidents, they are more passive than active, merely responding to rather than bringing about the various events. In *Finnegans Wake*, goal-directed actions give way entirely to internal thought processes—and to wholly involuntary, subconscious thought at that. It is the ultimate fictional realization of what Rand characterized as the "primacy-of-consciousness" mentality.

Samuel Beckett

Many of the tendencies of Joyce's late fiction are evident to a more extreme degree in the work of another acclaimed Irish-born author, Samuel Beckett (1906–1989)—whom Louis Sass has characterized in *Madness and Modernism* as one of several "markedly schizoid" artists prominent in twentieth-century culture. (367) Awarded a Nobel Prize in 1969 for his fiction and drama, Beckett was the seminal figure of the postwar avant-garde, best known for his play *Waiting for Godot*. His death, in 1989, was announced on the front page of the *New York Times*, which devoted more than a full-page spread to his obituary by theater critic Mel Gussow.[12] Calling Beckett "a towering figure . . . who altered the course of contemporary theater," Gussow (who subsequently published an account of conversations he had had with the playwright in Beckett's final decade) also deemed his novels among both the "most experimental" and the "most profound" in Western literature. In a similar vein, Richard W. Seaver, an editor who helped to promote Beckett's work from the 1950s on, had predicted that he would ultimately be ranked as "one of the giants not only of contemporary but of all literature."[13]

Turning to Beckett's work, one enters a world so bleak, so unremittingly hopeless and meaningless, that his critical acclaim may well seem inconceivable. As Sass points out, the helpless protagonists of his fiction and drama" often resemble schizophrenics in their profound detachment from reality.[14] Though theater was for Beckett "mainly a recreation from working on the novel,"[15] it was his stage pieces, beginning with *Waiting for Godot*, that brought him fame. Labeled "a tragicomedy in two acts," *Waiting for Godot* is a piece in which, as the title suggests, there is almost no action. The main characters, two feckless tramps named Vladimir ("Didi") and Estragon ("Gogo") pass their time in aimless conversation on a "country road" in the middle of nowhere, while awaiting the arrival of a would-be savior, Godot—who never arrives and whose identity is never disclosed. Apart from a messenger boy who appears briefly at the end of each act to say that Godot cannot come that evening but will surely come tomorrow, there are only two other characters, Lucky and Pozzo, who encounter Didi and Gogo in each of the two acts, first with Pozzo drawing Lucky beastlike on a leash, then with their roles reversed. The first act ends with Gogo saying "Well, shall we go?" and Didi replying "Yes, let's go," while neither of them moves. The second act ends with the same lines, their speakers reversed; Didi and Gogo remain immobile as the curtain falls. In effect, the action of the play could be characterized by a line of Gogo's near the end of the first act: "Nothing happens, nobody comes, nobody goes, it's awful!"[16]

The other primary element of drama, the spoken word, is also reduced to the absurd in *Waiting for Godot*. Peppered with tired vaudeville jokes, bits of Beckett's much-vaunted gallows humor (at one point Didi and Gogo actually contemplate hanging themselves), and the incoherent bombast of Lucky and Pozzo, it is largely repetitive and puerile— much of it pertaining to Didi's preoccupation with his unreliable penis and Gogo's with his aching feet. As noted by John Simon (who, in a rare lapse of critical judgment, considers *Godot* one of Beckett's "four supreme plays"), these preoccupations reflect the fact that Didi and Gogo "epitomize respectively the intellectual and the common man."[17] One of the play's most famous passages is a lengthy monologue delivered by Lucky near the end of act one. Purporting to be a parody of academic discourse, it is (to quote Sass) "a similacrum of schizophrenic speech so filled with vagueness, empty repetition, and stereotyped or obscure phrases that it achieves nearly total incoherence."[18]

Godot was "an evening's entertainment compared with what followed," as Morris Dickstein observes. Beckett's work grew "ever more austere and minimal," taking literature "as close to silence as we can imagine."[19] "Setting and character . . . steadily dwindled until . . . we have only portions of people, as in *Play*, where only heads protrude from urns," Seaver notes. (589) The "four noble cornerstones" of Beckett's theatrical achievement, in Simon's view, include *Endgame* (1957), in which elderly parents sit resignedly in trash cans while two master and servant characters (reminiscent of Lucky and Pozzo) await a "final solution"; and *Krapp's Last Tape* (1959), a one-act "play" in which a seedy old man sits musing over the playback of a tape recounting memories of his past, and ends by staring motionless before him, as the tape runs on in silence. In the fourth, *Happy Days* (1961), a woman buried up to her waist in a mound of sand sinks deeper and deeper as she chronicles her life and daily routine, until only her head is visible. (This "important play," Simon observes, "is probably the last of Beckett's stage works to maintain a minimal hold on what makes a play a play in the traditional sense. There is still a sliver of a plot, a hit of dramatic progression, a sprinkling of dialogue amid the monologizing, a bit of ghostly characterization, and a wraith of a conflict."[20] Why call it a play at all? we would ask.) In Beckett's ultimate theatrical representation of what Sass terms "disembodied consciousness"—*Not I* (1972)—the "protagonist" is simply a woman's mouth, highlighted on a darkened stage, emitting a tortured monologue so fragmented that is barely coherent.[21]

Like Joyce, Beckett has inspired a veritable industry of academic and critical commentary. "If the present rate of exegesis continues," Seaver predicted in 1976, "by the end of the century Beckett's *oeuvre* will have been the subject of more scholarly probes than that of any other writer in the history of the English language with the exception of Shakespeare." To judge from the lengthy review articles that regularly appear in various publications, it was no exaggeration. What is it that critics see in Beckett's work? According to Simon, the four major plays "embrace the fundamental themes of existence and, like no others in English since Shakespeare's, wrestle them to the ground. For each of mankind's major defeats—by faith, love, society, and mortality—Beckett conjures up a tremendous theatrical master image that, supported by subsidiary images and dialogue, achieves a reduction to the absurd."[22] Seaver similarly admires Beckett's "vision of the world, his painfully honest portrayal thereof, his anti-illusionist stance." (xi) As for his characters—"errant pilgrims, in search of a meaning which . . . constantly eludes them"—it is "their very impotence and lack of success [that] touch and move us as few figures in modern literature ever have." (xxxii) "For in his dimming landscape, peopled with clowns and misfits, has-beens and ne'er-do-wells, the malformed and the deformed," Seaver concludes, Beckett has, in effect, created "[o]ur world." In particular, *Waiting for Godot*, initially perceived by the general public as an "obscure and silly hoax," can now be seen as "a meaningful parable of the human condition," according to Clive Barnes.[23]

When Beckett died, a *New York Times* editorial declared that he had "understood what could not be understood," and that the "uncertainty principle in physics found its counterpart in his plays and novels, allegories in randomness."[24] (That fatuous claim parrots a common fallacy in twentieth-century criticism, which assumes that the behavior of human beings is governed by the same set of natural laws as subatomic particles.[25]) As Beckett clearly indicated on innumerable occasions, however, he lacked any clear knowledge of anything, much less on so universal a scale. To questions regarding the meaning of his own work, he repeatedly said that he knew no more than was on the printed page. More telling, when asked about the purported influence of Joyce (with whom he had been closely associated for many years in Paris), Beckett replied that Joyce had been able to make "words do the absolute maximum of work," whereas

> I'm not the master of my own material. . . . [Joyce tended] toward omniscience and omnipotence as an artist. I'm working with impotence, ignorance. . . . My little exploration is the whole zone of being that has always been set aside by artists as something unusable—as something by definition incompatible with art.[26]

On another occasion, Beckett alluded to the anxiety aroused in him by the act of writing as the paradox of the artist for whom "there is nothing to express, nothing with which to express, no power to express, no desire to express, together with the obligation to express."[27] Such statements should not be regarded as mere tokens of false modesty but, rather, as signs of a deep psychological disturbance all too transparently reflected in Beckett's work. This "bard of a condition of nearly terminal detachment" (to quote Sass again) presented a "vision of meaninglessness . . . so taken for granted [that] any alternative view [was] out of the question from the outset."[28] It was a vision that stemmed not from any profound insight on his part but from his own schizoid tendencies, so dysfunctional that he had to struggle against them all his life,[29] even undergoing a two-year course of treatment at the Tavistock Clinic in London in the early 1930s.

To those who nonetheless insist that Beckett's work presents a true picture of the human condition, we can only reply that, were such the case, mankind would never have made its way out of the caves.

As the London theater critic Charles Spencer observed of Beckett's *Endgame*:

> [M]ost critics argue that Beckett's bleak vision is the achievement of a heroic and honest artist. Beckett, we are asked to believe, had courage. What he really had was an illness. Anyone who has ever suffered from depression will immediately recognise Beckett's dramatic world—the listlessness and despair, the blank horizon, even the outbreaks of gallows humour that grow from the death, rather than the resilience, of the human spirit. This may be of psychiatric interest, but frankly it is inadequate as art. I'm not suggesting that all

plays should aim for a spurious spiritual uplift, but Beckett's despair is too all-embracing, and too facile. He has given up before he has started, and his view of life is woefully incomplete. . . . All that is left is grim endurance. You can pity the dramatist for this, but during the interminable course of *Endgame* you find yourself resenting him, too. Depression is as infectious as flu and the . . . relentless drip, drip, drip of misery [in the play] is like Chinese water torture. By the end you've been reduced to Beckett's level of hopelessness. It is only as you emerge from the theatre and notice that the trees are in bud, the pubs are open and lovers are walking down the street that you re-acquaint yourself with the fact that life has far more to offer than the playwright suggests.[30]

John Ashbery

Since the middle of the twentieth century, no body of work purporting to be poetry has been simultaneously as critically acclaimed and as unintelligible as that of John Ashbery.[31] Rare is the review that does not cite both facts, in virtually the same breath, without discerning any contradiction. One writer notes his "enormous literary prominence," for example, while adding that he has "both delighted and confounded critics, some of whom claim his cerebral code is a bit too hard to crack." [32] Another observes that though he is "often regarded as the most original poet" of his time, he is "difficult, hard to understand."[33] While Ashbery's work is "extremely difficult, if not impenetrable," Richard Kostelanetz declares, his fame is by now such that "even those anthologists and [literary] historians unable to comprehend his difficult poetry feel obliged to acknowledge it.[34] And Mark Ford, to cite yet another example, refers to "the ever-shifting but unabridgeable gap between the words and meanings charted by Ashbery's poetry," whose "indirectness takes on many forms"—"slippery syntax, elusive personae, narrative uncertainy, the blending of incongruous dictions," among others.[35] None of these writers ever considers the possibility that Ashbery's work may not qualify as poetry.

　　Ashbery was inspired by the avant-garde work of the 1950s, from the paintings of Jackson Pollock to the musical compositions of Elliot Carter.[36] Not suprisingly, no figure influenced him more than the ubiquitous John Cage. On one pivotal occasion, Ashbery, who had for two years been experiencing writer's block, happened to attend a performance of Cage's "Music of Changes." As he relates, he was "jolted" out of his long depression by the piece. "It was a series of dissonant chords, mostly loud, with irregular rhythm. It went on for over an hour and seemed infinitely extendable. I felt profoundly refreshed after listening to that. I started to write again shortly afterwards. I felt that I could be as singular in my art as Cage was in his."[37] Ashbery further explains: "The actual mechanics of [Cage's] method escaped me then as it does now;

what mattered was that chance elements could combine to produce so beautiful and cogent a work. It was a further, perhaps . . . ultimate proof not so much of 'Anything goes' but 'Anything can come out'"[38]—a meaningless distinction in our view. Ford comments that "Cage's autonomous tone-clusters served both as a paradigm for future innovations and as a revelation of the virtues of experimentation *per se.*"[39]

Some idea of the sort of work that resulted from such inspiration can be gleaned from the first three stanzas of a "poem" entitled "Theme," in the collection *Can You Hear, Bird* (1995): "If I were a piano shawl / a porch on someone's house / flooding the suave timbre . . . // Then forty, he, / a unique monsieur— / and yet he never wanted to look into it. // 'Have you forgotten your little Kiki?' / Smoke from the horses' nostrils / wreathed the pump by the well." [40] In a review of *Can You Hear, Bird*, the poet Wlliam Logan observes: "Reading such stanzas, you feel they might have been arranged in another way without loss, that a typesetter might have jumbled two or three poems together without anyone noticing—without even Ashbery noticing!"[41]

According to Kostelanetz: "The real key to Ashbery's genius lies . . . in the 'sound' of his poetry; it is also the quality most likely to elude the hasty reader of his works. His poetry initially communicates, as music communicates, at levels that defy conceptual definition. Ashbery's poetry demands not only reading with highest concentration but persistent rereading; the mastering of it becomes a kind of spiritual experience."[42] Kostelanetz's self-serving encomium to Ashbery, which is yet another instance of the counterfeit elitism pervasive among modernist and postmodernist critics, not very subtly faults the poor reader who dismisses the poet's rantings as incomprehensible by suggesting that he lacks sufficient concentration and persistence to "master" the deep complexities of Ashbery's work.

Kostelanetz's emphasis on the "sound" emanating from Ashbery is echoed by essayist and poet Dana Gioia in *Can Poetry Matter?*[43] For Gioia, Ashbery's pieces "often seem arbitrary," and their unity is "mainly stylistic"; their "meaning is in their method." They are

mainly the surface play of words and images. One never remembers ideas from an Ashbery poem, one recalls the tones and textures. If ideas are dealt with at all, they are present only as faint echoes heard remotely in some turn of phrase. Ideas in Ashbery are like the melodies in some jazz improvisations where the musicians have left out the original tune to avoid paying royalties. They are wild variations on a missing theme. [44]

In her only theoretical statement on the subject, Rand observed that the "basic attributes of poetry are theme and style."[45] Her crucial term *theme* is synonymous with "abstract meaning." Thus something purporting to be poetry must have more than style; it must have a discernible meaning. Or, as one reader of the *Times Literary Supplement*, who was disturbed by mere "words posing as poetry" in several numbers of that periodical, dared to suggest: "One prime qualification of a poem has to be, doesn't it, that is makes some sense?"[46] Thrall, Hibbard, and Holdman, too, maintain that poetry "must have significance . . . a meaning, an attitude." It is the "existence of an idea, a significance, a meaning, an attitude, or a feeling" they emphasize, that "distinguishes *poetry* from doggerel."[47]

A decade ago, Gioia lamented (in what later became the title essay of *Can Poetry Matter?*)[48] that the "general reader" no longer cares about contemporary poetry. As he explained:

> Decades of public and private funding have created a large professional class for the production and reception of new poetry, comprising legions of   [poet-]teachers, graduate students, editors, publishers, and administrators. Based mostly in universities, these groups have gradually become the primary audience for contemporary verse. . . . The situation has become a paradox. . . . Over the past half century, as American poetry's specialist audience has steadily expanded,[49] its general readership has declined. [2]

"How does one persuade justly skeptical readers, in terms they can understand and appreciate, that poetry still matters?" Gioia asks. (18) His fervent wish is that "poetry could again become part of American public culture," (22) and he offers six modest proposals for achieving his goal, such as mixing poetry readings with music performances, and spending less time on analysis of poetry in high-schools and colleges, and more on readings. (22–23) Echoing poet Robert Bly's view (in *American Poetry: Wildness and Domesticity*), Gioia maintains that much of the problem lies in the proliferation of *mediocre* poetry, and in the virtual absence of objective criticism. As Bly observed, "although more bad poetry is being published now than ever before . . . , most of the reviews are positive"—which is confusing to some young poets and readers, "who end up doubting their own critical perceptions."[50] In our view, the main problem lies not with bad poetry, but with the legions of poet-teachers, many of whom—like Ashbery, who teaches at Bard College— write inscrutable "experimental" work in the name of poetry.

For poetry to "matter," it must be more than doggerel or gibberish. But Gioia fails to make that connection. He deems Ashbery "a marvelous minor poet," for example, though "an uncomfortable major one." (186) We argue that Ashbery is not a poet at all. Any work that is "arbitrary," whose "meaning lies in its method," and that is impenetrably "difficult," to borrow Gioia's words, cannot be art—which, as Rand emphasized, is always more than mere style—or (to quote Gioia again) "surface play."[51]

The Art of Film

In insisting that "literature is *the* ruler and term-setter" of motion pictures (as we noted in Chapter 4), Rand clearly challenged the prevailing view in the film industry. "Film is a visual medium," declares screenwriting theorist Syd Field. "You must find ways to reveal your character's conflicts *visually*."[52] So, too, film critic Andrew Sarris has argued, regarding the now-dominant "*auteur* theory" that the director is the prime "author of a film, the person who gives it any distinctive quality": "Because so much of the American cinema is commissioned, a director is forced to express his personality through the visual treatment of material rather than through the literary content."[53] Novelist E. L. Doctorow echoes the prevailing view in declaring that film "has begun to affirm its essentially nonliterate nature and to make of its conventions an art form detached and self-contained, like painting."[54]

Yet, as Field notes (8), and scarcely anyone would dispute, film is preeminently a form of *story-telling*. If the art of film were essentially visual, the story could be told primarily through pictures. But anyone who has ever tried to watch a film without the sound knows how difficult it is to follow the sense of the action without benefit of the dialogue, whereas one could readily grasp the gist of the story by listening to the sound track alone. Storytelling on any but the most minimal level requires *words*: narration to set the context in which the characters act, and dialogue to help establish their individuality and motivation. As Rand emphasized in "Basic Principles pf Literature," all fictional characterization requires both action and dialogue. (A major factor in the success of the recent spate of films based on the novels of Jane Austen, for example, lies in the brilliance of her dialogue, which tells the story with a minimum of narration, and which the filmmakers have wisely not much tampered with.) Since the chief significance of any story lies in the values that motivate the characters, and since values are abstractions, storytelling is fundamentally conceptual in nature. It is only through words that the complexities of value-conflicts within or between characters can be clearly conveyed, thereby indicating the logical connection between the events of the plot. Without such a connection, there is no story, or plot, in the proper sense of these terms. Even in silent films a verbal scenario was necessary to establish the story for the actors and directors; and title cards were interspersed with the visual images in the finished film to clarify the action for the audience.[55]

Only two years after Rand expressed her maverick view on the essentially literary nature of film in "Art and Cognition," much the same argument was compellingly developed by Douglas Garrett Winston in a book entitled *The Screenplay as Literature*, now regrettably out of print. Explicitly reacting against the *auteur* theory, Winston maintained that the key to successful film-making is the screenplay. He cited, admiringly, the rather audacious proposition of John Gassner thirty years earlier that "the 'screenplay' could be considered not only as a new form of literature but also as a very important form in its own right." (13) Winston had noticed that the films of foreign directors such as Ingmar Begman and Frederico Fellini excited him in the same manner as "the great masterworks of literature." In particular, he was impressed by "the completeness of their characterizations, the subtleties and nuances of their dialogue, and the complex way in which many of them were constructed." (9) A film, Winston concluded, "can be no better than the idea from which it has sprung"—and the idea (or theme) is embedded in the screenplay. No amount of editing (or, presumably, direction), in his view, "could compensate for, or cover up, the all too prevalent deficiencies of slipshod writing—poorly drawn characters, weak structures, inane dialogue and fuzzy (or, in some cases, non-existent) thinking." (19)

So, too, Robin Russin and William Missouri Downs (both of whom are successful screenwriters) argue, in their superb new guide *Screenplay: Writing the Picture*, that "all good movies depend upon well-structured screenplays." (89) As Rand would no doubt have applauded, Russin and Downs recommended that all screenwriting students "begin their study of structure with Aristotle's *Poetics*, the first known treatise on how to plot a dramatic story." In their analysis of Aristotle, they emphasize the importance of elements that Rand, too, stressed: thematic integration, meaningful selectivity, and a logical progression of events—all subsumed under Aristotle's concept of "unity," which they summarize, in part, as follows:

> [C]haracter, thought, diction, etc., [must] come together to bear on a single subject or "spine." . . . Unity also comes from the "likelihood" and "necessity" of each incident . . . [T]he incident must be both probable and essential to the story. [Their] probability [comes] . . . from the internal logic of the story . . . [which] does not slavishly copy nature but rather imitates it . . .
>   Unity also comes from the cause-and-effect relationship between incidents." [90-91]

Rand, who worked as a much-respected screenwriter in Hollywood for long periods in the 1930s and 1940s, considered the most difficult aspect to be devising a plot, a "concrete story," that would convey an "abstract theme."[56] She wrote to Henry Blanke (producer of *The Fountainhead*):

> A real dramatic plot is the one surefire element for a great popular success, in a novel, a stage play or a picture—most particularly in a picture. . . . [P]*lot*

is the one absolute *must* in a story. Characterization, dialogue, mood and all the rest . . . have value *only* when based on a good plot. Without it—they are worthless. The plot of a movie is its motor. It is not an accident that people call pictures "vehicles" for stars. A vehicle has to move. A plotless story is like an expensive car with a wonderful body design, luxurious seats, upholstery, headlights (production, direction, cast)—and no motor under its hood. That is why it gets nowhere.[57]

As Rand emphasized in "Basic Principles of Literature" (88), an essential element in creating a logical plot is supplying the characters' *motivation*—their guiding aims and values. Her own screenplay for *Love Letters*, far more effective than the novel by Chris Massie from which it was adapted, clearly demonstrates the difference between a story line dependent on accident and one that develops organically, from the virtues and vices, the values and disvalues, of the characters.[58]

The literary foundation necessary to effective filmmaking is often acknowledged, if only implicitly, by critics. In a review of the 1992 film starring Gérard Depardieu as Christopher Columbus, for example, Vincent Canby wrote:

> *1492* is not a terrible film. Yet because it is without any guiding point of view, it is a lot less interesting than the elaborate physical production that has been given it. Only a very great writer could do justice to all the themes the Columbus story suggests. [Screenwriter Roselyne] Bosch may be a very good researcher, but she's not a very great writer. She can't even squeeze in many relevant facts, much less define the relevance of those she does include.[59]

So, too, Peter Rainer—reviewing *Runaway Bride*, starring Richard Gere and Julia Roberts—has noted: "In Hollywood's Golden Age of romantic comedy, even stars like Cary Grant and Katharine Hepburn needed a strong story and sharp dialogue in order to shine. But celebrity is its own reason for being now." He added, in a metaphor Rand would have appreciated: "We're not supposed to worry if these star vehicles have any gas in their tanks."[60]

Characteristic of the old school of movie-makers, writer, director, and producer Joseph L. Mankiewicz, for example, is remembered as "a meticulous craftsman who preferred words to images, who stressed dialogue and reaction to it in a highly theatrical style."[61] As Vincent Canby said of Mankiewicz—best known for his Academy Award–winning films *A Letter to Three Wives* (1949) and *All about Eve* (1950), both of which were written as well as directed by him—he "'always possessed a singular gift for humane, well-rounded, literate dialogue,' and his best films had 'the scope of novels.'"[62]

Also relevant here is Bernard Weinraub's observation that prime-time television today is often superior to motion pictures. Because the Hollywood studios "seem obsessed with trying to appeal to younger audiences and to the lucrative foreign market," Weinraub suggests, "films are far safer in terms of subject matter, as well as more derivative and more action-driven, dealing almost entirely in fantasies and spectacles." Moreover, in the view of many, he notes, "the most significant reason television has surpassed movies . . . is that it is a writer's medium, while films are dominated by directors."[63]

No one has offered a more eloquent analysis of the anti-intellectual, anti-literary trends in recent filmmaking than novelist, essayist, and film critic Phillip Lopate, in an anthology of essays on the "dumbing down" of American culture.[64] "Much of what dumbs down movies today," he argues, "starts with the screenplay." To an unprecedented degree, screenwriting "has become coded into a step-by-step convention"[65]—which takes as its basic premise the idea "that movies are above all a visual medium." Therefore,

> dialogue must be kept to a minimum, or you risk sounding 'literary'; a voiceover is a 'literary device' and a form of 'cheating'; 'literary' is bad. Translation: words and ideas are bad. The result is a fearfulness that creeps into the screen-writer's intestines whenever his characters start to speak up for more than two sentences. [172]

When today's studio executives see a large block of type, indicating a long speech in a screenplay, Lopate explains, they often demand that it be trimmed "without even bothering to read it."[66] (173) In contrast, even in quite ordinary films of the 1930s and 1940s, "characters were allowed to talk to each other! Scenes went on and on between them . . . and in those confrontations one's sympathies would shift from one character to another, as each struggled to make clear his point, his perspective, his worldview." (173)

As Lopate further observes, movies are no longer "allowed to breathe"; they have become increasingly "hyperkinetic." In the 1960s, new (or newly rediscovered) technologies such as the zoom, slow motion, freeze-frame, and split screen—all of which emphasized the visual aspect of film—"began to be used like toys, puncturing the stately space of the classical composition. The era of fragmentation and rapid cutting had arrived"—a trend exacerbated by the MTV generation. The triumph of quick cutting, or "montage," over a more old-fashioned mise-en-scène aesthetic, has resulted in "fricasseed visuals"—all of which is related to the anti-intellectual mentality of recent American films. In Lopate's view, if we are no longer invited to enter an image on the screen and dwell there inwardly for more than three seconds; if our eye is not given the time to travel from one character's face to another's and then to the objects and scenery behind or to the side of them; if we are being presented with too many close-ups that show us a very small amount of visual information, which make one point and only one point per shot; if we are not encouraged to develop *fidelity* to a shot—then we do not make as deep a commitment to understand and interpret the material presented to us. A scene is no longer, properly speaking, a scene; a shot is less than an image. All is underselected: the necessity for rigorous composition is negated; we are in a perpetual, perspectiveless flux, a flux which defers judgment to a later, saner time, which never comes. [174–75]

In such a climate, few films rise above the level of entertainment (and not very good entertainment at that) to the level of art.

"Harrow Alley"

In the early 1960s, an original screenplay was written that exemplifies the high standards Rand had envisioned for the medium—standards rarely, if ever, met by contemporary film, as Lopate's analysis suggests. Though never produced, and therefore probably unknown to Rand, *Harrow Alley,* by Walter Brown Newman (d. 1993),[67] has been judged by many film professionals one of the best screenplays ever written, if not *the* best. In the words of one admirer, it is "a truly remarkable epic with wonderful characters, hilarious dialogue, and absorbing drama."[68]

Set in London during the horrific Great Plague of 1664–65, *Harrow Alley* is filled with scenes of disease and death. But neither of these was Newman's subject. As he explained: "I was simply writing about how do we live under such conditions."[69] And further

I'm interested in how you meet life, how you meet death, how you meet love, how you meet hate, how you express these things, what you do about them, what you do about dignity, your own, what you do about integrity, how you hang on to it, when you let go, what does it mean to compromise, is it wise, ever? I have a feeling these things engaged people while they were building the pyramids. And without being stuffy about it and not by any means thinking of myself in terms of the great Greeks or anything like that, I find naturally that these are the things that interest me. [118]

Newman's script (which he wrote an speculation because the theme deeply interested him) offers compelling evidence that the screenwriter, not the director, is the creative artist, the true *author,* of a film. He spent over seven months researching the background, combing secondhand bookstores and academic libraries for material that would give him a sense of the life of the time. One likely source was Daniel Defoe's historical fiction *A Journal of the Plague Year* (1722). Written as if it were a firsthand account of the Great Plague, Defoe's work actually included episodes in Harrow Alley.

While based on such sources, Newman's settings—the primary *visual* element in film—are, ultimately, his conception. And, like a good novelist, he re-creates the scenes in vivid detail. Harrow Alley, for example, is "a narrow refuse-strewn way hemmed in on both sides by three- and four-story buildings. A few are tenements. The rest, occupied by merchants, tradesmen and artisans, are shops below and homes above, with gardens and stables in the rear." At one end there is "Barnabas Gate, an archway in the old City wall leading to open fields." Newman even adds this appropriately ominous detail: "A wooden figure of Death—an hourglass in one hand, a dart in the other— appears to strike the hour" from the clocktower of the parish church. (64)

In dramatizing the different ways in which inhabitants of Harrow Alley respond to the calamity that befalls them, Newman creates a richly woven tapestry of characters of every age and station, from the fashionable nobility taking flight in their carriages to a gentle young mute who goes about rescuing children orphaned by the plague. The three principal characters are Gamaliel Ratsey, Harry Poyntz, and the physician Nathaniel Hodges. Ratsey, a "burly, vigorous ruffian" (who provides comic relief in this somber tale), is about to be hanged by the city authorities as the story begins, but is saved by Harry — an honest tailor and an alderman of the local parish—who puts him to work transporting the ever increasing dead to the burial pits outside the city. Ratsey and Harry are both good men, whose lots are dramatically reversed at the end in unexpected fashion. The real hero of the story, however, is the aging doctor, Hodges, "a corpulent giant, cynical, irreverent, humane and misanthropic."

In a key scene, Harry, conscientious in the fulfillment of his responsibilities as an alderman, seeks advice in vain from Sir Edward Alston, the President of the College of Physicians—a benighted and unprincipled dignitary, whom he finds preparing to flee to Oxford to escape the plague. After counseling Harry to "burn noxious materials" and "sprinkle the walls and floor daily with vinegar and horses' urine" to ward off infection, he leaves. The narrative portion of Newman's script then directs: *"In a few seconds, his coach is heard rumbling across the courtyard outside. Someone chuckles drily and, turning, Harry sees Dr. Hodges at a bookshelf in a far corner.*

HODGES: The best cure Sir Edward ever worked was upon his own purse. When he began it was lean and sickly and now it is one of the fattest in the profession.

Hodges takes down a few books and blows the dust from them.

HODGES (*continuing*): Look at that. They haven't been touched since the day I loaned them to the College. Too unorthodox. Ah, well, I'm not surprised. When I first showed them to Sir Edward I rather expected him to put them to his nose, like the ape, and ask me whether they were something to eat. If your child is a son and one day decides to be a physician, be sure to send him to an English university. They'll stuff his head properly with the writings of doctors dead three thousand years and he'll never be confused by facts as I was, studying at Montpellier in France.

HARRY: You have no trust in Sir Edward's recommendations?

HODGES: Who am I to doubt the words of Procopius who devised those same . . . effective measures six hundred years before Christ? And applied them, too, with tremendous effect—until the Black Death killed him. And twenty million more. How can we combat the plague, Harry, when we cannot say what causes it? . . . [77]

Hodges urges Harry to flee, as he himself plans to do. But Harry remains. And for all his misanthropy, Hodges himself is pulled back, in a later scene (though he has one foot *"in the stirrup, preparying to mount"*), drawn in by the dread sight of the first person to fall victim to the plague in Harrow Alley. (79) Hodges remains, not only to care for the dying but, ultimately, to perform an unprecedented autopsy in an attempt to discover the cause of the disease. In the process, he describes his findings, while Betty, a stalwart resident of the parish, writes down what he says. (105)

In a later scene, Betty sees the doctor as she is leaving church with Ratsey. Hodges, who is growing blind, calls out to her: "Betty, Betty Buckworth. Where are you?" She is horrified by what she sees. Newman describes the scene:

Hodges stands outside his open front door, barefoot and naked but for his shroud. Clutched under his arm is a manuscript. He would appear comical but for the tokens and blotches that pepper his face and neck. Passersby and inhabitants of the Alley shrink from him. [107]

Hodges and Betty exchange words. We quote just his to her: "I remind you of your promise. The reports, Betty. Promise me you'll send them off. . . . One to Montpellier. . . . One to Oxford and one to Cambridge. One to the medical faculty at the school in Salerno. I forget where the others go, but I've written it all down. And there's money there, too, for the posting. . . . That's all, then, and goodbye to you. (*Looking blindly about*) Are there any University men within hearing? If there are, sing with me, my brothers. Sing with me for the last time. *And, staggering toward and through Barnabas Gate, Hodges lifts a surprisingly true voice in song.*" What he sings is *Gaudeamus igitur*, the famous ancient student drinking song in Latin, dating perhaps to the thirteenth century (the melody of which has been made familiar to modern ears by Brahms's *Academic Festival Overture*). Hodges, the aging man of learning and science, sings of the youthful rejoicing of students, as he staggers toward death:

HODGES: 'Gaudeamus igitur, / Juvenes dum sumus; / Gaudeamus igitur, / Juvenes
    dum sumus; / . . . Vivat academia, / Vivant professores; / Vivat academia, /
    Vivant professores; / Vivat membrum quodlibet, / Vivant membra quaelibet,
    / Semper sint in flore, / Semper sint in flore. . . .'

As Betty weeps, comforted by Ratsey, Hodges leaves the highway, "with its traffic streaming toward the gate" and "cuts across the grass toward the pits," all the while continuing in song. "At the pits there are still dead-carts, Bearers and Buriers," who "glance at him briefly . . . then proceed with their work." He is still singing as "*his strength leaves him and he sinks to his knees at the edge of one of the pits.*" . . .

Clutching his manuscript to him, he topples forward on his face and lies still. And a Burier hurrying past, almost without pausing, puts a foot against the body and sends it rolling down out of sight. Field birds rise from the pit, screeching protest, then settle back again to resume eating." [108]

In a final brief scene, normal life is resuming in Harrow Alley, as Ratsey returns from a trip outside the parish. To the coachman's "Fine day, ain't it?" Ratsey responds: "Yes. (*With absolute conviction*) Yes, it is." He then disappears into the crowd in Harrow Alley, as the clock in the bell-tower of St. Barnabas Church strikes the hour. At Newman's "FADE OUT" life is flourishing once again. (112)

We trust that this brief synopsis conveys, albeit imperfectly, some measure of *Harrow Alley*'s literary virtues, which admirably illustrate the principles of screenwriting as an art. We found it deeply moving, even in written form, and can imagine how powerful it could be if fully realized. Given the present tenor of the film industry, however—in which directors, producers, and even influential movie stars think nothing of tinkering with screenplays without the writer's approval—the likelihood of a faithful production is slim indeed. We shudder to think of the gratuitous scenes of sexual intimacy that would surely be added to increase box-office appeal, for example—perhaps between Harry's young wife, Jem, and the boy she loved before her marriage to Harry was arranged. Only when the day arrives that this work could be billed as "*A Film by Walter Brown Newman*," or "*Walter Brown Newman*'s '*Harrow Alley*'" would its integrity be ensured. As the late George C. Scott (who had purchased the rights to the screenplay in 1968) told *Scenario* magazine in 1995, the only stumbling block to obtaining financing had been his unwillingness to alter Newman's work. "'This is a piece,'" Scott rightly insisted, "'and it's got to go like this.'"

14

Postmodernism in the "Visual Arts"

Rand never wrote about postmodernism as such. That she was aware of some of the phenomena now covered by that term is suggested by the following item, however—it was published, without comment, in the May 1968 issue of *The Objectivist*:

> "A grave in Central Park, dug by two grave-diggers for the customary fee of $50 each and then filled in, has become New York's latest work of art—'invisible sculpture' or 'unsculpture,' city officials call it. Claes Oldenburg, a leading pop artist, at whose request the grave was dug behind the Metropolitan Museum of Art yesterday, calls it 'underground sculpture.' . . . Mr. Sam Green, New York's consultant on sculpture, said: 'Everything is art if it is chosen by the artist to be art. You can say it is good art or bad art, but you can't say it isn't art. Just because you can't see a statue doesn't mean that it isn't there.'"
> *Daily Telegraph* (London), 3 October 1967.

Under the rubric "Esthetics," this item was a fitting addition to the "Horror File," an occasional feature of *The Objectivist* that aimed to "illustrate the tie . . . between the present state of our culture and its philosophical roots."[1] And it was emblematic of the phenomena we will consider in this chapter.

Though Rand referred to all avant-garde work as "modern," Oldenburg's "invisible sculpture" would now be termed *postmodernist* by most scholars and critics. As we indicated in our discussion of dance in Chapter 12, the concept of postmodernism is a problematical one, however, with no clear definition. In the view of one scholar, it is so "diffuse, fragmentary, multi-dimensional, and contestable" that it may not constitute a "clear and coherent object of study" at all.[2] Nonetheless, the artworld has routinely used the term *postmodern* to refer to work it classifies as visual art since the mid-1950s, when a deliberate reaction set in against modernism's cultural hegemony,[3] particularly abstraction.

Beginning with the first stirrings of Pop art in the mid-1950s, postmodernism in the "visual arts" was a deliberate rejection of previous modernist practice, theory, and criticism—in particular, of Abstract Expressionism and the formalist criticism of Clement Greenberg. Reaction followed reaction in rapid succession: happenings, conceptual art, photorealism, earth art, assemblage, video art, performance art, installation art, and appropriation art, to name but a few. Often the results have not been discrete *visual* objects at all. And much of the work has been so violently transgressive of common-sense standards of reason and decency as to make the "underground sculpture" cited above seem innocuous by comparison.

Just as abstract art was theory-driven, the characteristic features of postmodernism have been predicated on a series of mistaken ideas. Whereas the spurious notions on which abstract art was ultimately based were primarily metaphysical, pertaining to the fundamental relationship between spirit and matter, postmodernism's original frame of reference was mainly esthetic. That is, postmodernism has developed in direct response to a series of false assumptions about the nature of art itself. Chief among these is the notion that (as Sam Green remarked regarding Oldenburg's hole in the ground) "Everything is art if it is chosen by the artist to be art. You can say it is good art or bad art, but you can't say it isn't art."

The Long Shadow of Duchamp

More than any other figure, the French-born artworld eccentric Marcel Duchamp (1887–1968) is credited with legitimizing the notion that anything can be art.[4] As Arthur Danto has observed, "'The story of the avant-garde in the [late] twentieth century, whether in America or in Europe, seems largely to be the story of Duchamp.'" To quote another philosopher, it is Duchamp's *readymades*, in particular, that "'have become the central hurdle over which any attempt to define art must leap.'"[5] According to the *Dictionary of Art*, Duchamp's "conception of the ready-made decisively altered our understanding of what constitutes an object of art."[6] While that major reference work defines the readymade as "an existing manufactured object deemed to be a work of art simply through its selection by the artist." Duchamp himself confided toward the end of his life: "'The curious thing about the readymade is that I've never been able to arrive at a definition or explanation that fully satisfies me."[7] Among the so-called readymades on which Duchamp's fame rests are: *Bicycle Wheel* (1913), a bicycle wheel set on its inverted fork on a wooden stool; *In Advance of the Broken Arm* (1915), a snow shovel on which he placed his signature; and *Fountain* (1917), a porcelain urinal positioned on its back, on which we comment below.[8]

Virtually all the facts surrounding their origin, as well as his own statements about them, make clear that he regarded these objects—which the artworld regards as irrevocably changing the course of art history—as little more than a private joke. "Distraction" and "amusement" were the terms he most often used to characterize them; and his titles for them, as for other works, were mostly childish wordplay, ranging from sheer nonsense to sophomoric sexual allusions—mere exercises in what he thought of as the "chess game of language." In this game, he was inspired by the example of Raymond Roussel, a writer whom Louis Sass characterizes as "profoundly schizoid or perhaps even schizophrenic."[9] Roussel's method of composition, which Duchamp emulated, employed puns and other word games based mainly on the sounds of words, and emphasized verbal ambiguity, without regard to the contextuality of meaning.

Duchamp was quick to point out that, on the whole, he had not intended the readymades for exhibition or sale. Most were given away to friends and relatives, or simply lost. "Please note that I didn't want to make a work of art out of [the readymade]," he emphasized in an interview two years before his death. Moreover, it seems clear that his most notorious readymade—the urinal he dubbed *Fountain* and submitted, under the assumed name "R. Mutt," for exhibition by the Society of Independent Artists in New York in 1916— was a huge practical joke, a lighthearted provocation by insiders, in which his friend and major collector, Walter Arensberg, was complicit. A fact rarely cited is that Duchamp and Arensberg were among the organizers of the exhibition and that Duchamp himself was head of the Hanging Committee. Arensberg had accompanied Duchamp to the plumbing supply showroom where it was purchased, and willingly abetted the deception. When the painter George Bellows, a society member, protested that the name sounded "fishy" and that "someone must have sent it in as a joke," Arensberg proclaimed, with an air of great seriousness: "A lovely form has been revealed, freed from its functional purpose, therefore a man has clearly made an aesthetic contribution." He further argued: "This is what the whole exhibit is about: an opportunity to allow the artist to send in anything he chooses, for the artist to decide what is art, not somebody else." To which Bellows angrily replied—more prophetically than he could have guessed: "You mean to say, if a man sent in horse manure glued to a canvas that we would have to accept it!" Arensberg responded, with feigned regret: "I'm afraid we would." According to Duchamp's biographer Calvin Tomkins, Duchamp and Arensberg had "obviously planned the whole thing as a deliberate provocation" and "milked it for all it was worth," going so far as to publish an ephemeral little magazine, *The Blind Man*, for the express purpose (as Duchamp later explained) of defending *Fountain*. As Tomkins argues, the whole "brouhaha over *Fountain* was played out in a key of larky humor." (193)

Despite extravagant claims regarding his "rigorous intellect" (André Breton called him "the most intelligent man of the twentieth century"), Duchamp suffered from a lifelong paucity of ideas, which explains his extremely limited output. He prided himself on cultivating the "beauty of indifference" (*Ma position est l'absence de position*, he once said). Moreover, his life and thought were a mass of contradictions. The man who could not tolerate boredom in real life (he had divorced his wife of a few months, for example, because he found marriage too "boring") conceived the readymade as "a visually indifferent object," whose distinction lay precisely in its essential lack of interest, its boredom. "'Doubt in myself, doubt in everything, . . . never believing in truth': this was . . . Duchamp's characterization of his own fundamental attitude," as Sass notes. (139) Duchamp's whole career, he observes, was devoted "to a series of mockeries, of ironic comments on art and its purported relationship to life." (36) Like the irony characteristic of schizophrenia, Duchamp's irony is "totalizing . . . all-encompassing, not a criticism of one thing in favor of another but a universal mockery." (113) "Further, this spirit of ironic negation—of detachment, subversion, and unremitting criticism—has been turned not just on 'life' but on 'art' itself." (36)

Pop Art

Two seminal figures in the transition to postmodernism from the "high modernism" of the Abstract Expressionists were Robert Rauschenberg (b. 1925) and Jasper Johns (b. 1930). Both of them began as painters but subsequently expanded their activities to other media. Together they ushered in the Pop art movement in the United States, and they continue to serve as models for the contemporary artworld, which never tires of lavishing attention and praise upon them. Their work exemplifies many of the major postmodernist trends. Rauschenberg, in particular, brought the postmodernist anti-esthetic promoted by John Cage into the realm of the visual arts.[10] To quote Michael Kimmelman: "[A]s much as anyone else during the last 50 years, [he] helped to erase all the old dividing lines: between painting and sculpture, painting and photography, sculpture and dance, sculpture and technology, technology and performance art, not to mention art and life."[11] In an adulatory American Masters program aired on PBS in 1999, Rauschenberg was touted as an "inventive genius," the Michelangelo or Leonardo of the twentieth century.

Claiming to work in the "gap" between art and life,[12] Rauschenberg employs found objects, chance methods, absurd juxtapositions, and mechanical means of creating images directly from life or of reproducing existing images. His early "inventions" included lifesize "monoprints" made by shining a sun-lamp over a nude model reclining on architectural blueprint paper. His technique for making what he called "transfer drawings," by applying solvent to mass-media images and then rubbing them onto paper, similarly minimized the creative role of the artist. When one also considers his *Erased de Kooning Drawing*—which came from his "wanting to know if a drawing could be made out of erasing"—one may well doubt not only his concept of "drawing" but his sanity as well.[13] Other reputed Rauschenberg breakthroughs include his "combines"—works which purported to be part-sculpture, part-painting, but were really three-dimensional equivalents of collage. In one such work, *Bed* (1955), Rauschenberg combined an old patchwork quilt, framed canvas-like on a stretcher, with a sheet and a pillow, on which he dripped and slathered paint in Abstract Expressionist fashion. In his even more bizarre *Monogram* (1955–59), perhaps his best-known work, he slipped an automobile tire onto the body of a stuffed Angora goat had bought in a secondhand store, daubed some paint on the goat's snout, and mounted the ensemble on a paint-smeared platform made up of fragments of old boards and signs.

Random juxtapositions of disparate borrowed elements also characterize Rauschenberg's "silk-screen paintings" (more accurately, they are "prints"), consisting of random patchworks of pre-existing photographic images of virtually anything, from astronauts to parts of Old Master paintings. For the oversized silk-screened works he made as part of his ambitious "Rauschenberg Overseas Cultural Exchange," a series of works created in the late 1980s based on visits to various countries, he simply appropriated photographs from newspapers and magazines, which he transferred, along with his own snapshots of the places visited, onto the canvas, by the essentially mechanical process of silk-screening—alongside swatches of fabric, and overlain in places with brightly colored areas of paint. According to one curator, Rauschenberg's silk-screens demonstrate "how to receive and process information and how to find order and connectivity in an apparently haphazard and discontinuous environment."[14] On this claim, Rauschenberg remarked: "You mean I had a direction? It's a damned good thing I didn't know that before I did the painting. When I know what I'm doing, I don't do it."[15] Finally, on another occasion, he observed: "It's never bothered me a bit when people say what

I'm doing is not art,";"I don't think of myself as making things that will turn into art."[16]

While Rauschenberg has probably had the greater influence on artworld practice, Jasper Johns enjoys the more inflated reputation. His works consistently fetch record prices at auction, and (unlike Rauschenberg) he was recently voted one of the top ten living artists in an *ARTnews* magazine poll of museum directors, curators, and critics around the world.[17] Johns first stunned the artworld in the 1950s with his "breakthrough" paintings of the American flag and targets. When the Metropolitan Museum of Art purchased Johns's *White Flag* (1955) for an undisclosed sum in 1998 (the painting had been sold at auction for a record-breaking $7 million a decade earlier), Philippe de Montebello, the museum's director, characterized this monochrome version of the American flag as "an authentic masterpiece . . . as good as they come."[18]

Johns's choice of emblematic signs and symbols as his "subject matter" (in addition to flags and targets, he used the alphabet, numbers, and maps) was a simple expedient. Largely self-taught and of limited ability, he could not even win a merit scholarship at the commercial art school he briefly attended. "Using the design of the American flag took care of a great deal for me," he once explained, "because I didn't have to design it. So I went on to similar things like the targets—things the mind already knows. That gave me room to work on other levels." Promising though the phrase may sound, Johns's "other levels" pertained mainly to technical matters, not to meaning. In contrast with Rauschenberg's alternately slapdash or mechanical approach to execution, he devotes painstaking craftsmanship to his stupefyingly banal subjects. Often employing especially demanding media, such as encaustic, he has elicited critical encomiums such as the following: "[Johns's] *Flag* is a magnificently variegated surface, an intensely *made* thing, a dense amalgam of newspaper, encaustic, and paint. It does not occur to you, when you encounter it in the flesh, to contemplate its metaphysics— . . . you are too busy soaking up the sense data."[19] Another critic takes the rather different view that "Johns has made us look at 'things which are seen but not looked at,' as he put it."[20] The question we would ask is, Do Johns's abstract signs and symbols and banal "things" warrant being "looked at," in and of themselves, divorced from a larger context of meaning?

The art historian Leo Steinberg has argued that many of Johns's inventions "are interpretable as meditations on the nature of painting."[21] But "meditations" of any kind seem to have been far from his habits of mind. According to Johns, "artists work out of rather stupid kinds of impulses and then the work is done."[22] His sketchbooks contain such vacuous jottings as "Put a lot of paint & a wooden ball or other object on a board. Push to the other end of the board. Use this in a painting." And "Take a canvas. / Put a mark on it. / Put another mark on it."[23] To his painted "images" of signs and symbols,[24] Johns added sculptures of everyday objects in the same spirit of banality. His *Painted Bronze* (1960), for example, is a "sculptural" representation of two cans of Ballantine ale.[25] Contrary to frequent speculation, the piece was not intended as social or philosophic comment of any kind. As Johns told an interviewer, it was inspired by a chance comment a fellow painter had made about Johns's dealer, Leo Castelli: "'That son-of-a-bitch; you could give him two beer cans and he could sell them.'"[26]

Johns's later work displays an equal poverty of visual ideas. His "crosshatch" paintings and drawings, for example—to which he devoted himself for a decade—consist of an overall pattern of crosshatches at various angles, rather like the texture of tweed, greatly enlarged. Reverting to almost total abstraction, they are relieved only by occasional references to the everyday world, such as the shapes of irons in his pretentiously titled *Weeping Women*. According to Mark Rosenthal (who organized an exhibition of Johns's work after 1974 for the U. S. Pavilion at the 43rd Venice Biennale in 1988), "a dramatic new direction" was signaled for the painter by his critically acclaimed series of autobiographical paintings. *The Seasons* (1985–86), for example, consist of collage-like pastiches of elements copied from his own early paintings (notably, his flag series), famous works of art (among others, the *Mona Lisa* alluding to Duchamp's famous send-up of that masterwork), and perceptually ambiguous drawings like those discussed by E. H. Gombrich in *Art and Illusion*—as well as the crudely drawn outline of his own form, which someone traced for him directly from his shadow on the ground (one critic absurdly refers to this as Johns's "first explicit self-portrait"[27]). These elements are merely juxtaposed, as in Rauschenberg's work, with no attempt at integration. In Rosenthal's view, the "wholeness" of this cycle of paintings can be understood in the context of these lines, written by Johns: "The condition of a presence. / The condition of being there. / its own work / its own / its / it / its shape, color, weight, etc. / it is not another (?) / and shape is not a color (?) / Aspects and movable aspects. / To what degree movable? / Entities / splitting."[28] Wholeness? Not quite. We would argue that these lines are the verbal counterpart of the mental confusion and lack of integration reflected in Johns's painting.[29]

The term "Pop art" (which originated in Britain) refers to an international movement in the visual arts. It was, essentially, a deliberate reaction against the counterfeit elitism of abstract art, in favor of a more accessible imagery drawn from popular culture.[30] As an essay by one of its principal theorists indicated, however, the movement recognized no distinction between "culture" in the broadest sense (including consumer products and the mass media) and "art," or between art and entertainment. All "hierarchical" arrangements of knowledge were rejected, and a sonnet, a newspaper, and the behavior of a crowd were considered equivalent.[31]

Pop artists were right to reject the pretentious inscrutability of Abstract Expressionism—its claims to conveying deep meaning and profound personal emotion through mere abstract forms and the artist's sometimes idiosyncratic brushstrokes. But the alternative they embraced was equally false. While accessible, their imagery did not derive primarily from the direct observation and experience of life itself. Instead, it was an often mechanical recycling of banal mass-media images and vulgar commercial products. Like Rauschenberg and Johns, leading Pop artists such as Andy Warhol and James Rosenquist generally appropriated such elements directly, using mechanical processes of modern technology. The result is imagery that, despite its familiar content, is strangely (and intentionally) remote and dehumanized, devoid of depth or intensity. Andy Warhol's silk-screen images of various celebrities are as bland as his paintings of Campbell's Soup cans. And, despite their enlarged scale, Roy Lichtenstein's simulations of Mickey Mouse cartoons and true-romance comic strips seem far more vacuous than the originals.

Some critics and scholars have read grave significance into the remoteness and detachment of Pop art, seeing it variously as an ironic comment on contemporary life or, ludicrously, as an investigation into the nature of art itself.[32] According to philosopher-critic Arthur Danto, for example, Andy Warhol (1928–1987), the most notorious and influential of the Pop artists,

> possessed a philosophical intelligence of an intoxicatingly high order. He could not touch anything without at the same time touching the very boundaries of thought, at the very least thought about art. . . . [It] was among Warhol's chief contributions to the history of art that he brought artistic practice to a level of philosophical self-consciousness never before attained. . . . [He] violated every condition thought necessary to something['s] being an artwork, but in so doing he disclosed the essence of art.[33]

For Danto, Warhol's *Brillo Boxes*, which are virtually indistinguishable from supermarket Brillo cartons, "made plain that one cannot any longer think of distinguishing art from reality on perceptual grounds, for those grounds have been cut away."[34] The validity of Danto's weighty proposition, however, is based on the premise that the Warhol work *is* art—a premise that he merely asserts.

In any case, Warhol's own words render Danto's suggestion preposterous. They reveal that the anonymous, mechanical character of his work stems not from philosophic profundity but, rather, from psychological dysfunction—from an almost total anomie and emotional deadness. Nor is the detachment of his work intentionally ironic (as some critics have suggested); it is merely a reflection of his aberrant psychology. "I always thought that I was more half-there than all-there," he wrote in 1975, "that I was watching TV instead of living life."[35] Moreover, his robotlike lack of passion stemmed from an absence of values that chillingly recalls the extreme indifference of the schizoid personality, as described by Louis Sass.[36] In Warhol's words: "Everything is nothing." (183) "The reason I'm painting this way," he told one interviewer, "is that I want to be a machine."[37] He had begun making collages, he explained on another occasion, because he didn't "love roses or bottles or anything like that enough to want to sit down and paint them lovingly and patiently." "And it's threatening too," he confided, "painting something without any conviction about what it should be." (119) Remarkably, his work as a commercial artist was often more inventive and stylistically distinctive than his independent "artwork"—because others imposed a "feeling" upon him. As he noted: "I'd do anything they told me to do, correct it and do it right. I'd have to invent and now I don't; after all that 'correction,' those commercial drawings would have feelings, they would have a style. The attitude of those who hired me had feeling or something to it; they knew what they wanted, they insisted; sometimes they got very emotional."[38]

The "quintessential master of Pop painting"[39] Roy Lichtenstein (1923–1997) has been credited with creating "artworks that explore the complex connections between popular culture and the fine arts."[40] (This would, in any case, be a task for philosophy, not for visual art.) In fact, however, Lichtenstein's images were essentially abstract formal designs to him. "I paint my . . . pictures upside down or sideways," he declared. "I often don't even remember what most of them are about," he is reported to have said.[41] His paintings, based on such mass-media images as comic strips and ads from the yellow pages of the telephone book, seemed but a continuation of his former work as a commercial artist. Lichtenstein's "defining stroke of genius" (to quote the novelist John Updike) was to enlarge the "Ben Day" dots of commercial photogravure into a design motif, which he subsequently reproduced using mechanical stencils.[42] Much like Warhol, he wanted his "painting to look as if it [had] been programmed."[43] In 1991, Lichtenstein tellingly remarked on his recent painting: "It seems not to have any important content—which is true of all my work."[44]

Conceptual Art

No other aspect of postmodernism has more profoundly or pervasively undermined the practice of the visual arts in the years since the early 1960s than the notion of so-called *conceptual art*. As defined in the *Oxford Dictionary of Art* (1988), the term refers to "various forms of art in which the idea for a work is considered more important than the finished product, if any." Like Pop art, conceptual art was initially a reaction against the meaninglessness of abstraction. Whereas Pop artists mainly rejected the expressionist pretensions of recent abstract art, conceptual artists are more concerned with repudiating the formalist view of abstraction promulgated by Clement Greenberg. In a perverse kind of dialectic, however, they embrace the opposite pole of a false dichotomy. Greenberg's formalism had mistakenly predicated esthetic forms emptied of ideas and meaning. Conceptual art abandons esthetic[45] forms entirely—in favor of "ideas."

Like other purported twentieth-century innovations in the arts, conceptual art rests on a set of false assumptions, about human perception and cognition, about the nature (and purpose) of art, and about the properties of the various art forms. In the earliest theoretical statement on the subject, for example, Henry Flynt (a self-styled philosopher and practitioner of the movement) wrote: "*Concept art* is . . . an art of which the material [medium] is *concepts*, as the material of music is sound. Since *concepts* are closely bound up with language, concept art is a kind of art of which the material is language."[46] What he ignored of course is that such an art form already existed—that is, *literature*. Nonetheless, Flynt acknowledged that the notion of a wholly "nonaesthetic" art form is rather contradictory; and he even suggested that it might be better to seek another term, and "*to recognize my activity as an independent, new activity, irrelevant to art*" (emphasis ours). In effect, he was admitting that his "new activity" did not really qualify as art. All the same, he retained the term *art*, in part because, as he explained, "the antecedents of concept art are commonly regarded as artistic, aesthetic activities." To use the term *art* for work that flouted the concept's defining attributes, however, was but another of the artworld's many instances of what Rand referred to as the "fallacy of the stolen concept."

Another brief but influential essay was "Paragraphs on Conceptual Art" (1967), by the former Minimalist[47] Sol LeWitt. In conceptual art, LeWitt wrote, "all of the planning and decisions are made beforehand and the execution is a perfunctory affair. The idea becomes a machine that makes the art."[48] Moreover, "What the work of art looks like isn't too important," since the "idea itself, even if not made visual is as much a work of art as any finished product." Yet the ideas need be neither "complex" (as LeWitt's own work amply testified) nor "logical"—he often resorted to random procedures in devising the arrangement of forms in a work. Nor does it "really matter if the viewer understands the concepts of the artist by seeing the art." Finally, at the core of LeWitt's notions of conceptual art lay his profoundly mistaken assumption that "the functions of conception and perception are contradictory," and his related claim that conceptual art "is made to engage the mind of the viewer rather than his eye or emotions." What he failed to grasp was that perception and conception are *complementary* phases of awareness, that human cognition requires "dancing back and forth" between the two (as Rand emphasized[49]), and that visual art has always engaged the mind *through the eye*, and the emotions *through the mind*, by presenting value-laden images.

Muddled thinking also marks another influential essay on conceptual art— "Art after Philosophy" (1969), by Joseph Kosuth, an essay which anthologist Gregory Battcock selected as "perhaps the best example" of the early writing on the subject.[50] To his credit, Kosuth (unlike LeWitt) was explicitly critical of "'Formalist' art," as "the vanguard of decoration," and of Clement Greenberg, as "the critic of taste." He also argued, quite reasonably, that the traditional emphasis on "beauty" in esthetics had detracted attention from consideration of art's function. Formalist critics "always bypass the conceptual element in works of art," he aptly suggested, because formalist abstract art is "mindless"—mere "'visual *Muzak*'"—only superficially resembling earlier works of art. (77–79)

When Kosuth proceeded to analyze the function of art, however, he was deeply mistaken. To begin, he declared that esthetic considerations are "*always* extraneous to an object's function or 'reason-to-be,'" unless the object's "reason-to-be is strictly aesthetic . . . [or] decorative."[51] Thus he did not understand that a work of art cannot fulfill its function without first catching and focusing the viewer's attention (so that he can then perceive its content), and that esthetic elements play a crucial role in this process. Like LeWitt, moreover, Kosuth misses the main purpose of art, which is, as it has always been, to concentrate vital meaning in a *perceptually* immediate form—to bring value-laden concepts "to the perceptual level of consciousness," as Rand put it. Instead, he argues that the function of art now is "to question the nature of art." Conceptual art is "inquiry into the foundations of the concept 'art,' as it has come to [be understood]."[52] Kosuth also argued that "questioning the nature of art" requires rejecting "the European tradition of a painting-sculpture dichotomy."[53] (79) Further, in contrast with Rand's idea that every work of art in effect declares: *This is life as I (the artist) see it*, Kosuth holds that each art work is "a comment on art," an implied "definition of art." Finally, according to Kosuth, every artist's implied definition "is true a priori"—in other words, (borrowed from the minimalist "sculptor" Donald Judd), "'if someone calls it art, it's art.'" (83)

Apart from the obvious absurdity of such a claim, and of his implication that painting and sculpture belong merely to "the European tradition," Kosuth's argument rests on a basic epistemological error, one which pervades postmodernism. He attempts to reify the abstraction *art*, without regard to the basic attributes of its original referents. "Art" in the abstract has no material existence, however; only works in specific art forms, such as painting and sculpture, exist. The only legitimate way to "question" the nature of art, therefore, is to analyze the nature of such individual works, including their function. (And that is a task for philosophers, not artists.) To present something essentially different from them as art is not to "question" art but to invent something new, which logically requires a new name—as Flynt had earlier suggested. Nor do we accept Kosuth's further claim that the first works of conceptual art were Duchamp's readymades because they "questioned the nature of art." Such a claim assumes that Duchamp intended them as art in the first place—a dubious assumption at best. Ironically, Kosuth himself insists that an artist's intentions are crucial considerations in interpreting his work.

The "conceptual art" Kosuth's theory attempted to justify includes his series of "Definition works," in which he presented the enlarged text of a dictionary definition of an everyday object, often accompanied by a photograph of the object and a real specimen of the object itself. His 1965 piece *One and Three Chairs (Etymological)*, for example, incorporates a nondescript folding chair, a lifesize black-and-white photograph of an identical chair, and an enlarged dictionary entry on "chair." (Just how such a work questions the nature of art is not at all apparent to us.) Art historians not only accept such banal exercises as art but freely parrot the confused ideas behind them. Thus Lisa Phillips, in her catalog for the Whitney Museum's landmark exhibition *The American Century, 1950–2000*, refers to works such as that just described as symptomatic of the "emergence of language as a medium for advanced art." (Using "language as a medium" entails more than merely reproducing dictionary entries, of course, but she is apparently unaware that the use of any artistic medium entails meaningful transformation.) In her discussion of conceptual art, in a section entitled "Questioning the Canon," Phillips further notes that such "art was no longer about morphological characteristics but about an inquiry into what art means," and that it "had a long lineage, beginning with Marcel Duchamp"—remarks mindlessly echoing Kosuth.[54]

Assemblage Art and Installation Art

Like many works of so-called conceptual art, Kosuth's *One and Three Chairs (Etymological)* is an "assemblage" or "installation"[55]—a three-dimensional construction or arrangement of various nonartistic materials and everyday objects, akin to a three-dimensional collage. Installations differ from assemblages mainly in their size and their relation to the viewer's space. Assemblages are small-scale and relatively self-contained, while installations are more spatial and usually ephemeral arrangements, which often invite the viewer to walk through them and may appeal not only to the sense of sight but to those of hearing and smell as well (such installations are sometimes termed "environments"). Typically, assemblages and installations do not employ pictorial or sculptural re-creations of reality, but instead incorporate real-life objects, furniture, and other paraphernalia—or slipshod simulations of them. An early example is Oldenburg's *The Store* (1961), a mixed-media environmental installation. In a rented storefront on New York's Lower East Side, he offered for sale more than a hundred crude plaster re-creations of everyday consumer goods such as food, clothing, and jewelry." Like much other early conceptual art, this project was intended to "play off the idea of art as commodity," as Lisa Phillips puts it.

By taking their work out of the customary gallery and museum contexts, and by making ephemeral and amorphous pieces that were not saleably or collectibly discrete (the items in Oldenburg's *Store* were somewhat atypical in this respect), installation artists aimed, or so they insisted, to free art from the commerce of the artworld. Ironically, though what they made was surely not art, it was soon eagerly absorbed by the art establishment. It was as if a shoemaker, disgruntled at having to sell his wares through the usual retail channels, had protested by making shoes without soles, only to find that people nonetheless clambered to possess them.

Since no artistic skill and very little imagination is required to produce assemblages and installations, they have been a preferred form of expression for would-be artists since the late 1950s. One simple installation-art "tactic" noted by critic Roberta Smith is to display "a lot of just one thing,"[56] as in Felix Gonzales-Torres's 1991 piece *Untitled (Portrait of Ross in L.A.)*, a pile of "multicolored candies individually wrapped in cellophane." A similar work was aptly satirized in an episode of the *Murphy Brown* show some years ago.[57] In another installation, Ann Hamilton stacked 800 men's white shirts, "folded, starched, singed and gilded," as part of a Whitney Museum exhibition entitled *Dirt and Domesticity: Constructions of the Feminine*.[58] Walter de Maria's *New York Earth Room* (1977) at the gallery of the Dia Arts Foundation consists, simply, of a "pristine-white gallery space filled with a deep layer of dirt."[59]

The principal theorist behind such work was a former painter, Allan Kaprow (b. 1927), who studied "musical composition" with John Cage in the late 1950s. Kaprow's 1958 essay "The Legacy of Jackson Pollock" performed the prodigious intellectual feat of providing a theoretical link between Abstract Expressionist painting and the installations and assemblages that would dominate the artworld into this century.[60] For Kaprow, Pollock's historic achievement was his near disregard of the limits of a painting's rectangular field "in favor of a continuum going in all directions simultaneously, *beyond* the literal dimensions of any work." His mural-scale drip paintings thus "ceased to become paintings and became environments" in which the viewer was "confronted, assaulted, sucked in." Artists who did not wish to continue in the same vein as Pollock could only "give up the making of paintings entirely," Kaprow argued (true to the avant-garde mindset, he could not entertain the possibility of a return to "traditional" painting and sculpture).

As the logical outgrowth of Pollock's "advanced" abstract painting, Kaprow promulgated a "new concrete art," which would be "preoccupied with and even dazzled by the space and objects of our everyday life" and would utilize virtually everything as its materials: not merely paint, but "chairs, food, electric and neon lights, smoke, water, old socks, a dog, movies, . . . happenings and events, found in garbage cans, police files, . . . in store windows and on the streets"—in short, anything at all, from the "odor of crushed strawberries" to "a billboard selling Drano."[61] The dazzling everyday objects Kaprow employed included a heap of used automobile tires, with which he filled the backyard of a New York art gallery, for his 1961 piece entitled *Yard*.[62]

Since such work is "as open and fluid as . . . everyday experience" (to quote Kaprow again), it of course blurs the boundary between art works and life experience—a persistent theme of his, as indicated by his collected *Essays on the Blurring of Art and Life*. It also obliterates the identity of the various art forms. "Young artists of today need no longer say, 'I am a painter' or 'a poet,'" declared Kaprow. "They are simply 'artists.'"[63] Moreover, both the viewer's and the would-be artist's relationship to the "new concrete art" radically differs from that toward "traditional" art. One does not "come to look *at* things," Kaprow explained. Instead, "We simply enter, are surrounded, and become part of what surrounds us, passively or actively, according to our talents for 'engagement.'"[64] Echoing avant-gardists from the abstract pioneers to Duchamp, Kaprow further argued that such work places more responsibility for the "'success' of a work" on the viewers than ever before.[65]

Performance Art

In her thorough survey, *Performance Art: From Futurism to the Present*, RoseLee Goldberg traces the history of the form from its roots early in the twentieth century through 1986. According to Goldberg, "performance became accepted as a medium of artistic expression in its own right in the 1970s" (7), as a tangible outgrowth of conceptual art. More than any other postmodern form, it was used to "[break] down the categories and [indicate] new directions in twentieth-century art. It became, she says, "an avant avant garde."

The history of performance art in the twentieth century is the history of a permissive, open-ended medium with endless variables, executed by artists impatient with the limitations of more established art forms. For this reason its base has always been anarchic. By its very nature, performance defies precise or easy definition beyond the simple declaration that it is live art by artists. Any stricter definition would negate the possibility of performance itself. . . . Indeed, no other artistic form of expression has such a boundless manifesto, since each performer makes his or her own definition in the very process and manner of execution. [9]

Performance, Goldberg concludes, "has one overriding and peculiar character, which is that it still can be anything at all: for the artist, it represents the possibility of working without rules and guidelines." As an advocate of performance art, Goldberg, naturally, does not allude to the psychopathology which we argue is inherent in the form (as it is to virtually all avant-garde art from the first decade of the twentieth century to the present). Performance art is, as she notes, at root anarchic and confrontational, often resorting to violent or sexually transgressive behavior. Like conceptual art, with which it is closely associated, it paradoxically grew out of a *visual art* context—ostensibly as a reaction against the gallery system and the arts establishment. Since it recognizes no boundaries of form or content, and the performer is the autonomous "artist," performance art appears to constitute, however illusorily, the ultimate bastion of artistic freeedom.

Coined in the early 1960s, the term "performance art" was first applied to live events staged by disaffected members of the "avant-garde" artworld—events such as the daffily senseless "Happenings" Allan Kaprow had begun organizing in the late 1950s and the bizarre "concerts" promoted by various members of Fluxus, inspired in part by John Cage's 1952 multimedia event at Black Mountain College.[66] Later varieties of performance art included the self-mutilating "body art" of individuals such as Chris Burden—whose 1971 piece *Shoot* consisted of having a friend shoot him in the arm, and whose street performance entitled *Through the Night Softly* (1973) entailed his crawling bare-skinned over broken glass.[67]

Once on the fringe of contemporary culture, performance art has now become a mainstream form, welcomed even into the artworld institutions its makers formerly scorned. Lisa Phillips, respectfully documents its history (through photographs and texts, owing to its ephemeral nature)—including several of its most insanely outrageous examples, such as Carolee Schneemann's piece *Interior Scroll* (1975), in which the performer, her face and naked body partially covered in streaks of paint, "pulled a long scrolling text from her vagina and read from it." (242) In 1997, Schneeman's work was also featured in a special "Performance Art" issue of the *Art Journal*, published by the College Art Association. Reviewing a Schneemann exhibition at the New Museum of Contemporary Art in New York, Robert C. Morgan, professor of the history and theory of art at the Rochester Institute of Technology, praised the museum for "presenting an artist of such significance." "To understand *Interior Scroll* [which Schneemann performed again for the exhibition]," he maintained, "is to place it in the context of the [art] of the 1970s and to understand the artist's feminism as being about the body, in contrast to the insular protectiveness of the masculine brain. By pulling the scroll from her sex and reading it aloud, the artist is stating that what is inscribed on or within the sexual body is a discourse inseparable from that body."

We doubt that this is what students from a freshman class at a local private school, for example, would have thought on the day we saw them visiting the *American Century* exhibition (which included a photograph of Schneemann's act). Since the text read by Schneemann makes little sense, and since neither it nor the intended meaning of her actions can elude the titillating effect the public sight of a naked female body (even in a photograph) is likely to have in a culture in which nudity is customarily a private affair, *Interior Scroll*, is likely to be seen by the ordinary person as a form of exhibitionism, verging on pornography.[68] The same is true of other sexually explicit "performance art," despite the purported nobility of its intentions. Yet the *Encyclopedia of Aesthetics* devotes serious attention to "professional sex worker" Annie Sprinkle's *Post Porn Modernist* performances (in which she invites audience members to examine her cervix).[69]

As one might expect, the theory of performance art is as confused as the practice. Martha Wilson, a leading performance artist who edited the special issue of *Art Journal*, observes that, though performance art is "the opposite of theater," it has "raided literature, music, dance, and theater traditions . . . , [thus] spreading confusion."[70] What is distinctive about it, she suggests, is that "performance artists remind their audiences: *There is no artifice here; this is happening now, in 'real' time*."[71] Through performance art, Wilson declares, the body has become "the new art medium of this century." Such a claim mistakes the nature of an artistic medium, however. The body is the *instrument* in performance art; its *medium* is language and movement, sometimes with music added. But those elements are not new. They have been the stuff of drama and dance since prehistory. Moreover, precisely speaking, the verb "perform" connotes "an act for which a process or pattern of movement has already been established, esp. one calling for skill or precision," as in the phrase to "*perform* a dance."[72] The content and value of a work of performance art ultimately depends not on the mere fact of its execution by a live body in "'real'" time, therefore, but on the meaning and quality of the performer's words and actions. Since performance artists expressly reject the "artifice"—the rules and "limitations"—of the established art forms that employ these media, their work cannot rise to the level of art.

Though Kaprow repeatedly advocated blurring the boundary between art and life, he occasionally recognized the inherent contradiction this involved— much as abstract artists have continually feared their work might be mere "decoration" and Henry Flynt questioned whether his "concept art" might, in fact, be something other than art. "I am not so sure whether what we do now is art or something not quite art," Kaprow wrote of his Happenings in 1961. "If I call it art," he then hedged, "it is because I wish to avoid the end-less arguments some other name would bring forth."[73] That was a rather disin-genuous claim, of course, since another name would never smell as sweet, could never confer the status that "art" magically conveys. Like all his fel-low members of the avant-garde, Kaprow wants to have it both ways—to destroy art, yet retain its aura.[74]

Video Art

Since the late 1960s, when Sony first introduced an inexpensive, portable video camera, video has been a preferred medium in the postmodernist art-world. "Whether you like it or not, video art marks the twenty-first century," a Manhattan art dealer informed *Forbes* magazine in 1996. "Young people who want to be artists aren't interested in painting anymore. They grew up captivated by TV, not paintings."[75] There is another, perhaps more important, reason, of course: *anyone can make a video*—though (as the appalling qual-ity of most "video art" attests) few people can make one worth anyone else's time to look at.

Like other postmodernist forms, video art is virtually impossible to define. According to the *Dictionary of Art*, it employs "the apparatus and processes of television and video" and can take many forms—from "recordings that are broadcast . . . or distributed as tapes or discs" to "sculptural installations, which may incorporate one or more television receivers or monitors, displaying 'live' or recorded images and sound" to "performances in which video representa-tions are included."[76] The pioneer video artist Nam June Paik's installation *Megatron/Matrix*, for example, is a 12' by 33' stack of 215 television sets, which emit a deafening sound and a pulsating kaleidoscope of rapidly chang-ing images ranging from the Seoul Olympics to a David Bowie concert.[77]

Most video art makes no attempt at narrative or story-telling of any kind— when one remembers that, as Rand emphasized, "story" (or plot) implies a *logical* progression of events. Consider the work of Bruce Nauman, for example—a leading postmodernist (one of the "top ten living artists" in the *ART-news* poll we cited above) who frequently uses video in his installations.[78] A typical Nauman video piece is *Poke in the Eye/Nose/Ear* (1994), an endless video loop showing him sticking his finger in the stipulated orifices. In Nauman's *Clown Torture* (1987), a clown is shown sitting on a toilet, reading, and howling furiously. Such pieces make no sense in themselves, and their cumulative effect, as in the huge Nauman retrospective we attended a few years ago, evokes an insane asylum. As the novelist Francine Prose admiringly observes: "To attend an exhibition of his work, is to recapture some of the danger and excitement of hanging out with the most inventive, creative, and charismatic kid on the block—the one who, of course grew up to be the criminal or the psycho."[79]

For the past few years, the video artist most in demand has been Matthew Barney, another of the *ARTnews* poll's "top ten." Barney first seduced the art-world in 1990 (a year after graduating from Yale), with his video *Field Dressing (Orifill)*—in which he climbed, naked, up a pole and cables, and "applied dollops of Vaseline to his orifices." As Michael Kimmelman recently observed, in a feature article for the *New York Times Magazine*: "It helped that Barney was marketable apart from his art, with Yale connections and model good looks."[80] In 1991, Barney galvanized critics with a video of himself climbing—naked, of course—across the ceiling of the art gallery that sells his work.[81] Since then, he has been producing and performing in an elaborate series of videos, entitled *Cremaster* (the name of a muscle on the male genitals).

According to Kimmelman, Barney's work—which uses a "mythological language" that seems "willfully irrational"—tells wordless "stories." Reviewing *Cremaster 4* a few years ago, however, Kimmelman noted that its story line "is as difficult to describe as it is to follow," as even this partial summary testifies: "The movie is set on the Isle of Man, with Mr. Barney playing a dandyish, primping, henna-haired satyr, attended by three androgynous fairies. He tap-dances a hole through the floor of a pier, walks along the sea bed and wriggles through a narrow, gooey tunnel that is like the intestines, or birth canal." Regarding the point of it all, Kimmelman had no clue. Most viewers would probably be equally clueless regarding Barney's more recent effort, *Cremaster 2*—which involves, among other things, serial killer Gary Gilmore's grandmother, Houdini, the Mormon doctrine of blood atonement, Utah's Bonneville Salt Flats, the Columbia ice field in Canada, a re-creation of the World's Columbian exposition, ballroom dancing, and bull-riding. Kimmelman now claims to "get it," however, and he anoints Barney "the most important artist of his generation," because "his imagination is so big." It may be that, in this case, as so often with "cutting-edge" art, the critic's imagination exceeds even that of the artist himself.

Postmodernism and Photography

An especially lamentable aspect of the postmodernist goal of blurring the boundary between art and life is that the essential distinction between photography (as a literal means of recording reality) and art (as a selective re-creation of reality) is deliberately flouted in a variety of ways. As we noted in Chapter 9, the curators of the landmark 1987 exhibition, *Photography and Art: Interactions since 1946*, argue that "the integration of photography and the other visual arts has advanced to the point that it no longer seems appropriate to distinguish them as two categories of expression, or to view photography as a medium unto itself."[82] Since modernism emphasized the "totally separate agendas" of the media, so the postmodernist reasoning goes, such distinctions can have no value.

Women have been particularly drawn to using the camera for "personal expression and visual experimentation." Representative of this trend is the photographer-impersonator Cindy Sherman, who first gained attention in the 1970s with her *Untitled Film Stills*, a series of black-and-white photographs simulating Hollywood movie stills—for which she posed in various settings and guises, employing wigs, ingenious makeup, prosthetic devices, and costumes. In 1997, when the Museum of Modern Art bought a complete set of the series (69 photos in all) for $1 million, its chief photography curator, Peter Galassi, called it "a landmark body of work" in both the photographic and the broader artistic tradition.[83] Contrary to that exalted claim, however, the work is unexceptional as photography. Sherman—who failed her introductory photography course in college, and was saved only by discovering "conceptual art"—did not even shoot all the pictures herself (which she ordinarily does).[84] In any case, photography is not art, for all the reasons we discussed in Chapter 9. The only "artistic" element in the series lies in the ingenuity of Sherman's impersonations, which became even more elaborate in her series of "History Portraits" (1988–1990), which included images alluding to various portraits by Ingres and earlier master painters. Sherman's impersonations are really a variety of "performance art." Moreover, like much postmodernist work, they are not re-creations of reality but imitations of re-creations of reality. Feminist scholars and critics have woven intricate theories about Sherman's photographs as "explorations" of female identity in relation to conventions of mass-media representation.[85] But such ideas are completely external to the pictures themselves—being arbitrarily *read into them*. Such themes are in any case far too abstract to be dealt with in images alone, even if that were Sherman's intent. In and of themselves, without a dramatic or narrative context, they can convey little.[86]

Just as Sherman reverses the proper relationship of photography to reality by using its mechanical means to present imitations of imitations, *photorealist* "artists" have used the creative media of painting and sculpture to generate mechanical copies of reality. Rather than "selectively re-create reality," painters such as Chuck Close began in the mid-1960s to work directly from photographs, slavishly replicating them with the use of enlargements, proportional grids, and other mechanical means.[87] The result is strangely remote and, even in his greatly enlarged "portraits," essentially dehumanized. Close is the only photorealist to depict the human face exclusively, but his approach is inhumanly abstract. His explicit intent is "to make something that was so large that it could not be readily seen as a whole and [thereby to] force the viewer to scan the image in a Brobdignagian way, as if they were Gulliver's Lilliputians crawling over the surface of the face, falling into a nostril and tripping over a mustache hair."[88]

Though a recent series of paintings look less photographic than his early work, they continue to be based directly on photographs, and remain equally remote from the usual concern of artists with the physiognomy of the face, exploring instead "our perception of shape" (a task of science, not art). After photographing his subject, Close draws a grid onto the photo, then copies the areas in each segment onto a greatly enlarged grid on canvas, by filling each segment with abstract daubs of roughly the same color, but not the same form, as in the photo.[89] As Michael Kimmelman has observed, in such work Close "is revealing himself to be more and more an abstract painter, at heart. His grids are now containers for lozenges, blips and teardrops in vivid color combinations. . . . The faces themselves, especially with their affectless expressions, are almost incidental. . . . Close's style creates an effect like looking through water, or through thick glass."[90] The object of portraiture is to reveal character, however, not to obscure it. Thus Deborah Solomon's reference to Close as the "reigning portraitist of the Information Age" is dubious praise indeed.[91]

The Future: Art and Technology

As Johanna Drucker approvingly observed a few years ago in an issue of *Art Journal*[92] (of which she was guest editor) devoted to the visual arts and technology, "the ready availability of digital manipulation in a wide variety of media . . . has put the tools of electronic art within reach of an ever growing number of artists." She further noted that the personal computer, "a novelty fifteen years ago, is now a standard item . . . in art schools, professional studios, and, increasingly, galleries and museums." Drucker regarded this as progress. During the decade she considered, however, so-called *electronic art*, under whatever rubric—whether computer art, internet art, cyber art, web art, digital art, interactive art, interface art, video art, or robotic art—produced nothing that qualifies as art, in the sense defined by Rand and presented here. As Drucker concludes, "art making remains the same no matter what the medium," and the "age-old functions of art . . . remain what they have always been." Or, as the old song by Herman Hupfeld reminds us: "The fundamental things apply / As time goes by."[93] What "applies" in the case of *art* are its defining attributes. The arts of the infinite future, regardless of technological advances, will not differ essentially from what they were in prehistory when man painted images of animals on the walls of caves, carved the human figure, told stories, and made music on flutes. They will, above all, be intelligible. To *be* art, the art of the future must make sense. We are optimistic that at some near time in the twenty-first century the arts will undergo a renaissance, as the bogus forms of the twentieth, and the empty theories that have sustained them, recede into the background. If *What Art Is* plays some small role in hastening that renaissance, our efforts will have been worthwhile.

15

Public Implications

Although Ayn Rand's esthetic theory focuses on the profoundly personal role of art, she did not ignore the complex ways in which art interacts with broader aspects of the culture. When she touched on such questions, however, as she frequently did in her fiction and essays, it was mainly to criticize what she viewed as the growing moral void in the popular arts, as evidenced in contemporary works of detective fiction, television drama, and the movies.[1] Our emphasis in this chapter is somewhat different. To conclude our application of Rand's theory to a critique of the "avant-garde," we examine its implications in four main areas of public concern and policy: government subsidy, corporate support, law, and education. Though Rand herself did little more than briefly allude to some of the specific issues we raise here, we draw upon broader principles of her philosophy in our analysis.

Government Subsidy of the Arts

In considering the issue of government subsidies for art, we focus on the National Endowment for the Arts (NEA), which serves as a model for state and local government initiatives—as well as for private support of the arts—and thus exerts an influence far beyond its relatively modest fiscal allocations.[2] Our criticisms of NEA programs, therefore, also apply in large measure to other governmental as well as major foundation programs.[3] Though Rand correctly argued, on principle, against *any* direct government support of the arts,[4] we limit ourselves here to a consideration of how federal programs have undermined both the concept and the contemporary practice of art—since *What Art Is* is a study not in political philosophy but in the philosophy of art.

The most vehement objections to the NEA in recent years have been raised by cultural conservatives justifiably outraged at the obscene or blasphemous character of certain government-funded projects. Our objection is more fundamental. We contend that much of the contemporary work funded by the endowment since its inception is not art at all. Though arts advocates attempt to minimize the part played by so-called nontraditional work in the NEA's 35-year history, bizarre projects have been funded since the endowment's early years, particularly in the "Visual Arts" category—as a former deputy chairman of the agency has candidly recounted.[5] Surely, if government continues to allocate public funds for support of "the arts," taxpayers have a right to expect that at the very least "the expenditure [will] be on *art*, and not on some substitute pretending to be art"—to quote the philosopher Oswald Hanfling.[6]

As NEA advocates are well aware, the ordinary person takes "art" to mean the *fine arts*, or the forms traditionally included under that term. Thus a 1998 public address by NEA chairman Bill Ivey, for example, notes that the endowment is "charged with bringing music, dance, theatre, literature and painting to the American people."[7] Similarly, a press release on grants for the year 2000 refers to fostering the creation of new works "in music, dance, visual arts, theater, literature, and film."[8] And the rhetoric by which government support of art was initially justified—in terms such as "high civilization" and "great branches of man's . . . cultural activity"[9]—implies the benefits works in these forms can provide. But NEA support for new work (or for presentation and exhibition of recent work) flows mainly to artists working in the spurious art forms generated by the artworld, from "media art" and "video art" to "installations," "ceramic art," and "artists' books."[10]

Artworld influence is, in fact, endemic to the agency's operations. To escape the charge that government support would lead to government control, the endowment has from its inception employed a "peer-panel" review process, in which all substantive decision-making—on grant awards, programs, and policy—is guided by allegedly qualified members of the arts community. This process purportedly ensures both artistic freedom and a maximum diversity of creative expression. In truth, however, the government's inescapable dependence on recognized "experts" has resulted in a *de facto* entrenchment of avant-gardism in national arts policy and practice, since the prominent "artists" and "experts" in the contemporary artworld are modernists or postmodernists of one stripe or another. Vanguard assumptions have therefore pervaded government involvement in the arts, beginning with the very language of the law establishing the NEA in 1965. In dealing with the key term, *the arts*, the legislation eschewed a formal definition. Instead, it enumerated a laundry list of purported art forms, including—but "not limited to" (the ultimate "open sesame")—not only the time-honored primary and performing arts (music, dance, drama, painting, sculpture, and so-called creative writing—presumably fiction and poetry) but also utilitarian, or applied-art, categories such as industrial and fashion design, architecture and "allied arts," and electronic communications media such as radio and television. Moreover, the original legislation indiscriminately referred to all of these as "major art forms."[11]

While the NEA has undoubtedly assisted many worthwhile exhibitions and productions of the great art of the past, its synergistic relationship with the arts establishment has had a deleterious influence on the contemporary practice of art. Although current application guidelines no longer stress innovation, and controversial grants to individuals of the sort that caused a public furor a decade ago have been discontinued,[12] the pattern of grant-making is no less far removed from the domain of art. Projects in the "Media Arts," for example, have included documentary films on subjects such as "the private and public spaces" of Madison Square Garden (the nation's "pre-eminent sports and entertainment arena") and "the power, meaning, and mystery of people's names"—as well as radio documentaries on "people who live on the edge of society" and on "the art of the radio documentary."[13] A Tallahassee, Florida, gallery was awarded $5,000 to support "a national juried exhibition entitled *H2O*, examining the aesthetic, recreational, and environmental issues associated with water." The Community Architexts Association won a $16,500 grant for "a public design installation . . . to develop communication infrastructures for disadvantaged women. The result will be an installation of the women's statements onto a prominent building's facade and signage that will eventually be available for local business use." Finally, San Francisco Camerawork will employ its $20,000 grant toward an exhibition entitled *Timekeepers*, and a related issue of the journal *Camerawork*. "Work in the exhibition, which will be predominantly new media, will question and expand the ways in which we conceive of time."[14]

Nor do awards in other categories inspire confidence. In the field of dance, for example, one of the largest NEA grants in 1999 ($100,000) went toward the creation and presentation of two new works by Merce Cunningham, whose avant-garde approach to dance we analyzed in Chapter 12. "Creation and Presentation" awards for the year 2000 include grants to the Alex Theatre in Glendale, California, in part for performances by Momix and Meredith Monk, as well as to the Cunningham company; and to Dance Umbrella Boston for work by Pilobolus, among other groups we have also discussed.[15]

Recent grants to museums have included support to Illinois State University for *Post-hypnotic*, a touring exhibition "addressing the resurgence of optical effects in the work of abstract artists throughout the United States"; to the San Francisco Museum of Modern Art for a touring retrospective of the work of Sol LeWitt (whose spurious ideas on art we noted in Chapter 14); and to the Guggenheim Museum for a retrospective exhibition of the work of video artist Nam June Paik (also cited in Chapter 14). Far more disturbing is the rarely cited fact that NEA support for museums and new exhibitions has implicitly sanctioned, and directly or indirectly underwritten, postmodernist transgressions against both art and public propriety in exhibitions such as *Sensation* and *The American Century* (both of which we cited in Chapter 14). A $50,000 award to the Whitney Museum in 1999, for example, was for "training for primary and secondary school teachers nationwide in conjunction with *The American Century*"—an exhibition that included such works as Kiki Smith's *Tale* (a crudely sculpted naked female figure, crawling on the floor, with a ten-foot-long piece of excrement issuing from her anus) and Robert Mapplethorpe's black and white photograph, *Man in Polyester Suit*, (showing a close-up of the subject from the bottom of his jacket lapel and buttoned up vest to just above the knees, but with his penis prominently exposed).[16]

Work of this kind can scarcely be said to "nourish the human spirit"—to borrow a phrase from the Preamble to the NEA's original Statement of Mission. Yet it is apparently through such "art" that the endowment judges we can best "understand ourselves and our potential" and by which we hope to "be understood and remembered by those who will come after us" (again quoting from the Preamble). Nor can such work be said to meet the NEA's professed goal of fostering "excellence" in the arts—a goal that must ring hollow in the absence of an objective definition either of art or of the standards by which it is to be judged. As Supreme Court Justice Anthony Scalia has argued, the fact that a federal agency "charged with making grants under a statutory standard of 'artistic excellence' . . . has itself thought that standard met by everything from the playing of Beethoven to a [photograph] of a crucifix immersed in urine" should raise serious doubts about its constitutional validity, in view of the basic rule against legislative vagueness.[17]

The endowment's purported goal of excellence has been further undermined by the simultaneous goal of "diversity" in recent years—reflecting the movement toward "multiculturalism" in the arts, politics, and education. Departing from the original legislative focus on "*national* progress" in the arts and "*American* artistic creativity," amendments to Public Law 80-209 in 1980 and 1985 shifted concern to "cultural diversity" and "minorities"—as well as to "supporting the cultivation of community spirit" and to helping "address the concerns of America's communities through the arts." Lip service is still paid to "artistic excellence and artistic merit," and to "selecting individuals and groups of exceptional talent"; but the pattern of grant-making clearly reveals that the goal of "diversity" is uppermost— calling to mind the "modern tribalism" that Rand warned against more than two decades ago.[18] The NEA's recent agenda is evident on the endowment's web page sampling some of the 1998 Creative Writing (or "Literature") Fellowship winners and boasting "a variety of ethnic backgrounds"—a "diversity [deemed] all the more remarkable when we consider that they are selected by panelists who make their decisions based solely on a writing sample."[19] Though the term "Creative Writing" once meant the writing of poems, fiction, or plays, it is now used by the NEA as a catch-all category for projects with an ethnic emphasis. One award of $20,000 for the year 2000 went for the translation from Spanish of a book-length essay, *Usos Amorosos de la Post guerra Española* (Courtship Customs in Postwar Spain), for example; another, for the translation from the French of a novel by a "Caribbean" author, about the "migration and memory of the Caribbean people at the end of the twentieth century"; and yet another for a translation from Spanish of the complete works of an Argentine writer.[20] Such projects surely give the lie to Bill Ivey's claim, in the press release for awards in the year 2000, that a "broad spectrum of *American* creativity will be supported by . . . new grants" (emphasis ours).

Corporate Support

The picture is as dismal in the realm of corporate funding for the arts, although for somewhat different reasons. Where "excellence" and "quality" were once the focus,[21] now "innovation" is the key word, without regard to whether the work is even art, much less to its quality or value. It is enough that it be perceived as "innovative." Corporations seeking to present themselves as forward-thinking in today's rapidly changing global marketplace eagerly identify themselves with the avant-garde, while ignoring its fundamental irrationality.[22] Thus the catalog for *The American Century* exhibition at the Whitney Museum of American Art (which we cited in Chapter 17) begins with a self-serving "Statement of Collaboration" from the chairman of the Intel Corporation, comparing the "spirit of inventiveness" and the "intellectual rigor found in the work of American artists" in the exhibition to the "dynamics that . . . propel the American high-technology industry."[23] When one considers that the Whitney exhibition included, in addition to the pieces already cited, such works as a postminimalist "scatter piece" by Barry Le Va, consisting of scraps of felt and glass strewn over a corner of the museum floor; a "sound installation" of cats purring by Terry Fox; and Matthew Barney's *Drawing*

Restraint 7 (a silent video showing, in part, two men in the guise of satyrs grappling in a stretch limousine), the Intel chairman's statement seems preposterous indeed.[24]

Equally inane are the claims made by the chairmen and co-chief executive officers of Citigroup, in a letter announcing the corporation's "proud" sponsorship of an exhibition devoted to the work of minimalist painter and sculptor Ellsworth Kelly—"a major American artist" who "represents artistic innovation in the United States in the twentieth century." The corporate connection is predictable: "Our company," the executives explain, "reflects that same innovative spirit."[25] As for exactly what sort of innovations Kelly achieved, the accompanying press release from the Art Institute of Chicago, notes that his development of a "radically inventive and stubbornly impersonal" minimalist style depended, in part, on "the principles of chance"—an approach he shared with John Cage, on whom we have already commented at length in Chapter 12.[26]

A corporate trail-blazer in support for "the spirit of innovation and experimentation" in the arts is Philip Morris, which launched its efforts in 1965 by funding the exhibition *Pop & Op*.[27] In the same spirit, a two-page magazine spread by the company for the Guggenheim Museum's Robert Rauschenberg retrospective in 1997 (on which, see Chapter 14) proclaimed in typical art-world rhetoric: "Defy convention. Shatter boundaries. Redefine the art of our time." This "contemporary American master," the ad continued, is but one of the many "visionary individuals and pioneering organizations" that Philip Morris has supported over the years "who enhance the quality of our world." A line across the bottom of the page reads: "Supporting the spirit of innovation."[28] In a public display of their embrace of the avant-garde, executives from Philip Morris and dozens of other major corporations had amiably sat through the 1986 American premiere of Merce Cunningham's *Roaratorio* with its cacophonous "score" by John Cage—the opening night gala of which their companies had generously funded—at the Brooklyn Academy of Music's "Next Wave Festival."[29]

Among those present at the Cunningham premiere were executives from AT&T, which had begun seeking "to distance itself from [its] stodgy-old-phone-company image" of the past by affiliating with "high-tech inventiveness, diversity and creativity" in the arts.[30] In keeping with this goal, AT&T announced its "proud" sponsorship of Cage's "Rolywholyover[:] A Circus," for example—the press release for which explained:

> With many activities in the museum occurring simultaneously (the "circus" of the title) and the location of many objects in constant flux, guided by a computerized process of random selection, this project breaks with traditional

approaches to museum exhibition programming and is itself a new work of art. [According to a director of public relations for AT&T:] "John Cage's multimedia approach, integrating traditional art forms with new technologies, parallels our own multimedia vision for the convergence of communications, computing, information and entertainment. Because we encourage research and development in the arts just as we do in business, we hope . . . audiences will learn from the discoveries of this modern genius."[31]

The suggestion that this major American corporation hopes to learn from John Cage is preposterous, of course, as any company guided by Cage's principles would not long survive.[32]

Fifteen years ago, most companies hesitated to support public exhibitions of avant-garde work. Now, however, many seek to attract younger customers by creating a "hip" image through the funding of "cutting-edge art"—often, the more outrageous the better. Beck's Beer, for example, has sponsored the controversial British postmodernists Damien Hirst, famed for his installations of livestock preserved in formaldehyde, and Rachel Whiteread, whose resin plaster-cast of a water-tower on a rooftop in the SoHo neighborhood of New York was a dubious contribution to the city's public art in 1998. Whiteread's life-size plaster cast of a row house in London a few years ago, also funded by Beck's, had to be bulldozed following complaints from local officials.[33]

Art and the Law

The burgeoning field of art law is plagued by inconsistencies and contradictions—owing not only to varying emphases dependent on the particular legislative context but also to the fact that the objective standards essential to the law are virtually nonexistent in today's artworld. Symptomatic of the problem is the ambivalence evident in the textbook *Law, Ethics, and the Visual Arts* by John Henry Merryman and Albert E. Elsen.[34] In their introduction, the authors seem to accept the artworld view that art cannot be defined, for they suggest that art is a "creative act . . . that transcends boundaries, defies conventions, breaks the rules," whereas law and ethics constitute "a system of boundaries, conventions and rules, maintained by an established order" (1: xiv). Yet, in a subsequent chapter, they challenge the artworld dictum "'If it is made by an artist it is art'" by observing that such a claim leaves open the question of whether the maker is indeed an artist. "If we answer that an artist is one who makes art," they properly note, "we are running in a circle" (1:318). Thus they imply that a definition of art is necessary after all.

As we have argued, art, like any concept, can be defined. It observes its own "boundaries, conventions, and rules," just as law and ethics do. Moreover, what it is does not depend, as Merryman and Elsen mistakenly suggest, on anyone's alleged "right to define" it (1:316).[35] As Rand insisted, the boundaries of any concept are not determined by individual fiat, but by logical, disinterested analysis of reality: "Who 'decides'? In politics, in ethics, in art, in science, in philosophy—in the entire realm of human knowledge—it is *reality* that sets the terms, through the work of those . . . who are able to identify its terms and to translate them into *objective* principles."[36] Despite their ambivalence, Merryman and Elsen concede that the question Is it art? must be faced if the law is to continue to afford works of art special protection (1:317). They also quote the observation by Stephen E. Weil—an attorney specializing in art law, and deputy director of the Hirshhorn Museum in Washington D.C.— that "'the law cannot accord a special status to art without also providing some mechanism for tracing its boundaries.'"[37] That mechanism, we suggest, can be found in the esthetic theory of Ayn Rand.

Historically, three areas of the law have been particularly concerned with the definition of art: international trade, artists' rights, and freedom of expression. In each of these areas, the definition has been tailored to the distinctive legislative purpose. Case law in each area graphically demonstrates the difficulty the courts have had in grappling with the concept of art, as the art-world itself has adopted an increasingly open-ended view. The courts, in turn, have no doubt contributed to further public confusion regarding the nature of art.

The question of whether an object qualifies as art is particularly relevant to the law governing duties on imported items. Consistent with the purpose of such duties—which is to protect American manufacturers from undue competition—commercial products are taxed, while works of art are exempted. Early customs cases clearly defined "art" as the traditional fine arts (specifically painting and sculpture), as distinguished from the utilitarian industrial arts.[38] The chief criteria were entirely objective: to be exempt from duty, the work had to be wholly nonutilitarian, representational, and individually fashioned, not factory-produced. In 1892, for example, the U.S. Supreme Court defined the fine arts as those "'intended solely for ornamental [i.e., nonutilitarian] purposes, and including paintings in oil and water, upon canvas, plaster, or other material, and original statuary of marble, stone, or bronze."[39]

In 1916, the customs court further clarified the Supreme Court's distinction between merely artistic objects and "works of [fine] art," defining the latter as "only those productions of the artist which are something more than ornamental or decorative and which may be properly ranked as examples of the free fine arts, *natural objects as the artist sees them*, and appealing to the emotions through the eye alone."[40] The court further established a clear representational test for art by defining the art of sculpture as

> that branch of the free fine arts which chisels or carves out of stone or other solid material or models in clay or other plastic substance for subsequent reproduction by carving or casting, *imitations of natural objects, chiefly the human form,* and represents such objects in their true proportions of length, breadth, and thickness, or of length and breadth only [i.e., in relief]."[41]

In 1928, however, in a lawsuit concerning Constantin Brancusi's abstract sculpture *Bird in Flight*, the customs court acceded to modernist theory by setting aside the objective representational test, in favor of more subjective criteria. Following expert testimony, it conferred legitimacy on "a so-called new school of art, whose exponents attempt to portray abstract ideas rather than to imitate natural objects," and argued that Brancusi's work qualified as fine art because it is "beautiful," made "for purely ornamental [i.e., nonutilitarian] purposes," and "the original production of a professional sculptor."[42]

In 1958, standards were further relaxed when the Tariff Act of 1930 was amended to allow free entry to art works "in other media" than those previously stipulated. Since then, most purported art objects have been admitted duty-free, with the notable exception of articles reproduced by mechanical processes—or of obviously utilitarian objects, such as vases, cups, plates, and trays. In this area, the court has appropriately retained its original distinction between "fine art" and the decorative or utilitarian arts, as well as a corresponding distinction between "artists" and "artisans."[43] In determining whether someone qualifies as an artist, however, substantial weight is given to artworld recognition—which we have argued is of dubious validity in today's cultural climate.[44]

The legal definition of art developed differently in the area of copyright and patent law. This body of law is not designed to protect the interests of American manufacturers, but rather, to protect the economic interests of creators and inventors—and to advance the "public good" by promoting creativity.[45] In a landmark Supreme Court case in 1903, *Bleistein v. Donaldson Lithographing Co.*, Justice Oliver Wendell Holmes argued for the majority that, in defining the "useful arts" which Congress is empowered to promote, the Constitution "does not limit the useful to that which satisfies immediate bodily needs."[46] Clearly "useful" in this context did not mean the same thing as "utilitarian" in the area of customs law, but simply reflects Holmes's recognition that the fine arts, too, have a function—albeit not a practical, or physical, one—as Rand argued.

In reaching his conclusion in *Bleistein,* Justice Holmes appropriately emphasized the idiosyncratic quality of art. Such a quality inevitably emerges, even in a drawing done directly from nature, as "the personal reaction of an individual," he stressed, since "[p]ersonality always contains something unique" (635). It is this distinctive quality that copyright law recognizes and protects. Such *originality* is distinguished from mere "novelty or invention," as another landmark case, *Mazer v. Stein* (1954), clearly established.[47] Copyright protects the distinctive expression of an idea, not the idea itself. "Absent copying," the court insisted, "there can be no infringement of copyright."[48] (These important distinctions contrast sharply with views prevailing in the artworld since the ascendancy of "conceptual art" and other postmodernist tendencies in the 1960s.) Unlike the customs exemption, however, copyright protection is not limited to objects of fine art, but extends to other instances of "artistic" originality as well. In *Mazer,* for example, the court ruled that statuettes designed and used as lamp bases were copyrightable—though such an object would more properly qualify as decorative art.

Following *Mazer,* the copyright office implemented new regulations in 1959. These regulations distinguished between utilitarian objects that are merely "unique and attractively shaped" and those that incorporate "artistic" features. Only the latter—in the form of a "sculpture, carving, or pictorial representation, which can be identified separately and are capable of existing independently"—are copyrightable.[49] The implications of this distinction were clarified in a 1985 case, in which the court ruled that clothing mannequins shaped like partial human torsos "did not possess artistic or aesthetic features that were physically or conceptually separable from their utilitarian dimension and therefore were not copyrightable."[50]

Alluding to the artworld's authoritarian (or institutional) definition of art, the court further noted: "Almost any utilitarian article may be viewed by some separately as art, depending on how it is displayed." Yet, "Congress has made it reasonably clear," the court emphasized, "that copyrightability of the object should turn on its ordinary use as viewed by *the average observer.*" (419*n*5, emphasis ours) A dissenting opinion by Judge Jon O. Newman also espoused this common-sense test. To qualify as "conceptually separable," he argued, the design features of an object must stimulate in the mind of the beholder an idea distinct from that evoked by the object's utilitarian function; and "the relevant beholder must be that most useful legal personage—*the ordinary, reasonable observer.*" (422, emphasis ours) Most significantly, Newman stressed that

In endeavoring to draw the line [between copyrightable and non-copyrightable designs], courts will inevitably be drawn into some minimal inquiry as to the nature of art. . . . Of course, courts must not assess the *quality* of art, but a determination of whether a design engenders the concept of a work of art, separate from the concept of an article's utilitarian function, necessarily requires some consideration of whether the object is a work of art.[51] [423]

The inescapable need to consider whether an object is a work of art— recognized by Judge Newman—becomes all the more apparent in cases following the 1990 amendment to federal copyright law—the Visual Artists' Rights Act (VARA). Intended to protect works in certain categories of visual art from intentional "distortion, mutilation or other modification" that would harm an artist's reputation or that would seriously damage works "of recognized stature,"[52] VARA, like many other areas of art law, is impaired by vague and inconsistent definition of its scope—that is, "works of visual art." As defined by copyright law, such works include paintings, sculpture, drawings, small-edition prints (less than 200 copies), and photographs produced for exhibition.[53] Not only is the law's inclusion of photographs questionable (see our discussion of photography in Chapter 9), the precise nature of the other categories is left undefined.[54]

The need for greater definition became apparent in the first case under VARA. In question was a purported work of sculpture, described by the *New York Times* as "an eye-popping *sculptural installation* made of recycled materials, scrap and abandoned appliances reconfigured into a huge silver fish, a moon that opens up to reveal an astronaut with a trash-can head, a bathtub sun and much more."[55] According to the *Wall Street Journal* the work was a "scrap-yard Wonderland" in which "Sculptures crafted from an estimated 50 tons of junk hang from the ceiling, fill the elevators, crawl up the walls and even sprout from the elaborate floor mosaics of recycled glass."[56]

The plaintiffs in the case were three alleged artists, who had created the contested installation on commission for a partnership that was leasing the building but had not obtained permission for the installation from the owner, represented by Helmsley-Spear, a prominent New York real-estate management firm. When the leaseholders went bankrupt, Helmsley-Spear sought to remove the installation, which it deemed a nuisance and a safety hazard to tenants and visiting members of the public. Among other offensive features of the work were a 500-pound metal gong which emitted an ear-splitting sound, as well as an elevator button shaped like a penis, which set the letters flapping in an overhead sign that spelled "start licking."[57]

In concluding that removal of the work was barred under VARA, the district court relied on the testimony of "expert witnesses," who testified that the installation was a work of "recognized stature." The court specifically cited the art historian and critic Robert Rosenblum's testimony that the work was "like almost nothing I've ever seen before"[58] and was "staggering in its lunatic *invention*."[59] Other witnesses also testified to the novelty of the work. However, the district court failed to consider whether the work possessed a uniquely personal "signature"— a requisite characteristic of art as defined by Justice Holmes in *Bleistein*.. The district court also ignored the clear distinction emphasized by the Supreme Court (in *Mazer*) between artistic "originality," which is protected under copyright law, and mere "invention," which is not. Further, it appears that no one connected with the case (including Hilton Kramer, who testified for Helmsley-Spear, disputing the alleged merit of the work) questioned whether the installation was indeed a work of "sculpture"— the category under which it purported to warrant protection—much less whether it was "art" of any kind. Helmsley-Spear's counsel merely claimed that, as a "work done for hire," the installation was not protected under VARA. Ultimately, the case was decided in Helmsley-Spear's favor, on that ground. Had such a technical consideration not been involved, however, the owner's property rights would have been nullified by the testimony of "expert witnesses" from the artworld—though, as we have suggested throughout this book, their views on the nature of art are deeply flawed, and fundamentally at odds with those of Judge Newman's "ordinary, reasonable observer." The lower court's decision, prior to Helmsley-Spear's successful appeal, had in fact been for the plaintiffs, based mainly on artworld testimony that their work was "of recognized stature" and would be damaged by removal.[60] Moreover, the lower court judge explicitly preferred the views of witnesses "who are intimately familiar with *evolving standards* in the area of contemporary art"[61] to Kramer's dissenting testimony—a preference whose very phrasing suggests its mistaken premises.

The concept of art is also crucially relevant to lawsuits in which purported art works may have exceeded the legal limits of free expression. Two areas in which the courts allow abridgment of First Amendment rights are desecration of the American flag and obscenity, or pornography. Since the antiwar movement of the 1960s, the flag has frequently been used in politically motivated works of "installation art" that appear to flout statutes barring its desecration. Litigation pertaining to such work has been confounded by an inadequate definition of art, in particular a blurring of the distinctions between art and other forms of "expression." One such a case involved the owner of a Manhattan art gallery, Stephen A. Radich, who had been convicted by a New York City court for having publicly displayed the flag in a "defiled and mutilated" condition, in violation of state law.[62] Though his conviction was upheld by the New York State Court of Appeals and by the State Supreme Court, it was subsequently overturned by a federal district court. While upholding the constitutionality of the law itself, the federal court held that the application was violative of First Amendment Rights.

As characterized by the appeals court, the work in question consisted of "certain 'constructions,' comparable to sculptures, which had been fashioned by an artist [Marc Morell]" as a protest against the Vietnam war.[63] One of the pieces displayed the flag "in the form of the male sexual organ, erect and protruding from the upright member of a cross."[64] In overturning the conviction, the federal district court perpetuated a category error contained in the state appeals court's decision. Similarly referring to "the Morell constructions" as "sculptures," the federal court held that they warranted equal protection with so-called "ornamental picture[s]," which are clearly exempt from prosecution under the anti-desecration statute. (300, 299) That analysis, developed at length in a dissenting opinion by Chief Judge Fuld of the appeals court,[65] ignores a fundamental distinction, however: "pictures" are modes of pure *representation*, whereas Morell's "constructions" (works of "installation art," on which see Chapter 17) are composed of actual flags and other real objects.

Such a distinction is not a trivial one. As one Korean war veteran astutely observed—regarding another politically motivated installation piece, in which a flag was placed on the floor so that people would walk on it: "'It would be different if it was [an artistic] rendering of the flag. *But it was a real flag*. And it belongs to the American people.'"[66] Similar objections by ordinary people were provoked by a 1996 exhibit devoted to "flag art" at the Phoenix Art Museum. Entitled *Old Glory: The American Flag in Contemporary Art*, the exhibition featured such pieces as a "flag made of dried strips of human skin" and a real flag "stuffed into a gleaming porcelain toilet bowl . . . in a mockup of a jail cell."

First Amendment protection in such cases is based on the presumption that the disputed works are a form of "symbolic speech or conduct having a clearly communicative aspect" (295–96). To so qualify, they must meet the test established by the Supreme Court for distinguishing between mere "conduct" (which is not protected) and "pure speech," which is safeguarded by the First Amendment: there must be both "an intent to convey a particular message" and "a likelihood that the message would be understood by those who observed it."[67] In most assemblage and installation pieces, however, the purported intent is anyone's guess. What, for instance, is the "particular message" of the flag stuffed into the toilet bowl? As one *New York Times* reporter pondered, regarding the Phoenix exhibition: "But is it art? Or is it politics? Or is it just plain desecration and exploitation of that greatest of all American icons, under the guise of artistic freedom?"[68] In response to the museum director's claim that "'the test of a good museum exhibit is both to entertain and [to] encourage people to think and react,'" one Navy veteran reasonably demurred: "You don't preserve freedom and speech, . . . and you don't entertain or teach anybody anything, by making a flag of human skin, like Hitler's people did in concentration camps[, or by] putting a flag in a commode."[69]

Finally, we come to one of the most controversial of all recent lawsuits involving the concept of art—the Mapplethorpe obscenity case of a decade ago. In this much-publicized lawsuit, municipal authorities charged the Contemporary Arts Center of Cincinnati and its director, Dennis Barrie, with "pandering obscenity" and the "illegal use of a minor in nudity-oriented material" (i.e., child pornography) in connection with seven photographs in an exhibition, entitled *The Perfect Moment*, devoted to Robert Mapplethorpe's work. Five of the photographs were of men engaged in homoerotic acts characterized as "sadomasochistic" by the exhibition's curator.[70] The remaining two were of young children with their genitals exposed.[71] Apart from the media interest customarily generated by First Amendment cases, the lawsuit was closely watched for its potential repercussions for the National Endowment for the Arts, which had provided support for the exhibition.

Conviction for obscenity requires that a jury find beyond a reasonable doubt the following: (1) that the disputed material appeals to the prurient interest, (2) that it depicts and describes in a patently offensive way sexual conduct specifically defined by applicable state law, and (3) that, taken as a whole, it is without serious literary, artistic, political, or scientific value. All three criteria must be met to deprive a work of First Amendment protection.[72] While the first and second criteria are to be decided by reference to a consensus of local community standards, the crucial third criterion of "serious. . . value" may be determined by "'a minority view among reasonable people.'"[73] In this regard, "expert testimony" by a critic or other artworld representative may suffice.[74] Child pornography is held to a stricter standard, however. It need not meet the three-part test for obscenity. The Supreme Court has ruled that it lies entirely outside First Amendment protection and may be banned by the state even if it is deemed to have "serious value" and is not considered to be obscene.[75]

Jurors in the Mapplethorpe case readily determined that the five "S&M" photographs (as they were referred to at the trial) appealed to prurient interests and depicted sex in a patently offensive way. On the question of "artistic value," however, they considered themselves bound to capitulate to the overwhelming weight of testimony offered by a wide range of artworld experts for the defense—all of whom testified to the brilliance and seriousness of Mapplethorpe's work as art. "'If the prosecution could have come up with just one credible witness—a sociologist, a psychologist, somebody, anybody—maybe we would have voted differently,'" lamented one juror after the trial.[76] All of the expert witnesses "'were so certain it was art,'" said another. "'We had to go with what we were told.'"[77] As we have argued, however, *no photography* (regardless of its subject matter) *is art.* Moreover, the very nature of the photographic medium, as a means of literal transcription of actual persons and things, may render sexually explicit subject matter "inherently pornographic."[78]

The most disturbing aspect of the Mapplethorpe case is the ease with which the charge of child pornography was dismissed. Press coverage largely ignored this issue. One media account perfunctorily noted that the mothers of the two children pictured had testified that they had authorized the taking of the photographs.[79] The account also quoted a Cincinnati art critic, one of the defense's expert witnesses, as having described the images as "a perfect illustration of the phrase 'evil is in the eye of the beholder.'"[80] While presumed art status offers no legal shield for child pornography, the aura of "art" such critics and artworld representatives have created around Mapplethorpe's photography may well have colored the jurors' perception regarding the character of the images in question, just as it may have prompted poor judgment on the part of the children's mothers in authorizing the taking of the pictures. That none of these questions appears to have been broached in the Mapplethorpe case disconcertingly suggests that the cause of alleged art readily preempts the state's interests in protecting minors from pornographic exploitation in today's culture.[81]

Teaching the Arts to Children

However disturbing the late twentieth-century trends in government, corporate, and foundation involvement in the arts may appear, and however confusing the legal response may be to cases touching on the nature of art, the public arena in which Ayn Rand's theory of art should stimulate the most profound debate and concern is the educational system, for here the irrationality rampant in the contemporary artworld works its destructive influence on a captive audience of young minds in their most formative stage.

Rand did not write about arts education per se, but one of her strongest polemics, an essay entitled "The Comprachicos" (1970), was on the subject of "progressive" pedagogy, and her critique may be applied to recent approaches to teaching the arts. Despite the bitterness of her invective and her sometimes shocking metaphors, Rand's argument is compelling. Modern-day educators, she charged, ignore the basic principle that should inform all teaching and learning: that man is a being of conceptual consciousness. She compared them to the seventeenth-century "comprachicos" whose vicious practices

Victor Hugo had excoriated in his novel *The Man Who Laughs*. Whereas those Spanish nomads had purchased young children from their parents and had surgically disfigured their faces—so that they could be sold for profit as court jesters or side-show freaks—teachers entrusted with the education of children, Rand maintained, often stunt their cognitive capacities. She regarded such teachers as "comprachicos of the mind" [82] (155).

Focusing on "progressive" nursery schools, but casting a wider net by implication, Rand charged that the dominant view of a child's needs is "militantly anti-cognitive and anti-conceptual."[83] (155) With lamentable consequences, so-called progressive schools ignore that "the process of forming, integrating and using [higher-level] concepts is not automatic, but a volitional process . . . not an innate, but an acquired skill; it has to be *learned*" (158). "This skill," Rand emphasized, "does not pertain to the particular *content* of [a person's] knowledge at any given age, but to the *method* by which he acquires and organizes knowledge—the method by which his mind deals with its content" (158). The "progressive" approach to pedagogy, however, "conditions [the child's] mind to an anti-conceptual method of functioning that paralyzes his rational faculty"[84] (168). In particular, Rand faulted John Dewey, "the father of modern education," because he "opposed the teaching of theoretical (i.e., conceptual) knowledge, and demanded that it be replaced by concrete, 'practical' action, in the form of 'class projects' which would develop the students' social spirit"[85] (172).

Rand's thesis was elaborated fourteen years later by her philosophic disciple Leonard Peikoff, who substantiated it with examples gathered in a series of classroom visits to some of New York City's leading public and private schools, from kindergarten through college. Having observed the most highly regarded teachers, in order to judge the system "at its best," Peikoff reported that the anti-conceptual approach characterized teaching in every subject at every level—from the "Look-Say" method in early reading instruction (which Rand, too, had criticized) to the study of literature, science, and history, and pedagogical theory itself.[86] In all cases, Peikoff noted, the tendency was to present and discuss concretes in and of themselves, "without connection to any wider issue," as if the mind were stuck on the perceptual level. (211)

The "crucial philosophic point" stressed by Peikoff was that, while human knowledge "begins on the perceptual level, with the use of the five senses, . . . what makes us human is what our mind does with our sense experiences. What makes us human is the *conceptual* level, which includes our capacity to abstract, to grasp common denominators, to classify, to organize our perceptual field." (211) On the perceptual level, "there is no need of logic, argument, proof; a man sees what he sees, the facts are self-evident, and no further cognitive process is required. But on the conceptual level, . . . we need a method of validating our ideas; we need a guide to let us know what conclusions follow from what data. That guide is logic." Moreover, the formation of abstractions "requires a definite order," proceeding from the simple to the more complex, and an understanding of "a specific context at each stage." (212)

A proper pedagogy, Peikoff stressed, would lead a child "to make connections, to generalize, to understand the wider issues and principles involved in any topic . . . by presenting the material to him in a calculated, conceptually proper [i.e., hierarchical] order, with the necessary context, and with the proof that validates each stage."[87] (212) Instead, many contemporary educators "regard concepts as mental constructs without relation to reality"—that is, as "a mere human convention, a ritual unrelated to knowledge or reality, to be performed according to arbitrary social fiat" (218). Rand, too, had deplored this tendency, ascribing it to the influence of the philosophic school of "Linguistic Analysis," which she condemned for declaring "that words have no specific referents, but mean whatever people want them to mean."[88]

Discipline-Based Art Education

The anti-conceptual methods deplored by Rand and Peikoff pervade arts instruction today. Nowhere is this more evident, for example, than in the pedagogical approach adopted by the influential Getty Education Institute for the Arts.[89] As outlined by Stephen Mark Dobbs in the Getty publication *Learning in and through Art: A Guide to Discipline-Based Art Education (DBAE),*[90] this approach was independently conceived in the 1980s, in order to establish art on an equal footing with such core subjects such as English, science, and mathematics. A purportedly "comprehensive approach to teaching and learning in art," DBAE has already had a major impact on pedagogical theory and practice.[91] It aspires to rigor by offering instruction in (or, as Dobbs puts it, "exposure to, experience with, and acquisition of content from") four related disciplines: art-making, art criticism, art history, and esthetics. Instruction in these disciplines is said to contribute to "the creation, understanding, and appreciation of art, artists, artistic processes, and the roles and functions of art in cultures and societies." (3)

Such claims for DBAE sound impressive, but in the absence of clear conceptual understanding, they lack substance. Dobbs loosely characterizes (though not quite defines) each of DBAE's four disciplines.[92] On the core concept of *art* itself, however—the *basic subject matter* of all the disciplines— the reader searches in vain for a coherent statement of its nature and purpose. Though Dobbs declares, early on, that DBAE engages students "in the *rigorous study of art*" (5, emphasis in original), nowhere does he define the key term, *art*. And there is surely no rigor in his claim that DBAE "is not a monolithic system with a single conception of art," but an "evolving approach" that is "flexibly configured" to meet the needs "of young persons and others for a general understanding of art as a basic form of human culture and as a basic means of human communication" (6–7).

Dobbs further obfuscates the central question of what art is when he notes that DBAE is "arts-pluralistic" (63), making "no distinction between 'fine arts' and 'popular' or 'applied arts'" (66), and "drawing upon imagery and ideas from a variety of art sources, including folk arts, ceramics, jewelry, crafts, industrial and applied arts, fashion design, and photography and electronic media, in addition to painting, sculpture, printmaking, and architecture" (63). To make matters worse, "[s]uitable content for study" may also include video, earthworks and installations, and "contemporary experimental forms such as performance art" (66). Indeed, purported examples of art can be found even in the "students' own homes"—"a quilt in the bedroom," for instance, or "a teapot on the stove"[93] (57), presumably even the proverbial kitchen sink. How students are to make any sense of this conceptual flea-market Dobbs does not say. Nonetheless, he does not hesitate to assert that DBAE meets children's "need for higher-order thinking skills " (93–94).

Equally ill-considered is the Getty's notion of "learning *in* and *through* art," which implies that art is to serve as a tool for learning. According to Dobbs, "works of art educate children about the world," helping them to understand "how the many different communities of this increasingly interdependent world, both past and present, live and think and feel about their lives, their cultures, and their place in the world" (4). Such educational goals pertain mainly to disciplines such as history, sociology, and anthropology, not to art. Nor does one study art history in order to "better understand the human condition," as Dobbs suggests (4). Despite a nod to the "essentialist argument" that "art should exist in the curriculum for what it provides, not for its subordinate or contributory purpose in advancing nonart kinds of knowledge" (9), he clearly favors the "instrumentalist (or utilitarian)" view that art be studied to foster such general skills as "communication, critical thinking, and problem-solving," while also allowing opportunities for instilling "awareness of a multicultural society"[94] (9–10). In fact, a politically correct,[95] multiculturalist agenda lies at the very core of DBAE. As Dobbs explains:

> DBAE supports the larger goal of creating a society in which there is opportunity and fulfillment for all its citizens . . . by providing a receptive . . . place for cultural diversity in the school program. . . .
>   [This] diversity has helped to expand the range of curricular opportunities in art. The previous focus in the art disciplines on a primarily Western or Eurocentric tradition has shifted to global possibilities. . . . This, in turn, sup-

ports the societal goal of building understanding and appreciation for the diverse communities that make up the United States.[96] [10–11]

In sum, discipline-based art education offers "an emancipation . . . from the old boundaries of cultural thinking." (11)

Dobbs's claims regarding the four key disciplines are also dubious. Art criticism, for example, purportedly helps "the general public know something about and better understand contemporary art, . . . whose meanings and significance [are] difficult to access." (34) In their study of this discipline, students will not only identify the subjects and themes of art works, and consider what these say about the "intentions, interests or social or political concerns of the artist," and will also also ponder the "meaning of the objects, nonobjects, or visual effects" in the work. Surely students will fail to meet these goals with regard to abstract art and the other forms of nonart we have criticized in preceding chapters. Thus they will have to fall back upon "what . . . critics [or their teachers] say the work means" (38)—surely not a promising prospect in today's climate.

Dobbs's account of how art criticism has evolved as a field offers further evidence that DBAE proponents embrace a politically correct view of art and culture. He uncritically accepts the influence of so-called critical studies—such as deconstructionist theory and feminist, Marxist, and other postmodernist approaches. "The net impact of these perspectives has been to challenge some basic assumptions about the roles, functions, and sources of criticism, history, and philosophy," he declares. "For example, . . . deconstructionist theory and semiotics have exposed the limitations to which language is subject." (37) "Nontraditional approaches" of this kind are "in increasing favor" in art history, "because they allow teachers and students to explore the history of art in many different, flexible ways," with an emphasis "not on *preexisting* knowledge" but on "discovering and *re-creating* knowledge" (42, emphasis ours). In other words, the Western "tradition" (discipline) of art history is being replaced by the "new perspectives" of postmodern theory—not because they yield greater access to objective *truth* (a concept that is itself rejected by postmodernists) but because they are more "flexible." So, too, Dobbs deemphasizes the high achievements of "traditional" Western art, in favor of "nontraditional" (avant-garde) contemporary work; yet he considers the "traditional" art of ethnic minorities and non-Western cultures worthy of study.[97]

The flawed epistemology at the base of such cultural views was identified by Ayn Rand nearly three decades ago. The growing emphasis on "ethnicity" in American culture was simply a form of *cultural racism*, she argued, and racism in all its forms is a manifestation of the "anti-conceptual mentality," since it involves judging individuals according to an unvarying set of concrete assumptions about a group—which precludes testing those assumptions against actual experience.[98] Ethnicity merely stresses "the traditional [cultural], rather than the physiological characteristics of a group."[99] As Rand further noted, the emphasis on ethnic values for their own sake (as in today's "multiculturalism" or "cultural pluralism") is blatantly one-sided. "'Tolerance' and 'understanding'" must flow from the majority[100] to any given minority's values and customs—but not the other way. In short, "we are asked to study, to appreciate and to respect . . . any sort of culture except our own" (143). As Rand emphasized, such cultural balkanization undermines the "community of values," necessary to any successful relationship among diverse human beings (134).[101]

An interview with philosopher Marcia Eaton on the Getty's Arts Ed Net website offers further evidence of the mingling of conceptual obfuscation with a socio-political agenda in contemporary art education. One of the most influential philosophers in this area, Eaton advocates, for example, that "art education should . . . deal with not just works of art but with the environment as well" and should ask such questions as: "To what extent does knowing that a landscape is ecologically unhealthy change our aesthetic evaluation of it?" In Eaton's view: "It's very easy to get students to understand the ecological, ethical, economic, and biological implications of the aesthetic choices we make. In this way, aesthetics also connects to character, or values, education."[102]

On the question of what art is, Eaton (whose authoritarian theory of art we examined in Chapter 6) often meets with teachers and engages them in philosophic speculation on such questions as whether a simple object such as a cake pan is art, whether hanging it in a museum and calling it *Women's Destiny* would make it art, and why or why not. Claiming that "people have been struggling with [such questions] for thousands of years," Eaton maintains that it is "liberating for both teachers and students to learn that nobody has the truth sewn up."

Eaton's remarks seem rather disingenuous, however, since she herself emphatically declared in another context that "[something] is a work of art if . . . " and specified the conditions which must be met.[103] Thus Eaton herself seems to have "sewn up" the truth, or at least her version of it. In any case, people have surely not been struggling with these questions for millennia, since the concept of art at issue was not articulated until the eighteenth century; and only in the twentieth century did anyone attempt to extend it to ordinary objects. What is most disturbing about Eaton's approach, however, is her suggestion that it is "liberating" for teachers to learn that "nobody has the truth sewn up" about what art is. At the very least, ought not every teacher understand the basic nature of the subject he teaches? Can one imagine a science teacher not knowing the difference between science and magic, for example? Or a math teacher not knowing what mathematics is?

The lamentable (if sometimes amusing) character of what actually transpires in American classrooms in the name of arts education may be further gleaned from Internet "shop talk" among elementary school teachers nationwide, on the Getty's ArtsEdNet website.[104] A teacher in rural Pennsylvania, for example, relates that she devotes two 45-minute classes to a "Jackson Pollock lesson" with her seventh-graders, in which "they gain an understanding of the man and his way of creating art." "Most kids in this age group don't like his work and think they could do it with no problem," notes the teacher. "But after the lesson, I usually hear when can we do it again! . . . It is a cooperative project in which the kids work in groups of four. They choose an emotion to depict . . . , [then] decide what 'tools' to use . . . , then what colors to paint with (one color per person). Their marks from the tools and paint must reflect the emotion." Another earnest instructor begins: "Hi, fellow art educators! I am thinking about inspiring my 5th graders to create a George Segel-style lifesize figure in plastercraft (the plaster impregnated gauze that you wet, mold and that hardens as it dries). Once my 6th graders created an Egyptian Sarcofficus by covering a volunteer in the class with plastercraft. The model was lying on his back, so the form was only the front half of the model. I'm thinking about 2x4s and chicken wire for this full-figure armature. Does anyone have any other ideas?"[105] A third teacher reports: "We just began discussing Marcel Duchamp and Andy Warhol in my eighth grade classes. My students decided anything is art if . . . you will it to be so." Her post elicits the comment—from an art teacher in upstate New York—that "the whole philosophy surrounding Duchamp and his 'Fountain' is a fun and open-ended discussion with any age group" ("fun" crops up frequently in these communiqués).[106]

As if such pointless activities were not cause enough for concern, professors of philosophy (or of art education) are sometimes invited to teach—indoctrinate would be the more accurate term—the children. The participation of one "philosopher of art," Robert Sitton, was reported in the Getty Center's newsletter as one of DBAE's early successes. Through a program called Artists in the Schools, partly sponsored by the National Endowment for the Arts, Sitton (though not an artist) regularly visited public elementary school classes in Portland, Oregon, and engaged his young charges in esoteric discussions about the meaning and value of art. At the end of the school year, one fifth-grader wrote this note of appreciation to her philosopher-mentor:

Art can be good in any way. . . . Art can be anything with line, shape and color. Art doesn't have to be a picture. Art can be anything in the world. Anything is art. Thanks for coming to teach us about art.[107]

Such testimony encouraged Sitton to boast: "'[We] are on the right track. We have a long way to go, but it's the right way, because we are going to produce generations of people who think totally differently about art. . . . These kids . . . are more tolerant of . . . cultural points of view and of opinion. We are moving toward a more enlightened society.'" Sitton's fatuous presumption that teaching children "art can be anything" is a step toward a more enlightened society reveals an appalling ignorance of what such a society most requires—that is, the cultivation of reason (and all that entails), which his approach to art education directly undermines. Astonishingly, although the sexual abuse of children by a teacher would arouse universal public outrage, such cognitive abuse of the young is, instead, institutionalized.

Like the seventeenth-century children disfigured by the comprachicos, the fifth-grader seems blissfully unaware of what has happened to her. As Rand wrote:

The ancient comprachicos hid the operation, but displayed its results; their heirs have reversed the process: the operation is open, the results are invisible. In the past, this horrible surgery left traces on a child's face, not in his mind. Today, it leaves traces in his mind, not on his face. In both cases, the child is not aware of the mutilation he has suffered. But today's comprachicos do not use narcotic powders: they take a child before he is fully aware of reality and never let him develop that awareness. . . . To make you unconscious for life by means of your own brain, nothing can be more ingenious.[108]

Nineteen Eighty-Four: *A Cautionary Tale*

There is an eerie, Orwellian[109] quality to the little girl's note, with its robotic cadence and its repetition of the word "art"—a quality reflecting the regurgitation of undigested ideas. Indeed, Orwell's *Nineteen Eighty-Four*, though written half a century ago with a specifically political focus, is a cautionary tale relevant to our critique of contemporary arts education. The child's words, echoing the meaninglessness of artworld discourse (aptly termed "Artspeak" by many), is disturbingly reminiscent of *Newspeak*—the official language of the dystopian society Orwell envisioned in the novel. The purpose of Newspeak was to express the accepted orthodoxy of thought, and to eliminate the possibility of competing systems.[110] In some instances its function was not to express meaning at all, but to eliminate it; in others, it was to render speech on any controversial topic "as nearly as possible independent of consciousness." (253) In time, it was hoped, articulate speech might be made to issue directly "from the larynx without involving the higher brain centers at all" (253–54).[111]

In the novel, Orwell's protagonist, Winston Smith, struggles to understand, and to resist, the manipulation of his mind (something young children are ill-equipped to do): "It was as though some huge force were . . . battering against your brain, frightening you out of your beliefs, persuading you, almost, to deny the evidence of your senses. In the end [they] would announce that two and two made five, and you would have to believe it. . . . The heresy of heresies was common sense." (68–69) Later, a still-defiant Winston, clinging to his diminishing capacity for independent, rational thought, reflects:

> [They] told you to reject the evidence of your eyes and ears. It was their final, most essential command. . . . And yet he was in the right! They were wrong and he was right. The obvious, the silly, and the true had got to be defended. Truisms are true, hold on to that! The solid world exists, its laws do not change. Stones are hard, water is wet, objects unsupported fall toward the earth's center. . . . With the feeling . . . that he was setting forth an important axiom, he wrote [in his secret diary]: *Freedom is the freedom to say that two plus two make four. If that is granted, all else follows.* [69]

As an adult who had grown up in the pre-Newspeak era, Orwell's protagonist could still hold heretical thoughts such as these. In contrast, the fifth-grader who unthinkingly uttered that "art can be anything in the world" had been made to believe, in effect, that two and two can add up to five.

The "Core Knowledge" Program

Anti-conceptualism is not limited to arts education efforts pursuing a politically correct agenda. It also mars more tradition-bound approaches such as the "Core Knowledge" initiative, promulgated by the philosopher E. D. Hirsch, Jr.[112] One could scarcely argue with Hirsch's aim—"to define, in a coherent and sequential way, a body of widely used knowledge [which] forms a necessary foundation for the higher-order reading, writing, and thinking skills that children need for academic and vocational success." However, the proposed methods and materials of the program's arts education component fall far short of these goals. Not only is the information presented often shockingly inaccurate; little or no attempt is made to show the conceptual relationships between facts, which are instead presented as isolated concretes—in much the same manner Rand and Peikoff had criticized in their analyses of American education. As in the DBAE materials we have examined, conceptual confusion is rife in the Core Knowledge program—most fundamentally, with the concept of art itself. In the "Introduction to the Fine Arts" (for parents and teachers) in each volume, for example, the term "fine arts" is used interchangeably with "the arts" and "art," but no definition is offered. Further, many of the illustrations used in the lessons do not qualify as art at all. Naming the section for children "Fine Arts," rather than simply "The Arts," seems especially pointless. Even more important, in our view, the program's emphasis on objective "knowledge" about (rather than on personal experience of) the arts is fundamentally misguided.

The chapters on the "fine arts" in the series (and the literature sections of the "language arts" chapters) are riddled with errors of logic and common sense, artworld rhetoric, and outright misinformation. A brief introduction to a chapter on the "visual arts" for *kindergarteners* wisely counsels parents that, at this level, the emphasis should be on "*doing*," while looking at art, and thinking and talking about it, are also important. Yet they are urged to think of their child as a practicing artist—a pretension which is encouraged in the child as well, in a section entitled "What Do Artists Do?" and throughout the series.[113] An age-appropriate goal of this chapter is learning about color. And the suggested activity demonstrating the effects of combining colors[114] would be justified—as a science lesson. Telling the child that the result is a "color painting," however, and asking him to give it a title, blurs the essential distinction between science and art and introduces him to the notion of abstract art (though that term is not used). (158) The child is subsequently told:

> Some artists use color in their paintings, but they don't include people or things. Helen Frankenthaler's *Blue Atmosphere* [illustrated in color] is a painting made up of colors. The colors seem to float in the air because of the special way the artist put the paint on the canvas. Though the artist called this painting *Blue Atmosphere,* there's a lot of red in it. The fiery red seems to be pushing back the cool, deep blue. What name would *you* give this painting?[115]
> [160]

Inescapable similarities between the Frankenthaler work and the child's "painting" further encourage him to consider himself an artist. The passage quoted serves as an early indoctrination not only in the idea that such work is a legitimate form of art, but also in the meaningless formalist discourse it so often engenders.[116] Finally, the mistake is made of interpreting the painting for the child, rather than allowing him to respond to it on his own terms, and then eliciting his reactions to it.

While *first-graders* learn that "art is another word for painting, drawing, and sculpture" (a statement which reflects conventional usage regarding the visual arts), other forms of "art" are introduced with no further explanation. A lesson on "symmetry and pattern in arts and crafts," for example, sounds promising enough, until one discovers that the term *craft* does not appear again, and that both an Egyptian headrest ("a small sculpture—actually used for a headrest!") and American Indian pottery, rugs, and blankets are discussed as if they were art.[117] (153) Architecture, too, is called "art":

> It can mean the art of design of buildings—buildings like your school, your church or temple, your library, even your house or apartment building. Tall buildings like the Empire State Building . . . are [also] architecture. The igloos that Eskimos build out of ice and the tepees of American Indians, as well as grass huts and log cabins, are all kinds of architecture. [155]

In addition to the fact that architecture is not art, because it is primarily utilitarian (as we argued in Chapter 10), these remarks are fraught with conceptual confusion. The child is told that the term architecture "can mean" (which implies that it need not mean) "the art of design of buildings" (an awkward phrase that muddles the concepts of art and design). Are some buildings, then, not architecture? How can one tell? A clear definition differentiating *architecture* from *building* would help, we think, as would the omission of such simple, strictly utilitarian dwellings as igloos, tepees, grass huts and log cabins.

In *second grade* the conceptual confusion regarding architecture increases. While the "visual arts" are defined as "art that we look at" (169), correctly implying that they have no utilitarian function, the child is informed that "A building can be a work of art too" and that "The art of planning buildings is named architecture." When is a building not art? Since all buildings are to some degree planned, and "creating buildings is [said to be] an important art," it is impossible to tell. Not to mention that the function of architecture is not primarily to be "looked at," as even proponents of architecture-as-art agree. Thus how can the child reconcile his concept of architecture with the definition he was given for "visual art"? Finally, to add to his confusion, he is told that "some people think that architecture is like a sculpture, but a sculpture that has space inside it and is so big you can walk around in it."[118] (174)

The *third-grade* lessons on art further blur the distinction between art and utilitarian objects—as well as between more basic perceptual categories. In a comparison of an American Indian cornhusk mask with a Byzantine mosaic, for example, children are told:

> This is a work of art that is meant to be worn! It is a mask made by an Iroquois artist. . . . Can you almost imagine how the squares of glass [in the

mosaic] and the corn braids [of the mask] would feel if you ran your hands over them? Do you think one would feel colder than the other? When you answer these questions, you are describing the *texture* of the artworks. Artists use the word texture to describe how the surface of an artwork feels, or how we imagine it feels when we look at it. [190–91, emphasis ours]

No other examples are given, but some bright children might remember that they were previously told that art is meant to be *looked at*—not worn. They might also wonder about Halloween masks and costumes, or about their own clothing—familiar things in their universe that are "worn." And what is the third grader to make of the claim that *cold* is an instance of *texture*?

Regarding the teaching of poetry, the *fourth-grade* guide begins with sound advice, which ought to be extended to the other arts as well: "Until children take pleasure in the sound and sentiment of poetry, there is little reason to study it technically. . . . A child's knowledge of poetry . . . should come first from pleasure and only later from analysis"—though simple terms such as "line" and "stanza" should be introduced to facilitate discussion. (42)

Far less felicitous is the note recommending Kenneth Koch's "two fine books on helping children write poetry and teaching poetry to children." (42) In our view, Koch— like John Ashbery, an avant-garde poet of the "New York school"[119]—has wrought more havoc in the teaching of poetry to children over recent decades than any other figure we know of. In *Wishes, Lies, and Dreams: Teaching Children to Write Poetry* (one of the two books cited in the Core Knowledge volume), Koch outlined his method, and reprinted many of the "poems" produced by elementary school children under his tutelage. The book's title refers to devices he used to inspire students to write—such as suggesting that they begin every line with "I wish." The products are, on the whole, fragmented and incoherent. Most are simply lists of one-line ideas or images, unified only by the repetition of (or variations on) Koch's formula phrases: "I wish . . ." or "I dreamed. . ." or "If I was. . . ." Some of the samples are undisguised prose, not even arranged to resemble poetry. One of Koch's favorite techniques was to have children collaborate on their writing in pairs or groups, often with each child contributing lines without knowing what the other lines were. In Koch's view, the finished product was "one poem—interesting, beautiful, funny, and sometimes even making sense."[120]

Music is perhaps the most difficult art to teach because it presents no discernible subject matter or theme, and is so difficult to talk about. Because each listener creates his own context, largely subconsciously, it is also the most purely personal of art forms. Any pedagogical practice that ignores this principle ill serves the child. The Core Knowledge approach makes the all-too-common mistake of suggesting the "appropriate" response before students have listened to the music. A *fourth-grade* lesson on the baroque composer Antonio Vivaldi, for example, introduces *The Four Seasons* (in itself an apt choice) by telling them that "much of his music has a bouncy feel in the bright parts, and a sad, haunting sound in the slow parts," and that

> *The Four Seasons* . . . captures in music the feeling of the seasons: spring, summer, autumn, and winter. When you listen to it, try to feel each of the times of the year. Does the *Winter* concerto remind you of winter? Why? In the great *Spring* concerto, Vivaldi gave the violas the sounds of "a barking dog," and the violins the sound of spring's "sweet rustling of leaves." Can you hear them? [223]

Although *The Four Seasons* was an early example of programmatic music, composed by Vivaldi to "illustrate" four sonnets about the seasons, it is virtually impossible for instrumental music to achieve such specificity. To discuss one of the first pieces of classical music children are introduced to in so literal terms sets up largely inappropriate expectations. Such detailed characterization in terms of specific concretes robs the child of the chance to respond to the piece on his own terms and belies the essential nature of music. Moreover, for students who would answer No to the question of whether the *Winter* concerto reminds them of the season, the follow-up question, *Why?* can only confuse them or undermine their confidence in their natural responses.

The *fifth-grade* component of music education pursues the same misguided approach. Students are told that Beethoven's Third Symphony, the *Eroica*, "makes you feel heroic and grand" (234); that his Fifth Symphony "begins with a melody like a knock on the door that promises to bring something either very wonderful or terrible into your life" (234); and that his Sixth Symphony (the *Pastoral*) is "like a long walk through woods and fields in the country. If you listen closely, you can hear birds calling, a storm coming up, and many other things" (234–35).

Another lamentable aspect of the Core Knowledge series is its treatment of *abstract art*, an example of which was first introduced in kindergarten—albeit without mention of the term—as we have noted. In the *sixth-grade* curriculum, the concept is dealt with explicitly for the first time. But both the terminology and the discussion are hopelessly muddled. In the "Introduction to the Fine Arts" for parents and teachers, for example, the authors explain that they will "discuss art traditions that led into the modern period, focusing on realism in particular," and will then "show how artists began breaking away from realism with abstract styles, including those that came to be known as impressionism, expressionism, and cubism." (228) Students are subsequently informed: "When an artist represents objects by simplifying and exaggerating shapes or colors, we say that he or she is working in an abstract style." (245) They are also told that Picasso's *Ladies of Avignon* (*Les Demoiselles d'Avignon*) was "in an abstract style," and that the African masks that inspired him were "abstract images of the human face." (249) An African headpiece with a stylized representation of a human face is similarly characterized as an "abstract sculpture." (247) The student is here faced with a conceptual meltdown. "Realism," in fact, commonly refers to all *representational* art, and therefore includes *impressionism* and *expressionism* (unless one specifies "abstract expressionism"). *Cubist* works such as the Picasso painting cited, while highly stylized, are not "abstract" in the usual sense, which means *nonrepresentational*.[121] To speak of an "abstract image" of anything, therefore, is a contradiction in terms, since images are, by definition, representations.

Not until the section entitled (misleadingly) "Back to Basics" is abstract art at last discussed under the accurate, if less common, designation "nonrepresentational art." But the content of the lesson is far from satisfactory. Presented with an illustration of Mondrian's *Broadway Boogie-Woogie*,[122] students are told that it

> was not painted in order to express Mondrian's reactions to the world around him. Instead, Mondrian is known for a style that we call nonrepresentational: that is, not representing objects at all. (Some people don't agree. They point out that even nonrepresentational art does represent such things as motion and vibration.)
>
> Mondrian wanted mainly to show the visual effects that are made by putting lines and colors together. He said that what was important to him was to show the *relationships* between the most basic elements of art. Some of the paintings that Mondrian is best known for use only horizontal and vertical lines and the colors red, yellow, blue, black, and white. [251–52]

Since we discussed Mondrian's work at length in our chapter on abstract art, we will not comment further here, except to insist that nonrepresentational painting is not a "style" of art, since it is not art at all. Nor are motion and vibration "things," in the sense of *objects*; they are *attributes* of objects. Detached from a human context, they are abstractions of interest mainly to physicists—of little relevance to the sphere of art, since they gain human value and significance only in a specific context.

"The Educated Child"

The flaws of the Core Knowledge approach to arts education are largely perpetuated in *The Educated Child*, written by William J. Bennett, Chester E. Finn, Jr., and John T. E. Cribb, Jr., as a guide for parents. Though the book offers much sound general advice on what a good elementary school program should include, on basic pedagogical principles, and on contentious educational issues such as multiculturalism, its recommendations on arts education (which the authors regard as an important part of the curriculum) leave much to be desired.[123] While they emphasize that children should be taught "to think logically and clearly" (11) and "to think for themselves" (93), their own treatment of the arts often belies these precepts.

Many of the specific suggestions in *The Educated Child* are based directly on the Core Knowledge program, which the authors deem "the best content guide for the elementary grades" that they have seen. They further note that this "well-tested" curriculum is being used successfully in several hundred U.S. schools, and that it "engages and stimulates . . . children while supplying them with important knowledge and valuable skills." (100)

Although Bennett, Finn, and Cribb maintain that a "fully educated person knows something about the arts"[124] (262), they themselves, though highly educated, appear to know very little about the subject. For example, they accept without question the many non-art forms included in the Core Knowledge program—from mobiles, mummy cases, and architecture, to Navajo blankets, ceremonial masks, photography, and the abstract paintings of Jackson Pollock. They also perpetuate spurious claims such as the notion that musical compositions (namely, Tchaikovsky's *1812 Overture* and Copland's *Appalachian Spring*) "can depict a nation's identity." (272–73)

As to *why* children should learn about the arts, *The Educated Child* offers a cornucopia of reasons—among others, that they

> reveal the esthetic dimension of the human mind . . . train young eyes and ears to appreciate the world around us . . . help children express themselves . . . [give them] practice imagining, experimenting, solving problems, thinking independently, and making their own decisions . . . [instill] pride in accomplishment . . . boost overall academic achievement . . . [link] students with the past . . . [aquaint them with] the traditions and cultures that have shaped our society . . . teach them to discriminate between what is fine and what is mediocre, between the sublime and the mundane . . . [and] cultivate in their hearts a love for beauty. [263]

Once again, we are reminded of Jacques Barzun's sage advice—in this case: "There do not have to be eighteen reasons to justify art in the school. One is enough."[125]

A Radical Alternative

The approaches to teaching the arts to children that we have examined are all attempts to fill a lamentable gap in American schooling. In most schools, from kindergarten through college, music and the visual arts are sorely neglected, often relegated to elective studio courses or mere extracurricular activities. Of the major arts, only literature has been a regular component of the curriculum, primarily because of its integral relation to the study of English. For the reasons we have outlined above, however, to follow the DBAE and Core Knowledge programs are worse than not teaching art at all, since they undermine the very concept of art and do not afford students the kinds of cognitive and emotional benefits that the arts uniquely provide.

In the light of Ayn Rand's theory of art, we propose a radically different approach to "arts education" or, more accurately, to teaching the arts—an approach that has been successfully applied in the classroom, albeit on a small scale.[126] To begin, we suggest as far as possible dispensing with the much-abused terms "education" and "educator." As Barzun argued more than two decades ago, *teaching* refers to the process of "leading a child to knowledge, whereas *education* properly refers to a completed development, or the whole tendency of the mind toward it. A person is taught by a teacher but educates him- or herself, partly by will, partly by assimilating experience."[127] Surely this distinction is particularly relevant with respect to the arts.

The design of a detailed curriculum is of course far beyond our scope here. What we present are a few basic principles and a simple methodology which may be adapted for use in a single classroom, or as part of a comprehensive, sequential program. Though we are mainly concerned with the teaching of visual art and music in the elementary schools, the approach we propose can be equally adapted to the teaching of literature, and to any age group or instructional setting.

First, we insist that the teaching of all the arts, including literature, must be based on an objective understanding of *what art is*: the works studied as art in the early years must clearly *be* art. Examples of non-art should be introduced in later grades only after students have formed a clear concept of genuine art. The primary goal should be to offer students an enriched awareness and understanding of the kinds of experience the arts uniquely provide. To quote Barzun again: "The benefits of teaching art to the young will consist mainly in the pleasure that comes of being able to see and hear [and read] works of art more sharply and subtly, more consciously, to register that pleasure in words, and compare notes with other people similarly inclined." (113)

As we have emphasized throughout this book, the experience of art draws upon the deepest cognitive and emotional levels of the *individual* psyche. It therefore involves each student's unique constellation of values and associations. Consequently, the arts ought not—cannot—be taught according to the same principles as, say, history or math, where the goal is the acquisition of objective knowledge, detached as far as possible from emotional predispositions. The arts, by their very nature, involve the emotions, which are a mainly private affair. The *initial* experience(s) of any work of art should be with the work on its own terms. Difficult though it may be to refrain from *teaching* on such occasions, the teacher should allow the work to speak for itself. Tangential issues, whether historic, biographical, technical, or esthetic, should be deferred until a later time. During the early stages of viewing or hearing a work, students should reflect upon three core questions: *Do I like it? How much?* And *Why or why not?* The learning process thus begins with *focused attention*—on the art work itself and, simultaneously, one one's response to it.

For works of visual art, the teacher instructs students to jot down in their notebooks their *immediate* response, in the form of answers to these core questions. Students should be told, for example, that there are no "right" or "wrong" answers, and that they may express mixed feelings, such as "not sure," or "yes" to some parts or aspects of a work and "no" to others. The teacher also instructs students that their answers should be in the form of brief sentences, phrases, or even single words. They may change their minds at any time while viewing the work, during class discussion, or after learning more about the work from the teacher. No cross-outs are allowed, however, and all notes must be saved, so that students will become aware of their own patterns of response and their reasons for them, and will be able to draw upon their notes for subsequent writing assignments.

After these basic instructions are given, a slide of a work of painting or sculpture is projected in a semi-darkened room. The private process of *contemplation*—and of *introspection*, a crucial element, and something which can be taught—then begins. (The selection of slides shown may be chronological or thematic, but should comprise high-quality, age-appropriate works from a variety of cultural traditions and periods.) While students' reactions to a given work will inevitably vary, all will necessarily relate to one or more of the fundamental attributes of visual art: *subject, style, theme* (meaning), *form,* or *composition* (arrangement of parts). These technical terms, and any others relevant to the discussion, should be introduced by the teacher only after students have begun to articulate their responses to the work. Many such terms will be implied by the students, as will basic concepts relevant to the definition of art such as "reality," "selection," and "re-creation."

The stage is then set for further questioning by the teacher and guided discussion (using the Socratic method) to help students sharpen their observations, articulate their responses more clearly, identify the underlying emotions and value-judgments, and relate them to features of the work. The teacher points out additional details that the students may not have yet noted, and introduces relevant background information. In time, students will grasp that one's reaction to any work of art is based on one's personal context: that is, on what one values, on what one thinks is important—which may or may not coincide with what others think and feel.

In teaching music, the basic principles are the same. Age-appropriate recordings—of classical music—are played in a semi-darkened room, to minimize visual distractions. (Students may even be asked to close their eyes on occasion.) Since music is a dynamic and temporal form, and is often difficult to verbalize, students are instructed to record as best they can two aspects of their experience, in any order or combination: their response to the music at any given moment, and a brief characterization of the musical passage producing that response. In addition to the do-I-like-it-or-not-how-much-and-why considerations involved in responding to visual art, students record *whatever they are aware of, experience, feel, think, or imagine while the music is playing.* Inevitably, they will cite ideas, thoughts, emotions, moods, imagined scenes or events, physical responses (such as swaying, tension, foot- or finger-tapping, and so on)—though none of these should be suggested to them in advance.[128] If the piece is long, the teacher should indicate how many movements it consists of, so that students can more readily identify the passages their responses refer to. Notes should be taken in especially abbreviated form, since the music is constantly evolving. Needless to say, short works (or single movements from longer compositions) are most practicable, particularly for young students with a limited attention span. In addition, short pieces can more easily be repeated, in a single class session or over a period of several days or weeks. For upper grades (junior and senior high school), longer works such as a complete concerto or symphony should be included as well. As in the case of the visual arts, the teacher introduces relevant terms (the names of instruments and parts of the orchestra, tempo designations, and so on), as well as relevant biographical and historical information, only after students have begun to articulate their personal responses.

The primary "academic" component in this approach to teaching the arts consists of expository writing assignments (for students at all levels from first grade on), ranging from single paragraphs to longer essays, in which students articulate their experience with a particular work (or works), in the context of what they have learned about it. Since all the communication skills—speaking and listening as well as writing—are essential to this approach, teachers should be experienced in all these areas. They should also be knowledgeable about the basic nature and function of art, and be familiar with a variety of works of visual art and music (primarily, though not exclusively, of Western origin), as well as with the main elements of each art form. Ideally, the same teacher should be involved during the entire process. At the junior-high and high school levels, English teachers with broad knowledge about the arts would be the best qualified, since they are trained to teach the skills enumerated above. In any case, the instructors in this new specialty should be referred to as "arts teachers," not "arts educators."

The approach we have outlined is designed to impart to students what is uniquely valuable about the arts. By introducing them to exemplary works, and by helping them to sharpen their perceptions and articulate their responses, it will, we trust, help prepare them for a lifetime of meaningful personal engagement with all the arts.

Appendix A

New Forms of Art

Following are some of the alleged art forms invented since the beginning of the twentieth century. As a rule, if the term art is preceded by qualifiers such as conceptual, incendiary, *or* Pop, *one can be reasonably certain that the work in question is not art by the standards outlined in this book.*

Abstract art
Anti-art
Appropriation art
Artists' book
Assemblage art
 (Assemblage)
Billboard art
Body art (Tatooing,
 Piercing, Body
 Modification, etc.)
Book art (also Offset-book
 art)
Byte art (see Computer art,
 Web art)
Cartography (see Map art)
Ceiling piece (see Floor
 piece, Wall piece)
Ceramic art
Circus art
Collage
Combines
Computer Art (also Byte
 Art, Web art)
Conceptual art
Construction
Crop Art (wheat field, for
 example, seen from the
 air)
Cyber-art(also Net art,
 Web art)
Dance piece
Designated art
Digital art
Diorama
Documentary film
Earth art (also Land art)
Electronic art
Environmental art
Environmental theater
Environment(s)

Experimental art (dance,
 fiction, poetry, theater,
 etc.)
Fashion
Floor piece (also Ceiling
 piece,Wall piece)
Found object
Fountains (also Hydraulic
 art, Water sculpture)
Fractal art
Furniture art
Glass art
Goth art
Graffiti (also Tag art)
Happenings
Hydraulic art (also
 Fountains, Water
 sculpture)
Incendiary art (Fireworks)
Installation art
Interactive art
Interface art
Internet art
Junk art
Kinetic sculpture
Land art (also Earth art,
 Environmental art)
Light sculpture
Lighting design
Literary translation
Magic
Mail art (also Postal art)
Map art (also Cartography)
Media art
Memoir
Minimal art (Minimalist
 painting and sculpture)
Mixed media
Mobiles
Monologue
Net art (also Cyber
 art,Web art)

Op art
Organic sculpture
Participatory art
Participatory installation
 (also Installation).
Performance art
Photography
Pop art
Postal art (also Mail art)
Procedural art
Process art
Puppetry (Puppet art)
Quilt art
Radio art
Robotic art (Robot art)
Scanned art
Sculpture installation
Sculptural simulacra art
Site-specific art
Sonic art
Stage lighting
Street art
Tag art (also Graffiti art)
Telecommunications art
Telematic art
Telepresence art
Television
Text intensive painting
Theater piece
Verbatim art
Video art
Virtual art
Wall piece (also Ceiling
 piece, Floor piece)
Water sculpture (also
 Fountains, Hydraulic
 art)
Weather art
Web art (also Cyber art,
 Net art)

Appendix B
Artworld Buzz Words

What follows are examples of some of the more common buzz words and critical cliches of the artworld. One can safely infer that whenever these buzz words are used in arts criticism, the work in question is not art by any objective standard. Unless otherwise indicated, the emphasis in all cases is ours. For additional examples, see Louis Torres, "Blurring the Boundaries at the NEA" in the Selected Bibliography.

Blur the Boundaries

"While a child disregards the reality of the broom when turning it into a fantasy horse, the Cubist collage deliberately retains the reality of the object in a continuum that *breaks down the boundary between what is real and what is 'art.*'" Jonathan Feinberg, "Modernism and the Art of Children," *Chronicles of Higher Education*, 27 March 1998.

"When Dario Fo was awarded the Nobel Prize in Literature last week, it was the first time the honor had been given to an actor and clown. . . . His primary distinction is in combining all his diverse theatrical roles—[performer] . . . director . . . designer—into a single act of comic self-creation. . . . By recognizing Mr. Fo, the Swedish Academy *expands the boundaries of literature.*" Mel Gussow, Critic's Notebook, "The Not-So-Accidental Recognition of an Anarchist," *New York Times*, 15 October 1997.

"The New York City Opera . . . strive[s] to present opera 'as exciting theater,' and [Paul Kellogg, its general director] remains unapologetic about *pushing boundaries*. 'If we are going to reach contemporary audiences with contemporary reactions and contemporary feelings,' he said, 'then we have to do things in a contemporary way. This will require education. Innovation always does.'" Anthony Tommasini, "Realism Unvarnished For Gluck's Bonded Males," *New York Times*, 3 October 1997.

"The great paintings of Piet Mondrian . . . *tease all customary judgments of what constitutes pictorial form.*" Julian Bell, "Nature's Leading Edge." Review of "Mondrian: Nature to Abstraction" (Exhibition at the Tate Gallery), *Times Literary Supplement*, 8 August 1997.

"Even the center's more conventionally art-focused show . . . includes several pieces that *straddle the boundary between art making and mass production, between art and junk.*" Tessa DeCarlo, "Putting a Mixer in a Museum and asking, What Is Art?," *New York Times*, 22 June 1997.

"'What is so great about all these artists is that they are really *pushing the limits not only of perception but of the existential question: "What am I doing here?*'" Louise Neri, (co-curator, 1997 Whitney Museum of American Art Biennial), quoted by Michael Kimmelman, "Narratives Snagged On the Cutting Edge," *New York Times*, 21 March 1997.

"*The elasticity of drawing* is always a central issue at the Drawing Center in SoHo. . . . This impressive show introduces three talented young artists, each of whom *stretches drawing* to create different kinds of hybrids, whether physical, intellectual or cultural. . . . The inaugural show . . . introduces the work of . . . a young English artist who *pushes drawing toward film.* . . . One is . . . made aware . . . of *drawing's uncanny resiliency. Pushed in new directions,* it still retains its inherent immediacy and magic." Roberta Smith, "Drawing That Pushes Beyond the Boundaries," *New York Times,* 21 March 1997.

"*Fudging the boundaries between the arts* is not a bad idea, though you can wonder what motivated the curators in . . . Forsythe's case, since his work refers to the formal possibilities of dance, not [visual] art." Michael Kimmelman, "Narratives Snagged On the Cutting Edge," *New York Times,* 21 March 1997.

"Alvaro Siza [in Portugal] is not alone in *pushing the boundaries of conventional practice [in architecture] . . .* the *exploration of new directions.* . . . the *expansion of the art of architecture* itself . . . *reinventing architecture . . . stretching the limits of the art.* . . . Gehry is *pushing the very idea and definition of architecture to its limits* in a very dangerous but exhilarating game. . . . There are always architects who seek ways to achieve revelations that will *break through custom to new kinds of vision and design, to new definitions of art and use.*" Ada Louise Huxtable, "The New Architecture," *New York Review of Books,* 6 April 1995.

"After the innovative astonishments of fiction writers like . . . Jorge Luis Borges and Donald Barthelme (and Thomas Pynchon and John Barth and Robert Coover)—writers who have *exploded the received boundaries of the form*—the novel would seem to have few large surprises in store. Jonathan Baumbach, review of "You Can Read It Across or Down," review of *Landscape Painted with Tea, New York Times Book Review,* 16 December 1990.

"*Some art seeks the edge, tries to break the boundary.* And other art struggles to refine, integrate, bring the past forward into the present. Who, in the end, can say with assurance which is the more valuable?" Robert Hughes, *Time,* 13 August 1990.

"In previous books such as *Great Expectations* (1984) and *Don Quixote* (1986), Kathy Acker not only set out to work variations on classic literary texts, but also to *subvert all our traditional expectations* concerning causality, narrative form and moral sensibility. Michiko Kakutani, review of *Literal Madness,* by Kathy Acker, *New York Times,* 30 December, 1987.

Break Down

"'A desire to *break down the barrier between art and life* inspired [avant-garde artists around 1960]. So they made art using real objects, real space and time, and live human beings. They brought the audience into their art." Edward M. Gomez, "Modern Art's Missing Link: The Jersey Scene," *New York Times,* 21 February 1999.

"[The goal of Schoenberg's atonality] was to *break down whatever expectations of melody and harmony listeners might have retained* through centuries of evolution of an ever more complex tonal system." James R. Oestreich, "How Does Music Turn the Century?" *New York Times,* 27 December 1997.

Redefine (Reinvent)

"Theory can *redefine architecture* or derail it." Ada Louise Huxtable, "The New Architecture," *New York Review of Books*, 6 April 1995.

Challenge

"Follow the development of American art [from Abstract Expressionism] to the present day and discover *how each new generation challenges the definition of art*." From the description of "Modern Art at the Met," course listed in the 92nd Street Y, of New York City, Winter/Spring 1999 catalog.

"One of the functions of art is to *stir the pot*, to *make us think*, to *challenge complacency and fixed beliefs*. Art *can* [emphasis in original] be a threat." Richard Philp, "Success" (editorial), *Dance Magazine*, August 1995.

"Orlan [the 'multimedia/performance artist' who 'transforms' herself through plastic facial] surgery *challenged both religious traditions and art-world assumptions*, the former through blasphemous imagery, the latter with real time/real place actions identifying art with life." Barbara Rose, *Art in America*, February 1993.

Confront

"[Ann] Hamilton is not a creator of purely visual installations. Rather, she *confronts and overwhelms her viewers*. Rank odors and sweet, the grotesquerie of live vermin and rotting carcasses, the spectacle of 47,000 blue uniforms piled neatly on a platform, the artist hypnotically kneading and chewing dough. . . ." Steven Henry Madoff, "After the Roaring 80's in Art, a Decade of Quiter Voices," *New York Times*, 2 November 1997.

Disturb (see also "Provoke")

"[Barbara] Kruger's art is in essence a quick take that *disturbs and provokes thought*, like a politically conscious advertisement. 'It's about the power and the use and abuse of language,' said . . . Kruger." Carol Vogel, "Three Aphorism Shows Are Better than One," *New York Times*, 30 October 1997.

Cutting Edge

"[Martha] Schwartz's urban gardens—one of which prompted outraged neighbors to call the police—are important for their *cutting-edge design* [but] . . .a predominance of hardware and a shortage of plants make them unsuitable for weekend pottering. "Where the Bagels Blow," *Times Literary Supplement*, 26 September 1997.

Provoke

"Robert Gober [has a] . . . reputation for . . . uncannily *provocative sculptures and installations*, at once witty and disturbing. A leg, replete with hair, trouser, sock and shoe, juts from a wall." Steven Henry Madoff, "After the Roaring 80's in Art, a Decade of Quieter Voices," *New York Times*, 2 November 1997.

Elevate

"Gehry has constructed a furniture museum in which the utilitarian is *elevated to high drama and fine art.*" Ada Louise Huxtable, "The New Architecture," *New York Review of Books*, 6 April 1995.

Experimental

"'The ephemeral work that I do is a form of *experimentation*,' [Andy] Goldsworthy explains. 'Often I go out and don't have an idea what I'm going to do. So I tend not to use tools, because I don't know what I'm going to make, and I do love using my hands.'" Kenneth Baker, "Searching for the Window into Nature's Soul," *Smithsonian*, February 1997.

Explore

"A client's site, his budget and his program—how many bedrooms . . . the need for such things as a home office . . . —obviously play a fole in determining the final form. But these things must be fit into [Charles] Gwathmey and [Robert] Siegel's continuing quest to *explore the nature of architectural space*." Paul Goldberger, "The Masterpieces They Call Home," *New York Times Magazine*, 12 March 1995.

Investigate

"[T]he show ['Wordrobe,' at the Metropolitan Museum of Art's Costume Institute] is *an investigation* of the use of letters, words, numbers, and printed messages in the clothes of the twentieth century. Tobi Tobias, "Read My Clothes," *New York*, 15 September 1997.

"Recent paintings that *investigate spatial ambiguity* through the juxtaposition of patterns. . . ." Art (Gallery Listings), *New York*, 15 September 1997.

Quirky

"The films and videos are more integrated with the rest of the biennial than usual, and *quirkier* than much of it. David Hammons's short video of a man kicking a bucket down a street is a wry dirge." Michael Kimmelman, "Narratives Snagged On the Cutting Edge." *New York Times*, 21 March 1997.

Seductive

Techno-Seduction exhibition co-sponsored by the College Art Association—*CAA News*, Vol. 22, No. 2, March/April 1997. Michael Kimmelman, "Inventing Shapes To *Tease the Mind and Eye*," *New York Times*, 26 September 1997.

Appendix C

The *New York Times*—"The Arts"

Promiscuous use of the term "arts" is nowhere more rampant than in the New York Times *section entitled "The Arts." Following are titles (and brief summaries where the headline is not self-explanatory) of representative articles that have appeared on the front page of this section over the past decade. Readers will note that the editors of the* Times *implicitly consider* television, documentary film, and biography, *among other things, as art forms—on a par with painting, sculpture, dance, music, and theater.*

"An Ugly Legacy Lives On, Its Glare Unsoftened by Age" (by Roberta Smith), 16 January 2000.

> About an exhibition of professionally shot photographic postcards depicting lynchings (mostly of black men and women, and mostly in the South) which took place between 1883 and 1960. Dramatically llustrated by an enlarged sepia-toned photograph, from 1920, of a 16-year-old boy hanging from a tree branch above a crowd of whites, including children, facing the camera.

"Essay Winner from Moscow Gauges Time in Definitions" (by Alan Riding), 13 December 1999.

> About an international essay contest on a millennial theme about the past and future.

"My Dear Sir: Letters by a Reluctant Commander" (by Adam Nagourney), 1 December 1999.

> About an exhibition of letters, documents, maps, and artifacts commemorating the 200th anniversary of George Washington's death.

"Two Cities, Two Leaps of Faith: Columbus [Ohio] Pins Its Dreams on a Jazzy New Science Center" (by Bruce Weber); and "In Kansas City, Few Trains, but New Life in the Station" (by Shirley Christian), 15 November 1999.

> An account of two efforts to revitalize urban areas—in the first, a theme park and interactive laboratory intended to instill a love of science and learning in . . . children of all ages; in the second, a train station transformed as a public space, including restaurants, shops, offices, and a science-recreation facility.

"Game Shows, Greedy and Otherwise,"Caryn James, 18 November 1999.

> Review of two new prime time television shows, "Who Wants to Be a Millionaire" and "Greed."

"Seeing Anew in a World of Light and Darkness," Dinitia Smith, 1 November 1999.

Article about *Twilight: Losing Sight, Gaining Insight,* the autobiography of Henry Grunwald, former editor-in-chief of Time, Inc., and his experience of going blind.

Ralph Blumenthal, "Collecting Facts for Fun and Profit: A Publisher Keeps a Keen Eye on the Antiques World," 14 September 1999.

A profile of a family-run newspaper, *The Maine Antique Digest.*

Anita Gates, "Vying for Guys' Remote-Control Finger," 25 January 1999.

Discussion of some of the most popular television shows among 18-to-34-year-old males.

"Revisiting a Watershed Era: Photo Show Reflects Turmoil of the Civil Rights Battle" (by Felicia R. Lee), 18 January 1999.

About a historical exhibition, "America and the Civil Rights Movement, 1954-1968," at the 92nd Street Y in New York City.

"When He Shot, He Soared: Jordan the Man and Athlete" (by Michiko Kakutani), 19 January 1999.

Review of a book about the former Chicago Bulls basketball star Michael Jordan.

"13 Years and Counting for a Reagan Biography: A High-Profile Project Meets Another Delay" (by Doreen Carvajal), 28 September 1998.

About writing of the biography *Dutch: A Memoir of Ronald Reagan.*

"A Holocaust Memoir in Doubt: Swiss Records Contradict a Book on Childhood Horror" (by Doreen Carvajal), 3 November 1998.

Controversy over a memoir of a Jewish childhood in the concentration camps of Poland.

"Once a Fear Beyond Fear Itself" (by Stephen Holden), 4 March 1998.

A review of the documentary film *A Paralyzing Fear: The Story of Polio in America.*

"He Knows If You've Been Good, for Goodness' Sake" (by Alex Witchel), 11 December 1997.

Interview with a "mentalist" who performs such feats as telling audience members "where they spent their last vacation, and which part they liked best."

"A Survivor's Legacy, to the Highest Bidder: Documenting a Secret Life Amid the Nazis" (by Ralph Blumenthal), 3 December 1997.

About the auction by Sotheby's (London) of "hundreds of pages of German letters, photographs and Nazi records" belonging to a survivor of the holocaust.

"Cursive, Foiled Again: Mourning the Demise of Penmanship" (by Edward Rothstein), 7 April 1997.

Historical account of the Palmer method of teaching penmanship to children.

"In the Trenches: How Civil Rights Were Won" (by Kevin Sack), 26 March 1997.

Review of 26-part, 13-hour oral history of the civil rights movement aired on public radio stations.

"Laughing at Big Government, and Crying, Too" (by Richard Bernstein), 1 August 1991.
About political humorist P. J. O'Rourke and his new book *Parliament of Whores*.

"3 Queens of Talk Who Rule the Day" (by Walter Goodman)," 29 July 1991.

Review of the television talk shows of Oprah Winfrey, Joan Rivers, and Sally Jessy Raphael.

"The Value of Pigs and Other Insights At Mead Film Festival" (by John Noble Wilford), 24 September 1990.

Review of documentaries shown at the 14th annual festival in honor of anthropologist Margaret Mead at the Museum of Natuaral History in New York City.

Notes

Introduction

1. Cubism and abstract painting are the best known of the unprecedented "innovations"of early modernism. For some of the less familiar departures from traditional art, see RoseLee Goldberg, *Performance Art*. Although such developments had precursors in Symbolist poetry, in the second half of the nineteenth century, it was not until the twentieth that they took hold in all the fields of art. On fundamental similarities between modernist art and insanity, see Louis Sass, *Madness and Modernism*, esp. 28–39. For early twentieth-century examples of fraud in art, see Curtis D. Mac-Dougall, *Hoaxes*, 266–275; and Jeffrey Weiss, *Popular Culture of Modern Art*, esp. 109–163. Regarding fraud in the arts in recent decades, see Roger Scruton, "The Philosophical Hedonist: Arthur C. Danto on Art," *New Criterion*, September 1990, 71; and Danto, *Encounters and Reflections*. On the phenomenon of fraud, or charlatanism, in other fields, see James Randi, *The Faith Healers* (Buffalo: Prometheus Books, 1987), and *Flim-Flam!* (New York: Lippincott and Crowell, 1980). Though it is difficult to prove that some self-styled artists are, in fact, charlatans or frauds (as Randi has done for "faith healers"), there is no reason to believe that the arts are any more immune to such deceit than any other sphere of human endeavor.

2. See, for example, Kenyon Cox, *Three Papers on Modernist Art*; F. W. Ruckstull, *Great Works of Art*, Preface; and H. Wayne Morgan, *Keepers of Culture*.

3. Though the trends we note have been most pronounced in the visual arts (see, for example, Torres, "New Dawn of Painting," and Kamhi, "R. H. Ives Gammell"), they have affected the other arts as well.

4. We use the term "artworld" (as a single word) pejoratively, to refer to the arts establishment which rejects "traditional" contemporary art in favor of avant-garde work.

5. A word is merely an arbitrary visual-auditory symbol used to stand for a concept, whereas a concept is a mental abstraction which represents its referents. See Rand, *Introduction to Objectivist Epistemology*, 13 and 40. Rand defines a concept as "a mental integration of two or more units [referents] possessing the same distinguishing characteristic(s), with their particular measurements omitted." (13)

6. The evolution of the concept of (fine) art is traced in detail by Paul Oskar Kristeller, "The Modern System of the Arts," in *Renaissance Thought and the Arts*, 163–227; and by Wladyslaw Tatarkiewicz, in *A History of Six Ideas*—though both accounts contain errors and inconsistencies which we note in subsequent chapters.

7. Regarding our use of the term "avant-garde," see below, Ch. 8, n. 8.

8. On the concept of mimesis, and its fundamentality to the arts, see Chapter 7.

9. Harvey Mudd, letter to the editor, *New York Times*, 23 October 1988. Mudd refers to those who "have slipped by the gatekeepers" as "self-promoters, . . . illusionists, and . . . outright cons."

10. Bill Zopf, letter to the editor, *Smithsonian*, April 1989.

11. Joan Higgins, letter to the editor, *New York Times*, 30 June 1991.

12. Morton I. Teicher, letter to the editor, *New York Times*, 16 May 1993.

13. Si Lewen, letter to the editor, *New York Times*, 1 January 1989. Lewen's observation on the displacement of art by rhetoric recalls Tom Wolfe's thesis in *The Painted Word*.

14. Roberta Smith, "A 24-Hour-a-Day Show, on Gaudy, Bawdy 42nd Street," *New York Times*, 20 July 1993.

15. Malvine Cole, letter to the editor, *New York Times*, 4 February 1990.

16. Clarence Stark, letter to the editor, *Investment Vision*, November–December 1990.

17. Cartoon by A. Bacall, *Wall Street Journal*, 27 April 1994.

18. Cartoon by Schwalb, *Wall Street Journal*, 4 June 1993.

19. Cartoonist and source unknown.

20. Cartoon by H. Bosch, *Wall Street Journal*, 25 November 1992.

21. Cartoon (signature illegible) in *Wall Street Journal*, February or March 1993.

22. Cartoon by Ed Fisher, *Chronicle of Higher Education*, 28 September 1994. Another vein of postmodernism was the subject of a *New Yorker* cartoon some years ago—in which a suburban housewife serves tea to two friends, while the lifelike figure of a man in business attire, with briefcase in hand, stands in a corner of the living room. She explains: "That's Robert, done in polyester resin, standing on the platform waiting for the eight-twelve, and watching me as I drive off in the station wagon waving goodbye." A leading practitioner of the brand of hyper-realist "sculpture" alluded to was Duane Hanson, who cast his works directly from live models (see Chapter 14).

23. Regrettably, the signature on this delightful cartoon is illegible, and the exact date is unknown.

24. Bill Watterson, Universal Press Syndicates, 1990. See <http://www.calvinandhobbes.com> for more information about this engaging comic strip.

25. Irving Kristol, "It's Obscene but Is It Art?" Wall Street Journal, 7 August 1990.

26. George Will, "Washington's Works of Art," *Newsweek*, 10 January 1994, 64–65.

27. William Rusher, "Remember the Fine Arts?" *Washington Times*, 21–27 September 1998.

28. Thomas Sowell, "Random Thoughts on the Passing Scene," *New York Post*, 14 July 1995.

29. R. Emmett Tyrrell, Jr., "Politics and Art: Traditionalists to the Fore," *New York Post*, 3 June 1995.

30. John Leo, "The Backlash against Victim Art," *U.S. News & World Report*, 16 January 1995, 22.

31. Dave Barry, "Call It Art for Air Compressor's Sake—But Be Sure To Label It," *Los Angeles Daily News*, 7 September 1997; also published as "It's Either Bad Art or Good Ventilation, *New York Daily News*, 6 September 1997. Barry is on the staff of the *Miami Herald*; see <http://www.herald.com/tropic/barry> for more information on his syndicated column.

32. Jeff Jacoby, "How the NEA Pollutes American Culture," *Boston Globe*, 24 January 1995; online (along with related columns) at <http://www.bigeye.com/jj_nea.htm>. Jacoby's *Globe* columns, from August 1998 on, are also archived (under different titles) at the *Jewish World Review*: <http://www.jewishworldreview.com>. On the NEA, see the "3/27/99" link.

33. Jeff Jacoby, "Don't Cave in to the NEA," *Boston Globe*, 4 March 1999; archived under "Is Art Less Sacred Than Rock Music or B-Ball?" at the *Jewish World Review* (see n. 32, above).

34. Morley Safer, "Yes . . . But Is It Art?" *60 Minutes*, CBS News, aired 19 September 1993.

35. For one critic's feeble defense of this inane work, see Michael Kimmelman, "A Few Artless Minutes on '60 Minutes,'" *New York Times*, 17 October 1993.

36. On the *Charlie Rose* show of 25 October 1993, Safer was confronted by a stacked deck of artworld representatives—philosopher-critic Arthur Danto, Whitney Museum director David Ross, and "installation artist" Jenny Holzer. Several months after its original broadcast, *60 Minutes* repeated Safer's piece, which he introduced by stating: "'Yes . . . But Is It Art?' generated more mail than anything we've broadcast for years, and it's still coming! Art seems to strike a powerful nerve in the American psyche." On 5 October 1997, Safer hosted "Yes . . . But Is It Art II"—observing: "We made a discovery here a few years ago. Forget politics, religion or sex as subjects. If you want to set people's hearts on fire, really get them steamed, try art, modern art. And if you thought that some of the things we showed you then were pretty outrageous, let me assure you, they've gotten worse, or, depending on your point of view, even better."

37. Murphy Brown, CBS-TV, 17 January 1994. See Torres and Kamhi, "Yes . . . But Is It Art?"

38. Duchamp's pervasive influence on postmodernism will be discussed in Chapter 14.

39. Manchester *Guardian*, 10 February 1993. According to the *Guardian*, a "blob"-like painting by a four-year-old child was bought by a collector for £295 after being exhibited in the annual show of the Manchester Academy of Fine Arts. The child's mother had submitted the painting as a joke, and a panel of six experts, unaware of the age of the "artist," had selected it from among more than 1,000 works, because they thought it displayed "a certain quality of colour balance, composition, and *technical skill*" (emphasis ours). When informed that the work was that of a four-year-old, the president of the Academy was unperturbed. "The art of children often has a very uncluttered quality which adults often strive to gain," she explained, "so I don't feel in the least embarrassed about it." She then added, without flinching at her implicit contradiction of the expert panel's judgment: "Technical skill can get in the way of instinctive response."

40. In "Pottery . . . But Is It Art?" (*New Zealand Herald*, 1989, month and day unknown), Denis Dutton argues that well-crafted pottery should be considered art. See also Michael Kimmelman, "Tattoo Moves from Fringes to Fashion. But Is It Art?" *New York Times*, 15 September 1995; Alexandra Peers, "It May Not Always Look Like Art, But It's Definitely Cutting Edge," *Wall Street Journal*, 4 May 1995; Roberta Smith, "Comics, Furniture, Etc.: Nearly Art and Gaining," *New York Times*, 30 August 1991; Richard B. Woodward, "It's Art. But Is It Photography?" *New York Times Magazine*, 9 October 1988; and Michiko Kakutani, "Is It Fiction? Is It Non-fiction? And Why Doesn't Anyone Care?" *New York Times*, 27 July 1993. See also nn. 44 and 45, below.

41. Publisher's press release for *But Is It Art?*, 16 December 1994. The book is edited by Nina Felshin, an independent curator and writer.

42. Andy Grundberg, "If It's Commercial, Is It Really Art?" *New York Times*, date unknown.

43. Suzanne Slesin, "Sottsass' Oversize Collection: Is It Furniture or Art?" *New York Times* (Home Section), 29 October 1987.

44. Bruce Weber, "Just Stuff. Just Art?" *New York Times*, 10 May 1995.

45. Julia Llewellyn Smith, "Art—Or Just a Hollow Sham?" *Times* (London), 3 February 1994, emphasis ours.

46. H. W. Janson, *History of Art*, 2nd ed., 9, emphasis ours. Since Janson's book has sold several million copies worldwide, it is worth quoting his introductory paragraph in its entirety: "'Why is this supposed to be art?' How often have we heard this question asked—or asked it ourselves, perhaps—in front of one of the strange, disquieting works that we are likely to find nowadays in museums or art exhibitions. There usually is an undertone of exasperation, for the question implies that we don't think we are looking at a work of art, but that the experts—the critics, museum curators, *art historians* (emphasis ours)—must suppose it to be one, why else would they put it on display? Clearly, their standards are very different from ours; we are at a loss to understand them and we wish they'd give us a few simple, clear-cut rules to go by. Then maybe we would learn to like what we see, we would know 'why it is art.' But the experts do not post exact rules, and the layman is apt to fall back upon his final line of defense: 'Well, I don't know anything about art but I know what I like.'" Janson's use of "we" in this passage seems rather disingenuous, however, since

as an art historian he was clearly among the "experts," not one of the perturbed laymen.

47. Anthony Janson's answer to the question "What is art?" is itself senseless. After stating that art is an "aesthetic object," and that "aesthetic" means "that which concerns the beautiful," he adds: "Of course not all art is beautiful to our eyes, but it is art nonetheless."

48. Frederick Hartt, *Art: A History of Painting, Sculpture, Architecture*, 1st ed. (1975), 14, emphasis ours.

49. Both "contemporary" art museums and the "twentieth-century" wings of comprehensive museums invariably exclude work in a traditional style, although *contemporary*, properly speaking, simply means "occurring at the same period of time."

50. Hartt, *Art*, 15; 2nd ed., 14, emphasis ours.

51. Gombrich, *Story of Art*, 15. In Gombrich's view, "art with a capital A has come to be something of a bogey and a fetish. You may crush an artist by telling him that what he has just done may be quite good in its own way, only it is not 'Art.' And you may confound anyone enjoying a picture by declaring that what he liked in it was not the Art but something different." Another eminent art historian, Erwin Panofsky, in his classic volume of essays on iconology and iconography, *Meaning in the Visual Arts*, asks "[W]hat is a work of art?" and answers that it is a "man-made object demanding to be experienced aesthetically" (10, 14)—which is a far from adequate definition.

52. John Canaday, *What Is Art?*, 3, emphasis ours. This book is based on The Metropolitan Seminars of Art, a series of twelve monographs by Canaday, published by the Metropolitan Museum of Art in 1958 and widely distributed by the Book-of-the-Month Club.

53. Janson does not even mention the work of realist painter Andrew Wyeth (b. 1917), for instance, much less that of such traditional American sculptors as Daniel Chester French (1850–1931) and Anna Hyatt Huntington (1876–1973), though he does include the British abstract sculptor Barbara Hepworth (1903–1975).

54. We do not mean to suggest that there is no room for improvement upon the standard surveys of art history. We would prefer less emphasis on purely "esthetic" or stylistic concerns per se, for example, and more on the meaning conveyed by artworks in their totality.

55. The Fall 1995 issue of the *Art Journal*, published by the College Art Association, was devoted to a reconsideration of introductory art history surveys.

56. Bradford R. Collins, "Rethinking the Introductory Art History Survey: A Practical, Somewhat Theoretical, and Inspirational Guide," *Art Journal*, Fall 1995, 23; and Mitchell Schwarzer, "Origins of the Art History Survey Text," *ibid.*, 28. Also included among the standard survey texts to be "rethought" is Helen Gardner's *Art Through the Ages* (first published in 1926).

57. Marilyn Stokstad, *Art History*, notice in *Times Literary Supplement*, 10 November 1995. See also Larry Silvers, *History in Art* (1993), cited by Graham (see below, n. 58).

58. Mark Miller Graham, "The Future of Art History and the Undoing of the Survey," *Art Journal*, Fall 1995, 30–34, emphasis ours.

59. James Elkins, "Art History and Images That Are Not Art," *Art Bulletin*, December 1995, 553–571, esp. 553–54, 570–71, emphasis ours. Typical of the new approach was an undergraduate introductory course instituted by Harvard's Fine Arts Department (now the History of Art and Architecture Department) in the fall of 1994, entitled "Art and *Visual Culture*" (emphasis ours)—which replaced the traditional survey course, and included lessons such as "The Body as a Vehicle of Expression" and "Against Quality." Irene J. Winter and Henri Zerner, "Art and Visual Culture," *Art Journal*, Fall 1995, 42–43.

60. As we note in Part II, a few critics do dare on occasion to maintain that a given work is not art—among others, Arlene Croce, John Simon, and Tobi Tobias.

61. Roberta Smith, "It May Be Good But Is It Art?" *New York Times*, 4 September 1988. Although Smith strikes an independent pose in this article by concluding that "being good . . . is not the same as being art," her discussion of four controversial exhibitions is equivocal; and implicit in her subsequent body of criticism is the premise that there are no objective criteria for determining whether something is a work of art; that if an expert (whether Smith herself or some other critic or scholar) says it's art, it's art.

62. Jack Anderson, "Just What Is This Thing Called Dance?" *New York Times*, 12 August 1990. Anderson maintains that "'[b]allet,' 'dance' and 'choreography' resist easy definition, in part because the arts to which they refer are constantly developing."

63. Rita Reif, "Ask Not 'Is It Art?' Ask 'Did an Artist Make It?'" *New York Times*, 21 February 1992.

64. Grace Glueck, "Art on the Firing Line," *New York Times*, 9 July 1989.

65. Jacques Barzun, *Use and Abuse of Art*, 18 and 7.

66. Eliseo Vivas, "The Objective Basis of Criticism," in *Creation and Discovery*, 191–92.

67. John Simon, interviewed by film critic Annette Innsdorf, the 92nd Street Y, New York City, 6 December 1984.

68. Stephen Davies, *Definitions of Art*, 74–75. On the definition of art, see Ch. 6.

69. Margaret P. Battin, position paper presented for the American Society for Aesthetics (ASA) to the American Council of Learned Societies, *ASA Newsletter*, Winter 1993, 5–7. According to the official statement of the ASA (printed in each issue of the *Journal of Aesthetics and Art Criticism*): "The term 'aesthetics' . . . is understood to include all studies of the arts and related types of experience. . . . 'The arts' include the visual arts, literature, music, and theater arts." But the expanded definition offered on the journal's website <http://www.temple.edu/jaac/main.html> more accurately reflects the society's confusion regarding the concept art: "The 'arts' are taken to include not only the traditional forms such as music, literature, landscape architecture, dance, painting, architecture, sculpture, and other visual arts, but

also more recent additions including photography, film, earthworks, performance and conceptual art, the crafts and decorative arts, contemporary technical innovations, and other cultural practices, including work and activities in the field of popular culture."

70. Although many philosophers include architecture and dance among the fine arts, Rand treats them separately from what she terms the "primary" arts.

71. The late James W. Tuttleton, for example, resorted to the customary conservative appeal to authority in defense of traditional artistic values in a review of two books on modernism. Although he correctly observed that "what the Futurists produced was inane nonsense, deliberately at war with logic, causality, temporality, grammar, syntax, and referentiality itself," he nevertheless concluded with an appeal not to these objectively grounded values but rather to "[d]uty, responsibility, prescription, obedience, authority, [and] the past." "Revolution in Technology, the Arts, and Politics," *Chronicles*, May 1988.

72. "[I]n a free, civilized society citizens accept ideas and products because they are true and/or good—*not* because they are old *nor* because their ancestors accepted them." Rand, "Global Balkanization," 119. "The plea to preserve '*tradition*' as such, . . . [is] particularly outrageous here, in America, the country based on the principle that man must . . . live by his own judgment." "Conservatism: An Obituary," in *Capitalism*, 198. See also her letter to Isabel Paterson, 4 August 1945, in *Letters*, 180–82.

73. Consistent with this view, Rand considers movies (film) to be, at base, a literary form, governed by the same fundamental principles as fiction and drama. See Chapters 4 and 13.

74. On the interconnectedness of Rand's ideas, see esp. Sciabarra, Ayn Rand, 126; and David Kelley, *Truth and Toleration*.

75. Rand, "Philosophy: Who Needs It," in *Philosophy*, 3–4.

76. Hegel began his *Introductory Lectures on Aesthetics* by stating (as abridged by Henry Paolucci): "These lectures deal with *Aesthetics*. . . . The word . . . in its literal sense is perhaps not quite appropriate here, for it means, strictly speaking, the science of sensation or feeling. Yet it is now commonly used in our more specialized sense, and may therefore be permitted to stand. We should bear in mind, however, that a more accurate expression for our science is the 'Philosophy of Art,' and better still, the 'Philosophy of Fine Art.'" For an unabridged but less idiomatic English version, see the Bosanquet translation (Penguin ed.), 3.

Hegel also explained that he would exclude from consideration the *beauty of nature* (which had figured prominently in Kant's esthetics), because the beauty of art is "higher" than that of nature, for art is a "product of mind [Ger. *Geist*, often trans. as 'Spirit']." Paolucci, 2; Bosanquet, 4. Contemporary usage of the term *esthetics* (we follow the spelling adopted by Rand) tends to be much more inclusive than Hegel's or Rand's.

77. Rand once summarized the basic content of Objectivism as follows: "1. Reality exists as an objective absolute—facts are facts, independent of man's feelings, wishes, hopes, or fears. 2. Reason (the faculty which identifies and integrates the material provided by man's senses) is man's only . . . source of knowledge, his only

guide to action, and his basic means of survival. 3. Man—every man—is an end in himself, not the means to the ends of others. He must exist for his own sake, neither sacrificing himself to others nor sacrificing others to himself. . . . 4. The ideal political-economic system is *laissez-faire* capitalism . . . a system where men deal with one another . . . as *traders*, by free, voluntary exchange to mutual benefit. . . . The government acts only as a policeman that protects man's rights. . . ." "Introducing Objectivism," *The Objectivist Newsletter*, August 1962, 35.

For an excellent brief overview of Rand's life and work, see Sciabarra, *Ayn Rand: Her Life and Thought*. For a more comprehensive account, see Sciabarra's *Ayn Rand: The Russian Radical*. Peikoff's *Objectivism* provides a systematic presentation of her philosophy, albeit from an uncritical perspective. Also useful for reference is *The Ayn Rand Lexicon*, edited by Binswanger, which culls Rand's principal statements on key terms, concepts, and issues—with one conspicuous omission, as we note in a later chapter.

78. Both the Reason Foundation (which has led the move toward privatization of nonessential government functions) and the Cato Institute acknowledge their intellectual debt to Rand. Alan Greenspan, chairman of the Federal Reserve, is the most prominent public figure to openly credit Rand with having had a major influence on his thought.

79. On the tradition of intellectual activism outside the academy in Russia, see Sciabarra, *Ayn Rand*, 10.

80. See Kamhi and Torres, "Critical Neglect of Ayn Rand's Theory of Art," *Journal of Ayn Rand Studies*, Fall 2000.

81. In the early years of Objectivism, the Nathaniel Branden Institute sponsored lectures and other educational activities. Since Rand's death, two new organizations have been founded to study and further her philosophy: the doctrinaire Ayn Rand Institute—headed, in effect, by its Chairman emeritus, Leonard Peikoff (who is also Rand's "intellectual heir" and executor of her estate); and The Objectivist Center (formerly the Institute for Objectivist Studies), which advocates the open exchange of ideas, and is directed by its founder, David Kelley, a former associate of Rand's. See Marci McDonald, "Fighting over Ayn Rand: A Radical Individualist's Followers Can't Get Along," *U.S. News & World Report*, 9 March 1998, and letters to the editor, 30 March 1998.

82. Among the recent texts that consider Rand's ideas are *Reason and Responsibility: Readings in Some Basic Problems of Philosophy*, 10th ed., edited by Joel Feinberg and Russ Shafer-Landau (Wadsworth, 1998); *Moral Philosophy: A Reader*, edited by Louis Pojman (Hackett, 1993); *Philosophy: The Quest for Truth*, 4th ed., edited by Louis Pojman (Wadsworth, 1998); *Twenty Questions: An Introduction to Philosophy*, 4th ed., edited by G. Lee Bowie, Meredith W. Michaels, and Robert C. Solomon (Harcourt Brace Jovanovich, 2000); and *Ideology and Political Life*, edited by Kenneth R. Hoover, 2nd ed. (Wadsworth, 1994).

83. For a summary of Sciabarra's achievements, see Roger Donway, "Chris Sciabarra: Objectivism's Matchmaker," *Navigator* (newsletter of The Objectivist Center, Poughkeepsie, N.Y.), January 2000. See also Sciabarra's website, under "Internet Sources" in the Selected Bibliography, below.

84. Jeff Sharlet, "Ayn Rand Has Finally Caught the Attention of Scholars," Chronicle of Higher Education, 9 April 1999, <http://www.chronicle.com/colloquy/99/rand/background.htm>; and Scott McLemee, "Has Objectivism Gone Subjective?" *Lingua Franca*, September 1999, archived at <http://www.linguafranca.com>.

85. On Rand's subordination of her philosophy of art to her literary esthetic, see our article cited above, n. 80.

86. We have had to limit ourselves to Rand's published work. Our request for access to unpublished materials in the archive of the Ayn Rand Institute was denied by Leonard Peikoff, the executor of Rand's estate. More troubling, we were unable to obtain access to the original manuscripts for Rand's essays on esthetics, which were placed on the auction market in the fall of 1998 by their owner, Robert Hessen (a former friend and associate of Rand's), who refused to make them available to us.

Chapter 1 "The Psycho-Epistemology of Art"

1. In arguing that the earliest human beings had "art," Rand is not speaking of the concept but, rather, of its referents. Early man did not require a concept of art in order to paint, sculpt, create myths, or make music. See also Stephen Davies's observation: "The universality of art from the earliest times suggests that art answers to some deep human needs, and that art might serve those needs for so long as the fundamental character of human nature remains unchanged." In Cooper, *Companion to Aesthetics*, s.v. "'end of art,'" 141.

2. Rand's essay "The Psycho-Epistemology of Art," first appeared in *The Objectivist* (April 1965), which she co-founded and co-edited with Nathaniel Branden. The term "psycho-epistemology" was coined by Barbara Branden. See Sciabarra, *Ayn Rand*, 194–95.

3. In "Art and Cognition" (see our Chapter 4), Rand refers primarily to literature, painting, sculpture, and music. Though these forms are generally subsumed by the term "fine arts" (see our Introduction), she never uses that term, instead characterizing them as "the major branches of art" or "the primary arts." (64) Rand regards the "performing arts" (in which she includes dance) as subordinate to these primary arts. Her position on the status of architecture is equivocal and will be discussed by us in Chapters 4 and 10.

4. Elsewhere Rand argues that "[m]etaphysically, *life* is the only phenomenon that is an end in itself." "The Objectivist Ethics," in *Virtue of Selfishness*, 7.

5. Clive Bell, "The Aesthetic Hypothesis" (1912), in *Art*, 28; emphasis ours. In this essay, Bell also maintained: "To appreciate a work of art we need bring with us nothing from life, no knowledge of its ideas and affairs, no familiarity with its emotions." (27) In contrast with such views, Objectivism holds that "Art is not 'for art's sake,' but for *man*'s sake." Peikoff, *Objectivism*, 442.

6. By *spiritual*, Rand means "pertaining to man's consciousness"—which includes not only cognition but also values and emotions. "Objectivist Ethics," 28.

7. In the first of her *Lectures on Fiction-Writing* (1958), Rand noted that art is "an end in itself" only as distinguished from utilitarian objects, since nothing is truly

an end in itself but man. In stressing that art (in the sense of the "fine arts") is not "utilitarian," she maintains a distinction that was first fully articulated by Aristotle. According to Aristotle, the "practical," or utilitarian, arts are those which "supply the [material] deficiencies of nature in regard to man," who comes into the world in a more helpless state than the other animals—without clothing, means of defense, and so on. In contrast, he held the purpose of the "imitative arts" (later termed the "fine arts") to be "pleasure," in the sense of "rational enjoyment." (See Butcher, *Aristotle's Theory of Poetry and Fine Art*, 115–16, 118, 121, 198ff., and 207; and Halliwell, *Aristotle's Poetics*, 62–81.) The view of fine art as nonutilitarian was elaborated in the eighteenth century—albeit with an inappropriate focus on beauty as the source of pleasure, a focus that deflected attention from the broader cognitive function of art envisioned by Aristotle and more fully, if somewhat differently, articulated by Rand. On the eighteenth-century view, see Kristeller, "Modern System of the Arts," in *Renaissance Thought and the Arts*, 200, 202, 209; and our discussion in Ch. 10.

8. In this context, Rand distinguishes between two main types of abstractions, or concepts, that human beings must form. *Cognitive abstractions* simply "identify the facts of reality" and "deal with that which *is*"—e.g., girl, teacher, chair, food. *Normative abstractions* are more complex in origin, for they involve *evaluating* the facts of reality and prescribing a code of action-guiding principles; they "deal with that which *ought to be* (in the realms open to man's choice)"—e. g., honesty, justice, and courage. According to Rand, normative abstractions, which are the province of ethics or morality (she uses these terms interchangeably), are "derived from and dependent on" cognitive abstractions, because "to prescribe what man ought to do, one must first know *what* he is and *where* he is—i.e., what is his nature (including his means of cognition) and the nature of the universe in which he acts." (18) For Rand's view of *esthetic abstractions*, see Chapter 3.

9. Rand's emphasis on art's relation to the cognitive need for unit-economy bears comparison with Susanne Langer's view of art as *symbolic* in nature (see, for example, *Feeling and Form*, Ch. 3). Langer, too, stresses the importance of selectively condensing vital experience in art. But her term "symbol" (which implies an arbitrary, conventional sign) does not suggest the all-important mimetic character of art, which Rand's theory properly emphasizes.

10. Rand uses the term "metaphysical" in the purely philosophic sense—pertaining to the nature of reality, without quasi-religious or mystical implications of any kind.

11. Note that the last of the questions posed by Rand is clearly normative in content. In another context, she poses a similar series of questions to be answered by philosophy: "Are you in a universe which is ruled by natural laws and, therefore, is stable, firm, absolute—and knowable? Or are you in an incomprehensible chaos, a realm of inexplicable miracles, an unpredictable, unknowable flux, which your mind is impotent to grasp? Are the things you see around you real—or are they only an illusion? Do they exist independent of any observer—or are they created by the observer? Are they the object or the subject of man's consciousness? Are they *what they are*—or can they be changed by a mere act of your consciousness, such as a wish?" In Rand's view, these are the crucial philosophic questions, because "The nature of your actions—and of your ambition—will be different, according to which set of answers you come to accept." "Philosophy: Who Needs It" (originally deliv-

ered as an address at the United States Military Academy at West Point, 6 March 1974), 2–3. Rand frames these questions in the broadest, most abstract terms, focusing on epistemological concerns.

12. According to Rand, *metaphysical value-judgments* are of primary importance because they "determine the kind of *ethics* men will accept and practice." (19) This dubious premise—that an individual's morality is *determined* by his fundamental view of reality—recurs at several points in her analysis of art. As we shall argue in Chapter 2, we consider such a view overly simplistic.

13. As Rand argues in her subsequent essays, the subconscious plays a crucial role in the formation and retention of these fundamental metaphysical abstractions, which are largely held implicitly rather than explicitly.

14. For an image of Jacques-Louis David's *Death of Socrates*, see the website of the Metropolitan Museum of Art.

15. For further discussion of "core evaluations," see Ch. 2.

16. We offer an extended analysis and appraisal of Rand's definition of art in Chapter 6.

17. Rand's language is less than clear when she states that the art work "represents an embodied abstraction." It might be clearer to say that the art work "concretizes, or objectifies, an abstraction."

18. In arguing that the Greek and medieval sculptures are "concretized representations of the philosophy of their respective cultures," Rand does not imply the Hegelian notion of a *Zeitgeist* which uniformly imbues an entire culture. Rather, her view is that in every culture certain fundamental ideas and values are widely accepted and are therefore generally (but not inevitably) shared by each artist and reflected in his work.

19. Rand's reduction of the complexity of Greek and medieval culture to such simple terms is an effective didactic device to illustrate her thesis that "art is a concretization of metaphysics," reflecting the basic premises of the artist's culture. But one should not regard so stark a characterization as the final word on the subject, as some of her unthinking followers tend to do. Greek culture for them is reduced to an endless parade of "godlike" images, and medieval culture is regarded as utterly devoid of beauty or dignity or value. The result is an impoverishment of both historical thought and esthetic appreciation. See, for example, Ch. 4, n. 36.

20. "Man's senses are his only direct cognitive contact with reality and, therefore, his only *source* of information." Rand, "Kant Versus Sullivan," in *Philosophy*, 90. Rand regards percepts as the basic form of sensory contact with reality. She defines a perception as "a group of sensations automatically retained and integrated by the brain of a living organism, which gives it the ability to be aware, not of single stimuli, but of *entities*, of things." "Objectivist Ethics," 10.

21. The principle Rand formulates here is similar to Hegel's view that "the work of art ought to bring a content before the mind's eye, not in its generality as such, but with this generality made absolutely individual, and sensuously particularized." *Introductory Lectures on Aesthetics*, 56. Schopenhauer, too, maintained that the visual and literary arts give perceptual embodiment to "Ideas"—but in Plato's sense of the

"the permanent essential forms of the world," which he explicitly differentiated from *concepts*. See, for example, *The World as Will and Representation*, 1:233 and *passim*: also Patrick Gardiner, in Turner, *Dictionary of Art*, *s.v.* "Schopenhauer, Arthur." Rand rejects the idealist metaphysics of both Hegel and Schopenhauer (which she regarded as rooted in a false mind-body dichotomy), and explains the essentializing character of art in purely epistemologocal, or cognitive, terms.

22. In her *Fiction-Writing* course (Lecture 1), Rand states: "All art is the objectivization [*sic*] of values." Her subsequent discussion suggests that by "values" she means what she later characterized as *metaphysical value-judgments*, in the sense of a view of life.

23. Rand's reference to "entities" in this context departs from her usage in *Introduction to Objectivist Epistemology* (6, 157), where she treats entities as solid, perceptible *objects*. Conceived in that way, entities would not include music and literature. (Perhaps Rand ought to have said here that "art converts man's metaphysical abstractions into the equivalent of *entities*, into specific *concretes* open to man's direct perception.") In "Art and Cognition," she commits a similarly careless error regarding the nature of literature, when she refers to a book as a "physical object" comparable to a work of painting or sculpture. See our discussion in Ch. 5, n. 1.

24. In stating that the adage "'art is a universal language' is not any empty metaphor, it is literally true," Rand does not mean that art corresponds to language in every respect.

25. Rand, *Fiction-Writing*, Lecture 1. Regarding the "re-creation of reality," Rand adds: "Conscious and deliberate fantasy is a legitimate method, . . . but one has to know how to use it within a rational framework. . . . [T]here 'fantasy' is used not in a metaphysical sense, but in a purely literary, inventive sense, and proper fantasy, again, has to be consonant with metaphysically proper reality." Rand warmly praises a passage from one of Isak Dinesen's *Seven Gothic Tales*, describing a herd of unicorns grazing in a field. Rand emphasizes that, while unicorns are fantastic creatures, their physical appearance (a composite of characteristics known from various real animals) is familiar through mythology, and Dinesen describes them in such concrete terms that the reader can vividly imagine them. *Ibid.*, Lecture 10; see also Rand, *Art of Fiction*, 125–27, 169–72. Similarly, Leonardo da Vinci advised artists that to "create imaginary animals [that] appear natural," each part should be based on resemblance to that of an existing creature. Notebooks, extracted in Goldwater and Treves, *Artists on Art*, 53, 52.

26. Plato, *Republic* (tr. Cornford), Book X. On Aristotle's different view, see Butcher, 121–22; and Halliwell, *Aristotle's Poetics*, 125.

27. Rand notes that Babbitt exemplifies a mainly *cognitive* abstraction, rather than a *normative* one—an implicit contrast with her own fictional protagonists, who do embody normative abstractions.

28. An even more illuminating instance of the "selective re-creation of reality" in fiction is the genesis of Ellsworth Toohey, the unforgettable villain of *The Fountainhead*, who is one of Rand's most effective characterizations. As she related to her biographer, she had already formed the broad idea of Toohey as a "leftist intellectual," when she happened to hear a talk by the influential British socialist Harold

Laski. "When I saw Laski I knew I was seeing the soul of Ellsworth Toohey in the flesh," Rand recalled. "Thereafter, I just had to remember how Laski lectured—his mannerisms, the pseudo-intellectual snideness, the whole manner of speaking on important subjects with inappropriate sarcasm as his only weapon, acting as though he were a charming scholar in a drawing room, but you could sense the bared teeth behind the smile, you could feel something evil—and I would know how Toohey would act in any circumstance. . . . Even [Laski's] appearance was ideal. I drew a sketch during the lecture, with the narrow cadaverous face and glasses and big ears, and I gave all of it to Toohey." Quoted in B. Branden, *Passion of Ayn Rand*, 139. To have depended exclusively on one model for the character would have yielded a "journalistic" rather than truly fictional result, however, as Rand further explained. It would have been too literal, too biographical. She drew inspiration for added details of Toohey's persona from several other prominent intellectuals of the time. All these exemplars helped her to concretize a concept that had previously been vague and undefined in her mind, "like an abstract drawing." (139–40)

29. In another context, Rand characterized religion as "an early form of philosophy" in that "the first attempts to explain the universe, to give a coherent frame of reference to man's life and a code of moral values, were made by religion, before men graduated or developed enough to have philosophy." Interview with Alvin Toffler, *Playboy*, March 1964, 40.

30. See also below, n. 38.

31. Rand adds that "without a conceptual theory of ethics, an artist would not be able successfully to concretize an image of the ideal." Thus her focus here is on *moral* values, pertinent only to the field of literature. Yet Rand's fundamental distinction between art, on one hand, and religion or philosophy, on the other, is relevant to all the arts: whereas a work of art conveys abstractions (universals) *implicitly*, they are *explicitly* stated in religious doctrine or philosophy. This distinction is further analyzed in Chapters 2 and 3.

32. Rand, Introduction to the 25th anniversary edition of *The Fountainhead*, viii; reprinted in *The Objectivist*, March 1968, 4.

33. Regarding Hegel's influence on art history, theory, and criticism, see E. H. Gombrich, "'The Father of Art History'," in *Tributes*, 51–69. It is characteristic of Rand that she does not mention Hegel in this context. She rarely cites any philosopher, save for occasional references to Aristotle. Yet Hegel's influence on Russian intellectual life during her formative years was pervasive; see Sciabarra, *Ayn Rand*, esp. 25–31, 34–35, 42, 48, 52. Sciabarra argues that the profoundly dialectical quality of Rand's thought (with respect to methodology, but not to metaphysics) has its roots in the Hegelian tradition. Since the phenomena of art, religion, and philosophy form a central focus of Hegel's thought, Rand's comments constitute an implicit rebuttal of Hegel's "phenomenology of spirit."

Rand's analysis of art, religion, and philosophy is strikingly similar to that of the French literary historian and critic Hippolyte Taine. In his *History of English Literature*, he wrote that "art is a kind of philosophy made sensible, religion a poem taken for true, philosophy an art and a religion dried up, and reduced to simple ideas. There is, therefore, at the core of each of these three groups, a common element, the conception of the world and its principles." Quoted by Joseph Carroll, *Evolution and Literary Theory*, 36. On Taine, see also below, Ch. 2, n. 14.

34. Hegel uses the German word *Geist*, which is variously translated.

35. Nathaniel Branden emphasizes that mind is "a complex architecture of structures and processes. It includes more than the verbal, linear, analytic processes popularly if misleadingly described sometimes as 'left-brain' activity. It includes the totality of mental life, including the subconscious, the intuitive, the symbolic, all that which is sometimes associated with the 'right brain.' Mind is all that by means of which we reach out to and apprehend the world." "What Is Self-Esteem?" paper delivered at the First International Conference on Self-Esteem, Asker/Oslo, Norway, 9 August 1990.

36. Hegel's philosophy of art inspired Arthur Danto to argue more than a decade ago that art "really [was] over with, having become transmuted into philosophy." "The End of Art," in *Philosophical Disenfranchisement of Art*, 8. The absurdity of his proposition is evident when one considers that the work he regards as having achieved "absolute knowledge" is represented by, among other things, Andy Warhol's re-creations of Brillo boxes. Anthony Haden-Guest aptly satirizes Danto in a cartoon depicting the two philosophers next to a "Brillo box"; the caption reads: "Professor Arthur Danto showing the peak of late 20th-century philosophy to his colleague, Dr. Hegel." Recently, Danto has explained, with characteristic opacity, that "it was not his view "that there would be no more art, . . . but that whatever art there was to be would be made without benefit of a reassuring sort of narrative in which it was seen as the appropriate next stage in the story." *Art after the End of Art*, Introduction. Cartoons by Haden-Guest (including the one cited here) may be viewed at <http://www.artcity.com>. On Warhol see Ch. 14.

37. Rand, "What Is Romanticism?" in *Romantic Manifesto*, 122.

38. Ralph Waldo Emerson similarly observed: "The philosopher has a good deal of knowledge which cannot be abstractly imparted, which needs the combinations and complexity of social action to paint it out. . . . [S]o [he] avails himself of the drama, the epic, the novel, and becomes a poet; for these complex forms allow for the utterance of his knowledge of life by *indirection* as well as in the didactic way, and can therefore express the fluxional quantities and values which the thesis or dissertation could never give." Quoted from Joel Porte, *Emerson in His Journals* (Cambridge, Mass.: Harvard University Press, 1982), 217, in Ruth Anna Putnam and Hilary Putnam, "The Quarrel between Poetry and Philosophy," *Bulletin of the Santayana Society*, No. 14 (Fall 1996): 1. The Putnams (1–2) also quote William James, from his essay "The Moral Philosopher and the Moral Life": "[Philosophic] books upon ethics, . . . so far as they truly touch the moral life, must more and more ally themselves with a literature which is confessedly tentative and suggestive rather than dogmatic,—I mean with novels and dramas of the deeper sort."

39. Although Rand is stressing *moral* values in this passage, it goes without saying that mythology also serves to concretize the *metaphysical* views of primitive cultures.

40. As an example of art's power to project a moral ideal in a readily graspable form, Rand recounts an experience related to her by some readers of *The Fountain-*

head. Faced with a difficult moral choice, these readers found that envisioning what the novel's hero, Howard Roark, might do in that situation, quickly led them to understand the principles involved and to identify an appropriate course of action. (22) Such a process requires abstracting the appropriate moral principle from the fictional instance and correctly applying it to the individual's concrete context.

41. Rand's dictum "Art is the technology of the soul" closely resembles Stalin's characterization of the writer as the "engineer of the human soul." On this similarity, see Sciabarra, *Ayn Rand*, 208. Sciabarra points out that Stalin's phrase echoed the beliefs of Nietzschean Marxists, "who saw art as the prime mover of . . . social transformation."

42. Peikoff, *Objectivism*, 420–21, emphasis ours. Few novels exhibit a "whole code" of virtues, of course. Rand's *Atlas Shrugged* is a notable exception, to which Peikoff is probably alluding.

43. Rand's insistence that the primary function of art is not moral instruction has its counterpart in Aristotle's thought. As we have indicated above, n. 17, Aristotle maintained—contrary to many ancient writers—that the principal purpose of poetry, as of all the "imitative arts," was to provide emotional delight and pleasure. Also holding that poetry and even music might be used in the moral education of the young, however, Aristotle (like Rand) did admit a moral function as a "secondary consequence," to borrow Rand's words. See Butcher, *Aristotle's Theory of Poetry*, 215–22. Hegel, too, argued against the notion that the purpose of art is primarily moral. "Against this [view]," he maintained, "it is necessary to maintain that art has the vocation of revealing *the truth* in the form of sensuous artistic shape, of representing the reconciled antithesis [between spirit and matter]." *Introductory Lectures on Aesthetics*, 61.

44. Rand's phrases "is to seek" and "is to achieve"—both of which imply a normative standard or code of action—seem to contradict her prior contention that "art is not the means to any didactic end."

45. Rand's analysis of Romanticism and Naturalism is similar in important respects to at least one standard account. According to Thrall, Hibbard, and Holman, *Romanticism* emphasizes "faith in the individual and in his freedom from rules," whereas *Naturalism* views man as merely another "animal in the natural world, responding to environmental forces and internal stresses and drives, *over none of which he has either control or full knowledge*" (emphasis ours). They further observe: "*[N]aturalism* shares with *Romanticism* a belief that the actual is important not in itself but in what it can reveal about the nature of a larger reality; it differs sharply from *Romanticism*, however, in finding that reality not in transcendent ideas or absolute ideals but in the scientific laws which can be revealed through the action of individual instances." *Handbook to Literature, s. v.* "Naturalism." Rand, too, acknowledges that the Naturalist writers had to exercise a degree of abstraction and selectivity: "in order to reproduce 'real-life' characters," they had to differentiate between 'essential' (fundamental) and 'non-essential or accidental' characteristics. In her view, "they were led to substitute statistics for values as a criterion of selectivity: that which is statistically prevalent among men, they held, is metaphysically significant and representative of man's nature; that which is rare or exceptional, is not." "What Is Romanticism?" 117.

Thrall, Hibbard, and Holman further note that *Romanticism* "tends to see the individual at the very center of all life and all experience, and it places him, therefore, at the center of art, making literature most valuable as an expression of his unique feelings and particular attitudes. . . . It places a high premium upon the creative function of the imagination, seeing art as a formulation of intuitive imaginative perceptions that tend to speak a nobler truth than that of fact, logic, or the here and now. . . . [I]t always seeks to find the Absolute, the Ideal, by transcending the actual, whereas *Realism* finds its values in the actual, and *Naturalism* in the scientific laws which undergird the actual." *Handbook to Literature*, *s.v.* "Romanticism." See also Jaques Barzun's analysis of Romanticism as "an effort to create order [and values] out of experience individually acquired." *Classic, Romantic, and Modern*, 94.

46. Rand, *Fiction-Writing*, Lecture 1.

47. *Ibid.* In Rand's words: "The literary form expressing the essence of [volitional] action is the *plot*." "What Is Romanticism?" 100.

48. Rand herself emphasizes that moral values can be *concretized* only through action. She observes that, if a writer merely presents the thoughts of his character, for example, "he has not really objecti[fied] his story. It might be a very interesting psychological [thesis]—it is not a work of art. Because to be a work of art it has to be presented in terms of reality; . . . [that is,] in terms of *action*, because *that* is the only way values exist or are perceivable in reality." *Fiction-Writing*, Lecture 1. Rand also states that "Romantic literature concerns itself primarily with the issue of the role of values in man's life, and presents man's existence in terms of men's pursuit of values and [the] conflict of their values. The formal expression of that will be a plot structure." With respect to Rand's "principle of volition," which can be concretized only through characters in action: the visual arts can suggest character, and music can suggest movement and action (in a highly abstract fashion); but neither painting, sculpture, nor music alone, without an associated literary text, can represent characters engaged in purposeful action.

49. In arguing that Rand's *definition* of Romanticism applies exclusively to narrative and dramatic literature, we are not suggesting that there is no such thing as "Romantic" painting, sculpture, or music, or that Rand says nothing of value on the subject of Romanticism in literature. Our point is simply that her definition is too narrow to encompass all art forms.

50. "Romanticism is a product of the nineteenth century—a (largely subconscious) result of two great influences: Aristotelianism, which liberated man by validating the power of his mind—and capitalism, which gave man's mind the freedom to translate ideas into practice (the second of these influences was itself the result of the first)." Rand, "What Is Romanticism?" 103. Nonetheless, Objectivists often use the term "Romantic" to characterize art from any period that projects strongly positive qualities or a heroic, inspiring view of man. In so doing, they lapse into an ahistoricism Rand clearly deplored in principle.

51. Notwithstanding our criticism of particular points of Rand's argument, we wholeheartedly agree with her charge that "today's esthetic spokesmen"—the contemporary arts establishment—typically exhibit a profound antipathy toward the embodiment of positive values.

Chapter 2 *"Philosophy and Sense of Life"*

1. Rand's definition of *sense of life* is, to our knowledge, entirely original. Though the term has long been used in English, it is not defined in any of the unabridged dictionaries we have consulted, including the *Oxford English Dictionary* and *Webster's New International Dictionary* (2nd and 3rd editions).

On other writers who applied the term *sense of life* to psychological and cultural phenomena, see below, n. 5; and Jeff Riggenbach, "Philosophy and Sense of Life, Revisited," in *Reason*, November 1974, 37–42. Riggenbach was mistaken, however, in stating that Arthur Mizener "applied the idea to fiction in a Randian way at least three years before Rand made any public statements on that subject." Mizener's *The Sense of Life in the Modern Novel* was published in 1964; but Rand had delivered a paper entitled "Art and Sense of Life" in October 1962, at the annual meeting of the American Society for Aesthetics. According to John Hospers, this paper was published in substantially the same form in *The Romantic Manifesto*. "Memoir: Conversations with Ayn Rand," part 2, *Liberty*, September 1990, 52; and letter to the authors, 23 July 1996.

Also discussed by Riggenbach is the Spanish philosopher Miguel de Unamuno's *Tragic Sense of Life*, first published in English in 1921. On 10 October 1946, Rand wrote to Frank Lloyd Wright: "No, I have not read *The Tragic Sense of Life* by Unamuno, but I shall get it and read it." *Letters*, 118. Given Rand's admiration for Wright, who had apparently recommended that she read Unamuno's work, it seems likely that she would have done so.

2. Nathaniel Branden, *Psychology of Self-Esteem*, 213; and *Psychology of Romantic Love*, 98.

3. José Ortega y Gasset, *On Love*, 92–93; we are indebted to Peter Saint-André for calling this passage to our attention. Since Ortega's work was published in English in 1958, Rand may very well have read it. She had previously read his *Revolt of the Masses*, and commented on it critically in a journal entry dated 15 May 1934. *Journals*, 70–73.

4. Ortega y Gasset, *On Love*, esp. 85, 90, and 93. According to Ortega, in the formation of metaphysical sentiment, "the role of the will and, in general, of the mind, is not creative, but merely corrective." (90) In contrast, Rand regards sense of life as the product of the individual's *volitional* responses to reality. Evidence from the field of psychology suggests that the truth lies somewhere between the extremes suggested by these two views. See Chapter 7.

5. As Sciabarra emphasizes, the emotional sum that constitutes one's sense of life, in Rand's view, is not logically derived: it is not a product of rational deliberation. From infancy on, it is formed automatically and spontaneously "as an unintended consequence or by-product of the child's contact with reality." *Ayn Rand*, 191. Rand's concept bears comparison with Susanne Langer's reference to a "personal 'sense of life' or 'sense of identity'" that arises from the individual's experiences, and to a "continuity of thought that systematizes our emotional reactions into attitudes with distinct feeling tones." *Feeling and Form*, 372.

6. N. Branden, *Self-Esteem*, 214; and *Romantic Love*, 99.

7. N. Branden, *Self-Esteem*, 214–16; *Romantic Love*, 99–102. Anne Frank's poignant declaration in her diary, shortly before her capture by the Nazis, that at heart she still believed in the basic goodness of people, surely qualifies as a sense-of-life evaluation.

8. Edith Packer, "Understanding the Subconscious," *The Objectivist Forum*, February 1985, esp. 2–6.

9. As Packer emphasizes, however, not all core evaluations actually "correspond to the fundamental facts of reality and as such provide an individual with a sound psychological framework for his development." Examples of mistaken core evaluations cited by her are: "'People are such that sooner or later they will hurt me.' 'Life is a power struggle, and, being weak, I will always be defeated.' 'The real me is bad.' 'Life does not hold the possibility of happiness for me.'" In contrast, Packer cites the following as correct evaluations: "'People are not born good or bad. Each individual creates his own character and values. And that includes me.' 'Values are achievable and happiness is possible.'" *Ibid.*, 3.

10. Note that Packer, unlike Rand, uses the verb "influence," not "determine," to characterize the relationship between one's core evaluations (or sense of life) and one's actions (or morality).

11. Rand, "The Age of Envy," in *New Left*, 2d ed., 152. This essay, which did not appear in the original edition of *The New Left*, was first published in *The Objectivist*, July and August 1971. See also n. 13 below.

12. Nathaniel Branden, *Six Pillars of Self-Esteem*, 287–88.

13. "A nation, like an individual, has a sense of life, which is expressed not in its formal culture, but in its 'life style'—in the kinds of actions and attitudes which people take for granted and believe to be self-evident, but which are produced by complex evaluations involving a fundamental view of man's nature. . . . [This] does not mean that every member of a given nation shares it, but only that a dominant majority shares its essentials in various degrees. . . . A nation's sense of life is formed by every individual child's early impressions of the world around him: of the ideas he is taught (which he may or may not accept) and of the way of acting he observes and evaluates (which he may evaluate correctly or not). And although there are exceptions at both ends of the psychological spectrum—men whose sense of life is better (truer philosophically) or worse than that of their fellow-citizens—the majority develop the essentials of the same subconscious philosophy. This is the source of what we observe as 'national characteristics.'" Rand, "Don't Let It Go,"in *Philosophy: Who Needs It*, 205–206.

14. "At certain times there appears an original form of mind, which produces philosophy, a literature, an art, a science, and which, having renewed human thought, slowly and infallibly renews all human thoughts." Hippolyte Taine, *History of English Literature*, quoted by Joseph Carroll, *Evolution and Literary Theory*, 34. Taine's proposition strikingly calls to mind Rand's theme in *The Fountainhead*. She may very well have learned of Taine's ideas during her studies at the University of Leningrad, as he was frequently quoted in the work of G.V. Plekhanov, who may have taught one of the courses she took in her history studies. See Chris Matthew Sciabarra, "The Rand Transcript," *Journal of Ayn Rand Studies*, Fall 1999, 1–26. Our thanks to George

Kline for generously providing information on Plekhanov's references to Taine. Since Rand was fluent in French, she might have also read Taine in the original.

15. Rand uses the verb "invoke," which is clearly inappropriate to the context.

16. Popular culture offers many apt illustrations of the process of emotional generalization which Rand describes—from the children in J. M. Barrie's *Peter Pan*, who are instructed by Peter to "think happy thoughts," to the Rodgers and Hammerstein song "My Favorite Things" in *The Sound of Music*.

17. On the importance of individual context in cognition and valuation, see Rand, "Objectivist Ethics," in *Virtue of Selfishness*, 21: "One must never make any decisions, form any convictions or seek any values out of context, i.e., apart from or against the total integrated sum of one's knowledge." In our view, temperament, or innate disposition, should probably be added to the contextual factors Rand regards as relevant to individual values and emotional response. See the section on "The Psychology and Physiology of Emotion" in Chapter 7.

18. On "context-dropping," see Rand, "The 'Conflicts' of Men's Interests," in *Virtue of Selfishness*, 60.

19. Rand's regrettable tendency to regard her personal preferences and tastes as virtual absolutes has been emulated all too often by Objectivists who fail to grasp the principles at issue. Even Peikoff has deplored this tendency. "Understanding Objectivism," Lecture 10.

20. See above, Ch. 1, n. 12. Rand's proposition is unduly categorical, since (as she herself elsewhere argues) many individuals profess and practice ethical precepts that are inconsistent, even in direct conflict with, their implicit sense of life. See her observations in "Art and Sense of Life," 41–42; and "Introduction to *Ninety-Three*," in *Romantic Manifesto*, 159–60.

21. Rand uses the term "values" rather than "value-judgments" in this context—a usage inconsistent with her view that sense of life is an "implicit *metaphysics*" (not an implicit axiology or ethics). On this point, see our critique of her definition in Chapter 6. In addition, she interpolates a series of items that also seem to slip into the ethical realm. "'It is important to understand things'—'It is important to obey my parents'—'It is important to act on my own'—'It is important to please other people'—'It is important to fight for what I want'—'It is important not to make enemies'—'My life is important'—'Who am I to stick my neck out?'" Rand adds: "It is of such conclusions that the stuff of [one's] soul [i.e., consciousness] is made." Again, contrary to her implication, the moral significance of her examples would depend on the context. For instance, for a very young child, it might be entirely appropriate to think "it is important to obey my parents," though unquestioning obedience would no doubt indicate excessive dependence in the case of an adolescent.

22. According to Rand, an individual's sense of life can undergo change, even in adulthood, but only through a "long process of psychological retraining"—in which, presumably, one would internalize new philosophic premises. (31) Nathaniel Branden argues that "to a profound degree" the sense-of-life attitudes formed early in childhood "prove remarkably tenacious and resistant to change"—a judgment no doubt informed by his experience as a psychotherapist. *Romantic Love*, 99.

23. In contrast, Rand elsewhere suggests that sense of life influences, but does not necessarily determine, one's values, emotions, and actions. She states that an individual's sense of life—his "unidentified philosophy"—"affects his choice of values and his emotional responses, influences his actions, and, frequently, clashes with his conscious convictions." "Don't Let It Go," 205.

24. Peikoff, "The Philosophy of Objectivism" (1976), Lecture 2; quoted in Binswanger, *Ayn Rand Lexicon, s.v.* "Character." The instances of Rand's usage of the term that are cited in the *Lexicon* are consistent with the definition given by Peikoff. On Peikoff, see above, Ch. 1, nn. 75 and 79.

25. For a philosophic perspective relevant to the complex etiology of moral values, see David Kelley, *Truth and Toleration*, esp. 30–37. Although Kelley's discussion pertains to the consequences of philosophic ideas in a society, his comments are equally applicable to the complexities involved in an individual's formation of moral values.

26. Unlike *character*, the term *personality* does not connote moral qualities.

27. Rand's tendency to interpret romantic love solely in terms of a response to *moral* values has been rejected by both Nathaniel Branden and Edith Packer, each of whom argues that a mutually fulfilling romantic relationship is based on far more than shared moral values. See Branden, *Romantic Love*, Ch. 3. In Lecture 11 of Peikoff's "Understanding Objectivism" series, Packer similarly notes that shared moral values are a necessary but not a sufficient basis for romantic love. Regrettably, that lecture is no longer being distributed with the series, owing to Peikoff's repudiation of Packer.

28. Rejecting Rand's view as "grossly inadequate to the complexity of the actual facts," Branden argues: "Many factors contribute to who we become as human beings: our genes, our maturation, our unique biological potentials and limitations, our life experiences and the conclusions we draw from them, the knowledge and information available to us, and, of course, our premises and philosophical beliefs, and the thinking we choose to do or not to do. And even this list is an oversimplification." "The Benefits and Hazards of the Philosophy of Ayn Rand: A Personal Statement," *Journal of Humanistic Psychology* 24 (1984): 61–62.

29. Branden further argues: "Just as we need to know more than a human being's philosophical beliefs in order to understand that human being; so we need to know more than a society's or culture's philosophical beliefs to understand the events of a given historical period. . . . [T]he [O]bjectivist method of historical interpretation is guilty of the same gross oversimplification that is manifest at the level of explaining individual behavior." Yet, as Sciabarra argues, Rand's view of history often exhibited greater compleity. *Ayn Rand*, 360–63.

Chapter 3 "Art and Sense of Life"

1. Rand's concept of sense of Life is the only aspect of her theory of art that has elicited published comment from estheticians. John Hospers (who knew Rand in the early 1960s) briefly mentioned it in his introductory text *Understanding the Arts*.

(255–56) In a review of that book, moreover, Francis Sparshott cites Rand's ideas on sense of life as one of only two points that might be "of interest to anyone versed in aesthetics or in general philosophy." *Journal of Aesthetics and Art Criticism* 41 (1983): 335.

2. Although Rand implies that an art work conveys the artist's "view of life" in the broadest sense, no single work or body of work, however comprehensive, can concretize so wide and complex an abstraction.

3. For a critique of the various meanings ascribed to the term "expression" in relation to art, see Hospers, "The Concept of Artistic Expression," in *Introductory Readings*, 142–67.

4. Leo Tolstoy, *What Is Art?*, tr. Maude, 43. In a more idiomatic English edition by Richard Pevear (Penguin Books), the relevant passage reads (39–40): *"To call up in oneself a feeling once experienced and, having called it up, to convey it by means of movements, lines, colours, sounds, [or] images expressed in words, so that others experience the same feeling—in this consists the activity of art. Art is that human activity which consists in one man's consciously conveying to others, by certain external signs, the feelings he has experienced, and in others being infected by those feelings and also experiencing them."* For Tolstoy, the "feelings" conveyed by art are "most various," from the "raptures of lovers" to the "merriment evoked by a dance" to the "feeling of quietness transmitted by an evening landscape" or the "admiration evoked by a beautiful arabesque" (tr. Maude, 42–43). They thus include both *feeling-states* (such as "quietness") and *emotions* ("merriment," "admiration," etc.). Tolstoy's definition of art is so broad, of course, that it would encompass phenomena normally considered outside the realm of art.

5. Reacting against the obscurity of French avant-garde poetry, in particular, Tolstoy wrote: "to say a work of art is good, but incomprehensible to the majority of men, is the same as saying of some kind of food that it is very good but that most people can't eat it." *What Is Art*, tr. Maude, 87. His extreme view led him to reject as beyond the pale of art not only the hermetic poetry of the French Symbolists (especially Baudelaire) but also the work of Shakespeare, Dante, Goethe, Beethoven, Michelangelo, and, incredibly, even his own novels. As Stanley Bates has astutely observed, however, Tolstoy raised a number of legitimate questions about certain disturbing modernist trends in the arts, as well as about the then-prevailing assumption that the main purpose of art is the creation of beauty. "Tolstoy Evaluated," in Dickie, Sclafani, and Roblin, *Aesthetics*, 66.

6. In the view of Stephen Mulhall, who offers a useful summary and critique of the Croce-Collingwood theory, "[t]he idea that the concept of 'expression' might be central to a philosophical understanding of the nature of art derives much of its contemporary force" from this theory's influence. In Cooper, *Companion to Aesthetics*, *s.v.* "expression."

7. R. G. Collingwood, "Art as the Expression of Emotion," in Dickie, Sclafani, and Roblin, 111–12.

8. According to the Croce-Collingwood theory, the "completed" art work exists in the mind of the artist, as a product purely of his creative imagination; and the craft

or technique required to externalize it are considered foreign to the artistic process itself. Whereas a *craftsman* knows in advance exactly what he intends to make and follows precise rules of technique to achieve his end, the *artist* is engaged in a process of discovery and clarification, gradually working out his initially vague, confused feeling or emotion until he has arrived at a clear understanding of it.

9. Susanne Langer, *Problems of Art*, 15. Langer subsequently defines the *process* of art-making as "the creation of perceptible forms expressive of human feeling," and frankly acknowledges that the key terms of her definition ("creation," "forms," "expressive," and "feeling") are imprecise. (80) In *Feeling and Form*, published four years earlier, she defined art-making as "the creation of forms *symbolic* of human feeling." (40, emphasis ours) As these few citations indicate, her theory of art underwent considerable modification over time. Her misplaced emphasis on the "expressive" or "feeling" content of art no doubt stemmed from her initial focus on music, and her subsequent generalization from music to the other arts.

10. Langer, *Problems of Art*, 22.

11. Of all the arts, it is music that most appears to "express" or objectify emotion. On Rand's analysis of music, see Chapter 5.

12. A similar emphasis on reference to external reality is explicit in Chinese esthetics. With respect to Chinese literature, for example, Li Zehou (a leading scholar of Chinese philosophy and art) observes that "not every work that expresses the author's feelings can be considered art. . . . [S]ubjective feelings must be made objective . . . through reference to external scenes or objects." They must be transformed into "an artistic image coloured by reason and emotion." *The Path of Beauty*, 53. See also Kenneth J. DeWoskin, "Chinese and Japanese Aesthetics," in Cooper, *Companion*.

13. The philosopher Louis Arnaud Reid, too, was critical of characterizing the arts as a form of "communication." *Study in Aesthetics*, 181.

14. To *communicate* means to transfer information or knowledge. It implies not only that the communicator aims to present his message in a manner accessible to another but also that it be grasped. It stresses the *result* of the transfer. *Webster's Dictionary of Synonyms* (1st ed.), *s.v.* "communicate." Although Rand herself sometimes uses the term in relation to art, she intends it loosely, not in its precise sense. On the inappropriateness of characterizing art as a form of "communication," see also Dipert, *Artifacts, Art Works, and Agency*, 178–79. As he argues, an emphasis on communication risks turning the artist into a mere "propagandist and manipulator."

15. Rand's concept of "objectification" in art differs from Langer's. For Langer, art "objectifies" human feeling ("the subjective realm"), while for Rand art objectifies values and a view of life.

16. Rand, "Philosophical Notes on the Creative Process," 4 May 1946, in *Journals*, 479.

17. Such a view of the artist is not confined to modern Western culture. A colophon by the Chinese painter Wu Li (1632–1718), for example, quotes an artist of the Sung dynasty as saying: "I write in order to express my heart, I paint in order to comfort my mind. I may wear rough clothes and eat coarse food, but I would not ask support

from others." Wu Li comments: "Neither kings nor dukes or nobles could command these painters; they were unattainable by worldly honors." Quoted in Meyer Schapiro, "Diderot on the Artist and Society"(1964), in *Theory and Philosophy of Art,* 203.

18. The life of the American writer Jack Schaefer (1907–1991)—author of *Shane,* among other works of fiction and nonfiction—testifies to the basic truth of Rand's story. After twenty years of writing inspiring fiction about the men and women who settled the American West, Schaefer became disillusioned, concerned about the destructive impact of settlement on the environment, and began to write works of natural history, focusing on creatures of the Southwest whose survival he believed was in jeopardy. Try as he might, however, he could not be "downbeat" about his own "species," he later recalled. Inevitably, his fundamental "romanticism [would] creep in"—the optimistic sense of life he had formed in his youth. Despite all his intentions, his "ultimate faith in mankind" would assert itself. Schaefer, "A New Direction," in *Shane: The Critical Edition,* 428–30; quoted in Torres, "Jack Schaefer, Teller of Tales," Part II, *Aristos,* December 1996.

19. That Rand refers to the "viewer" or "reader," but not to the "listener," suggests that she is here focusing on the visual arts and literature, not music. For her analysis of music, see Chapter 5.

20. Langer, too, emphasizes the indirect nature of artistic "communication." *Feeling and Form,* 393–95.

21. This principle has often been ignored by the avant-garde, as we shall argue in Part II.

22. Rand, *Fiction-Writing,* Lecture 5; and *Art of Fiction,* 55.

23. Rand, "Art and Cognition," 65. On the stylization that inevitably occurs in any visual representation by different individuals, see E. H. Gombrich, *Art and Illusion,* 64.

24. In characterizing *esthetic abstractions* as pertaining to "what is *important,*" Rand is referring to the content of works of art, not to such concepts as "beauty" and "harmony."

25. With regard to art as "creation," Ronald W. Hepburn notes that, in the view of many contemporary theorists and artists, "'creative imagination' is that power by which, in a display of freedom that echoes the divine prerogative of creation *ex nihilo,* we summon up to actuality possible worlds—worlds that God has not created but has, as it were, left for us to create. . . . Art [is] freed from dependence on appearances. . . . Originality and individuality become criteria of high merit." In Cooper, *Companion to Aesthetics, s.v.* "Theories of Art," 424. Kristeller points out that the term "creation" has been widely applied to the production of art only since the late eighteenth century. In its original sense, it denotes the bringing of something new into being out of nothingness, and was formerly used almost exclusively in relation to the work of God in the biblical account of Genesis. "Afterword: 'Creativity' and 'Tradition,'" in *Renaissance Thought and the Arts,* 247–58.

26. Rand, "The Metaphysical Versus the Man-Made," in *Philosophy* 25. In another context, Rand refers to the novelist as a "creator," to emphasize that he is more than a "recording secretary" of life exactly "as it is." "The Goal of My Writing," 164–65.

See also Langer's contention that a work of art is "more than an 'arrangement' of given things. . . . Something emerges from the arrangement . . . , which was not there before." _Feeling and Form_, 40. Rand would no doubt have agreed.

27. Rand implicitly recognized that the arts vary in scope when she emphasized that "nothing can take the place of art, and _specifically fiction_," in the "concretization of values"—by which she meant, primarily, moral values. _Fiction-Writing_, Lecture 12, emphasis ours.

28. In another context, Rand emphatically rejected the notion that anyone could accurately infer her sense of life from her fiction, even though it is "all over every page" and one would therefore have "some grasp of it." Even a novel as complex and comprehensive as _Atlas Shrugged_, she implied, cannot fully reveal its author's sense of life—which is "enormously private." Question period following Lecture 12 of Peikoff's course "The Philosophy of Objectivism." As Rand emphasized in "Philosophy and Sense of Life" (32), one's sense of life is also a "very complex sum."

29. Aristotle, _Poetics_ (tr. Butcher), Ch. 8.

30. Kenyon Cox, _What Is Painting?_ 109.

31. Langer, _Problems of Art_, 95.

32. Contrary to Rand's implication, not all the sculptors of ancient Greece depicted man as a "god-like" figure, nor did Greek culture, in general, ignore the darker aspects of humanity. Rand (unlike Nietzsche) tends to ignore or deny its Dionysian aspect. Similarly, her sweeping reference to "the sculptors of the Middle Ages" blurs the long and complex cultural history of the era, which included its own periods of classical renewal, and at times manifested an inspiring vision of man. Nonetheless, her broadly drawn contrast does convey the dominant spirit of the art and thought of these two cultures. See also above, Ch. 1, n. 19.

33. Rand, _Fiction-Writing_, Lecture 1. According to Rand, the artist subconsciously internalizes many of the values and meanings which are later concretized or expressed in his work. During the process of creation, he may not be fully aware of the meaning of a particular element or detail but may select it because it "feels right" to him (based on the subconscious integrations he has performed over a lifetime)—even if he does not articulate the reasons why. See also _Art of Fiction_, esp. 51–54, 83–86, and 132.

34. We use the generic term "responder" in place of the more specific terms "viewer" (or "beholder"), "reader," and "listener," since those more common terms are applicable only to particular art forms. Further, "responder" better conveys the active quality of experiencing art than does the generic term "perceiver" (or Langer's "percipient").

35. For Rand's term "application" (which suggests moral principles that could be actively "applied" to one's life) we would substitute "relevance." We would also note that "human interest" news stories, not unlike fiction, imply a presumption of universality.

36. According to Rand, an individual with a "malevolent sense of life" subscribes to what she terms the "malevolent universe premise"—i.e., the metaphysical view

that man, "by his very nature, is helpless and doomed—that success, happiness, achievement are impossible to him—that emergencies, disasters, catastrophes are the norm of his life and that his primary goal is to combat them." "The Ethics of Emergencies," *Virtue of Selfishness*, 55.

37. It seems to us that some "irrational" individuals might very well think that the world is "benevolently" disposed toward them, that everything will turn out well without any conscious effort on their part. Conversely, some "rational" and "moral" individuals might have a dark, pessimistic (what Rand would call "malevolent") sense of life.

38. For Rand's "view" of "irrationality," see "The Objectivist Ethics," in *Virtue of Selfishness*, 20, where she characterizes it as the deliberate "rejection of man's means of survival [i.e., of reason]." Nathaniel Branden has criticized Rand for failing to distinguish between the "irrational" and the "nonrational," and between the "rational" and the "reasonable." See "The Benefits and Hazards of the Philosophy of Ayn Rand," *Journal of Humanistic Psychology* 24 (1984): 39–64.

39. Peikoff, "Understanding Objectivism," Lecture 10.

40. Such confusion is evident in Hosper's rather patronizing claim: "When someone who isn't accustomed to contemporary art . . . [says] '*That's* not art!' . . . he isn't really denying that it's art. . . . What his remark means is that in his opinion it isn't good art." *Understanding the Arts*, 29–30. Rand would no doubt have argued, as do we, that Hospers is mistaken here.

41. Aristotle held that the "objects of imitation" in all the arts, not merely dramatic or narrative poetry, are "men in action." *Poetics* (tr. Butcher), Ch. 2. On the principle that literature "has to be about people," see also novelist Mark Helprin's "Against the Dehumanization of Art," in *Aristos*, May 1995; also in *The New Criterion*, September 1994 <http.//www.newcriterion.com/archive/13/sept94/helprin.htm>.

42. Rand, "Art and Sense of Life," 40.

43. Rand, "The Goal of My Writing," 166, emphasis ours.

44. Though Rand fails to cite specific theories, it is true that much modernist criticism does focus on the attribute of style, often to the complete neglect of subject matter. See our discussion in Chs. 8 and 13 for examples.

45. The concept of *theme* must be differently characterized with respect to music, which has no explicit or clearly identifiable "subject" comparable to that in literature or visual art.

46. Surely Rand would have admired the heroic implications of these two paintings, if she had troubled to learn of their existence—which she could have easily done, since Vermeer's total oeuvre numbers fewer than 30 works and had been widely illustrated.

47. Art historian Erwin Panofsky also confuses "subject matter" with "meaning," or "content." In his seminal essay "Iconography and Iconology," he proposes "to define the distinction between *subject matter or meaning* on the one hand, and form on the other." In *Meaning in the Visual Arts*, 26, emphasis ours. See also n. 50, below.

48. L.A. Reid notes that "the term 'content' is in ordinary usage taken to be very much the same thing as 'subject-matter,' and . . . the idea of 'subject-matter' is apt to be full of confusion." *Study in Aesthetics*, 229. Reid is rarely cited by contemporary theorists, no doubt because his essentially Aristotelian, realist perspective leads him to reject (just as Rand does) the modernist trend toward nonobjective values in the arts. Our thanks to Jacques Barzun for recommending his work to us.

49. Rand similarly observes, in "Art and Cognition," that there is no "clear, conceptual distinction and separation of object from subject in the field of musical perception."

50. In contrast with Reid, Panofsky analyzes "primary" and "secondary" subject matter in relation to meaning discernible in the finished work of art, rather than to the creative process. For Panofsky, "primary," or "natural," subject matter consists of forms whose meaning is directly discernible without any special cultural knowledge—e.g., images of human beings and aspects of pose and facial expression that are universally intelligible. "Iconography and Iconology," 28.

51. Reid notes (*Study in Aesthetics*, 236) that, in identifying and focusing upon the subject in representational art, "we are apt to regard it for its own sake and to separate it from its . . . embodiment"—which is what Rand tends to do.

52. Rand, *Fiction-Writing*, Lecture 8.

53. Though Rand uses the term *element* here, in "Basic Principles of Literature" (93) she more accurately characterizes style as an *attribute* of the novel, emphasizing that it is not a "separable part" (as the term *element* might imply).

54. Rand, *Fiction-Writing*, Lecture 8.

55. For considerations of artistic style as a manifestation of different ways of thinking, see esp. Erich Auerbach, *Mimesis*, Ch. 20; Emmanuel Loewy, *The Rendering of Nature in Early Greek Art*, Introduction and Ch. I; Meyer Schapiro, "Style" (1962), in *Theory and Philosophy of Art*, 83–84; Ian Watt, "The First Paragraph of *The Ambassadors*," reprinted in *Henry James*, edited by Tony Tanner (London: Macmillan, 1968), 291ff.; Heinrich Wölfflin, *The Sense of Form*, Ch. VIII, "Clarity and the Subject in Art: Visibility and Objectivity," and his "Conclusion"; and Susan Sontag, who argues ("On Style," in *Against Interpretation*, 35) that "every style embodies an epistemological decision, an interpretation of how and what we perceive."

56. On the importance to Rand of articulating implicit values and ideas, see Sciabarra, *Ayn Rand*, 210–15, 358–67, 371.

57. Art historian James Ackerman properly emphasizes the importance of considering the complexity of the "total context" in interpreting works of art. "Style," in *Art and Archeology*, ed. James S. Ackermann and Rhys Carpenter (Englewood Cliffs, N.J.: Prentice-Hall, 1963), 185–86. On the difficulty of drawing broad inferences from the limited evidence provided by a single work or part of a work, see also Schapiro, "Style," 90–92, 96–99. Finally, Gombrich admonishes that it is "extremely hazardous to make inferences from [a single] manifestation [of style] . . . even when we know the context and conventions extremely well." "Style," in *International Ency-*

clopedia of the Social Sciences, ed. David Sills (New York: Macmillan, 1968), Vols. 15–17, 358.

58. Joan Mitchell Blumenthal—a painter who was a close friend and associate of Rand's—offers an illuminating analysis of how formal elements contribute to the ultimate meaning of paintings in "The Ways and Means of Painting" (videotape—see Bibliography).

59. As Rand notes, the writer's "'choice of words' will convey the emotional implications or connotations, the value-slanting, of the particular content he has chosen to communicate." "Basic Principles," 94. On style and content, philosopher Jenefer Robinson observes: "It used to be a commonplace of literary theory that the subject-matter of a text is *what* the writer writes about, whereas the style is *how* she writes about it. This distinction has recently been questioned by several writers." "Style and Personality in the Literary Work," in Dickie, Sclafani, and Roblin, 467. One of those writers, philosopher Nelson Goodman, argues that "some notable features of style are features of the matter rather than the manner of the saying." "The Status of Style," 799. According to Robinson, a feature of subject-matter has "stylistic relevance" when "it is expressive of the implied author's personality"; that is, of his "qualities of mind, attitudes, interests," as well as of "his moral qualities and deep-seated character traits"—in short, of all those qualities that constitute his psychological individuality. "Style and Personality," 467, 456, and 458, emphasis ours. On the interrelatedness of style and meaning, see Robinson, "Style and Significance in Art History and Art Criticism," *Journal of Aesthetics and Art Criticism* 40 (1981): 5–14, although her analysis is marred by illustrations from abstract painting—which, we argue in Chapter 8, has no meaning.

60. Rand, *Fiction-Writing*, Lecture 8.

61. Predictably, reviewers of *The Romantic Manifesto* were critical of Rand for her praise of Spillane. See for example, Richard J. Cattani, "Ayn Rand and All That," *Christian Science Monitor*, 5 February 1970.

62. Rand mistakenly writes "subjective."

63. On denotation versus connotation, see Rand, *Fiction-Writing*, Lecture 9; and *Art of Fiction*, 107–108 and 123–24.

64. Rand, *Fiction-Writing*, Lecture 9.

65. Barbara Branden testifies that Rand repeatedly condemned as "irrational" responses to art that she deemed inconsistent with her esthetic principles. *The Passion of Ayn Rand*, 241. Branden relates: "Ayn . . . convinced me [of Thomas Wolfe's failings]—as she was to convince me that the paintings of Vincent Van Gogh were too undisciplined, too chaotic and wild to be considered great art[;] . . . that Somerset Maugham's *Of Human Bondage* propounded a deeply malevolent view of life[;] . . . that Wagner's *Tristan and Isolde* was profoundly tragic. She convinced me, as, over the years, I would see her convince so many others, of the invalidity of their artistic tastes. . . . [W]e were to hear Ayn excoriate the 'grim, unfocused malevolence' of Rembrandt—to a painter; Shakespeare's 'abysmal failure' to present human beings with free will—to a writer; Beethoven's 'tragic sense of doom'—to a musician. And we were to see the painters, the writers, the musicians [among us], fail

hopelessly to refute her arguments and unhappily grant the logic of her position
. . . . [F]rom then on their work reflected the air-tight underground into which they
had placed their aesthetic emotions; in the name of reason, their work became thin,
and tight, and without originality." (243)

66. Contrary to Rand's assumption, Michael Polanyi argues that an "unbridled
lucidity"of details can sometimes impede one's grasp of the whole. "Scrutinize closely
the particulars of a comprehensive entity and their meaning is effaced, our conception of the entity is destroyed. . . . [T]he belief that, since particulars are more tangible, their knowledge offers a true conception of things is fundamentally mistaken."
The Tacit Dimension, 18–19.

67. In another context, however, Rand suggests that one cannot easily infer the
reasons for another individual's emotions. "In regard to judging the emotional responses
of others," she states, "it is extremely difficult to tell their reasons in a specific case."
"The Age of Envy," *The New Left*, 132. As Nathaniel Branden has emphasized, Rand's
often judgmental attitude is psychologically unsound as well as philosophically mistaken. Since the nature of one's response to art, like any emotional response, is automatic and spontaneous, not under conscious control, it is outside the moral sphere.
See his "Benefits and Hazards," 39, 52–56.

68. Erich Auerbach's classic literary study *Mimesis: The Representation of Reality in Western Literature* offers some support for Rand's proposition, at least with
respect to some twentieth-century fiction. Most illuminating in this regard is his chapter ("The Brown Stocking," 525–53) analyzing a passage from Virginia Woolf's *To
the Lighthouse*. Auerbach emphasizes that almost everything presented in the passage is portrayed "by way of reflection" in the various characters' minds, so that there
is no longer any sense of "an objective reality"—that is, a reality apart from the consciousness of the characters themselves. (534) In employing the stream-of-consciousness style, Woolf and other similar modernist writers "hesitate to impose upon
life . . . an order which it does not possess in itself." (548) If, as Auerbach argues
(551–52), their method is, at least in part, a symptom of their confusion, helpless-
ness, and doubt, it may lend credence to Rand's proposition that style reflects the
artist's view of the "efficacy or impotence" of human consciousness.

69. By "efficacy of consciousness" in this context, Rand appears to mean a generalized capacity to grasp reality, rather than any particularized skill. On this distinction, see Sciabarra, *Ayn Rand*, 215–17.

70. For readers unfamiliar with Francis Bacon's paintings, something of their
flavor may be suggested by the following passage from Rand's essay "Bootleg Romanticism": "The composite picture of man that emerges from the art of our time is the
gigantic figure of an aborted embryo whose limbs suggest a vaguely anthropoid shape,
who twists his upper extremity in a frantic quest for light that cannot penetrate its
empty sockets, who emits inarticulate sounds resembling snarls and moans, who
crawls through a bloody muck, red froth dripping from his jaws, and struggles to
throw the froth at his own non-existent face, who pauses periodically and, lifting the
stumps of his arms, screams in abysmal terror at the universe at large." (130) Though
there is no evidence that Rand was familiar with Bacon's work, this general comment (however immoderate) on certain modernist tendencies readily applies to the
sense of life projected by his paintings.

71. For Rand, "esthetic" as she uses it here has a more inclusive meaning for her than in customary usage. It pertains not only to the formal qualities of art but to the work as a whole, encompassing meaning as well.

72. The principle Rand articulates here recalls a similar view stated by Henry James in his essay "The Art of Fiction": "We must grant the artist his subject, his idea, his *donnée*; our criticism is applied only to what he makes of it. . . . The execution belongs to the author alone; it is what is most personal to him, and we measure him by that."

73. In "The Psycho-Epistemology of Art," for example, Rand declares: "The greater a work of art, the more profoundly universal its theme" (22).

74. Rand, "What Is Romanticism?" 107. In her ranking of Romantic writers, however, Rand mistakenly implies that only those in the "top rank" are concerned with "profound value-conflicts" and the "fundamental, universal, timeless issues of man's existence."

75. Reid, *Study in Aesthetics*, 238–43.

Chapter 4 *"Art and Cognition"*

1. "Art and Cognition" did not appear in the original edition (1969) of *The Romantic Manifesto*. First published in *The Objectivist* (April–June 1971), it was reprinted in the second, revised paperback edition of *The Romantic Manifesto* in 1975.

2. According to Kristeller, "the irreducible nucleus of the modern system of the [fine] arts" consists of "the five major arts of painting, sculpture, architecture, music and poetry." "Modern System of the Arts," in *Renaissance Thought and the Arts*, 164–65. This classification corresponds to Rand's in all but two respects. First, Kristeller refers only to poetry (he subsequently notes that theater, opera, eloquence, and prose literature "are sometimes added," along with gardening, engraving, and the decorative arts). In contrast, Rand clearly includes fiction and drama (as forms of imaginative literature) among the arts. She also differs from Kristeller in being somewhat equivocal on the status of architecture, as we shall see.

That the term *fine arts* appears nowhere in Rand's essays on art is perhaps significant. Since it is intimately associated with the eighteenth-century's emphasis on the creation of *beauty* as the principal purpose of art (as indicated by the original French term, *beaux arts*, "beautiful arts"), it has misleading connotations. For this reason, we avoid using the term wherever possible. See our further discussion of this concept in Chapter 10.

3. Although Rand here refers only to "abstractions" in the acquisition of knowledge, her developed theory of epistemology assigns an important role to perception as well. Rand adds that art also "tells man, in effect, which aspects of his experience are to be regarded as essential, significant, important" and "teaches [him] how to use his consciousness"—a claim that appears to undercut, however unwittingly, her emphatic declaration in "The Psycho-Epistemology of Art" that "art is not the means to any didactic end." (22)

4. We omit the adjective "physical," which Rand employs in error here. The medium of literature—language—is not *physical*, properly speaking. See Ch. 5, n. 2.

5. Rand declares that "the future of sculpture depends to a large extent on the future of architecture," since "one of its most effective functions is to serve as architectural ornament." (50) Her statement gives short shrift to the role of free-standing sculpture in both public and private settings not dependent on architecture, however; it also blurs the distinction between sculptural art and "ornament."

6. Rand defined an entity as "that which you can perceive and which can exist by itself," as contrasted with "[c]haracteristics, qualities, attributes, actions, [and] relationships" which "do not exist by themselves." *Introduction to Objectivist Epistemology*, 264. In *The Evidence of the Senses*, which develops a realist theory of perception based on Rand's epistemology, David Kelley extends the concept of an entity to include nonsolid objects of sensory perception such as sounds and smells (45–46)—an extension which has important implications for Rand's analysis of musical perception, which we discuss in Chapter 5.

7. By "entities themselves," we do not mean Kant's concept of "things in themselves," but simply physical objects located in space, which constitute the primary objects of perception for any living organism.

8. Rand, *Objectivist Epistemology*, 5. The fundamentality of visual and tactile perception in human cognition, we might add, is revealed by the metaphorical roots of numerous idioms signifying understanding—for example: "to have in*sight*," "I *see* what you mean," "to *grasp*," "*seeing* is believing."

9. Rand readily acknowledged that poetry was a subject about which she knew little and which did not interest her. When asked on one occasion to name her favorite poets, she replied: "I am not an admirer of poetry. I react to it only [on a] sense-of-life [basis]. I have no particular theories about it, or very few." She subsequently characterized Swinburne and the Russian Symbolist Aleksandr Blok as "magnificent poets" despite their "ghastly" sense of life—an esthetic judgment that suggests an implicit theory, however. She also noted that she admired the poems of Kipling, "both in form and . . . in content." Question period following Lecture 11 of Peikoff, *Philosophy of Objectivism*. As Stephen Halliwell observes, Aristotle, too, paid little attention to lyric poetry, instead valuing dramatic and, secondarily, narrative poetry. *Aristotle's Poetics*, 68–69, 128, and Ch. 8.

10. Rand's analysis of fiction in "Basic Principles of Literature" is based on a series of twelve informal private lectures on fiction-writing she delivered in her home to friends and acquaintances. The lectures have recently been published as *The Art of Fiction*, edited by Tore Boeckmann. But this edition cannot be relied on as an accurate transcript of the lectures, since it incorporates substantial revisions (beyond eliminating the "awkwardness, . . . repetition, . . . obscurities, and . . . grammatical lapses" noted by Leonard Peikoff in his Introduction). For a critique of Boeckmann's textual changes, see Chris Matthew Sciabarra, "Orthodox Interpretations of Ayn Rand," *Full Context*, January-February 2000; online at <http://www.nyu.edu/projects/sciabarra/essays/oioar.htm>.

11. Rand's usage is consistent with Thrall, Hibbard, and Holman's definition of *fiction* as "[n]arrative writing drawn from the imagination of the author rather than from history or fact," and with their observation that the term "is most frequently associated with novels and short stories, though drama and narrative poetry are also forms of *fiction*."

12. Stephen Cox, "Literary Theory," IOS Study Guide #6, published by the Institute for Objectivist Studies (now The Objectivist Center), Poughkeepsie, N.Y.,1994.

13. Harry Binswanger writes, for example, in a further distortion of Aristotle: "The credo of the Romantic school of art is Aristotle's principle that art presents life as it 'could be and ought to be.'" "Ayn Rand's Philosophic Achievement," Part 4, *The Objectivist Forum*, December 1992, 7. Note that Binswanger not only mistakenly extends Aristotle's alleged principle to include all art, he also refers, misleadingly in this context, to the "Romantic school of *art*," although, as we have argued, Rand's definition of Romanticism applies only to literature. See "Romanticism and Naturalism," in Chapter 1, above.

14. On Rand's misquotation of Aristotle, see Stephen Cox, "Ayn Rand: Theory versus Creative Life," *Journal of Libertarian Studies* 8 (1986): 20; and Torres and Kamhi, "Ayn Rand's Philosophy of Art," *Aristos*, September 1992, 6. We attribute Rand's error to carelessness or wishful thinking, not to deliberate misrepresentation.

15. Rand refers to "fiction" (a modern term), where Aristotle uses the Greek word for "poetry," since all types of imaginative literature (dramatic as well as narrative) were in poetic form in antiquity.

16. Aristotle, *Poetics* (tr. McKeon), Ch. 9, emphasis ours. Rand's misquotation of this passage seems to echo the interpretation (but not the translation) proposed by S. H. Butcher in *Aristotle's Theory of Poetry and Fine Art*, esp. 151ff.

17. According to Aristotle: "The poet being an imitator just like the painter or other maker of likenesses, he must necessarily in all instances represent things in one or other of three aspects, either as they were or are, or as they are said or thought to be or to have been, or as they ought to be." Later in the same chapter, Aristotle adds: "If the poet's description be criticized as not true to fact, one may urge perhaps that the object *ought to be* as described—an answer like that [given by] Sophocles, who said that he drew men as they ought to be, [while] Euripides [drew them] as they were. If the description, however, be neither true nor of the thing as it ought to be, the answer must be then, that it is in accordance with opinion." *Poetics* (tr. McKeon), Ch. 25, emphasis ours.

18. We would argue, however, that such a work may not merely be a "bad novel" (as Rand states); it may not be a novel, in the sense of literary art, at all.

19. Aristotle *Poetics* (tr. Butcher), Ch. 6. Aristotle further emphasized (*ibid.*) that "without action there cannot be a tragedy."

20. Rand's definition is more precise than, for example, E. M. Forster's: "A plot is . . . a narrative of events, the emphasis falling on causality." *Aspects of the Novel*, 86. In any case, the principle of logical causality is central to both Rand's and Forster's concept, as well as to the discussion of plot in Thrall, Hibbard, and Holman's *Handbook to Literature*, which emphasizes that the actions of a plot progress "through a logically related sequence to a logical and natural outcome." (Rand's phrase "the resolution of a climax" is confusing, however. Whereas *resolution*—also termed *dénouement* or "falling action"—usually refers to the events following the climax, her syntax could mean that the resolution is *part of* the climax.) The principle of logical connection between the events of a plot is also implicit in Aristotle's oft-cited analysis (*Poetics*, Ch. 7) of a proper "beginning, middle, and end" in tragedy.

21. Contrary to Aristotle, Rand properly applies the concept of *final causation* only to conscious beings capable of choosing goals and taking the actions necessary to achieve them. "Causality Versus Duty," in *Philosophy*, 99.

22. In contrast with Rand's emphasis on essentials, Thrall, Hibbard, and Holman vaguely define characterization as the "creation of images of . . . imaginary persons so credible that they exist for the reader as real within the limits of the fiction[al] story]."

23. On *characterization*, Thrall, Hibbard, and Holman (81) similarly observe: "Ultimately every successful character represents a fusion of the universal and the particular and becomes an example of the *concrete universal*." As they further explain: "Our minds may delight in abstractions and ideas, but it is our emotions that ultimately give the aesthetic and dramatic response, and they respond to the personal, the particular, the concrete. This is why a novel speaks to us more permanently than an allegory."

24. Rand's emphasis on dialogue as well as action in characterization is significant. Surprisingly, Thrall, Hibbard, and Holman do not include dialogue among the "three fundamental methods of *characterization* in fiction." Aristotle, however, does refer, in discussing the creation of fictional characters, to "how a person of a certain type will . . . speak or act." *Poetics* (tr. Butcher), Ch. 9.

25. E. M. Forster, too, argues that a fictional character becomes "real" only when the novelist knows everything about him, and that the novelist's function is to reveal the character's "hidden life at its source." *Aspects of the Novel*, 45ff. Unlike Rand, however, Forster refers mainly to the emotional dimensions of that life, rather than to its "basic premises and values," which she emphasizes as the source of emotions.

26. Since *style* is "the means by which the other three [elements] are presented," it, too, must be thoroughly integrated with them. Rand, "Basic Principles of Literature," 94, 80.

27. According to Rand's theory of perception, human beings normally experience sensations not as isolated phenomena but, rather, as aspects or attributes of perceptual entities. She defined a *perception* as "a group of sensations automatically retained and integrated by the brain of a living organism, which gives it the ability to be aware, not of single stimuli, but of *entities*, of things." "The Objectivist Ethics," in *Virtue of Selfishness*, 10. On Rand's concept of *entities*, however, see above, n. 6.

28. Music, like "abstract art," does not represent objects or entities. As we will argue in Chapter 5, however, it does not "reduce" the auditory field to "mere sense data" but, rather, integrates sounds into meaningful combinations.

29. Note that Rand's use of the term *abstraction* differs markedly from its use in the term "abstract art"; see Ch. 8, n. 1.

30. Rand's idea that visual art mirrors the process of concept-formation bears comparison with the psychologist J. J. Gibson's theory of pictorial representation, which we discuss in Chapter 7.

31. Painter, teacher, and critic R. H. Ives Gammell (1893–1981) offers a more instructive view than Rand's regarding the goals of impressionism. He explains that, whereas the ordinary person tends to see things "in a series of piecemeal observa-

tions," the impressionist painter "grasps the scene before him as a whole and seeks to transcribe to his canvas the impression which that entity makes upon him." In contrast, the literal realist "paints his vision of each separate object and his picture ends up as a compilation of separate observations which are in reality incompatible. That is to say, no human eye could see at one time all of those objects with an equal degree of definition and coloration." Gammell further argues that "the great original contribution of the nineteenth-century impressionists lay in their full realization of our perception of color and all its implications for the painter's art," but that they did not seek "to make an exaggerated statement of the individual painter's optical reactions." *Twilight of Painting*, 84, 89, 82. See also Kamhi, "Gammell."

32. Striking instances of inlaid work to simulate eyes are extant in several ancient Greek bronzes—most notably, the splendid fifth-century "Charioteer" of Delphi.

33. In the case of all but the simplest objects, an entity can be recognized from its basic form or outline alone. Only in the case of simple geometric shapes or forms—a spherical object, say—is color or texture (and relative size within a given context) an essential clue to identification. Regarding the greater importance of form than color in painting, see also Aristotle's observation that "the most beautiful colours laid on without order will not give one the same pleasure as a simple black-and-white sketch of a portrait." *Poetics* (tr. McKeon), Ch. 6.

34. On the comparative merits of painting and sculpture, the Florentine sculptor Benvenuto Cellini argued that "the art of sculpture is eight times as great as any other based on drawing, because a statue has eight views and they must all be equally good." Letter to Benedetto Varchi, 28 January 1547, in Goldwater and Treves, *Artists on Art*, 87.

35. Considerations of the distinctive characteristics and relative virtues of the various art forms (in particular, of poetry and painting) have a long history. The most famous treatise of this kind is Gotthold Lessing's *Laocoon*. See also E. H. Gombrich, "The Diversity of the Arts: The Place of the *Laocoon* in the Life and Work of G. E. Lessing (1729–1781)," in *Tributes*, 28-49.

36. For "a discussion of sculpture's means" of expressing a view of existence, Rand refers readers to an article by Mary Ann Sures, "Metaphysics in Marble," *The Objectivist*, February and March 1969. That article does not discuss the sculptural medium as such, however; rather, it expands on a thesis Rand briefly articulated in "The Psycho-Epistemology of Art" and "Art and Sense of Life"—arguing that a particular "metaphysical view of man" is discernible in the characteristic way the human figure is rendered in sculpture in various eras. Sures makes the mistake of interpreting the work of vastly different cultures from a narrowly ahistorical, contemporary Western perspective. In focusing on what she characterizes as the ancient Egyptians' "obsessive preoccupation with life after death," for instance, she ignores the well-documented fact that it grew out of their love of life on earth and their wish to extend its pleasures into eternity—positive values clearly reflected in their art. See, for example, Barbara Sewell, *Egypt Under the Pharaohs* (which begins: "The Ancient Egyptians loved life."); and the Introduction to Lange and Hirmer, *Egypt*.

37. See Michael Richman, *Daniel Chester French*; Beatrice Proske, "Harriet Whitney Frishmuth: Lyric Sculptor," *Aristos*, April 1984; Kamhi, "Anna Hyatt

Huntington's 'Joan of Arc,'" *Aristos*, March 1988; and John H. Dryfhout, *The Work of Augustus Saint-Gaudens*, esp. 253–58.

38. By "primary arts," Rand means literature, music, painting, and sculpture. Of these, only literature and music serve as the basis for the performing arts.

39. As we argue later in this chapter, dance does more than merely "translate" music into existential action. Rand also states, somewhat inaccurately, that in the performing arts "the medium employed is the person of the artist." (64) More accurately, the *instrument* employed is the person of the artist (in all the performing arts but nonvocal music, in which the musician actually performs upon an instrument); the *media* employed are words and movement, in acting; pitched sound, in music; and movement, in dance.

40. To clarify the distinction between a circus performer and a performing artist, Rand explains: "The performance of an aerialist, for instance, demands an enormous physical skill—greater, perhaps, and harder to acquire than the skill demanded of a ballet dancer—but what it offers is merely an exhibition of that skill, with no further meaning"; it is merely "a concrete," not a concretization of an abstraction. (71) Ironically, since Rand wrote that statement, the concept of art has become so debased that one liberal arts college has offered a "circus arts" course for "fine art" credit. See Kamhi and Torres, "Revaluing the Liberal Arts." See also our discussion of circus-like entertainments in Chapter 12.

41. Rand neglects to mention that performing artists are sometimes called upon to supply even more substantial instances of their own creativity. As Stephen Davies observes, the indications provided by the primary artist are often minimal. "To the extent that performers, in presenting the work, must go beyond that with which they are provided by the work's creator, performance is essentially creative." In Cooper, *Companion to Aesthetics, s.v.* "performance." Such creativity is especially important in the improvisatory passages of many musical works of the baroque and early classical periods, as well as in jazz, which is largely improvisatory.

42. Complex issues are involved in determining the primary artist's intended meaning and in effectively realizing it for an audience. Though such issues are not considered by Rand, they have been discussed at length by other writers. As those writers emphasize, the further removed a performer (and his audience) is from the culture in which a given work was created, the greater the difficulties of interpretation. On this issue, see, for example, Dipert, *Artifacts, Art Works, and Agency*, Ch. 11; and Davies, in Cooper, *s.v.* "performance."

43. Rand's view of dance as dependent on music (and not among what she considers to be the "primary arts") offers a logical answer to a long-standing question of esthetics regarding the proper classification of this art form. While some theorists hold that dance is, as David Best has asserted, "a fine art in its own right" (*Expression in Movement and the Arts,* xii), Francis Sparshott has observed that, historically, it "was not generally considered one of the fine arts" (*Off the Ground,* 32). Aristotle and other early thinkers did consider dance among the "imitative arts," however—which some later writers equated with the "fine arts." See *Poetics* (cited below, n. 47); and Abbé Charles Batteux, *Les Beaux Arts,* 78, 86–87. Perhaps the exclusion of dance from the "fine arts" by many later theorists was owing to their sense that (as Rand argues) it is not a self-sufficient form of artistic expression.

44. Regarding Rand's problematical view of how music "presents a stylized version of man's consciousness in action," see our discussion in Chapter 5.

45. Rand similarly proposes that music "presents an abstraction of man's emotions in the context of his cognitive processes." Although her phrase "in the context of" is even less clear here than in her parallel proposition about dance, it is important to note that her proper stress on the emotional content of music in this passage belies the emphasis she places on its purely *epistemological* significance in her analysis of music, which we critique in Chapter 5.

46. Rand's full characterization of the goal of dance reads: "the projection of metaphysical value-judgments, the stylization of man's movements by the continuous power of a fundamental emotional state—and thus the use of man's body to express his sense of life." (67) In summarizing her statement, we omitted her reference to "metaphysical value-judgments," because we consider that "sense of life" better conveys what is involved in dance. See, further, our discussion of Rand's definition of art, in Chapter 6.

47. Aristotle notes that it is by "rhythmical movement" that the dancer "imitates character, emotion, and action." *Poetics* (tr. Butcher), Ch. 1. The various dictionaries and encyclopedias we have consulted—ranging from the definitive *Oxford English Dictionary* to the *World Book Dictionary* (intended for school children)—all cite rhythm as a defining attribute of dance. See also Rand's observation, in relation to tap dancing, that rhythm is the "common element crucial to music and to man's body." (69) Nonetheless, Sparshott argued in the first of his two volumes on the philosophy of dance: "Dance is [simply] the art of meaningful movement. . . . Saying that such movement must be inherently musical or rhythmical adds little or nothing." *Off the Ground*, 151. For his subsequent equivocations on this point, see below, Ch. 12, nn. 82 and 89.

48. Fokine's *Les Sylphides* is set to music by Chopin; MacMillan's *Romeo and Juliet*, to Prokofiev's score for the ballet.

49. Norman dello Joio, in "Composer/Choreographer: A Symposium" (1963), reprinted in Cobbett Steinberg, *Dance Anthology* (143)—an invaluable collection of essays by critics, philosophers, and others. For additional examples illustrative of the complex relationship between music and dance, see our discussion in Chapter 12.

50. Gunther Schuller, "Composer/Choreographer" (cited above, n. 49,), 144. Schuller cites Balanchine's *Episodes*, set to music by Anton Webern, as a remarkable example of the extra dimension added by choreography at its best.

51. Dello Joio, *ibid.*, 141–42. Further testimony is offered by William Carter, who describes how Graham worked with him on the role of the minister in *Letter to the World* (her work based on the life and poetry of Emily Dickinson): "We were in a studio, alone, with the pianist, and she said, 'All right, let's hear the music,' and she put both hands over her face, I guess to block out any exterior interferences, and she tilted her head down, closing her eyes, and she listened to the music. Then she said, 'Could I hear it again, please?' And she listened again, and I suppose certain images must have come to mind, and she said, 'Try doing this,' and she demonstrated." Quoted by Tobi Tobias, "Bill Carter: An Interview," *Dance Magazine*, June

1975, 56. See also Carter's views which we cite in our discussion of "Dance: The 'Silent Partner of Music'" in Chapter 12.

52. If Rand's categorical rejection of "random movements" would (as we suspect) have excluded from the realm of dance a work such as Paul Taylor's *Esplanade* (1975), we think her conception far too narrow. Though *Esplanade* contains no conventional dance movements, and employs only "natural" movements such as running, skipping, and sliding, the movement is *stylized*. Instead of using an established "system of motion," Taylor stylized everyday movement by extending and intensifying it, and by organizing it into dance rhythms and patterns. Most important, the dance is completely integrated with the music to which it is set (parts of the E major and d minor violin concertos by J. S. Bach), and is highly expressive in its own right: its allegro sections project the sheer energy and joyous exhilaration of youthful vitality, while the intervening slow movement is brooding and melancholic in feeling. *Esplanade* well merits its status as a classic of the modern dance repertoire. See *The Paul Taylor Dance Company* (video), which includes *Esplanade*. See also below, Ch. 12, n. 90.

53. As dance critic Don McDonagh has observed (in a book that is much more substantial than its modest title indicates), romantic ballets like these "exalted the passionate, emotional side of personal expression." *How to Enjoy Ballet*, 13–14.

54. Clarke and Vaughan, *Encyclopedia of Dance and Ballet, s.v.* "Romeo and Juliet." The pas de deux in the first scene of Act Three of MacMillan's ballet expresses the young lovers' ecstatic passion, while Romeo's agonized dance with the lifeless body of Juliet in the final scene projects the grief of love bereft by death. See, for example, the exquisite performance by Britain's Royal Ballet, starring Rudolf Nureyev and Margot Fonteyn, happily captured for posterity on film and video. While the choreography owes much of its expressive power to the revitalizing influence modern dance has had on classical ballet, it remains wholly within the ballet idiom.

55. Balanchine's *Bugaku*, for example, as well as his *Rubies* (the second act of *Jewels*), also project sexuality.

56. Regarding Hindu dance, what Rand views as "an image of man as infinitely pliable," for example, may actually represent deities possessing extraordinary powers. Her further claim that it cannot express "positive emotions" such as "joy or triumph" (68) is also inaccurate. According to the *Natya Shastra*—the primary manual on traditional Indian dance, drama, and music (the three art forms were long considered inseparable)—eight sentiments, or emotional states, can be expressed: love, humor, pathos, anger, heroism, terror, disgust, and wonder. See R. Massey, "Asia," in Clarke and Vaughan, 26; and R. Massey and J. Massey, *Dances of India*, esp. xiv and xvii. Contrary to Rand, the latter source also cites a type of dance, called *Ananda*, which expresses joy (xiv).

57. Though Rand implies that the music for tap dance is continuous, extended passages of tap in performance are often driven only by the dancer's inner rhythmic sense.

58. Rand remarks that tap dancing "is of American Negro origin" (68)—a claim that is correct in spirit, if not in detail. In its developed form, tap dancing owes its expressive characteristics mainly to the syncopated rhythms and freedom of move-

ment derived from African tribal dance. But its percussive nature derives from European clog and step dancing. See James H. Siegelman, "Tap Dancing," in Clarke and Vaughan, 332. Siegelman defines tap as "a style of dance in which the percussive sound of the footwork is the distinguishing characteristic." He also implies that, as we would argue, it is a form of entertainment, not art.

59. Dance critic Joan Acocella, too, notes that tap "has been a limited form," and also calls attention to its "traditional elegance and gaiety." "On Tap," review of *Bring in 'da Noise, Bring in 'da Funk, New York Review of Books*, 6 June 1996, 4. In recent years, tap dancer Sabian Glover (the star of that show) has employed the form to express a more somber, dramatic mood, however.

60. Postmodernist theater is replete with examples of the sort of directorial "vision" that strays too far from the original work. Peter Sellars's setting of Mozart's *Così fan Tutte* in a diner is but one such example.

61. Rand's emphasis on the visual aspect of film is perhaps more appropriate to silent films than to those with sound. In the latter, dialogue (and, therefore, the screenplay) becomes far more important than visual effects in carrying the story. For further discussion, see Chapter 13.

62. Although Rand is correct in arguing that feature films are dependent for their substance on a literary text (the screenplay), she may be somewhat off the mark in considering the screenplay a species of drama. As Susanne Langer suggests, the structure of film is closer to narrative fiction than to drama. "A Note on the Film," in *Feeling and Form*, 411–15. See Chapter 13.

63. In regard to opera, however, Rand held that the primary "esthetic base" is music, not the libretto. "Art and Cognition," 71. By that she no doubt meant that the music, both instrumental and vocal, is the predominant element in projecting the emotional and thematic core of the opera—the greatest works of which (as she would probably have agreed) have strong librettos as well as superb musical scores.

64. Rand does not define what she means by "modern art." She uses the term loosely and idiosyncratically to refer to twentieth-century genres that she has previously argued do not qualify as art—such as "non-objective" (abstract) painting and sculpture, and "music" that has been reduced to noise (i.e., that is "made of sounds produced by anything"). *Romantic Manifesto*,128, 64, 78. We prefer to use the terms *modernist* and *modernism* in that pejorative sense, and reserve the adjective *modern* for work that rejects the *conventions* of traditional art, but not the fundamental characteristics of art itself. Thus we refer to the choreography of Martha Graham, for example, as "modern," not "modernist."

65. The anti-conceptual animus of radical modernists has often been quite explicit. The painter Jean Dubuffet, for instance, while never embracing total abstraction, nonetheless claimed: "I break down the partitions raised by the mind . . . between different systems of objects, between different registers of facts and of things, and the different levels of thought." Cited in Robert Payne, *World of Art*, 512. Dubufett's crude, often brutal work imitated *graffiti* and the inchoate art of young children and the insane. Payne observes that Dubuffet "produced paintings deliberately intended to be senseless" and that he "pronounced a sentence of death on all human values." On Payne's insightful survey of art, see Kamhi, "Robert Payne."

66. Even critics sympathetic to, or tolerant of, abstract painting confirm, however inadvertently, Rand's charge that such work reduces consciousness "to the level of sensations." Hilton Kramer, for example, has written of the abstract work of Morris Louis: "The eye is ravished by an experience of color. . . . There is nothing 'hidden' or mysterious in these paintings and nothing metaphysical in our experience of them. They capture the eye . . . and hold it by eliminating everything but a naked appeal to the kind of optical pleasure that color, and color alone, can offer." *Revenge of the Philistines*, 201. In another vein, Kay Larson, reviewing a retrospective exhibition of Robert Ryman's lifelong output of virtually blank all-white canvases, has objected to his "expectation that the eye, stripped of all the distractions urged on it by the mind, offers an experience rich enough to sustain itself through . . . 30-odd years of patient elaboration"—though she does not, as we do, exclude Ryman's work from the category of art. "A Paler Shade of White," *New York*, 11 October 1993. For further discussion of "abstract art," see Chapter 8.

67. Rand's apparent implication that all "modern" artists have been anti-conceptual in their *intent* is mistaken. As she herself subsequently observes, most practitioners of "modern art" probably do not grasp its true nature. Indeed, over the years, numerous practitioners and advocates have promulgated elaborate, if ill-founded, theories ascribing high intellectual purpose and spiritual significance to modernist work. For examples, see Chapter 8.

68. E. H. Gombrich, *The Story of Art*, 15. On the "institutional theory" of art, see our Chapter 6.

69. John Cage, "On Robert Rauschenberg, Artist, and His Work" (1961), in *Silence*, 101.

70. John Cage, "Composition as Process" (1958), in *Silence*, 51; and "Lecture on Nothing" (1959), *ibid.*, 109. As the most influential practitioner of "aleatory music," Cage epitomizes the anti-rational, anti-conceptual character of the "avant-garde." For more on Cage, see Chapter 12.

71. Samuel Beckett (in *Disjecta*, ed. Ruby Cohn [New York: Grove Press, 1984]), quoted by Morris Dickstein, "An Outsider in His Own Life," *New York Times Book Review*, 3 August 1997.

72. Among other honors, Cage delivered the prestigious Charles Eliot Norton Lectures on art at Harvard in 1988; he was the subject of a respectful "American Masters" documentary on public television; and he was a member of the American Academy of Arts and Letters—perhaps this country's highest nongovernmental recognition of artistic merit.

Chapter 5   Music and Cognition

1. Rand states that "the other arts create a physical object (i.e., an object perceived by [the] senses, be it a book or a painting)," misleadingly implying that the work of literary art consists of the physical book as such. We regard this as a careless misstatement, not to be taken literally. Rand surely knew that what one "perceives" (in the imagination) in the act of reading fiction, are the concrete characters, events, and other phenomena described in the text, not the book itself. As one critic

has observed: "[T]he physicality [of books] dissipates in our hands as we engage with . . . the speech and actions of their characters. Once a book is begun, . . . its material presence is largely overlooked. Reading *Crime and Punishment*, we see [in our imagination] Raskolnikov's axe rather than the typeface." Oliver Reynolds, "Reading the Leaves," review of "Artists' Books" Exhibition at the Tate Gallery, London, *Times Literary Supplement*, 15 September 1995. Reynolds's reference to "see[ing] Raskolnikov's axe" should not be taken too literally either, however, since in the course of reading fiction, one does not pause to visualize every detail.

2. Rand's view of the difference between music and the other arts has precedents in nineteenth-century thought, with which her early education in Russia very likely familiarized her. (Regarding that education, see our Introduction, Ch. 2, n. 14, and Ch. 15, n. 85; and Sciabarra, *Ayn Rand*, Ch. 3.) The Austrian dramatic poet Franz Grillparzer argued (*Complete Works*, 9:142.), for example, that the "essential difference between music and poetry [i.e., literature]" is that "music primarily affects the senses and, after rousing the emotions, reaches the intellect last of all. Poetry, on the other hand, first raises up an idea which in its turn excites the emotions, while it affects the senses only as an extreme result. . . . They, therefore, pursue an exactly opposite course, for one spiritualizes the material, whereas the other materializes the spiritual." Grillparzer is approvingly quoted by Eduard Hanslick (*Beautiful in Music*, trans. Cohen, 8*n*1).

3. Regarding the importance of such a nonverbal mode of cognition, see our discussion of mimesis in Chapter 7.

4. See n. 14, below.

5. For a view combining elements of both cognitive and arousal theories, see n. 16, below.

6. On the arousal side, Rand declares, for instance, not only that music "induces an emotional state" (51) and that it is experienced "as if it had the power to reach man's emotions directly" (50) but also that it "evokes . . . emotions" (54), and that the listener "experiences an emotion without existential object" (57). On the cognitive side, she states that "emotions [are] projected by the music" (51); that "men hear the same emotional content in a given piece of music" (60–61); and that "one grasps the suggestion of a certain emotional state" (53). For a discussion of "arousal" theories, see Peter Kivy, *Corded Shell*, Chs. 3 and 4; and *Music Alone*, Ch. 3; and Stephen Davies, *Musical Meaning*, 184–99. For various cognitive views, see *Corded Shell*, *passim*; *Music Alone*, esp. Chs. 5, 8, and 9; and Davies, 221–240.

7. We omit Rand's clause "it [music] cannot deal with concretes," which could be misleading. In an earlier passage, she states that music "does not deal with entities." (46) The term *concretes* (in contrast with *entities*), in Rand's usage, does not signify "physical objects" but, rather, *the referents of any concept*, however abstract or intangible—including emotions. *Introduction to Objectivist Epistemology*, 156–58; see also Kelley, *Art of Reasoning*, 14–15. The category *concretes* therefore subsumes the sort of mental and emotional phenomena music does "deal with," in the sense of "have to do with" or "pertain to."

As we suggested in Chapter 4, Rand at times misleadingly implies that all art must present *entities*, rather than *concretes*. Art must indeed "concretize" abstractions, or universals, by presenting particular instances; those instances (*concretes*) need not be limited to solid entities, however. Rand herself seems to imply this distinction in "The Psycho-Epistemology of Art" when she observes: "Abstractions as such do not exist: they are merely man's epistemological method of perceiving [i.e., grasping] that which exists—and that which exists is concrete." (23)

In a chapter entitled "The Myth of Storytelling in Music," the conductor David Randolph—for many years an inspiring teacher of music appreciation at the New School in New York City—argues that "an approach based on the alleged storytelling or descriptive powers of music is not only misleading, it is actually harmful, in that it encourages the listener to look and listen for the wrong satisfactions." *This Is Music*, 29.

8. The full title of Liszt's composition is "St. Francis de Paul Walking on the Waters," from his *Deux Légendes*. The view Rand expresses in this passage may be compared to that of J. W. N. Sullivan—a mathematician and a philosopher of science as well as a music critic and amateur pianist—who argued that music can express neither philosophic nor scientific ideas nor religious beliefs; rather, it can suggest only the "states of consciousness" arising from such thoughts. *Beethoven*, 34–35 and 81–83.

Regrettably, Rand did not always honor this principle, however. In response to a question following one of her lectures which Louis Torres attended at the Ford Hall Forum in Boston in the 1970s, for example, she wrongheadedly asserted that the music of Beethoven projected a sense of life diametrically opposed to that projected by her novels—one which reflected "*man's struggle against his own destiny, and his defeat,*" an interpretation that is not only too philosophically explicit to be expressed in music but that also belies the predominant spirit of Beethoven's music and its inspiring effect on most listeners. In contrast, Sullivan (167) characterizes the spiritual content of Beethoven's most representative and best-known work as "achievement through heroism in spite of suffering"—a characterization which, though itself perhaps too specific, surely comes closer to the heart of the music.

9. Rand's terms in this passage are less than precise. For "convey," we would substitute "suggest." And we would characterize *serenity, defiance,* and *exaltation* as states of mind, rather than "emotions." We would also argue that "*dedicated* struggle" (emphasis ours) is, no less than "revolution," too specific a concept to be expressed musically.

10. Kivy, *Corded Shell*, 56; and *Music Alone*, 176.

11. Langer, *Feeling and Form*, 27, emphasis ours. Davies observes that music "presents emotion characteristics. . . . [W]e experience the dynamic character of music as like the actions of a person; movement is heard in music, and [it] is heard as purposive and as rationally organized. . . . [Since] the composer contrives and controls the expressiveness of the music . . . music can properly be understood as referring to, or being about, the world of human feelings." *Musical Meaning*, 277.

12. If by a "piece of music" Rand means an entire composition, regardless of its length, her statement can be somewhat misleading, since most compositions of more than brief duration contain contrasting passages or movements that differ greatly in their emotive tenor, and would therefore be difficult to characterize with such simple adjectives as "gay or sad or violent or solemn." If her statement is taken to refer

to such passages or movements (or to very brief works), however, it is no doubt valid. As reported by John Sloboda, various studies show that, "by and large, adults in a given culture agree on the broad characterization of a musical passage." "Empirical Studies of Emotional Responses to Music," in Jones and Holleran, *Cognitive Bases of Musical Communication*, 36. See also Kivy, *Corded Shell*, 60.

13. In a subsequent passage, Rand more accurately indicates that music conveys the "suggestion of . . . emotional state[s]." (53) Randolph similarly observes that music "is a means of communication of emotional states." *This Is Music*, 27.

14. Rand's view that the listener's emotional response ultimately depends on a personal affinity with the composer's musical expression has been adumbrated by other authors. For example, Deryck Cooke notes: "People can only react to the emotions expressed in a work of art according to their own capacity to feel those emotions." *Language of Music*, 21. Similarly, Aaron Copland observes: "A masterwork awakens in us reactions of a spiritual order that are already in us, only waiting to be aroused." *Music and Imagination*, 26. And Alan Walker refers to "a highly selective principle at work . . . which predetermines our basic responses toward music . . . a principle of unconscious identification." *Anatomy of Musical Criticism*, 89. Finally, Schonberg observes that in the appreciation of any art (including music, of course) "the responder's identification with the mental processes of the [artist] is critical: the closer the identity, the greater the appreciation." *Lives of the Great Composers,* 46.

15. Although Rand sometimes seems to imply that perception and conception are entirely separate phases of cognition, Davies's observation regarding their interrelationship probably comes close to Rand's own view of a mature consciousness at work. According to Davies, "perception itself is irreducibly cognitive; . . . seeing or hearing is a thoughtful experience. . . . We do not (always) perceive things *before* bringing them under concepts; (usually) we perceive them under concepts from the outset. The eyes and ears are educated by experience. We see tables and chairs, not uninterpreted patches of color, even if we do not say to ourselves as we see that it is tables and chairs we see." *Musical Meaning*, 335.

16. Note that Rand's initial verb, "conveys," suggests a cognitive view of the expressive quality of music, while her subsequent verb, "experience," misleadingly implies an arousal view. See above, n. 6. What she seems to mean by "experience" in this context, however, is "grasp" or "understand," perhaps implying a degree of empathy as well. Rand may be assuming a two-step process: in the first step, listeners who hold widely divergent views of life would subconsciously "grasp" the same emotional content in the music, but the subsequent full-blown emotional response of each would vary according to the individual's sense of life.

17. Note that Rand here refers to "grasp[ing] the suggestion of a certain emotional state"—a phrase more appropriate than her previous claim that music "conveys emotions." See also Sullivan's reference to music as expressive of "states of consciousness," cited above, n. 8.

18. Similarly, Hanslick observed that the listener's "imaginative faculty" might supply the requisite "concrete notions and conceptions" to transform "an indefinite feeling" into "a definite one." *Beautiful in Music* (tr. Cohen), Ch. 2; in Kennick, *Art and Philosophy*, 191–92.

19. Rand implies that this subconscious process occurs *because* the listener "knows" (at least implicitly) "that he cannot experience an actually causeless and objectless emotion." (51) We would argue that such a process need not depend on "knowledge" of this kind, however. Instead, the subconscious perception of the emotive character of the music might act as a direct stimulus, or "trigger"—perhaps by activating areas of the brain in which analogous emotionally charged memories or assocations are stored. Indeed, neurological research suggests that just such a triggering process may be one mechanism involved in the generation of emotion. See Joseph E. LeDoux, "Emotion, Memory and the Brain," *Scientific American*, June 1994, 50–57; and *Emotional Brain*.

20. Jacques Barzun similarly suggests that, when we listen to music, a multitude of "associations" and "other influences stream through our consciousness along with the stream of sound." "The Meaning of Meaning in Music," in *Critical Questions*, 92.

21. Ironically, Rand's claim is not borne out by her own musical tastes. She had little use for baroque music—its complexity and intricacies notwithstanding—and she loved the simple, lighthearted strains of certain popular songs of her youth, which she affectionately referred to as her "tiddlywink music." See B. Branden, *Passion of Ayn Rand*, 7–8, 46, and 386.

22. Since Rand also maintains that musical integration "is a physiological process . . . performed unconsciously and automatically," and that one "is aware of the process only by means of its results" (57), it is not at all clear in what sense one can be said to "experience" the process itself.

23. For an understanding of the errors in Rand's analysis of music in relation to the work of Helmholtz, we are indebted to Roger E. Bissell, who developed this point in an unpublished monograph, "Esthetics Objectively" (1971). See also his "Music and Cognition," *Journal of Ayn Rand Studies*, Fall 1999, 59–86. We disagree, however, with his emphasis on the cognitive (as contrasted with the emotional) aspect of musical experience, among other points.

24. In addition, Helmholtz praised Hanslick for having "triumphantly attacked the false standpoint of exaggerated sentimentality, from which it was fashionable to theorise on music," and for having emphasized "the simple elements of melodic movement." *On the Sensations of Tone*, 2. Though both writers objected to the Romantic tendency to assign specific narrative or depictive meaning to music, neither of them denied that it possesses emotionally suggestive qualities.

25. According to Bissell (see n. 23, above), Helmholtz's error in characterizing the experience of tones as "sensations" stems from his holding a *representational* (as opposed to a *realist*) theory of perception. (On the fundamental difference between these views of perception, see our discussion in Chapter 7.) Though Rand subscribed to a realist theory, she failed to note Helmholtz's error.

26. Rand herself refers (61) to the integration of sounds into a "musical entity" that "one perceive[s]."

27. Rand, question period following Lecture 11 of Peikoff, *Objectivism* (1976). Randolph observes that melody is the "subject matter" of music. *This Is Music*, 18.

28. *Webster's Third New International Dictionary*. *The New Grove Dictionary of Music* (1980) defines *melody* as "pitched sounds arranged in musical time in accordance with given cultural conventions and constraints." But the concise edition (1988) defines it, more clearly, as a "series of musical notes arranged in succession, in a particular rhythmic pattern, to form a recognizable unit." "Melody" is not synonymous with "tune," however, which properly refers to a simple melody that can be easily remembered and reproduced.

29. Rhythm is widely acknowledged to be an essential attribute of music. Randolph terms it "basic" (*This Is Music*, 14); and Copland, "essential" (*What to Listen for in Music,* 33). Langer observes that rhythm is the "most characteristic principle of vital activity" and argues that the essence of all musical composition is "the semblance of *organic* movement," which rhythm contributes to. *Feeling and Form*, 126.

30. Only at the end of her hypothetical analysis (61) does Rand make a passing reference to the "rhythmic characteristics" of music, and she subsequently notes that the scientific research necessary to prove her hypothesis would entail investigating, among other things, "the relationship of tones to rhythm."

31. By the same token, the enjoyment and appreciation of music requires no theoretical or technical knowledge. As Davies persuasively argues in the concluding chapter of *Musical Meaning*, depth of "musical understanding" (i.e., meaningful enjoyment) is not necessarily correlated with technical sophistication. Copland similarly observes that "[m]ere professionalism . . . is not at all a guarantee of intelligent listening. . . . The sensitive amateur, just because he lacks the prejudices and preconceptions of the professional musician, is sometimes a surer guide to the true quality of a piece of music." *Music and Imagination*, 19. In the same vein, Schoen cites the responses of a "professional musical listener," who suppresses the "intrasubjective and associative aspects, . . . all personal feelings, activities and imaginations, . . . in favour of the objective aspect, the critical, analytical standpoint." *Effects of Music*, 18. Randolph similarly argues that the serious "amateur listener," rather than the trained musician, "is most likely to experience the deepest enjoyment of a musical work." *This Is Music*, 10. The principle underlying these observations about music applies to *all* the arts, we would add.

32. H. Gardner, *Frames of Mind*, 126–27.

33. Contrary to Rand's claim that the "modern diatonic scale used in Western civilization is a product of the Renaissance" (63), diatonic music has far more ancient origins (see our discussion in Chapter 7), though it has had its fullest development in the West in the modern era.

34. An eloquent testament to the universality of Western music was the simultaneous performance of the "Ode to Joy" from Beethoven's Ninth Symphony by choruses in Beijing, Sydney, Cape Town, Berlin, and New York (at the United Nations) for the opening of the 1998 Winter Olympics.

35. While Rand's overly broad characterization of "primitive and most Oriental music" may suffer from cultural myopia, there is no doubt that some music can have a "narcotic effect" on the listener. Certain rates of drumming, for example, are thought to work in phase with the natural frequency of brain waves, thereby amplifying them and producing hallucinations and trancelike feelings of dissociation. Pfeiffer,

Creative Explosion, 212. Such an effect may also be relevant to the hypnotically boring effect of twentieth-century Western "minimalist" compositions—aptly dubbed
"wallpaper music" by composer and critic Virgil Thompson. On minimalism, see
Ch. 12.

36. Copland, *Music and Imagination*, 26. Copland adds "or that aspect of [the
composer's being] reflected in the particular work in question"—a qualification suggesting, as we did in Chapter 3, that even the most comprehensive work of art is of
finite scope.

37. Copland, *What to Listen for in Music*, 265; pb., 158.

38. Cooke adds that the emotions "expressed" in music must be woven into "an
intellectually and emotionally coherent statement," for the creation of all art "is guided
both by the feelings and the intellect." *Language of Music*, 31.

39. Storr, *Music and the Mind*, 186–87.

40. In considering Rand's conception of the composer's viewpoint, we would
be remiss if we failed to comment on a scene from *Atlas Shrugged* (781–84; pb.,
727–29)—depicting a conversation between the composer Richard Halley and the
novel's heroine, Dagny Taggart—which was excerpted, under the heading "The
Nature of an Artist," in *For the New Intellectual* (139–41; pb., 114–17). The excerpt
purportedly presents, in monologue form, the composer's views on the creative
process and on the sort of appreciation he wishes for his music. But Rand herself
acknowledged (in the first of her lectures on fiction-writing in 1958) that Halley's
speech actually represents her own thoughts as a novelist. If one were to re-read the
passage, substituting herself for Halley, and literature for music, she suggested, it
would provide considerable insight into the basic premises informing her own
approach to writing fiction. She was mistaken to attempt so literal a translation of
ideas from one art form to another, however. The sort of explicit identifications that
are appropriate to fiction are impossible in music. Any interpretation of the passage
must also consider that, in the context of the novel, it served more as an encomium
to the creativity of industrialists and businessmen than as a quasi philosophic explication of the artist/composer's viewpoint. Even so, it is surely one of the less felicitous passages in the novel. At one point, Halley characterizes the sort of artist who
relies on spontaneous inspiration as a "flabby, loose-mouthed, shifty-eyed, drool-
ing, shivering, uncongealed bastard!" whose work comes out of him "like vomit out
of a drunkard." At another, he exclaims "emotions be damned!" In any case, both
in its negation of emotion and in its insistence on "conscious judgment" and "rational
identification," the passage belies insights Rand subsequently brought to the subject of music in "Art and Cognition"—in particular, her emphasis on the role of
both subconscious and implicit emotional associations and integrations in musical
experience.

41. In discussing the characteristics of art in his *Introduction to Aesthetics* (50),
for example, George Dickie argues: "[I]t is impossible to show that every work of
art imitates; for example, much music and, by definition, nonobjective painting do
not imitate."

42. On the essential differences between music, painting, and literature, see
Barzun, "Meaning of Meaning in Music"; Cooke, *Language of Music*, Ch. 1; Davies,

Musical Meaning, Ch. 2; and Scruton, "Representation in Music," in *Aesthetic Understanding*, 62–76.

43. One obvious respect in which music can re-create reality is in the direct imitation of specific sounds of nature. Examples abound, such as the "thunder" of the kettle drums in the fourth movement of Beethoven's "Pastoral" Symphony, the song of birds simulated in Respighi's *Pines of Rome*, or the braying of an ass suggested in Mendelssohn's incidental music for *A Midsummer Night's Dream*. While such direct imitation has been felicitously exploited by many serious composers, it is a relatively trivial, incidental effect, not musical expression proper.

44. Detailed accounts of the mimetically expressive aspects of music can be found in Arnheim, "Perceptual Dynamics in Musical Expression," in *New Essays*, 214–27; Cooke, *Language of Music*, Ch. 2; Davies, *Musical Meaning*; and Kivy, *Corded Shell*.

45. According to Hanslick: "[M]usic is a kind of kaleidoscope, though its forms can be appreciated only by an infinitely higher ideation. . . . The main difference consists in the fact that the musical kaleidoscope is the direct product of creative mind, whereas the optic one is but a cleverly constructed mechanical toy." *Beautiful in Music* (tr. Cohen), Ch. 3; in Kennick, *Art and Philosophy*, 202.

46. See, for example, Andrew Kagan, who notes that through "the invention of new, purely instrumental forms, such as the symphony and concerto, divorced from song and dance," among other factors, music "was the first of the arts to be 'freed' . . . from th[e] Aristotelian task of imitating nature." "Ut Pictura Musica, I: to 1860," *Arts Magazine* 60 (May 1986): 87.

47. Storr, *Music and the Mind*, 67. Aristotle observed that, like epic poetry, tragedy, comedy, and dithyrambic (lyric) poetry, "the music of the flute and of the lyre in most of their forms are all in their general conception modes of imitation." *Poetics* (tr. Butcher), Ch. 1.

48. Susanne Langer attributes the phrase "felt life" to Henry James but does not cite a precise source in his work. *Feeling and Form*, 292; and *Problems of Art*, 48, 60, 67.

49. Hanslick, *Beautiful in Music*, Ch. 2; in Kennick, *Art and Philosophy*, 193, emphasis ours. Hanslick's music criticism clearly demonstrates that he was by no means insensitive to the emotive content of music. See, for example, his review of the première of the First Symphony of Brahms, quoted in Kivy, *Music Alone*, 185. The formalist emphasis in Hanslick's theoretical writing is best understood as a reaction against what he regarded as the excessively literal programmatic tendencies in nineteenth-century music (in particular, the theory and practice of Wagner), as well as against the then widely held arousalist view of emotional expression in music. See Morris Weitz, Introduction to *The Beautiful in Music*; and Malcom Budd, "Hanslick, Eduard," in Cooper, *Companion to Aesthetics*. Moreover, as its title indicates, Hanslick's treatise was primarily concerned with the *beauty* of music, not its *meaning*.

50. Regarding the shared neurological basis of motor and vocal components of emotional expression, see our discussion of Manfred Clynes's work in Ch. 7, n. 76.

51. In the early decades of the twentieth century, the psychologist Max Schoen investigated the "elusive changes in muscular tension which accompany the hearing of music," as well as "the bodily movements, which consciously or unconsciously, every listener to a melody exhibits." He observed: "Not every one taps his foot or sways his body to the rhythm of the music: but every listener who is at all musical, everyone to whom the succession of tones means anything, responds by exhibiting very slight but characteristic changes of muscular tonicity." *Effects of Music*, 5–6.

52. Storr, *Music and the Mind*, Ch. 1.

53. It seems more than a mere holdover from vocal music that the term "voice" is applied to the various melodic lines in contrapuntal instrumental compositions. Like many other musical metaphors, it is profoundly indicative of a basis in extramusical experience. Nor is this metaphor unique to Western culture. In the Gola language of West Africa, for example, there is no general term for "music"; instead, one refers to the "voice" or "speech" (*míé*) of each instrument. Warren d'Azevedo, "Sources of Traditional Artistry," in *Traditional Artist*, 314.

54. See, for example, Hanslick, *The Beautiful in Music*, Ch. 2: "no feeling can be shown to form the subject of the forty-eight preludes and fugues of J. S. Bach's *Well-Tempered Clavichord*." In Kennick, *Art and Philosophy*, 195. The tendency to regard Bach's contrapuntal compositions as abstract patterns of sound, devoid of expressive or emotional meaning, is evident even among those who do not subscribe to a strict formalist view of all music. Hence, Anthony Storr attributes to them "the icy grandeur of the impersonal." *Music and the Mind*, 180. Although Kivy acknowledges that some music exhibits expressive qualities, he regards Bach's *Well-Tempered Clavier* as a prototypical instance of "profundity in music" that is dependent entirely on formal features, rather than on any expressive or referential meaning. *Music Alone*, Ch. 10. Ultimately arguing that such music is "pure sonic design," Kivy actually proposes that it "be understood as a decorative rather than a fine art." "Is Music an Art?" *Journal of Philosophy* 88 (1991): 553. Needless to say, we find his proposition utterly untenable.

55. Schonberg, *Lives of the Great Composers*, 47.

56. Landowska, Commentaries on Bach's *Well-Tempered Clavier*. The pianist Charles Rosen attributes much of the "expressive power" of Bach's music to his understanding of the "emotional possibilities inherent in counterpoint." "The Great Inventor" (review of *Bach and the Patterns of Invention*, by Laurence Dreyfus), *New York Review of Books*, 9 October 1997. The pianist Peter Serkin notes that many of Bach's seemingly unemotional pieces were intended as pedagogical exercises. "Complex Uses of Simplicity," *New York Times*, 1 September 1997.

57. Allan Blumenthal, a psychiatrist and pianist who was a longtime friend and associate of Rand's, provides an illuminating account of the development of Western music in his audiotaped series of lectures *Music: Theory, History, Performance* (originally delivered in 1974 under Rand's auspices), which he prepared with his wife, painter Joan Mitchell Blumenthal. His account of the expressive richness of Romantic music is particularly instructive.

58. Percy A. Scholes, *Oxford Companion to Music*, s.v. "Instruments." Oddly, Scholes here compares the voice not to the strings, but only to the wind instruments,

although in a discussion of vocal sound-production (*s.v.* "Voice") he draws an analogy between the vocal cords and the strings of a violin.

59. Further, the four principal strings that gradually evolved for orchestral use—violin, viola, cello, and double-bass—correspond roughly to the main divisions in the range of the human voice (a pattern more or less duplicated in the "choirs" of woodwinds and brasses as well). Also significant, no doubt, the string quartet—that most intimately and intensely expressive of instrumental musical groups—employs two violins, a viola, and a cello, thus incorporating the most commonly occurring vocal ranges. In addition, musicians and critics often refer to the "singing" tone of a string player or instrument.

60. It is telling that instrumental compositions are divided into sections termed *movements*, and the earliest examples of music so divided (in the seventeenth century) were suites of dances. The term *orchestra* itself derives from the ancient Greek word for "dancing-place." Richard Franko Goldman, in *Collier's Encyclopedia* (1974), *s.v.* "Orchestra."

61. Nor are such developments limited to the West. According to Goldman (*ibid.*), large orchestras were maintained in China as early as the seventh century.

62. Thus it was possible, for example, for one of my students in a high school class in music appreciation to report, on first hearing the complete Beethoven's Fifth Symphony, that "something important [was] happening" during a particular passage—though she did not specify what it was, nor was she expected to.—*L.T.*

63. Nor does Leonard Bernstein, in his Norton lectures, *The Unanswered Question*, do much to illuminate musical meaning, for he focuses on the "syntax" of music, without considering the expressive import of the various elements that are syntactically related—an approach that yields as little understanding as studying the meaning of verbal statements by analyzing their grammatical structure without any knowledge of the semantic significance of the words or phrases involved. In contrast, though Bernstein began the first of his popular Young People's Concerts by declaring that "music is never *about* anything [else]"—"it's about notes"—he ended by saying that "most music is about feelings" and that "what music means . . . is the way it makes you feel when you hear it." "What Is Music?" (1958).

64. Leonard Meyer, "Toward a Theory of Style," in *Style and Music: Theory, History and Ideology* (Philadelphia: University of Pennsylvania Press, 1989), similarly emphasizes the importance of "biological constraints" on musical composition. See also Robert Jourdain, *Music, the Brain, and Ecstasy*: "Music beyond our grasp is not music at all. . . . Our brains fail to draw together underlying relations, and we experience little more than high-quality noise" (259).

Chapter 6 The Definition of Art

1. Though Rand gives little direct evidence of having read the contemporary philosophic literature, much less that pertaining specifically to the definition of art, she was certainly broadly aware of philosophic trends. Moreover, in the early 1960s, around the time she began articulating her theory of art, she had lengthy conversations on the subject with the philosopher John Hospers, who arranged for her to

deliver a paper on "sense of life" at the annual meeting of the American Society for Aesthetics in 1962. See Kamhi and Torres, "Critical Neglect of Ayn Rand's Theory of Art."

2. George Dickie, "Definition of 'Art,'" in Cooper, *Companion*, 111.

3. Morris Weitz, "The Role of Theory in Aesthetics" (1956), 90, *Journal of Aesthetics and Art Criticism* 15 (1956); reprinted in Coleman, *Aesthetics*, 90.

4. William E. Kennick, "Does Traditional Aesthetics Rest on a Mistake?" (1958), reprinted in Coleman, 411–27.

5. Wladyslaw Tatarkiewicz, *History of Six Ideas*, 33. On skepticism among contemporary estheticians regarding a definition of art, see also Eaton, *Art and Nonart*, 15.

6. For other seminal statements of the "anti-essentialist" view, see Paul Ziff, "The Task of Defining a Work of Art" (1953), reprinted in Coleman, 94–111; and John Passmore, "The Dreariness of Aesthetics" (1951), reprinted in Coleman, *Contemporary Studies*, 427–43. According to Stephen Davies (*Definitions of Art*, 22), it was Weitz who "persuaded many that artworks could not be defined in terms of their perceptible, intrinsic properties."

7. There is no relationship between "analytical," or essentialist, definitions and the "analytic" school of contemporary philosophy. Indeed, as noted below (n. 12), that school eschews the analytic approach to definition.

8. Regarding essentialist approaches to defining art based on "expression," see our discussion of "Emotion and 'Expression' in Art" in Chapter 3. As Davies notes (*Definitions*, 22), it was, in particular, the effort to define art in terms of "certain aesthetic properties, such as beauty," that anti-essentalists rejected. Since beauty is neither a necessary nor a sufficient attribute of art works, it should never have been the focus of a definition. As Davies explains, rather than continue the search for a valid essentialist criterion, philosophers adopted a "contextualist" approach, attempting to define art in relation either to its social function or to the "procedures" by which art works are brought into being. The "procedural" definitions to which Davies refers, however, bear no similarity to the creative process implied in Rand's definition; his prime example of a procedural definition pertains to the "institutional theory" of art, which we discuss later in this chapter.

9. As noted by Dickie (in Cooper, *Companion*, 111), many philosophers have even gone so far as to argue that works of art need not be artifacts.

10. For a persuasive refutation of Wittgenstein's claim that an essentialist definition of *game* is impossible, see Kelley, *Art of Reasoning*, 47–51.

11. On Wittgenstein's pervasive influence, see Dickie, in Cooper, *Companion*, *s.v.* "definition of 'art'"; and Hanfling, "Definition" (see below, n. 55), 14–16.

12. The emphasis on linguistic analysis in contemporary American and British philosophy was an outgrowth of *nominalism*, the view that concepts are merely mental constructs bearing no objective relation to reality. According to nominalists, a definition is simply an arbitrary stipulation as to how a word will be used, and is therefore neither true nor false. For a succinct analysis and refutation of this position, see Ruby,

Logic, 114–18. See also Rand's rebuttal of various nominalist claims in her *Introduction to Objectivist Epistemology*, 36–38, 47–48, 50, and 77–78.

13. Dickie's earliest formulation of an "institutional" definition of art was the following: *"A work of art in the descriptive sense is (1) an artifact (2) upon which some society or some sub-group of a society has conferred the status of candidate for appreciation."* "Defining Art," *American Philosophical Quarterly* 6 (1969): 254.

14. Dickie's 1974 definition, quoted by him in *Introduction to Aesthetics*, 83. Dickie's phrase "status of candidate for appreciation" seems an unnecessarily convoluted way of saying "status of *art*," which is, presumably, what he meant. The latter phrase would, of course, have rendered his definition even more evidently circular. On the concept "artworld," see below, n. 17.

15. After noting the "dictionary definition" of *artifact*—"'An object made by man, especially with a view to subsequent use'"—Dickie argues that a piece of driftwood "picked up and displayed in the way that a painting or a sculpture is displayed" would be "an artifact of an art-world system." He further maintains that the urinal Marcel Duchamp presented as an art work entitled *Fountain* "can be understood along the same lines." *Introduction to Aesthetics*, 87. Regarding Duchamp's work and its influence, see our Chapter 14. Randall Dipert observes that, though *artifact* is a key concept in Dickie's definition, it is inadequately developed and explained by him. *Artifacts, Art Works, and Agency*, 8n6 and 110. For an analysis of the concept, see esp. 29–33. Contrary to Dickie's claim regarding the piece of driftwood treated as art and the urinal appropriated by Duchamp, Dipert argues, in part, that *any* artifact (not least a work of art) should be recognizable as intended for the purpose it serves. He then constructs a definition by refining Dickie's concept of artifactuality so as to specify the distinctive nature of artistic intentionality. Though the approach seeks to identify an essential aspect of art, the resulting definition ("An art work is an artifact that is not con-ceived to have been made with an unsubordinated intention other than one that is such that its recognition implies its fulfillment" [112]) is unclear, owing to its dependence on a complex series of clauses and a double negative.

16. For comments by Dickie on his original definition, see, for example, his recent book, *Introduction to Aesthetics*, 83.

17. Regarding the concept *Artworld*, Dickie ("Defining Art," 254) quoted Danto's 1964 article in the *Journal of Philosophy*, which argued: "To see something as art requires something the eye cannot decry [*sic*]—an atmosphere of artistic theory, a knowledge of [the] history of art: an artworld." As Davies observes, Danto's discussion "shifted attention from the artistically relevant properties of artworks to the social context without which they could not take on and present such properties. That shift of attention prepared the ground for an institutional account of the definition of art." *Definitions*, 81.

18. Dickie, *The Art Circle* (1984), 80–82; cited in his *Introduction to Aesthetics*, 92. As implied in n. 17, above, the term "artworld public" does not refer to the public at large, but to a relatively small segment of it whose members are knowledgeable about, and receptive to, "avant-garde" contemporary work and the theories supporting it.

19. A review of Dickie's *Introduction to Aesthetics*, in the Newsletter of the American Society for Aesthetics (Spring 1998), makes the mistake of quoting the

later version of his definition without comment, while omitting the four supporting definitions he himself treats as, in effect, integral to it. The reviewer, Sarah Worth (co-editor of the *ASA Newsletter*), recommends the book, reporting that she has used it in an introductory esthetics course.

20. We will not attempt to analyze here Eaton's broader theory of art which includes her definition, for to do so would take us too far afield.

21. In Eaton's 1989 version, the work must be "discussed in such a way that information about [it] directs the viewer's attention to features that are considered worthy of attending to in aesthetic traditions (history, criticism, theory)." Quoted in Ralph A. Smith, *Excellence II*, 69. More recently, Eaton has replaced "discussed" with "treated" because, as she explains, colleagues pointed out that her emphasis on *discussion* was appropriate only to "Eurocentric art." "Reply to Symposiasts," *Journal of Aesthetic Education*, Summer 1995, 29. We would offer a different criticism, however, arguing that Eaton's definition, like all versions of the institutional theory, is mistakenly predicated upon the spurious art of the twentieth-century avant-garde.

22. According to Eaton, "aesthetic value is the value a thing or event has [owing] to its capacity to evoke pleasure that is recognized as arising from features in the object traditionally considered worthy of attention and reflection." Quoted by Smith, in *Excellence II*, 69. Eaton's phrase "traditionally considered" alludes, as Smith suggests, to the sort of critical and theoretical discussions of art that lie at the center of the institutional theory.

23. Smith, *Excellence II*, 70.

24. Davies views the debate over the definition of art as a conflict between "functional" and "procedural" accounts of the nature of art. On "procedural" approaches, see above, n. 6. Davies leans toward a procedural approach, which is characteristic of the institutional theory. *Definitions*, 22.

25. Incredibly, Davies concludes: "Had the Artworld never arisen, there never would have been any artworks." *Definitions*, 219. Contrast that view, all too commonly held, with Tatarkiewicz's observation: "Art exists not only where its name is to be found, where its concept has been developed and where there is a ready theory. These were not present in the caves at Lascaux, yet works of art were created there. Even were the concept and the institution of art to perish in obedience to certain avant-garde precepts, we may still suppose that people would go on singing and wittling [*sic*] figures in wood, imitating what they see, constructing forms and giving symbolic expression to their feelings." *Six Ideas*, 49.

26. Other groups subsumed by the term "artworld" include philosophers of art, administrators and impresarios, dealers, collectors, and art historians. See, for example, Wollheim, *Painting as an Art*, 13; and below, n. 31. Only those individuals within these groups who are receptive to avant-garde work and theories would be bona fide "artworld" members, however. The absurd pretentiousness of this term is apparent when one considers that nothing comparable exists in any other sphere of human activity. On this point, see Dipert, *Artifacts*, 110.

27. As just one example of the countless individuals, worldwide, who today hold, and act on, the belief that they have the "authority" to "confer art status" on virtu-

ally anything—consider the example of Christine Hill, who declares that the *used clothing store* she created on a side street in an old neighborhood in the former East Berlin "is being perceived as art, *because [she has] chosen to call it that.*" She further explains: "I want to illustrate to people . . . that *art becomes art in the way it is perceived and considered.*" Interview with Janet A. Kaplan, Executive Editor, *Art Journal,* Summer 1998, 43–44, emphasis ours.

28. Enjoyment is an important aspect of experiencing art; but, as we shall argue in Chapter 7, it is a *by-product,* not a metaphysical *primary.* An analogy may be drawn with the experience of eating food, the primary function of which is nourishment, not pleasure.

29. Amei Wallach, "Is It Art? Is It Good? And Who Says So?" *New York Times,* 12 October 1997.

30. Furthermore, McEvilley argued "that issues of art are just as difficult as issues of molecular biology," and are therefore beyond the understanding of ordinary people.

31. Rosenblum further claims that the only criterion for a work's status as art, as well as for the determination of its quality, is "consensus . . . among *informed people*—[that is,] artists, dealers, curators, collectors" (emphasis ours)—in other words, among members of the artworld. That basic assumption of the "artworld," in this era of impoverishment in the visual arts, is ironically at odds with the view widely held in Renaissance Italy, that an educated layman was fully qualified to judge works of art. See Sir Anthony Blunt, *Artistic Theory in Italy,* 56.

32. On the fallacy of the "appeal to authority," see Ruby, *Logic,* 132–34; and Kelley, *Art of Reasoning,* 118–20. Kelley (109) characterizes fallacies as "a class of arguments . . . so weak that the premises do not support the conclusion at all."

33. On this point, see the absurd claim of one artworld authority in n. 30, above.

34. Barzun, "Philosophy and the Arts," in *Critical Questions,* 258. On the importance of intelligibility in discourse about art, see also Barzun's "A Little Matter of Sense: Thoughts on the Language of Criticism," *Aristos,* March 1988; reprinted from *New York Times Book Review,* 21 June 1987.

35. The 1948 edition of the *Encyclopaedia Britannica* lists the following rules, *s.v.* "definition." (1) *The definition must be equivalent or commensurate with that which is defined;* . . . (2) *[It] must state the essential attributes;* . . . (3) *[It] must be [in terms of] genus [and] differentia. . . .*" Three "minor rules" include the admonition that "[o]bscure and figurative language must be avoided." The most recent edition of the *Britannica* (1997), reflecting the contemporary eschewal of analytic definition, contains no entry on *definition* as such. The index does include a reference to "definition by genus and differentia," but it is keyed to a cursory mention of *genus* and *differentia*—buried deep in the article on "Aristotelianism," in a section entitled "Relationship to Neoplatonism"—which merely lists them as two of five concepts "that had been much used by Aristotle" (the other three being *species, property,* and *accident*). No hint is given of the emphasis placed on definition by genus and differentia in the long tradition of classical logic originated by Aristotle.

36. Ruby's inclusion of architecture is inappropriate, in our view; see Ch. 10.

37. Whereas Ruby implies that a definition of art is possible, though he does not himself offer one, Kelley is less sanguine. He begins inauspiciously with the following speculation: "Suppose that an artist puts an egg on top of a brick, and exhibits the arrangement as his latest sculpture. Would this be a case of art? Some people would doubtless argue that it is; others would argue with equal vehemence that it is not. . . . The only way to settle the issue would be to find a definition of *art* that both sides could agree to." (34–35) In so stating, he makes the fundamental mistake of assuming that an individual who would exhibit an egg on top of a brick as his latest "sculpture" might agree to an objective definition. Such an "artist" would *ipso facto* subscribe to the authoritarian theory of art, and would therefore reject out of hand what Kelley means by "definition." More troubling with regard to Rand's definition, however, is Kelley's subsequent remark: "It won't always be easy to find a definition—in the case of *art*, people have been trying for a long time—but even the effort to find one can clarify our understanding of a concept." (35) Notwithstanding any misgivings he may have about Rand's definition, it is regrettable that, as a leading interpreter of her work, he did not at least cite and critique her attempt, so rare in the twentieth century, at the sort of definition he extolls in his text. See Kamhi and Torres, "Critical Neglect."

38. As Sciabarra explains: "The definition implies *all* of the concepts' differentiated units. But a definition is only an identification that satisfies the cognitive need for 'unit-economy'; it is not a description. Since people cannot grasp every characteristic of every existent in a single act of consciousness, they must utilize definitions that focus on essence within a specific context or level of generality." *Ayn Rand*, 175. Kelley points out that a definition serves to clarify the *boundaries* of a concept, to clarify the relationships between concepts, and to provide a summary statement about the referents of a concept. *Art of Reasoning*, 32–35.

39. Although Rand does not discuss the process of classification as such, she clearly implies that a meaningful definition presupposes that the referents of the concept being defined are similar in some fundamental respect—i.e., that they have been rationally grouped or classified. In her *Objectivist Epistemology*, she notes, for example, that "concepts represent classifications of observed existents according to their relationships to other observed existents" (47); "concepts represent a system of cognitive classification" (66); and "conceptual classification of newly discovered existents depends on the nature and extent of their differences from and similarities to the previously known existents" (73). See also her comments on the *genus* and *species* of the category "art works," in "Art and Cognition," 78. It is also significant that, in *The Art of Reasoning*, Kelley precedes his discussion of definitions (Ch. 3) with a discussion of classification (Ch. 2)—whereas Ruby's discussion of classification is relegated to the context of "scientific methodology," in his penultimate chapter. Moreover, Kelley emphasizes that things should be *classified* according to their "*essential* [i.e., fundamental] *attributes*" (19)—an explicit statement of a principle clearly implicit in Rand's epistemology.

40. With respect to the original referents of the term *art*, it is important to recognize that the idea of *skill* underlies the root concept of *art*, in its widest sense, which derives from the Latin *ars*, the equivalent of the Greek term *technê*, meaning

"craft, technique." For Aristotle and other Greek writers, the "mimetic arts" (corresponding to the modern "fine arts") are among the diverse products of human *technê*—that is, of practical, productive skill requiring the application of systematic knowledge. According to Aristotle's conception, the mimetic arts inevitably involve *technê*. This root meaning persists in the background of modern-day discussions of art, though the "artworld" often ignores it in the indiscriminate granting of art status to works involving little or no skill. When someone objects that something isn't art, because "anyone could do it," the notion of skill is clearly implicit. As novelist and critic Anthony Burgess observed: "Art begins with craft, and there is no art until craft has been mastered." "A Deadly Sin—Creativity for All," in *But Do Blondes Prefer Gentlemen?* (New York: McGraw-Hill, 1986); quoted in editorial, *Aristos*, March 1987.

41. See Rand, *Introduction to Objectivist Epistemology*, 13–14.

42. Dickie, *Introduction to Aesthetics*, 84, cites the twentieth-century examples we quote, and affirms that "both versions of the institutional theory have quite consciously been worked out *with the practices of the artworld in mind*—especially developments of the last hundred years or so" (emphasis ours). Thus his focus is on the avant-garde, rather than on traditional work. Davies devotes considerable attention to "hard cases" with respect to the definition of art. See *Definitions*, 39ff.

43. For the rules of definition, see Ruby, *Logic*, 102–108; and Kelley, *Art of Reasoning*, 36–43.

44. Note that while Rand's definition refers to "art" in the sense of *art works*—that is, the artistic *products*, not the process or activity—it also implies the essential nature of the creative process.

45. On the concept of *mimesis* in Greek thought, see the highly illuminating analysis in Halliwell, *Aristotle's Poetics*, 109–137; and his subsequent article, cited below, n. 46. Rand's genus is far more informative than that of Dickie's institutional definition—"an artifact." In specifying art works as a particular kind of *mimesis*, moreover, Rand's definition answers a major objection raised by Dickie ("Definition of 'Art,'" 109–110), who notes that the idea of art as imitation (*mimesis*), which persisted for 2,000 years after Plato, "flouts the traditional approach [to definition] by specifying only *one* condition rather than *two*" and thus implies that all imitations are works of art. Rand supplied the missing differentia.

46. As Halliwell notes, Aristotle (*Poetics* 1448b4–9, on "the instinct of imitation . . . implanted in man from childhood") seems to view the play-acting of children as an example of non-artistic mimesis. "Aristotelian Mimesis Reevaluated," *Journal of the History of Philosophy* 28 (1990): 490n5.

47. Dipert, too, argues that the ultimate function of art is less apt to be held in conscious awareness than is the function of other artifacts, especially practical ones. *Artifacts*, 111.

48. As we noted in Chapter 3, the precise manner in which a given artist concretizes what he deems important may be influenced to a large degree by the expressive and stylistic conventions of his time and place; but this does not alter the fact that it is *his* view which he projects in his work.

49. Note that Rand's term "re-creation" is general enough to encompass the diverse arts, whereas a term such as "embodiment," say, could not apply to all art forms, since its implication of physicality would exclude literature and music. Dickie, however, argues that some works of art "are not imitations in any way," citing as examples "many pieces of instrumental music and non-objective paintings." Contrary to his view, we have argued (Chapter 5) that all music is fundamentally mimetic. For our arguments against regarding nonobjective (wholly abstract) paintings as art, see Chapter 8.

50. In contrast with contemporary theorists such as Weitz and Dickie, Rand clearly holds that artistic "creativity" is delimited by the perceptual, cognitive, and emotional requirements of human nature. We explore some of those requirements in Chapter 7. Responding to Weitz's argument that an essentialist definition would foreclose creativity, Dickie sanguinely considers that "this danger is now a thing of the past." *Introduction to Aesthetics*, 85–86. For an instance of the sort of "creativity" Dickie's theory helps to legitimize, see above n. 27; for other examples, see our Introduction and Part II.

51. On the basic objections to essentialist definitions, see Davies, *Definitions*, 6, 8, 15, 20, and 21. One obvious problem was the assumption that the diverse forms of art could share directly perceptible properties. Rand's definition is framed at a sufficiently abstract level to avoid this problem.

52. See Merrill, *Ideas of Ayn Rand*, 125; and our discussion in Kamhi and Torres, "Critical Neglect."

53. As Kelley observes, "the essential attribute of a man-made object is usually its function. Such objects are created to serve a purpose, and the purpose explains why they are designed the way they are." *Art of Reasoning*, 21. Unfortunately, he comments no further, and cites no particular exceptions to the general rule.

54. Historically, functional definitions of art have been flawed, because they have incorrectly identified the ultimate purpose of art. Lacking the understanding of art's cognitive function that Rand provides, theorists have proposed definitions based on various misconceptions. Perhaps the most common of these (at least since the eighteenth century) is the idea that art is created solely for the "pleasure of contemplation"—in other words, that the primary function of art is to give pleasure. In contrast with Rand's theory, such accounts offer no adequate explanation regarding the source of that pleasure.

55. As Hanfling notes ("The Problem of Definition," in *Philosophical Aesthetics*, 27), for example, Kennick (see above, n. 4) cites ancient Egyptian funerary art, intended to provide magical benefits for the deceased, as evidence that the attempt to define art in terms of function is "doomed."

56. The enduring appeal of work from past centuries and distant cultures is potent testimony that true art often transcends the specific circumstances of its origins.

57. Neither "maker" nor "creator" is appropriate for every kind of art work. One does not speak of "making" a novel, for example, though choreographers often refer to "making" a dance. Regarding the problematic implications of the term "creation" (and its cognates), see above, Chapter 3, n. 25.

58. The term *value-judgments* is familiar enough in contemporary discourse, in the sense of "an assessment of someone or something in terms of personal values, such as whether it is good or bad, worthwhile or troublesome; a subjective judgment or appraisal"—as defined in the *World Book Dictionary* (1981), for example—or "a judgment attributing a value (as good, evil, beautiful, desirable) to a thing, action or entity" (*Webster's Third New International Dictionary*, 1967). While the primary meaning of *metaphysical* corresponds to Rand's sense of "pertaining to the fundamental nature of reality," however, the term is often differently construed in common usage—as pertaining to the spiritual, the occult, or the supernatural, to that which cannot be accounted for by physical science, for instance, or to that which is "highly abstract, hard to understand."

59. "Art is a re-creation of reality accoding to one's values." Rand, *Fiction-Writing*, Lecture 1. Similarly, in a lecture at the 1961 Creative Arts Festival at the University of Michigan, she defined art as follows: "Art is a re-creation of reality according to the artist's values. It is not a creation our of a void, but a *re-creation*, a selective rearrangement of the elements of reality, guided by the artist's view of existence." Quoted by N. Branden, *Who Is Ayn Rand?* 90.

60. Rand, "Objectivist Ethics," in *Virtue of Selfishness*, 5.

Chapter 7 Scientific Support for Rand's Theory

1. Although Rand, to our knowledge, never characterized her theory of art as "biocentric," she did apply the term to Aristotle's philosophy, since "[l]ife—at its highest form, man's life—is the central fact in [his] view of reality." Review of *Aristotle* by John Herman Randall, Jr., *Objectivist Newsletter*, May 1963; reprinted in *Voice of Reason* 6–12.

2. As Jeffrey Friedman has observed (in the lead essay of the spring 1997 issue of *Critical Review*, devoted to "Nature and Culture"), "data have become available that enable us to go far beyond the casual empiricism that was the only recourse of such students of human nature as Aristotle." Various sciences "have produced ample information about the nature of 'man' that often stands in sharp contrast to the . . . conclusions reached by classical philosophers—conclusions that have, in our day, hardened into dogmas. . . . [I]t would seem imperative to bring these new data to bear."

3. For Rand's assumptions regarding the ubiquity of art in prehistory, see her comments in "Psycho-Epistemology of Art," 15; and "Art and Cognition," 73.

4. We use the term *literature* loosely here, to include the oral forms of story-telling, drama, and poetic expression found in primitive cultures.

5. As Rand emphasizes in her *Introduction to Objectivist Epistemology* (235–38), the basic meaning of a concept is its *referents*—that is, the kinds of "existents it refers to in reality." Thus, the relevant question here is not, Did prehistoric man *have a concept* of art? but, rather, Did he *create* art (paintings, sculpture, etc.)? Steven Mithen, among other writers, misses such a distinction when he claims that "the definition of art is culturally specific" and adds that "many societies wh[ich] create splendid rock paintings do not have a word for art in their language." *Prehistory of the Mind*, 154–55.

6. The term "prehistoric art" is often equated with Paleolithic cave paintings—and, to a lesser degree, with widely disseminated, voluptuously modeled female figurines such as the famed "Venus of Willendorf."

7. On prehistoric flutes, see Marshack, *Roots of Civilization*, 383; Dissanayake, *What Is Art For?*, 56; the display on "Ice Age Art" in the Hall of Human Evolution, American Museum of Natural History (New York City); and Pfeiffer, *Creative Explosion*, 180–82. The recent discovery of a flutelike bone object in a Neanderthal site suggests that the origins of music lay at an even earlier stage of evolution, anywhere between 43,000 and 82,000 years ago. John Noble Wilford, "Playing of Flute May Have Graced Neanderthal Fire," *New York Times*, 29 October 1996. No evidence has yet been found of Neanderthal visual art, however. Marshack, 368.

8. On the musical characteristics of the early flutes, see Pfeiffer, 180–82; and "Ice Age Art," cited above, n. 7. According to John Sloboda, the diatonic scale "can be traced back to the most ancient tuning systems thus far deciphered from archeological evidence." *Musical Mind*, 257.

9. Payne, *World of Art*, 21. Alternatively, Pfeiffer suggests that the remains of flutes and other musical instruments in the caves, as well as footprints indicative of dance, are evidence of ceremonial activities incorporating all the arts, including painted and engraved images. *Creative Explosion*, 177ff.

10. Regarding prehistoric depictions of dance, see Dissanayake, 56, 58; and *World Book Encyclopedia* (1981), *s.v.* "Dancing." Howard Gardner emphasizes the relative frequency of such depictions in cave art. *Frames of Mind*, 222. On footprints attributed to dancers, see Marshack, 243; and Pfeiffer, *Creative Explosion*, 177–80.

11. Marshack, 237. A comparable example is the "Sorcerer" image, from the Trois Frères cave in France, depicted wearing a reindeer mask and a lion's skin with a horse's tail. *Ibid.*, fig. 150a. The likelihood that a "storied" meaning underlies such prehistoric images can be extrapolated from known practices in present-day nonliterate societies. See Mithen, *Prehistory*, 47–48, 164–67. Marshack also suggests (114) that the use of fire by prehistoric peoples probably involved story-telling about it as well. Recently discovered anatomical evidence indicates that human speech may have evolved more than 400,000 years ago. John Noble Wilford, "Ancestral Humans Could Speak, Anthropologists' Finding Suggest," *New York Times*, 28 April 1998.

12. One striking bone engraving, for example, depicts a series of stags viewed in profile, with salmon leaping about them and nipping at their legs and haunches, suggesting an event that would occur only in spring: migratory reindeer crossing a river full of salmon swimming upstream to spawn. Similarly, representations of fighting stags and bellowing bison suggest the fall rutting season. Numerous other seasonal scenes occur, some including much smaller forms of life, such as a budding flower or a grasshoppper. Marshack, 172–91, 210.

13. Marshack, 261, 119. For further images suggesting a story, see also 274–76. More enigmatic scenes also suggest a myth or story of some sort—as in a much-cited painting from the Lascaux caves, in which a bird-headed man with a conspicuously erect penis is depicted falling or supine in front of a powerfully drawn wounded bison, whose entrails spill out in bold black loops. (277 and fig. 155) See also Donald, *Origins of the Modern Mind*, 281–82. As is often the case in Paleolithic paint-

ings, the human form is reduced to a mere stick figure, while the animal is skillfully rendered with striking realism. On the often schematic rendering of the human form in prehistoric art, see below, n. 17.

14. The practices of present-day hunter-gatherer societies indicate that, for purposes of magic, the animals would simply have been scratched in the sand or on an open rock surface, and the rite performed swiftly, with minimal effort. See Marshack, 231; also Gombrich, "The Miracle at Chauvet" (review of *Dawn of Art: The Chauvet Cave, The Oldest Known Paintings in the World*, by Jean-Marie Chauvet, Eliette Brunel Deschamps, and Christian Hillaire; and *The Cave Beneath the Sea: Paleolithic Images at Cosquer*, by Jean Clottes and Jean Courtin), *New York Review of Books*, 14 November 1996, 10. In addition, while animal remains found at prehistoric sites provide fairly precise information about which creatures were commonly consumed as food or used to supply other physical needs, the cave art often depicts other creatures—among them, bears, lions, hyenas, owls, and rhinos. Marshack also notes (265) that, in a period when reindeer were a major food source, they were rarely depicted. Furthermore, many of the images (including the seasonal scenes noted above, n. 12) do not suggest any killing. Finally, even when animals are represented as killed, they are often not those that were commonly consumed. Regarding the broad diversity of animals depicted in cave art, see Marshack, 237–39, 244, 248–49, 265, and 274; Robert Hughes, "Behold the Stone Age," *Time*, 13 February 1995, 60; Marlise Simons, "Prehistoric Art Treasure Is Found in French Cave," *New York Times*, 19 January 1995; Simons, "Newly Found Cave Paintings in France Are the Oldest, Scientists Estimate," *ibid.*, 8 June 1995; and John Noble Wilford, "Homo Artisticus," *ibid.*, 11 February 1995.

15. On the skill and power of much prehistoric art, see Marshack, 279–83; Gombrich, *Art and Illusion*, 108–109; Mithen, *Prehistory*, 155–56; Payne, *World of Art*, 19–27; John Noble Wilford, "Scholars Say First Atelier Was in a Cave," *New York Times*, 15 May 1990; Marlise Simons, "In a French Cave, Wildlife Scenes from a Long-Gone World," *ibid.*, 24 January 1995; and Simons, "Newly Found Cave Paintings."

16. Marshack, 169 and figs. 62a, 62b, and 76.

17. Mithen, *Prehistory*, 162. See also Marshack, 253–54 and 248–49. When Mithen compares the work of the Paleolithic artists to that produced "by the great artists of the Renaissance," however, his judgment must be considered in context. As Gombrich has noted, lifelike representations of the human form (which are the crowning achievement of Renaissance art) are few and far between in the prehistoric record— perhaps, at least in part, because they require far greater technical mastery than do depictions of animals. "Miracle at Chauvet," 12. Such differences could also be due to a disparity of focus and interest.

18. See, for example, Mithen, 170–73; and Donald, Ch. 8.

19. Henry de Lumley, director of the National Museum of Natural History, Paris, commenting on the Chauvet cave; quoted in Hughes, "Behold the Stone Age," 62. (His remarks are consistent with Rand's view that both the selectivity and the stylization of art reflect what the artist regards as *metaphysically* important—in particular, his fundamental values.) Further, Donald observes that the typically remote

locations of prehistoric cave paintings suggest that they were ritual images invested with "great religious significance." *Origins*, 280.

20. See Torres and Kamhi, "Homo Artisticus," *Aristos*, May 1995.

21. Gombrich, "Miracle at Chauvet," 12.

22. Payne, 22, emphasis ours. Payne is mistaken in some particulars, however, as when he implies that all the creatures represented in Paleolithic art supplied "fur and food and bone, sinew and hide and horn." Yet his sensitive evocation of "the first artists" seems for the most part well-informed, and is eminently worth reading. See also Kamhi, "Robert Payne," *Aristos*, December 1993.

23. The quote is from "Ice Age Art" in the Hall of Human Evolution, American Museum of Natural History.

24. Marshack clearly distinguishes between pictorial representations and abstract markings such as sets of engraved lines or hachures, which he interprets as early "calendars," recording the lunar cycle. Other abstract symbols found on prehistoric artifacts or on the cave walls include gridlike forms and regular patterns of incised or painted dots. See also Donald, *Origins*, 198. Mithen (155), however, maintains (mistakenly, we think) that "[m]embership in the elite group of artifacts that we call 'art' must go to those which are either representational or provide evidence for being part of a symbolic code."

25. For the understanding in Greek antiquity that mimesis is central to the arts, see Stephen Halliwell's insightful scholarly account in "Mimesis," Ch. 4 of *Aristotle's Poetics*; and "Aristotelian Mimesis Reevaluated," *Journal of the History of Philosophy* 28 (1990): 487–510.

26. The definition we offer in italics is a condensed paraphrase of Donald's account (168–69). In "Reflections on Aesthetics and Evolution," *Critical Review* 11 (1997): 193–210, the psychologist Nathan Kogan considers Donald's theory of "mimetic culture," but mistakenly attributes to him a view of *"Homo erectus* as the first artist" (203). To our knowledge, Donald does not argue that these ancestors of modern man actually created art; what he proposes is that they possessed a mimetic mode of representing reality that was the *precursor* for the later development of the arts in *Homo sapiens*. Thus Donald's theory regarding the evolution of art is not as "strikingly different" from Steven Mithen's as Kogan suggests (205). Both theorists regard art as a product of the special capacities of *Homo sapiens*; they differ mainly in the mechanism they postulate for its emergence: Donald regards it as due to the higher level of conceptual consciousness made possible by the acquisition of language and all its cultural consequences, while Mithen attributes it to a greater "cognitive fluidity" made possible by an opening up of the "architecture" of the brain, permitting interaction between formerly isolated areas and functions.

27. As a simple example of a mimetic gesture, Donald cites holding one's hand to one's heart to *represent* grief—which derives its intelligibility from its basis in spontaneous expressions of grief. A more dramatic example might be clenching one's fist to represent anger. In contrast, snoring, to indicate fatigue or boredom, is a mimetic action often employed humorously.

28. Among the important characteristics shared by mimesis and speech, in Donald's view, are intentionality and a clear differentiation between representations and their referents. *Origins,* 171–77.

29. Donald argues that mimesis constitutes the basic medium of human communication and is therefore crucial in social interchange (189). However, he also observes that it "is not absolutely tied to external communication" and may simply serve the purpose of representing an event to oneself (169)—a proposition that recalls Rand's emphasis on the importance of artistic representations of reality for the *individual,* apart from any *social* or interpersonal function.

30. As evidence of human cognition without language, Donald cites the ability of prelinguistic children and illiterate deaf-mutes, among others, to "perform a variety of difficult cognitive functions without language, without even the possibility of internal speech." He maintains that the "range of their cognitive competence is impressive: it includes intentional communication, mimetic and gestural representation, categorical perception, various generative patterns of action, and above all the comprehension of social relationships, which implies a capacity for social attribution and considerable communicative ability." (166–67)

31. Donald adds: "And those who preserve and regulate myth—priests and shamans—hold positions of great power in the collective cognitive hierarchy." (258) In Rand's view, of course, one of the great achievements of Western civilization has been to dismantle such a cognitive hierarchy, allowing its power to reside instead in each individual. Regarding the importance of personally constructed narratives, see below, n. 75.

32. Rand, "Art and Cognition," 47. On this point, see also Donald's observation that "we have many ways of representing the same reality. An artist might draw his conception of an idea . . . while a dancer [or] an actor might each capture the same idea in a different way." Donald characterizes these various means of representation as "domain-general"—that is, as cutting across and integrating various specialized cognitive and perceptual modules of the brain. "The Prehistory of the Mind: An Exchange," *New York Review of Books,* 14 May 1998, 61.

33. C. R. Hallpike argues—contrary to many anthropologists, who tend to eschew the term—that modern-day hunter-gatherer societies may be accurately characterized as "primitive," since they have retained many of the features characteristic of the early stages of human life: small-scale impermanent settlements, decentralized social organization, hunting and gathering rather than agriculture, the use of human and animal labor, and non-literate (oral) language and culture, all of which practices profoundly influence their thought processes. *Foundations of Primitive Thought,* v–vi. Hallpike also differs from most anthropologists in his insistence that the *individual* mind plays an active role in the creation and transmission of culture in primitive societies. See his Ch. 2: "Collective Representations and the Thought Processes of Individuals."

34. Anthropomorphic and totemic tendencies survive, of course, in various practices and traditions in civilized cultures—ranging from the mythology of ancient Greece to modern-day children's literature and the perennial appeal of teddy bears and other stuffed animals among adults as well as children.

35. Lévi-Strauss, quoted in Mithen, 165.

36. See also Dissanayake, *What Is Art For?*, 46–47. As an anthropologist, Dissanayake is concerned primarily with the human behaviors involved in art, and therefore tends to refer to artistic *activities*, rather than to their *products*. Subsequent citations to this author in the text are to this volume.

37. On Dissanayake's concept of art as "making special," see *What Is Art For?*, 92–103; and *Homo Aestheticus*, Ch. 3.

38. For Dissanayake's view that the "present-day Western concept of art is a mess," see *What Is Art For?*, 5; and *Homo Aestheticus*, 222, where she contrasts the practice of "art for life's sake" in primitive societies with the Western notion of "art for art's sake." Cf. Peikoff's proposition that "art is not 'for art's sake,' but for *man*'s sake." *Objectivism*, 442.

39. On the origins of the idea of "art for art's sake" and its relation to eighteenth-century concepts of *fine art*, see David Whewell, "[A]estheticism," in Cooper, *Companion*, 6–9; Bell-Villada, *Art for Art's Sake and Literary Life*, Introduction and Ch. 1.; and Woodmansee, *The Author, Art, and the Market*.

40. Similarly, the anthropologist Warren d'Azevedo considers an "artistic object" to be "any combination of visual, auditory, tactile, olfactory, or other sense impressions conveyed through a permanent or impermanent medium." "Structural Approach to Esthetics," *American Anthropologist* 60 (1958): 102. In speculating on a definition of art for anthropology, therefore, he, too, fails to distinguish between "decorative" arts and major art forms.

41. See Dissanayake, *What Is Art For?*, esp. Chs. 1 and 5. In contrast with her view of art as an evolved adaptive behavior (involving both the making and the experiencing of a variety of objects and activities), cognitive psychologist Steven Pinker regards the arts as "nonadaptive by-products" of mental capacities that evolved to meet various material needs of human survival. Arguing that the arts (as well as religion and philosophy) are "biologically functionless," he views them as simply another form of "pleasure technology," comparable to strawberry cheesecake and pornography—"megadoses of agreeable stimuli . . . concocted for the express purpose of pressing our pleasure buttons." *How the Mind Works*, 524–25. Such a fatuous notion is bound up with his failure to distinguish between genuine art forms and spurious art such as "modern and postmodern works . . . intended to baffle the rubes in Peoria," pulp fiction, "paintings on black velvet," and mere entertainment. *Ibid.*, 522–23. Given the vacuousness of his examples (to say nothing of his ill attempt at humor), it is not surprising that he neither considers that art might fill a profound *psychological* need of human consciousness nor reflects that it could thereby contribute to the long-range survival of the species. For a review critical of Pinker's "oversimplification" of mental processes, see Herrnstein Smith. "Is It Really a Computer?" *Times Literary Supplement*," 20 February 1998.

A reasonable alternative to Pinker's view that the arts are a "nonadaptive by-product," may be that they are an *adaptive* by-product of the conceptual form of human consciousness. That is, even if no specific *genetic* mechanism gave rise to them directly, the arts could have emerged as a universal *cultural* adaption to satisfy the psychological need for conceptual concretization (objectification), arising from the nature of human consciousness. Such an evolutionary view seems consistent with Rand's theory, though she did not deal directly with this issue.

42. The innate human preference for sweets, for example, though highly adaptive in a natural environment (since naturally occurring sweet foods—fruits and berries, as well as human milk—provide substantial nutritional benefits), has quite the opposite effect in an environment of highly processed foods with added sugars. By the same token, Dissanayake seems to imply, individuals in modern society may find a spurious pleasure in so-called art that does not, in the long run, contribute to human well-being.

43. Dissanayake mistakenly regards the question of differentiating the "fine" from the "decorative" arts as "evaluative" (rather than ontological) in nature. Nonetheless, we think that the answer Rand offers to that question is one compatible with her own views.

44. Much like Dissanayake, Lévi-Strauss has been outspokenly critical of avant-garde movements in twentieth-century art, from "abstract art" to serial music. He also makes the mistake of viewing such tendencies as representative of Western art and culture—rather than regarding them (as Rand does) as fundamentally disjunctive, since they have failed to gain broad popular acceptance, in spite of their institutional entrenchment. For a summary of Lévi-Strauss's views on "contemporary art," see H. Gardner, *Art, Mind, and Brain*, 35–37. See also Lévi-Strauss's comments on the "wreckage of non-figurative art," in *Look, Listen, Read*, 65ff.

45. Rand argued that "the differences in the music produced by various cultures in the various eras of history are deeper than those among the other arts. . . . Western man can understand and enjoy Oriental painting; but Oriental music is unintelligible to him, it evokes nothing, it sounds like noise. In this respect, the differences in the music of various cultures resemble the differences in language; a given language is unintelligible to foreigners." "Art and Cognition," 54.

The relationship between music and spoken language, which we touched on in Chapter 5, has understandably been the subject of extensive philosophic reflection as well as scientific investigation. Perceptual studies in the past two decades have illuminated the close connection between music and the tonal characteristics of human speech. According to Diana Deutsch, a leading researcher in the field, these studies suggest that, in the formative years of language acquisition, the individual learns not only the verbal components of his native dialect but also its characteristic pitch "template," its tonal range and pattern. Such a tonal template would have an obvious biological value, for it would provide a framework within which the emotional nuances of a speaker's voice can be detected in that language or dialect. Since it is likely that such a tonal template for speech becomes neurally embedded in the mind in early childhood, it could provide a deeply ingrained tonal framework for the indigenous music of that culture. Such a phenomenon would clearly help to explain the highly idiosyncratic character of ethnic music. "Paradoxes of Musical Pitch," *Scientific American*, August 1992. We would add that, of course, individuals can, and do, subsequently learn other musical "dialects"—or even the "lingua franca" of Western music—just as it is possible for them to learn, with varying fluency, other languages.

46. Rand, "Art and Cognition," 64. Regarding the natural determinants of musical intelligibility, see also Fred Lerdahl, "Cognitive Constraints on Compositional Systems," in Sloboda, *Generative Processes*, 231–59.

47. Sloboda, *Musical Mind*, 254. He notes that fixed "*reference* pitches" are common to various musical traditions, and serve as a tonal center, at least for the duration of a given piece. In addition, the interval of the *octave* is a prominent feature of most scales, and its subdivisions into regular scale steps tend to follow "common principles" that enhance perception. (254–55) The number of subdivisions is always relatively small (most commonly five or seven notes); and the scale steps are almost always unevenly distributed (that is, the pitch intervals between adjacent notes are rarely the same for every succeeding pair). Sloboda suggests that this ubiquitous principle of unevenly stepped tones probably serves a "fundamental psychological purpose" by allowing the listener to "get tonal bearings" on subsets of notes within a given sequence. The uneven spacing gives the listener a clear and continual sense of where the music is within the given framework. The dynamic effects essential to tonal music—the sense of motion and rest, tension and resolution—are largely dependent on this relationship to the tonal framework. Roger Shepard, quoted in Sloboda, *Musical Mind*, 255. In contrast, the chromatic and whole-tone scales are symmetrical and regularly stepped: since they confer equal status on every tone, they allow no clear sense of location or motion—which fact may help to explain why such scales have never been widely employed.

48. Shepard, "Structural Representations of Musical Pitch," in Diana Deutsch, *Psychology of Music*, 379.

49. Just as scales are usually made up of unequal *pitch* intervals or steps, selected from a larger series of equal pitch intervals, so rhythmic patterns are made up of unequal *time* intervals, selected from a larger series of equal time intervals. Such irregular spacing serves to give the listener a well-defined sense of temporal location within the metrical unit.

50. For a defense of tonality and melody as "time-honored traditions" in music, see, for example, "The Prince and the Cellist" (editorial), *Wall Street Journal*, 18 February 1998.

51. Robert Efron, "What Is Perception?" *Boston Studies in the Philosophy of Science* 4 (1969): 137. As he further notes, the study of perception therefore has "a unique significance for philosophy and science."

52. While arguing that Rand's "broad view" of perception was essentially correct, we do not deny that she was mistaken in certain details. We have already noted (in Ch. 5), for example, her error in regard to some aspects of musical perception.

53. Semir Zeki, "Visual Image in Mind and Brain," *Scientific American*, September 1992, 69.

54. According to early models of perception, the "sensing" of visual reality was thought to consist in "an image . . . 'impressed' on the retina, much as it would be on a photographic plate." *Ibid.* For example, Newton stated in his *Opticks* (1730) that "the Light which comes from the several points of the Object is so refracted as to . . . paint the Picture of the object upon that skin called the *Retina* . . . . And these

Pictures, propagated by motion along the Fibres of the Optick Nerves into the Brain, are the cause of Vision." Quoted in James Gibson, "Information Available in Pictures," *Leonardo* 4 (1971): 28. In such perceptual models, the faculty of "understanding," had to "interpret" the retinal image for perception to be complete.

55. Zeki, 76. For the psychologist Rudolph Arnheim's view of perception as a mode of understanding, or cognition, see "The Intelligence of Visual Perception," (i) and (ii), in *Visual Thinking*, 13–53; and n. 58, below. See also Stephen Davies's remarks above, Ch. 5, n. 15; and Oliver Sacks, "To See and Not See," in *Anthropologist on Mars*, 108–152.

56. For J. J. Gibson's theory, see *The Perception of the Visual World*, "A Theory of Direct Visual Perception," in *The Psychology of Knowing*, edited by J. Royce and W. Rozeboom (New York, 1972), 215–27; *The Senses Considered as Perceptual Systems* (his best theoretical work); and "New Reasons for Realism," *Synthese* 17 (1967): 162–72. among other works. For an overview of his theory, see Michaels and Carello, *Direct Perception*. For answers to criticisms of his theory, see Kelley, *Evidence*, 67–78.

57. B. Taylor, *Linear Perspective* (London, 1715); quoted in Gibson, "Information in Pictures," 27.

58. Gibson, "Information in Pictures," 30. See also the exchange between Gibson and Arnheim in *Leonardo* 4 (1971): 197–99, in which Arnheim claims that "an image can be true without presenting any version of what meets the eye in the outside world," while Gibson counters that "an image *cannot* be true unless it presents *some* version of what meets the eye in the outside world."

59. Gibson, "Information in Pictures," 31–34. For a philosopher's appreciation of Gibson's distinctive view, see David Blinder, "In Defense of Pictorial Mimesis," *Journal of Aesthetics and Art Criticism* 45 (1986): 19–27. For Gibson's further explication of his view, see his reply to E. H. Gombrich (*Leonardo* 4:197–98), whose work is informed by the premise that pictorial intelligibility depends largely on cultural conventions. The psychologist Robert Solso briefly considers Gibson's view of pictorial perception, but surely misses the point, for he proceeds to claim that "[w]hen we study a piece of art, the complex object is initially sensed as a series of primitive light signals," which "are integrated into a composite picture, in which the mind adds interpretation." Moreover, the illustration he provides—a seventeenth-century "trick drawing" that we are likely to understand only "if we already know what to look for"—is so schematic that it is relevant neither to perception of the real world nor to the experience of art. *Cognition and the Visual Arts*, 79.

60. Gibson's distinction between perceptual information and underlying physical stimuli reveals the error implicit in the notion that the practice of contour drawing is unnatural and conventional, since "there are no outlines in nature." According to Gibson's theory, the lines of a drawing correspond to a crucial feature of the information provided in the optic array, for they indicate the boundaries of objects or forms. As Blinder explains: "Pictorial realism is not based on structural *identity* between the two optic arrays, but on informational *equivalence*." As he also notes: "A realistic picture produces a *delimited* optic array that contains some of the same information that would be found in the ambient array from the environment it depicts." "In Defense of Pictorial Mimesis," 26 and 25.

61. Gibson, reply to E. H. Gombrich, *Leonardo* 4 (1971): 198.

62. For Rand's account of visual abstraction, see "Art and Cognition," 47–48, and our discussion in Ch. 4.

63. The neuroscientist Gerald Edelman proposes a biological theory of consciousness that, like Gibson's theory of perception, posits fundamental neural links between perceptual experience and evaluation of the experience with respect to the organism's needs. See, for example, *Remembered Present*, 151–55. For a summary of Edelman's theory, see John Searle, "Mystery of Consciousness: Part II," *New York Review of Books*, reply to Daniel C. Dennett, 21 December 1995. See also Richard S. Lazarus, "Thoughts on the Relations between Emotion and Cognition," in Klaus Scherer and Paul Ekman, *Approaches to Emotion*, 247-57; LeDoux, *Emotional Brain*; and A. Damasio, *Descartes' Error*.

64. The psychologist Magda Arnold's seminal study *Emotion and Personality* (1960) has been credited as a catalyst in the general shift toward viewing emotion as a product of subconscious cognitive evaluation. LeDoux, *Emotional Brain*, 49–50. Nathaniel Branden reports that Rand learned of Arnold's work through him, but that she "had already formed her theory of emotions long before." Personal communication, 20 March 1998. Rand's conviction that emotion depends on cognition is evident in *Atlas Shrugged* (1033, pb. 959), for example: "An emotion is a response to a fact of reality, an estimate dictated by your standards. . . . An emotion that clashes with your reason, an emotion that you cannot explain or control, is only the carcass of that stale thinking which you forbade your mind to revise." Following Arnold's work, a growing consensus has developed among psychologists and neuroscientists that no fundamental dichotomy exists between reason and emotion and that they are, instead, integrally related. That principle was adumbrated by Rand, however, as early as 1928, when she wrote in her journal that a "perfect, clear understanding also means a *feeling*. It isn't enough to realize a thing is true. The realization must be so clear that one *feels* this truth. For men act on feelings, not on thoughts [alone]." *Journals*, 24. On Rand's view of reason and emotion, see also Sciabarra, *Ayn Rand*, Ch. 7.

65. Contrary to Rand's view, most theorists hold that the stored information involved in emotion may include certain "hard-wired" (i.e., genetically determined) responses, such as an innate fear of snakes. See Lazarus, 251; LeDoux, "Reply," 366; and Damasio, 131–34. Damasio distinguishes between such "primary emotions" and "secondary emotions," which involve "experiencing feelings and forming *systematic connections between categories of objects and situations, on the one hand, and primary emotions, on the other* " (134). It is the second category of emotion that is most relevant to art.

66. LeDoux, *Emotional Brain*, 211–12. Rand may have anticipated such a view as early as the 1950s, when she wrote a note in her journals that began: "The 'emotional' epistemology of the 'perceptual' level [mentality] works as follows: instead of storing conceptual conclusions and evaluations in his subconscious, a man stores concrete memories plus an emotional estimate." *Journals*, 674. As Rand emphasized, however, such stored emotional estimates are often not a reliable basis for judging situations or issues of a complex nature.

67. Daniel Alkon, chief of the Neural Systems Laboratory at the National Institutes of Health, quoted in Sandra Blakeslee, "In Brain's Early Growth, Timetable May Be Crucial," *New York Times*, 29 August 1995.

68. Joseph E. LeDoux, "Emotion, Memory and the Brain," *Scientific American*, June 1994, 50–57. See also Sandra Blakeslee, "Tracing the Brain's Pathways for Linking Emotion and Reason," *New York Times*, 6 December 1996.

69. On the survival value of the emotions, see, for example, LeDoux, *Emotional Brain*, 121–25; Pinker, *How the Mind Works*, 370; and Klaus Scherer, "On the Nature and Function of Emotion: A Component Process Approach," in Scherer and Ekman, *Approaches to Emotion*, 293–317.

70. Ross Buck, "The Psychology of Emotion," in LeDoux and Hirst, *Mind and Brain*, 291–92.

71. On universals in facial expression and recognition, see Paul Ekman, "Biological and Cultural Contributions to Body and Facial Movement," in Blacking, ed., *Anthropology of the Body*.

72. Since autistic individuals conspicuously lack this normal human capacity to recognize or express emotion, they are now thought to suffer from an impairment of relevant area[s] of the brain. See Sacks, *Anthropologist on Mars*, 247–48 and 289.

73. Of considerable interest regarding universal aspects of emotional expression is the work of Manfred Clynes, a neurophysiologist who has also had a career as a concert pianist. Assuming that each basic emotion is generated by a characteristic neural impulse or brain pattern—which triggers internal hormonal and cardiovascular changes as well as the appropriate external expressive features, whether vocal, postural, or facial—Clynes has attempted with some success to identify characteristic dynamic forms expressive of various basic "emotions." In a simple yet ingenious series of experiments, he has quite persuasively abstracted the dynamic essence of these emotions in the form of simple line graphs, in which the horizontal axis represents time and the vertical axis represents energy input. *Sentics*, 15. The graphs generated for each emotion are remarkably consistent, not only over repeated experiments with individual subjects but also from subject to subject in the same culture and even for those in widely disparate cultures.

Moreover, Clynes proposes intriguing (if not all equally convincing) examples of the use of these expressive contours in works of visual art ranging from Michelangelo's *Pietà* and Giotto's *Epiphany* to dancing figures depicted by an Australian aborigine artist. (plates 4–8) As if mirroring Clynes's thesis that the diverse modes of expression for a given emotion share a common dynamic form, the music critic Harold Schonberg, writing on Monteverdi's opera *Orfeo*, calls attention to "the psychological penetration of the piercing sadness when the Messenger announces the death of Euridice: a simple, hushed, chromatic droop that has a Giotto-like purity." *Lives of the Great Composers*, 21. Clynes emphasizes that the dynamic forms expressive of emotion are best captured by music—which, as a temporal art, is capable of conveying "the onset and decay, repression and changes of intensity" of emotional experience. For the application of his research techniques to the study of elements of musical expression, see Manfred Clynes and Nigel Nettheim, "The Living Quality of Music: Neurobiologic Patterns of Communicating Feeling," in *Music, Mind and*

Brain, 47–82. As evidence of the universality of emotional expression, they report (69–71) that the experimental responses (identifications of the basic character of various emotionally expressive musical sounds) by Central Australian aborigines bore a "high degree of similarity" to those of white urban students.

74. As Rand observed in "The Psycho-Epistemology of Art" (16), the pleasure of experiencing art is "so intense, so deeply personal" that it is felt as "a self-sufficient, self-justifying primary" pertaining to "[one's] identity, [one's] deepest, essential self."

75. Sacks elsewhere notes that each of us has "a life-story, an inner narrative—whose continuity, whose sense, *is* our lives. It might be said that each of us constructs and lives a 'narrative,' and that this narrative *is* us, our identities. . . . A man *needs* such a narrative, a continuous inner narrative, to maintain his identity, his self." (*Man Who*, 110–11) That an individual's experiences of art may help him to "construct," or at least to clarify and maintain, just such an inner narrative, seems to us to be strongly implicit in Rand's esthetic theory, as indicated by the phrases quoted in the preceding note—and by her metaphor of art as "the technology of the soul," which helps man to discover his values and can give him the "experience of seeing the full, immediate concrete reality of his distant goals." Rand, "Goal of My Writing," 169–70. An individual's responses to art can make him more aware of the deepest levels of his being, bringing to the surface thoughts and values that are often implicit and unarticulated.

76. Even for severely retarded individuals, sequences of movements that would normally be beyond them suddenly become possible in the presence of music. "What we see, fundamentally," Sacks observes, "is the power of music to organise—and to do this efficaciously (as well as joyfully!) when abstract or schematic forms of organisation fail." *Man Who*, 185.

77. On this principle, see also above, Ch. 5, n. 14.

78. Oliver Sacks, letter to the authors, 22 December 1992.

79. Sacks, *Man Who*, 176, 174.

80. *Ibid.*, 207. Sacks's observation recalls a statement of much the same principle by Rand; see above, n. 75.

81. On the following page (18), Sacks hedges his judgment, musing whether Dr P. might have gained, in his "cubist" phase, an "almost Picasso-like" power of vision. Yet, in the final pictures, Sacks saw "only chaos and agnosia."

82. See, for example, Sacks, *Anthropologist on Mars*; Gardner, *Frames of Mind*; and A. Damasio, *Descartes' Error.*

83. For various "modular" views of the brain and mind, see, for example, Fodor, *The Modularity of Mind*, 38–101; Pinker, *How the Mind Works*, 27–37; and LeDoux, *Emotional Brain*, 106, 196–98. Mithen (37–45) offers an overview of the principal theories.

84. On Cunningham's use of random methods for choreographing movement, see especially pages 55–57 in the interview "Choreography and the Dance," in Cobbett Steinberg, *Dance Anthology*, 52–62. See also our Chapter 12.

85. Further, Gardner (196) notes that the shop talk of artists has long dwelled on how best to capture on canvas the perceptual qualities of reality, and he cites a letter from Vincent van Gogh to his brother, in which the painter declares that, without the knowledge involved in drawing well, "one never brings forth anything."

86. The profound relevance of Sass's book for Rand's view of modern art was noted by us in a lecture sponsored by the Institute for Objectivist Studies (The Williams Club, New York City, 16 October 1993). The cultural implications of *Madness and Modernism* were more fully explored by Leonard Peikoff in a lecture delivered at Ford Hall Forum, Boston, 7 November 1993, and published in *The Intellectual Activist*, November 1994.

87. Sass, *Madness and Modernism*, 29. On the kinship between modernism and postmodernism, see also Kamhi, "Kandinsky and His Progeny." For our further views on postmodernism, see Chapters 12 and 14.

88. Brief review of the paperback edition of Sass, *Madness and Modernism*, *Times Literary Supplement*, 27 January 1995, emphasis ours.

89. For an insightful account of Rand's view of reason, see Sciabarra, *Ayn Rand*, 166–68.

90. Remarkably, the "anti-art" thrust of much modernist and postmodernist work has been openly acknowledged, yet such work is still regarded as art. Anthony Janson, for example, refers to the "deliberately antiart approach" of so-called conceptual art and of the early twentieth-century Dada movement, yet he includes them in his editions of *History of Art*.

Chapter 8 The Myth of "Abstract Art"

1. By *abstract art* we mean painting and sculpture that do not depict discernible persons, places, or things. The term is less than ideal: since *abstraction* (from the Latin *abstrahere*, "to draw from, to separate") means the "act or process of leaving out of consideration one or more qualities of a complex object so as to attend to others," all art involves a degree of abstraction, as Rand emphasized. Though *abstract art* is less precise than the synonyms *nonrepresentational* or *nonobjective art* (which Rand used), it is both simpler and more familiar. In addition, it has the virtue of not being cast as a negative, and of conveying these highly appropriate connotations of the adjective *abstract*: "difficult to understand: abstruse, . . . having no reference to a thing or things—opposed to concrete." In prior chapters, we have set the term off in quotation marks to indicate that we regard it as an invalid concept; for the sake of simplicity, however, we will omit them in our discussion from this point on.

2. Peter and Linda Murray claim, as a purported precedent for abstract art, that "[the view] that specifically artistic values reside in forms and colours and are entirely independent of the subject of the painting or sculpture . . . is of great antiquity . . . and also prevails in Moslem countries." *Dictionary of Art and Artists, s.v.* "Abstract Art." Such a claim blurs the fundamental distinction between decorative and artistic uses of abstract forms. See our discussion in Chapter 11.

3. In his comprehensive catalog for the Guggenheim Museum's 1996 exhibition *Abstraction in the Twentieth Century: Total Risk, Freedom, Discipline*, Mark Rosenthal (curator of twentieth-century art at the National Gallery of Art in Washington, D.C.) suggests that the invention of abstract art was a "startling, previously unimaginable rupture with the past . . . [as] dramatic in its way as the achievement of manned flight or the invention of the computer." (1) We, of course, take a less sanguine view of its value to mankind, as does most of the public. At the press preview for the exhibition, Rosenthal himself acknowledged that abstract art still meets with "a certain amount of skepticism." When we asked why this is so, he replied: "You're asking me to be a sociologist, more than an art historian, and I would only be guessing in the same way you could guess. So it's not information that I know better than you." He then quickly excused himself, cutting off further dialogue.

4. Mondrian, in particular, explicitly advocated the vanguard position of painting, claiming that, of all the arts, it is the freest in its portrayal of "pure relationship" and therefore the best suited to serve as an example to mankind. Blotkamp, *Mondrian*, 128.

5. Blotkamp argues (11) that, for Mondrian, "practice often followed theory."

6. Rosenthal cites Kandinsky, Malevich, and Mondrian as the "true pioneers" of abstraction, noting that, "while certain [other] prophetic innovators may be named, their works were either experiments or little known"—and therefore of little historical importance. *Abstraction*, 11. For a very brief introduction to the three seminal figures, with samples of their work, see "The Pioneers" at <http://www.artnetweb.com/abstraction/pioneer.html>.

7. Blotkamp notes, for example, that Kandinsky sought to create a "system of signs whereby it would be possible to express feelings . . . without any reference to visible reality," whereas Mondrian attempted to distill "visible phenomena . . . [into] the common denominators that formed the essence of reality, the true reality behind the illusions that [in his view] make up the visible world" (94).

8. We use the term "avant-garde" in the combined sense of the definitions offered by *Webster's Third New International Dictionary*, with our modifications indicated in brackets: "Those who [purport to] create, produce, or apply new, original, or *experimental* ideas, designs, and techniques . . . in the arts; [especially] a group . . . that is *[anti-]orthodox* and *[anti-]traditional* in its approach . . . *[often] extremist and bizarre*" (emphasis ours). We substitute "anti" for Webster's "un." Whereas self-described "new" movements in the arts had occurred at various times in prior centuries, the twentieth-century "avant-garde" is unprecedented in its radical break with established forms and in its pretensions to total originality.

9. Crispin Sartwell, writing on "abstraction" in the Blackwell *Companion to Aesthetics* (ed. Cooper), for example, supposes that "hardly anyone will at this point be perverse enough to deny" that "abstract works can be art."

10. "Check your Premises" was the title Rand gave to her column in *The Objectivist Newsletter*. She had first used the phrase in *Atlas Shrugged*. When Dagny Taggart is struggling to understand the seemingly uncharacteristic behavior of her former lover Francisco d'Anconia (who has, without her knowledge, joined the strike of the producers of the world), he tells her: "Contradictions do not exist. Whenever you

think that you are facing a contradiction, check your premises. You will find that one of them is wrong" (Part 1, Ch.7). The admonition reappears frequently in the novel and in Rand's nonfiction.

11. Kandinsky, quoted in Rosenthal, 33. Similarly, Mondrian referred to a "turning point of culture." "Neo-Plasticism: The General Principal of Plastic Equivalence" (1920), in Holtzman and James, *The New Art*, 137.

12. On Mondrian's embrace of mind over matter, see Holtzman and James, 30 and 324. Rosenthal writes that each new movement in early modern art was "a kind of religious crusade, with materialism always the enemy" (39). Regarding the fundamental philosophic question of the relationship between consciousness (mind) and existence (reality—the world we are aware of), Rand characterized the two basic theoretical positions as "the primacy of consciousness" and "the primacy of existence." *For the New Intellectual*, 151; and "The Metaphysical Versus the Man-Made," in *Philosophy*, 24. The *primacy of consciousness* view holds that reality is "all in the mind," that the mind (consciousness), in effect, *creates* "reality"—as suggested by Descartes's famous statement "I think, therefore I am." The *primacy of existence* view holds that reality exists independent of anyone's awareness of it, and that the mind merely *perceives* it. Broadly speaking, every philosophic school can be classified according to its position on this basic issue, which has profound implications for art and esthetics. Although the vast majority of Western philosophers, from Plato on, have assumed the primacy of consciousness in one form or another, Aristotle and the philosophers he influenced—including Rand—have assumed that existence is primary, and that consciousness is simply the faculty for apprehending what exists (reality).

13. Kandinsky, *Concerning the Spiritual in Art*, 2. Regarding this early treatise, the abstract painter and critic Michel Seuphor wrote: "No book has done so much for the dissemination and understanding of the new ideas. . . . It is, and will remain, one of the foundation stones of twentieth-century art." *Abstract Painting*, 42.

14. Mondrian, letter to the architect J. J. P. Oud (1925), quoted in Holtzman and James, 198; and "Purely Abstract Art," *ibid.*, 200. Similarly, Malevich aspired to an "objectless creation." "From Cubism and Futurism to Suprematism: The New Realism in Painting" (1916), quoted in Rosenthal, 21.

15. Mondrian, "Neo-Plasticism" (1923), in Holtzman and James, 176–77; "Pure Abstract Art" (1929), *ibid.*, 223–25; and "Art without Subject Matter"(1938), *ibid.*, 303.

16. Blotkamp, *Mondrian*, 15.

17. On the influence of Theosophy on the early abstract artists, see n. 34, below.

18. Xenophon, *Memorabilia* III.x.1–8. See also the ancient Chinese view that "Things are apprehended by means of their appearances,/and the mind responds by the application of reason." Liu Hsieh, *Literary Mind*, 158. As Joseph Frank has emphasized, the mistake of modern art is its attempt "completely to negate its contact with the tangible and visible world of human meaning." "The Dehumanization of Art," in *Widening Gyre*, 176.

19. Malevich, *The Non-Objective World*, 58. See also Mondrian, "The New Plastic in Painting" (1917), in Holtzman and James, 28ff. Given the anti-individualist

animus of the first abstract artists, it is particularly ironic that contemporary critics who completely reject collectivism in the political sphere consider Mondrian and Kandinsky to be among the supreme artists of the twentieth century, ignoring these painters' perverse denial of everything personal and individual in the realm of art.

20. Manifesto of *De Stijl*, quoted in Holtzman and James, 24.

21. Malevich, "From Cubism and Futurism to Suprematism: The New Realism in Painting" (1916), quoted in Rosenthal, 21.

22. Mondrian, letter to H. P. Bremmer, January 1914; quoted by Martin S. James, in Holtzman and James, 14–15.

23. Mondrian, "Purely Abstract Art" (1926), in Holtzman and James, 199.

24. Mondrian, "Natural and Abstract Reality" (1920), quoted by Blotkamp, 161; and "Pure Abstract Art" (1929), in Holtzman and James, 225.

25. Kandinsky, *Spiritual in Art*, 11. See also similar ideas of Mondrian, in Blotkamp, 79, and Holtzman and James, 303.

26. Kandinsky, *Spiritual in Art*, 32.

27. "Sensation[s]" may be a more appropriate English equivalent for the Russian term customarily translated as "feeling[s]" in Malevich's text. See Norbert Lynton, "What's In, What's Art" (review of *The Language of Twentieth-Century Art*, by Paul Crowther), *Times Literary Supplement*, 24 April 1998. Either term implies a subjectivist viewpoint in the given context, however.

28. Malevich's reference to the geometric forms he used as a "vocabulary"— and to his nonrepresentational painting of a black square on a white field as a "picture"—were but two of many instances of "stolen concepts" in relation to abstract art, on which we will comment later in this chapter.

29. John Canaday aptly observed: "[S]ince the aim of suprematism was to create the ultimate work of art, [Malevich's] black square on a white ground was the supreme suprematist composition. . . until in 1918 [he] conceived a white square on a white ground. Beyond that not even he could go. . . . [I]n two paintings he had exhausted the possibilities of suprematism as a theory, and there was not much left to do with it except to defend it in dialectics." *Mainstreams of Modern Art*, 489–90. Although Malevich's Suprematist paintings (which include compositions incorporating the other shapes we cited above) are less well known than the work of Kandinsky or Mondrian, they are historically significant (and therefore merit attention here) as precursors of the numerous "monochrome" paintings by highly reputed American painters such as Ad Reinhardt, Robert Ryman, and Robert Rauschenberg, as well as work by the French painter Yves Klein, and Joseph Albers's *Homage to the Square* series. To the delight of audiences in America and abroad in recent years, such work is satirized in Yasmina Reza's popular comedy *'Art'*—in which two friends bitterly quarrel over the value of an all-white painting one of them has purchased for an exorbitant sum.

30. Mondrian, "Art without Subject Matter" (1938), in Holtzman and James, 302, emphasis ours; Mondrian similarly claimed, in an earlier context, that the "fundamental function of art is to express beauty plastically."

31. Mondrian, letter to the critic and editor H. P. Bremmer, 29 January 1914; quoted by Martin S. James, "Piet Mondrian: Art and Theory to 1917," in Holtzman and James, 15.

32. Mondrian, "Purely Abstract Art" (1926), in Holtzman and James, 199.

33. Kandinsky, *Spiritual in Art*, 2, emphasis ours.

34. Kandinsky, 27–45. See also Whitford, *Understanding Abstract Art*, 85–89. Kandinsky was no doubt influenced by Theosophical speculations regarding the spiritual significance of forms and colors. A book entitled *Thought-Forms*, published in 1905 by the Theosophists Annie Besant and Charles W. Leadbeater, had maintained, for instance, that form-giving constitutes the highest spiritual undertaking, and had proposed that a symbolic language of "thought-forms" be devised for the expression of spiritual concepts. Rosenthal, 34. Kandinsky's early debt to Theosophy—a late nineteenth-century spiritualist movement founded by Helena Blavatsky and Henry Olcott—is explicit in his references to Mme. Blavatsky in *Concerning the Spiritual in Art*, 13–14. Mondrian was even more strongly influenced by Theosophy, in which he maintained a lifelong active interest. The unwholesome influence of occult philosophy does not diminish the admiration of critics such as Kramer for these modernists, however, as noted in Kamhi, "Kandinsky and His Progeny."

35. On the failure of abstract artists to develop a consistent "language" of color, see Rosenthal, *Abstraction*, 34.

36. For a common-sense view that whatever value abstract painting may have lies in the realm of decoration or design, see novelist Mark Helprin's essay "Against the Dehumanization of Art"—which, on that and numerous other points, offers a powerful indictment of the modernist position propounded in Ortega y Gasset's 1925 essay "The Dehumanization of Art." Helprin's essay, originally delivered as the 1994 Duncan Phillips Lecture, under the auspices of the Phillips Collection in Washington, D.C., was reprinted in *Aristos* (May 1995). It was also reprinted in Kramer's journal *The New Criterion* (September 1994)—notwithstanding his persistent championing of abstract painting and sculpture as "high art."

37. See our discussion of "decorative art" in Chapter 11.

38. More recent abstract artists, though no longer necessarily claiming profound metaphysical meaning for their work, nonetheless remain defensive regarding the issue of art vs. decoration. See, for example, Helen Frankenthaler's remark that color "doesn't work unless it works in space. . . . Color alone [without some suggestion of space] is just decoration—you might as well be making a shower curtain." Quoted by Deborah Solomon, "Helen Frankenthaler: Artful Survivor," *New York Times*, 14 May 1989, 62. Yet Frankenthaler, too, reveals the widespread "obsess[ion] with the idea of 'beauty'" when she admits that what concerns her when she paints is not what her "picture" represents but "did [she] make a beautiful picture?" *Ibid.*, 68. (Note, again, the inappropriate use of the term *picture* with respect to intentionally nonobjective work.) In any case, for all her protestations, Frankenthaler's paintings—some of which bear no small resemblance to a free-form watercolor done by our grandnephew Ben at the age of three—would be well-suited to shower curtains.

39. Kandinsky, *Spiritual in Art*, 47, emphasis ours. See also Rosenthal, 37. It is ironic that contemporary champions of early abstract work exhibit just the sort of focus on "the idea of 'beauty'" that Kandinsky disdained. For example, Roger Kimball maintains that, although artists such as Kandinsky, Malevich, and Mondrian heavily invested their work with earnest spiritual claims, "their primary claim on our attention has always been an artistic [esthetic] claim: [w]e care chiefly about the *beauty* of their art"—and "beauty remains the touchstone of art." "Russia's Pioneer of Abstract Art," review of "Kazimir Malevich, 1878–1935" at the National Gallery of Art, *Wall Street Journal*, 2 October 1990, emphasis ours.

40. Kandinsky, *Spiritual in Art*, 52. See also Rosenthal, 21. Ironically, in the view of Solomon R. Guggenheim (whose foundation was a prime force in promoting abstract, or "non-objective," art in America), the virtue of Kandinsky's work lay precisely in the fact that it "doesn't mean a damn thing.'" Quoted by Judith Selkowitz, "Art Incorporated: Images with Art," *Horizon*, January–February 1983.

41. Blotkamp, *Mondrian*, 80, 113, and 204. See also Rosenthal, 36–37.

42. Mondrian, in Holtzman and James, 29. See also his comment "Just as pure abstract art is not dogmatic, neither is it decorative" and his advice that architecture, painting, and sculpture must "perfect [themselves] separately," lest each of them "degenerate into decorative or applied art." "Pure Abstract Art" (1929) and "Art without Subject Matter" (1938), in Holtzman and James, 224 and 304, respectively.

43. In 1924, Mondrian actually severed all ties with his friend and associate Theo van Doesburg and their magazine *De Stijl* because van Doesburg wanted to insert a diagonal line into their system of forms. Meyer Schapiro, "Mondrian: Order and Randomness in Abstract Painting" (1978), in *Modern Art*, 233. In the early 1930s, Mondrian devoted himself to what he weightily referred to as his "new research into painting with double lines." Quoted in Blotkamp, 215.

44. See, example, Yves Saint Laurent's dress designs inspired by Mondrian, in Bennett Schiff, "For Mondrian, Art Was a Path to the Universal," *Smithsonian*, June 1995.

45. Charlotte Douglas, "Biographical Outline," in Malevich et al., *Malevich: Artist and Theoretician*, 14.

46. Malevich, "Through My Experience as a Painter," in Malevich et al., 201.

47. See Martin S. James, "Piet Mondrian: Art and Theory to 1917," in Holtzman and James, 18; also Rosenthal, 34.

48. Mondrian, "Introduction to 'The New Art—The New Life'" (1932), in Holtzman and James, 277–80.

49. Mondrian, "Purely Abstract Art," in Holtzman and James, 200. Mondrian's claim that "pure equilibrium . . . engenders the *joie de vivre*" is especially bizarre, since the joy of living would more normally be associated with energy and activity than with the stasis of "pure equilibrium." On the utopianism of the pioneers, see Rosenthal, 40.

50. Kramer, "Tom Wolfe and the Revenge of the Philistines" (review of *The Painted Word*), *Commentary*, May 1975; in *Revenge of the Philistines*, 304.

51. Umberto Boccioni, "La Pittura Futurista" (1911), quoted in Charlotte Douglas, "Malevich and Western European Art Theory," in *Malevich*, 58. Douglas also notes the influence of the philosophic theories of Henri Bergson and Bishop George Berkeley regarding the role of sensation.

52. Regarding the influence of a contemporary physician who claimed, for instance, that "our world consists of sensations," see Douglas, "Malevich and Art Theory," 58.

53. Rand emphasized in "Art and Cognition" (75–76): "Color as such (and its physical causes) is . . . an *attribute* of entities and cannot exist by itself." In the art of painting, unlike the decorative arts, the primary function of color and shape is not merely one of sensual appeal; they serve a representational purpose.

54. Boccioni, quoted by Douglas, in Malevich et al., 59.

55. Kandinsky, *Spiritual in Art*, 28 and 29.

56. Malevich, quoted by Douglas, in Malevich et al., 59–60.

57. Mondrian, "The Grand Boulevards" (1920), quoted in Blotkamp, 133.

58. Mondrian wrote: "The less the forms, lines, and colors creating limiting and particular forms, the purer is the expression of their relationships. . . . Neo-Plastic [painting] reduces particular form to its fundamental elements, that is, to straight lines in rectangular opposition. . . . [It] annihilates limited form and creates pure relationships. For in Neo-Plastic composition, the straight lines constantly intersect each other, so that the rectangles apparently formed are not asserted as such. . . . *Color is primary*." "Neo-Plastic" (1938), in Holtzman and James, 305, emphasis ours.

59. What is remarkable is not that such ideas were held early in the century, when the scientific understanding of perception was not yet far advanced, but that they have continued to influence thinking and writing about art.

60. Titian, quoted in Goldwater and Treves, 77.

61. Ingres, quoted in Goldwater and Treves, 216.

62. Kandinsky, *Spiritual in Art*, 19. While Kandinsky was justified in regarding music as an "expression of the [composer's] soul," his claim that it does not "reproduc[e] natural phenomena" misleadingly implies that no mimesis is involved. On the mimetic nature of music, see above, Chapter 5. In any case, he was mistaken to assume that what is appropriate to music would necessarily be appropriate to other art forms.

63. Richard Cytowic, a physician who has studied the condition in depth, points out that the often misused term *synesthesia*—derived from the Greek *syn* (union) and *aisthesis* (sensation)—literally means "a joining of the senses": it is an "*involuntary* joining in which the real information of one sense is accompanied by a perception in another sense" so that the additional "perception" is felt by the synesthete to have real, not merely imaginary, existence. *Synesthesia*, 1. In genuine synesthesia, then, such correspondences are not merely metaphorical and imaginary; they are neurological.

64. See, for example, Kandinsky, *Spiritual in Art*, 56–57.

65. E. H. Gombrich, "The Vogue of Abstract Painting" (first published as "The Tyranny of Abstract Art" in *The Atlantic Monthly*, April 1958), in *Meditations*, 148. As Gombrich adds (148–49): "But how good is [even] the best chord in isolation?"

66. Though Chinese scroll painting sometimes conveys a sense of movement across a landscape, it is a rare and limited exception to the primarily static quality of painting. In contrast, as Stephen Davies has observed, music "has a dynamic vitality that justifies our thinking of it as . . . presenting the emotional life of an agent. Musical expressiveness has both purposiveness and coherence. . . . We experience . . . [a musical work] as an organic, living whole [that evokes our] human involvement and response . . . as *no static image of feeling would." Musical Meaning*, 291, emphasis ours.

67. Mondrian, letter to H. P. Bremmer (29 January 1914), quoted in Holtzman and James, 14; and in Blotkamp, 81.

68. Mondrian, "Pure Abstract Art" (1929), in Holtzman and James, 224.

69. Boccioni, quoted in Douglas, "Malevich and Art Theory," 59.

70. Douglas, "Malevich and Art Theory," 58–59.

71. Kandinsky, *Spiritual in Art*, 6–9. As an example of an artist who "stood . . . solitary and insulted" in his lifetime Kandinsky cites Beethoven (6)—a claim that is grossly inaccurate.

72. Mondrian, quoted by Blotkamp, 79. See also n. 74 below.

73. Mondrian, "The New Plastic in Painting" (1917), in Holtzman and James, 32. What Mondrian and others have characterized as simply a new "style" is, in fact, an attempt to alter the essential nature of painting.

74. Mondrian, unpublished letter to a friend (ca. 1930), quoted in Blotkamp, 16. Blotkamp observes (167) that Mondrian's "small elite" comprised "himself, a few kindred artists and several non-artists capable of assessing his work at its true value."

75. As Robert Hughes notes, abstract art is "elitist . . . by nature." "Golden Oldies—An Overambitious Survey of the Century's Distinctive Movement: Abstraction" (review of the Guggenheim Museum's *Abstraction in the Twentieth Century*), *Time*, 4 March 1996. Yet Hughes fails to recognize that abstract art's elitism is ill-founded, just as Ortega y Gasset ignored the errors at its base in *The Dehumanization of Art*. In contrast, Rand impugned nonobjective painters as a "self-appointed elite of mystics." *Art of Fiction*, 10.

76. See, for example, Kramer's collection of essays entitled *The Revenge of the Philistines*.

77. Rosenthal notes: "Abstraction as a personal quest reached its supreme purpose and grandest claim in the artists' discussions of freedom" (36). Stressing that the abstract artists sought an "exalted state of freedom to act, at least on the artistic plane" (1), he also quotes the American abstract painter Stuart Davis's declaration (in 1939) that abstract art "is here to stay because the progressive spirit it represents is here to stay. A free art cannot be destroyed without destroying the social freedoms it expresses." (93) For the subtitle of his exhibition of abstract art, Rosenthal chose

the motto of the abstract "sculptor" Eva Hesse, "Total Risk, Freedom, Discipline." (1, 238*n*2) "Risk-taking" and total "freedom" were also emphasized by the abstract expressionists Adolph Gottlieb, Barnett Newman, and Mark Rothko, discussed later in this chapter. (117) Yet these concepts are fundamentally incompatible, since the idea of *risk* inevitably entails the possibility of failure—which, in turn, implies (as does *discipline*) an objective standard of value, thereby nullifying a condition of "total freedom."

78. Mondrian, for example, claimed that "[p]ure abstract art becomes completely emancipated, free of naturalistic appearances" and could attain the "spontaneity of the child." "Pure Abstract Art" (1929), in Holtzman and James, 224. He further insisted that it is "a free aspect of life . . . *[n]ot . . . bound* by physical or material conditions." "Liberation from Oppression in Art and Life" (1939–40), *ibid.*, 320.

79. "Implied is the need for freedom *from* . . . the conditions of material culture and everyday existence." Rosenthal, 36.

80. To illustrate this "pathological freedom," Sass reproduces a drawing by a schizophrenic (fig. 4.1) in which a bizarrely attenuated human figure is shown with flowers sprouting from its ribbon-like "arm." Such *art brut* has long been celebrated by modernist artists as a source of inspiration and imitation, and has become fashionable among collectors.

81. Elie Bontzolakis, a Paris physician who had treated scores of abstract artists, reported that many of them are, indeed, mentally ill, and that "the more abstract, the sicker they are." The doctor further noted that, in addition to those who were "passionately sincere" and truly sick, there were "the poseurs attracted by snob appeal, laziness, money or mere lack of talent." Quoted in *Time* (Medicine section), 9 March 1959, 60, based on a report in the weekly *Arts*. Among the abstract artists discussed later in this chapter, both Mark Rothko and Jackson Pollock exhibited psychological pathology—ending in suicide for Rothko, and in a fatal accident regarded by many as suicidal, for Pollock. When the subject of mental illness in art arises, defenders of modern art often cite instances of insanity among earlier artists such van Gogh and Robert Schumann. Such an argument ignores an essential difference, however: whereas van Gogh and Schumann struggled *against* their madness in their art, modernist artists deliberately apply themselves to developing precisely those aspects of their "art" most symptomatic of mental aberration. See also our discussion of the obsessive tendencies in Barnett Newman's work, later in this chapter.

82. Kramer, "Paintings by Mondrian Shown at Guggenheim," *New York Times*, 8 October 1971.

83. Remarkably, critics who value abstract art sometimes recognize the dubious assumptions at its base. In his review of a major Malevich exhibition (cited above, n. 39), for example, Kimball points to the "occultist sentiments" that inspired not only the work of the "pioneers of abstract art" but also that of later abstract painters such as Mark Rothko and Barnett Newman, both of whom we discuss later in this chapter. Though Kimball tends to dismiss such sentiments as irrelevant, Hilton Kramer emphasizes that the "espousal of occult doctrine" by the early abstract artists was fundamental to their work. "Mondrian and Mysticism: 'My Long Search Is Over,'" *The New Criterion*, September 1995, 5. Moreover, Kramer notes that the

"uneasy mystical foundation" on which Mondrian built his "absolutist aesthetic of abstraction" was itself based on the painter's existential "anxiety about nature." (13) Yet, despite all this, Kramer insists that Mondrian's "fateful leap into abstraction" (4) was one of the high achievements of twentieth-century culture. Similarly, Robert Hughes, art critic of *Time* magazine, comments at some length on the "bizarre" and "singular" implications of Mondrian's avowed abhorrence of nature, yet praises him as an "artist of extreme importance, not only because of the historic inventiveness of his pictures and the daring leaps of consciousness they embody, but because of their beauty as art." "Purifying Nature: A Superb Exhibition Traces Mondrian's Quest for Images that Express a Universal Order," *Time*, 23 October 1995. (Note that Hughes refers to Mondrian's work as "pictures" though, in fact, they de*pict* nothing.) Blotkamp, too, observes that, although the philosophy Mondrian "was striving to express in his work has been largely ignored, or dismissed as an oddity," the paintings it helped shape constitute "one of the most impressive bodies of work in twentieth-century art" and continue to "stand tall, splendid and unapproachable." (17)

84. While abstract art has in recent years been losing critical and academic ground to the postmodernists, who reject it as essentially meaningless, the alternative forms they promulgate are, if anything, farther removed from being art and are even less worthy of institutional support, as we shall argue in Chapter 14.

85. Alfred Barr characterized the two modes of abstract art as the "intellectual" and "geometrical" style, as in Mondrian, and the "intuitional and emotional" style, which is "organic or biomorphic" in form, as in Kandinsky's early abstractions. *Cubism and Abstract Art*, 19.

86. Meyer Schapiro's reputation and influence within the cultural establishment can be partly gauged from his obituary in the *New York Times* (4 March 1996), which began on the front page and ran for 47 inches in all—as compared, for example, to Ayn Rand's 20 inches, wholly relegated to the obituary page (7 March 1982).

87. Meyer Schapiro, "The Apples of Cézanne: An Essay on the Meaning of Still-Life," in *Modern Art*, 15, 19, and 22.

88. When "The Nature of Abstract Art" was reprinted in Schapiro's Selected Papers, mention of its original publication in *The Marxist Quarterly* was conspicuously omitted—although prior publication information is included for other essays.

89. Linda Nochlin, "Meyer Schapiro's Modernism," review of Schapiro's *Modern Art, Art in America*, March–April 1979, 29.

90. Though Schapiro does not doubt the abstract artist's "sovereignty over objects," Sass (32) cites this passage from Schapiro's essay as indicative of the similarity between abstract art and schizophrenia, and comments: "Often this sovereignty over objects amounts to a kind of solipsism, with experiential objects seeming dependent on the perceiving self or the self expanding to fill the world"—a phenomenon corresponding to what Rand termed a "primacy of consciousness" mentality.

91. That abstract work by adults resembles the efforts of children is, in our view, evidence that it is not art. For an amusing perspective, see "Art or Just Crap" <http://twws1.vub.ac.be/studs/tw15120/graphics/jwz/art.htm>. For other views, see

Fineberg, *Discovering Child Art*; and Howard Gardner, *Art, Mind, and Brain*, and *Artful Scribbles*. See also above, Introd., n. 39; and Ch. 8, n. 38.

92. Schapiro mentions the term "freedom" or its synonyms and cognates no fewer than sixteen times, and the concept of "spontaneity" at least seven times.

93. According to Schapiro: "The architect does not have to tell stories with his forms; he must [only] build well and build nobly." And "[t]he musician need not convey a statement about particular events and experiences or articulate a moral or philosophical commitment." "Recent Abstract Painting," in *Modern Art*, 225. First delivered as an address to the American Federation of Arts in 1957. Architecture (which, we argue in Chapter 13, is not art) need not "tell stories" or convey meaning in other ways because its primary function, unlike that of art, is physical and practical. And music does not convey "statements about . . . events" or "articulate" a philosophic viewpoint because it conveys meaning in another way—that is, through its essentially *expressive* nature as a medium based (unlike painting) directly and primarily on the mechanisms of human emotional expression.

94. Schapiro, "Nature of Abstract Art," in *Modern Art*, 195.

95. Schapiro, "Recent Abstract Painting," 215.

96. Such usage is but one of the many "stolen concepts" frequently employed by the champions of abstract work.

97. Schapiro, "Nature of Abstract Art," 223. In the essay "On the Humanity of Abstract Painting" (the title of which contradicts the fundamental intentions of the early abstract artists), in *Modern Art*, 227–32, Schapiro observed: "The best in art . . . must be discovered in a sustained experience of serious looking and judging, with all the risks of error."

98. Clement Greenberg, "Avant-Garde and Kitsch," in *Collected Essays*, 1:5–22. In 1991, Greenberg declared: "'Avant-Garde and Kitsch' embarrasses me now: it's so crude and the writing is so bad, and it's so full of simple-minded Bolshevism. . . . I can't stand [it] today." Interview with Peter Fuller, in *Modern Painters*, Winter 1991, 19.

99. Greenberg attributes this "formulation" to the influential abstract painter and teacher Hans Hofmann. "Avant-Garde and Kitsch," 9*n*2.

100. Greenberg, "The Case for Abstract Art," in *Collected Essays* 4: 82–83. Yet he had written that he was "still able to enjoy a Rembrandt more for its expressive qualities than for its achievement of abstract values—as rich as it may be in them." "Toward a Newer Laocoon," in *Collected Essays* 1: 37. He also stated, late in life: "All other things being equal I prefer figurative art." Quoted by Deborah Solomon, "Catching Up with the High Priest of Criticism," *New York Times*, 23 June 1991.

101. Greenberg, "'American Type' Painting," in Ross, *Abstract Expressionism*, 235-53. Greenberg also claimed—disingenuously, in our view—that, in the long period when most art was commissioned by patrons who stipulated the subject (prior to the advent of capitalism and "bourgeois society"), the artist "concentrate[d] on [his] medium" and devote[d] all his energy to formal problems." "Avant-Garde and Kitsch," 17–18. He thereby implied that the "medium" and the "formal problems"

were dealt with abstractly, for their own sake, rather than in relation to the task of representing the required subject in a striking and emotionally compelling way. And he conveniently ignored the fact that those artists, working at a time when cultural values tended to be relatively homogeneous, were likely to share the fundamental religious and moral values of their patrons, and could therefore fulfill a commission while remaining true to their own sense of life. (For a better-informed view than Greenberg's, see Schapiro, "On the Relation of Patron and Artist: Comments on a Proposed Model for the Scientist," in *Theory and Philosophy*, 227–38.) No one can doubt, for example, that Giotto's profoundly inspired Arena Chapel frescoes, albeit created at the behest of the Scrovegni family, were the authentic expression of his own view of the human significance of the life and Passion of Christ.

102. For Greenberg's phrase "ineluctable flatness" see "Modernist Painting," in *Collected Essays*, Vol. 4, 87; reprinted in Kostelanetz, *Aesthetics Contemporary*. For Wolfe's comments, see *The Painted Word*, 50ff. In an interview a few years before he died, Greenberg claimed, as if in answer to Wolfe, that his emphasis on the flatness of the picture plane was merely descriptive, not prescriptive; that he never intended it to dictate the course of all future painting. Further avowing a "prejudice . . . towards realistic art," he protested as "hearsay" the idea that he was "for abstract art." *Modern Painters*, Winter 1991, 20, 22.

103. Greenberg, "Modernist Painting," 85.

104. Rosenthal, 122. See, for example, the claims of Mark Rothko and Barnett Newman, discussed later in this chapter.

105. Sass further observes that one implication of the emphasis placed on flatness in painting by the formalist school of painting and criticism "is to declare that the representation of some external object, scene, or event is not necessary in order to justify the existence of artist or artwork. In this sense we might say that the flat, formalist painting is a kind of symbol of mind, conceived of as a self-sufficient and reflexive entity. Pervading many such works, it seems to me, is a distinctive combination of superiority and impotence, though sometimes one may also sense at least a hint of desperation." (171)

106. Greenberg, interview in *Modern Painters*, 22.

107. Kramer, for example, considers Greenberg "the greatest art critic of his time." "The Passion and the Resentment" (review of *Clement Greenberg: A Life*, by Florence Rubenfeld), *Times Literary Supplement*, 22 May 1998, 22. For Kimball, he is "one of the greatest art critics America has yet produced." "My Darling Clement: The Art of Writing about Art," *The Weekly Standard*, 18 May 1998, 45. According to Charles Harrison, Professor of the History and Theory of Art at the Open University, Greenberg was "unquestionably the most influential critic of modern art writing in the English language during the mid-twentieth century." Introduction to Greenberg, *Homemade Esthetics*, xiii.

108. Greenberg's 1955 essay on the Abstract Expressionists ("'American Type' Painting") abounds in the formalist banalities that have become commonplace in modernist criticism, larded with "stolen concepts" appropriated from the realm of representational painting. Thus Hans Hofmann—second only to Pollock in Green-

berg's estimation of these painters—is "never so lucid as when he consigns a picture to thicknesses of paint, nor . . . has any artist of this century outdone him in the handling of such thicknesses." (240) There is no "picture," properly speaking, however, since Hofmann does not *depict*, or *represent*, anything. His canvases typically consist of rectangular blotches of color variously arranged. Similarly, the "drawing" praised by Greenberg—"a sudden razor sharp line" or "thick globs of paint, without support of a firm edge"—is not drawing at all, since it does not represent anything. In short, Hofmann's "pictures" are, to borrow one of Greenberg's typical circumlocutions, essentially "devoid of pictorial incident."

109. Hilton Kramer, "30 Years of the New York School," *New York Times Magazine*, 12 October 1969.

110. The work of Rothko, Pollock, and Newman will be discussed later in this chapter.

111. Barnett Newman, "On Modern Art: Inquiry and Confirmation" (1944), reprinted in O'Neill, *Barnett Newman*, 69.

112. Barnett Newman, "The Plasmic Image" (1943–45), excerpted in Ross, *Abstract Expressionism*, 127.

113. Shapiro and Shapiro, *Abstract Expressionism*, 2.

114. Newman, "Plasmic Image," 127. Rand regarded as one of the "signs and symptoms of the Dark Ages . . . rising again" the fact that artists "announce that they do not paint objects, they paint *emotions*." "Faith and Force" (1960), in *Philosophy*, 71.

115. The Abstract Expressionists' artistic "breakthroughs" remind us of the advice given to the young Gypsy Rose Lee in *Gypsy*, the musical based on her life. As the seasoned strippers counsel the eager young newcomer: "[Y]ou gotta get a gimmick [title of song]/If you wanna get ahead." Book by Arthur Laurents, lyrics by Stephen Sondheim, music by Jule Styne, act 2, scene 2.

116. Essentially a form of verbal doodling (see Murray, *Dictionary of Art and Artists*, *s.v.* "automatism"), "automatic writing" was a technique originated by the Surrealist André Breton, purporting to provide "'a true photograph of thought'" and to free verbal expression from all rational and communicative constraints. Sass, *Madness and Modernism*, 194.

117. Shapiro and Shapiro, 2.

118. Canaday is correct, of course, in arguing that the work of animals (and similar work by humans) is not art. For views pro and con, see Dick George, *Ruby: The Painting Pachyderm*; Bil Gilbert, "Once a Malcontent, Ruby Has Taken Up Brush and Palette, " *Smithsonian*, December 1990; Thierry Lenain, *Monkey Painting*; Gorilla Paintings" <http://www.gorilla.org/Art>; and Frans de Waal, "Apes with an Oeuvre" <http://chronicle. com/free/v46/i13/13b00601.htm>.

119. John Canaday, "Happy New Year: Thoughts on Critics and Certain Painters as the Season Opens," *New York Times*, 6 September 1959; reprinted in Shapiro and Shapiro, 119–21.

120. John Canaday, "The City and the New York School," *New York Times*, 22 May 1960; reprinted in Ross, *Abstract Expressionism*, 272–73.

121. "A Statement on Modern Art" (1950), reprinted in Ross, 230–33. The principal signatories to the document were James S. Plaut, Director of the Institute of Contemporary Art, Boston; René d'Harnoncourt, Director of the Museum of Modern Art, New York; and Hermon More, Director of the Whitney Museum of American Art, New York.

122. This argument, which is raised again and again in defense of the avant-garde, misses a crucial distinction. Prior to the twentieth century, artistic "innovation" confined itself to changes of style and subject matter; unlike the later avant-garde, it did not attempt to alter the essential nature of the art forms—by claiming, for instance, that visual art can be nonrepresentational.

123. Adolph Gottlieb, quoted by Selden Rodman, *Conversations with Artists*, 89. On the Abstract Expressionists' hostility toward the public, see also Rosenthal, 122; and n. 131 below. Nonetheless, as documented by Bradford Collins, many of them were capable of relaxing that hostility when it was in their economic interest to do so. "*Life* Magazine and the Abstract Expressionists, 1948–51: A Historiographic Study of a Late Bohemian Enterprise," *Art Bulletin*, June 1991, 283–308.

124. Shapiro and Shapiro, *Abstract Expressionism*, 18.

125. Rothko was the subject of major retrospectives at the Guggenheim Museum in 1978 and the Whitney Museum of American Art in New York City in 1998. For illustrations and commentary on his work and life, see print sources cited in the subsequent notes. See also the following Internet sources: National Gallery of Art, Washington, D.C. <http://www.nga.gov/feature/rothko/rothkosplash.html> (includes *Untitled*, 1948, *Untitled*, 1949, and *Untitled* [Seagram Mural], c. 1958); ArtLex <http://www.artlex.com>, under "Abstract Expressionism"—includes *Untitled (Red, Black, White on Yellow)*, 1955, and *Yellow Band*, 1956; *Orange Yellow Orange* (1969) at <http://www.aiusa.com/satire/rothko.htm> (follow "Mark Rothko" link for commentary on him and on *Yellow Band*).

126. Rosenthal, 104. The specific works cited by him are *Blue over Orange*, 1956, and *No. 207 (Red over Dark Blue on Dark Grey*, 1961).

127. Janson, *History of Art*, 3rd ed., 713 and colorplate 148 (*Earth and Green*).

128. Michael Kimmelman, "Rothko's Gloomy Elegance in Retrospect," *New York Times*, 18 September 1998.

129. Dore Ashton, "Rothko's Mystery Remains," review of *Mark Rothko: The Works on Canvas* (comp. David Anfam), in *Modern Painters*, Winter 1998, 109.

130. Rebecca Butterfield, in Rosenthal, 284. See also the extensive discussion of Rothko's lifelong emotional and psychological problems in the biography by James E. B. Breslin.

131. Rothko, quoted by Breslin, 358. See also the painter's declared intention, regarding his projected murals for the Seagram Building in New York, "'to paint something that will ruin the appetite of every son of a bitch who ever eats in that

room.'" Quoted *ibid.*, 3, from John Fischer, "Mark Rothko: Portrait of the Artist as an Angry Man," *Harper's Magazine*, July 1970, 16–23.

132. Mark Rothko, quoted by Simon Morley, "Fields of Colour, Fields of Despair," review of *Mark Rothko: A Biography*, by James E. B. Breslin, *Times Literary Supplement*, 3 June 1994, 18. Breslin is a professor of English at the University of California, Berkeley.

133. Breslin, quoted by Morley. Regarding the issue of transcendence in Rothko's work, Dore Ashton astutely observes: "[O]nce that prefix 'trans' appears, the work of the iconographer goes up in smoke, and the commentator is left with the uncomfortable task of either merely describing (boring) or responding (personal and not verifiable)." "Rothko's Mystery Remains," 110. Contrary to Morley, and ignoring Breslin's tendency toward poetic hyperbole, Hilton Kramer considers Breslin's book "the best life of an American painter that has yet been written, . . . a biographical classic," and claims that he is "scrupulous in . . . resisting the temptation of fanciful interpretation." "The Passion of Mark Rothko," *New York Times Book Review*, 26 December 1993.

134. As Peter Plagens observed in his review of the 1998 Rothko exhibition, "a lot of abstract painters, fearing their work will be put down as mere decoration, like to hint at the presence of profound subject matter." "Darkness into Light: A Gorgeous Rothko Retrospective in Washington Shows Off the Luminous Power of His Painting," *Newsweek*, 1 June 1998. See also our discussion of this point earlier in this chapter.

135. On Rothko's fears that his paintings might be viewed as "decorative"—fears that increased with the growing sales of his work—see Breslin, 340 and 357. Greenberg claims that the issue of "just where the pictorial stops and the decorative begins" is surmounted in Rothko's work, but he never says how. "'American Type' Painting," 248.

136. James E. B. Breslin, quoted by Laurel Graeber, "Art History without Permission" (sidebar), *New York Times Book Review*, 26 December 1993, 21.

137. Hilton Kramer, "Rothko Retrospective," in *Revenge of the Philistines*, 147.

138. Kramer's impersonal reference to "the eye" misleadingly generalizes his own experience, implying that all viewers are similarly affected by Rothko's color. See above, Ch. 4, n. 66, for his similar remark on the paintings of Morris Louis.

139. Kramer's unblinking acceptance of the primacy of color in Rothko's art, and of the absence of external subject matter in abstract art, is oddly contradicted by the description for a projected book by him which was never published, entitled *Abstract Art: A Cultural History*. According to the publisher's catalog entry, Kramer's historical and critical narrative was to explore "the concrete meanings and powerful implications of an often misunderstood form," and he would lucidly demonstrate "that abstract art was never purely abstract: it was always 'about' the ideas, problems, and manners of contemporary life." Free Press, Fall–Winter 1992 catalog.

140. James Gardner, "Altogether Rothko," *National Review*, 23 November 1998, 58. According to Gardner, "one is left with an almost overpowering sense of being in proximity to something throbbingly real and important," though he can point only

to their "chromatic harmonies" and notes that even in this respect many of the works "fall just short."

141. Calvin Tomkins, "The Escape Artist: A New Rothko Retrospective at the Whitney," *The New Yorker*, 28 September 1998, 102.

142. According to Tomkins, Rothko preferred that viewers stand precisely eighteen inches away from his paintings. *Ibid.*, 103.

143. Kimmelman, "Rothko's Gloomy Elegance in Retrospect," 34. Kimmelman's reference to Rothko's "images" (a common "stolen concept" in writing about abstract art) is inappropriate, since this term implies pictorial representation.

144. Rothko, quoted by Rodman, *Conversations with Artists*, 93.

145. Hilton Kramer, "Was Rothko an Abstract Painter?" *The New Criterion*, March 1989, 1.

146. For illustrations and commentary on Pollock's life and work, see print sources cited in subsequent notes, and the following Internet sources: National Gallery of Art, Washington, D. C. <http://www.nga.gov/cgi-bin/psearch> (search for Pollock); WebMuseum, Paris <http://sunsite.unc.edu>, which features reproductions of Pollock's early work as well as of one in his "signature" style; and the Museum of Modern Art in New York <http://www.moma.org>, which contains a page on the 1998–99 retrospective exhibition *Jackson Pollock*.

147. Part I of a two-part article about the Abstract Expressionists by Dorothy Seiberling, "Baffling U.S. Art: What It Is About," in *Life*, was devoted exclusively to Pollock; Part II, to "four other giants of the movement: Willem de Kooning, Clyfford Still, Mark Rothko and Franz Kline." A subsequent article about Pollock, also by Seiberling, was entitled "Is He the Greatest Living Painter in the United States?" *Life*, 8 August 1949. The 33-cent stamp, titled "Abstract Expressionism," depicts Pollock in the process of creating one of his "drip" paintings. Based on a famous photograph of him by Martha Holmes for *Life*, the image was retouched by the U. S. Postal Service to eliminate the characteristic cigarette dangling from Pollock's mouth—an ill-advised attempt to sanitize Pollock's image. Rebecca M. Knight, "Helping Pollock Quit, Even Posthumously," *New York Times*, 6 February 1999.

148. Greenberg, interview in *Modern Painters*, 21.

149. Kramer offers a rare contrarian view; but in the absence of reasons his assertion that Pollock's work is "scarcely comparable to the greatest painting of the modernist era," rings hollow—as do most critical assessments of abstract art, since they lack an objective standard. "Jackson Pollock and the New York School," *New Criterion*, January 1999.

150. Michael Brenson, "Divining the Legacy of Jackson Pollock," *New York Times*, 13 December 1987.

151. Kay Larson, "Jackson Whole," *New York*, 21 May 1990, 76.

152. Holland Cotter, "Prospecting in the Jumble of Pollock's Earliest Work," *New York Times*, 21 October 1997.

153. Robert Hughes, "Jackson Pollock," in *Nothing If Not Critical*, 217. The phrase "broke the ice" is borrowed from a remark Willem de Kooning made about Pollock.

154. James F. Cooper, "Jackson Pollock: The Right Stuff," *American Arts Quarterly*, Winter 1999, 3.

155. Kirk Varnedoe, "Comet: Jackson Pollock's Life and Work," in Varnedoe and Karmel, *Jackson Pollock*, 48 and 17.

156. Brochure for *Jackson Pollock*, Museum of Modern Art, 1 November 1998–2 February 1999. The term "allover," commonly used to characterize Pollock's work, normally pertains to repetitive patterns in design or decorative art, not to fine art.

157. According to Greenberg, Pollock was "alone in his power to assert a paint-strewn or paint-laden surface as a single synoptic image. . . . Moreover, when . . . he began working consistently with skeins and blotches of enamel paint, the very first results he got had a boldness and breadth unparalleled by anything seen in [his predecessors]." "'American Type' Painting," 242–43. Through digital imaging, Pepe Karmel claims to have discovered deliberately obscured figurative imagery in the so-called drip paintings. In any case, even if such forms were present, they would be invisible to the naked eye, and therefore irrelevant to the viewer.

158. Sarah Boxer, "The Photos That Changed Pollock's Life," *New York Times*, 15 December 1998. See also Pepe Karmel, "Pollock at Work: The Films and Photographs of Hans Namuth," in Varnedoe and Karmel, *Jackson Pollock*. No doubt more people were impressed (and still are) by Namuth's photographs and films than by the paintings themselves. See Barbara Rose's comment: "'What stuck in people's minds was less Pollock's work than Namuth's images of him making it.'" Quoted by Karmel, *ibid.*, 92.

159. Rosenthal, 95. *Lavender Mist* (which measures approximately 7 x 10 feet and is painted in oil, enamel, and aluminum), is in the collection of the National Gallery of Art in Washington, D.C. (see website above, n. 146). If considered as "decorative art," it does have a certain sensory appeal, owing to its delicate palette and lace-like pattern.

160. Bob Morris, "Now Playing at House Museums: The Tell-All Tour," *New York Times*, 1 October 1998. Pollock's studio, re-created with the fidelity suggestive of a shrine, was the centerpiece (along with the Namuth films and photographs cited below, n. 169) of the 1998–99 retrospective—a key element in the mythologizing of Pollock.

161. Kay Larson, "Jackson Whole," *New York*, 21 May 1990, 76.

162. Ratcliff, *Fate of a Gesture*, 3.

163. Steven Neifeh and Gregory Smith, "Jackson in Action" (excerpts from *Jackson Pollock: An American Saga*), *Mirabella*, November 1989, 188.

164. Michael Kimmelman, "How Even Pollock's Failures Enhance His Triumphs," *New York Times*, 30 October 1998, emphasis ours.

165. Varnedoe, "Comet," 17. Pollock's paintings may indirectly *reveal* the way they were made, but that is not to say that they are *about* how they were made. To say that a work of art is "about" something means that it represents or pertains to something outside itself—to an aspect of external reality. Contrary to frequent claims by contemporary critics, a work of art is never about itself.

166. Rosalind Krauss and Yve Alain-Bois, quoted by Varnedoe, "Comet," 54.

167. Robert Hughes, *Shock of the New*, 311.

168. Ratcliff, *Fate of a Gesture*, 3. Reviewers of Ratcliff's book uncritically cited the Whitman-Pollock analogy. See, for example, Michiko Kakutani, *New York Times*, 17 December 1996; and Michael Peppiatt, "Splash," *New York Times Book Review*, 16 February 1997. For other allusions to the Whitman connection, see Mark Stevens, "Pour Soul," *New York*, 14 September 1998, 125; and "Painter's Punch," *New York*, 9 November 1998, 65.

169. Namuth's brief films of Pollock in action (one in his studio in black and white; the other, outdoors in color) were featured in the 1998–99 Museum of Modern Art retrospective.

170. Pollock, Interview with William Wright (1950), in O'Connor, *Jackson Pollock*, 80; reprinted in Ross, *Abstract Expressionism*, 141. Adding that "the modern artist is . . . expressing his feelings rather than illustrating" (*ibid.*), Pollock implied a false alternative that is all too commonly posed in modernist art theory. True painting is never mere illustration.

171. Varnedoe, "Comet," 73.

172. Equally troubling is O'Connor's allusion to heroic qualities in relation to Pollock's paintings—which, he suggests, "have entered modern mythology by virtue of a *heroism of character* that transcends both tradition and tragedy." "Jackson Pollock," in Turner, *Dictionary of Art*, 168, emphasis ours. There is nothing heroic in Pollock's work—except perhaps the size of the canvases—and there is certainly nothing heroic in the life of a man whose final act of irresponsibility was to take not only his own life (in a drunken driving accident) but that of a woman with him at the time, as well as injuring her friend.

173. For a color image of *Voice of Fire*, see Barber, Guilbaut, and O'Brian, *Voices of Fire*, xx; or the National Gallery of Canada's website at <http://cybermuse.gallery.ca/ng>.

174. Sarah Jennings, "Canada's National Gallery Under 'Fire,'" *Wall Street Journal*, 19 April 1990.

175. *Ibid.* The source of Jennings's quotation was Shirley Thomson, then the National Gallery's director, whose pretentious claim for Newman's painting as having a comforting effect not only presumed everyone's everyday life to be burdened by "'devastating cares'" but absurdly belied her prior implication that the work, like all "'great art,'" was fulfilling its role, which is "'to provoke.'"

176. Transcript of Global Television Network News Report, 7 March 1990; reprinted in *Voices of Fire*, 56.

177. "MP Wants Art Gallery to Explain $1.8M Choice," *Ottawa Citizen*, 10 March 1990; reprinted in *Voices of Fire*, 58.

178. *Saskatoon Star-Phoenix*, quoted in *Voices of Fire*, 29; and "All in the Eye of the Taxpayer," *Kamloops Daily News*, 9 March 1990; reprinted *ibid.*, 57.

179. "All in the Eye of the Taxpayer" (see preceding note), 57.

180. Stephen Godfrey, "Can This Voice Put Out the Fire?" *Globe and Mail*, 30 March 1990; reprinted in *Voices of Fire*, 67–69. Following the *Voice of Fire* controversy, Brydon Smith took a one-year sabbatical—far short of what we would have recommended—and returned to the National Gallery in 1994 as curator of twentieth-century art.

181. Bronwyn Drainie, "*Voice of Fire*'s Elitist Message Sure to Make Canadians Burn," *Globe and Mail*, 21 April 1990; reprinted in *Voices of Fire*, 75–78. The quote Drainie attributes to Newman—which actually reads not "drained of . . ." but "We are freeing ourselves of . . ." etc.—is from his essay "The Plasmic Image," in *Barnett Newman*, ed. by Thomas B. Hess (New York: Museum of Modern Art, 1971), 37–39; excerpted in Ross, *Abstract Expressionism*, 127. (Paul Crowther, *Language of Twentieth-Century Art*, 244n19, mistakenly attributes this passage to Newman's "The Sublime Is Now.") In any case, Drainie's inference about the essentially antisocial animus of the Abstract Expressionists is entirely valid. Several of them were quite explicit on this score, as we have noted; see above, nn. 123 and 131.

182. Cartoon by Peter Lazulak, *Toronto Star*, 14 March 1990; reprinted in *Voices of Fire*, 106.

183. Bruce Barber, "Thalia Meets Melpomene: The Higher Meaning of the *Voice of Fire* and *Flesh Dress* Controversies," *Voices of Fire*, 106.

184. Cartoon by Brian Gable, *Globe and Mail*, 17 March 1990; reprinted in *Voices of Fire*, 106–107.

185. In one of the more absurd footnotes to modernist art history, a dispute arose in the 1970s between British and American abstract painters as to who should be credited with "discovering" *stripes*. See the interview with Clement Greenberg in *Modern Painters*, 25. Rosenthal (63) finds an "uncanny precedent for [Newman's] work" in *Untitled (Green Stripe)* by Olga Rozanova, one of the early Russian abstract painters.

186. See Rebecca Butterfield on Ad Reinhardt and Robert Ryman, in Rosenthal, 285 and 293.

187. Cartoon by Adrian Raeside, *Sudbury Star*, 17 March 1990; reprinted in *Voices of Fire*.

188. The incident is recounted by the art historian Thierry de Duve in his essay "Vox Ignis Vox Populi," in *Voices of Fire*.

189. De Duve is properly critical of the "cultural élite whose code and scale of values are . . . incomprehensible" to ordinary people such as Czupryniak. (92)

190. Even the critic Harold Rosenberg questioned Newman's claim that his minimalist paintings pertained to such "sublime" themes as (in Rosenberg's words) "the

creation of man, the division between night and day, . . . and the anguish of man's abandonment." "How could all these grandiloquent dramas be seen in the repeated image of a rectangle with stripes?" Rosenberg asked. "Newman: Meaning in Abstract Art, II" (originally published in *The New Yorker*, 1972), reprinted in Shapiro and Shapiro, 345.

191. Another guard, José Rafael Heredia, while choosing his words more "tactfully" than Sologob, had this to say about *Vir Heroicus Sublimis*: "Well, it's a big colorful painting with a few stripes. I can't say that I like all the paintings here, but we protect them all. You do hear people insulting this one." He then admitted that he would not want to hang the Newman work in his own home.

192. Kramer similarly observes that "what has come to be regarded as 'classic' Pollock is . . . maddeningly repetitious." "Jackson Pollock and the New York School, II," *The New Criterion*, February 1999, 15.

193. While Moore's work tends to retain at least a faint suggestion of human or animal figures, albeit highly abstracted, some of Brancusi's pieces (such as his many versions of *Endless Column*, and *Socrates*) are essentially geometric in form.

194. The leading Constructivists were Vladimir Tatlin, Naum Gabo, and Antoine Pevsner. See Canaday, *Mainstreams*, 498–99.

195. For examples of work by Judd and Andre, see ArtLex <http://www.artlex. com>.

196. Smith's work is included on the National Gallery of Art website, <http://www.nga.gov>. His *Cubi XXVI* (1965) was loaned by the gallery for exhibition in the Jacqueline Kennedy Garden of the White House in 1998–99 <http://www.whitehouse.gov/WH/Tours/Garden_Exhibit2/smith.html>. For various print sources, see the following notes.

197. See Chilvers and Osborne, *Oxford Dictionary of Art*, s.v. "Smith, David"; and Karen Wilkin, *David Smith*, 107.

198. For Kramer's inflated assessment of Smith—echoing an earlier tentative judgment by Clement Greenberg (in a review of the exhibition *American Sculpture of Our Time* in 1943)—see "A Critic Calls David Smith 'Greatest of All American Artists,'" the cover article of the *New York Times Magazine*, 16 February 1969. (Subsequent references to Kramer in this section are to this article.) See also Kramer's laudatory remarks about Smith, dating from 1984, in *Revenge of the Philistines*, 417.

199. Wilkin, *David Smith*, 7.

200. Constructions much like Smith's are typical of the sculptor Mark di Suvero, whose work is discussed by Thomas Schlotterback in "Two Public Monuments a Century Apart," *Aristos*, May 1988.

201. David Smith, quoted in Kramer, 44.

202. For Kramer, who notes that cubism became the "vital center" of Smith's art, his main distinction lay "in embracing the modern movement in all its diversity" (49–50). On the influence of cubism and constructivism on Smith, see also his interview with Katharine Kuh, in *The Artist's Voice*, 219–233.

203. For examples of Smith's drawings, see the catalogue raisonné prepared by Rosalind Krauss, esp. nos. 44–49 (nudes) and figs. 756–762 (abstract "drawings"); and Paul Cummings, *David Smith: The Drawings* (New York: Whitney Museum of American Art), fig. 73. That such examples are seriously exhibited and discussed as *drawings* is not only one of the many absurdities of Smith's inflated reputation but is symptomatic of a tendency in twentieth-century criticism and scholarship in general—as evidenced in the Guggenheim Museum's 1997 exhibition *From Dürer to Rauschenberg: A Quintessence of Drawing*, which equated the master drawings of Dürer with "transfer drawings" made by Rauschenberg from impressions of wet newsprint. See also Wilkin's unblinking reference, in her article on Smith for the *Dictionary of Art*, to Smith's "sprayed drawings," which he made by spraying paint or enamel around objects placed on paper—a technique that some readers may recall with amusement from "arts and crafts" experiences in summer camp.

204. David Smith, quoted by Kramer, 44–46.

205. On Smith's *Hudson River Landscape*, see Craven, *Sculpture in America*, 628, and fig. 16-4.

206. In any case, landscape is scarcely an appropriate subject for sculpture, since insubstantial, shifting forms such as foliage, water, and clouds—not to mention the all-important effects of light and atmosphere—can only be captured pictorially, not sculpturally.

207. Michael Kimmelman, "At Home in the Fields a Sculptor Called Home," *New York Times*, 18 May 1997.

208. Karen Wilkin, "Smith, David," in Turner, *Dictionary of Art*. For an image of Smith's *Two Circle Sentinel* (1961), see the website of the Houston Museum of Fine Arts <http://mfah.org/garden/artists/smith.html>.

209. Craven, *Sculpture in America*, 393–94. The contrast between Smith's "personages" and Daniel Chester French's *Minute Man* drives home the marked imbalance in the space (in number of columns) allocated by the recent *Dictionary of Art* to Smith (more than four) in comparison to French (one) and to other outstanding American sculptors, such as Augustus Saint-Gaudens (three), Anna Hyatt Huntington (less than a half), and Harriet Whitney Frishmuth, who is entirely omitted. On these underrated artists, see Richman, *Daniel Chester French*; Alexandra York, "Daniel Chester French—Public Monuments and Private Passions," *Aristos*, October 1983; Dryfhout, *Augustus Saint-Gaudens*; Michelle Marder Kamhi, "Anna Hyatt Huntington's 'Joan of Arc,'" *Aristos*, March 1988; and Beatrice Gilman Proske, "Harriet Whitney Frishmuth—Lyric Sculptor," *Aristos*, June 1984.

210. On the *Cubis*, see Craven, 628–29; Janson, *History of Art*, rev. ed., 552; and Kramer, 60. Regarding Janson's claim, a toddler's construction of building blocks (which the *Cubis* most nearly resemble) might as readily represent a "triumph over gravity," yet it would not be art, much less a masterpiece. In any case, such an abstractly impersonal concept as gravity is a subject for physics, not sculpture.

211. David Smith, "Tradition and Identity," speech given at Ohio University, 17 April 1959; in Ross, *Abstract Expressionism*, 185.

212. On the incoherence of much twentieth-century criticism, see Jacques Barzun's "A Little Matter of Sense," and our editorial on it, in *Aristos*, March 1988.

213. Craven, 684–85. For examples of Judd's work, see the website of the Sheldon Memorial Art Gallery <http://sheldon.unl.edu/html/artist/judd_d/ss.html> and the "Art in Context" website <http://www.artincontext.com>. A typically inanimate piece by Judd (like all his pieces, it is titled *Untitled*) consisting of six identical black aluminum cubes, four feet high, is featured on the jacket of Craven's book; see also, p. 685 and fig. 17.11. Its selection, over the countless figurative works illustrated in Craven's tome on the entire history of American sculpture, speaks volumes.

214. On the concept of "anti-art," see ArtLex <http://www.artlex.com>.

215. Kramer admiringly notes, for example, that Smith's *Cubi* series "almost overnight, formed the basis of an entirely new movement in sculpture, the movement known as 'minimal' sculpture or 'primary structures'" (59).

216. Carmi Weingrod, "Art by Census: Should People Get Exactly What They Ask For?" *American Artist*, October 1995, 14–18.

217. The survey was repeated in Denmark, Finland, France, Germany, Holland, Iceland, Italy, Kenya, Portugal, Russia, Turkey, Ukraine, and China (the one locale in which it was conducted in a door-to-door canvas, rather than by phone). For the results, see "Komar & Melamid: The Most Wanted Paintings on the Web" <http://www. diacenter.org/km/homepage.html>.

218. As Edward Rothstein notes, for example, a number of the questions posed false alternatives, such as: "Art should be relaxing to look at, not all jumbled up and confusing." "Class Lessons: Who's Calling Whom Tacky?" *New York Times*, 25 July 1998. Rothstein is mistaken, however, in suggesting that Komar and Melamid aimed, in part, "to poke fun" at middle class taste. Though the kitschy juxtaposition of incongruous elements in *America's Most Wanted* prompts such an inference, it is clear both from interviews and from other projects by them that it was not their intent.

219. On "conceptual art," see Chapter 14. We regard the "conceptual" projects of Komar and Melamid as a form of visual satire—not as art.

220. Both paintings are reproduced in Richard B. Woodward, "The Perfect Painting," *New York Times Magazine*, 20 February 1994; and in *American Artist* (see above, n. 216).

221. The only country in which the majority of respondents indicated a preference for abstract painting was Holland, the home of Mondrian.

222. Arthur C. Danto, "Can It Be the 'Most Wanted Painting' Even If Nobody Wants It?" in JoAnn Wypijewski, *Painting by Numbers*, 138. See Melamid's admission that "it's not the best picture in the world,'" quoted by Woodward, "The Perfect Painting."

223. "Painting by Numbers: The Search for a People's Art," interview with Alex Melamid, *The Nation*, 14 March 1994, 337; <http://www.diacenter.org/km/ nation.html>. The survey questions and responses accompany the print version.

224. Wypijewski similarly observes: "I've been occasionally stunned by just how seriously . . . uncredentialed citizens seem to take art." "Notes on a Public Conversation," in *Painting by Numbers,* 81.

225. Modesty prevents us from citing a book that might fill the bill.

226. Ross's remark is typical of the patronizing attitude of artworld representatives towards the general public.

227. See the Dia Center website: <http://www.diacenter.org>.

228. David Halle, *Inside Culture: Art and Class in the American Home.* Halle is now professor of sociology and director of the Neiman Center for the Study of American Society and Culture at the University of California, Los Angeles.

229. Most of the art created during the past 150 years that is displayed in museums (such as Impressionist paintings), Halle emphasizes (1), came from collectors who had purchased it for their own homes.

230. Noting that conventional "definitions of art are fraught with controversy," Halle chose to include in his study "the full range of artistic items" (20) found in people's homes—among them, not only abstract art and landscape paintings, the two categories most relevant to our discussion, but also images and objects not ordinarily regarded as art yet serving some of the same functions (for example, reproductions and prints, works by unknown artists, "ordinary" photographs, and mass-produced religious icons).

231. For this study, Halle astutely defined *abstract art* as work that was not only nonrepresentational (i.e., that "eschewed easily recognizable images of the external world") but was also "presented as 'art'"—for example, "framed, hung on a wall, and considered of aesthetic value" (121). The latter part of his formulation alludes to the institutional, or "authoritarian," theory of art, which we discuss in Chapter 6.

232. An interesting historical footnote to the popularity of abstract art as "decoration" is Halle's highly plausible suggestion that it was due in large measure to the declining use of wallpaper. Owing to the influence of modern designers such as the Austrian architect Adolph Loos, who had condemned decorative elements such as wallpaper as a "crime" against taste, whitewashed walls became *de rigueur* in the twentieth-century home. Colorful abstract paintings may well have offered welcome relief from such austerity.

233. Such a comment on Frankenthaler's work is particularly ironic, given her express intention to be more than merely decorative; see above, n. 38.

234. Halle defines landscapes as "paintings over half of whose content is land, water, or sky"; he thus includes what are usually termed "seascapes."

235. Danto ignores the obvious alternative explanation that the reason landscape scenes are commonly depicted on calendars is because people prefer them.

236. Eakins's *Max Schmitt in a Single Scull* is in the collection of the Metropolitan Museum of Art.

237. Bradford's *Coast of Labrador* is in the collection of the Art Institute of Chicago.

238. Roger Kimball, "Home Is Where the Sociologist Is," review of *Inside Culture* by David Halle, *Times Literary Supplement,* 10 June 1994. Though Kimball (who is managing editor of *The New Criterion*) is an astute cultural critic, and we agree with him on many issues—from multiculturalism and political correctness to postmodernist "art"—we consider his position on abstract art to be completely mistaken, and were dismayed by his treatment of Halle.

239. As noted by Lionel Ruby (*Logic,* 136), the ad hominem argument—seeking "to discredit a proposition by discrediting the speaker"—is "an evasion of the law of rationality because it fails to provide relevant evidence against the proposition it seeks to disprove."

240. Maureen Corrigan, "What Does New York Like to Put Over Its Sofas? (and Why?)," review of *Inside Culture* by David Halle, *New York Observer,* 21 February 1994.

Chapter 9   Photography: An Invented "Art"

1. A recent introductory esthetics text not only treats photography as an art but argues that it "could replace painting." Graham, *Philosophy of the Arts,* 85. Many art history textbooks, too, now treat photographic images on a par with painting and sculpture. Although the first edition of H. W. Janson's classic *History of Art* (1962), for example, contained only scattered references to photography—in relation to discussions of painting, not as an art form in its own right—the third edition (1986), edited by his son, Anthony Janson, devotes its entire final chapter to photography as one of "the arts." In his Preface, he explains that, "though its status is still challenged, photography now merits treatment as a legitimate field of art historical investigation." Marilyn Stokstad's more recent *Art History* (1995) *begins* with an extended comparison of painting and photography, claiming that "Photographs can be powerful works of art." Recent editions of Honour and Fleming, *Visual Arts*; and Adams, *History of Western Art,* also treat photography as an art.

2. Rand, "Art and Cognition," 74. Rand acknowledges that there is "an artistic element in some photographs, which is the result of such selectivity as the photographer can exercise"; but, in adding "and some of them can be very beautiful" and comparing them to "many utilitarian products," she seems to imply that the only value that can be conveyed by a photographic image is beauty. We would argue that photographs can suggest a much broader, and more fundamental, range of human values—though they do so not because the photographer is an "artist" but, rather, because he is able to capture what Henri Cartier-Bresson termed "the decisive moment" expressing the character of a person or event. Significantly, as we note later in this chapter, the acclaimed photographer does not consider his own work to be art. See below, n. 25.

3. Rand, *Fiction-Writing,* Lecture 1. In the same vein, the art historian Edgar Wind observed: "What precludes photography, as [philosopher Benedetto] Croce put it, from becoming 'entirely art,' although it may have 'something artistic about it' [*Estetica* (1958 ed.), I, ii, 20], is the crucial surrender of the pictorial act to an optical or chemical agency which, however carefully set up and controlled by the photographer, must remain automatic in its operation." Wind, *Art and Anarchy,* 138n140.

See also André Bazin's remarks on the "essentially objective character of photography": "For the first time an image of the world is formed automatically, without the creative intervention of man. The personality of the photographer enters into the proceedings only in his selection of the object to be photographed. . . . Although the final result may reflect something of his personality, this does not play the same role as is played by that of the painter. *All the arts are based on the presence of man*, only photography derives an advantage from his absence." "The Ontology of the Photographic Image," in *What Is Cinema?* 1:13, emphasis ours.

4. Roger Scruton similarly emphasizes that a photograph of a person reveals how the subject appears *at a given moment*, whereas a painted portrait aims to convey the enduring essence of the sitter's character. "Photography and Representation," *Critical Inquiry* 7 (1981): 586–87.

5. The phrase "mechanical and mindless" is from John Szarkowski, the former director of the photography department at the Museum of Modern Art; see his *Photographer's Eye*, Introduction.

6. Susan Sontag, *On Photography*, and Scruton, "Photography and Representation" (see above, n. 4). Neither Sontag nor Scruton defines or comments on the crucial term "art." Sontag's view is implicit in her uncritical observation that the museums' "naturalization of photography as art is the conclusive victory of the century-long campaign waged by modernist taste on behalf of an open-ended definition of art." (131) Her muddled concept of art is further apparent in the following statement: "Although photography generates works that can be called art—it requires subjectivity, it can lie, it gives aesthetic pleasure—photography is not, to begin with, an art form at all. Like language, it is a medium in which works of art (among other things) are made. . . . Photography is not an art like, say, painting and poetry." (148) For indications of Scruton's concept of art, see Ch. 10.

7. On this point, see Louis Torres, letter to the *New York Times*, 13 August 1989. [Though I was unaware of it at the time, the same idea is explicit in Stephen Sondheim's lyric for his 1984 musical, *Sunday in the Park with George* (Act II): "Bit by bit, / Putting it together . . . / Piece by piece— / Only way to make a work of art. / Every moment makes a contribution, / Every little detail plays a part. / Having just the vision's no solution, / Everything depends on execution: / Putting it together— / That's what counts." Letters from three readers disagreeing with my conclusion that photography is not art were published in the *Times*, 27 August 1989. See *Aristos*, November 1989, for a reprint of my original letter, and my comments on the responses.—*L.T.*]

8. As emphasized by John Kouwenhoven in a highly illuminating essay: "Photographs record only unstoried instants of ever-changing reality, while paintings include aspects of that reality that were perceived over a period of time and were deliberately selected by the painter for their significance. . . . [The photographer] cannot select some details and ignore others visible at that instant, nor can [he] incorporate details that were visible at other moments no matter how significant [he] might consider them to be. A continuing process of selection determines what details are included in a painting, and the painting's [meaning emerges from] that sustained process." "Living in a Snapshot World," in *Half a Truth*, 158. The extent to which painters modify the details of a scene even when they are painting from nature is

readily discernible in photos *American Artist* magazine occasionally publishes showing painters at work—illustrating, in effect, Rand's concept of "a selective recreation of reality."

9. William Fox Talbot, *The Pencil of Nature*, quoted in Haworth-Booth, *Photography*, 21. Talbot's use of the verb "depict" here is not quite accurate, however, since it implies intentional representation—which does not occur in the essentially mechanical process of photography. For an early photograph by Talbot, *Articles of Glass* (1843), see <http://www.artlex.com> under "photography."

10. On the issue of intention, see Scruton, "Photography and Representation," esp. 581, 586, and 593. Profound meaning has sometimes been mistakenly inferred from entirely accidental aspects of photographs. John Kouwenhoven justly objected to the historian Michael Lesy's claim (eventually published in his book *Wisconsin Death Trip* [New York: Pantheon, 1973]) that the staring eyes in photos of small-town midwesterners in the 1890s evinced suffering and mental illness. "Those images of staring eyes are not 'primary data' for the psychic history of a community," Kouwenhoven argued, "they are visual documentation of specific people's difficulties holding still during the long exposures required by available lenses and emulsions." "Photographs as Historical Documents," in *Half a Truth Is Better Than None*, 197. The same circumstances were responsible for the dour facial expressions of sitters in portraits by the acclaimed nineteenth-century photographer Julia Cameron—expressions that have been portentously ascribed to such emotions as "sorrow, resignation, composure, solemnity, and . . . determined love." See Janet Malcolm, "The Genius of the Glass House," review of *Julia Margaret Cameron's Women*, by Sylvia Wolf et al. (New Haven: Yale University Press, 1998), *New York Review of Books*, 4 February 1999, 10.

11. Sontag observes that, "despite their reluctance to say so, most photographers have always had—with good reason—an almost superstitious confidence in the lucky accident." *On Photography*, 117. No doubt their reluctance stems from the knowledge or suspicion that, as Rand emphasized, the accidental has no place in art.

12. In the creative act of painting, however, merely looking at a photograph is *not* a substitute for looking at the thing itself. Paintings based primarily or exclusively on photographs are not art, because they are a selective re-creation not of reality but of an image of reality. (On this practice, see Christopher Willard, "Paintings from Photographs," *American Artist*, March 1999, 12–18; and other issues of this magazine.) Such paintings lack what is implicit in all art: the artist's response to life itself—to real people, places, and things. Yet Gerhard Richter's *Seascape* (1969), a "romantic composition based on two photographs," sold for $2.5 million in 1998. Carol Vogel, "Gamble Pays Off for Christie's," *New York Times*, 4 June 1998.

13. Hans Koning, "Notes on the Mirror with a Memory," *Atlantic Monthly*, July 1990, 89–90, emphasis ours. In contrast, see Robert Atkins, "Photography Becomes Art," review of exhibition *Photography and Art: Interactions since 1946*, *Horizon*, June 1987.

14. Haworth-Booth, *Photography*, 25.

15. Quoted *ibid.*, 73.

16. Though the commissioners of the international exhibition to be held at South Kensington, London, in 1862, initially classified photography with machinery, they reclassified it as "an independent art" to mollify photographers and their advocates, who had vehemently protested that the previous classification demeaned their work. *Ibid.,* 78–79.

17. For an image of Stieglitz's classic photograph *The Steerage* (1907) on the Internet, follow the link "photography" at <http://www.artlex.com>.

18. On Alfred Stieglitz, see Peter Blank, "Which History of Photography: The Modernist Model," *Art Documentation,* Winter 1994, 19.

19. Vicki Goldberg, "Ethnologists' Data Turn Out to Be Art," *New York Times,* 13 September 1996.

20. Guggenheim Museum, Press Release, 3 December 1992, emphasis ours. In exchange for a bequest of $2 million in cash and more than two hundred of Mapplethorpe's "finest photographs," the Guggenheim trustees agreed to incorporate a "strong, in-depth selection of [his] work into the [museum's] permanent collection of twentieth-century masters." According to the museum's director, Thomas Krens: "For the Guggenheim Museum, which has to date been exclusively focused on painting and sculpture, this is an historic event. Photography is one of this century's most significant artistic pursuits." *Ibid.*

21. The Khmer Rouge exhibition provoked a storm of protest in the media. The *New York Times* commented on its editorial page: "[I]t is certainly fair to ask what these sensational photographs are doing in an art museum. Does this imply that the killers who took them are artists? Can genocide be art? And does the book from Twin Palms, so glossily produced, estheticize and exploit the dead?" *New York Times,* 20 June 1997.

22. "In the past decade photography has attained a prominence in the art world that is unprecedented in its 150 years of existence." Grundberg and Gauss, 7.

23. Grace Glueck,"Art on the Firing Line," *New York Times,* 9 July 1989.

24. Hilton Kramer, "Is Art above the Laws of Decency?" *New York Times,* 2 July 1989.

25. Anthony Janson, after stating that Cartier-Bresson "thinks of himself primarily as [a photojournalist]," then declares that his "purpose and technique are nevertheless those of an artist." *History of Art,* 3d ed., 770. For Cartier-Bresson's disclaimer, see *New York Times,* 14 November 1990. On Dorothea Lange, see <http://sheldon.unl.edu/HTML/ARTIST/Lange_D/AS.html>.

26. Cartier-Bresson, quoted by Michel Nuridsany, "The Moment That Counts: An Interview with Henri Cartier-Bresson," *New York Review of Books,* 2 March 1995.

27. Deborah Solomon, "But Is It Art?" *New York Times Magazine,* 4 October 1998.

28. What Solomon terms "folk photography" is also known as "vernacular photography," or "unpremeditated art." See the *Wall Street Journal* article (by Eileen Kinsella) about collecting snapshots, entitled "Accidental Art," 2 October 1998.

29. Hambourg also managed to persuade the trustees of the Ford Motor Company to vote a gift of $1.8 million dollars to purchase a major private collection of photographs—which Solomon characterizes as "the largest corporate gift ever made in this country to acquire *art*." Solomon, "But Is It Art?", 66, emphasis ours.

30. Grundberg and Gauss, Introduction to *Photography and Art*, 17. Art critic Christopher Knight considered this a "landmark exhibition." See his review in *Last Chance for Eden*, 286.

Chapter 10 Architecture: "Art" or "Design"?

1. Regarding Rand's research on architecture for *The Fountainhead*, see B. Branden, *Passion of Ayn Rand*, 143–44; *Journals of Ayn Rand*, chap. 5; and Peter Reidy, "The Ideal Made Real," *Navigator* (Institute for Objectivist Studies), July–August 1998. To judge from her *Journals*, Rand's primary focus was on contemporary practice, not on the history and philosophy of architecture.

2. Rand, *Journals*, 189.

3. Preliminary notes on Roark's characterization, under the heading "Artistically," *Journals*, 189. Rand further wrote of architecture as "Changing the face of nature, man's background, that against which his whole life is played." *Ibid*. Yet it is important to recognize that she did not regard the arts as the sole arena for spiritual values or human creativity. See n. 7, below. It is also worth noting that Kira, the heroine of Rand's semi-autobiographical first novel, *We the Living*, was portrayed as another type of creator—an engineer, whose goal was, in Kira's words, to "build" bridges.

4. *The Fountainhead*, 505–506. The metaphor "music in stone" is inapt in view of the contradictory attributes of its two components. Rand's extended comparison of architecture to music is less than satisfactory even in purely literary terms. If Roark is to be considered a primary artist, then the "variations on a single theme" represented by the homes he designed should be compared to a symphony *composed* by "an inexhaustible imagination," not "played" by one. There is, of course, a long, if unfortunate, tradition of similarly flawed figures of speech, the most famous of which is Goethe's reference to architecture as "frozen music," a phrase echoed by Rand's "music in stone"—metaphors which ignore that the essence of music is melodic *movement*.

5. Imitation of real objects rarely occurs in architecture. And even when it does occur—as, for example, in the exterior of the Opera House in Sydney, Australia, which is in the form of a sail, inspired by its marine setting—the primary intention and effect are symbolic, not *representational*. That is, as Scruton explains (*Aesthetics of Architecture*, 187–91), awareness of the object imitated is not essential to the architectural experience; the building does not focus or develop *thought* upon the object—it is merely a visual allusion on the periphery of one's consciousness.

6. John Gillis, an architect with a particular interest in Rand's philosophy of art, mistakenly argues that, according to her theory, the "two categories [of] art and utilitarian object . . . are not mutually exclusive." Letter to the Editor, *Full Context*, November 1992. His claim ignores her statement that "utilitarian objects cannot be classified as works of art" (74).

7. Years before she wrote her essays on esthetics, Rand used an equally problematic locution when she explained to an admirer that she had chosen architecture as the profession of the hero of *The Fountainhead* because "it is a field of work that *covers both art and a basic need of men's survival*" and "one cannot find a more eloquent symbol of man as creator than a man who is a builder." Letter to Helen Blodgett, 28 August 1943, in *Letters*, 92, emphasis ours. Rand's phrase "man as creator" need not be limited to the sphere of art, however, since she elsewhere explicitly characterized creators as including thinkers, scientists, and inventors as well. *For the New Intellectual*, 77.

8. Conspicuously, *The Ayn Rand Lexicon* (a "compilation of key statements"), edited by Harry Binswanger, does not include an entry on Architecture, although it lists entries for forty-one topics under "Philosophy: Esthetics." These include all the art forms and related topics Rand discussed in her essays, from Art, Decorative Arts, Literature, and Motion Pictures, to Music, Painting, Photography, and Sculpture. See the "Conceptual Index," xvii–xviii. Given Rand's explicit statements on architecture in "Art and Cognition," its omission from the *Lexicon* is troubling—the more so since Binswanger reports that Rand "helped [him] define appropriate standards for . . . topic selection," and that she was able to review the entries under the letter "A" before her death. Editor's Preface, ix.

9. Batteux, *Les Beaux-Arts,* Preface to the first edition, translation ours.

10. Batteux clearly implies that this third category (combining utility with pleasure) comprises more than just architecture and rhetoric (*l'éloquence*), however—in contrast with Rand's claim that architecture is "in a class by itself." We suspect that he included only these because rhetoric had since antiquity been a focus of interest in philosophic considerations of the liberal arts and the arts in general, and because architecture had been prominent in such discussions since the Renaissance.

11. Batteux's implication that architecture came into being at a later date than the fine arts brings to mind yet another respect in which Rand's theory suggests that it should not be classified with them: her argument that "all the arts were born in prehistoric times" as a means of "unify[ing] man's consciousness and offer[ing] him a coherent view of existence." "Art and Cognition," 73. Even Gillis, who argues that architecture is art (see above, n. 6), implies that it was not born of this need, since it "originated in the human need for shelter."

12. Batteux's term "poetry" (*la poésie*) subsumed imaginative literature, as contrasted with *l'éloquence* (rhetoric), which applied to expository literature and argumentation.

13. Gordon Graham, *Philosophy of the Arts*, 131.

14. As we have noted, Batteux's designation of this category referred to "pleasure" (not "beauty") and "utility."

15. The *Oxford Companion to Art* (ed. Osborne, 1970), on which the *Oxford Dictionary of Art* is based, presents an even more muddled account of the classification of architecture. It claims that Nicolas Blondel's *Cours d'Architecture* (1675) anticipated the eighteenth-century classification system in arguing that the pleasure of architecture is based on the same principle (i.e., "'uniformity of harmony'") as

that of "poetry, eloquence, comedy, painting, sculpture, and the like." Lest too much be made of this comparison, however, we note that Blondel (who was a military engineer as well as an architect) also compared "the beauty of the harmonies of music" with those of "an army ranged in battle" (785). Like its successor volume, the *Companion* misrepresents the principles underlying Batteux's classification system, claiming them to be "beauty" and "utility," rather than "pleasure" and "utility."

16. D'Alembert's entry on the "Arts" for the *Encyclopedia* did not even discuss the fine arts, focusing instead on the liberal and, more especially, on the mechanical, arts.

17. D'Alembert, *Preliminary Discourse*, 37.

18. The value of the traditional classification of the "imitative arts" (which omitted architecture but included music) is insufficiently recognized by the principal scholars who have traced the origins of the concept "fine art." Paul Oskar Kristeller, in his landmark essay "The Modern System of the Arts" (1951-52), is critical of the classical philosophers' omission of architecture from the category. "The Modern System of the Arts," in *Renaissance Thought and the Arts,* 171–72. See also n. 22 below. Wladyslaw Tatarkiewicz, in his book-length study *A History of Six Ideas* (1975), notes that architecture was omitted from "the 'imitative' or 'mimetic' arts" prior to the mid-eighteenth century; but he mistakenly claims that music was omitted as well (22), and he is ultimately critical of Batteux for omitting architecture and including music (see below, n. 24). In contrast, the value of the concept of mimesis as a basis for conceptualizing the fine arts is emphasized by Stephen Halliwell in *Aristotle's Poetics* and "Aristotelian Mimesis Reevaluated," *Journal of the History of Philosophy* 28 (1990): 487–510. That concept was perpetuated in the most complete Renaissance system of the fine arts—compiled from the notebooks of Leonardo (in the *Paragone*, edited by Irma A. Richter). Leonardo compares painting with sculpture, poetry, and music, but not with architecture. Other treatises similarly omit architecture: Gotthold Lessing's classic and highly influential study *Laocoon* (*Laokoön* in some editions), focuses on a comparison of poetry and the visual arts; and Rensselaer Lee's *Ut Pictura Poesis* explores the long tradition of such comparisons since antiquity, while Andrew Kagan's "Ut Pictura Musica" surveys sources comparing music to painting and the other arts. "Ut Pictura Musica, I: to 1860." *Arts Magazine* 60 (May 1986): 86–91.

19. Susanne Langer commits a comparable error when she accepts Le Corbusier's claim that in architecture man "creat[es] his own universe . . . *in the image of nature"*—adding, by way of explanation, "not, indeed, by simulating natural objects, but by exemplifying 'the laws of gravity, of statics and dynamics.'" *Feeling and Form*, 97, emphasis ours. To argue that an "image" does not *simulate natural objects* but, rather, *exemplifies physical principles* not only places esthetic concerns on a remote, abstract plane but also robs the concept "image" of its essential meaning and of its fundamental relevance to the visual arts—yet another instance in twentieth-century esthetics of what Rand termed a "stolen concept." We have commented on similar instances with regard to abstract painting and sculpture in Chapter 8.

20. For d'Alembert's comparison of the fine arts, in which he does not mention architecture, see Denis Diderot's *Encyclopedia* (Selections), ed. Gendzier, 16.

21. As early as 1769, for example, Saverio Bettinelli, the author of *Dell'Entusiasmo delle Belle Arti*, listed the fine arts (*belle arti*) as poetry, eloquence, painting, sculpture, architecture, music, and dance, and cited the *Encyclopedia*, among other sources. Kristeller, "Modern System," 189n130.

22. Kristeller, "Modern System," 202. Kristeller's essay, though a landmark contribution to the scholarship on the subject, is marred in several important respects. First, he downplays the importance of the ancient concept of "mimetic art" (in part, because it ignored architecture) in the genesis of the concept "fine art." He also faults the writers and thinkers of antiquity both for their inability or unwillingness "to detach the aesthetic quality of . . . works of art from their intellectual, moral, religious and practical function or content" and for their failure "to use . . . aesthetic qualit[ies] as a standard for grouping the fine arts together or for making them the subject of a comprehensive philosophical interpretion." *Ibid.*, 174. Such criticisms imply that he considers "aesthetic" qualities (such as beauty, presumably), rather than meaning, to be of *primary* importance in art. What Kristeller thus represents as a flaw in early theories of art, we regard as a major virtue—one revived and strengthened in Rand's philosophy of art. Also regrettable is Kristeller's uncritical acceptance of d'Alembert's *inclusion* of architecture among the "imitative arts"—Kristeller fails to question, or even mention, d'Alembert's inadequate argument for that departure from long-established practice. *Ibid.*, 170–71, 202. He also erroneously claims that "Diderot and the other authors of the *Encyclopédie* . . . followed Batteux's system of the fine arts" (200), although Batteux had unequivocally placed rhetoric and architecture in a separate category. See also n. 18, above.

23. See, for example, the comprehensive article by Sidney Colvin *s.v.* "Fine Arts" in the classic 11th edition of the *Encyclopedia Britannica* (1910). It notes (under the rubric "Non-imitative character of architecture"): "As music appeals to our faculties for taking pleasure in non-imitative combinations of transitory sound, so architecture appeals to our faculties for taking pleasure in non-imitative combinations of stationary mass." With mimesis thus discarded as a defining attribute of art, the door was opened to the eventual acceptance of abstract painting and sculpture.

24. Tatarkiewicz, for example, mistakenly claims that "Batteux included architecture . . . among the imitative arts." *Six Ideas*, 276; see also 273–74 and 22. He also mistakenly characterizes music as "non-imitative" and unfairly faults Batteux for including it (274). At one point, he vaguely alludes to Batteux's placement of architecture and rhetoric in a *separate* category ("Batteux listed five fine arts—painting, sculpture, music, poetry and dance—plus two related ones, architecture and eloquence"), but then misleadingly adds: "This list [of the seven arts] came to be universally accepted." *Ibid.*, 21. On Kristeller's errors, see nn. 18 and 22, above.

25. For readers interested in a less theoretical approach than that offered by Scruton, Steen Eiler Rasmussen's *Experiencing Architecture* offers a lucid analysis of the basic elements involved in the perception of architectural form and value.

26. Note, for instance, Scruton's suggestion that the "concept of art" involving "such distinctions as that between art and craft" is "inadequate . . . to the discussion of architecture." *Aesthetics of Architecture*, 259.

27. Despite his characterization of painting and sculpture as "representational arts" here, Scruton does not appear to reject the notion of "abstract art." See, for example, his uncritical references to "the abstracts of Mondrian" (179) and "abstract art" (181–82).

28. The "'sculptural' view of architecture" that Scruton alludes to can refer only to abstract sculpture.

29. The example of Wright's Guggenheim Museum is instructive here. While the building's spacious central interior, with its spiral ramp, is visually exciting, it has been justly faulted by critics for ill serving the needs of museum exhibition. Only in the adjoining rooms can museumgoers view art in an undistracted state of physical equilibrium. In the main exhibition space along the ramp, the viewer either feels the effort of ascending or the subtle pull of gravity downward.

30. G. L. Hersey, "Architecture," *World Book Encyclopedia*, 1981 ed., 566. Ironically, many of Wright's structures are badly built and have proved to be "maintenance horrors." See Reidy (cited above, n. 1). See also Timothy D. Schellhardt, "This Office Building Is a Work of Art, Unless It's Raining," *Wall Street Journal*, 18 February 1997, which reports on the physical problems of Wright's acclaimed Johnson Wax Building in Racine, Wisconsin—which has been preposterously characterized as not merely America's "greatest piece of twentieth-century architecture" but "possibly, the most profound work of art that America has ever produced" (Kenneth Frampton, Introduction to *Frank Lloyd Wright and the Johnson Wax Buildings*, by Jonathan Lipman, xii). The building's structural problems include a leaky roof and a haven for mice, as well as excessive noise in corner offices whenever it rains.

31. Lescaze, in Centeno, 141. See also Hersey, 566–67. As the critic Brendan Gill observed in a 1998 PBS documentary on Wright, "there's no point in being an architect unless you get to build." A contemporary house constructed in the 1990s in Bordeaux, France, dramatically illustrates the sorts of problems that an architectural design must solve in response to the client's needs. Since the owner had lost the use of his legs in an automobile accident, the architect designed an elevator room as both the dramatic and the functional core of the house. Herbert Muschamp, "Living Boldly on the Event Horizon," *New York Times*, 19 November 1998.

32. On this point, Rand's discussion of the scene in *The Fountainhead* describing the emotional impact of Roark's Monadnock Valley village is highly misleading. While it is true that works of architecture can afford inspiration through "the sight of human achievement," it does not follow that they are *art*, as Rand claims. "The Goal of My Writing," 170.

33. Wright's Guggenheim Museum provides a stark illustration of this principle. Originally designed for a site surrounded by trees and landscape, the building's spiral exterior is incongruous amidst the urbane uniformity of Fifth Avenue's rectilinear apartment buildings. See also the examples cited by Scruton in his discussion of "localized quality" (i.e., site specificity) in *Aesthetics of Architecture*, 10–12.

34. Wright, *Future of Architecture*, 19.

35. *Fallingwater*—the vacation home Wright designed for the Kaufman family in Bear Run, Pennsylvania—was voted the most outstanding work of architecture of

the past 125 years. Regarding Wright's "Organic Architecture," see his London lectures under that title in *Future of Architecture*.

36. On the complex influence of such practical considerations, see Scruton, 26–30. Michael Frank emphasizes, for example, that "the need for light and air [largely] determined the form of early skyscrapers." "New York Skyscrapers as Ancient Temples," *New York Times*, 4 July 1997.

37. Here Scruton's remark pertains only to figurative sculpture, whereas an earlier comparison by him pertained only to abstract sculpture. See above, n. 28.

38. Roark asks the sculptor for the figure of "a naked woman" that will express "The human spirit. The heroic in man. . . . Seeking God—and finding itself. Showing that there is no higher reach beyond its own form." *The Fountainhead*, 332. See also Rand's brief remarks on the close relationship between sculpture and architecture in "Art and Cognition," 50; cited above, Ch. 4, n. 5.

39. See, for example, the scene between Dagny Taggart and the composer Richard Halley which was excerpted in *For the New Intellectual*, and our objections in Chapter 5, n. 40.

40. Contrary to Rand's claim in *The Fountainhead* (519), a building alone cannot convey a "sense of joy."

41. For a particularly egregious example of architecture criticism that elevates buildings to fine art despite their "functional rationale," see Ada Louise Huxtable, "The New Architecture," *New York Review of Books*, 6 April 1995, in which phrases such as "poetic force," "eloquently expressive masonry," "sculptural shapes," and "high art" are repeatedly employed.

42. See Rosenthal, *Abstraction*, 5–7 and 91; and the "Chronology" section at the end of the volume, which includes biographical sketches on such architects as Walter Gropius, Mies van der Rohe, and Le Corbusier, though the bulk of the section pertains to abstract painters and sculptors.

43. Denise McColgan, in Rosenthal, *Abstraction*, 276.

44. H.W. Janson, *History of Art,* rev. ed., 552; and 3rd ed., 741. See also Michael Benedikt, "Sculpture as Architecture," in Battcock, *Minimal Art*, 61-91.

45. Kimmelman, "The Museum as Work of Art," *New York Times*, 20 October 1997. To Gehry's credit, however, when he was asked if he thinks of himself as a "sculptor" as much as as an architect, he replied that, while architecture, as a three-dimensional object, is sculptural, "it's different." He explained that his work "has to do with buildings that are functional and have budgets and have people using them and relate to different kind[s] of constraints. In the end, after you solve all the functional problems, there's a moment of truth, I call it, where you're like the artist. You're making decisions of scale and form and composition and color and texture and so on. But I think it's different. I've been invited to make sculptures, and I've fantasized it. . . . [But] no, I'm an architect, pure and simple." "The Newest Guggenheim," interview with Elizabeth Farnsworth on the PBS "NewsHour," 21 October 1997 (for the text of the interview and related material, see <http://www.pbs.org/newshour>). Yet Kimmelman argues that "the persistent question [about the Bilbao museum] has been

whether any art can thrive in what is really a monumental sculpture." "Richard Serra: A Spectacular Meeting of Sculpture and Space," *New York Times*, 29 August 1999.

46. Alan Riding, "Guggenheim Opens in Spain under Shadow of Militants," *New York Times*, 19 October 1997.

47. The basic sense of *disegno* in the Italian term *Arti di disegno* is "drawing"— on which all the visual arts depend. As defined in the classic *Enciclopedia Italiana* (Rome, 1939), it means "the graphic representation of forms." See also Murray, *Dictionary of Art and Artists*, *s.v.* "Disegno." In English, however, "design" and "drawing" are not synonymous.

48. Leon Battista Alberti, *De Re Aedificatoria* (trans. by Bartolo and Leoni as *Ten Books on Architecture*), Book X; quoted by Scruton, *Aesthetics of Architecture*, 23–24. Ironically, the principle articulated by Alberti seems to anticipate the modernist dictum that "form follows function," though the architectural results in each case could not be more disparate.

49. In addition, Scruton further implies that architecture is a "decorative art"— thereby ignoring the distinction between that concept and "design." While we agree that architecture is a species of *design*, we would not term it a "decorative art."

So-called *landscape architecture* is also a species of design. Regrettably, the *Art and Architecture Thesaurus* prefers this dubious term over its more appropriate synonyms *landscape design* and *landscape gardening* (defined as "the development and decorative planting of gardens and grounds"). Though "gardening" was sometimes erroneously included among the fine arts in the eighteenth century, the pretentious designation "landscape architecture" is of late and rather spurious origin. It is ironic that the individual often credited with raising the practice to a "high art"—Frederick Law Olmstead (1822–1903), the brilliant co-designer, with the architect Calvert Vaux, of New York's Central Park and countless other urban parks in America— never considered himself an artist, and employed the term "landscape architecture" only reluctantly. It was Vaux who pressed this exalted designation upon him, with the explicit intent of enhancing the prestige of their project and thereby increasing public support for it. Laura Roper, *FLO*, 292. Rather than "post [him]self in the portals of art," a presumption he deemed "sacrilegious," Olmstead conceived of his work as an undertaking which would improve the surroundings of the urban populace, and thereby promote human well-being, physical as well as spiritual. *Ibid.*, 315–16. He recognized that landscape and garden design differ fundamentally from (fine) art, because the designer depends on nature to "realize his intentions." The primary materials of landscape design are the living products of nature which the designer merely selects and arranges rather than re-creates. That the term *art* applies to the realm of the *man-made*—as contrasted with the realm of nature, absent human intervention— is a fundamental distinction now largely ignored, however, as evidenced by two important monographs on the garden as an "art" form: Miller, *The Garden as an Art* (1993); and Ross, *What Gardens Mean* (1998).

50. The late architecture critic Reyner Banham, quoted by Martin Filler in "The Big Rock Candy Mountain," review of three books on the Getty Center, *New York Review of Books*, 18 December 1997, 32.

51. Andrew Ballantyne, "Where Once Taliesin Shone," review of *The Architecture of Frank Lloyd Wright*, by Neil Levine, *Times Literary Supplement*, 8 November 1996, 4, emphasis ours.

52. Witold Rybczynski, "Gentlemen, Here Is the Winner," review of *Architectural Competitions*, by Cees de Jong and Erik Mattie, *Times Literary Supplement*, 11 August 1995, 19.

Chapter 11 Decorative Art and Craft

1. The concepts of "decorative art" and "craft" overlap considerably in recent usage: both subsume objects that combine utilitarian function with attention to esthetically pleasing visual and, often, tactile properties. The *Art and Architecture Thesaurus* defines *decorative arts* as the "[t]raditional Western designation for those arts involving the creation of works that serve utilitarian as well as aesthetic purpose, or involving the decoration and embellishment of utilitarian objects." As this definition indicates, the term sometimes refers only to the applied decorative elements themselves (Rand's sense), sometimes to the decorated object as a whole. Synonymous terms are *applied arts* and *minor arts*. In contemporary usage, the term *decorative art* is rapidly being replaced by *craft* (a shortened form of *handicraft*), a term which in its original and most concrete sense means simply "the activity, and its products, of forming handmade articles," while *craftsmen* (or *artisans*) are "persons who practice or are highly skilled in a craft." *Art and Architecture Thesaurus*. Though their etymology and connotations differ, *decorative art* and *craft* are now often used interchangeably, resulting in considerable conceptual confusion. As noted by Larry Shiner (in Kelly, *Encyclopedia of Aesthetics, s.v.* "Craft"), the term *craft* has two related meanings: "human ability in production or performance" (comparable to the original concept of "art"—*techne* or *ars*—in antiquity) and "a class of activities or objects that result from such abilities" (a sense that could apply to both decorative and fine art). See also n. 5 below, and our further discussion of these concepts under "Historical Influences" later in this chapter.

2. Roberta Smith, "Conference Ponders Nature of Crafts," *New York Times*, 22 January 1990. Smith's reference to the attending craftsmen as "artists" is symptomatic of a widespread trend. Where curators, critics, and journalists once wrote of "design" and "designers," "craft" and "craftsman," or "artifacts" and "artisans," they increasingly refer to "art" and "artists," often alternating in their choice of terms in a given context.

3. In its broad generic sense meaning "skill in the adaptation of things in the natural world to the uses of human life" (*Webster's New International Dictionary*, 2nd ed.), the concept of art could conceivably "embrace the whole range of man-made things"; but that is not the sense in which one would expect an art historian to construe it, since the profession of art history has traditionally dealt with art in the narrow sense of the visual "fine arts."

4. For a reproduction of Jusepe de Ribera's *St. Peter* on the Internet, search under the painter's name at <http://www.spectrumvoice.com/art/index.html>.

5. Patterson Sims, curator of modern art at the Seattle Art Museum, quoted by Smith (cited above, n. 2).

6. The term "decorative art," which Rand employed, is now in such disrepute among art scholars that the purportedly comprehensive *Dictionary of Art* (1996) altogether omits an entry on it, offering in its place only a passing mention, under "Classification of the Arts." Ironically, references to the "Decorative Arts" of various cultures nevertheless appear in the dictionary's index. The recent *Encyclopedia of Aesthetics* (ed. Kelly) also omits a definition or discussion under the term "Decorative Arts"—though it does refer the reader to related entries, such as "Craft" and "Morris, William." One drawback of the term is that it connotes surface beauty devoid of meaningful or expressive content (see n. 9 below), while many objects classified as decorative art do possess such content. See, for example, the splendid Scythian ornaments and objects illustrated in the cover article, "Scythian Gold," *Smithsonian*, March 2000.

7. We focus in the text on what we consider to be Rand's valid propositions on decorative art. But she also claims, mistakenly, that the "psycho-epistemological base of the decorative arts is . . . *purely sensory*" (emphasis ours); that they employ only "colors and shapes in nonrepresentational combinations conveying no meaning other than visual harmony"; and that any "representational element is a detriment in the decorative arts; it is an irrelevant distraction, a clash of intentions." "Art and Cognition," 75. She further argues that "although designs of little human figures or landscapes or flowers are often used to decorate textiles or wallpaper, they are artistically [esthetically] inferior to the nonrepresentational designs (74–75)." In so claiming, she is once again generalizing her own esthetic preference into a universal rule. (Rand's bias against realistic representation in the decorative arts echoes the view of numerous design theorists in the nineteenth century, who regarded the direct imitation of nature as "the chief vice" in the decorative arts of the day. E. H. Gombrich, *The Sense of Order*, 36.)

Contrary to Rand's assertion, of course, many highly developed traditions of decorative art have employed floral, human, and animal motifs and forms to admirable effect, in realistic as well as stylized treatments. See the many examples in Gombrich and in Rhys Carpenter, *Esthetic Basis of Greek Art*, esp. 16–20. Furthermore, even decorative elements that are entirely abstract and nonrepresentational are not experienced in a purely "sensory" fashion, but as attributes of the object they decorate—which is perceived as a whole, according to Rand's own views on the nature of perception. Indeed, in subsequently arguing that their "meaning or purpose is concrete and lies in the specific object they decorate," she seems to acknowledge this— though her use of the term "meaning" is inappropriate with respect to nonrepresentational elements.

8. We revise Rand's proposition here, because her literal claim, that the meaning or purpose of the decorative arts "lies in the specific object which they decorate," is misleading. Decorative art which incorporates symbolic or representational motifs *can* have meaning beyond the specific object.

9. As we noted in Chapter 8, many of the leading abstract artists rightly feared that, in the absence of perceptible meaning, their work would be perceived as "merely decorative." In the same vein, Steven Blake Shubert argues that, at root, the term *dec-*

orative pertains to "the embellishment or ornamentation of an object in order to evoke visual satisfaction or delight, *without any pretense of expressing meaning or emotion.*" "The Decorative Arts: A Problem of Classification," *Art Documentation*, Summer 1993, 78, emphasis ours. (Shubert's paper—which received the 1993 Gerd Muehsam Award from the Art Libraries Society of North America—offers a much-needed survey of the subject, but is riddled with errors of both fact and interpretation, some of which are noted below, n. 14.)

10. The most esthetically satisfying figured Greek vases, for example, are, in our view, those in which the figurative decoration is most stylized. See our brief review of *The Amasis Painter and His World*, in *Aristos*, March 1986. On the controversial question of whether Greek vases qualify as art, see Jasper Griffin, "Vases or Pots?" (review of *Artful Crafts: Ancient Greek Silverware and Pottery*, by Michael Vickers and David Gill), *New York Review of Books*, 8 June 1995. Vickers and Gill rightly argue in favor of their status as craft, not art.

11. Created in 1911 by Edward Clark Potter, the lions for the New York Public Library were intended by the sculptor to be "icons of nobility" (though some critics faulted their gentle appearance). Additional qualities—ascribed to them by the public—include patience and fortitude, for which they have been named. Margot Gayle and Michele Cohen, *Manhattan's Outdoor Sculpture* (New York: Prentice Hall Press, 1988), 156.

12. Rand's view, which we have summarized and briefly expanded upon here, contrasts sharply with the extreme (and, in our view, vacuous) formalist position articulated by the contemporary minimalist artist Frank Stella, who insists that a painting is nothing but "an object," devoid of any values "besides the paint on the canvas." Quoted by Karsten Harries (*Bavarian Rococo Church*, 252) from Bruce Glaser, "Questions to Stella and Judd," in Battcock, *Minimal Art*, 157–58. Stella is correct with regard to his own abstract work, of course.

13. Though it is often said that the distinction between "(fine) art" and "decorative art" arose in the eighteenth century, the fundamental classification of the arts into those "directed to the necessities of life" (the utilitarian) and those that "aim at giving pleasure" (the non-utilitarian) is clearly indicated in Aristotle *Metaphysics* (tr. McKeon) 1. 1. 981b.

14. The idea that (fine) art presents "beauty" for its own sake, while decorative art combines "beauty with utility," is sometimes mistakenly attributed to the eighteenth-century theorist Charles Batteux (whose treatise on the fine arts we cited in Chapter 10). The entry for "fine arts" in the *Oxford Companion to Art* (edited by Harold Osborne, a prominent British esthetician) states, for example, that Batteux's was a "systematic attempt to classify [the] arts in terms of beauty" and that he divided them into "the useful arts, the beautiful arts . . . , and those which combine beauty and utility." As the passage we quoted in Chapter 10 makes clear, however, Batteux's criteria were *pleasure* (not "beauty") and *utility*. Nonetheless, in mistakenly positing beauty as the main *source* of pleasure in art, he foreshadowed later theorists who exacerbated his error by claiming that beauty "for its own sake" is the *purpose* of art. Steven Blake Shubert ("The Decorative Arts") perpetuates the *Oxford Companion*'s misattribution of the idea to Batteux. Although Shubert cites Batteux's treatise

as his source, his statement that Batteux classified the arts as "either useful, beauti-ful . . . , or combining utility and beauty" (77) clearly echoes the *Oxford Companion* (which he cites in connection with another point, from a seventeenth-century treatise on architecture, also misquoted by both authors—see Ch. 10, n. 11). "The Decorative Arts: A Problem in Classification," *Art Documentation*, Summer 1993, 77–81.

15. See Norman Kelvin, "Morris, William," in Kelly, *Encyclopedia of Aesthetics*.

16. Alan Crawford, "Arts and Crafts Movement," in Turner, *Dictionary of Art*.

17. The mistaken assumptions of Aestheticism are still evident in contemporary criticism. In a review of three exhibitions of Asian carpets, for example, Holland Cotter claims that, "while we have come to associate great art with museum walls, it can also be found rolled up in the corner or spread out on the ground underfoot." Prais-ing carpets mainly for their *beauty*, Cotter observes not only that they serve various practical functions but also that their representations of nature are typically "distilled and abstracted"—characteristics that, in our view, confirm their status as decorative art. "Of Beauty Beneath the Feet," *New York Times*, 29 November 1996.

18. Clive Bell, "The Aesthetic Hypothesis," in *Art*, esp. 17–18.

19. The generic term *artifact* refers to any "objects made, modified, or used by man." *Art and Architecture Thesaurus*. It most often refers to objects from the past, whose purpose may or may not be known. According to the anthropologist Warren d'Azevedo: "The artistic [or esthetic] object detached from the producer or from the sociocultural matrix of its production is, in a real sense, an artifact." "Structural Approach to Aesthetics," in *Traditional Artist*, 710. See also n. 22 below.

20. The exhibition, entitled "Visions of the People: A Pictorial History of Plains Indian Life," was "the largest and most comprehensive" of its kind ever staged, and was funded by the National Endowment for the Arts. From the Minneapolis Insti-tute of Arts, it traveled to the St. Louis Art Museum and the Joslyn Art Museum in Omaha. Henry Adams, "The Enduring Vitality of Plains Indian Art," *Smithsonian*, November 1992, 124. Similar artifacts are featured in the George Gustav Heye Cen-ter, the first of three facilities in the Smithsonian Institution's National Museum of the American Indian, and are characterized as "Native works of art" by Joseph Bruchac, "The Heye Center Opens in Manhattan with Three Exhibitions of Native Arts," *Smith-sonian*, October 1994, 40.

21. A rare exception to the craft objects in the exhibition was a sensitively carved quartzite buffalo effigy from Alberta—which does qualify as art. For an illustration of this wonderful little sculpture, see Adams, "Enduring Vitality," *Smithsonian*, November 1992, 132.

22. Bruchac, "Heye Center," 40. Bruchac's frequent reference to the purported works of art as "objects" and "artifacts" indicates their real status, however. These are also the terms employed by a representative to the Six Nations Iroquois Con-federacy in lamenting the "difficulties [they] have had in preventing [their] sacred objects from being sold and becoming someone's 'art.'" Doug George-Kanentiio, letter to the editor, *New York Times*, 28 November 1994. By an ironic twist, the let-ter's heading, "Indian Art," belies the point made by the writer.

23. On the predominantly conventional, symbolic character of American Indian styles of visual representation, see Turner, *Dictionary of Art, s.v.* "Native North American Art," esp. pp. 558, 560, 561, and 590–91. Nancy J. Parezo emphasizes that the renowned sand paintings of the Navajo, for example, are essentially *mnemonic* in nature, employing a variety of symbolic motifs. "Designs are formal, geometric and abstract, and . . . standardized with little room for variation; they have to be exact in order to become efficacious, and no significant style changes have been noted since they were first recorded in the mid-1880s." *Ibid.*, 591.

24. According to the publisher's catalog description for Torrence's book, the parfleches constitute "one of the great traditions of abstract imagery created by American Indian artists" and should be of interest to scholars concerned with "modern abstract art"—a dubious claim to significance in our view.

25. Roderick Kiracofe and Mary Elizabeth Johnson, *The American Quilt: A History of Cloth and Comfort, 1750–1950*, quoted by Patricia T. O'Conner, "Art to Snuggle Under," *New York Times Book Review*, 15 December 1993.

26. For images of quilts from the Renwick Gallery—a division of the National Museum of American Art (a constituent of the Smithsonian Institution)—see <http://smithsonian/si.edu/smithsonian/issues96/nov96/quilts>.

27. O'Conner, "Art to Snuggle Under."

28. Virginia Hall, quoted by Patricia Leigh Brown, "Life's Thread Stitched into Quilts" (captioned "An African-American art form is revived"), *New York Times*, 4 April 1996.

29. Broude and Garrard, *Feminism and Art History*, 12–13.

30. Patricia Mainardi, "Quilts: The Great American Art," *Feminist Art Journal*, Winter 1973; reprinted in Broude and Garrard, 331–46, which we cite.

31. On the latter two neglected artists, see Michelle Marder Kamhi, "Anna Hyatt Huntington's 'Joan of Arc,'" *Aristos*, March 1988; and Beatrice Gilman Proske, "Harriet Whitney Frishmuth—Lyric Sculptor," *Aristos*, June 1984.

32. The largest exhibition of African art and artifacts ever held, *Africa: The Art of a Continent* was hailed as a turning point in the West's understanding and recognition of African art, according to Alan Riding, quoting William Packer, who wrote in *The Financial Times*: "'This is great art, all of it, and this is one of these rare exhibitions that change perception and understanding forever. . . . We shall never look at African art in our old innocent, patronizing naïveté again.'" The exhibition was unprecedented, Riding emphasized, because "objects made by African hands [were] separated from their cultural context and [could] be judged simply as art. "'Primitive' No More, African Art Finds a Proper Respect," *New York Times*, 29 October 1995.

33. Kwame Anthony Appiah, "Why Africa? Why Art?" in Phillips, *Africa: The Art of a Continent*, 7 and 8. Appiah is chairman of the Committee on African Studies, and Professor of African-American Studies and Philosophy, at Harvard University. The title of his essay reflects the dual irony he emphasizes: the objects exhibited were made by people who did not think of themselves as "Africans," and they were

not intended to serve the function of "art" (7). Our subsequent citations are to an expanded version of that essay that was published as "The Arts of Africa," *New York Review of Books*, 24 April 1997.

34. Appiah's refreshing insistence that "a weight is a weight" echoes Aristotle's "A is A" (a thing is what it is, and not just what someone *thinks* it is). Since this principle is axiomatic to Rand's philosophy, she adopted it as the title of Part III of *Atlas Shrugged*.

35. In a review of the exhibition, John Ryle similarly argues, regarding the *nkisi* figures—"anthropomorphic or zoomorphic sculpture[s] covered in congealed blood and honey, with nails and hoe blades hammered into [them]": "Whether you call these Kongo sculptures fetishes or power objects or ritual tools, one thing they are not is art. . . . To treat them as such is a category mistake; it is to fetishize the fetish." "The Anxiety of Exoticism: How the Western Idea of Art Impedes Our Understanding of Africa," *Times Literary Supplement*, 20 October 1995, 19. Ryle, the journal's ecology and anthropology editor, nonetheless mischaracterizes the portable furniture featured in the exhibition as "work[s] of art you carry with you." *Ibid.*

36. Although the precise use of the splendid life-sized Yoruba portrait heads (dating from the 11th–12th centuries) is uncertain, they may have been representations of kings that were used to display the royal regalia in a ritual setting. Drewal and Pemberton, *Yoruba*, 65–66. Though this is a nominally "practical" function, its spiritual focus is consistent with the function of art. In any case, these compelling sculptures—which possess an aura of dignified composure and benevolent strength that clearly transcends any practical function—merit classification as art. Puncture holes around the mouth probably served to attach a beaded veil for the lower face, in keeping with Yoruba tradition, which dictated that kings cover their mouths when eating or speaking. Though the mouth would not then have been visible, it is sculpted with great care and sensitivity—much as ancient Greek sculptors perfectly finished parts of figures that would not be visible in their final architectural setting. While these heads are akin to classical Greek sculpture in style, quality, and power of execution, they are thought to belong to a wholly indigenous tradition of representation.

37. Appiah's specialties are African philosophy and literature, not esthetics. Yet he echoes the contemporary artworld in declaring that "it is no longer helpful to try to explain what art has come to be for us by offering a definition." And he never explicitly questions the validity of contemporary Western notions about the nature of art, though he refers almost ruefully at one point to the artworld's "denizens whose work is to challenge every definition of art, to push us beyond every boundary, to stand outside and move beyond every attempt to fix art's meaning" (48).

38. See, for example, the following essays in d'Azevedo, *Traditional Artist*: Robert Farris Thompson, "Yoruba Artistic Criticism"; William Bascom, "A Yoruba Master Carver"; James Fernandez, "The Exposition and Imposition of Order: Artistic Expression in Fang Culture"; and Warren d'Azevedo, "Sources of Gola Artistry."

39. Curators and critics somewhat missed the point in emphasizing that the spirit figures and other works of Baule art differ from Western art in that they are not intended to be publicly displayed or gazed upon. See Roberta Smith, "Objects of Wonder That Are Too Potent for Mere Display," *New York Times*, 11 September 1998.

The crucial consideration is that they are self-contained visual embodiments of important values, not that they are displayed publicly or privately.

40. *Baule: African Art/Western Eyes*, Museum for African Art, New York City, 11 September 1998–3 January 1999.

41. Similarly, Warren d'Azevedo writes of the Gola, another West African society, that "there is in Gola culture a role similar to that of the artist in our own culture, though it is not so clearly differentiated by concepts and terminology." "Sources of Gola Artistry," in *Traditional Artist*, 334.

42. This point was emphasized in the exhibition of Baule art cited in n. 40, above. See also Daniel J. Crowley's comment that "Chokwe masks are essentially dance regalia, theatrical costuming designed to be seen in motion in combination with music, dance, and social, political, and/or religious activities." "Aesthetic Value and Professionalism in African Art: Three Cases from the Katanga Chokwe," in d'Azevedo, *Traditional Artist*, 247.

43. Jane Adlin, quoted by William L. Hamilton, "Handmade to High Style: Crafts Take Pride of Place," *New York Times*, 25 February 1999.

44. Whereas a well-conceived object of craft or decorative art conforms to the design principle Gombrich terms "explanatory articulation" (*Sense of Order*, 163–65), today's craft "artists" are concerned mainly with maximizing "visual expression." In the case of a contemporary tea service commissioned by the Newark (New Jersey) Museum, for instance, the forms do not serve to articulate the handle, spout, base, and lid; instead, they are largely arbitrary and free-flowing, and the result looks more like an abstract metal sculpture than a tea service. Rather than being defined and enhanced, the functional object is, in effect, camouflaged. For an illustration of the tea service, see Robert Mehlman, "High Tea, High Style," *Art & Auction*, November 1995. For other outlandish examples of contemporary teapots, see Marion Burros, "The Fine Art of Teapots (Hold the Tea)," *New York Times*, 18 April 1996.

45. Franklin Parrasch, quoted by Suzanne Slesin, "Art or Furniture? A Little of Both," *New York Times*, 19 March 1992.

46. "Tradition Defied: Artist Wendell Castle Questions Accepted Notions of Furniture Design," *Detroit Monthly*, DIA (Detroit Institute of Arts) section, December 1989, 2A and 3A.

47. Made of purpleheart (wood), cowhide, and aluminum, Wendell Castle's *Bench* (1987–88) carries bad design and pretentious tastelessness to new extremes. For an image and discussion of it, see the Detroit Institute of Arts website <http://www.dia.org/galleries/1988-19.html>. Not all members of the "studio furniture" movement share Castle's disdain for functionality and good design, however. Some are mindful that "providing support for the body, as well as pleasure for the eye, remains at the center of the furniture maker's art." Witold Rybcznski, "If a Chair Is a Work of Art, Can You Still Sit on It?" *New York Times*, 5 May 1991.

48. "Tradition Defied" (see above, n. 46), 2A.

49. Donald Kuspit, "Delirious Glass: Dale Chihuly's Sculpture," in Donald B. Kuspit and Jack Cowart, *Chihuly*, 31–32.

50. Of Chihuly's Glass Forest (consisting of some hundred stalks of opaque white milk-glass, six to nine feet tall, resting upon the flattened mass of molten glass from which they were blown), Kuspit declares, that it is "a fully realized statement of Chihuly's sense of the contradictory character of glass as both morbid residue and libidinously expressive line. . . . [Hi]s sense of glass as residue suggests the 'suicidal' character of the medium—it begins to 'die,' as it were, as soon as it leaves the fire." *Ibid.*, 34. While Kuspit recognizes, at least, that art must convey meaning, the meanings he ascribes to Chihuly's work derive more from the characteristics of the medium than from any ideas conveyed through form by their maker. Chihuly's forms are far too simple to support even a modicum of the significances Kuspit attributes to them. In contrast with such critical inflation, Peter Lane, a New York ceramist, unaffectedly declares: "I make decorative, functional work. . . . It's not sculpture. When contemporary craftspeople move away from design into art—and higher prices—it creates a new category that I don't find appealing." Peter Lane, quoted by Hamilton, "Handmade to High Style," *New York Times*, 25 February 1999.

51. See Dissanayake's *What Is Art For?* and *Homo Aestheticus*, which we discussed in Chapter 7.

52.. An exemplary approach seems to be offered by the Bard Center for the Decorative Arts in New York City, which aims to emphasize the relationship of objects to their historical and practical context. According to the school's founder, Susan Soros, the principal questions are "Who used the object? Why does it look the way it does, and what does it tell us about how people lived?" Susan Soros, quoted by Dinitia Smith, "A Private Life, a Public Passion," *New York Times*, 7 March 1996.

53. Reported by Roberta Smith (see above, n. 2).

Chapter 12 Avant-Garde Music and Dance

1. On the term "avant-garde," see Ch. 8, n. 8.

2. In recent years, music theorists have increasingly stressed the role of perceptual and cognitive constraints in the experience of music. See, for example, Leonard Meyer, "The Arguments for [and against] Experimental Music," in *Music, the Arts, and Ideas*, 245–65; Robert Erickson, "New Music and Psychology," in Deutsch, *Psychology of Music*, 517–535; and John A. Sloboda, "The Musical Mind in Context: Culture and Biology," in *The Musical Mind*, 239–268.

3. *Chromaticism* employs the "chromatic" scale, comprising all twelve halftones of an octave—in contrast with the "diatonic" seven-tone scales (comprising both whole and half-tones) characteristic of Western music since Greek antiquity. Because the chromatic scale lacks a clear central keynote, it contributes to a restless, unstable musical effect. Of the nineteenth-century composers, Wagner made the most extended use of it in *Tristan and Isolde*, as exemplified in the familiar "*Liebestod*."

4. Arnold Schoenberg, quoted in Schonberg, *Lives of the Great Composers*, 596. See also Paul Griffiths, "Schoenberg, Arnold," in Arnold, *New Oxford Companion to Music*, 1636.

5. Schoenberg, quoted in Schonberg, *Lives of the Great Composers*, 601.

6. Regarding Schoenberg's *Pierrot lunaire*, Terry Teachout has aptly observed: "Atonality makes sense only when intended to serve as a musical representation of nonsense [or pathology]—that is, [of] psychosis or some other dire mental disturbance. . . . [T]he ear registers it not as a separate musical language but as a deliberate distortion of the normal vocabulary of tonality." "Masterpieces of the Twentieth Century," *Commentary*, April 1999; and 6 May 1999 <http://www.commentarymagazine.com/9905/teachout.html>. For a study documenting listener response to atonal music, see J. David Smith and Jordan N. Witt, "Spun Steel and Stardust: The Rejection of Contemporary Compositions," *Music Perception*, Winter 1989, 169–86.

7. Paul Griffiths, "Serialism," in Sadie, *New Grove Dictionary of Music*; and Schonberg, *Lives*, 606–607.

8. Teachout's observation on atonal music (see above, n. 6) applies equally to serialism.

9. Schonberg, *Lives*, 620.

10. Milton Babbitt, "The Composer as Specialist," in Kostelanetz, *Esthetics Contemporary*, 280–81; first published as "Who Cares If You Listen?" in *High Fidelity*, February 1958.

11. Schonberg, *Lives*, 621.

12. Bernard Holland, "New York Premiere of Violin Concerto from Elliott Carter," *New York Times*, 3 December 1991.

13. Terry Teachout, "Masterpieces of the Century: A Finale," *Commentary*, June 1999; and <http://www.commentarymagazine.com/9906/teachout.html>. See also Teachout's "Holy Minimalism," *ibid.*, April 1995, 50–53.

14. Reich, for example, has referred to the "'harmonic ambiguity'" of early pieces such as *Come Out* (1966) and *It's Gonna Rain* (1965), and has emphasized that the chords in *The Desert Music* (1984) can't "'be positively nailed down.'" Quoted in Mark Dery, "The Reich Stuff," *Ovation*, May 1987, 14. Similarly, Glass has characterized his Symphony No. 2 (1994) as "'a study in bitonality,'" explaining that he is "'interested in the ambiguous qualities that can result from polytonality . . . how what you hear depends on how you focus your ear, how a listener's perception of tonality can vary in the fashion of an optical illusion.'" Quoted in K. Robert Schwarz, "Symphonic Film Score, Antisymphonic Symphony," *New York Times*, 10 January 1999. Smith and Witt (see n. 6 above) recognize the atonality of minimalism yet argue, mistakenly in our view, that a "focus on mood, atmosphere, and . . . referential program[s]" makes this music "'romantic'" (183–84).

15. According to K. Robert Schwarz (author of *Minimalists*), however, Reich's *Different Trains* is "a work of such astonishing originality that breakthrough seems the only possible description," and one that has for him an "absolutely harrowing emotional impact." "For Steve Reich, War and Rediscovery," *New York Times*, 28 May 1989. In the *Stagebill* for Lincoln Center Festival 99 (which featured seven events on Reich and his work), Schwarz counts him as one of the artistic "giants who live among us."

16. Peter G. Davis, "Star Drek" (review of *The Voyage*, by Philip Glass), *New York*, 26 October 1992, 91. The scatological pun of the review's title alludes to the Yiddish word *dreck*.

17. See Harold Schonberg, "Plumbing the Shallows of Minimalism," *New York Times*, 21 February 1985 (characterizing minimalism as "pseudo-classical music written for listeners who . . . never liked classical music"); and Bernard Holland, "Listening to Philip Glass and Hearing Links to Rock," *New York Times*, 15 December 1997.

18. Terry Teachout, "Holy Minimalism," *Commentary*, April 1995, 51.

19. Terry Riley, quoted in Ed Ward, "Terry Riley: Maximizing Minimalism," *Wall Street Journal*, 12 February 1997.

20. Rand, "Art and Cognition," 62. Though many cultures employ repetitive "music" of this kind (see Ch. 5, n. 35), particularly in connection with trance-inducing "dance," they also possess more expressive musical forms, and probably distinguish between the two categories, as they distinguish between varieties of dance. According to some anthropologists, cultures that employ dance-like movements to achieve a state of trance or of shamanistic "possession" by spirits appear to distinguish between such instances and true "dance," in which the performer controls his movements with the intention of creating an "aesthetic" effect for an audience. Erica Bourguignon, "Trance Dance," in Cohen, *International Encyclopedia of Dance*, 186.

21. Alex Ross, "Of Mystics, Minimalists and Musical Miasmas," *New York Times*, 5 November 1993. Edward Rothstein similarly observes that John Tavener's *The Protecting Veil* (for solo cello and string orchestra) "doesn't go anywhere or resolve anything; it seems to float in melodic space." "How Long Will Melody Linger On?" *New York Times*, 18 April 1993.

22. It is possible that some of the holy minimalists' popular appeal is due to extraneous factors such as relief from the dissonance of serialism or identification with the religious connotations of their work.

23. Rothstein, "How Long Will Melody Linger On?" *New York Times*, 18 April 1993.

24. Astonishingly, Rothstein (see preceding note) claims that "[m]elody is not usually associated with plainchant or madrigals . . . [or] with sacred music of the Renaissance . . . [or] with Beethoven's major compositions."

25. Scholes, *Oxford Companion to Music*, s.v. "plainsong," 821.

26. Many contemporary critics share the view of Richard Kostelanetz that "No American has done more [than Cage] to forge an esthetics for post–World War II advanced art." Richard Kostelanetz, "Intoduction to Contemporary American Esthetics," *Esthetics Contemporary*, 23.

27. In the epigraph to the reprint of his essay on Rauschenberg (cited above, Ch. 4, n. 69) in *Silence*, 98, Cage wrote: "The white paintings came first; my silent piece came later." John Rockwell referred to this work as "conceptual art with a vengeance." "Cage Merely an Inventor? Not a Chance," *New York Times*, 23 August 1992.

28. Richard Kostelanetz in the *New York Times*, 17 May 1969; quoted by Virgil Thomson, "Cage and the Collage of Noises," in *American Music*, 67; see also Charles Hamm, in Sadie, *New Grove* (1980), *s.v.* "Cage, John," 601. For examples of early twentieth-century Futurist theatrical "experiments" in a similar vein, see Goldberg, *Performance Art*, Ch.1.

29. On the "schizoid personality" syndrome, as distinct from fully developed schizophrenia, see Sass, 76–82. According to Sass, "[not] all schizoid individuals eventually develop a schizophrenic psychosis (most, in fact, do not)."

30. John Cage, quoted in Tomkins, 67 and 70.

31. *Ibid.*, 72. The prepared piano constituted a major step in Cage's shift toward his "esthetic" of indeterminacy. As one critic noted: "The 'Prepared' sound, . . . may not only bear no relationship in timbre to its unprepared piano counterpart, but its tonality, pitch, and whole position in the piano range territory may be totally unexpected. The sound may jump up three octaves, down one, up a second, down a ninth, all while the fingers are playing notes adjacent to each other in a simple scale passage." Peggy Glanville Hicks, *Music Courier*, September 1948; quoted in Scholes, *s.v.* "Cage, John."

32. See Hamm (cited above, n. 28), 598.

33. Cage's abandonment of melody, the essential attribute of music, did not prevent the National Academy of Arts and Letters from honoring one of his compositions for "prepared piano" (*Sonatas and Interludes*, 1949), for having "'extended the boundaries of musical art.'" Quoted *ibid.*, 598.

34. Tomkins, *New Yorker* profile on Cage, 76.

35. "I wrote a sad piece, and people hearing it laughed," Cage confided in one interview, excerpted in Kostelanetz, "Cagean Esthetics," *Esthetics Contemporary*, 295.

36. Cage was not the first to use chance methods of composition. The American modernist composer Henry Cowell, for example, with whom Cage had studied briefly in the 1930s, had also done so. But Cage carried chance procedures to unprecedented extremes, the "common denominator" of all his work being, he said, to "find ways of writing music where the sounds [were] free of [his] intentions." Quoted in Bill Shoemaker, "The Age of Cage," *Down Beat* (December 1984), excerpted in Kostelanetz, "Cagean Esthetics," 296.

37. John Cage, Interview with Roger Reynolds, *Generation*, January 1962; excerpted in Kostelanetz, "Cagean Esthetics," 296. See also Cage's remarks quoted in the concluding section of chapter 4, above.

38. On the likelihood of such a defense-mechanisim in schizoid individuals, see below, n. 46.

39. N. Branden, "Alienation," in Rand, *Capitalism* 283. Branden argues: "The alienated man is fleeing from the responsibility of a volitional (*i.e.*, self-directing) consciousness: the freedom to think or not to think, to initiate a process of reason or to evade it, is a burden he longs to escape. But since this freedom is inherent in his

nature as man, there is no escape from it. . . . The man who does not want to think, does not want to bear responsibility for the consequences of his actions nor for his own life."

40. Cage, Interview with Reynolds, in Kostelanetz, 296. One of the pieces Cage intended to increase awareness was *0'0"* (1962)—which, as performed by him in the mid 1960s, "consisted in his preparing and slicing vegetables, putting them in an electric blender and then drinking the juice, with the sounds of these various actions amplified throughout the hall." Hamm (see above, n. 28), 601. Not surprisingly, such performances, Hamm notes, "were taken by many to be the actions of a madman or a charlatan." Cage's explanation—Hamm nonetheless adds without objection—"was that distinctions between life and art should be broken down, that he as a composer should, through his compositions, make his audiences more aware of the world they were living in." *Ibid.*

41. Cage, quoted by Tomkins, 64. If, however, as Cage implies, music has no particular identity, it does not exist, and the term is meaningless. As Rand emphasized: "To exist is to be something, . . . it is to be an entity of a specific nature made of specific attributes." *Atlas Shrugged*, 1016. Francis Sparshott argues that a "definition of music whereby Cage's *4'33"* [were] decreed not to be music would be defective, but not nearly so defective as the one whereby that work figured as normal or standard music." *Off the Ground*, 202. Contrary to Sparshott's implication, the Cage piece does not even qualify as a "marginal case," since in both its intent and its attributes it is the antithesis of music, objectively defined.

42. Alan P. Merriam, "The Bala Musician," in D'Azevedo, *Traditional Artist in African Societies*, 272. The principle cited is yet another confirmation of Aristotle's axiom "A is A."

43. For Rand's view of the "concrete-bound" mentality, see *Introduction to Objectivist Epistemology*, 76–77.

44. Cage, quoted by Joseph H. Mazo, "John Cage Quietly Speaks His Piece," *Bergen Sunday Record*, 13 March 1983; excerpted in Kostelanetz, "Cagean Esthetics," 293.

45. Cage, quoted by Cole Gagne and Tracy Caras, "John Cage [1980]," in *Soundpieces: Interviews with American Composers* (Metuchen, N.J.: Scarecrow, 1982); excerpted in Kostelanetz, "Cagean Esthetics," 300.

46. Sass, 77 and 79; on similar symptoms in schizophrenic individuals, see *ibid.*, 23. Sass also cites the psychiatrist Ernst Kretschmer's observation that there often lies "'behind the affectless, numbed exterior" of schizoid individuals, "a tender personality-nucleus with the most vulnerable nervous sensitivity which has withdrawn into itself'"—an observation that also seems relevant to Cage. *Physique and Character*, tr. W. J. H. Sprott (New York: Harcourt Brace, 1925), 153; quoted by Sass, 81.

47. E. Kraepelin, *Lectures on Clinical Psychiatry*, 2nd ed. (New York: William Wood, 1906), 22; quoted in Sass, *Madness and Modernism*, 24.

48. H. C. Rümke, "The Nuclear Symptom of Schizophrenia and the Praecoxfeeling (1941)," in *History of Psychiatry*, I (1990), 337; quoted in Sass, 112.

49. See, for example, the opening segment of the "American Masters" television program on Cage, *I Have Nothing to Say and I Am Saying It*; and the photograph of Cage with Tim Page's laudatory article "American Composers: John Cage— The Savant of Avant," *Washington Post*, 16 August 1998; and <http://www. washingtonpost.com/wp-srv/style/music/features/cage16.htm>.

50. See, for example, dance critic Anna Kisselgoff's reference to the "discontinuity" in Cunningham's work (under Cage's influence) as reflecting his "belief that 'anything can follow anything,' a Zen-inspired acknowledgment of the randomness in life." "Ceaseless Novelty in a Lifetime of Dance," *New York Times*, 18 July 1999.

51. Rand's polemical assertion—at the conclusion of "The Esthetic Vacuum of Our Age" (*Romantic Manifesto*, 128)—that "the apostles of irrationality, the existentialists, the Zen Buddhists, [and] the non-objective artists, have not achieved a free, joyous, triumphant sense of life, but a sense of doom, nausea and screaming, cosmic terror" is certainly not an accurate representation of most Zen art. For examples of Zen-inspired painting, see Lee, *History of Far Eastern Art*, esp. Ch. 16.

52. Regarding these principles, see Zeami Motokiyo, *On the Art of the No Drama*, esp. 10–11, 13, 27, 38–39, 43, 46, 55, 62, 81, and 96. See also Kenneth J. DeWoskin, "Chinese and Japanese Aesthetics," in Cooper, *Companion*, 72–73; and *Zen and Japanese Culture*, by Daisetz T. Suzuki, whom Cage claimed to haved studied with in the late 1940s.

53. Cage, Interview with Laura Fletcher and Thomas Moore (1983); excerpted in Kostelanetz, 291.

54. Hamm (cited n. 28), 597, where Cage is identified as an "American composer, philosopher, and writer on music." The pathological implications of Cage's thought also appear to have escaped music critic John Rockwell when he admiringly declared: "Even if I remain fairly guarded about the music, . . . [his] ideas are seminal." *John Cage: I Have Nothing to Say and I Am Saying It*, American Masters, Thirteen/WNET, PBS, 17 September 1990. (The program title is a line from Cage's "Lecture on Nothing," in *Silence*, 109.) See also Rockwell's article cited above, n. 27.

55. In a lengthy entry on Cage in the *International Encyclopedia of Dance*, Roy M. Close claims that his contribution to both music and the performing arts was "to free them from the constraints of convention. Over a five-decade career he systematically stripped his music of elements long deemed essential to the form, substituting noise for pitched tones, silence for sound, and the workings of chance for self-expression." Since the elements of which Cage stripped music are not merely "deemed essential" but are in fact essential to music as such, one cannot reasonably claim that Cage made a contribution to *music*. What he promoted was non-music.

56. Goldberg, *Performance Art*, 126–27. Astonishingly, Goldberg says nothing about the insanity of the event, but comments that "it suggested endless possibilities for future collaborations"—an absurd claim, since "collaboration" implies a cooperative effort toward achieving an intentional common goal. Simply "doing your own thing" alongside others doing theirs does not constitute collaboration.

57. David Vaughan, in Cohen, *International Encyclopedia of Dance*, *s.v.* "Cunningham, Merce," 288.

58. Bernard Holland, reporting on the Seventh Annual John Cage Birthday Tribute in New York City. "Summoning the Spirits of Minimalist Musicians," *New York Times*, 7 September 1999.

59. When an audience member at a public interview with Cunningham asked why he bothered to use music at all if there were no connection between the dance and the music, Cunningham offered his stock reply (which comes straight from Cage): since many unrelated things go on simultaneously in life, art can do the same thing. "Merce Cunningham in Conversation with Trisha Brown," Lincoln Center Festival 99, 22 July 1999. As a rejoinder to Cunningham's inadequate explanation, his questioner—an elderly art lover—appropriately retorted that he expected art to do more than simply replicate the confusion in life.

60. See Marcia B. Siegel, "Come in, Earth. Are You There?" (1970), in Kostelanetz, *Merce Cunningham*, 72, 75; and Roy M. Close, "Music for Dance: Western Music since 1900," in Cohen, *International Encyclopedia of Dance*, 519; also Cunningham's description in Steinberg, 61.

61. Carolyn Brown, "Winterbranch," in Cohen, *International Encyclopedia of Dance*. According to Brown (one of the performers), the dance took place in darkness: "the dancers' movements [were] often barely visible, caught as if by accident by abruptly changing lights similar to automobile headlights suddenly illuminating objects or animals on a road at night." The "tape-recorded sound played at an extremely high volume" alternated the noise produced "by scraping ashtrays against a mirror" and by "rubbing pieces of wood against a Chinese gong."

62. Siegel, "Come in, Earth," 71. Siegel's suggestion that Cunningham could be "good-natured" while engaging in the metaphorical rape of an audience is preposterous.

63. In the New York City Ballet revival of *Summerspace* at the New York State Theater, 21 July 1999, the piece was performed without the scrim that had been used in the original production. Though this gave greater visibility to the "dance" movements, they nonetheless appeared arbitrary and unmotivated.

64. See our discussion of Mark Rothko's work in Ch. 8.

65. Cunningham, quoted in Klosty, 101.

66. Cunningham, in Steinberg, 57–58, and 55. Cunningham's idea of dance as "experimenting with movements" reflects a long-standing modernist fallacy: the view of avant-garde art as "experimental." John Dewey argues, for example: "[O]ne of the essential traits of the artist is that he is born an experimenter. . . . Only because the artist operates experimentally does he open new fields of experience and disclose new aspects and qualities in familiar scenes and objects." *Art as Experience*, 144. The basic fallacy involved is neatly identified by E. H. Gombrich: "When we speak of 'experiments' in science . . . there are public standards by which the success or failure of experiments can be judged. If words like 'exploration' or 'experiment' are to be more than vague prestige words in art, aimed at spuriously imparting to the stu-

dio the aura of the laboratory, we have to find our way back to some standard of success *or failure.*" "The Vogue of Abstract Art" (1956), in *Meditations on a Hobby Horse*, 146–47. Avant-garde artists have, of course, no such standard.

67. Merce Cunningham, "Choreography and the Dance," in Steinberg, 52–62, see esp. 57 and 59. According to a source who has observed the Cunningham company at close hand and has interviewed its members, Cunningham's extreme emotional detachment coupled with the dehumanized quality and complexity of his choreography, contributes to exceptional psychological stress among the young dancers, many of whom experience rapid "burnout." Personal communication following "Merce Cunningham in Conversation with Trisha Brown" (see n. 59, above).

68. Cunningham, in Steinberg, 52–53.

69. Clive Barnes, "Merce Cunningham at Seventy-Five," *Dance Magazine*, May 1994, 122. According to another observer, Cunningham's work "has so thoroughly shed any vestiges of emotional derivation that it comes as close to being 'abstract' as a medium whose material is the human body can come." Erica Abeel, "The New New Dance," in Nadel, *Dance Experience*, 118; quoted by Julie van Camp, "The Definition of 'Dance,'" Ch. 2 of Ph.D. dissertation *Philosophical Problems of Dance Criticism* (1981), n. 49; <http://www.csulb.edu/~jvancamp/diss2.html>. Abeel views this as the "triumph of the Cunningham idiom"; we regard it as indicative of its illegitimacy.

70. Cunningham was by no means the first choreographer to claim that dance has no need of music. The early modern dancer-choreographer Mary Wigman (who had the greatest influence on modern dance in Europe), for example, insisted that dance can be created and performed without music. Many prominent twentieth-century choreographers (Balanchine, Robbins, Taylor, etc.) have attempted pieces set to silence, but soon abandoned this approach. (See examples listed by van Camp, cited in n. 155.)

71. Anna Kisselgoff, "Dissociation in Merce Cunningham Premiere," *New York Times*, 2 March 1989.

72. David Littlejohn, "'Ocean' Fills Gym," *Wall Street Journal*, 8 May 1996.

73. See, for example, Kisselgoff's reviews of Cunningham's work in the *New York Times* on 3 March 1991, 15 March 1992, 20 March 1992, 11 March 1993, and 17 October 1997.

74. Cunningham, *Dancer and the Dance*, 133. Cunningham's rejection of "linear" organization echoes a common fallacy of contemporary thought. See our discussion in Ch. 16. And just as he mistakenly rejects sequential ordering of events, he also abandons spatial ordering. "The idea of a single focus to which all [elements of a dance] adhere is no longer relevant," he claims—since, in "the paintings of Jackson Pollock, the eye can go any place on the canvas. No one point necessarily leads to another." *Ibid.*, 140. We of course have argued that Pollock's "allover" paintings are not art either.

75. In 1944, reviewing Cunningham's first solo recital as a dancer-choreographer to percussion music by Cage, the esteemed critic Edwin Denby praised his

remarkable "gifts as a lyric dancer," adding: "I have never seen a first recital that combined such taste, such technical finish, such originality of dance material, and so sure a manner of presentation." Yet Denby also detected a certain "remoteness and isolation," which he hoped Cunningham would outgrow in time. From Denby's *Looking at the Dance*, in Klosty, *Merce Cunningham*, 213. As it turned out, however, those qualities were to define Cunningham's style.

76. Deborah Jowitt, for example, observes that Cunningham training has "always produced dancers who appear calm, alert, quick on their feet, and able to achieve a state of equilibrium in almost any position." "Merce Cunningham," in Cohen, *International Encyclopedia of Dance*, 441. "[H]is dancers are as superb, majestic, and consummately trained as any in modern dance." Bill Deresiewicz, "Derry Swan: A Year with Merce," *Dance Magazine*, October 1997, 64.

77. Arlene Croce, "The Avant-Garde on Broadway," reprinted in *Afterimages*, 339.

78. Arlene Croce, "The Big Click" (1 April 1974), reprinted in *Afterimages*, 51. Croce's view was confirmed for us by the audience's response at a revival of Cunningham's *Sounddance* at the New York State Theater, 21 July 1999. Despite the technical skill of the dancers, we found the work a punishing experience, and offensive in the extreme. Accompanied by a "music" score by David Tudor, consisting of ear-splitting electronically amplified noise relentlessly blasted from all sides of the theater, the choreography was essentially incoherent in its intricacy. To our dismay, the piece was greeted by a standing ovation (perhaps not surprising, since the majority of the audience members were probably Cunningham enthusiasts). When we asked the young woman next to us, who was ardently applauding, what it was she admired, she replied "the virtuosic dancing." "What about the score?" we asked. "It's abominable. I hated it," she responded. "I had to hold my fingers in my ears." When we suggested that dance should integrate movement with music, she demurred: "Oh, but he's changed all that."

79. Sorell, *Dance through the Ages*, 249. For example, both Tobias ("Golden Pond," *New York*, 9 August 1999) and Acocella ("Cunningham Takes a Bow," *Wall Street Journal*, 28 May 1997) admire Cunningham as the "grand old man" of modern dance. Yet even they seem uneasy about his work at times. Tobias (who elsewhere emphasizes the importance of humanistic values in dance—see below, n. 116) sees in his *Biped* (1999) "a fathomless . . . and quite possibly dehumanizing outer space," in which dancers "move with the spasmodic angularity attributed to robots, their faces expressionless masks." And Acocella (who "didn't like Mr. Cunningham's work at first"—a natural enough reaction) frankly suggests that "modernism's snob value" may have been a factor in her coming to like, even "love," it. She also acknowledges that Cunningham's *Sounddance*, as a work of "High modernism, of the Joyce and Picasso variety, . . . is something that we'll probably be scratching our heads over for many years. Why did we want our world shattered? . . . We don't know."

80. Croce, *Afterimages*, 130. According to Kisselgoff, for example, Cunningham's *Cargo X* could be seen, "depending on the critic, as either funereal or festive." "Movement Toward Death? If You Like," *New York Times*, 11 March 1993.

81. Martha Graham, "A Modern Dancer's Primer for Action" (1941), reprinted in Steinberg, 47, 45–46.

82. Rand, "Art and Cognition," 69. Non-Western sources also stress the essential connection between dance and music. For example: "[D]ancing is truly impossible without the strength of [musical] sound behind it." Zeami Motokiyo, *On the Art of the No Drama*, 79. In the Pacific Islands, composite performances comprise "structured sound [music], structured movement [dance], and poetry—all of which are integrally related." "Music for Dance," in Cohen, *International Encyclopedia of Dance*, 495. "Music in sub-Saharan African societies is [also] closely bound with dance." *Ibid.*, 483. Sparshott devotes an entire chapter to "Dance and Music" (*Measured Pace*, Ch. 12), but takes no clear position. Though he tantalizingly suggests, for example, that music "is the dance of the inner life, and its outward manifestation is dance . . . the objective counterpart of music" (222), he ultimately hedges the question—see below, n. 89. And he raises no objection to the idea that the music in a piece by Cunningham can be "*independent* of the dance" (499*n*29).

83. Norman dello Joio, "Composer/Choreographer: A Symposium," in Steinberg, 140. Dello Joio collaborated with Martha Graham and José Limon, among other choreographers.

84. Marian Horosko, "Balanchine's Guide to a Young Choreographer," *Dance Magazine*, December 1996, 87.

85. George Balanchine, "The Dance Element in Stravinsky's Music," in Steinberg, 149. Like many twentieth-century choreographers, Balanchine attempted (only once, to our knowledge) to set a "dance" without music. But he swiftly departed from this dead end.

86. Close, "Music for Dance," 518.

87. Susan Gould, "La Carla Nazionale: Carla Fracci," *Dance Magazine*, August 1993, 36.

88. William Carter, quoted by Tobi Tobias, "Bill Carter: An Interview," *Dance Magazine*, June 1975, 54. Carter—who died in 1988, at the age of 56—was one of the twentieth century's extraordinary dance figures. As a leading dancer with the New York City Ballet, American Ballet Theater, and the companies of Martha Graham and Pearl Lang, and as a partner to such Spanish dancers as Maria Alba, he gained the respect, admiration, and affection of many of the most eminent choreographers, dancers, and critics of his time—as well as of the dance lovers fortunate enough to see him perform. That he was not known to a larger public was, ironically, due to the very qualities that made his work so exceptional. A profound sensitivity and depth of feeling, coupled with the desire to realize his own inner vision, led him to become something of a nomad in the dance world. Forgoing financial security and potential fame, he spent much of his career touring the world with his own small companies. Carter's interview with Tobias in *New York* magazine (which she had the inspiration to publish as a monologue) stands as a moving tribute to his life and thought, and ought to be required reading for every student of dance. On every major point regarding the nature of the art, Carter's views are the virtual antithesis of Merce Cunningham's. In contrast with Cunningham's application of perfect technique to movements devised by chance procedures, for instance, Carter held that, while "there has to be

an enormous concern with the technical aspect of [dance] . . . there has to be an equal concern with the reason a gesture is made" (52). For him, "as an art form, dance really does have to do with life, the consciousness and meaning of life"; art is created "when the essence of feeling and the essence of thinking come together to make a form" (55). For an example of Carter's choreography, see the video of his brief one-act ballet *In a Rehearsal Room* (set to the Pachelbel *Canon*), danced by Cynthia Gregory and Ivan Nagy, and documented in a book of the same title, with photographs by Susan Cook. Sadly, this work has, to our knowledge, never been added to any company's repertory.

89. Moira Shearer, quoted by Sparshott, *A Measured Pace*, 217–18. Although Sparshott objects that "[d]ance without music is not only possible but quite common," he nonetheless admits that "the absence of music . . . tends to strike us as artificial or uncanny" and that "a practice in which dancing was *always* done in dead silence, or to the accompaniment of casual ambient noise, would be downright creepy. . . . So thoroughly intertwined are the arts of music and dance as we know them that, throughout this work, I keep falling back on musical analogies and structures when aspects of dance itself seem inadequately articulated." *Ibid*.

90. Morris's "most ambitious and glorious" work to date is his *L'Allegro, Il Penseroso, ed Il Moderato* (1988), set to baroque music—Handel's song cycle based on poems by John Milton. Tobi Tobias, "Marquee Mark," *New York*, 31 July 1995. It is an extraordinarily rich and deep work that seems to encompass the whole of mankind and the full range of human emotional experience. Yet its sense of clarity and order demonstrates that, as Tobias observed in her review of its New York premiere, "For all his irreverence and catholicity of taste, Morris is intrinsically a classicist." "Paradise Regained," *New York*, 29 October 1990. Two of Paul Taylor's finest works—*Esplanade* (see above, Ch. 4, n. 52) and *Airs* (1978)—are also inspired by baroque music. For still photographs and video information on *Esplanade*, see his company's website at <http://www.ptdc.org>.

91. Acocella, *Mark Morris*, 171. Arlene Croce, too (notwithstanding her admiration for Cunningham's work independent of music), emphasizes Morris's musicality, noting that he usually "derives [his dance] structure from music and, as [Paul] Taylor does, creates a correspondingly organic choreography." *Sight Lines*, 315. Taylor's musically "organic" choreography is evident in *Esplanade* (see preceding note).

92. Anna Kisselgoff, "What Jerome Robbins Heard in Bach," *New York Times*, 25 January 1992. In Robbins's obituary, Kisselgoff reported that he had once said: "'Dance is about relationships.'" Thus, she adds, "he imbued his ballets, no matter how plotless, with human insights and emotions that had a universal resonance." "Jerome Robbins, 79, Is Dead; Giant of Ballet and Broadway," *New York Times*, 30 July 1998.

93. Jerome Robbins, interview with Deborah Jowitt, quoted by Marilyn Hunt, "Robbins Speaks!" *Dance Magazine*, September 1997, 40.

94. Boris Eifman, quoted by Nina Alovert, "Fantasies of a Dreamer," *Dance Magazine*, April 1998. See also Robert Johnson, "A Traditionalist Who Seeks to Update the Russian Soul," *New York Times*, 5 April 1998; and Clive Barnes, "The Eifman Cometh," *Dance Magazine*, July 1998.

95. Twyla Tharp, *Push Comes to Shove*, 95. She further explains: "We rehearsed and performed in silence because music communicates emotion-structure more easily to most people than movement, and *it was movement we wanted to explore*" (99, emphasis ours). Yet, even then, she relates, she would begin her day by improvising to music. In 1971, soon after the birth of her first child, Tharp re-choreographed a silent piece, *The History of Up and Down,* into *Eight Jelly Rolls,* set to jazz piano pieces by Jelly Roll Morton. She recalls thinking: "'Yes, letting music play with the dance is old hat, but, hey, having babies isn't too original either, is it? But it's still one of the wonders of life so let's keep the music.'" *Ibid.,* 155–56.

96. Kisselgoff observes: "For the past three decades, most of her works have been about dance itself. Now these formal essays are veering toward [a] metaphysics about life and death, even life after death." "Twyla Tharp's Metaphysical Muse," *New York Times,* 30 April 1995.

97. Tharp, *Push Comes to Shove,* 175.

98. Jack Anderson, "In Sync with Beethoven's Joy and Thunder" (review of Tharp's *Grosse Sonate*), *New York Times,* 5 July 1999. Just as dance is inspired by music, however, it can be impeded by compositions that offer too little rhythmic or emotional support. Lar Lubovitch's *Othello* (1998), for example, fails in its dramatic impact largely because of the relentlessly percussive score by Elliott B. Goldenthal. The music provides no lyrical expression of Othello and Desdemona's love, and without that contrast the danced drama lacks tragic proportions. In contrast with Prokoviev's masterly score for *Romeo and Juliet,* for example, which interweaves lyricism with percussion and dissonance, Goldenthal's music is almost unrelievedly jarring in its effect. "Too *loud*," complained one ballet lover at the performance we attended (Metropolitan Opera House, 9 June 1998). "I wasn't moved by the dance," she added, "because the music didn't move me."

99. "Everything is permitted if zero is taken as the basis. That's the part that isn't often understood. If you're nonintentional, then everything is permitted." Cage, quoted by Rob Tannenbaum, "A Meeting of Sound Minds: John Cage + Brian Eno," *Musician,* September 1985; excerpted in Kostelanetz, "Cagean Esthetics," 291. Van Camp (cited above, n. 69) lists as defining characteristics of dance cited by "[m]any dance critics, writers, and philosophers over the last several centuries" (and systematically "challenged" by the avant-garde) the following: "(1) human movement, that is (2) formalized (e.g., by being stylized or performed in certain patterns), with (3) such qualities as grace, elegance, and beauty, (4) to the accompaniment of music or other rhythmic sounds, (5) for the purpose of telling a story and/or (6) for the purpose of communicating or expressing human emotions, themes, or ideas, and (7) with the aid of mime, costumes, scenery, and lighting." As van Camp makes clear, however, not all writers include all of these characteristics. "The Definition of Dance," 22, 30ff. With the exception of item (3), which Rand would (properly) not have regarded as a *defining* characteristic, all these attributes are explicit or implicit in Rand's analysis, which we discussed in Chapter 4. Van Camp offers a well-documented overview of the ways in which "avant-garde experiments . . . play havoc with [these] traditional definitions and concepts," but her own equivocal position regarding the legitimacy of such "experiments" is troubling.

100. David Vaughan, in Cohen, *International Encyclopedia of Dance, s.v.* "Cunningham, Merce," 290–91. Vaughan's claim that Cunningham remained "firmly in control" of his work is rather hollow, however, given Cunningham's heavy dependence on chance procedures in the choreographic process. (See also Croce's claim, quoted above in Chapter 12, that Cunningham's work did not depend on chance.) The remaining attributes cited by Vaughan ("technical finish" and "theatricality") are of secondary importance, insufficient to compensate for the absence of musically based movement conveying emotional significance.

101. On the seminal workshops at the Cunningham studio, see Goldberg, *Performance Art*, 140.

102. Yvonne Rainer, in *Work 1961–1973* (New York, 1974); quoted in Goldberg, *Performance Art*, 141.

103. According to esthetician Noël Carroll and dance critic and theorist Sally Banes, the point of these "task dances" is "to make ordinary movement *qua* ordinary movement perceptible." "Working and Dancing: A Response to Monroe Beardsley's 'What Is Going on in a Dance?'" *Dance Research Journal* 15 (1982): 37–42; reprinted in Dickie, Sclafani, and Roblin, 645–46.

104. According to Marcia Siegel, this was "the most spectacular in a group of studies in which Brown placed the performer in a distorted, *even deranged* relationship to the environment." "Avant-garde dance," in Clarke and Vaughan, 36, emphasis ours.

105. Philosopher Francis Sparshott speculates at length as to the possible intentions and implications of this piece; but, astonishingly, he seems more critical of Horst than of Taylor. *Off the Ground*, 245–46. Happily, this phase of Taylor's career was brief.

106. Deborah Jowitt, "Ice Demons, Clicks and Whispers," *New York Times Magazine*, 30 June 1991, 18.

107. Meredith Monk, quoted by Jack Anderson, "Entering a World Only Meredith Monk Can Map," *New York Times*, 16 June 1996.

108. Tobi Tobias, "Arrivals and Departures," *New York*, 31 May 1993, 64–65.

109. See Anderson (cited above, n. 107). Of Monk's early multimedia work *Education of the Girlchild*, Tobias (cited above, n. 108) writes: "Monk calls her work an opera . . .; I'd call it an incantation." Even the latter term is inaccurate, however, since culturally based incantation operates in a functional context of serious import to the societies that practice it. Monk's pseudo-chants have no such import. In any case, the fundamental meaning of *opera* is "drama set to music." *Drama* requires the telling of a story through the actions and dialogue (which, in opera, is at least partly sung) of the characters portrayed. As both Tobias's and Anderson's descriptions suggest, none of these essential elements are present in any meaningful sense in Monk's work.

110. Anderson (see above, n. 107).

111. Tobi Tobias, "Postmodern Medley," *New York*, 8 May 1995, 75.

112. Tobi Tobias, "Failure to Thrive," *New York*, 11 January 1993, 64.

113. As Clive Barnes has observed, many of the "so-called cutting-edge works of art . . . could actually have been created any time within the past seventy-five years." "Backward with the Avant-Garde," *Dance Magazine,* March 1998, 138. Contrary to the widely held view (see, for example, n.124 below) that Cunningham represents the "classic" tradition of modern dance, David Vaughan appropriately suggests that in its "Dadaist quality"—in particular, its "general iconoclasm"—his work is more closely linked to the early twentieth-century avant-garde ballets than to American "modern dance." "Cunningham, Merce" (287), in Cohen, *International Encyclopedia of Dance.*

114. Tobi Tobias, "Heart and Craft," *New York,* 1 April 1996.

115. Tobi Tobias, "New Revelations" (review of Alvin Ailey American Dance Theater), *New York,* 22–29 December 1997, 138, emphasis ours. Tobias's observation that in classic modern dance "the world is knowable" and "makes sense" calls to mind one of the metaphysical questions Rand argues are at the base of all art: "Is the universe intelligible to man, or unintelligible and unknowable?" "The Psycho-Epistemology of Art," 19. See our discussion of "metaphysical value-judgments" in chapters 1 and 6, above.

116. Tobi Tobias, "Oh, the Humanity," *New York,* 8 January 1996. Ironically, despite her insistence on the importance of humanistic values, Tobias praises Cunningham, "the grand old man of modern dance," for his "persistent iconoclasm" and his "unceasing pursuit of new ways to consider space and human motion." "Golden Pond" (review of Cunningham program danced at Lincoln Center's New York State Theater), *Dance Magazine,* 9 August 1999. Since Tobias also cites the "sophisticated invention" and "stunning beauty" of his work, we suspect that, like other critics, she is won over mainly by his technical virtuosity, and therefore disregards its lack of any message regarding human character or relationships.

117. The term "dance theater" refers to a bogus hybrid art form in which there is relatively little *dance,* and no real *theater*—in the sense of "*dramatic* literature or performance [thereof]" (*American Heritage Dictionary*). On the meaning of *drama,* see above, n. 108.

118. Tobi Tobias, "A Few Steps Removed," *New York,* 17 November 1997, 104. Tobias further observes that a segment of the public "*with a yen to be found at the cutting edge*—enjoys the spectacle (especially when it's transgressive) and imbues it, as it is prompted to do, with notions about the human condition and the meaning of life" (emphasis ours). That segment, we would argue, belongs to the "artworld" public (see our discussion of this concept in Ch. 8). In contrast, Tobias elsewhere alludes to a more authentic audience response (one based on sense of life, Rand would have said) to the work of Bausch and others like her, when she observes: "Their kind of thing is welcomed enthusiastically in Europe, where . . . pessimism is integral to reality, but less so in the States." "Endgame," *New York,* October, 1995.

119. Tobias, "A Few Steps Removed," 104. See also Clive Barnes's indictment of the "'Look, Ma, I'm Emoting' follies" of Bausch and De Keersmaeker. "Backward with the Avant-Garde," *Dance Magazine,* March 1998, 138. Yet Tobias does not go far enough here toward explaining what should prompt one to say that some-

thing is not dance. Missing is any mention of intelligibility or fundamantal human concerns, which she emphasizes elsewhere (see above, nn. 114 and 115).

120. Tobias, "A Few Steps Removed," 104. In an earlier review of the work of Maguy Marin—a French choreographer who, like Bausch and DeKeersmaeker, "specialize[s] in angst-ridden theater-without-words"—Tobias properly insisted that "what they were doing isn't dancing, and it isn't even effective theater." "Endgame," *New York*, October, 1995. We would insist that it is not even "theater," as that term is precisely understood. See n. 108, above.

121. Anna Kisselgoff, "Dance: New Group from Dartmouth," *New York Times*, 31 December 1971.

122. On the distinction between *entertainment* and *art*, see our discussion in Ch. 16. Momix, a spin-off group formed by Moses Pendleton, one of the founders of Pilobolus, belongs in that category as well.

123. A recent dance series sponsored by Yale University featured Pilobolus as "one of the most superb dance companies in the world." Brochure for the 1999-2000 season of the Shubert Theater, New Haven, Connecticut. The Yale-sponsored series also included Momix.

124. Jennifer Dunning, "Forgoing Surprises for the Sake of Fun," *New York Times*, 3 July 1996. See also Dunning, "More Savvy-Seeming, but Still Loyal to the Founders," *New York Times*, 5 July 1996. For a more discriminating view, see Tobi Tobias, "Downward Mobility," *New York*, 21 July 1997, 50.

125. Sana Siwolop, "For a Choreographer, a Chance to Leap out of Debt," *New York Times*, 20 July 1997.

126. Anna Kisselgoff, "The Air as Stage, Bungees and All," *New York Times*, 18 December 1997. On the concept of "experimental" art, see above, n. 66. Not surprisingly, Cunningham has praised Streb for her discovery and investigation of certain "movement possibilities." *The Dancer and the Dance*, 142.

127. Robert Johnson, "Tethering Newton's Apple to a Bungee Cord," *New York Times*, 14 December 1997.

128. Elizabeth Streb, quoted *ibid.*

129. Anna Kisselgoff, "A Topsy-Turvy Beauty in Anxious Encounters," *New York Times*, 8 March 1999.

130. As an example of "aerial choreography"—reviewed under the caption "Dance Review"—Kisselgoff notes that a former Bausch dancer knows how to "create metaphors for love as dancers swing in embraces while suspended in the air." "Mystery, Aggression, and Mating Rituals," *New York Times*, 25 October 1996. On "trapeze dances," see Jennifer Dunning, "Invoking the Mystery of Flight," *New York Times*, 26 June 1996. See also Iris M. Fanger, "Meister Eckhart Flies in Boston," *Dance Magazine*, April 1990, 21–22.

131. John Rockwell, "France's Summer Hit Is a Circus. Sort Of," *New York Times*, 8 August 1994.

132. Bartabas, quoted *ibid.* To Bartabas's list, we would add "a little flim flam."

133. Stephen Holden, "Magical World of Man and Beast," *New York Times*, 19 September 1996. For another theater critic's review (under the caption "Dance") of Zingaro, see Alan Riding, "Using the Horse to Hold a Mirror to the Human," *New York Times*, 6 September 1998.

134. Vincent Canby, "*Chimère* and *Area Boy*," *New York Times*, 27 October 1996. See also Tobi Tobias, "Hoofing It," *New York*, 14 October 1996, 101; and Joan Acocella, "The Wisdom of the Beast," *Wall Street Journal*, 25 September 1996. For Tobias, the Zingaro show, "essentially a chain of vignettes, is not theater or dance or even—despite the uncanny equine feats—circus but, rather, *spectacle*" (emphasis ours). Acocella, too, properly deflates the troupe's pretensions, characterizing their performance as "two hours of horse acts"—mostly "movement plays in which horse and human meet and do a little something together."

135. One example of bodily constrained choreography is a duet for two female ballet dancers wearing straitjackets. Jack Anderson, "Straitjackets, and Speaking with the Feet," *New York Times*, 20 April 1996. See also Jennifer Dunning, "States of Mind, with Emphasis on Professionalism," *New York Times*, 30 April 1999 (about a solo in which the dancer "tended to stay in one place, letting out short bursts of breath," her means of expression limited mostly to "suppressed jitters" of her arms).

136. Tobi Tobias, "Keeping Still," *Village Voice*, 13 June 1995. Tobias's acceptance of a "dance for the face" is surprising, in view of her insistence—with regard to Pina Bausch's work—that dance, at a minimum, involves "rhythmic motion and a sense of the body in space and time." See above, n. 118.

137. Francis Sparshott, *A Measured Pace*, 131–33. Sparshott's proposition is all the more preposterous given the title of his book. It is certainly difficult to imagine eyes *pacing*.

138. Eleanor Blau, "She Cannot Walk, Yet She Can Dance," *New York Times*, 20 July 1997.

139. Margaret Willis, "Britain's Can*do*Co: The Little Company That Could," *Dance Magazine*, January 1995, 78. Willis is a *Dance Magazine* contributing editor and London correspondent. Her article is captioned "London troupe of performers in wheelchairs redefines the meaning of *dance*." For a similarly uncritical view of "wheelchair dance," see Anna Kisselgoff, "Taking Wing from the Confines of a Wheelchair," *New York Times*, 8 February 1993.

140. Because it is virtually impossible to suspend such compassion and awareness, these factors become an important element in the response to a performance, and thus a distraction from whatever it is the performers are attempting to project.

141. Joan Acocella, "What Critics Do," *Dance Ink*, Summer 1992; see also *Ballet Alert!* online, at <http://www.balletalert.com/reviews/acocella2.htm>.

142. Arlene Croce, "Discussing the Undiscussable," *New Yorker*, 26 December 1994/2 January 1995. *Dance Connection*, at <http://www.canuck.com/Esalon/dance/Croce.html> reprints the essay.

143. The literature on Bill T. Jones and *Still/Here* is extensive. In addition to the articles we cite in other notes, see the PBS website page at <http://pbs.org/ktca/alive/still-here.html>, which includes photographs and textual, audio, and video excerpts from the work. For a laudatory article about Jones, published prior to Croce's piece, see Henry Louis Gates, Jr., "The Body Politic," *New Yorker,* 28 November 1994.

144. Croce, "Discussing the Undiscussable," 54, emphasis ours. See also John Leo, "The Backlash against Victim Art," *U.S. News and World Report,* 16 January 1995.

145. In a sympathetic review that predated Croce's essay, for example, Tobias, emphasizes that the words, movements, and faces of the people "captured on video . . . constitute the raw material of *Still/Here,*" and she praises Jones's "sheer technical feat of taking these unmediated words and images, ideas and feelings, and evolving them into an immensely sophisticated theatrical construct"—a product of his "vision, editorial and directorial skill, avid imagination, nerve, and persistence." "Heaven Can Wait," *New York,* 12 December 1994. In contrast with Tobias's view, Dale Harris concludes: "[W]hile Mr. Jones's themes . . . are large and troubling, his choreography is trite and his conception of theater unadventurous. . . . *Still/Here* [is] cheap in conception and shoddy in realization, [and] lacks any of the complexities of serious art." "The Patron Saint of Suffering," *Wall Street Journal,* 6 January 1995. To our mind, the unimpressive quality of Jones's choreography suggests that this piece, like the multimedia works Tobias has criticized (see above, n. 108), relies on the video material to communicate meaning that he could not convey through dance.

146. Joyce Carol Oates, "Confronting Head On the Face of the Afflicted," *New York Times,* 19 February 1995.

147. Clive Barnes, "Critics and Their Expectations," *Dance Magazine,* December 1995.

148. "Ice dancing" is a genre of figure skating expressively choreographed to music. Though the term is usually reserved for duets, we include in our discussion here solo skating as well.

149. Anna Kisselgoff, "Torvill and Dean Opt for Pure Dance, and Lose," *New York Times,* 22 February 1994. Though Kisselgoff's remarks are captioned "Critic's Notebook," not "Dance Review," she identifies herself as a "dance critic" in her lead sentence. In an earlier piece, Kisselgoff alternated between accepting a skating troupe's designation as "a *dance* company on ice" and referring to skating as a "*sport* in which children start practicing at an early age." "Modern Choreography Plus the Speed of Ice," *New York Times,* 1 November 1991. See also her "Athleticism Leavened with Artistry" (captioned "Review / Ice Skating"), *New York Times,* 4 March 1991.

150. Susan Reiter, "Ice Dancing: A Dance Form Frozen in Place by Hostile Rules," *Dance Magazine,* March 1995, 46, emphasis added. Its contradictory subtitle notwithstanding, this article is highly informative about the constraints imposed by all those "fine-print" rules—which dictate, for example, "how often, and for how long, the two dancers may separate."

151. "Artistry on Ice" (Editorial), *New York Times,* 26 March 1996.

152. Sarah Montague, "Curry, John," in Cohen, *International Encyclopedia of Dance*.

153. Gary Beacom, quoted by Daniel Gesmer, "Gary Beacom: Figure Skating's First Modernist," *Dance Magazine*, March 1995, 52.

154. Janice Rio, quoted in Sparshott, *Off the Ground*, 225–28.

155. Clive Barnes, "'Ice Follies' Good Example of Genre," *New York Times*, 27 September 1974; quoted by Julie van Camp, "The Definition of 'Dance,'" Ch. 2 of Ph.D. dissertation *Philosophical Problems of Dance Criticism* (1981), 53–54; <http://www.csulb.edu/~jvancamp/diss2.html>.

156. Van Camp (*ibid.*) compares figure skates to toe shoes, but misses this crucial distinction: toe shoes merely enable the dancer to extend and stylize natural movement, while ice skates produce an entirely artificial repertoire of movement.

157. Charles and Stephanie Reinhart, quoted by Susan Reiter, "Finding the Edge Where Sport Ends and Dance Begins," *New York Times*, 19 July 1998. Not surprisingly, some critics contend that swimming, too, is dance. See, for example, Anna Kisselgoff, "The Human Condition Portrayed in Water," *New York Times*, 24 June 1988; and Elizabeth Zimmer, [no title], *Dance Magazine*, May 1988, 41. In contrast, Frank Litsky's article on synchronized swimming, "Competing, Perfectly in Sync, across Gender Gap," *New York Times*, 16 July 1998, is in the sports section, where it belongs; and quotes what former film star Esther Williams (who introduced the public to synchronized swimming in the 1940s) said to Bill May, the only male participant in "waterballet" competition: "'You bring a new romance to this *sport*'" (emphasis ours).

Chapter 13 The Literary Arts and Film

1. As Stephen Cox has observed, Rand's considerable "comic and satiric skill" has been too little appreciated. Stephen Cox, "Ayn Rand: Theory versus Creative Life," *Journal of Libertarian Studies*, 8 (1986): 24.

2. For information on Joyce and his work, see the website of the International James Joyce Foundation: <http://www.cohums.ohio-state.edu/english/organizations/ijjf/main.htm>.

3. J. I. M. Stewart, in *Collier's Encyclopedia* (1974), *s.v.* "Joyce, James Augustine," 646.

4. Stuart Gilbert, *James Joyce's* Ulysses, Preface to the 2nd ed, v–vi.

5. Stewart, "Joyce," 648. In contrast, Rand censured Joyce as "the ultimate in nonobjective writing," because "he uses words from different languages, makes up some words of his own, and calls that literature." She continued: "When communication by language is discarded, . . . [w]riting becomes inarticulate sounds." *Art of Fiction*, 11.

6. James Joyce, quoted by Daniel J. Boorstin, in *The Creators*, 710.

7. Stewart, "Joyce," 648. Excerpts from *Finnegans Wake* are available online at <http://www.robotwisdom.com/jaj/shortwake1.html> and <http://www.mailbag.com/users/bjork/b1494.htm>.

8. Anthony Burgess, quoted by Boorstin, 711.

9. In 1932, Joyce wrote to Bennett Cerf at Random House (publisher of the first American edition of *Ulysses*): "You are surely aware of the difficulties I found in publishing anything I wrote from the very first volume of prose I attempted to publish: *Dubliners* [a collection of short stories]. Publishers and printers alike seemed to agree among themselves . . . not to publish anything of mine as I wrote it. No less than twenty-two publishers and printers read the manuscript of *Dubliners* and when at last it was printed some very kind person bought out the entire edition and had it burnt in Dublin—a new and private *auto-da-fé.*" The letter is reprinted in full in the Modern Library edition of *Ulysses*.

10. Harry Levin, Introduction to *The Portable James Joyce*, 12.

11. "Writing excellent stuff in conventional patterns, [Joyce] had got very little attention and was so hard up that he had to go on teaching languages to keep alive, but from the moment he took to the literary bizarreries of Greenwich Village and began to push them even further than Greenwich Village (or even the Left Bank) had ever dared, he was a made man." H. L. Mencken, quoted in "Mencken, Dead, Has More to Say," *New York Times,* 2 November 1991.

12. Mel Gussow, "Samuel Beckett Is Dead at 83; His 'Godot' Changed Theater," *New York Times*, 27 December 1989.

13. Richard W. Seaver, Introduction to *Samuel Beckett*, ix.

14. On the schizophrenic nature of Beckett's protagonists, see Sass, *Madness and Modernism*, 58, 297, 303–304, 344–45, 367; and Richard Stephensen, *The Insanity of Samuel Beckett's Art*. (See also n. 27, below.) For a sample of Beckett's work, see *Fizzle 4*, one of eight single-paragraph, single-sentence monologues (or "stories") he wrote between 1960 and 1975: <http://www.msu.edu/user/sullivan/BeckettFizzle4.html>.

15. Samuel Beckett, quoted by John Banville, "The Painful Comedy of Samuel Beckett" (review of six books by or about him), *New York Review of Books*, 14 November 1996, 29.

16. Ironically, billionaire financier George Soros's Open Society Institute chose to support a production of *Waiting for Godot* in Budapest a few years ago. Such philanthropy seems sadly misguided, since Beckett's dismal depiction of man as utterly helpless, irrational, and dependent on salvation from some unknown source belies the virtues of rationality, and independence essential to a free society.

17. John Simon, "The Master's Epitaph," *New York*, 19 August 1996.

18. Sass, *Madness and Modernism*, 189; see also Sass's additional comments on Lucky's monologue, 208. Regarding the play's meaning, Glen Newey claims that, like Beckett's other works, *Godot* "both invites and resists semantic recovery. . . . Pinning down the meaning does violence to the text" (more directly put, it is unin-

telligible). "Afterthoughts on an Old Muckball," review of *Waiting for Godot* at the Old Vic Theatre, *Times Literary Supplement*, 11 July 1997. As Newey notes, Beckett told director Peter Hall that "it means what you want it to mean."

19. Morris Dickstein, "An Outsider in His Own Life," review of *Samuel Beckett: The Last Modernist* by Anthony Cronin, *New York Times Book Review*, 3 August 1997.

20. John Simon, "Hapless Hours," *New York*, 28 September 1987. The attributes Simon lists are not simply "traditional"; they are defining elements of drama. Since they are minimal even in Beckett's supposed masterpiece *Waiting for Godot*, and virtually nonexistent in all his other stage works, we suggest that it is indeed "time to reassess [his] theatrical achievement," to borrow Simon's own words. "Holograms Might Be Better," *New York*, 6 February 1995. See also n. 22, below.

21. Similarly, Sass (419*n*78) finds in Beckett's *Endgame* the depiction of "a disembodied consciousness that [can] only helplessly endure all that it perceives." Disembodiment is total in Beckett's *Breath* (1969)—a 35-second stage piece in which sound and light fall on "'miscellaneous unidentifiable muck'" while the sound of a single breath is heard. (Gussow absurdly refers to this as a "wordless and actorless . . . play." "The Beckett Canon: So Little Is So Much," *New York Times*, 27 July 1996.) Beckett's fictional protagonists also suffer paralysis, dismemberment, and bodily incapacity.

22. John Simon, "The Master's Epitaph," 50. Since Beckett's "reduction to the absurd" is antithetical to art, however, it scarcely constitutes an achievement.

23. Clive Barnes, "The Intimate 'Godot' You've Been Waiting For" (review of production by the Classic Stage Company), *New York Post*, 20 November 1998.

24. "What 'Godot' Hath Wrought" (editorial), *New York Times*, 29 December 1989. For a revealing account of the intensely negative initial reception of *Godot*, and the subsequent manipulation of public opinion by the London theater critics Kenneth Tynan and Harold Hobson, see Deirdre Bair, *Samuel Beckett*, 453–60.

25. Even so astute a scholar as Joseph Frank refers to "uncertainty about the ultimate nature of reality created by the discoveries of modern physics" as an influence upon twentieth-century thought and art. Introduction to Erich Kahler, *The Tower and the Abyss*, xiv.

26. Beckett, quoted by Seaver, xxii, from interview with Israel Shenker, *New York Times,* 6 May 1956.

27. Beckett, "Three Dialogues," quoted by Stephenson, *Insanity of Beckett's Art*, 7. Stephenson (who holds a Ph.D. in psychology, is trained in psychoanalysis, and studied French literature at the Sorbonne and the University of Besançon) aptly characterizes Beckett's widely cited remark as his "autistic-artistic credo" (28), and argues that "the extraordinary story of twentieth century literature is that critics canonize Samuel Beckett's writings as works of genius when they are records of atrophy brought about by his mental illness." (1) Though Stephenson's privately published book might seem easy to dismiss, owing to its idiosyncratic style and typography, his provocative and well-documented (and indexed) analysis of Beckett's work from

a psychoanalytic perspective is broadly consistent with Louis Sass's observations. For further information, see Stephenson's website:<http://rjstephenson.com>.

28. Sass, *Madness and Modernism*, 36 and 56.

29. "I am finding it more and more difficult to write, but keep trying," Beckett wrote in a letter to H. O. White in 1959. Quoted by Seaver, xl, who attributes such sentiments simply to "the nature of [Beckett's] enterprise." After reading Beckett's minimalist novels *Molloy* and *Malone Dies* in 1952, Seaver had written in *Merlin* (a small English-language magazine in Paris): "Is it possible for Mr. Beckett to progress further without succumbing to the complete incoherence of inarticulate sound, or to . . . silence?" *Ibid.*

30. Charles Spencer, "This Is as Good as Beckett Gets," *Daily Telegraph* London, 19 April 1996.

31. Born in 1927, John Ashbery has written twenty books of poetry. In 1976, his *Self-Portrait in a Convex Mirror* won the Pulitzer Prize, the National Book Critics Circle Award, and the National Book Award. He is Charles P. Stevenson, Jr. Professor of Languages and Literature at Bard College, and in 1989–90 was the Charles Eliot Norton Professor of Poetry at Harvard University. He has been named a Guggenheim and a MacArthur Fellow, and is a chancellor of the American Academy of American Poets. Ashbery was a member of the so-called New York School of poets, which also included Frank O'Hara, James Schuyler, and Kenneth Koch (whom we discuss in Chapter 15). See David Lehman, *Last Avant-Garde*, for further information on Ashbery, also see the website of the American Academy at <http://www.poets.org>, and that of the *Encyclopaedia Britannica* <http://www.britannica.com>.

32. Sarah Bernard, "Little Darlings," *New York*, 5 April 1999, 14.

33. Robert Hass, "Poet's Circle," review of *The Last Avant-Garde: The Making of the New York School of Poets* by David Lehman, *Washington Post*, 11 October 1998.

34. Richard Kostelanetz, "How to Be a Difficult Poet," *New York Times Magazine*, 23 May 1976, 18.

35. Mark Ford, "Nothing and a Lot," review of *Can You Hear, Bird* by Josh Ashbery, Times Literary Supplement, 17 May 1996.

36. Mark Ford, "The Four Musketeers," review of *The Last Avant-Garde* by David Lehmen, *Times Literary Supplement*, 30 April 1999. 30.

37. John Ashbery, quoted by Kostelantez, "How to Be Difficult Poet," 20.

38. Ashbery, quoted by Ford, "Four Musketeers," 30.

39. Ford, "Four Musketeers," 30.

40. Ashbery, "Theme," in *Can You Hear, Bird*, 129–30.

41. William Logan, "Martyrs to Language," *The New Criterion*, December 1995.

42. Kostelanetz, "How to be a Difficult Poet," 31.

43. The emphasis by Kostelantez and Gioia on sound in Ashbery's work reminds us of Rand's satirical reference to Ellsworth Toohey's praise of "sound as sound, the poetry of words as words," quoted early in this chapter from *The Fountainhead*.

44. Dana Gioia, review of *Shadow Train* by John Ashbery, in *Can Poetry Matter?* 185–86.

45. Rand, "Basic Principles of Literature," 81.

46. W. Waller, "The Definition of Poetry," letter to the editor, 5 February 1999. As Waller further remarked, "the reader's emotions need to be involved, some association, some memory needs to be conjured up by the list of words presented as a poem; otherwise simply tell everyone to read the telephone directory."

47. Most writers (ourselves included) agree that the defining attributes of poetry also include meter and stanzaic organization-some add rhyme as well. In addition, poetry is often marked by some sort of "musical" quality. On the other hand, Jacques Barzun has argued that "it is not possible to name a set of requirements for poetry." See his letter in *Aristos*, December 1988. Regarding what poetry is, our focus is broader than such technical requirements, however. Since poetry is an *art* form, any work purporting to be a poem must, at the very least, be *intelligible*.

48. Dana Gioia, "Can Poetry Matter?" *Atlantic Monthly*, May 1991 <http://www. theatlantic.com/unbound/poetry/gioia/gioia.htm>.

49. Some two hundred graduate "creative-writing" programs in the United States, Gioia predicted, would produce about 20,000 largely unread "accredited professional poets" by century's end. *Can Poetry Matter?* 1–2
Much the same can be said of the numerous graduate "fine arts" programs across the land which add to the glut of postmodernist in the "visual art" categories we discuss in Chapter 14.

50. Robert Bly, *American Poetry: Wildness and Domesticity.* Quoted in Gioia, 8.

51. In any case, as the headline for a review by John Simon of Joyce Carol Oates's *Sunday Dinner* quipped, "Is the Inscrutable Worth Scruting?" *New York*, 16 March 1978.

52. Syd Field, *Screenplay*, 27.

53. Andrew Sarris, "Notes on the Auteur Theory" (1962), in Braudy and Cohen, 515–16. The definition of the *auteur* theory which Sarris cites and we quote here is from Ian Cameron, "Films, Directors, and Critics," *Movie*, September 1962. The theory originated with the French journal *Cahiers du Cinéma*, which became the leading film magazine in the world. Even Saris notes, however, that successful films can be made without a director, citing Marlon Brando's *One-Eyed Jacks* as an example.

54. E. L. Doctorow, "Quick Cuts: The Novel Follows Film into a World of Fewer Words," *New York Times*, 15 March 1999.

55. In Doctorow's view (see preceding note), the title cards of silent films told little more than was conveyed by the action itself, and dialogue in today's feature films increasingly tends to function in much the same minimalist fashion. Though

he is mistaken in thinking it characteristic of the medium as such, he aptly observes that the visual aspect of film "de-literates thought." Relying primarily on associations between visual impressions, it creates "a broad band of sensual effects that evoke your intuitive nonverbal intelligence." Contrary to his suggestion that you "understand what you see without having to think it through with words," however, such associative inferences are often unreliable avenues to understanding—as Rand often admonished, and as he himself implies when he laments that images may "eventually unseat linguistic composition as the major communicative act of our culture." For Rand's analysis of the fundamentally "anti-conceptual" nature of such thought by association, see her essays "The Missing Link" (1973), in *Philosophy*, 35–45; and "The Age of Envy" (1971), in *New Left*, ed. Schwartz, 130–158.

56. Rand, to Gerald Loeb, 21 August 1945, in *Letters of Ayn Rand*, 148. In the same letter, Rand wrote: "I seem to get along with Hal Wallis very well." The previous year, she had signed a five-year contract with Wallis when he left Warner Brothers to start his own independent company. Rand was the first writer he signed, and he had agreed, in what was an extraordinary concession in Hollywood, to allow her half of each year to pursue her own writing. Rand to Archibald Ogden (her editor for *The Fountainhead*), 19 July 1944. Wallis later said of Rand: "Ayn was a brilliant writer, and totally an individualist, in her person, her writing, and her ideas." Quoted by B. Branden, *Passion of Ayn Rand*, 191.

57. Rand, to Henry Blanke, 26 February 1949, in *Letters of Ayn Rand*, 428. Rand was trying to interest the studio in undertaking a remake of *The Isle of Lost Ships*, which she considered "one of the best screen stories of all time."

58. For a detailed comparison of the plot elements in Rand's screenplay for *Love Letters* and Massie's novel, as well as an analysis of the other films for which she wrote scripts (*You Came Along* and *The Fountainhead*), see Stephen Cox, "It Couldn't Be Made into a *Really* Good Movie: The Films of Ayn Rand," *Liberty*, August 1987, 5–10. Cox compares the relationship between Alan Quinton and the fellow soldier for whom he ghost-writes love letters to his girl friend to the "parasite-host relationship" between Howard Roark and fellow architect Peter Keating in *The Fountainhead*; but a more apt comparison, in our view, is to the relationship between Cyrano and Christian in Rostand's *Cyrano de Bergerac*—a play Rand greatly admired. In both cases, the relationship is not truly parasitical, since it is not entirely at the letter writer's expense; he derives vicarious pleasure in the process.

59. Vincent Canby, "Gérard Depardieu as Columbus: Idealist, Dreamer and Hustler" (review of *1492*), *New York Times*, 9 October 1992.

60. Peter Rainer, "Get Me Rewrite," review of *Runaway Bride*, starring Richard Gere and Julia Roberts, *New York*, 9 August 1999.

61. Peter B. Flint, "Joseph L. Mankiewicz, Literate Skeptic of the Cinema, Dies at 83," *New York Times*, 6 February 1993.

62. Vincent Canby, quoted *ibid.*

63. Bernard Weinraub, "In the Eyes of Many, TV, Not the Movies, Is the Higher Calling," *New York Times*, 14 February 1995.

64. Phillip Lopate, "The Last Taboo," in Washburn and Thornton, *Dumbing Down*, 164–178; an adapted version of this essay was published as "It's Not Heroes Who Have Bad Grammar; It's Films," *New York Times*, 18 June 1995.

65. The increasingly formulaic approach to screeenwriting is abetted by numerous "story development" software programs that "will almost write a screenplay for you." One such program, "Dramatica," begins by asking the user 250 questions about the story line; Dramatica's 'story engine' uses the answers to monitor and help structure the plot, add and delete characters, cross-reference their motivation, question their subconscious, and so on. Dana Kennedy, "Screenwriting @ Your Fingertips," *New York Times*, 9 January 2000.

66. Tampering with screenplays is nothing new of course. See Herbert Mitgang, "Hollywood's Writers Finally Have the Last Word," review of *Backstory 2: Interviews with Screenwriters of the 1940's and 1950's*, by Pat McGilligan, *New York Times*, 26 July 1991. Even when fidelity to the screenplay is contractually assured, changes can occur in the cutting room, as Rand painfully discovered with the final release of *The Fountainhead*—an experience which moved her to sever her working ties to Hollywood. See B. Branden, *Passion of Ayn Rand*, 211–13.

67. The only published version of Walter Brown Newman's screenplay *Harrow Alley* appeared in the Fall 1995 issue of *Scenario: The Magazine of Screenwriting Art*, to which our citations refer. Regrettably this issue is out of print. See <http://www. scenario.com>.

68. Glenn Erickson, "Movie Scripts As Research Tools," *DVD Savant, 1998*, <http://www.dvdresource.com/ savant/s46scripts.shtml>.

69. Walter Brown Newman, quoted by William Froug, "Writing *Harrow Alley*" (a 1972 interview with Newman), *Scenario*, Fall 1995, 116. The interview originally appeared in Froug's *The Screenwriter Looks at the Screenwriter* (New York: Macmillan, 1972; reprinted Sillman-James Press, 1991)

Chapter 14 Postmodernism in the "Visual Arts"

1. Rand, "An Answer to Readers: About the Horror File," *Objectivist*, March 1967, 12. As Rand explained, the feature in *The Objectivist*, consisting of examples from the popular press sent in by readers, had been inspired by the "Horror File" of research clippings she had kept while writing *Atlas Shrugged* (1957), and following its publication, to illustrate the deteriorating intellectual state of the culture and to reflect the influence of philosophy.

2. Daniel Herwitz, in *Encyclopedia of Aesthetics, s.v.* "Postmodernism," 58. See also above, chs. 12 and 13, as well as our discussion in ch. 7 of the fundamental similarities between modernism and postmodernism emphasized by Louis Sass in *Madness and Modernism*.

3. See Caroline A. Jones, "Post-modernism," in Turner, *Dictionary of Art*, 358; and Atkins, *Art Speak*, 131.

4. From 1915 on, Duchamp spent long periods in the United States, and eventually became a citizen, in 1954. His incalculable influence on the American artworld appears to have stemmed initially from his considerable personal charisma—he combined elegant good looks with a playful wit and a seductive coolness and reserve that probably suggested greater depth than he actually possessed—and his association with the European "avant-garde" as much as from his work and ideas. As his biographer Calvin Tomkins notes (13), he seemed to embody the ideal of the modern artist. See Roger Shattuck, "Confidence Man: Marcel DuChamp," in *Candor and Perversion*, 244–61.

5. Steven Goldsmith, quoted by John Brough, "Who's Afraid of Marcel Duchamp?" in *Philosophy and Art*, ed. Daniel O. Dahlstrom (Catholic University of America Press, 1991), 119. On Duchamp's readymades, see our Introduction, and Ch. 6, n. 15.

6. Francis M. Naumann, in Turner, *Dictionary of Art*, *s.v.* "Duchamp, (Henri-Robert-) Marcel," 354.

7. Duchamp, in Kuh, *The Artist's Voice*, 90.

8. For images of *Bicycle Wheel*, *Fountain*, and other works by Duchamp, see <http://www.artchive.com/artchive/D/duchamp.html>. An image of *In Advance of the Broken Arm* may be viewed at <http://theartcanvas.com/duchamp.arm.htm>.

9. Sass, *Madness and Modernism*, 488–89n107.

10. As we noted in Ch. 12, Rauschenberg participated in Cage's landmark multimedia event at Black Mountain College in 1952; and for more than a decade (1954–1965) he was closely associated with him in working as designer and stage manager for Merce Cunningham's dance company. Influence did not flow only from Cage to Rauschenberg, however; rather, their ideas and attitudes regarding art were mutually reinforcing.

11. Michael Kimmelman, "Clowning Inventively with Stuff of Beauty," *New York Times*, 19 September 1997.

12. Rauschenberg, quoted in Phillips, *American Century*, 83, from catalog for *Sixteen Americans* (New York: Museum of Modern Art, 1959), 58. The notion of working in the "gap" between art and life reminds us of the old joke about the father attempting to attract a potential suitor for his daughter, who assures the young man that she is "only a little bit pregnant." "Closing the Gap between Art and Life," as Phillips titles the section containing the Rauschenberg quote, can mean only one thing: eliminating art.

13. Rauschenberg's fellow painter Willem de Kooning had given him one of his drawings for the experiment, which took him "a month, and about forty erasers to do." In the end, "it really worked," he told his biographer. "I felt it was a legitimate work of art, created by the technique of erasing." Quoted in Tomkins, *Off the Wall*, 96–97.

14. Roni Feinstein, director of the Whitney Museum annex in Stamford, Connecticut, quoted by Grace Glueck, "Rauschenberg at 65, with All Due Immodesty," *New York Times*, 16 December 1990.

15. Robert Rauschenberg, quoted by Glueck, "Rauschenberg at 65."

16. Rauschenberg, quoted by Tomkins, *Off the Wall*, 183.

17. "The 10 Best Living Artists," *ARTnews*, December 1999, 137, 140.

18. Phillipe de Montebello, quoted by Carol Vogel, "Met Buys Its First Painting by Jasper Johns," *New York Times*, 29 October 1998. See also Rita Reif, "Johns's 'White Flag' Is Sold for Record Price," *New York Times*, 10 November 1998.

19. Louis Menand, "Capture the Flag: Jasper Johns' Own Private Icon" (review of *Jasper Johns: A Retrospective*, Museum of Modern Art, New York, 20 October 1996–21 January 1997), *Slate* magazine (online), 29 October 1996: <http://www.slate.com/Art/96-10-29/Art.asp>. See also "Jasper Johns: A Retrospective," at the New York Museum of Modern Art Website, <http://www.moma.org/johns/index.html>.

20. Lilly Wei, quoting Jasper Johns, "Complexity and Contradiction," *ARTnews*, December 1999, 140.

21. Leo Steinberg, "Jasper Johns: The First Seven Years of His Art," in *Other Criteria*, 48.

22. Jasper Johns, Interview with G. R. Swenson (1964), in Russell and Gablik, *Pop Art Redefined*, 83.

23. Jasper Johns, "Sketchbook Notes" (1965), in Russell and Gablik, 84–85.

24. As has often been pointed out, Johns's flat, decontextualized renderings of signs and symbols are indistinguishable from the signs and symbols themselves.

25. For Deborah Solomon, Johns's "cans of Ballantine Ale stand side by side with a dignity befitting Egyptian tomb figures." "The Unflagging Artistry of Jasper Johns," *New York Times Magazine*, 19 June 1988, 64.

26. Johns, Interview with Swenson, 83. On Castelli—the dealer most responsible for creating the inflated reputation of Johns, Rauschenberg, and the subsequent generation of Pop, minimalist, and conceptual "artists"—see the obituary by John Russell in the *New York Times*, 23 August 1999.

27. Solomon, "Unflagging Artistry," 66. Solomon reports that, when asked why he had "depicted himself as a quivering spook," he answered: "It was an easy solution to filling a large part of the canvas,' . . . letting loose one of his raucous laughs."

28. Jasper Johns, "Sketchbook Notes," *Art and Literature*, vol. 4 (Spring 1965), 192; quoted by Mark Rosenthal, *Jasper Johns*, 11.

29. "My experience of life is that it's very fragmented," Johns stated in 1978, adding that he wanted his work to provide "some vivid indication" of this. Quoted in wall text for *Jasper Johns: A Retrospective*, Museum of Modern Art, New York, 20 October 1996–21 January 1997.

30. While Rauschenberg and Johns introduced many of the elements employed in Pop art, they did not explicitly intend their work as a rejection of Abstract Expressionism as did Warhol, Lichtenstein, and Oldenburg. For this reason, it is somewhat misleading to regard them, as critics often do, primarily as Pop artists.

31. Lawrence Alloway, "The Long Front of Culture" (1959), reprinted in Russell and Gablik, 41–43. This essay was first published in a Cambridge University journal.

32. Some of these theories are summarized by Katy Siegel, in *Encyclopedia of Aesthetics, s.v.* "Pop Art."

33. Arthur C. Danto, "Aesthetics of Andy Warhol," in Kelly, *Encyclopedia of Aesthetics, s.v.* "Pop Art," 41.

34. Danto's conclusion regarding Warhol's *Brillo Box* has led him to postulate a series of highly unlikely philosophical conundrums based on hypothetical "indiscernibles"—that is, works of art indistinguishable from nonart objects.

35. Warhol, *Philosophy of Andy Warhol*, 91. See also Warhol's declaration that "[t]here's nothing behind" the surface of his work; quoted by Robert Hughes, "The Rise of Andy Warhol," *New York Review of Books*, 18 February 1982, 7.

36. Commenting on Alfred Jarry (the profoundly schizoid early twentieth-century French writer whose plays inspired the theater of the absurd), Sass equates his "robotlike persona" with "a sort of mechanical, *proto-Warholian* antipersonality who spoke in mock-heroic and periphrastic prose. In a peculiar, machinelike monotone he would emit his zany witticisms, generally expressing sudden ironic reversals that emanated from a position of utter emotional indifference and absolute disengagement from logic or practical realities." *Madness and Modernism*, 134.

37. Andy Warhol, interview with G. R. Swenson, in Russell and Gablik, 116–19; reprinted from "What Is Pop Art?" interviews with eight painters (Part I), *Art News*, November 1963. In time, by adopting the use of silk screens made from photographs, and by employing others to execute the work for him in his "Factory," Warhol did make the production of his "art" machine-like.

38. Warhol, interview with Swenson, 117.

39. Michael Kimmelman, "Roy Lichtenstein, Pop Master, Dies at 73," *New York Times*, 30 September 1997.

40. Clare Bell (assistant curator), brochure for *Roy Lichtenstein* retrospective, Guggenheim Museum, New York, 8 October 1993–16 January 1994.

41. Roy Lichtenstein, quoted from Michael Kimmelman, *Talking with Artists*, in book review by R. Cembalest, *New York Times*, 24 August 1998.

42. John Updike, "Big, Bright & Bendayed" (review of Guggenheim exhibition [see n. 21 above] and catalog), *New York Review of Books*, 16 December 1993, 4.

43. Lichtenstein, quoted *ibid.*

44. Lichtenstein, interview with Nan Rosenthal, 92nd Street Y, New York, 14 February 1991.

45. By "esthetic," we here mean forms designed with attention to their perceptual features.

46. Henry Flynt, "Concept Art" (1961), in Kostelanetz, *Esthetics Contemporary*, 429.

47. Minimalism, which we touched on briefly in relation to abstract art, in Ch. 12, served as a logical antecedent for conceptual art—since it was often fully conceived in advance as a systematic repetition of modular forms (as such, it was a visual counterpart of serial music).

48. Sol LeWitt, "Paragraphs on Conceptual Art" (1967), in Kostelanetz, *Esthetics Contemporary*, 432–35.

49. On Rand's idea of "dancing back and forth" between perception and cognition, see above, Ch. 3, n. 22.

50. Joseph Kosuth, "Art after Philosophy, I and II," in Battcock, *Idea Art*, 70–101; reprinted from *Studio International*, October and November, 1969.

51. See also his more recent claim: "Conceptual art, simply put, had as its basic tenet an understanding that artists work with meaning, not with shapes, colors, or materials." Joseph Kosuth, "Intention(s)," *Art Bulletin*, September 1996.

52. In considering what "art" has come to mean, Kosuth cites only the theoretical views of avant-gardists such as Judd, Duchamp, and LeWitt. Thus he violates the principle (identified by Rand) that, in tracing the meaning of a concept, one must examine the nature of its *original referents*.

53. "Being an artist now means to question the nature of art. . . . If an artist accepts painting (or sculpture) he is accepting the tradition that goes with it. . . . If you make paintings you are already accepting (not questioning) the nature of art." (79) Kosuth was referring, of course, only to visual art.

54. Lisa Phillips, *The American Century, 1950–2000*, 215. Phillips misleadingly poses these remarks immediately following a reference to LeWitt's essay, "Paragraphs on Conceptual Art." It was not LeWitt but Kosuth, however, who wrote of "morphological characteristics" and of Duchamp's influence.

55. Turner, *Dictionary of Art, s.v.* "Installation," 868; and Kaprow, *Assemblage, Environments, and Happenings*, 159.

56. Roberta Smith, "In Installation Art, a Bit of the Spoiled Brat," *New York Times*, 3 January 1993.

57. In that *Murphy Brown* send-up of the artworld, Murphy skeptically eyed an extravagantly priced pile of saccharin packets on a gallery floor and did a quick calculation of how more cheaply she could fabricate her own installation based on a quick trip to the supermarket. On other avant-garde work skewered in that episode, see Torres and Kamhi, "Yes . . . But Is It Art?" For an illustration of the Gonzales-Torres piece, see Phillips, *American Century*, fig. 581.

58. Roberta Smith, "A Conceptual Face-Off at 2 Whitney Branches," *New York Times*, 26 June 1992. "As a monument to women's labor in the home," Smith opines, the Hamilton piece "is hard to beat."

59. Turner, *Dictionary of Art, s.v.* "Installation," 869.

60. Allan Kaprow, "The Legacy of Jackson Pollock" (1958), in *Essays on the Blurring of Art and Life*, 1–9.

61. Kaprow acknowledged that his "new art" was a direct descendant of collage—the two-dimensional form (invented by Picasso in 1912) in which pre-existing materials or objects were incorporated into a painting by being glued to the flat surface of the canvas. For Kaprow, collage had led by "an almost logical progress" to the three-dimensional assemblages of the postmodernists. "Once foreign matter was introduced into the picture in the form of paper, it was only a matter of time before everything else foreign to paint and canvas would be allowed to get into the creative act, including real space." What had begun as mere pieces of paper on a flat canvas eventually grew into solid materials, "reaching out further into the room, [and] finally filled it entirely"—soon becoming what he referred to, all too aptly, as "rooms of madness" and "junk-filled attics of the mind." Since collage was *not* art, however—precisely *because* it was the first step across the boundary between the selective re-creation of reality and reality itself—none of its postmodernist extensions is art either. *Assemblage*, 165.

62. For a photograph of Kaprow's *Yard*, see Phillips, *The American Century*, fig. 141.

63. Kaprow, "Legacy of Jackson Pollock," 9.

64. Allan Kaprow, "Notes on the Creation of a Total Art" (1958), in *Essays*, 10–12.

65. "The work of art," Kaprow wrote, "must now receive its meaning and qualities from the unique, expectant (and often anxious) focus of the observer, listener, or intellectual participant." *Assemblage*, 173. What he envisioned differed fundamentally from Rand's view. The artist's task, as she saw it, is to concretize his values in an objectively appropriate form (from which the viewer can then grasp them)—a task requiring skill and discipline. In contrast, Kaprow denied that intentional, disciplined activity was required on the part of the artist; and the burden of "creativity," as it were, was shifted to the viewer.

66. *Fluxus* (meaning "flow") was an informal international avant-garde movement of individuals whose work, in the antirational spirit of John Cage (see above, Ch. 12), featured performances of everyday movement or activities and noise "music." See Michael Corris, "Fluxus," in Kelly, *Encyclopedia of Aesthetics*. Fluxus performers included Yoko Ono, Nam June Paik (who gained later fame as a "video artist"), and La Monte Young.

67. On Chris Burden, see Phillips, *American Century*, 247, 253, and figs. 405 and 406; on Happenings, *ibid.*, 94–102; and on Fluxus, *ibid.*, 103–107;

68. In a classic instance of impenetrable postmodernist feminist art criticism, Amelia Jones argues that through the action in *Interior Scroll* (which she, like us, knows only from descriptions and photographs), "which extends 'exquisite sensation in motion' and 'originates with . . . the fragile persistence of line moving into space,' Schneemann integrated the occluded interior of the female body (with the vagina as 'a translucent chamber') with its mobile exterior, refusing the fetishizing processs, which requires that the woman not expose the fact that she is not lacking but possesses genitals, and that they are nonmale." "'Presence' in Absentia: Experiencing Performance as Documentation," *Art Journal*, Winter 1997, 11–18.

69. Amelia Jones, "Feminist Performance Art," in Kelly, *Encyclopedia of Aesthetics*. According to Jones, Sprinkle "uses her body as an always already alienated (commodified) physical instantiation of herself." Jones elsewhere notes that Sprinkle, who "moved into the art world" in 1985, "has performed in art venues as a whore/performer turned art/performer, still with 'clients' to seduce and pleasure." "'Presence' in Absentia: Experiencing Performance as Documentation," *Art Journal*, Winter 1997, 11–18. Sprinkle's pretentious resumé on her Internet homepage <http://www.heck.com/annie/index.html> itemizes, along with nearly one hundred "porn films," numerous museum and university "teaching" and "lecturing" credits.

70. Martha Wilson, "Performance Art: (Some) Theory and (Selected) Practice at the End of This Century," *Art Journal*, Winter 1997, 2. Wilson was the founding director of Franklin Furnace, one of New York City's "cutting-edge" performance spaces. In contrast with her view, Allan Kaprow—whose ideas on Happenings helped to legitimize performance as an "art form"—argued that, while Happenings appeared "to go nowhere," made no "particular literary point," and had "no structured beginning, middle, or end," they should nonetheless be regarded as "essentially theater pieces," which could be best understood "by widening the concept 'theater' to include them." Kaprow, "Happenings in the New York Scene" (1961), in *Essays*, 16–19. As he acknowledged, however, Happenings differed from theater in certain "crucial" respects (shared by much performance art): they were essentially nonverbal and nonsensical, they lacked a plot, and they deliberately blurred the distinction between performers and spectators. Largely improvisatory, they also made liberal use of chance—in the Cagean tradition that inspired them—and were consequently devoid of intentional meaning. To consider them *theater* was not to "widen" that concept, therefore, but rather to flout or destroy it, since they were lacking in the very quality that renders theatrical art valuable: its ability to organize and clarify human experience.

71. Wilson, "Performance Art," 2, emphasis in original.

72. *Webster's Third New International Dictionary* (1966).

73. Kaprow, "Happenings in the New York Scene" (1961), 21.

74. See Kaprow, "The Meaning of Life" (1990), in *Essays*, 229.

75. Holly Solomon (Manhattan art dealer), quoted by Doris Athineos, "O, Brave New World," *Forbes*, 23 September 1996, 250.

76. Mick Hartney, in Turner, *Dictionary of Art*, s.v. "Video art," 419. See also *Video Art*, edited by John G. Hanhardt and Maria Christina Villaseñor, special issue of *Art Journal*, Winter 1995.

77. Diane M. Bolz, "A Video Visionary," *Smithsonian*, October 1997, 34. Since Paik's television monitors are surely not art, their emissions must be, if his work is to qualify as art. Video, like film, is not an art form in itself; it is only a medium for recording sounds and images that may or not constitute art. Paik's frenetic video emissions, which fragment and confound perception, clearly do not. Just as the irreducible basis of film as an art form is the screenplay, the only original "art" possible in video, as a temporal medium, is the video play.

78. On the *ARTnews* poll, see above, n. 17. On the Nauman retrospective, see Kamhi, "Kandinsky and His Progeny."

79. Francine Prose, "The Funny Side of the Abyss," *ARTnews*, December 1999, 143. On the schizoid character of Nauman's attitude toward his so-called sculptures of the 1960s, see Sass, *Madness and Modernism*, 171.

80. Michael Kimmelman, "The Importance of Matthew Barney," *New York Times Magazine*, 10 October 1999.

81. According to *ARTnews* contributing editor Barbara Pollack, Barney's piece forced viewers "to question the boundaries between sculpture, installation, body art, and video art." (Postmodernist work is often said to "force" viewers to question something.) Barney's "sculptures, which resemble prosthetic devices," are "maddeningly indecipherable," she adds. "The Wizard of Odd," *ARTnews*, December 1999, 138.

82. Grundberg and Gauss, *Photography and Art*, 15. In the view of *San Francisco Chronicle* critic Christopher Knight, "this exhibition is likely to be the standard by which its topic will be measured for a very long time." *Last Chance for Eden*, 289. See also the admiring review by Robert Atkins, "Photography Becomes Art," *Horizon*, June 1987, 38, 40.

83. Peter Galassi, quoted by Barbara Pollack, "Self-Denial," *ARTnews*, December 1999, 146.

84. Amanda Cruz, text from essay in *Cindy Sherman: Retrospective* (Thames and Hudson, 1997) online at <http://www.masters-of-photography.com>.

85. See, for example, Angela Smith's statement that Sherman's work, when brought into contact with psychoanalytic and postmodern understandings of identity, enters into the complexities of embodied subjectivity," and that her photo series from 1985 to 1992 "form a a graphic commentary on the intertwining of bodily surfaces and matter with our self-perceptions, . . . making space to contest hegemonic and misogynistic narratives of subjectivity." "The Abject Female Body: The Photography of Cindy Sherman," at <http://english.cla.umn.edu>.

86. Cruz sees Sherman's *Untitled Film Still #21*, for example, as "a young secretary in the city." But it might just as well be a foreign tourist or a suburban housewife on her way to lunch at a fashionable restaurant—just as the purported "perky B-movie librarian" in *Untitled Film Still #13* could as easily be a self-conscious college student or a buxom public library patron. For reproductions of these images, see Krauss, *Cindy Sherman*, 30–31, and 69; and <http://www.artcyclopedia.com/artists/ sherman cindy.html>.

87. In more recent work, Close has blown up Polaroid images and transferred them to paper using a digital ink-jet process. See his 1996 "self-portrait" on the cover of *Art & Auction*, November 1996.

88. Chuck Close, quoted by Denis Pelli, "An Artist's Work Blurs Lines between Art and Science," *New York Times*, 10 August 1999.

89. *Ibid.* "Can art be science?" asks Pelli, but never really answers the question, which ought to be "Can science be art?"

90. Michael Kimmelman, on Chuck Close exhibition at Pace Wildenstein Gallery, in "Art in Review," *New York Times*, 8 December 1995.

91. Deborah Solomon, "The Persistence of the Portraitist" (cover article), *New York Times Magazine*, 1 February 1998. Like Chuck Close's painting, the work of "sculptors" Duane Hanson (1925–1996) and John de Andrea (b. 1941) is not a selective re-creation of reality. It is a mechanical reproduction of the human form, made by casting from molds made directly on live human figures, and then painted in a slavishly realistic style, with real hair and real clothing added to complete the waxwork-like effect. Hanson's preference was for "stoical, often fleshy denizens of malls, tract houses, group tours and gyms." Roberta Smith, "Tenderly Replicating the Banal," *New York Times*, 18 December 1998. De Andrea tends toward younger, more attractive types, as in *The Artist and His Model* (1980). They are not art, any more than figures in Madame Tussaud's famous waxwork museum are. By the same token, "sculptor" George Segal's plaster figures, cast directly from live friends and family members , while less realistic-looking than Hanson's and De Andrea's work, is not art either.

92. *Digital Reflections: The Dialogue of Art and Technology*, edited by Johanna Drucker, special issue of *Art Journal*, Fall 1997.

93. "As Time Goes By," lyrics and music by Herman Hupfeld (1931), from the film "Casablanca." The complete lyrics of the song may be found online at<http://users.aol.com/ VRV1/astime.html>.

Chapter 15 Public Implications

1. See, for example, Rand's essays "The Esthetic Vacuum of Our Age" (1962), *Romantic Manifesto*, 123–28; "Bootleg Romanticism" (1965), *ibid.*, 129–41; "Art and Moral Treason" (1965), *ibid.*, 142–52; and "Our Cultural Value-Deprivation" (1966), *Voice of Reason*, 100–114. See also Sciabarra's interpretation of Rand's cultural analysis in *Ayn Rand*, 319–29. Although she generally lamented the decline of moral values in popular culture, Rand applauded the lingering traces of Romanticism in television series such as *The Twilight Zone* and *The Untouchables* and in popular fiction such as the early work of Mickey Spillane and Ian Fleming's James Bond thrillers.

2. Though annual NEA appropriations are now far below their peak levels, the endowment exerts an influence far beyond its limited budget—through its joint efforts with state and local arts councils and, more important, its "partnerships" with private foundations. Even a small NEA grant affords a halo of legitimacy, purportedly validating the worth of the funded individual or organization, thereby opening the door, almost automatically, to further sources of recognition and funding.

3. The Fellowships in the Arts program of the multibillion-dollar Pew Charitable Trusts in Philadelphia is indicative of large-scale private support of the arts. Instituted in 1991 to fill some of the gap left by the NEA's discontinuation of direct grants to "visual artists," it employs a definition of art as open-ended as the NEA's. Though the program aims to provide "nourishment and stimulation" for the "cultural community" through support of new work, 1999 fellows in the spurious category of

"media arts" (to cite but one example) produced work that appears to do neither. Their output ranged from "furniture art" and "fiber art" to inscrutable "installations" and abstract "craft" objects having neither meaning nor practical function. Information on recent Pew fellows, with samples of their work, is available on the foundation's website at <http://www.pewarts.org/abpfmaintext.html>.

4. Rand forcefully argued that man's rights do not include "economic rights" such as support for the arts and artists. The spurious theory of "economic rights," she maintained, "includes the 'right' of every would-be playwright, every beatnik poet, every noise-composer and every non-objective artist . . . to the financial support you did not give them when you did not attend their shows." "Man's Rights," in *Capitalism: The Unknown Ideal* (New York: Signet, 1967), 327; and *The Virtue of Selfishness* (New York: New American Library), 133. For early arguments against the NEA, see the Congressional "Minority Views" on its proposed establishment (H.R. 9460), charging that this "far-reaching bill, creating Federal czars over the arts" was "full of ambiguities"—"a maze of bureaucratic organizational structure with a minimum of light to comprehend what the provisions actually mean or are intended to achieve." The minority's admonition that such a federal program "may well result in a lowering, rather than an elevation, of the cultural level of our Nation" has proved prophetic. In Merryman and Elsen, 1:342.

5. In his memoir *Twigs for an Eagle's Nest: Government and the Arts, 1965–1978*, Michael Straight, deputy chairman under Nancy Hanks (the NEA's first chairman), describes some of the dubious proposals—ranging from "a series of paintings, ten to fifteen layers of paint deep, consisting entirely of extremely subtle gradations of grey," to a small-scale hippie commune—funded by the NEA's Visual Arts Office. See especially the chapters entitled "The Excrement of the Artist" (130–32) and "Reflections upon Receiving the Golden Fleece of the Month Award" (166–72). For an early critique of NEA writing programs, see Hilary Masters, "Go Down Dignified: The NEA Writing Fellowships," *Georgia Review*, Summer 1981, 233–245.

6. Oswald Hanfling, "The Problem of Definition," in *Philosophical Aesthetics*, 2.

7. Remarks by Bill Ivey, Chairman, National Endowment for the Arts, National Assembly of State Arts Agencies Annual Meeting, Portland, Oregon, 13 November 1998; <http://www.arts.endow.gov/endownews/news98/NASAASpeech.html>. Ivey aimed his remarks at "many business and civic leaders . . . , as well as [at] a television and radio audience." On attempts by arts advocates to exploit the public sense of what the term *art* means, see Michelle Marder Kamhi, "NEA grants: 'Is This Work Really Art?'" *Detroit News* 9 October 1990; online at <http://www.aristos.org/editors/kamhi-dn.htm>.

8. See <http://www.//arts.endow.gov/endownews/news99/Announce12-99.html>.

9. *National Foundation on the Arts and Humanities Act of 1965, U. S. Code*, sec. 952 (a); <http://www.law.cornell.edu/uscode/20/952.html>. See also Merryman and Elsen, 1:338.

10. Although the term "visual arts" means primarily *painting and sculpture*, these forms are absent from the website home page for the NEA funding category

"Museums and Visual Arts"—which is illustrated with a necklace, a structure of indeterminate nature, and what appears to be either two "performance artists" or puppet
figures; <http://www.arts.endow.gov/artforms/Museums/Museum1.html>. "Visual
artists" featured on the NEA website include Meg Belichick, whose "artist's books"
incorporate texts "by a process of physically building the words and breaking them
into sentences and pages as objects and not just letters on paper"; <http://www.arts.
endow.gov/explore/Gallery/Belichick.html>.
See also NEA grants announced for the year 2000.

11. *National Foundation on the Arts and Humanities Act of 1965* (see n. 9, above);
also Merryman and Elsen, 1:338. The federal Art-in-Architecture program, established in 1963 under the General Services Administration, suffers from a similarly
free-wheeling, open-ended definition of "fine art"—and from an implicit bias against
so-called traditional figurative painting and sculpture, in favor of avant-garde work.
The most notorious Art-in-Architecture project was Richard Serra's *Tilted Arc*, which
had to be removed five years after its installation outside a federal office building in
Manhattan because it so offended the public. See Kamhi, "Today's 'Public Art.'"

12. In 1989, members of Congress objected to NEA support for an exhibition
of Robert Mapplethorpe's photographs, some of which they deemed obscene, and
for a grant to the photographer Andres Serrano, whose *Piss Christ* they regarded as
blasphemous. As a result, Congress passed a 1990 amendment, § 954(d), to the statute
governing the endowment, requiring that the Chairman ensure consideration of "general standards of decency and respect for the diverse beliefs and values of the American public," and barring funding of obscene work. Based on this amendment, Chairman
John Frohnmayer vetoed grants to four controversial "performance artists" that had
been approved in the peer-panel review process. The four applicants subsequently
sued the endowment, charging in part that the amendment was unconstitutionally
vague. (The most notorious of the four was Karen Finley, best known for her act "We
Keep Our Victims Ready," in which she smeared her nude body with chocolate to
signify the degradation of women.) Though the Supreme Court eventually upheld
the constitutionality of the amendment, the endowment has, in effect, circumvented
the restrictions, as Justice Anthony Scalia observed in his concurring opinion. See
below, n. 17. On the original controversy, see Richard Bernstein, "Subsidies for
Artists: Is Denying a Grant Really Censorship?" *New York Times*, 18 July 1990.

13. See NEA Guidelines and Applications, Grants to Organizations: How to
Apply <http://www.arts.endow.gov/guide/Orgs01/How.html>; and Basic Facts about
the NEA: 1999 Grant Awards, Creation and Presentation <http://www.arts.endow.
gov/learn/99Grants/C-P1.html>. Documentaries are not art for the same reasons that
journalism and history are not art. See Rand's distinctions between these concepts,
discussed above, Ch. 3, under "Art and Reality," and Ch. 4, under "Literature."

14. See "Basic Facts about the NEA: 2000 Grant Awards" on the endowment's
website.

15. For grants cited in this paragraph, see <http://www.arts.endow.gov/learn/
99Grants/C-P1.html> and <http://www.arts.endow.gov/learn/00Grants/C-P2.html>.

16. For illustrations of Kiki Smith's *Tale* and Robert Mapplethorpe's *Man in
Polyester Suit*, see Phillips, *American Century*, 358 and 332.

17. The image of a "crucifix immersed in urine" Scalia referred to was Andres Serrano's controversial photograph, *Piss Christ.* Scalia mistakenly referred to it as a "depiction." Justice Anthony Scalia, concurring opinion in *National Endowment for the Arts, et al., Petitioners v. Karen Finley, et al.*, 524 U.S. 569 (1998); 1998 U.S. LEXIS 4211.

18. As early as 1977, Rand deplored the growing emphasis on ethnicity in America, and cited as one example a recent complaint by Hispanic groups insisting on their "'fair share'" of state arts support, "'to assure the growth of 'non-mainstream' art forms.'" Rand, "Global Balkanization," lecture delivered at Ford Hall Forum, 10 April 1977; in *Voice of Reason*, 124; quoting New York State Senator Robert Garcia, from an article entitled "Hispanic Groups Say They Are Inequitably Treated in Support for the Arts," *New York Times*, 17 January 1977. Rand feared that this "modern tribalism" of values could eventually lead to the downfall of Western civilization, since it fosters irrationalism and collectivism, both of which are anathema to a free society.

19. NEA, Writer's Corner, 1998 Creative Writing Fellowships Winners in Fiction & Prose—A Sampler <http://www.arts.endow.gov/explore/Writers/Fellows.html>. Contrary to the NEA's claim of blind review, a panelist need not know the individual's name or biography to surmise the background of an applicant in the spurious category of "creative nonfiction" (i.e., *memoir*, on which see Chapter 13), for example, whose writing sample—describing her childhood memories of jumping rope— reads in part: "Ten years before Air Jordans, I learned to fly. It's like the way brothers pimp-walk to a basketball hoop with a pumped-up ball and throw a few shots, hitting each on effortlessly." The winner, who identified herself in her application as the daughter of "black Latinos from Panama," envisioned that the fellowship of $20,000 would be "especially vital in terms of funding research trips to Miami, San Antonio, Chicago, and Panama," purportedly to "explore more of [her] Latino heritage." NEA, Writer's Corner, Excerpt from "Mama's Girl" by Veronica Chambers <http://www.arts.endow.gov/explore/Writers/Chambers.html>.

20. These grants are all listed online at <http://www.endow.gov/learn/00grants/lit. html>.

21. A Raytheon advertisement in *Smithsonian* magazine in 1986, for example, depicted American Ballet Theatre prima ballerina Cynthia Gregory at the barre, with the caption "Quality starts with fundamentals." The text of the ad read: ". . . At Raytheon, we admire people like Cynthia Gregory because we go about our business in the same way. . . . [O]ur commitment to quality . . . starts with fundamentals." Similarly, a 1986 AT&T advertisement declared: "From the beginning, we've been committed to achieving excellence in communications. It's only natural for us to support excellence in the arts that communicate."

22. As early as 1985, Donald M. Kendall, the chairman of Pepsico—whose corporate headquarters maintains an expansive sculpture park featuring work by leading modernists and postmodernists—declared: "'I don't think anybody could walk away from here without being impressed. . . . This makes us a first-class company.'" Quoted by Thomas J. Lueck, "More Corporations Becoming Working Museums," *New York Times*, 15 September 1985.

23. Andrew S. Grove, Chairman, Intel Corporation, "Statement of Collaboration," in Lisa Phillips, *The American Century*, 5. Grove adds that "Intel and the Whitney Museum will be working together . . . to design a range of new interactive and educational tools that will . . . extend the exhibition into homes and classrooms around the world." As museums have grown ever more dependent on corporate sources of funding, alliances of this kind are becoming all too frequent. Douglas C. McGill, "Art World Subtly Shifts to Corporate Patronage," *New York Times*, 5 February 1985.

24. For illustrations of Barry Le Va's "scatter piece," *Continuous and Related Activities: Discontinued by the Act of Dropping* (1967), and Matthew Barney's video, *Drawing Restraint 7* (1993), see Phillips, *American Century*, 188 and 362.

25. John S. Reed and Sanford I. Weill, undated letter on Citigroup letterhead, included in press kit for exhibition (see following note).

26. Press release for *Ellsworth Kelly: The Early Drawings, 1948–1955* (11 September–5 December 1999), the Art Institute of Chicago, 12 August 1999. On Cage's use of chance procedures, see Ch. 15.

27. "Philip Morris Companies Inc. Supporting the Spirit of Innovation and Experimentation," 1996 flier.

28. "Rauschenberg Revolution," Philip Morris advertisement for *Robert Rauschenberg: A Retrospective*, in *New York* magazine, 1997.

29. Cathleen McGuigan, "The Avant-Garde Courts Corporations," *New York Times Magazine*, 2 November 1986, 34. On Cunningham's and Cage's *Roaratorio*, see above, Ch. 12.

30. Bruce Weber, "Making a New Opera Fly Financially," *New York Times*, 11 August 1999.

31. "AT&T Sponsors John Cage 'Circus' at Guggenheim Museum Soho," AT&T Press Release, 1994.

32. Whether corporations deserve to receive tax exemptions for such support is a question that must be raised, since the premise for such tax relief is that the work supported furthers the public good.

33. Eileen Kinsella, "Cutting-Edge Art Does Business," *Wall Street Journal*, 12 February 1999. Both Hirst and Whiteread are cited above, Ch. 14.

34. Merryman and Elsen's *Law, Ethics, and the Visual Arts*, now in its third edition, is one of numerous titles that reflect the growing interest in art law, which has been designated as an area of specialization by the American Bar Association.

35. Merryman and Elsen are further mistaken in claiming that Supreme Court Justice Holmes was reluctant to have the courts answer the basic question of whether something *is* art (1:317). What he was wary of were judicial decisions regarding artistic *quality*, which he knew are necessarily subjective.

36. Ayn Rand, "Who Is the Final Authority in Ethics?" in *Voice of Reason*, 22, emphasis in original. See also our discussion of the definition of art, in Chapter 6.

37. Stephen E. Weil, "The 'Moral Right' Comes to California," *ARTnews*, December 1979, 88, 90; quoted in Merryman and Elsen, 1:170.

38. DuBoff, *Art Law in a Nutshell*, 1–2.

39. *United States v. Perry*, 146 U.S. 71 (1892), quoted in Merryman and Elsen, 1:317; see also DuBoff, 1–2. The phrase "intended solely for ornamental purposes" was infelicitous, since it suggests a decorative function, rather than the contemplative, nonutilitarian one that was clearly intended.

40. *United States v. Olivetti & Co.*, T.D. 363309, 7 Ct. Cust. App. 48 (1916), quoted in Merryman and Elsen, 1:317, emphasis ours; see also DuBoff, 2–3.

41. *Ibid.*, emphasis ours. The definition of sculpture adopted by the court was, on the whole, a satisfactory one, except for the phrase "in their true proportions," which might seem to exclude stylization of any kind.

42. *Brancusi v. United States*, T.D. 43063, 54 Treas. Dec. 428 and 430–31 (1928), quoted in Merryman and Elsen, 1:317–18; also DuBoff, 2–3. Brancusi made numerous versions of this work, some of which are called *Bird in Space*; see Artchive <http://www.artchive.com/archive/B/brancusi.html> and the Modern Art collection on the Metropolitan Musuem of Art's website <http://www.metmuseum.org>.

43. DuBoff, 4–7.

44. Members of the judiciary do not always agree with the artworld's assessments, however. In public hearings held to determine the fate of Richard Serra's *Tilted Arc* in 1985, for example, representatives of the artworld staunchly defended the work, but Judge Paul P. Rao of the U.S. Court of International Trade testified: "If [it] ever came before our court, and I was called upon to write an opinion, I would be obliged to state that it is not a work of art." Quoted in *New York Times*, 7 March 1985 (hearing held on March 6th).

45. The constitutional clause empowering Congress to enact laws regarding copyright and patents reads: "To promote the Progress of Science and useful Arts, by securing for limited Times to Authors and Inventors the exclusive Right to their respective Writings and Discoveries." U.S. Const. § 8 (8). The term "Authors" was understood to include "the creator of a picture or a statue as well"—as noted in *Mazer v. Stein*, 347 U.S. 201, 98 L Ed 630, 100 USPQ 325 (1954); in *Law of Copyright, Patent and Trademark*, 660, 662.

46. *Bleistein v. Donaldson Lithographing Co.*, 188 U.S. 239, 47 L Ed 460 (1903); in *Law of Copyright, Patent and Trademark*, 634, 635.

47. *Mazer v. Stein*, 347 U.S. 201, 98 L Ed 630, 100 USPQ 325 (1954); in *Law of Copyright, Patent and Trademark*, 660, 665. See also Merryman and Elsen, 1:180.

48. *Mazer v. Stein*, 665.

49. Copyright regulations, 37 C.F.R. § 202.10(c) (1959 [as amended 18 June 1959]); quoted in *Barnhart v. Economy Cover*, 773 F. 2d 416 (1985).

50. *Barnhart v. Economy Cover*, 411, emphasis ours.

51. Judge Newman made the mistake of comparing the mannequins in question to Michelangelo's *David*, however, arguing that the latter "would not cease to be

copyrightable simply because cheap copies of it were used by a retail store to display clothing" (*Barnhart*, 424). He thereby ignored that, unlike the plaintiff, Michelangelo had not created the *David* for such a purpose.

52. William Grimes, "Is It Art or Merely a Safety Hazard?" *New York Times*, 11 May 1994.

53. Copyright Law, 17 U.S. Code § 101.

54. Prior state laws in this area are also marred by overly broad definitions of art. Both the New York's Artists' Authorship Rights Act (1983) and a comparable 1985 Massachusetts law contain "not limited to" phrases in their definitions that recall the NEA's open-ended definition of art, which we cited above. See Merryman and Elsen, 1:166,167. The California Cultural and Artistic Creations Preservation Act (1982) is somewhat more precise, defining "Fine art" as "an original painting, sculpture, or drawing, or an original work of art in glass, of recognized quality, and of substantial public interest" (165), though it relies on subjective tests, and its inclusion of "glass" art is puzzling.

55. Grimes, "Is It Art," emphasis ours. On "installation art," see our discussion in Ch. 14.

56. Amy Gamerman, "Now Here's a Lobby I Could Love," *Wall Street Journal*, 9 August 1994.

57. *Ibid.* See also, by William Grimes: "Artists Win Round No. 1 in Dispute over a Sculpture," *New York Times*, 19 May 1994; "Ruling Prevents Removal of Warehouse Sculpture," *New York Times*, 1 September 1994; and "Court Rejects Sculptors' Case," *New York Times*, 2 December 1995; and Carol Vogel, "Inside Art: A Sculpture Suit," *New York Times*, 29 July 1994. Virtually all the newspaper accounts on the case mistakenly refer to Helmley-Spear as the owner of the building, rather than as the managing agents. For simplicity, we refer to Helmsley-Spear, though all the litigation involved "474431 Associates" as well.

58. Robert Rosenblum, quoted in *Carter, Swing, and Veronis v. Helmsley-Spear, Inc. and 474431 Associates*, 94 Civ. 2922 (DNE); 861 F. Supp. 303; 1994 LEXIS 12207. Another witness for the plaintiffs—Aedwyn Darroll, a professor teaching "two- and three-dimensional design" (a characterization that itself suggests an inappropriate view of the nature of sculpture)—similarly emphasized the "imagination" of the work.

59. Robert Rosenblum, quoted in Grimes, "Is It Art," emphasis ours.

60. *Carter, Swing, and Veronis* (see above, n. 56). Even a lawyer for the plaintiffs seemed surprised that the court had granted protection to such a work—which, he said, "'Congress, I'm sure, did not have in mind when the statute was passed.'" Richard A. Altman, quoted by William Grimes, "Ruling Prevents Removal of Warehouse Sculpture," *New York Times*, 1 September 1994.

61. Judge David N. Edelstein, *Carter, Swing, and Veronis*, emphasis ours. According to Edelstein, Kramer's testimony was "so colored by his disdain for contemporary art in general as to be of . . . little probative value." Kramer's testimony offered little solid basis for his disdain, but our entire book presents an objective argument against the "evolving standards" so readily accepted by the court in this case.

62. See Merryman and Elsen, 1:294.

63. *People v. Radich*, 26 N.Y. 2d 114 (1970), in Merryman and Elsen, 1:294.

64. In addition, the defendant testified that tassels at the base of the penis-like protrusion might be "'decorative or pubic hair, depending on what one decides it looks like to him.'" Quoted *ibid.* As summarized by Judge Gibson, the defendant's view was "that perhaps the penis represents the sexual act, which by some standards is considered an aggressive act; [and] that . . . the figure . . . seems to suggest that organized religion is supporting the aggressive acts suggested."

65. Chief Judge Fuld had referred to the disputed "'constructions'" as "sculptures" and "works of art," and had also implied that they qualified as "symbolic speech or conduct having a clearly communicative aspect." (295–96)

66. Robert Jones (an official of the Veterans of Foreign Wars), quoted by Isabel Wilkerson, "Veterans Protest Flag Exhibit at Art Institute," *New York Times*, 2 March 1989, emphasis ours. The work Jones referred to was *What Is the Proper Way to Display the American Flag?* by Scott Tyler—a student at the School of the Art Institute of Chicago, where the piece appeared in an exhibit of recent student work. As described by Wilkerson: "The flag was displayed beneath photographs of flag-draped coffins and flag burnings. Viewers were asked to record their impressions on a ledger. But to get to the ledger most people found that they had to step on the . . . flag." Regrettably, a petition filed by veterans' groups to close the exhibition was denied, because the work was deemed "'as much an invitation to think about the flag as to step on it.'" Judge Kenneth L. Gillis, Cook County Circuit Court, quoted in "Flag Exhibit Upheld in Chicago by Judge," *New York Times*, 3 March 1989.

67. *Spence v. Washington*, 418 U.S. 405 (1974), quoted in DuBoff, 256. The court further ruled that instances of flag desecration that qualify as "symbolic expression" approaching "pure speech" could be suppressed by the state only if the state could demonstrate its interest in (1) preventing a breach of the peace, (2) protecting the sensibilities of passersby, or (3) preserving the flag as an unalloyed symbol of our country.

68. B. Drummond Ayres, Jr., "Art or Trash? Arizona Exhibit on American Flag Unleashes a Controversy," *New York Times*, 8 June 1996.

69. Robert Reinhardt (who headed the Arizona branch of the American Legion), quoted *ibid.*, in response to statement by James Ballinger, director of the Phoenix Art Museum.

70. *City of Cincinnati v. Contemporary Arts Center, City of Cincinnati v. Barrie*, 57 Hamilton County Municipal Court, Ohio; Ohio Misc. 2d 15 (1990); 1990 Ohio Misc. LEXIS 12, IV, *n*6.

71. The College Art Association reproduced the children's photographs in a newsletter column celebrating the Mapplethorpe verdict as a "victor[y] for artists'-rights advocates." "The Fight for Rights," *CAA News*, January-February 1991, 8–9. The little girl, wearing a dainty dress but no underpants, is frontally posed on an elegantly carved stone bench, with one knee raised, exposing her vagina. The little boy— totally nude, though he seems past the age when children feel no embarrassment at

being naked—is also posed frontally (against the back of an easy chair), with his legs wide apart, in an awkward, unnatural position, so that his genitals are the focal point of the picture. The images seem deliberately and provocatively arranged by the photographer to titillate the viewer.

72. The three-part test for obscenity was established by the Supreme Court in *Miller v. California*, 413 U.S. 15 (1973); DuBoff *Art Law in a Nutshell*, 260–62.

73. Justice Byron White, affirming *Miller v. Calfornia*, in *Pope v. Illinois* (1987); quoted by Barbara Hoffman, "By Whose Values?" *CAA [College Art Association] News*, May-June 1990, 7.

74. Hoffman, "By Whose Values?" 7. The implication that artworld representatives hold "reasonable" views on contemporary art is ludicrous, of course.

75. *New York v. Ferber* (1980), 458 U.S. 747 (1982), in DuBoff, 265–67; see also Hoffman, "By Whose Values?" 7.

76. Anthony Eckstein, juror, quoted by Isabel Wilkerson, "Obscenity Jurors Were Pulled Two Ways," *New York Times*, 10 October 1990.

77. James Jones, juror, quoted *ibid.* The prosecution's sole "expert witness," who testified to the pornographic nature of the two pictures of children, was not an art expert but had merely done research for the American Family Association. "The Cincinnati Obscenity Case: It's Art," *Economist*, 13 October 1990, 98. On the crucial question of whether the disputed pictures were "works of art," even so conservative a critic as Hilton Kramer (who had not been called on to testify) supposed they were, since he knew "of no way to exclude them from the realm of art"—although he censured public financing of such work. "Is Art above the Laws of Decency?" *New York Times*, 2 July 1989.

78. See Roger Scruton, "Photography and Representation," *Critical Inquiry* 7 (1981): 603.

79. "Cincinnati Obscenity Case." Under Ohio law, Rev. Code Ann. § 2907.323 (A)(3)(b) (Supp.1989), parental consent is apparently sufficient defense against charges of child pornography.

80. Owen Findsen, quoted in "The Cincinnati Obscenity Case."

81. On the widespread cultural tendency to suspend moral judgment in the name of "art," a tendency which originated in the nineteenth-century fallacy of "art for art's sake," see Roger Shattuck, "The Alibi of Art," in *Candor and Perversion*, 116–129.

82. For a valuable summary of "The Comprachicos," and of Rand's views on education, see Sciabarra, *Ayn Rand*, 325–29.

83. The term *aconceptual* might be more apt in some cases than Rand's "anti-conceptual." See our further comment in n. 86, below.

84. On the widespread disregard for rationality in education, William A. Henry III (press critic for *Time* magazine) observed that in many elementary and secondary schools the emphasis is "not on . . . sharpening one's reasoning. Indeed, in some circles . . . rationality itself is argued to be a Western cultural artifact, no more legit-

imate than other and more intuitive or primal ways of knowing the world. I have in fact met quite a number of nominally educated, if doctrinaire, people for whom the word 'rational' is a withering insult, a debate-stifling dismissal." *In Defense of Elitism*, 5.

85. Rand also quotes ("Comprachicos," 172) Dewey's claim that the "mere absorbing of facts and truths is so exclusively individual an affair that it tends very naturally to pass into selfishness" and "there is no clear social gain in success thereat." *The School and Society* (Chicago: University of Chicago Press, 1956), 15. She probably first became familiar with "progressive" theories of education as a student at the University of Leningrad (1921–24). In a study of her university transcript, Sciabarra notes that the head of the commissariat which formulated educational policy "stressed progressive pedagogy, influenced heavily by the teachings of John Dewey." In addition, one of Rand's college courses was "History of Pedagogical Doctrines," probably taught by V. A. Zelenko, who also emphasized the "progressive" approach. Further, between 1918 and 1923, five of Dewey's books were translated into Russian. "The Rand Transcript," *Journal of Ayn Rand Studies,* Fall 1999, 16. Rand especially rejected Dewey's overemphasis on the provisional nature of human knowledge—which, she argued, unduly undermines cognitive confidence. (Ralph A. Smith, editor of the *Journal of Aesthetic Education*, for example, reflects this emphasis when he remarks: "From Dewey I learned that the most we can hope for in the way of knowledge are warranted assertions. . . . [A]bsolute certainty will always elude us." *Excellence II,* 147.) Like Dewey, Rand held that all knowledge is contextual; but she argued that knowledge based on a rational epistemology can usually be adequate within a given human context, requiring man to be "neither infallible nor omniscient." See her *Introduction to Objectivist Epistemology,* 78–79; and Sciabarra, *Ayn Rand,* 220–21.

86. Leonard Peikoff, "The American School: Why Johnny Can't Think," lecture delivered at Ford Hall Forum, Boston, 15 April 1984; published in *The Objectivist Forum,* October–December 1984; reprinted in Rand, *Voice of Reason,* 209–229. For Rand's remarks on the "Look-Say" method (she mistakenly referred to it as "Look-See") of reading instruction, see "The Comprachicos," 174. Unlike Rand, Peikoff recognizes that it is not the teachers who are basically at fault but, rather, the professors of education who train them in the anti-conceptual approach: "The ones I saw . . . seemed to take their jobs seriously; they genuinely liked their classes and wanted to educate them. But given the direction of their own training, they were unable to do it." "The American School," 227.

87. To those who doubt that the process of concept formation can be fostered even in very young children, we recommend an exemplary picture book, which could well serve as a basic primer in epistemology–*What Makes a Bird a Bird?* by May Garelick. Though it is available in a more recent edition, the original edition, with its finely rendered illustrations by Leonard Weisgard, is particularly recommended.

88. Rand, "Comprachicos," 190.

89. The Getty Education Institute for the Arts (formerly the Getty Center for Education in the Arts) was founded in 1983, as a division of the J. Paul Getty Trust in Los Angeles, to initiate and support programs related to art education advocacy, theory, curriculum, and professional development.

90. The complete text of *Learning in and through Art* is available online on the Getty website at <http://www.artsednet.getty.edu/ArtsEdNet/Read/Liata/index.html>.

91. According to the Getty Institute: "Over the past 15 years, discipline-based art education . . . has been incorporated into two-thirds of state curriculum frameworks, the national standards for art education, national student assessments, and many texts and instructional materials." "News from the Getty" (Press Release), 13 January 1998.

92. Implicitly acknowledging his less than rigorous characterization of the disciplines, Dobbs assures the reader that "any closed definitions will eventually be shown to be insufficient, as the boundaries of the disciplines change and (usually) expand" (4).

93. In contrast to DBAE's laundry list of purportedly visual art forms, Jacques Barzun urged art teachers to trust their "common sense" in considering "the idea of art." "What do *you* think it covers?" he asked, and then suggested: music, painting, sculpture, the dance, and literature. "But does Art [also] include acting, scene-painting, directing, film-making, journalism, broadcasting, photography, weaving, pottery, jewelry-making, batik, macramé?" "Occupational Disease: Verbal Inflation," lecture delivered before the National Art Education Association, Houston, 18 March 1978; published in *Art Education* and *Journal of Aesthetic Education*, October 1978; reprinted in *Begin Here*, 110.

94. Referring to similarly inflated goals for art education (such as "to transmit the cultural heritage . . . to acquaint the child with foreign cultures . . . to enhance achievement in other subjects"), Barzun noted: "These stated goals are bad enough, but trailing after them is a batch of slogans supposed to organize the lust for art: . . . engender general creativeness; build ethnic identity; enhance problem solving; humanise schooling; . . . achieve affective education. . . . It is all Inflation. It inflates the plausible or possible into the miraculous." "Occupational Disease," 105–106. Examples of such inflation abound on the Getty Institute's website (see n. 90 above). According to one report, teachers and students in Tennessee celebrated one of the state's "oldest art forms by designing and producing quilts and learning math, nutrition, social studies, geography, reading, and writing all at the same time. Third-graders, for example, decorated squares of white and wheat bread with peanut butter, jelly, fruit, and candy sprinkles and then feasted on these edible quilts."

95. The *Random House Webster's College Dictionary* (1999) defines "politically correct" as "marked by or adhering to a typically progressive orthodoxy on issues involving [especially] race, gender, sexual affinity, or ecology." We would substitute "left-wing" for the presumptuous term "progressive."

96. An emphasis on communal identity and social goals, rather than on the individual, is also evident in another monograph from the Getty Education Institute— *Celebrating Pluralism: Art, Education, and Cultural Diversity*, by F. Graeme Chalmers, professor of art education at the University of British Columbia. According to Anita Silvers, a prominent esthetician, Chalmers presents a case for DBAE as "an effective vehicle for social reconstruction and social action." "Multiculturalism and the Aesthetics of Recognition: Reflections on *Celebrating Pluralism*," *Journal of Aesthetic Education*, 33, no. 1 (Spring 1999): 96. Silvers adds: "Art education must not

be complicit in, and should help to alleviate, the oppression of groups of people who have no social authority by people who are socioeconomically dominant." She also notes, approvingly, that Chalmers urges art educators to create curricula "that combat elitism" (97). For information on *Celebrating Pluralism*, including excerpts and related on-line discussions, see <http://www.getty.edu/publications/titles/celeplur/index. html. For an eloquent demurral to such views, see Henry, *In Defense of Elitism*, esp. 2–4 and 173. Among other trends, he deplores that both public and private schools today "are far less concerned with the educational needs of the children they teach than with the political yearnings of the adults who lobby them" (4–5). Such objections are the more remarkable in view of Henry's own avowed "liberal Democratic" leanings (2).

97. Any student attempting to grasp the meaning of the concept "traditional" would be hard pressed to reconcile Dobb's implicit contradictions.

98. Rand, "The Age of Envy" (1971), in *The New Left* (ed. Schwartz), 142–43; "The Missing Link" (1973), in *Philosophy*, 42; and "Racism" (1963), in *Virtue of Selfishness*, 172–185.

99. Rand, "Global Balkanization," 119; see also n. 18, above. When Rand wrote of "ethnicity," the term "multiculturalism" had not yet been coined.

100. Rand does not define what she means by the "majority" in this context; but clearly implies both here and elsewhere that she is referring to those who, regardless of racial or ethnic background, have assimilated the core values of modern American culture, with its roots in the Enlightenment.

101. Perhaps surprisingly, criticisms similar to Rand's were also raised by philosopher of education Mary Anne Raywid, who was president of the John Dewey Society, in a 1973 symposium paper entitled "Pluralism as a Basis for Educational Policy: Some Second Thoughts," in *Educational Policy: Highlights of the Lyndon B. Johnson Memorial Symposium on Educational Policy* (Glassboro State College, 1973), ed. Janice F. Weaver (Danville, Ill.: Interstate, 1975), 81–99. Raywid warned that the anti-individualism implicit in the "new ethnicity" was threatening the very fabric of American society. In her view, cultural separatism and particularism should be replaced with "universalism"—that is, "the tendency . . . to stress the similarity and brotherhood of peoples, and to promulgate a common core of beliefs and common standards to which all can aspire and against which all can be judged." (Such universalism of course requires the conceptual capacity emphasized by Rand—the capacity to abstract characteristics shared by different cultural groups and individuals.)

Fifteen years later, historian of education Diane Ravitch similarly argued that an emphasis on ethnocentricity "contradicts the principles and values of the Western liberal tradition"—the Enlightenment ideas and values which were the very "purpose of American schools to transmit to the young." While holding that pluralism is a positive value, Ravitch insisted that we must nonetheless preserve "a sense of an American community—a society and culture to which we all belong." "Multiculturalism: E Pluribus Plures," *The American Scholar* 59 (Summer 1990): 337–54. On Raywid's and Ravitch's views and related issues, see also the valuable discussion in Smith, *Excellence II*, chs. 6 and 7. Oddly, their work is not cited in the extensive bibliography for *Learning in and Through Art*, which Smith himself prepared. Ravitch's distinction between a "positive" pluralism and the exclusionary determinism of some "multiculturalists" is echoed in *The Educated Child*, by Bennett, Finn, and Cribb— which we discuss later in this chapter—who note that at times multiculturalism "turns out to be just a cover for a left-leaning political agenda aimed at shaping students' opinions and transforming society" (591).

102. "Is It Art? A Conversation with Dr. Marcia Eaton," *ArtsEdNet Offline*, Winter 1996, 5 (some text is missing from this portion of the online version of the interview on the ArtsEdNet website).

103. Eaton, *Art and Nonart*, 99; quoted above, Ch. 6.

104. ArtsEdNet Talk, an online discussion list for teachers (and others), may be found at <http:\\www.artsednet.getty.edu>.

105. We have retained the original spelling throughout.

106. For teachers' ideas on classroom activities based on the work of Pollock, Segal, and Duchamp, search the archive of ArtsEdNet Talk for their names.

107. See "Rapping with the Scan Man," Getty Center for Education in the Arts, Newsletter, Winter 1990, 10.

108. Rand, "The Comprachicos," 154. Rand later suggests that the damage done to children's cognitive development by "progressive" methods of pedagogy in their early years may in some cases be partly reversible, though the "latest research on the subject shows that a child whose early cognitive training has been neglected will never catch up, in intellectual terms, with a properly trained child of approximately the same intelligence." (168) Unfortunately, as was her habit, she cites no sources.

109. As Joseph Epstein has remarked, the term "'Orwellian' has clearly left 'Kafkaesque,' 'Chekhovian,' and other literary eponyms far behind. . . . So much have the ideas extracted from Orwell's writing been in the air that one needs scarcely to have read him to have a strong notion of what these ideas are." "The Big O: The Reputation of George Orwell," *The New Criterion*, May 1990; archived at <http://www.newcriterion.com/archive/ summer99/bigo.html>. Epstein's essay persuasively argues that, while Orwell was not a great novelist, his achievement was nonetheless of a high order.

110. George Orwell, *Nineteen Eighty-Four*, 246.

111. Not for nothing has the impenetrable language of the many art critics and scholars we quote been dubbed "*artspeak*."

112. The "Core Knowledge Series" comprises seven "resource books" edited by Hirsch for kindergarten through sixth grade. Each carries a title such as *What Your First Grader Needs to Know: Fundamentals of a Good First-Grade Education*, except for the Kindergarten volume—published last, in 1996—which is subtitled "Preparing Your Child for a Lifetime of Learning." In that volume, for the first time, John Holden is listed as editor and E. D. Hirsch as editor-in-chief of the series. For the series, Hirsch acknowledges the "help, advice, and encouragement" of some *two thousand* people, of whom he mercifully names only about two hundred—including seventeen advisors on multiculturalism, as compared with twelve on elementary edu-

cation. Though individual "writers" are acknowledged (with their specialty, but no institutional affiliation), it is impossible to know who originated the ideas or the final formulations in any given case. The content of the series is based, in turn, on the *Core Knowledge Sequence*, "a grade-by-grade sequence of specific content guidelines in history, geography, mathematics, science, language arts, and fine arts," also prepared in an elaborate review process involving numerous individuals. For information on the Core Knowledge program, see the Core Knowledge Foundation website at <http://www.coreknowledge.org>.

113. A basic fallacy of much contemporary arts education is the premise that all children are "artists," capable of producing real works of art—such as painting or poetry. We do not call second-graders who study history, math, and science, *historians, mathematicians,* or *scientists*, for example. What children do in each of these subjects is acquire basic knowledge and practice basic skills appropriate to their age level. Few of them will actually become *artists* of any kind. On the mistaken tendency to view children as "poets," see Torres, "The Child as Poet."

114. In part, the child is told: "dip your brush in the paint and let the paint drip onto the paper. Do this with several colors." While Jackson Pollock's "drip paintings" are not mentioned, the similarity is difficult to ignore.

115. Hirsch, *What Your Kindergartner Needs to Know*, 160. On Frankenthaler, see above, Ch. 8, n. 38.

116. See above, Ch. 8, especially the section "Clement Greenberg."

117. On the distinction between *art* and such utilitarian objects, see above, Ch. 11.

118. Regarding the invalid analogy between architecture and sculpture, see our discussion in Ch. 10.

119. On John Ashbery and the "New York school" of poetry, see above, Ch. 13. For a brief biography of Kenneth Koch, see <http://www.poets.org/lit/poet/kkochfst.htm>.

120. Kenneth Koch, *Wishes, Lies and Dreams*; quoted by Torres, "Child as Poet," who contrasts Koch with a true poet, Langston Hughes (1902–1967). For conveying to young children an idea of the function of poetry, and by extension all art, we recommend Leo Lionni's charming picture book about an intrepid little mouse-poet, *Frederick*.

121. Even *The Dictionary of Cultural Literacy*, edited by Hirsch and others, notes that abstract art abandons the "representation of physical objects" (159). As for the claim that cubism is an "abstract style," its most famous practitioner, Picasso, never wholly abandoned at least nominal reference to the visible world—although for the brief period of his "Analytical Cubist" phase (1909–1912), alleged objects are virtually indiscernible, and the painting is, in effect, *abstract*. In any case, Picasso quickly retreated from that extreme, always insisting that visual art must deal with visible objects.

122. Mondrian's *Broadway Boogie* is in the collection of the Museum of Modern Art in New York City. For an image of the painting see <htpp://www.moma.org>.

123. Also regrettable is the authors' strong implication that religious adherence is the only sure path to moral development. Bennett, Finn, and Crib, *The Educated Child*, 539–540.

124. Bennett, Finn, and Cribb, like Hirsch, place undue emphasis on *knowledge*, rather than on *personal engagement with* the arts, as if the subject under discussion were science or history. Merely "knowing about" the arts is hardly the most important thing that distinguishes the truly educated, or cultured, individual.

125. Barzun, "Occupational Disease," 109.

126. As a teacher in the English department of Indian Hills High School, a public school in Oakland, New Jersey, I developed and taught an eleventh-grade elective humanities course in which I applied the approach outlined here to the study of the visual arts and music. It was inspired, in part, by an "experiment" Rand had conducted on occasion with guests, in which she would ask them "to listen to a recorded piece of music, then describe what image, action or event it evoked in their minds spontaneously and inspirationally, without conscious devising or thought (it was a kind of auditory Thematic Apperception Test)." "Art and Cognition," 52. I subsequently taught similar classes at the short-lived American Renaissance School (a small, private secondary school based on Rand's philosophy) in White Plains, New York, in the early 1980s.—*L.T.*

127. Barzun, "Occupational Disease," 105, emphasis ours. Barzun attributed the preference for the term *education* over *teaching* to the self-styled educators' "egotistical urge to blur this distinction."

128. Rand's suggestion that her guests "describe what image, action or event" the music "evoked" in their minds was too narrowly specific, we think.

Selected Bibliography

Books and Articles

Articles not included here are cited in the notes.

Acocella, Joan. *Mark Morris*. New York: Noonday Press, 1995.

Adams, Brooks, et al. *Sensation: Young British Artists from the Saatchi Collection*. London: Thames and Hudson, 1997.

Adams, Laurie Schneider. *A History of Western Art*. New York: Abrams, 1994.

Aiello, Rita, with John A. Sloboda, ed. *Musical Perceptions*. New York: Oxford University Press, 1994.

Aiken, Nancy E. *The Biological Origins of Art*. Westport, Conn.: Praeger, 1998.

Alperson, Philip, ed. *What Is Music? An Introduction to the Philosophy of Music*. University Park, Penn.: Penn State Press, 1994.

Ammer, Christine. *Harper's Dictionary of Music*. New York: Harper and Row, 1972.

Angeles, Peter A. *Dictionary of Philosophy*. New York: Harper and Row, 1981.

Arnheim, Rudolf. *Art and Visual Perception*. New version. Berkeley: University of California Press, 1974.

————. *New Essays on the Psychology of Art*. Berkeley: University of California Press, 1986.

————. *Toward a Psychology of Art: Collected Essays*. Berkeley: University of California Press, 1966.

————. *Visual Thinking*. Berkeley: University of California Press, 1969.

Arnold, Denis, ed. *The New Oxford Companion to Music*. New York: Oxford University Press, 1983.

Arnold, Magda B. *Emotion and Personality*. 2 vols. New York: Columbia University Press, 1996.

Arts Education and Americans Panel, The. *Coming to Our Senses: The Significance of the Arts for American Education*. New York: McGraw-Hill, 1977.

Ashberry, John. *Can You Hear, Bird*. New York: Farrar, Straus, and Giroux, 1995.

Ashton, Dore. *About Rothko*. New York: Oxford University Press, 1983.

Atkins, Robert. *ArtSpeak: A Guide to Contemporary Ideas, Movements, and Buzzwords, 1945 to the Present*. New York: Abbeville Press, 1997.

Auerbach, Erich. *Mimesis: The Representation of Reality in Western Literature*. 1946. Translated by Willard R. Trask. Princeton, N. J.: Princeton University Press, 1968.

Bair, Deirdre. *Samuel Beckett: A Biography*. New York and London: Harcourt Brace Jovanovich, 1978.

Barasch, Moshe. *Theories of Art: From Plato to Winckelmann*. New York: New York University Press, 1985.

Barber, Bruce, Serge Guilbaut, and John O'Brian, eds. *Voices of Fire: Art, Rage, Power, and the State*. Toronto: University of Toronto Press, 1996.

Barlow, Horace B., Colin Blakemore, and Miranda Weston-Smith, eds. *Images and Understanding: Thoughts about Images, Ideas about Understanding*. London: Cambridge University Press, 1990.

Barnes, Clive. Commentary for *Dance Scene U.S.A.: America's Greatest Ballet and Modern Dance Companies in Photographs*, by Jack Mitchell. Cleveland: World Publishing, 1967.

Barr, Alfred H., Jr. *Cubism and Absract Art*. New York: Museum of Modern Art, 1936.

Barron, Stephanie, et al. *"Degenerate Art": The Fate of the Avant-Garde in Nazi Germany*. Published in conjunction with the exhibition organized by the Los Angeles County Museum (1991). New York: Abrams, 1990.

Barzun, Jacques. *Begin Here: The Forgotten Conditions of Teaching and Learning*. Chicago: University of Chicago Press, 1991.

———. *Classic, Romantic, and Modern*. First published as *Romanticism and the Modern Ego*, 1943; 2nd ed., rev., published under the present title, 1961. Chicago: University of Chicago Press, 1975.

———. *Critical Questions: On Music and Letters, Culture and Biography, 1940–1980*. Edited by Bea Friedland. Chicago: University of Chicago Press, 1982.

———. *The Culture We Deserve*. Middletown, Conn.: Wesleyan University Press, 1989.

———. *The Energies of Art: Studies of Authors Classic and Modern*. New York: Harper and Brothers, 1956.

———. *The House of Intellect*. New York: Harper and Brothers, 1959.

———. *The Use and Abuse of Art*. The A. W. Mellon Lectures in the Fine Arts, 1973. Princeton: Princeton University Press, [1974] 1975.

———, ed. *Pleasures of Music: A Reader's Choice of Great Writing about Music and Musicians from Cellini to Bernard Shaw*. New York: Viking Press, 1951.

Battcock, Gregory, ed. *Idea Art: A Critical Anthology*. New York: Dutton, 1973.

———. *Minimal Art: A Critical Anthology*. New York: Dutton, 1968.

Batteux, Abbé Charles. *Les Beaux-Arts réduits à un même principe*. 1746. Edited by Jean Rémy Mantion. Paris: Aux Amateurs de livres, 1989. Excerpted (tr. by Robert L. Walters) in Feagin and Maynard, 102–104.

Bazin, André. *What Is Cinema?* Vol. 1. Translated by Hugh Gray. Berkeley: University of California Press, 1967.

Bazin, Germain. *French Impressionists in the Louvre*. New York: Abrams, 1958.

Beckett, Samuel. *Waiting for Godot*. A tragicomedy in two acts. Translated from the original French by the author. New York: Grove Press, 1954.

Bell, Clive. *Art*. 1913. Rev. ed. New York: Capricorn Books, 1958.

Bell-Villada, Gene H. *Art for Art's Sake and Literary Life: How Politics and Markets Helped Shape the Ideology and Culture of Aestheticism 1790–1990*. Lincoln: University of Nebraska Press, 1996.

Berenson, Bernard. *The Italian Painters of the Renaissance*. New York: Meridian, 1957.

Bernstein, Leonard. *The Unanswered Question.* Cambridge, Mass.: Harvard University Press, 1976.

———. *Young People's Concerts.* 1962. Edited by Jack Gottlieb. Rev. ed. New York: Anchor, 1992.

Best, David. *Expression in Movement and the Arts: A Philosophical Inquiry.* London: Lepus Books, 1974.

Biederman, Charles. *Art as the Evolution of Visual Knowledge.* Red Wing, Minn.: Charles Biederman, 1948.

Binswanger, Harry, ed. *The Ayn Rand Lexicon: Objectivism from A to Z.* New York: New American Library, 1986.

Blacking, John, ed. *The Anthropology of the Body.* New York: Academic Press, 1977.

Blondel, [Nicolas] François. *Cours d'architecture, enseigné dans l'académie royale d'architecture.* Paris: Lambert Roulland, 1675–83.

Blotkamp, Carel. *Mondrian: The Art of Destruction.* Translated from the Dutch by Barbara Potter Fasting. New York: Abrams, 1995.

Blunt, Sir Anthony. *Artistic Theory in Italy 1450–1600.* 1940. London: Oxford University Press, 1962.

Boixados, Alberto. *Myths of Modern Art.* Lanham, Md.: University Press of America, 1991.

Boone, Sylvia Ardyn. *Radiance from the Waters: Ideals of Feminine Beauty in Mende Art.* New Haven: Yale University Press, 1986.

Boorstin, Daniel J. *The Creators.* New York: Random House, 1992.

Bootzin, Richard R., and Joan Ross Acocella. *Abnormal Psychology: Current Perspectives.* 5th ed. New York: Random House, 1988.

Branden, Barbara. *The Passion of Ayn Rand.* New York: Doubleday, 1986.

Branden, Nathaniel. *The Disowned Self.* Los Angeles: Nash, 1971.

———. *Honoring the Self: The Psychology of Confidence and Respect.* New York: Bantam, 1985. First published as *Honoring the Self: Personal Integrity and the Heroic Potentials of Human Nature,* 1983.

———. *The Psychology of Romantic Love.* New York: Bantam, 1980.

———. *The Psychology of Self-Esteem: A New Concept of Man's Psychological Nature.* New York: Bantam Books, 1971.

———. *Who is Ayn Rand? An Analysis of the Novels of Ayn Rand.* With a Biographical Essay by Barbara Branden. New York: Random House, 1962.

Breslin, James E. B. *Mark Rothko: A Biography.* Chicago: University of Chicago Press, 1993.

Bring, Mitchell, and Josse Wayembergh. *Japanese Gardens: Design and Meaning.* New York: McGraw-Hill, 1981.

Bronowski, Jacob. *Science and Human Values.* 1956. New York: Harper Torchbooks, 1959.

Broude, Norma, and Mary D. Garrard, eds. *Feminism and Art History: Questioning the Litany.* New York: Harper and Row, 1982.

Brown, Milton W. *The Story of the Armory Show.* New York: Abbeville Press, 1988.

Bruce, Vicki, Patrick R. Green, and Mark A. Georgeson. *Visual Perception: Physiology, Psychology, and Ecology.* 3rd ed. Hove, East Sussex (U.K.): Psychology Press, 1996.

Bruner, Jerome S. *Acts of Meaning.* Cambridge, Mass.: Harvard University Press, 1990.

Bull, George Anthony. *Michelangelo: A Biography.* New York: Viking, 1995.

Butcher, S. H. *Aristotle's Theory of Poetry and Fine Art.* With a critical text and translation of *The Poetics.* 1894. 4th ed. New York: Dover, 1951. <http://libertyonline.hypermall.com/Aristotle/Poetics-Body.html>.

Cabanne, Pierre. *Dialogues with Marcel Duchamp.* Translated by Ron Padgett. New York: Viking Press, 1971.

Cage, John. *Silence: Lectures and Writings by John Cage.* Middletown, Conn.: Wesleyan University Press, 1961.

Calo, Mary Ann. *Bernard Berenson and the Twentieth Century.* Philadelphia: Temple University Press, 1994.

Canaday, John. *Mainstreams of Modern Art: David to Picasso.* New York: Simon and Schuster, 1959.

———. *What Is Art? An Introduction to Painting, Sculpture and Architecture.* New York: Knopf, 1980.

Carpenter, Rhys. *The Esthetic Basis of Greek Art of the Fifth and Fourth Centuries B.C.* 1921. Rev. ed. Bloomington, Ind.: Indiana University Press, 1959.

Carroll, Joseph. *Evolution and Literary Theory.* Columbia, Mo.: University of Missouri Press, 1995.

Cassou, Jean, et al. *Art and Confrontation: The Arts in an Age of Change.* Translation by Nigel Foxell. Greenwich, Conn.: New York Graphic Society, 1970.

Centeno, Augusto, ed. *The Intent of the Artist.* Princeton: Princeton University Press, 1941.

Chalmers, F. Graeme. *Celebrating Pluralism: Art, Education, and Cultural Diversity.* Los Angeles: J. Paul Getty Trust, 1996.

Chilvers, Ian, Harold Osborne, and Dennis Farr, eds. *The Oxford Dictionary of Art.* New ed. New York: Oxford University Press, 1997.

Chipp, Herschel B., ed. *Theories of Modern Art: A Source Book by Artists and Critics.* Berkeley: University of California Press, 1968.

Clarke, Mary, and David Vaughan, eds. *The Encyclopedia of Dance and Ballet.* New York: G. P. Putnam's Sons, 1977.

Clements, Robert J. *Michelangelo's Theory of Art.* New York: Gramercy Publishing, 1961.

Clynes, Manfred. *Sentics: The Touch of Emotions.* New York: Anchor Press, 1977.

———, ed. *Music, Mind, and Brain: The Neuropsychology of Music.* New York: Plenum Press, 1982.

Cohen, Selma Jeanne. *The Modern Dance: Seven Statements of Belief.* Middletown, Conn.: Wesleyan University Press, 1966.

———, ed. *International Encyclopedia of Dance.* New York: Oxford University Press, 1998.

Cole, Jonathan D. *About Face.* Cambridge, Mass.: MIT Press, 1998.

Coleman, Francis J., comp. *Aesthetics: Contemporary Studies in Aesthetics.* New York: McGraw-Hill, 1968.

Collingwood, R. G. *The Principles of Art.* Oxford: Clarendon, 1938.

Cook, Susan, and Robin Woodard. *In a Rehearsal Room.* New York: Modernismo, 1976.

Cooke, Deryck. *The Language of Music.* 1959. New York: Oxford University Press, 1962.

Coomaraswamy, Ananda K. *Christian and Oriental Philosophy of Art.* New York: Dover, 1956. First published as *Why Exhibit Works of Art?* (1943).

————. *The Transformation of Nature in Art.* 1934. New York: Dover, 1956.

Cooper, David E., ed. *A Companion to Aesthetics.* Blackwell Companions to Philosophy. Cambridge, Mass.: Blackwell, 1992.

Copland, Aaron. *Music and Imagination.* 1952. The Charles Eliot Norton Lectures, 1951–52. Mentor Books, 1959.

————. *What to Listen for in Music.* 1939. Rev. ed. New York: McGraw-Hill, 1988.

Cox, Kenyon. *Three Papers on Modernist Art.* New York: American Academy of Arts and Letters, 1924.

————. *What is Painting? Winslow Homer and Other Essays.* Introduction by Gene Thornton. New York: Norton, 1988.

Craig, Edward, ed. *Routledge Encylopedia of Philosophy.* New York: Routledge, 1998.

Craige, Betty Jean, ed. *Relativism in the Arts.* Athens, Georgia: University of Georgia Press, 1983.

Craven, Wayne. *Sculpture in America.* Cranbury, N.J.: Cornwall Books and Associated University Press, 1984.

Croce, Arlene. *Afterimages.* New York: Alfred A. Knopf, 1978.

————. *Sight Lines.* New York: Alfred A. Knopf, 1987.

Crowther, Paul. *The Language of Twentieth-Century Art: A Conceptual History.* New Haven, Conn: Yale University Press, 1997.

Cunningham, Merce. *The Dancer and the Dance: Merce Cunningham in Conversation with Jacqueline Lesschaeve.* New York: Marion Boyars, 1985.

Cytowic, Richard E. *Synesthesia: A Union of the Senses.* New York: Springer-Verlag, 1989.

Csikszentmihalyi, Mihaly. *The Art of Seeing: An Interpretation of the Aesthetic Encounter.* Malibu: J. Paul Getty Museum and Getty Center for Education in the Arts, 1990.

————. *Flow.* New York: Harper and Row, 1990.

Dabrowski, Magdalena. *Kandinsky Compositions.* New York: Museum of Modern Art, distributed by Abrams, 1995.

D'Alembert, Jean Le Rond. *Discours préliminaire de l'encyclopédie.* Database compiled by American and French Research on the Treasury of the French Language, 1984. <http://humanities.uchicago.edu/ARTFL/ARTFL.html>.

————. *Preliminary Discourse to the Encyclopedia of Diderot.* Translated by Richard N. Schwab. Indianapolis: Bobbs-Merrill, 1963. Excerpted in Feagin and Maynard, 105–108.

Damasio, Antonio R. *Descartes' Error: Emotion, Reason, and the Human Brain.* New York: G. P P. Putnam's Sons, 1994.

Danto, Arthur C. *After the End of Art: Contemporary Art and the Pale of History.* Princeton, N. J.: Princeton University Press, 1997.

————. *The Philosophical Disenfranchisement of Art.* New York: Columbia University Press, 1986.

————. *The Transfiguration of the Commonplace.* Cambridge, Mass.: Harvard University Press, 1981.

Davies, Stephen. *Definitions of Art.* Ithaca, N.Y.: Cornell University Press, 1991.

————. *Musical Meaning and Expression.* Ithaca, N.Y.: Cornell University Press, 1994.

D'Azevedo, Warren L., ed. *The Traditional Artist in African Societies.* Bloomington, Ind.: Indiana University Press, 1973.

Den Uyl, Douglas J. *The Fountainhead: A Reader's Companion.* New York: Twayne, 1999.

Den Uyl, Douglas J., and Douglas B. Rasmussen, eds. *The Philosophic Thought of Ayn Rand.* Chicago: University of Illinois Press, [1984] 1986.

Deutsch, Diana, ed. *The Psychology of Music.* New York: Academic Press, 1982.

Dewey, John. *Art As Experience.* New York: Capricorn Books, 1958.

Dickie, George. *Introduction to Aesthetics: An Analytic Approach.* New York: Oxford University Press, 1997.

Dickie, George, Richard Sclafani, and Ronald Roblin, eds. *Aesthetics: A Critical Anthology.* 2nd ed. New York: St. Martin's Press, 1989.

Diderot, Denis. *Lettre sur les sourds et muets.* Edited by Paul Hugo Meyer. Geneva: Librairie Droz, 1965.

Dipert, Randall R. *Artifacts, Art Works, and Agency.* Philadelphia: Temple University Press, 1993.

Dissanayake, Ellen. *Homo Aestheticus: Where Art Comes From and Why.* New York: Free Press, 1992.

———. *What Is Art For?* Seattle: University of Washington Press, [1988] 1990.

Dobbs, Stephen Mark. *Learning in and through Art: A Guide to Discipline-Based Art Education.* Los Angeles: Getty Education Institute for the Arts, 1998.

Donahue, Keith, ed. *Writing America.* Washington, D.C.: National Endowment for the Arts, n.d.

Donald, Merlin: *Origins of the Modern Mind: Three Stages in the Evolution of Culture and Cognition.* Cambridge, Mass.: Harvard University Press, 1991.

Drewal, Henry John, and John Pemberton III, with Rowland Abiodun. *Yoruba: Nine Centuries of African Art and Thought.* New York: The Center for African Art in association with Abrams, 1989.

Dryfhout, John H. *The Work of Augustus Saint-Gaudens.* Hanover, N. H.: University Press of New England, 1982.

DuBoff, Leonard D. *Art Law in a Nutshell.* St. Paul, Minn.: West Publishing, 1984.

Eagleton, Terry. *The Ideology of the Aesthetic.* Oxford: Basil Blackwell, 1990.

Eaton, Marcia Muelder. *Aesthetics and the Good Life.* Rutherford, N. J: Fairleigh Dickinson University Press, 1989.

———. *Art and Nonart: Reflections on an Orange Crate and a Moose Call.* Rutherford, N. J: Fairleigh Dickinson University Press, 1983.

Eco, Umberto. *Art and Beauty in the Middle Ages.* 1959. Translated by Hugh Bredin. New Haven: Yale University Press, 1986.

Edelman, Gerald M. *Bright Air, Brilliant Fire: On the Matter of the Mind.* New York: Basic Books, 1992.

———. *The Remembered Present: A Biological Theory of Consciousness.* New York: Basic Books, 1990.

Eliot, T. S. *The Sacred Wood: Essays on Poetry and Criticism.* 2nd ed. New York: Barnes and Noble, 1928.

Ellis, John, M. *Against Deconstruction.* Princeton: Princeton University Press, 1989.

Empson, William. *Seven Types of Ambiguity: A Study of Its Effects in English Verse.* 1930. 3rd ed. Norfolk, Conn.: New Directions, 1953.

Feagin, Susan L., and Patrick Maynard, eds. *Aesthetics.* New York: Oxford University Press, 1997.

Faigin, Gary. *The Artist's Complete Guide to Facial Expression.* New York: Watson-Guptill Publications, 1990.

Field, Syd. *Screenplay: The Foundations of Screenwriting.* 3d ed. New York: Dell Publishing, 1994.

Fineberg, Jonathan, ed. *Discovering Child Art: Essays on Childhood, Primitivism, and Modernism.* Princeton: Princeton University Press, 1998.

Fodor, Jerry A. *The Modularity of Mind.* Cambridge, Mass.: MIT Press, 1983.

Forster, E. M. *Aspects of the Novel.* 1927. New York: Harcourt Brace, 1985.

Frank, Joseph. *The Widening Gyre: Crisis and Mastery in Modern Literature.* Bloomington: Indiana University Press, 1968.

Freedberg, David. *The Power of Images: Studies in the History and Theory of Response.* Chicago: University of Chicago Press, 1989.

Freire, Paulo. *Pedagogy of the Oppressed.* Translated by Myra Bergman Ramos. Rev. ed. New York: Continuum, 1998.

Friedländer, Max J. *Landscape, Portrait, Still-Life: Their Origin and Development.* Translated by R.F.C. Hull. New York: Schocken Books, 1963.

Fry, Edward, and Miranda McClintic. *David Smith.* New York: G. Braziller, 1982.

Fry, Roger. *Vision and Design.* 1920. Edited by J. B. Bullen. New York: Oxford University Press, 1981.

Gammell, R.H. Ives. *Twilight of Painting.* 1946. Orleans, Mass.: Parnassus Imprints, 1990.

Gardner, Helen. *Art through the Ages.* 4th ed. Edited by Sumner McK. Crosby. New York: Harcourt, Brace, 1959.

Gardner, Howard. *Artful Scribbles: The Significance of Children's Drawings.* New York: Basic Books, 1980.

———. *Art, Mind, and Brain: A Cognitive Approach to Creativity.* New York: Basic Books, 1982.

———. *The Arts and Human Development: A Psychological Study of the Artistic Process.* New York: Wiley, 1973.

———. *Frames of Mind: The Theory of Multiple Intelligences.* Tenth-anniversary edition. New York: Basic Books, 1993.

Gardner, James. *Culture or Trash?: A Provocative View of Contemporary Painting, Sculpture, and Other Costly Commodities.* New York: Birch Lane Press, 1993.

Gardner, John. *On Moral Fiction.* New York: Basic Books, 1975.

Garrod, H. W. *Tolstoi's Theory of Art.* Taylorian Lecture. Oxford: Oxford University Press, 1935.

Gendzier, Stephen J., trans. *Denis Diderot's* Encyclopedia: *Selections.* New York: Harper Torchbooks, 1967.

George, Dick. *Ruby: The Painting Pachyderm of the Phoenix Zoo.* New York: Delacorte, 1995.

Gibson, James J. *The Senses Considered as Perceptual Systems.* Boston: Houghton Mifflin, 1966.

Gilbert, Stuart. *James Joyce's Ulysses: A Study.* 1930. New York: Vintage Books, 1960.

Gioia, Dana. *Can Poetry Matter? Essays on Poetry and Americvan Culture.* St. Paul: Graywolf Press, 1992.

Gladstein, Mimi Reisel. *The Ayn Rand Companion.* Westport, Conn.: Greenwood, 1984.

———. *The New Ayn Rand Companion.* Rev. ed. Westport, Conn.: Greenwood, 1999.

Goldberg, RoseLee. *Performance Art: From Futurism to the Present.* Rev. ed. New York: Abrams, 1988. First published as *Performance: Live Art 1909 to the Present,* 1979.

Goldfinger, Eliot. *Human Anatomy for Artists: The Elements of Form.* New York: Oxford University Press, 1991.

Goldman, Alan H. *Aesthetic Value.* Boulder, Colo.: Westview, 1995.

Goldwater, Robert, and Marco Treves, eds. *Artists on Art: From the XIV to the XX Century.* 3rd ed. New York: Pantheon, 1958.

Gombrich, Ernst H. *Art and Illusion: A Study in the Psychology of Pictorial Representation.* The A. W. Mellon Lectures in the Fine Arts, 1956. New York: Pantheon, 1960.

———. *Ideals and Idols: Essays on Values in History and in Art.* Oxford: Phaidon, 1979.

———. *Meditations on a Hobby Horse and Other Essays on the Theory of Art.* Phaidon Catalog, Spring, 1995.

———. *The Sense of Order: A Study in the Psychology of Decorative Art.* New York: Phaidon, 1979.

———. *The Story of Art.* 1950. 16th ed. London: Phaidon, 1995.

———. *Tributes: Interpreters of Our Cultural Tradition.* New York: Phaidon, 1984.

Gombrich, Ernst H., and Richard Gregory, eds. *Illusion in Nature and Art.* New York: Scribner's, 1973.

Gombrich, Ernst H., Julian Hochberg, and Max Black. *Art, Perception, and Reality.* Baltimore: Johns Hopkins University Press, 1972.

Gould, James A., ed. *Classical Philosophical Questions.* 7th ed. New York: Macmillan, 1992.

Graham, Gordon. *Philosophy of the Arts: An Introduction to Aesthetics.* New York: Routledge, 1997.

Grandin, Temple. *Thinking in Pictures: And Other Reports from My Life with Autism.* New York: Doubleday, 1995.

Greenberg, Clement. *Art and Culture.* Boston: Beacon Press, 1961.

———. *Clement Greenberg: The Collected Essays and Criticism.* 4 vols. Edited by John O'Brian. Chicago: Chicago University Press, 1986–1993.

———. *Homemade Esthetics: Observations on Art and Taste.* New York: Oxford University Press, 1999.

Ground, Ian. *Art or Bunk?* New York: St. Martin's Press, 1989.

Grudin, Robert. *The Grace of Great Things: Creativity and Innovation.* New York: Ticknor and Fields, 1990.

Grundberg, Andy, and Kathleen McCarth Gauss. *Photography and Art: Interactions since 1946.* 1st ed. New York: Abbeville Press, 1987.

Guggenheim Museum. *From Dürer to Rauschenberg: A Quintessence of Drawing—Masterworks from the Albertina and the Guggenheim.* New York: Guggenheim Museum, 20 June–24 August 1997.

Gurney, Edmund. *The Power of Sound.* 1880. New York: Basic Books, 1966.

Gussow, Mel. *Conversations with (and about) Beckett.* London: Nick Hern Books, 1996.

Guyer, Paul, ed. *The Cambridge Companion to Kant.* New York: Cambridge University Press, 1992.

Hagen, Margaret. *Varieties of Realism: Geometries of Representational Art.* New York: Cambridge University Press, 1986.

————, ed. *The Perception of Pictures*. 2 vols. New York: Academic Press, 1980–81.

Hale, John. *The Civilization of Europe in the Renaissance*. New York: Atheneum, 1994.

Halle, David. *Inside Culture: Art and Class in the American Home*. Chicago: University of Chicago Press, 1993.

Halliwell, Stephen. *Aristotle's Poetics*. London: Duckworth, 1986.

Hallpike, Christopher Robert. *The Foundations of Primitive Thought*. Oxford: Oxford University Press, 1979.

Hanfling, Oswald., ed. *Philosophical Aesthetics: An Introduction*. Cambridge, Mass.: Blackwell, 1992.

Hanna, Judith Lynne. *To Dance Is Human: A Theory of Nonverbal Communication*. Austin, Texas: University of Texas Press, 1979.

Hanslick, Eduard. *The Beautiful in Music*. 1854. Translated by Gustav Cohen. Edited by Morris Weitz. New York: Bobbs-Merrill, 1957.

————. *On the Musically Beautiful*. Translated and edited by Geoffrey Payzant. Indianapolis: Hackett, 1986.

Harries, Karsten. *The Bavarian Rococo Church: Between Faith and Aestheticism*. New Haven, Conn: Yale University Press, 1983.

Harrison, Andrew. *Philosophy and the Arts: Seeing and Believing*. Bristol: Thoemmes Press, 1997.

Hartt, Frederick. *Art: A History of Painting, Sculpture, Architecture*. 4th ed. Englewood Cliffs, N.J.: Prentice Hall, 1993.

Hauser, Arnold. *The Social History of Art*. Translated by Stanley Godman. 4 vols. New York: Vintage, 1951.

Haworth-Booth, Mark. *Photography: An Independent Art: Photographs from the Victoria and Albert Museum 1839–1996*. Princeton: Princeton University Press, 1997.

Hearn, Maxwell K. *Splendors of Imperial China: Treasures from the National Palace Museum, Taipei*. New York: Metropolitan Museum of Art, 1996.

Hegel, Georg Wilhelm Friedrich. *Introductory Lectures on Aesthetics*. Translated by Bernard Bosanquet. Edited by Michael Inwood. London: Penguin Books, 1993. First published as *The Introduction to Hegel's Philosophy of Fine Art*, 1886.

————. *On the Arts: Selections from G.W.F. Hegel's Aesthetics or the Philosophy of Fine Art*. Abridged and translated by Henry Paolucci. New York: Frederick Ungar, 1979.

Henry, William A., III. *In Defense of Elitism*. New York: Doubleday, 1994.

Hirsch, E. D., Joseph F. Kett and James Trefil. *The Dictionary of Cultural Literacy*. 2nd ed. New York: Houghton Mifflin, 1993.

Hisamatsu, Shin'ichi. *Zen and the Fine Arts*. Translated by Gishin Tokiwa. Tokyo: Kodansha International, 1971.

Hjort, Mette, and Sue Laver, eds. *Emotion and the Arts*. New York: Oxford University Press, 1997.

Holtzman, Harry, and Martin S. James, eds. *The New Art—The New Life: The Collected Writings of Piet Mondrian*. Boston: G. K. Hall, 1986.

Honour, Hugh, and John Fleming. *The Visual Arts: A History*. New York: Abrams; 1st ed., 1982; 3rd ed., 1991; 4th ed., 1995.

Hoover, Paul, ed. *Postmodern American Poetry: A Norton Anthology*. New York: Norton and Company, 1994.

Hospers, John. *Introduction to Philosophical Analysis*. Englewood Cliffs, N.J.: Prentice-Hall, 1953.

———. *Understanding the Arts*. Englewood Cliffs, N.J.: Prentice-Hall, 1982.

———, ed. *Introductory Readings in Aesthetics*. New York: Free Press, 1969.

Howell, Peter, Ian Cross, and Robert West. *Musical Structure and Cognition*. New York: Academic Press, 1985.

Hughes, Robert. *American Visions: The Epic History of Art in America*. New York: Knopf, 1997.

———. *Nothing If Not Critical: Selected Essays on Art and Artists*. New York: Knopf, 1990.

———. *The Shock of the New*. New York: Knopf, 1980.

Hurwitz, Al, and Michael Day. *Children and Their Art: Methods for the Elementary School*. 5th ed. New York: Harcourt, Brace Jovanovich, 1991.

Hutcheson, Frances. *An Inquiry Concerning Beauty, Order, Harmony, Design*. 1725. Edited by Peter Kivy. The Hague: Martinus Nijhoff, 1973.

Jaeger, Werner. *Paideia: The Ideals of Greek Culture*. Volume 1: *Archaic Greece, The Mind of Athens*. Translated by Gilbert Highet. 2nd ed. New York: Oxford University Press, 1965. First published in German, 1933; first English edition, 1939.

James, Liz. *Light and Colour in Byzantine Art*. Clarendon Studies in the History of Art. Oxford: Clarendon Press, 1996.

Janson, H. W. *History of Art*. 3rd ed. Revised and expanded by Anthony F. Janson. New York: Abrams, 1986.

Janson, H. W., with Dora Jane Janson. *History of Art: A Survey of the Major Visual Arts from the Dawn of History to the Present Day*. New York: Abrams, 1962; revised and enlarged, 1969.

———. *History of Art for Young People*. 3rd ed. New York: Abrams, 1987.

Jones, Mari Reiss, and Susan Holleran, eds. *Cognitive Bases of Musical Communication*. Washington, D.C.: American Psychological Association, 1991.

Jourdain, Margaret, trans. *Diderot's Early Philosophical Works*. Chicago: Open Court, 1916.

Jourdain, Robert. *Music, the Brain, and Ecstasy: How Music Captures Our Imagination*. New York: Morrow, 1997.

Joyce, James. *Ulysses*. New York: Modern Library, 1934.

Judd, Donald. *Complete Writings 1959–1975*. New York: New York University Press, 1975.

Kagan, Jerome. *The Nature of the Child*. New York: Basic Books, 1984.

Kahler, Erich. *The Disintegration of Form in the Arts*. New York: Braziller, 1968.

Kamhi, Michelle Marder. "Anna Hyatt Huntington's 'Joan of Arc.'" *Aristos*, March 1988.

———. "Ayn Rand's 'We the Living': New Life in a Restored Film Version." *Aristos*, December 1988.

———. "Kandinsky and His Progeny." *Aristos*, May 1995.: <http://www.aristos.org/backissu/kandinsk.htm>.

———. "The Misreading of Literature: Context, Would-Be Censors, and Critics," *Aristos*, October 1986.

———. "R. H. Ives Gammell." *Aristos*, May 1990.: <http://www.aristos.org/backissu/gammell.htm>.

————. "Robert Payne: Uncommon Guide to the World of Art." *Aristos*, December 1993.

————. "Today's 'Public Art': Rarely Public, Rarely Art." *Aristos*, May 1988.

————. "Victorian Treasures—Paintings from the McCormick Collection." *Aristos*, March 1987.

Kamhi, Michelle Marder, and Louis Torres. "Critical Neglect of Ayn Rand's Theory of Art." *Journal of Ayn Rand Studies*, Fall 2000.

————. "Revaluing the Liberal Arts." *Aristos*, June 1994.

————. *See also* Torres, Louis, and Michelle Marder Kamhi.

Kandinsky, Wassily. *Concerning the Spiritual in Art.* 1911. Translated by M.T.H. Sadler. New York: Dover Publications, 1977.

Kant, Immanuel. *Critique of Judgment.* Translated by J. H. Bernard. New York: Hafner Press, 1951. Excerpted in *Kant: Selections*, ed. by Theodore Meyer Greene (New York: Charles Scribner's Sons, 1957).

Kaprow, Allan. *Assemblage, Environments, and Happenings.* New York: H. N. Abrams, 1966.

————. *Essays on the Blurring of Art and Life.* Berkeley: University of California Press, 1993.

Kelley, David. *The Art of Reasoning.* New York: Norton, 1988.

————. *The Evidence of the Senses: A Realist Theory of Perception.* Baton Rouge, La.: Louisiana State University Press, 1986.

————. *Truth and Toleration.* Poughkeepsie, N.Y.: Institute for Objectivist Studies, 1990. See <http://www.objectivistcenter.org>.

Kelly, Michael, ed. *Encyclopedia of Aesthetics.* 4 vols. New York: Oxford University Press, 1998.

Kennick, William E., ed. *Art and Philosophy: Readings in Aesthetics.* New York: St. Martin's Press, 1964.

Kerst, Friedrich, and Henry Edward Krehbiel, eds. *Beethoven: The Man and the Artist, as Revealed in His Own Words.* 1905. New York: Dover Publications, 1964.

Kivy, Peter. *The Corded Shell: Reflections on Musical Expression.* Princeton: Princeton University Press, 1988.

————. *Music Alone: Philosophical Reflections on the Purely Musical Experience.* Ithaca, N.Y.: Cornell University Press, [1990] 1991.

Klosty, James, ed. *Merce Cunningham.* New York: Saturday Review Press, 1975.

Knight, Christopher. *Last Chance for Eden.* Los Angeles: Art Issues Press, 1995.

Knobler, Nathan. *The Visual Dialogue.* New York: Holt, Rinehart and Winston, 1966.

Koestler, Arthur. *The Ghost in the Machine.* New York: Macmillan, 1967.

————. *The Act of Creation.* New York: Dell, 1967.

Kostelanetz, Richard, ed. *Esthetics Contemporary.* Rev. ed. Buffalo, N.Y.: Prometheus Books.

————. *Merce Cunningham: Dancing in Space and Time.* Chicago: A Cappella, 1987.

Kostof, Spiro. *A History of Architecture: Settings and Rituals.* Revised by Greg Castillo. New York: Oxford University Press, 1995.

Kouwenhoven, John A. *Half a Truth Is Better than None: Some Unsystematic Conjectures about Art, Disorder, and American Experience.* Chicago: University of Chicago Press, 1982.

Kovach, Francis Joseph. *The Philosophy of Beauty.* Norman, Okla.: University of Oklahoma Press, 1974.

Kramer, Hilton. *The Revenge of the Philistines: 1972–1984.* New York: Free Press, 1985.

Krauss, Rosalind E. *Cindy Sherman, 1975–1993.* New York: Rizzoli, 1993.

———. *The Sculpture of David Smith: A Catalogue Raisonné.* New York: Garland Publishing, 1977.

Kristeller, Paul Oskar. *Renaissance Thought and the Arts: Collected Essays.* Expanded edition, with new Afterword. Princeton: Princeton University Press, 1990.

Kubler, George. *The Shape of Time: Remarks on the History of Things.* New Haven, Conn: Yale University Press, 1962.

Kuh, Katharine. *The Artist's Vision: Talks with Seventeen Artists.* New York: Harper and Row, 1962.

Kuspit, Donald B. *Clement Greenberg: Art Critic.* Madison, Wisc.: University of Wisconsin Press, 1979.

Kuspit, Donald B., and Jack Cowart. *Chihuly.* New York: Abrams, 1997.

Landowska, Wanda. Commentaries on J. S. Bach, *The Well-Tempered Clavier* (complete). Radio Corporation of America, 1958.

Lang, Berel, ed. *The Concept of Style.* 1979. Revised edition. Ithaca, N.Y.: Cornell University Press, 1987.

———. *The Death of Art.* New York: Haven Publishing Corp., 1984.

Lange, Kurt, and Max Hirmer. *Egypt: Architecture, Sculpture, Painting in Three Thousand Years.* Translated by R.H. Boothroyd. 3rd ed. London: Phaidon, 1961.

Langer, Susanne K. *Feeling and Form: A Theory of Art Developed from Philosophy in a New Key.* New York: Scribner's, 1953.

———. *Mind: An Essay on Human Feeling.* Abridged by Gary Van Den Hewel. Baltimore: Johns Hopkins University Press, 1988.

———. *Philosophical Sketches.* Baltimore: Johns Hopkins University Press, 1962.

———. *Philosophy in a New Key: A Study in the Symbolism of Reason, Rite, and Art.* 1942. New York: Penguin Books, 1948.

———. *Problems of Art: Ten Philosophical Lectures.* New York: Scribner's, 1957.

Larson, Gary O. *American Canvas: An Arts Legacy for Our Communities.* Introduction by Jane Alexander. National Endowment for the Arts, 1997.

LeDoux, Joseph E. *The Emotional Brain: The Mysterious Underpinnings of Emotional Life.* New York: Simon and Schuster, 1996.

LeDoux, Joseph E., and William Hirst, eds. *Mind and Brain: Dialogues in Cognitive Neuroscience.* New York: Cambridge University Press, 1986.

Lee, Rensselaer W. *Ut Pictura Poesis: The Humanistic Theory of Painting.* 1940. New York: Norton, 1967. First published in the *Art Bulletin,* 1940.

Lee, Sherman E. *A History of Far Eastern Art.* New York: Abrams, 1964.

Lehman, David. *The Last Avant-Garde: The Making of the New York School of Poets.* New York: Doubleday, 1998.

Lenain, Thierry. *Monkey Painting.* London: Reaktion Books, 1997.

Leonardo da Vinci. *Paragone: A Comparison of the Arts.* Edited by Irma A. Richter. New York: Oxford University Press, 1949.

Lessing, Gotthold Ephraim. *Laocoon: An Essay upon the Limits of Painting and Poetry.* Translated by Ellen Frothingham. Boston: Little, Brown, 1910.

Levin, Harry., ed. *The Portable James Joyce.* New York: Penguin, 1976.

Lévi-Strauss, Claude. *Look, Listen, Read.* Translated by Brian C. J. Singer. New York: Basic Books, 1997. First published as *Regarder, Écouter, Lire,* 1993.

———. *The Raw and the Cooked: Introduction to a Science of Mythology.* Translated by John and Doreen Weightman. New York: Harper and Row, 1969. First published as *Le Cru et le Cuit,* 1964.

———. *The Way of the Masks.* Translated by Sylvia Modelski. Seattle: University of Washington Press, 1982. First published as *La Voie des Masques,* 1975, 1979.

Lévi-Strauss, Claude, and Didier Eribun. *Conversations with Claude Lévi-Strauss.* Chicago: University of Chicago Press, 1991. Translated by Paula Wissing. First published as *De près et de loin,* 1988.

Levin, Kim. *Beyond Modernism: Essays on Art from the '70s and '80s.* New York: Harper and Row, 1988.

Levy, Mervin, ed. *The Pocket Dictionary of Art Terms.* London: Longacre Press, 1961.

Lieberman, William S., et al. *Twentieth-Century Art–Painting: 1945–1985.* New York: Metropolitan Museum of Art, 1986.

Lipman, Jonathan. *Frank Lloyd Wright and the Johnson Wax Buildings.* New York: Rizzoli, 1986.

Li Tuo. *China Avant-Garde: Counter-Currents in Art and Culture.* New York: Oxford University Press, 1994.

Liu Hsieh [Xie]. *The Literary Mind and the Carving of Dragons: A Study of Thought and Pattern in Chinese Literature.* Translated by Vincent Yu-chang Shih. New York: Columbia University Press, 1959.

Livingston, Myra Cohn. *The Child as Poet: Myth or Reality?* Boston: Horn Book, 1984.

Li Zehou [Tse-hou]. *The Path of Beauty: A Study of Chinese Aesthetics.* Translated by Gong Lizeng. New York: Oxford University Press, 1994.

Loewy, Emanuel. *The Rendering of Nature in Early Greek Art.* Translated by John Fothergill. London: Duckworth, 1907.

Lyle, Cynthia. *Dancers on Dancing.* New York: Sterling, 1977.

MacDougall, Curtis D. *Hoaxes.* Rev. ed. New York: Dover, 1958.

Malevich, Kasimir. *Malevich: Artist and Theoretician.* With contributions by Galina Demosfenova, Evgeniya Petrova, Charlotte Douglas, Irina Vakar, Evgeny Kovtun, Dmitry Sarabianov, Irina Karasik. Translated by Sharon McKee. Paris: Flammarion, 1991.

———. *The Non-Objective World.* 1927. Translated by Howard Dearstyne. Chicago: Paul Theobold, and Company, 1959.

Mandel, David. *Changing Art, Changing Man.* New York: Horizon Press, 1967.

Marcuse, Herbert. *The Aesthetic Dimension: Toward a Critique of Marxist Aesthetics.* Boston: Beacon Press, 1978.

———. *An Essay on Liberation.* Boston: Beacon Press, 1969.

Marshack, Alexander. *The Roots of Civilization: The Cognitive Beginnings of Man's First Art, Symbol and Notation.* 1972. Rev. ed. Mount Kisco, N.Y.: Moyer Bell, 1991.

Masheck, Joseph., ed. *Marcel Duchamp in Perspective.* Englewood Cliffs, N.J.: Prentice-Hall, 1975.

Massey, Reginald, and Jamila Massey. *The Dances of India: A General Survey and Dancer's Guide*. London: Tricolour Books, 1989.

Matravers, Derek. *Art and Emotion*. New York: Oxford University Press, 1998.

Mayer, Ralph. *A Dictionary of Art Terms and Techniques*. Toronto: Fitzhenry and Whiteside, 1969.

McBride, Henry. *The Flow of Art*. Edited by Daniel Catton Rich. New Haven, Conn: Yale University Press, 1997.

McDonagh, Don. *Martha Graham: A Biography*. New York: Praeger, 1973.

Meier-Graefe, Julius. *Vincent Van Gogh*. New York: Dover, 1987.

Meiss, Millard. *Painting in Florence and Siena after the Black Death*. New York: Harper and Row, 1951.

Melly, George and J. R. Glaves-Smith. *A Child of Six Could Do It! Cartoons about Modern Art*. Seattle: University of Washington Press, 1973.

Merrill, Ronald E. *The Ideas of Ayn Rand*. La Salle, Ill: Open Court, 1991.

Merryman, John Henry, and Albert E. Elsen. *Law, Ethics, and the Visual Arts*. 2 vols. 2nd ed. Philadelphia: University of Pennsylvania Press, 1987.

Meyer, Leonard B. *Emotion and Meaning in Music*. Chicago: Phoenix, 1956.

———. *Music, The Arts, and Ideas: Patterns and Predictions in Twentieth-Century Culture*. Chicago: University of Chicago Press, 1967.

Michaels, Claire F., and Claudia Carello. *Direct Perception*. Englewood Cliffs, : Prentice-Hall, 1981.

Mill, John Stuart. *Autobiography and Literary Essays*. Collected Works of John Stuart Mill, Vol. 1. Edited by John M. Robson and Jack Stillinger. Toronto: University of Toronto Press, 1981.

Miller, Mara. *The Garden as an Art*. Albany, N.Y.: State University of New York Press, 1993.

Mithen, Steven. *The Prehistory of the Mind: The Cognitive Origins of Art, Religion, and Science*. London: Thames and Hudson, 1996.

Mizener, Arthur. *The Sense of Life in the Modern Novel*. Boston: Houghton Mifflin, 1964.

Mondrian, Piet. See Holtzman and James.

Montesquieu [Charles de Secondat, Baron de]. *Essai sur le goût*. Introduction and notes by Charles-Jacques Beyer. Geneva: Librairie Droz, 1967.

Moran, Maya. *Down to Earth: An Insider's View of Frank Lloyd Wright's Tomek House*. Carbondale, Ill.: Southern Illinois University Press, 1995.

Morgan, H. Wayne. *Keepers of Culture: The Art-Thought of Kenyon Cox, Royal Cortissoz, and Frank Jewett Mather, Jr.* Kent, Ohio: Kent State University Press, 1989.

———, ed. *An American Art Student in Paris: The Letters of Kenyon Cox, 1877–1882*. Kent, Ohio: Kent State University Press, 1986.

Morgan, Robert C. *Conceptual Art: An American Perspective*. Jefferson, N. C.: McFarland, 1994.

Motherwell, Robert. *The Collected Writings of Robert Motherwell*. Edited by Stephanie Terenzio. New York: Oxford University Press, 1992.

Murray, Peter and Linda. *A Dictionary of Art and Artists*. Baltimore: Penguin Books, 1959.

National Foundation on the Arts and Humanities Act of 1965, U. S. Code, sec. 952 (a); <http://www.law.cornell.edu/uscode/20/952.html>. See also Merryman and Elsen, 1:338.

Newman, Walter. *Harrow Alley* (screenplay). In *Scenario*, Fall 1995, 56–112.

O'Connor, Francis V., ed. *Jackson Pollock: A Catalogue Raisonné of Paintings, Drawings, and Other Works.* 4 vols. New Haven, Conn: Yale University Press, 1978.

O'Neill, John P., ed. *Barnett Newman: Selected Writings and Interviews.* Berkeley, Calif.: University of California Press, 1992.

Ortega y Gasset, José. *The Dehumanization of Art and Other Essays on Art, Culture, and Literature.* 1925. Princeton: Princeton University Press, 1968.

———. *On Love: Aspects of a Single Theme.* Translated by Toby Talbot. New York: Meridian, 1958.

———. *Velazquez.* New York: Random House, 1953.

Orwell, George. *1984.* First published 1949. New York: New American Library, 1961.

Osborne, Harold, ed. *The Oxford Companion to Art.* Oxford: Clarendon, 1970.

Panofsky, Erwin. *Galileo as a Critic of the Arts.* The Hague: Martinus Nijhoff, 1954.

———. *Idea: A Concept in Art History.* Translated by Joseph J. S. Peake. Columbia, S.C.: University of South Carolina Press, 1968.

———. *The Life and Art of Albrecht Dürer.* Princeton: Princeton University Press, 1955.

———. *Meaning in the Visual Arts: Papers in and on Art History.* Garden City, N.Y.: Doubleday, 1955.

Passmore, John A. *Serious Art.* LaSalle, Ill.: Open Court, 1991.

Payne, Robert. *The World of Art.* Garden City, N.Y.: Doubleday, 1972.

Peikoff, Leonard. *Objectivism: The Philosophy of Ayn Rand.* New York: Dutton, 1991.

Perecman, Ellen, ed. *Cognitive Processing in the Right Hemisphere.* New York: Academic Press, 1983.

Pevsner, Nikolaus. *An Outline of European Architecture.* 7th ed. Baltimore: Penguin, 1963.

Pfeiffer, John E. *The Creative Explosion: An Inquiry into the Origins of Art and Religion.* New York: Harper and Row, 1982.

Phillips, Lisa. *The American Century: Art and Culture, 1950–2000.* Catalog of exhibition at the Whitney Museum of American Art, 26 September 1999–13 February 2000. New York: Norton, 1999.

Pinker, Steven. *How the Mind Works.* New York: Norton, 1997.

Plato. *Ion.* Translated by Paul Woodruff. In Dickie, Sclafani, and Roblin, 10–19.

Plekhanov, Georgi. *Selected Philosophical Works.* 5 vols. Moscow: Progress, 1976–77.

Poggioli, Renato. *The Theory of the Avant-Garde.* Translated by Gerald Fitzgerald. Cambridge, Mass.: Harvard University Press, 1968.

Polanyi, Michael. *Personal Knowledge: Towards a Post-Critical Philosophy.* Chicago: Chicago University Press, 1958.

———. *The Tacit Dimension.* New York: Anchor Books, 1967.

Pollock, Jackson. *Jackson Pollock: A Catalogue Raisonné of Paintings, Drawings, and Other Works.* Edited by Francis V. O'Connor. 4 vols. New Haven, Conn: Yale University Press, 1978.

Popper, Frank. *Art of the Electronic Age.* Translated by Bernard Hemingway. New York: Abrams, 1993.

Popper, Karl. *Unended Quest: An Intellectual Autobiography.* La Salle, Ill.: Open Court, 1985. First published as "Autobiography of Karl Popper," in *The Philosophy of Karl Popper,* 1974.

Proske, Beatrice Gilman. *Brookgreen Gardens Sculpture*. New ed. Brookgreen Gardens, S.C., 1968.

Raffman, Diana. *Language, Music, and Mind*. Cambridge, Mass.: MIT Press, 1993.

Rainey, Lawrence. *Institutions of Modernism: Literary Elites and Public Culture*. New Haven, Conn: Yale University Press, 1998.

Rand, Ayn. "The Age of Envy" (1971). In *The New Left* (ed. Schwartz), 142–43.

———. "Art and Cognition." In *The Romantic Manifesto*, 45–79.

———. *The Art of Fiction*. Edited by Tore Boeckmann. New York: Plume, 2000.

———. "Art and Sense of Life." In *The Romantic Manifesto*, 34–44.

———. *Atlas Shrugged*. New York: Random House, 1957.

———. "Basic Principles of Literature." In *The Romantic Manifesto*, 80–98.

———. *Capitalism: The Unknown Ideal*. New York: New American Library, 1967. With additional articles by Nathaniel Branden, Alan Greenspan, and Robert Hessen.

———. *The Early Ayn Rand: A Selection from Her Unpublished Fiction*. 1983. Edited by Leonard Peikoff. New York: Signet, 1986.

———. *The Fountainhead*. New York: Bobbs-Merrill, 1943; Signet paperback, 1971.

———. "Global Balkanization." Lecture delivered at Ford Hall Forum, 10 April 1977. In *Voice of Reason*, 115–29.

———. "The Goal of My Writing." In *The Romantic Manifesto,* 162–72.

———. *Introduction to Objectivist Epistemology*. 2nd ed. Edited by Harry Binswanger and Leonard Peikoff. New York: Meridian Books, 1990.

———. Introduction to the 25th Anniversary Edition of *The Fountainhead*. New York: Bobbs-Merrill, 1968.

———. *Journals of Ayn Rand*. Edited by David Harriman. New York: Dutton, 1997.

———. *Letters of Ayn Rand*. Edited by Michael S. Berliner. Introduction by Leonard Peikoff. New York: Dutton, 1995.

———. "The Missing Link" (1973). In *Philosophy*, 35–45.

———. *For the New Intellectual: The Philosophy of Ayn Rand*. New York: New American Library (paperback), 1961.

———. *The New Left: The Anti-Industrial Revolution*. 2nd ed. New York: New American Library, 1971. Reissued as *Return of the Primitive: The Anti-Industrial Revolution*, ed. Peter Schwartz (New York: Meridian, 1999).

———. *Philosophy: Who Needs It*. New York: New American Library, [1982] 1984.

———. "Philosophy and Sense of Life." In *The Romantic Manifesto*, 25–33.

———. "The Psycho-Epistemology of Art." In *The Romantic Manifesto*, 15–24.

———. *The Romantic Manifesto: A Philosophy of Literature*. Rev. ed. New York: New American Library, 1975.

———. *The Virtue of Selfishness: A New Concept of Egoism*. With additional articles by Nathaniel Branden. New York: New American Library, 1964.

———. *The Voice of Reason: Essays in Objectivist Thought*. Edited by Leonard Peikoff. New York: New American Library, 1988.

Randall, John Herman, Jr. *Aristotle*. New York: Columbia University Press, 1960.

Randolph, David. *This Is Music: A Guide to the Pleasures of Listening*. New York: McGraw-Hill, 1964.

Rasmussen, Douglas B., and Douglas J. Den Uyl. *Liberty and Nature: An Aristotelian Defense of Liberal Order*. La Salle, Ill.: Open Court, 1991.

Rasmussen, Steen Eiler. *Experiencing Architecture*. Cambridge, Mass.: MIT Press, 1959.

Ratcliff, Carter. *The Fate of a Gesture: Jackson Pollock and Postwar American Art.* New York: Farrar, Straus, Giroux, 1996.

Ray, Man. *Man Ray: Photographs.* Translated by Carolyn Breakspear. Based on an exhibition at the Pompidou Centre, Paris, December 1981–April 1982.

Read, Sir Herbert. *Icon and Idea: The Function of Art in the Development of Human Consciousness.* The Charles Eliot Norton Lectures, 1953. Cambridge, Mass.: Harvard University Press, 1955.

———. *The Meaning of Art.* 1931. Baltimore, Md.: Penguin, 1949.

———. *The Philosophy of Modern Art.* New York: Horizon Press, 1953.

Reid, Louis Arnaud. *A Study in Aesthetics.* 1931. Westport, Conn.: Greenwood Press, 1973.

Rentschler, Ingo, Barbara Herzberger, and David Epstein. *Beauty and the Brain: Biological Aspects of Aesthetics.* Basel: Birkhäuser, 1988.

Reza, Yasmina. *'Art.'* A one-act play. Translated by Christopher Hampton. London: Faber and Faber, 1996.

Richman, Michael. *Daniel Chester French: An American Sculptor.* New York: Metropolitan Museum of Art, 1976.

Ridley, Aaron. *Music, Value and the Passions.* Ithaca, N.Y.: Cornell University Press, 1995.

Rimbaud, Arthur. *Arthur Rimbaud: Collected Poems.* 1962. Edited by Oliver Bernard. New York: Penguin Books, 1986.

Rodman, Selden. *Conversations with Artists.* New York: Devin-Adair, 1957.

Rollins, Mark, ed. *Danto and His Critics.* Oxford: Blackwell, 1993.

Roper, Laura Wood. *FLO: A Biography of Frederick Law Olmstead.* Baltimore: Johns Hopkins University Press, 1973.

Rosenthal, Mark. *Abstraction in the Twentieth Century: Total Risk, Freedom, Discipline.* New York: Solomon R. Guggenheim Museum, 1996. [Unless otherwise noted, citations to Rosenthal are to this work.]

———. *Jasper Johns: Work since 1974.* New York: Thames and Hudson, 1988.

Ross, Clifford, ed. *Abstract Expressionism: Creators and Critics.* New York: Abrams, 1991.

Ross, Stephanie. *What Gardens Mean.* Chicago: University of Chicago Press, 1998.

Ruby, Lionel. *Logic: An Introduction.* 2nd ed. New York: J. B. Lippincott Company, 1960.

Ruckstull, F. W. *Great Works of Art and What Makes Them Great.* Garden City, N.Y.: Garden City Publishing, 1925.

Russell, John, and Suzi Gablik, eds. *Pop Art Redefined.* New York: Frederick A. Praeger, 1969.

Russin, Robin U., and William Missouri Downs. *Screenplay: Writing the Picture.* Fort Worth, Tex.: Harcourt College Publishers, 2000.

Rykwert, Joseph. *The Dancing Column: On Order in Architecture.* Cambridge, Mass.: MIT Press, 1996.

Sacks, Oliver. *An Anthropologist on Mars.* New York: Vintage Books, 1995.

———. *Awakenings.* 1973. New York: HarperPerennial, 1990.

———. *The Man Who Mistook His Wife for a Hat—and other Clinical Tales.* New York: HarperPerennial, 1990.

Sadie, Stanley, ed. *The New Grove Dictionary of Music and Musicians.* London: Macmillan, 1980.

Sass, Louis A. *Madness and Modernism: Insanity in the Light of Modern Art, Literature, and Thought.* New York: Basic Books, 1992.

Schapiro, Meyer. *Modern Art: 19th and 20th Centuries.* Selected Papers, vol. 2. New York: George Braziller, 1978.

―――. *Theory and Philosophy of Art: Style, Artist, and Society.* Selected Papers, vol. 3. New York: George Braziller, 1994.

Scherer, Klaus, and Paul Ekman, eds. *Approaches to Emotion.* Hillsdale, N.J.: Erlbaum, 1984.

Schiller, Friedrich. *On the Aesthetic Education of Man in a Series of Letters.* 1794–95. Translated with an Introduction by Reginald Snell. Network: Frederick Ungar, 1965.

Schoen, Max, ed. *The Effects of Music.* 1927. Freeport, N.Y.: Books for Libraries Press, 1968.

Scholes, Percy A. *The Oxford Companion to Music.* 9th ed. New York: Oxford University Press, 1960.

Schonberg, Harold C. *The Lives of the Great Composers.* Rev. ed. New York: Norton, 1981.

Schopenhauer, Arthur. *The World as Will and Representaion.* 1818. 2 vols. Translated by E. F. J. Payne. 2 vols. New York: Dover, 1969.

Schwarz, Arturo. *The Complete Works of Marcel Duchamp.* 3d ed. 2 vols. New York: Delano Greenidge, 1997.

Schweder, Richard A., and Robert A. LeVine, eds. *Culture Theory: Essays on Mind, Self, and Emotion.* Cambridge: Cambridge University Press, 1984.

Sciabarra, Chris Matthew. *Ayn Rand: Her Life and Thought.* [Poughkeepsie, N.Y.:] The Atlas Society, a division of The Objectivist Center, [1999]. Reprinted from "Ayn Rand," in *American Writers: A Collection of Literary Biographies,* edited by A. Walton Litz and Molly Weigel, Supplement IV, Part 2 (New York: Charles Scribner's Sons, 1996).

―――. *Ayn Rand: The Russian Radical.* University Park, Penn.: Pennsylvania State University Press, 1995. [Citations to *Ayn Rand* are to this volume unless otherwise indicated.]

Scruton, Roger. *The Aesthetics of Architecture.* Princeton: Princeton University Press, 1979.

―――. *The Aesthetic Understanding: Essays in the Philosophy of Art and Culture.* New York: Methuen, 1983.

―――. *Art and Imagination: A Study in the Philosophy of Mind.* 1974. London: Routledge and Kegan Paul, 1982.

Scully, Vincent Joseph. *Architecture: The Natural and the Man-Made.* New York: St. Martin's Press, 1991.

Seaver, Richard W., ed. *Samuel Beckett—I Can't Go On, I'll Go On: A Selection from Samuel Beckett's Work.* New York: Grove Press, 1976.

Sedgwick, John P., Jr. *Art Appreciation Made Simple.* Garden City, N.Y.: Doubleday, 1959.

Seigel, Jerrold. *The Private Worlds of Marcel Duchamp: Desire, Liberation and the Self in Modern Culture.* Berkeley, Calif.: University of California Press, 1995.

Seuphor, Michel. *Abstract Painting: Fifty Years of Accomplishment from Kandinsky to Jackson Pollock.* New York: Dell, 1964.

Sewell, Barbara. *Egypt under the Pharaohs.* New York: G. P. Putnam's Sons, 1968.

Shakespeare, William. *The Complete Plays and Poems*. Edited by William Alan Neilson and Charles Jarvis Hill. Boston: Houghton Mifflin, 1942.

Shapiro, David, and Cecile Shapiro, eds. *Abstract Expressionism: A Critical Record*. New York: Cambridge University Press, 1990.

Shattuck, Roger. *The Banquet Years: The Origins of the Avant-Garde in France 1885 to World War I*. Rev. ed. New York: Vintage Books, 1968.

———. *Candor and Perversion: Literature, Education, and the Arts*. New York: Norton, 1999.

———. *The Innocent Eye: On Modern Literature and the Arts*. New York: Farrar, Straus and Giroux, 1984.

Sheppard, Anne. *Aesthetics: An Introduction to the Philosophy of Art*. New York: Oxford University Press, 1987.

Sherry, Patrick. *Spirit and Beauty: An Introduction to Theological Aesthetics*. Oxford: Clarendon Press, 1992.

Shikes, Ralph E. *The Indignant Eye: The Artist as Social Critic in Prints and Drawings from the Fifteenth Century to Picasso*. Boston: Beacon Press, 1969.

Sirén, Osvald. *The Chinese on the Art of Painting: Translations and Comments*. 1936. New York: Schocken Books, 1963.

Sloboda, John A. *The Musical Mind: The Cognitive Psychology of Music*. Oxford: Clarendon Press, 1995.

———, ed. *Generative Processes in Music: The Psychology of Performance, Improvisation, and Composition*. Oxford: Oxford University Press, 1988.

———. *See also* Aiello, Rita.

Smith, Ralph A. *Excellence in Art Education: Ideas and Initiatives*. Reston, Virginia: National Art Education Association, 1987.

———. *Excellence II: The Continuing Quest in Art Education*. Reston, Va.: National Art Education Association, 1995.

Solso, Robert L. *Cognition and the Visual Arts*. Cambridge, Mass.: MIT Press, 1994.

Sontag, Susan. *Against Interpretation and Other Essays*. New York: Octagon Books, 1978.

———. *On Photography*. 1977. New York: Noonday Press, 1989.

———. *Styles of Radical Will*. New York: Farrar, Straus and Giroux, 1969.

Sorell, Walter. *The Dance through the Ages*. New York: Grosset and Dunlap, 1967.

Sparshott, Francis. *A Measured Pace: Toward a Philosophical Understanding of the Arts of Dance*. Toronto: University of Toronto Press, 1995.

———. *Off the Ground: First Steps to a Philosophical Consideration of the Dance*. Princeton: Princeton University Press, 1988.

Spencer, Paul, ed. *Society and the Dance: The Social Anthropology of Process and Performance*. New York: Cambridge University Press, 1985.

Steinberg, Cobbett, ed. *The Dance Anthology*. New York: New American Library, 1980.

Steinberg, Leo. *Other Criteria: Confrontations with Twentieth-Century Art*. New York: Oxford University Press, 1972.

Stella, Frank. *Working Space*. The Charles Eliot Norton Lectures, 1983–84. Cambridge, Mass.: Harvard University Press, 1986.

Stephenson, Richard J. *The Insanity of Samuel Beckett's Art*. Aurora, Colo.: Paint Brush Press, 1990.

Stokstad, Marilyn, et al. *Art History*. New York: Abrams, 1995.

Storey, Robert. *Mimesis and the Human Animal: On the Biogenetic Foundations of Literary Representation.* Evanston, Ill.: Northwestern University Press, 1996.

Storr, Anthony. *Integrity of the Personality.* Baltimore: Penguin, 1963.

———. *Music and the Mind.* New York: Free Press, 1992.

———. *Solitude.* New York: Ballantine Books, 1989.

Straight, Michael. *Twigs for an Eagle's Nest: Government and the Arts, 1965–1978.* New York: Devon Press, 1979.

Sullivan, J.W.N. *Beethoven: His Spiritual Development.* 1927. New York: Vintage Books, 1960.

Suzuki, Daisetz T. *Zen and Japanese Culture.* Princeton: Princeton University Press, 1959.

Szarkowski, John. *The Photographer's Eye.* New York: Museum of Modern Art, 1966.

Tatarkiewicz, Wladyslaw. *A History of Six Ideas: An Essay in Aesthetics.* Dordrecht: Kluwer, 1980.

Terenzio, Stephanie, ed. *Collected Writings of Robert Motherwell.* New York: Oxford University Press, 1992.

Tharp, Twyla. *Push Comes to Shove: An Autobiography.* New York: Bantam, 1992.

Thrall, William Flint, and Addison Hibbard. *A Handbook to Literature.* Rev. by C. Hugh Holman. New York: Odyssey Press, 1960.

Tilghman, Benjamin R. *But Is It Art? The Value of Art and the Temptation of Theory.* New York: Basil Blackwell, 1984.

Tolstoy, Leo. *What Is Art? What Is Religion?* 1899. Translated from the Russian. New York: Charles Scribner's Sons, 1913.

———. *What Is Art?* Translated by Richard Pevear and Larissa Volokhonsky. New York: Penguin Books, 1995.

Tomkins, Calvin. *Duchamp: A Biography.* New York: Henry Holt, 1996.

———. *Off the Wall: Robert Rauschenberg and the Art World of Our Time.* New York: Penguin Books, 1981.

Torrence, Gaylord. *The American Indian Parfleche: A Tradition of Abstract Painting.* Seattle, Wash.: University of Washington Press, 1994.

Torres, Louis. "Blurring the Boundaries at the NEA." *Aristos,* January 1991: <http://www.aristos.org/backissu/blurring.htm>.

———. "Boswell's Johnson: Branden's Rand: 'The Passion of Ayn Rand' in Historical Perspective." *Aristos,* May 1987.

———. "The Child as Poet: An Insidious and Injurious Myth." *Aristos,* January 1988.

———. "Jack Schaefer: Teller of Tales." *Aristos,* October and December 1996.

———. "A Jaundiced Eye: Modern Scholarship on Victorian Painting." *Aristos,* March 1987.

———. "The New Dawn of Painting." *Aristos,* March 1986.

Torres, Louis, and Michelle Marder Kamhi. "Ayn Rand's Philosophy of Art: A Critical Introduction" Parts I and II, *Aristos,* January 1991; Parts III and IV, September 1991; Part V, January 1992; Part VI and Conclusion, September 1992.

———. "Yes . . . But Is It Art?: Morley Safer and Murphy Brown Take on the Experts." *Aristos,* June 1994: <http://www.aristos.org/backissu/yesbutis.htm>.

Tuchman, Maurice, et al. *The Spiritual in Art: Abstract Painting 1898–1985.* New York: Abbeville, 1986.

Turner, Frederick. *Beauty: The Value of Values*. Charlottesville: University Press of Virginia, 1991.

———. *The Culture of Hope: A New Birth of the Classical Spirit*. New York: Free Press, 1995.

———. *Natural Classicism: Essays on Literature and Science*. Charlottesville: University Press of Virginia, 1992.

Turner, Jane, ed. *The Dictionary of Art*. New York: Grove's Dictionaries, 1996.

Unamuno (y Jugo), Miguel de. *The Tragic Sense of Life (in Men and in Peoples)*. 1921. Translated by J. E. Crawford Flitch. New York: Dover, 1954.

Varnedoe, Kirk, and Pepe Karmel. *Jackson Pollock*. Catalog of the exhibition at the Museum of Modern Art. New York: Abrams, 1998.

Venturi, Lionello. *History of Art Criticism*. Translated by Charles Marriott. 1936. Rev. ed. New York: E. P. Dutton, 1964.

Vivas, Eliseo. *Creation and Discovery: Essays in Criticism and Aesthetics*. New York: Noonday Press, 1955.

Vivas, Eliseo, and Murray Krieger, eds. *The Problems of Aesthetics: A Book of Readings*. New York: Holt, Rinehart and Winston, 1953.

Walker, Alan. *An Anatomy of Musical Criticism*. Philadelphia: Chilton Book Company, 1968.

Wallis, Brian, ed. *Art After Modernism: Rethinking Representation*. Edited by B. Wallis. New York: New Museum of Contemporary Art, 1984.

Walton, Kendall L. *Mimesis as Make-Believe: On the Foundations of the Representational Arts*. Cambridge: Harvard University Press, 1990.

Warhol, Andy. *The Philosophy of Andy Warhol: From A to B and Back Again*. New York: Harcourt Brace, 1975.

Washburn, Katharine, and John F. Thornton, eds. *Dumbing Down: Essays on the Strip Mining of American Culture*. New York: Norton, 1996.

Weightman, John. *The Concept of the Avant-Garde: Explorations in Modernism*. La Salle, Ill.: Open Court, 1973.

Weinberger, Martin. *Michelangelo: The Sculptor*. 2 vols. New York: Columbia University Press, 1967.

Weiss, Jeffrey. *The Popular Culture of Modern Art: Picasso, Duchamp, and Avant-Gardism*. New Haven, Conn: Yale University Press, 1994.

Wellek, René, and Austin Warren. *Theory of Literature*. 1949. 3rd ed. New York: Harcourt, Brace and World, 1962.

Wendorf, Richard. *The Elements of Life: Biography and Portrait-Painting in Stuart and Georgian England*. Oxford: Clarendon Press, 1990.

Weyergraf-Serra, Clara, and Martha Buskin. *The Destruction of* Tilted Arc: *Documents*. Cambridge, Mass.: MIT Press, 1991.

Whitford, Frank. *Understanding Abstract Art*. New York: E. P. Dutton, 1987.

Wiener, Philip P., ed. *Dictionary of the History of Ideas: Studies of Selected Pivotal Ideas*. 5 vols. New York: Charles Scribner's Sons, 1973.

Wilde, Oscar. *The Artist as Critic: Critical Writings of Oscar Wilde*. Edited by Richard Ellman. Chicago: University of Chicago Press, 1982.

Wilkin, Karen. *David Smith*. New York: Abbeville Press, 1984.

Willetts, William. *Foundations of Chinese Art*. New York: McGraw-Hill, 1965.

Wilson, Edward O. *Consilience: The Unity of Knowledge*. New York: Knopf, 1998.

Wind, Edgar. *Art and Anarchy.* 1963. 3rd ed. Evanston, Ill.: Northwestern University Press, 1985.

Winston, Douglas Garrett. *The Screenplay as Literature.* Cranbury, N.J.: Associated University Presses, 1973.

Wittkower, Rudolf. *Architectural Principles in the Age of Humanism.* 1949. New York: Random House, 1965.

Wolfe, Tom. *The Painted Word.* New York: Bantam Books, 1976.

Wölfflin, Heinrich. *Principles of Art History: The Problem of the Development of Style in Later Art.* 1932. New York: Dover Publications, n.d.

———. *Renaissance and Baroque.* Ithaca, N.Y.: Cornell University Press, 1967.

———. *The Sense of Form in Art: A Comparative Psychological Study.* Translated by Alice Muehsam and Norma A. Shatan. New York: Chelsea Publishing, 1958. First published as *Italien und das Deutsche Formgefühl* ("Italy and the German Concept of Form"), 1931.

Wollheim, Richard. *On Art and the Mind.* Cambridge, Mass.: Harvard University Press, 1974.

———. *Painting as an Art.* The A. W. Mellon Lectures in the Fine Arts, 1984. Princeton: Princeton University Press, 1987.

Woodmansee, Martha. *The Author, Art, and the Market: Rereading the History of Aesthetics.* Social Foundations of Aesthetic Forms Series. New York: Columbia University Press, 1994.

Worringer, Wilhelm. *Abstraction and Empathy: A Contribution to the Psychology of Style.* 1908. Translated by Michael Bullock. 3rd ed. New York: International Universities Press, 1953.

Wright, Frank Lloyd. *The Future of Architecture.* New York: Mentor, 1963.

Wypijewski, JoAnn, ed. *Painting by Numbers: Komar and Melamid's Scientific Guide to Art.* New York: Farrar, Straus and Giroux, 1997.

Xenophon. *Memorabilia.* Translated by Amy L. Bonnette. Ithaca, N.Y.: Cornell University Press, 1994.

Young, Julian. *Nietzsche's Philosophy of Art.* New York: Cambridge University Press, 1992.

[Zeami Motokiyo]. *On the Art of the No Drama: The Major Treatises of Zeami.* Translated by J. Thomas Rimer and Yamazaki Masakazu. Princeton: Princeton University Press, 1984.

Tape Recordings (Audio and Visual)

Unless otherwise indicated, the following titles are audiorecordings. Videorecordings are listed by subject, rather than by producer.

Balanchine, George. *Choreography by George Balanchine*, part 1. *Tzigane, Andante* from *Divertimento No. 15* (Mozart), and *Four Temperaments.* Video, 60 min. New York: WNET, Dance in America, 1977.

———. *Choreography by George Balanchine*, part 4. *Ballo della Regina, The Steadfast Tin Soldier, Elégie, Tchaikovsky Pas de Deux.* Video, 51 min. New York: WNET, Dance in America, 1978.

Beyond the Mainstream. [On choreographers Trisha Brown, Laura Dean, and Steve Paxton] Producers, Merrill Brockway and Carl Charlson. Director, Merrill Brockway. Writer, Faubion Bowers. WNET Great Performances, Dance in America. Video, 60 mins. Wilmette, Ill.: Films Incorporated, 1980.

Blumenthal, Allan, and Joan Mitchell Blumenthal. *Music: Theory, History, Performance.* 12 lectures. New York, [1974] 1987. Distributed by Laissez-Faire Books, San Francisco.

Blumenthal, Joan Mitchell. *The Ways and Means of Painting.* Video, 90 min. Distributed by Laissez-Faire Books, San Francisco.

Branden, Barbara. *Principles of Efficient Thinking.* 10 lectures. 1962. Distributed by Laissez-Faire Books, San Francisco.

Branden, Nathaniel. *Love and Sex in the Philosophy of Ayn Rand.* Lecture delivered in 1983. Distributed by Laissez-Faire Books, San Francisco.

———. *Objectivism: Past and Future.* Lecture delivered at the California Institute for Applied Objectivism, 23 November 1996. Distributed by Laissez-Faire Books, San Francisco.

Cage, John. *Cage/Cunningham.* A Film by Elliot Caplan. Video, 95 min. New York: Cunningham Dance Foundation, 1991. Distributed by Kultur International Films, West Long Branch, N.J.

———. *John Cage: Man and Myth.* Produced and directed by Mitch Corber. Video, 60 min. New York, 1990.

———. *John Cage: I Have Nothing to Say and I Am Saying It.* Produced and written by Vivian Perlis. American Masters. Video, 56 min. New York: The Music Project for Television, WNET and Lola Films, 1990. Distributed by Kultur.

Cunningham, Merce. *Changing Steps.* Directed by Elliot Caplan and Merce Cunningham. Video, 36 min. New York: Cunningham Dance Foundation, 1989.

———. *Points in Space.* Music by John Cage. New York: Cunningham Dance Foundation, 1986. Video, 55 min. Distributed by Kultur International Films.

———. *Walkaround Time.* A Movie by Charles Atlas, 1973. Video, 48 min.

———. *See also* Cage, John. *Cage/Cunningham.*

Dancing: The Individual and Tradition. Produced and directed by Muffie Meyer and Ellen Hovde. Video, 58 min. New York: WNET, 1993. Distributed by PMI.

Discovery Channel. *The Brain: Our Universe Within.* 3 video programs, approx. 45 min. each: "Evolution," "Perception," and "Matter over Mind." Discovery Communications, 1994.

Graham, Martha. *Martha Graham: An American Original in Performance.* Includes *A Dancer's World, Night Journey,* and *Appalachian Spring.* Produced by Nathan Kroll. Video, 93 min. Distributed by Kultur International Films.

———. *Martha Graham: The Dancer Revealed.* Produced by Dominique Lasseur. Video, 60 min. New York: WNET, 1994. Distributed by Kultur International Films.

———. *Martha Graham: Three Contemporary Classics.* Includes *Errand into the Maze, Cave of the Heart,* and *"Acts of Light."* Produced and directed by Thomas Grimm. Video, 85 min. Martha Graham Center for Contemporary Dance, 1984. Distributed by Video Artists International, New York, N.Y.

Kelley, David. *The Foundations of Knowledge: An Objectivist Perspective.* 4 lectures. Distributed by Laissez-Faire Books, San Francisco.

Mayhew, Robert. *Ayn Rand's Marginalia* (1995). Distributed by Second Renaissance Books, Oceanside.

McCloskey, Susan. *Was Shakespeare a Determinist?* Two audiotapes. Poughkeepsie, N.Y.: Institute for Objectivist Studies, 1998.

Peikoff, Leonard. *The Philosophy of Objectivism.* 1976. 12 lectures. Distributed by Second Renaissance Books, Oceanside.

———. *Understanding Objectivism.* 1983. Distributed by Second Renaissance Books, Oceanside.

Rand, Ayn. *Lectures on Fiction-Writing.* 1958. 12 lectures. Distributed by Second Renaissance Books, Oceanside.

[Rauschenberg, Robert]. *Robert Rauschenberg: Inventive Genius.* Video, 60 min. American Masters.

Romeo and Juliet (music. Music by Serge Prokofiev, choreography by Kenneth MacMillan). Performed by The Royal Ballet, with Rudolf Nureyev and Margot Fonteyn. Royal Academy Productions, 1966. Video, 124 mins. Distributed by Kultur.

Suzanne Farrell: Elusive Muse. Directed by Anne Belle and Deborah Dickson, 1997. Video, 105 min. Distributed by Direct Cinema Limited, Santa Monica.

[Taylor, Paul.] *The Paul Taylor Dance Company.* [tbc]

———. *Paul Taylor: Dancemaker.*

Tharp, Twyla. *Baryshnikov by Tharp.* Includes *The Little Ballet, Sinatra Suite,* and *Push Comes to Shove.* WNET, Great Performances, Dance in America, 1984. Video, 60 min. Distributed by Kultur.

World Music and Dance, Video Anthology of. Edited by Fujii Tomoaki. In collaboration with National Museum of Ethnology, Osaka. 30 videocassettes. Tokyo: JVC, Victor Company of Japan, 1990. Distributed by Rounder Records, Cambridge, Mass.

[Wright, Frank Lloyd.] *The House on the Waterfall: The Story of Frank Lloyd Wright's Masterpiece.* Video. WQED Pittsburgh.

Internet Sources

American Society for Aesthetics: <http://www.aesthetics-online.org>.

American Society of Classical Realism: <http://www.classicalrealism.com>.

Aristos: <http://www.aristos.org>.

Artchive: <http://artchive.com>.

Artcyclopedia: <http://www.artcyclopedia.com>.

ArtLex: <http://www.artlex.com>.

Arts Journal (links to articles and reviews): <http://www.artsjournal.com>.

Arts & Letters Daily (links to articles, book reviews, essays, and opinion): <http://www.cybereditions.com/aldaily>.

ArtsEdNet: <http://artsednet.getty.edu>.

Association for Art History: <http://www.indiana.edu/~aah.org>.

Association of Literary Scholars and Critics: <http://www.scoliast.com/ALSC>.

Bookfinder: <http://www.bookfinder.com>.

Brookgreen Gardens (outdoor sculpture): <http://www.brookgreen.org>.

Core Knowledge Foundation (education): <http://www.coreknowledge.org>.

EpistemeLinks (philosophy resources): <http://www.epistemelinks.com>.
Google! (search engine): <http://www.google.com>.
Solomon R. Guggenheim Museum: (New York City): <http://www.guggenheim.org/
    srgm.html>.
Journal of Ayn Rand Studies: <http://www.aynrandstudies.com>.
Matsuoka, Mitsuhara (literature resources): <http://lang.nagoya-u.ac.jp/~matsuoka/
    index.html>.
Museum of Modern Art (New York City): <http://www.moma.org>.
National Gallery of Art (Washington, D.C.): <http://www.nga.gov>.
National Endowment for the Arts: <http://www.arts.endow.gov>.
New York Times: <http://www.nytimes.com>.
New York Review of Books: <http://www.nybooks.com>.
The Objectivist Center: <http://www.objectivistcenter.org>.
Sciabarra, Chris Matthew: <http://www.nyu.edu/projects/sciabarra>.
Times Literary Supplement: <http://www.the-tls.co.uk>.
Voice of the Shuttle (humanities resources): <http://vos.ucsb.edu>.
Whitney Museum of American Art (New York City): <http:www.whitney.org>.

Index